T0213643

Lecture Notes
in Business Information Processing   256

More information about this series at http://www.springer.com/series/7911

Manfred Reichert · Hajo A. Reijers (Eds.)

Business Process Management Workshops

BPM 2015, 13th International Workshops
Innsbruck, Austria, August 31 – September 3, 2015
Revised Papers

 Springer

Editors
Manfred Reichert
Institute of Databases and Information
 Systems
University of Ulm
Ulm
Germany

Hajo A. Reijers
Department of Computer Science
Vrije Universiteit Amsterdam
Amsterdam
The Netherlands

ISSN 1865-1348   ISSN 1865-1356 (electronic)
Lecture Notes in Business Information Processing
ISBN 978-3-319-42886-4   ISBN 978-3-319-42887-1   (eBook)
DOI 10.1007/978-3-319-42887-1

Library of Congress Control Number: 2016944920

Printed on acid-free paper

This Springer imprint is published by Springer Nature
The registered company is Springer International Publishing AG Switzerland

Preface

Business process management (BPM) is an established research domain for computer science, information systems, and management scholars. The International Conference on Business Process Management (BPM 2015), which took place in Innsbruck from August 31 to September 3, 2015, was the 13th conference in a series that provides the most distinguished and specialized forum for researchers and practitioners in the BPM field. The conference has a record of attracting innovative research of the highest quality related to all aspects of BPM, including theory, frameworks, methods, techniques, architectures, and empirical findings.

It is a tradition that topical workshops accompany the main BPM conference in order to allow groups to coalesce around new research topics, to present emerging research issues, or to focus in-depth on a particular area of research. BPM 2015 was accompanied by seven workshops – some new, some well-established ones. The workshops attracted 104 submissions, out of which 44 were accepted as full papers by the respective Program Committees. This made a full paper acceptance rate of 42 %. In addition to these full papers, the present proceedings include the invited papers of the keynote speakers.

The following seven workshops were held in the context of the BPM 2015 conference on the campus of the University of Innsbruck, Austria, on August 31, 2015:

- 4th International Workshop on Adaptive Case Management and Other Non-workflow Approaches to BPM (AdaptiveCM 2015)
- 11th International Workshop on Business Process Intelligence (BPI 2015)
- 8th Workshop on Social and Human Aspects of Business Process Management (BPMS2 2015)
- 4th Workshop on Data- and Artifact-Centric BPM (DAB 2015)
- Third International Workshop on Decision Mining and Modeling for Business Processes (DeMiMoP 2015)
- First International Workshop on Process Engineering (IWPE 2015)
- 4th International Workshop on Theory and Applications of Process Visualization (TAProViz 2015)

We would like to express our sincere gratitude to the organizers of each workshop for arranging entertaining, high-quality programs that were well received by the attendees. We are grateful to the service of the countless reviewers who supported the workshop chairs and provided valuable feedback to the authors. Several workshops had invited keynote presentations that framed the presented research papers and we would like to thank the keynote speakers for their contribution to the workshop program. We would like to thank Ralf Gerstner, Viktoria Meyer, Alfred Hofmann, Eléonore Samklu, and the team at Springer for their support in the publication of this LNBIP volume.

Finally, we are grateful to Barbara Weber and her team members for all their efforts in organizing the BPM 2015 conference and BPM 2015 workshops.

December 2015   Manfred Reichert
                                                                          Hajo A. Reijers

Organization

BPM 2015 was organized in Innsbruck, Austria, by the University of Innsbruck.

General Chair

Barbara Weber   University of Innsbruck, Austria

General Workshop Chairs

Manfred Reichert   Ulm University, Germany
Hajo A. Reijers   VU University Amsterdam, The Netherlands

4th International Workshop on Adaptive Case Management and other Non-workflow Approaches to BPM (AdaptiveCM 2015)

Irina Rychkova   University of Paris, France
Ilia Bider   Stockholm University, Sweden and IbisSoft AB,
                                  Sweden
Keith D. Swenson   Fujitsu America, USA

11th International Workshop on Business Process Intelligence (BPI 2015)

Boudewijn van Dongen   Eindhoven University of Technology, The Netherlands
Diogo R. Ferreira   University of Lisbon, Portugal
Jochen De Weerdt   KU Leuven, Belgium
Andrea Burattin   University of Innsbruck, Austria

8th Workshop on Social and Human Aspects of Business Process Management (BPMS2 2015)

Rainer Schmidt   Munich University of Applied Sciences, Germany
Selmin Nurcan   Sorbonne School of Management, France and
                                  University of Paris, France

4th Workshop on Data- and Artifact-Centric BPM (DAB 2015)

Rik Eshuis   Eindhoven University of Technology, The Netherlands
Fabiana Fournier   IBM Research - Haifa, Israel
Marco Montali   Free University of Bozen-Bolzano, Italy

Third International Workshop on Decision Mining and Modeling for Business Processes (DeMiMoP 2015)

Jan Vanthienen   KU Leuven, Belgium
Bart Baesens   KU Leuven, Belgium
Guoqing Chen   Tsinghua University, China
Qiang Wei   Tsinghua University, China

First International Workshop on Process Engineering (IWPE 2015)

Mathias Weske   University of Potsdam, Germany
Stefanie Rinderle-Ma   University of Vienna, Austria

4th International Workshop on Theory and Applications of Process Visualization (TAProViz 2015)

Ross Brown   Queensland University of Technology, Australia
Simone Kriglstein   Vienna University of Technology, Austria
Stefanie Rinderle-Ma   University of Vienna, Austria

Contents

BPI Workshop

BPMS2 Workshop

DAB Workshop

DeMiMoP Workshop

IWPE Workshop

TAProViz Workshop

AdaptiveCM Workshop

Introduction to the 4th International Workshop on Adaptive Case Management and Other Non-workflow Approaches to BPM (AdaptiveCM 2015)

Irina Rychkova[1], Ilia Bider[2,3], and Keith D. Swenson[4]

[1] Universisty Paris 1 Pantheon-Sorbonne, Paris, France
irina.rychkova@univ-parisl.fr
[2] DSV, Stockholm University, Stockholm, Sweden
ilia@dsv.su.se
[3] IbisSoft AB, Stockholm, Sweden
ilia@dsv.su.se
[4] Fujitsu America, Sunnyvale, CA, USA
kswenson@us.fujitsu.com

1 Introduction

The sign of our time is the amazing speed with which changes in the business world happen. This requires from the enterprises of today, and even more of the future to become agile, e.g. capable of adjusting themselves to changes in the surrounding world, e.g. by using opportunities in the changed environment for launching new products and services.

Started by F. Taylor and H. Ford, a pursuit of process optimization, automation and efficiency resulted in creation of workflow concept, where a process is considered as a (predefined) flow of tasks, where the human involvement is minimized.

Agile enterprise means agile decision making on all levels to quickly react on changes in the world, and even be proactive. In BPM, it means greater importance of the role of knowledge worker who has an advantage over any automated workflow of being able to adapt to the unpredictable situations. A focus on agility requires a paradigm shift in BPM that promotes process execution rules being less prescriptive and supports knowledge workers, giving them the opportunity to creatively use their knowledge and experience in volatile environments.

2 Goal

The goal of this workshop is to bring together researchers and practitioners to discuss theoretical and practical problems and solutions in the area of non-workflow based approaches to BPM in general, and Adaptive Case Management (as a leading movement) in particular. This workshop is aimed to promote new, non-traditional ways of modeling and controlling business processes, the ones that foster collaboration and creativity in the frame of business processes.

3 Submissions, Organization, and Attendees

It is the fourth consecutive edition of AdaptiveCM workshop after successful events ACM'12 (joint event with BPM'12), AdaptiveCM'13 (joint event with OTM'12), AdaptiveCM'14 (joint event with EDOC'14).

AdaptiveCM defines the following submission categories: (i) Position (short) papers raising relevant questions in the workshop area; (ii) Idea papers exploring the history, challenges and providing the in-depth analysis of various non-workflow approaches to BPM; (iii) Experience reports presenting challenges encountered in practice and (iv) Research papers reporting original results in the area addressed by the workshop.

For this 4th edition of the workshop we received 18 submissions. Eight long papers (3 research papers, 4 idea papers, 1 experience report) and one short paper have been accepted for publication and presented during the workshop.

More then 20 participants attended the workshop.

4 Conclusion

This workshop paves a road for a line of reasoning and research into the areas of unpredictable (knowledge-driven) work that is hard to support with traditional work-flow oriented BPM approaches. The concluding discussion of the workshop was focused on modeling. The following questions were discussed: Can [Adaptive] Case Management be done without any modeling? Why do we model [for case management]? Who models and for whom? What should be modeled? How a modeling language should look like?

We expect that these and other questions will be further explored in our next editions. The detailed summary of the presentations and discussions raises can be found on the blog: http://social-biz.org/2015/08/31/adaptivecm-2015-workshop-summary/.

Case Management: An Evaluation of Existing Approaches for Knowledge-Intensive Processes

Mike A. Marin[1,2]([✉]), Matheus Hauder[3], and Florian Matthes[3]

[1] IBM Analytics Group, 3565 Harbor Blvd., Costa Mesa, CA 92626, USA
[2] University of South Africa (UNISA), Pretoria, South Africa
mmarin@acm.org
[3] Technische Universität München (TUM), Boltzmannstr. 3, 85748 Garching bei München, Germany
{matheus.hauder,matthes}@tum.de

Abstract. Process support for knowledge work is far from being mastered in existing information systems. Predominant workflow management solutions are too rigid and provide no means to deal with unpredictable situations. Various case management approaches have been proposed to support this flexibility for unstructured processes. Recently the Object Management Group published the Case Management Model and Notation (CMMN) as a standard notation for case management. In this paper we compare prominent definitions of case management over the last twenty-three years against characteristics of knowledge-intensive processes (KiPs). Our goal is to evaluate the applicability of case management and CMMN for KiPs. We provide requirements for execution environments implementing CMMN and delineate existing case management approaches to advance the understanding of this important domain. We concluded that CMMN seems to be a suitable approach to KiPs when combined with an appropriate execution environment.

1 Motivation

Today's work environments require highly trained experts that are able to perform many tasks autonomously. These experts are referred to as knowledge workers and their processes have a huge impact on the success of an organization [3,7]. Knowledge-intensive processes (KiPs) integrate data in the execution of processes and require substantial amount of flexibility at run-time [9]. Due to the lower level of predictability compared to routine processes, KiPs need to balance between structured elements for repetitive aspects and unstructured elements to allow creative solutions for complex problems. In addition to this *uncertainty* during the definition of the process, KiPs can also be characterized as *goal oriented, emergent,* and *knowledge creating* [18]. Process models for highly structured routine processes are not suitable for KiPs since they would become too complex to manage and maintain [23]. KiPs require more emphasis on collaboration and creativity compared to highly structured processes.

© Springer International Publishing Switzerland 2016
M. Reichert and H.A. Reijers (Eds.): BPM Workshops 2015, LNBIP 256, pp. 5–16, 2016.
DOI: 10.1007/978-3-319-42887-1_1

Based on initial ideas on case handling numerous other approaches have been proposed, e.g., Case Management [8,12,16,28], Adaptive Case Management [24], Dynamic Case Management [6], Production Case Management [17], and Emerging Case Management [4]. Every case management approach covers various aspects that can be discussed based on Fig. 1. Main purpose of case instances is to manage relevant data and actions that are processed by case workers to achieve a certain goal. Case templates capture best practice knowledge that can be reused in a particular context. Main difference between existing case management approaches is their support for the adaptation and instantiation directions that are marked with (a) and (b) [17]. In (b) case templates are predefined through case modelers. Alternatively or in addition to modeling, case templates emerge through adaptations of case workers in (a). Both directions can be integrated to support the entire knowledge work lifecycle presented in [18]. Hauder *et al.* [10] presented one solution that supports both directions with templates that are structured on wiki pages.

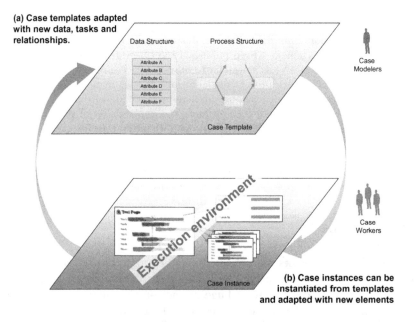

Fig. 1. Generic framework for the structuring of KiPs with case management

The goal of this paper is to evaluate how existing case management definitions compare against characteristics of generic KiPs and how CMMN [19] can be used to implement KiPs. Our methodology is based on the characterization of KiPs done by Ciccio *et al.* [9]. In the subsequent section definitions of case management from the last twenty-three years are presented for this purpose. We synthesize one definition of case management that covers the characteristics of KiPs commonly present in the definitions. Section 3 investigates to which extent the Case Management Model and Notation (CMMN) is suitable to support KiPs. Related work investigated applicability of CMMN to adaptive case management [14], without accounting for other definitions of case management or comparing against requirements for KiPs. Based on our comparison we identify important requirements for execution environments since not all requirements can be covered by a modeling notation like CMMN.

2 Defining Case Management

Definitions for the various case management approaches were searched in with Google Scholar, IEEExplore, ACM Digital Library, Google Search, and the library of our research institutions using the terms *case management* and *knowledge-intensive process* and trying to identify the first papers that provided definition. Papers in the legal or health care fields were excluded. Three types of definitions were extracted from the papers, first explicit definitions from papers that had them. Second for papers without formal definitions, the paragraph that better described and summarized case management was used as the definition. Third, for papers without a paragraph that could be used as definition, sentences that defined the term were extracted. Table 1 summarizes the resulting set of definitions with the comparison to the characteristics of KiPs[1].

The mapping of case management definitions to the KiP characteristics identified by Ciccio *et al.* [9] was done based only on the extracted definition. It relied on mapping the definition concepts and wording into the more specific characteristics identified by Ciccio *et al.* This approach assumes that we did correctly interpreted the meaning in the definition. In other words, it may be subjective in some instances, and there is no guarantee that we found all the papers with case management or case handling definitions in the area of business process.

Some of the first references to the term *Case Management* in the context of information technology (IT) and organizational processes were introduced by Berkeley and Eccles [3] in 1991, and Davenport and Nohria [7] in 1994. In both instances, case management was used to empower workers (case managers) to work across functional areas. It was recognized that case management was useful in processes that deal with customers, both internal and external to the organization. The goal was to make the back room and the front room indistinguishable from a customer perspective. Case management was seen as a way for organizations with complex customer processes to better service its customers. From an IT technology perspective, the challenge was to provide adequate tools for the case managers. Davenport and Nohria [7] concluded that the case manager role requires innovative thinking about business processes, their relationship to customers, the role of information in a process, and the power of individual employees. They acknowledged that case management may not be relevant to all business and all processes, but it has the potential to affect all the business organizations.

---

[1] The detailed analysis is available at: http://arxiv.org/abs/1507.04004.

Table 1. Comparison of case management with characteristics of KiPs

Definition	Date	C1	C2	C3	C4	C5	C6	C7	C8
Case management role [7]	1994	o	o						
Case handling [2]	2005	•		o	•	•			
Case management [12]	2006			—	—		—		—
Case management work [13]	2008	o	•	o	•				o
Dynamic case management [6]	2009	o	•				•	o	
Case management [28]	2009	•	•	o	o	•	•		o
Case management [16]	2010	•	•	•	•	•	•		o
Case management [8]	2010					•			
Case management [24]	2010								
Adaptive case management [25]	2010		o						
Adaptive case management [20]	2010	o							
Emerging case management [4]	2011	o	•	o					
Production case management [26, 17, 27]	2013	•		•	o	o			
Adaptive case management [26, 17, 27]	2013	•		•	•	o			o

Notes
- explicitly stated
- o Implicit in the definition
- — Precluded by the definition

2.1   From Case Handling to Case Management

Case Handling was first introduced by van der Aalst *et al.* [1] in 2001. It uses the case as the central concept for the process. Activities are less rigid than workflow activities and a balance between data-centric and process-centric is expected. The process is not driven just by the process flow, but the data helps drive the process. Workers do have more control, but they need to be aware of the whole case. The ability to execute, redo, and skip activities are important to provide the required flexibility. Four core features of case handling were identified by van der Aalst, *et al.* [2] in 2005:

1. Case handling avoids context tunneling (i.e. provide case workers with all the information about the case, instead of narrowing the information to the activity)
2. Case handling is data driven (i.e. enable activities based on the available information instead of only using control flow)
3. Case handling separates work distribution from authorization (i.e. query mechanisms can be used to navigate through active cases)
4. Case handling allows workers to view, add, and modify data outside an activity

The characteristics of case handling systems were described by Reijers *et al.* [22] as three, first the system's focus is on the case, second the process is data driven, and third parts of the process model are implicit. In a traditional workflow, the designer specifies what is permitted (explicit modeling). Modeling in case handling is less prescriptive where only the preferred or normal path is modeled (implicit modeling). Case handling treats both data and process as first class citizens [2]. Case handling concepts were implemented in a set of products that included FLOWer of Pallas Athena, the Staffware Case Handler, and the COSA Activity Manager [2].

Kaan et al. [12] in 2006 introduce Case Management as an alternative to Case Handling. The flexibility required by case handling do impair some of the advantages of the workflow technology [12]. The authors see case handling as an alternative to workflow [12,22]. Case Management as defined by Kaan et al. [12] enhances workflow technology by focusing on the tasks. The control flow between tasks is retained, but a task is decomposed into work content and activities. The work content provides the flexibility required by case management without compromising the control flow provided by the workflow. This initial definition of Case Management is at odd with current definitions, however it helps to clarify the distinction between case handling and case management. With the exception of Berkeley and Eccles [3] and Davenport and Nohria [7], until this moment in time definitions of case handling and case management were technology based and relied on particular tool implementations.

Further evolution of the term case management happened at the end of the 2000 decade, when market analysts started defining the term. The definition changed from an implementation definition into a more general market definition. The term case management evolved into a method or practice that could be implemented in multiple ways by different products. Several market analysts including Heiser et al. [11] in 2007 at Gartner Inc., Kerremans [13] in 2008 also at Gartner Inc., and White [28] in 2009 at Business Process Trends (BPTrends) popularized the term Case Management. They emphasized the collaboration nature of case management and the flexible interaction between humans, content, and processes. Kerremans defined case management work as collaborative and non-deterministic, where the work depends more on human decision making and content than in a predefined processes [13].

Clair et al. [6] in 2009 at Forrester Research introduced the term Dynamic Case Management. Clair et al. [6] define dynamic case management as highly structured but collaborative, dynamic, information intensive processes driven by events. The case folder contains all the information needed to process and manage the case. The definition is consistent the other market analyst definitions like [11,13,28]. Swenson [24] in 2010 popularized the term Adaptive Case Management. However, just in Swenson [24] there are five distinct definitions of case management by different authors. Three definitions of case management including the glossary [8,16,24], and two different definitions of adaptive case management [20,25]. Some authors [5] consider dynamic case management and adaptive case management as synonymous, while Pucher [21] distinguishes between the two based on a particular interpretation of Clair et al. [6] definition. Pucher [21] understand dynamic case management as being dynamic at runtime, versus adaptive case management in which the case is created just-in-time as needed. In addition, Pucher [21] view of adaptive case management implies case adaptation based on previous instances. *Emerging case management* defined by Bohringer [4] suggests a bottom-up view on case management that leverages social software techniques like micro-blogging, activity streams and tagging.

Swenson [26], Motahari-Nezhad and Swenson [17] distinguish between *Adaptive Case Management* (ACM) and *Production Case Management* (PCM). Both of them are compliant with a generic definition of case management. The distinction is based on who creates the case template and when it is created. In ACM, the case template is created by the knowledge worker at the moment that it is needed. In PCM, the case template is created by developers during a design phase, and it is then used by the knowledge workers. Both ACM and PCM, allow knowledge workers high degree of flexibility and discretion on how to complete the case.

Table 1 list the definitions discussed in this section and compares them to the KiP characteristics identified by Ciccio *et al.* [9]. The table seems to indicate little consensus on a common definition of case management. All five 2010 definitions are in the book edited by Swenson [24]. The two 2013 definitions by Swenson [24] introduce the distinction between adaptive case management and production case management. Taking the definitions as a whole, all the KiP characteristics are mentioned or implied, however C7 is only implied by one of the definitions by mentioning rules. With the terminology used by Ciccio *et al.* [9] for the KiP characteristics, and the analysis in Table 1, we attempt the following definition:

> Case management is a practice for knowledge-intensive processes with a case folder as central repository, whereas the course of action for the fulfillment of *goals* is highly *uncertain* and the execution gradually *emerges* according to the available *knowledge base* and expertise of knowledge workers.

3   CMMN for Knowledge-Intensive Processes

Kurz *et al.* [14] looked at the applicability of CMMN to adaptive case management, and concluded that for the most part CMMN fulfill the ACM requirements. In here, we look at the applicability of CMMN to knowledge-intensive process. For the analysis, we use the characteristics and requirements identified by Ciccio *et al.* [9], and compare them against a theoretical CMMN implementation.

CMMN is a modeling notation standard [19], and as such, avoids describing a particular implementation. The focus of the CMMN specification is the notation, the meta-model, interoperability between tools, and minimum execution semantics. Aspects like user interface, facilities for end users, user interaction with a case, tool usability, and others are considered implementation details and outside the scope of the specification. We divide a theoretical CMMN implementation, used to compare against Ciccio *et al.* [9] characteristics and requirements, into modeling and case worker environment. Modeling characteristics and requirements are those that a modeling tool should expose to support the ability of a case modeler to create case templates that satisfy knowledge-intensive process as defined by Ciccio *et al.* [9]. Case worker environment characteristics and requirements are those that an implementation should expose for case workers interacting with a case instance to support knowledge-intensive process as defined by Ciccio *et al.* [9]. Although, CMMN does not provides implementation details for the execution environment, Marin and Brown [15] have described an implementation of the information model. CMMN defines several levels of compliance with the specification. For this study we assume a CMMN complete conformance level of compliance [19].

Table 2. Comparing CMMN characteristics

Characteristic	Category		A CMMN implementation	
	Modeling	**Execution**	**CMMN Modeler**	**Case worker Environment**
C1 Knowledge-driven	✓		●	
C2 Collaboration-oriented		✓		◆
C3 Unpredictable	○	✓	◖	◆
C4 Emergent		✓		◆
C5 Goal-oriented	✓		◖	
C6 Event-driven	✓		●	
C7 Constraint/rule-driven	✓		◖	
C8 Non-repeatable	○	✓	◖	◆

Notes
- ✓ The characteristic is classified in the category
- ○ The characteristic contains elements of the category
- ● The CMMN specification provides full support
- ◖ The CMMN specification provides some support
- ○ The CMMN specification provides basic support
- ◆ A CMMN implementation can add support for the characteristic

3.1 Characteristics

Table 2 summarizes the comparison of the KiP characteristics defined by Ciccio *et al.* [9] with a theoretical CMMN implementation. The column labeled CMMN Modeler corresponds to the modeling environment that an implementation may expose for case modelers. The column labeled case worker environment corresponds to the implementation of an user interface for case workers to interact with case instances. We only rated the CMMN modeler for characteristics that involve some aspect of modeling, and we only marked as implementable by the case worker environment the characteristics that have some aspect of execution. With exception of *collaboration oriented, unpredictable, emergent and non-repeatable*, the remaining characteristics involve some aspect of modeling.

CMMN modeling ranked high in *knowledge driven* and *event driven*, because CMMN has a clear separation between the information model and the behavioral model that is bridged via events. The information model can be any type of structured or unstructured data (e.g. documents, correspondence, voice recordings, pictures, plain basic data fields, etc.) Activity in the information model generate events that can be used to enable tasks, stages, or milestones.

CMMN modeling ranked medium in *unpredictable, emergent, goal oriented, constraints, rules driven*, and *non-repeatable*. Ciccio *et al.* [9] makes very little distinction between the *unpredictable, emergent*, and *non-repeatable* characteristics. CMMN introduce discretionary elements used for execution time planning, providing the bases for *unpredictability*. CMMN provide the concepts of manual activation for tasks and stages, and manual completion for stages and the case instance itself that support the *emergent* characteristic. CMMN does not provide a global *case goal* definition, however it provides milestones that can be used to track intermediate goals. CMMN does not provide support for *rules*, although it provides the concept of sentries that can be seen an event-condition-action (ECA) rules, and are used as *constraints* to tasks, stages, and milestones.

3.2   Requirements

Table 3 summarizes our findings around the KiP requirements and a theoretical CMMN implementation. We only rated the CMMN modeler for requirements that involve some aspect of modeling, and we only marked as implementable by the case worker environment the requirements that have some aspect of execution. Most requirements are relevant for the execution environment.

CMMN modeling ranked high in *data-driven actions* and *late actions modeling*. For *data-driven actions*, CMMN has a concept of sentries that are used to define entry and exit criterion for task, stages and milestones. Entry and exit criterion are based on events from either the information model or the behavioral model, and are used to guide the execution of the model. CMMN provides the concept of discretionary items that can be added at execution time to the case plan by case workers and can be considered *late actions modeling*.

CMMN modeling ranked medium in *data modeling, late data modeling, goal modeling, flexible process execution*, and the *modeling of external events*. For *data modeling*, the CMMN meta-model provides a flexible information model that allow for the representation of a diverse set of data. The information model allows for the definition of folders and other structures that can be populated during execution with arbitrary data, and can be considered *late data modeling*. CMMN does not provides a global case *goal* definition, however provides milestones that can be used to track goals. For *flexible process execution*, CMMN discretionary items allow case workers to plan the case instance and to change those plans during execution. For *modeling of external events*, CMMN provide the ability to model events using event listeners, including two predefined type of events (human and timer events).

CMMN modeling ranked low in security *access to data*, formalization of *rules and constraints, resource and skill modeling*, and the definition of *worker priv-*

Table 3. Comparing CMMN Requirements

Requirement	Category		A CMMN implementation	
	Modeling	**Execution**	**CMMN Modeler**	**Case worker Environment**
R1 Data modeling	✓		◐	
R2 Late data modeling	○	✓	◐	◆
R3 Access to data	○	✓	○	◆
R4 Access to shared data		✓		◆
R5 Data-driven actions	✓		●	
R6 Late actions modeling	○	✓	●	◆
R7 Rules and constraints	✓		○	
R8 Late constraints		✓		◆
R9 Goal modeling	✓		◐	
R10 Late goal modeling		✓		◆
R11 Different modeling styles	✓	○	−	◆
R12 Visibility of knowledge		✓		◆
R13 Flexible execution	○	✓	◐	◆
R14 Unanticipated exceptions		✓		◆
R15 Migration of instances		✓		◆
R16 Learning from event logs		✓		◆
R17 Learning from data		✓		◆
R18 Resource/skill modeling	✓		○	
R19 Workers' interaction		✓		◆
R20 Workers' privileges	○	✓	○	◆
R21 Late resource modeling		✓		◆
R22 Late privileges modeling		✓		◆
R23 Workers' decisions		✓		◆
R24 Model external events	✓		◐	
R25 Late modeling of events		✓		◆

Notes
- ✓ The requirement is classified in the category
- ○ The requirement contains elements of the category
- ● The CMMN specification provides full support
- ◐ The CMMN specification provides some support
- ○ The CMMN specification provides basic support
- − The CMMN specification does not provide support
- ◆ A CMMN implementation can add support for the requirement

ileges. CMMN provides a concept of roles, but it is not related with the information model. For *access to data*, the case worker environment could use the role concept to impose access control over the case data. CMMN uses entry and exit criterion to model *constraints*. For definition of *workers privileges*, CMMN provides the ability to describe roles and the ability to describe how roles are allow to change the case plan, or which roles should execute some tasks. However CMMN does not define *security privileges*, as that is an execution consideration.

CMMN does not provides support for *different modeling styles*, because it is a declarative style of modeling. However, a CMMN implementation could include BPMN and in doing so provide both declarative and procedural modeling styles.

4   Discussion

Many different definitions for case management have been proposed, e.g., case handling, dynamic case management, adaptive case management, and emergent case management. Current definitions of case management are influenced by market analysts, which emphasized the collaboration nature and the flexible interaction between human decision making and processes, while early definitions were technology based. The definition of ACM focus on cases that are created just-in-time as needed with adaptations based on previous instances. Our analysis found little consensus between the definitions and the characteristics of KiPs. Nevertheless, we found every characteristic at least once in the analyzed case management definitions. Among all characteristics only C7 (Rules) is mentioned by only one definition whereas the other characteristics are mentioned at least four times. Based on this analysis we synthesize a definition that takes into account all characteristics of KiPs except for C7.

Regarding the characteristics of KiPs four of them were classified in the category of modeling. CMMN fully supports the knowledge-driven and event-driven characteristics. The goal-oriented and rule characteristics have some support in CMMN. The remaining four characteristics, collaboration, unpredictable, emergent, and non-repeatable need to be implemented within an execution environment for end-users.

We compared requirements for KiPs based on a fictional implementation of CMMN. For this purpose we divided the requirements into an execution and modeling category. Modeling requirements were compared against CMMN, while the execution requirements have to be supported by an execution environment. Regarding the modeling requirements CMMN seems suitable for data modeling, late data modeling, data-driven actions, and late actions modeling. We identified 18 of the 25 requirements for KiPs that have to be provided by an appropriate execution environment. CMMN seems to be a suitable approach to KiPs when combined with an appropriate execution environment.

5   Conclusion

Various case management approaches have been presented to support organizations with structured and unstructured processes. In this paper we compared their definitions against the characteristics of KiPs proposed by Ciccio *et al.* [9]. None of the definitions covered all the characteristics, therefore we proposed a synthesized definition based on the characteristics most commonly present in the definitions.

Our analysis revealed that CMMN matches most of the characteristics of KiPs that are related to the modeling of cases. Our comparison between CMMN and the requirements of KiPs proposed by Ciccio *et al.* [9] revealed that 18 of the 25 requirements need to be implemented by an execution environment. Therefore, it seems possible to support KiPs with a suitable CMMN implementation, and this paper provides a baseline for future research to develop CMMN execution environments to support KiPs.

References

1. Aalst, W., Berens, P.J.S.: Beyond workflow management: product-driven case handling. In: Proceedings of the 2001 International ACM SIGGROUP, pp. 42–51. ACM, New York (2001)
2. Aalst, W., Weske, M., Grunbauer, D.: Case handling: a new paradigm for business process support. Data Knowl. Eng. **53**(2), 129–162 (2005)
3. Berkley, J.D., Eccles, R.G.: Rethinking the Corporate Workplace: Case Managers at Mutual Benefit Life. Case N9–492-015, Harvard Business School, Boston, MA (1991)
4. Böhringer, M.: Emergent case management for ad-hoc processes: a solution based on microblogging and activity streams. In: Muehlen, M., Su, J. (eds.) BPM 2010 Workshops. LNBIP, vol. 66, pp. 384–395. Springer, Heidelberg (2011)
5. Burns, E.V.: Taming the Unpredictable, Real-world Adaptive Case Management: Case Studies and Practical Guidance, chap. Case Management 101: 10 Things You Must Know About Case Management, pp. 17–26. Excellence in Practice Series, Future Strategies Inc., Lighthouse Point, FL, USA (2011)
6. Clair, L.C., Moore, C., Vitti, R.: Dynamic Case Management An Old Idea Catches New Fire. Technical report, Forrester, Cambridge, MA (2009)
7. Davenport, T., Nohria, N.: Case management and the integration of labor. MIT Sloan Manage. Rev. **35**(2), 1123 (1994)
8. de Man, H., Prasad, S., van Donge, T.: Mastering the Unpredictable: How Adaptive Case Management Will Revolutionize the Way That Knowledge Workers Get Things Done, 1st edn. chap. Innovation Management, pp. 211–255. Meghan-Kiffer Press, Tampa, Florida, USA (2010)
9. Di Ciccio, C., Marrella, A., Russo, A.: Knowledge-intensive processes: characteristics requirements and analysis of contemporary approaches. J. Data Semant. **4**(1), 29–57 (2014)
10. Hauder, M., Kazman, R., Matthes, F.: Empowering end-users to collaboratively structure processes for knowledge work. In: Abramowicz, W. (ed.) BIS 2015. LNBIP, vol. 208, pp. 207–219. Springer, Heidelberg (2015)
11. Heiser, J., Lotto, R.J.D.: Introduction to Investigative Case Management Products. Techniocal Report April, Gartner, Stamford, CT (2007)
12. Kaan, K., Reijers, H.A., van der Molen, P.: Introducing case management: opening workflow management's black box. In: Dustdar, S., Fiadeiro, J.L., Sheth, A.P. (eds.) BPM 2006. LNCS, vol. 4102, pp. 358–367. Springer, Heidelberg (2006)

13. Kerremans, M.: Case Management Is a Challenging BPMS Use Case. Technical Report December, Gartner, Stamford, CT, gartner research number G00162739 (2008)
14. Kurz, M., Schmidt, W., Fleischmann, A., Lederer, M.: Leveraging CMMN for ACM: examining the applicability of a new omg standard for adaptive case management. In: Proceedings of the 7th International Conference on Subject-Oriented Business Process Management. pp. 4: 1–4: 9. S-BPM ONE 2015, NY, USA. ACM, New York (2015)
15. Marin, M.A., Brown, J.A.: Implementing a Case Management Modeling and Notation (CMMN) System using a Content Management Interoperability Services (CMIS) compliant repository, [cs.SE] (2015). arXiv:1504.06778
16. McCauley, D.: Mastering the Unpredictable: How Adaptive Case Management Will Revolutionize the Way That Knowledge Workers Get Things Done, chap. Achieving Agility 1st edn., pp. 257–275. Meghan-Kiffer Press, Tampa, Florida, USA (2010)
17. Motahari-Nezhad, H.R., Swenson, K.D.: Adaptive case management: overview and research challenges. In: Proceedings of the 2013 IEEE 15th Conference on Business Informatics, pp. 264–269. CBI 2013 (2013). http://dx.doi.org/10.1109/CBI.2013.44
18. Mundbrod, N., Kolb, J., Reichert, M.: Towards a system support of collaborative knowledge work. In: La Rosa, M., Soffer, P. (eds.) BPM Workshops 2012. LNBIP, vol. 132, pp. 31–42. Springer, Heidelberg (2013)
19. OMG: Case Management Model and Notation, version 1.0. Technical Report May, OMG, document formal/2014-05-05, May 2014
20. Palmer, N.: Mastering the Unpredictable: How Adaptive Case Management Will Revolutionize the Way That Knowledge Workers Get Things Done, chap. Introduction 1st edn., pp. 1–4. Meghan-Kiffer Press, Tampa, Florida, USA (2010)
21. Pucher, M.J.: The Difference between DYNAMIC and ADAPTIVE. https://acmisis.wordpress.com/2010/11/18/the-difference-between-dynamic-and-adaptive/. Accessed: Apr 29, 2015
22. Reijers, H.A., Rigter, J., Aalst, W.M.P.V.D.: The case handling case. Int. J. Coop. Inf. Syst. **12**(3), 365–391 (2003)
23. Strong, D.M., Miller, S.M.: Exceptions and exception handling in computerized information processes. ACM Trans. Inf. Syst. (TOIS) **13**(2), 206–233 (1995)
24. Swenson, K.D. (ed.): Mastering the Unpredictable: How Adaptive Case Management Will Revolutionize the Way That Knowledge Workers Get Things Done 1st edn. Meghan-Kiffer Press (2010)
25. Swenson, K.D.: Mastering the Unpredictable: How Adaptive Case Management Will Revolutionize the Way That Knowledge Workers Get Things Done, chap. The Nature of Knowledge Work 1st edn., pp. 5–28. Meghan-Kiffer Press, Tampa, Florida, USA (2010)
26. Swenson, K.D.: State of the Art in Case Management. white paper, Fujitsu (2013)
27. Swenson, K.D., Farris, J.: When Thinking Matters in the Workplace. Purple Hills Books, San Jose, CA, USA (2015)
28. White, M.: Case Management: Combining Knowledge With Process. Technical report, BPTrends (July 2009)

Comparing Declarative Process Modelling Languages from the Organisational Perspective

Stefan Schönig$^{(\boxtimes)}$ and Stefan Jablonski

University of Bayreuth, Universitätsstraße 30, 95447 Bayreuth, Germany
{stefan.schoenig,stefan.jablonski}@uni-bayreuth.de

Abstract. The spectrum of business processes can be divided into two types: well-structured routine processes and agile processes with control flow that evolves at run time. In a similar way, two different representational paradigms can be distinguished: procedural models and declarative models which define rules that a process has to satisfy. Agile processes can often be captured more easily using a declarative approach. While in procedural languages the organisational perspective can be modelled adequatly, in declarative languages, however, an adequate representation of organisational patterns is often still not possible. Agile processes, however, need to explicitly integrate organisational coherencies due to the importance of human decision-making. This paper presents a review of declarative modeling languages, outlines missing aspects and suggests research roadmaps for the future.

Keywords: Declarative process modelling · Organisational perspective · Process modelling languages

1 Introduction

A well accepted method for structuring the activities carried out in an organisation is business process management (BPM). BPM usually involves modelling, executing and analysing business processes [1]. The spectrum of business processes can be divided into two types [2]: well-structured routine processes with exactly predescribed control flow and agile processes with control flow that evolves at run time without being exactly predefined a priori. Agile processes are common in healthcare where, e.g., patient diagnosis and treatment processes require flexibility to cope with unanticipated circumstances. In a similar way, two different representational paradigms can be distinguished: procedural models describe which activities can be executed next and declarative models define execution constraints that the process has to satisfy. The more constraints are added to the model, the less possible execution alternatives remain. As agile processes may not be completely known a priori, they can often be captured more easily using a declarative rather than a procedural modelling approach [3–5].

Independent from a specific modeling paradigm different perspectives on a process exist [6]. The organisational perspective, often also referred to as resource

© Springer International Publishing Switzerland 2016
M. Reichert and H.A. Reijers (Eds.): BPM Workshops 2015, LNBIP 256, pp. 17–29, 2016.
DOI: 10.1007/978-3-319-42887-1_2

perspective deals with the definition and the allocation of human and non-human resources to activities [1]. In procedural process modelling languages like BPMN resource assignments can be expressed by extension languages with well-defined semantics like, e.g., the Resource Assignment Language (RAL) [7]. Furthermore, implementations like the YAWL system [8] provide rich support for the resource perspective, too. Lately, with RALph [9] even a graphical notation for defining human resource assignments in procedural process models with semantics defined in RAL has been introduced.

Due to the importance of human decision-making and expert knowledge, especially agile processes need to explicitly integrate the organisational perspective [5,10]. Unlike for procedural languages, however, the support of resource management in current declarative process modelling languages is ambiguous. While several studies of resource assignment approaches in procedural modelling languages exist [7,9], an in-depth analysis of the representation of organisational aspects in declarative process modelling languages is still missing. In this paper, we fill this gap by studying capabilities and expressiveness of existing executable declarative modelling languages and frameworks like Declare [3], the Declarative Process Intermediate Language (DPIL) [11] or the new declarative modelling standard Case Management Modelling and Notation (CMMN) [12] according to the well-known Workflow Resource Patterns (WRPs) [13]. Therefore, the contribution of this paper is a survey and comparison of modelling capabilities and insufficiencies of existing declarative process modelling languages. As an outlook we also suggest a solution approach to overcome existing issues.

The remainder of the paper is structured as follows: Sect. 2 describes the criteria, the evaluation framework and a running example. In Sect. 3, we give an in-depth analysis of the representation of the organisational perspective in well-known declarative process modelling languages. The results and possible solutions to the identified gaps are discussed in Sect. 4. Finally, Sect. 5 concludes this work.

2   Evaluation Framework and Running Example

In this section, we specify the evaluation framework that we will use for the analysis. Furthermore, we present a simplified example process to illustrate issues.

2.1   Evaluation Criteria

The expressiveness of modelling languages is assessed according to the well-known workflow resource patterns [13]. Specifically, we use the creation patterns, as they are related to resource selection. The patterns include:

- *Direct Allocation* is the ability to specify at design time the identity of the resource that will execute a task.
- *Role-Based Allocation* is the ability to specify at design time that a task can only be executed by resources that correspond to a given role.

- *Organisational Allocation* is the ability to offer or allocate activity instances to resources based their organisational position and their relationship with other resources.
- *Separation of duties* is the ability to specify that two tasks must be allocated to different resources in a given process instance.
- *Case Handling* is the ability to allocate the activity instances within a given process instance to the same resource.
- *Retain Familiar* is the ability to allocate an activity instance within a given process instance to the same resource that performed a preceding activity instance, when several resources are available to perform it. This pattern is also known as *binding of duties*.
- *Capability-Based Allocation* is the ability to offer or allocate instances of an activity to resources based on their specific capabilities.
- *Deferred Allocation* is the ability to defer specifying the identity of the resource that will execute a task until run time.
- *History-Based Allocation* is the ability to offer or allocate activity instances to resources based on their execution history.

Note that creation patterns Authorisation and Automatic Execution are not on the list. The former is excluded since it is not related to the definition of conditions for resource selection, and the latter since it is not related to the assignment language and is inherently supported by all Business Process Management Systems (BPMSs). Furthermore, we consider the direct allocation possible if a role-based allocation is supported.

In agile processes human participants are the main drivers of process execution [14]. For actors in different organisational groups frequently different rules apply. This results in different temporal dependencies between activities for different persons. In addition to resource assignment we also have to focus on patterns that relate to the control flow and the organisational perspective at the same time. These coherencies are called *cross-perspective* [15]. Cross-perspective patterns can be found in different application areas, e.g., in cases where the execution of certain process steps is bind to conditions only for certain actors. Examples are: (i) while in general work results like, e.g., documents, do not need to be checked before publication, the publication in case of trainees requires the work results to be checked in advance and (ii) while students in higher semesters can directly start lectures, new students need to complete a consulting dialogue before.

2.2   Running Example

Throughout this paper, we will use the simplyfied business trip process in a university as a running example. Some of the organisational patterns described above can be easily demonstrated by means of this simple example. For carrying out a business trip the applicant needs to fill out an application thats needs to be approved afterwards. Furthermore, at some point a flight needs to booked. Here, several organisational patterns can be identified:

- *Role-Based Allocation*: in any case the application needs to be checked and approved by an employee of the administration department.
- *Retain Familar*: the applicant himself knows circumstances and appointments best. Therefore, the flight must be booked by the applicant himself.
- *Cross-Perspective Pattern, Role-Based Sequence*: professors can book flights at any time and do not need to wait for the approval. Students, however, have to stick to a certain execution order of activities, i.e., they need to wait for the approval before a flight can be booked. Here, the control-flow is directly influenced by organisational circumstances.

3   Analysis

In this section, we analyse the capabilities of declarative process modelling languages w.r.t. the organisational patterns described in Sect. 2, i.e., resource assignment patterns as well as cross-perspective patterns. Our analysis comprises a selection of five well-known declarative process modeling languages, i.e., *Declare* [16], *DCR-Graphs* [17], *CMMN* [12], *DPIL* [11] and *EM-BrA^{2}CE* [18]. To the best of the authors knowledge this set contains the most recent *executable* and system supported rule-based process modelling languages. Recently also hybrid modelling approaches that combine procedural and declarative elements like, e.g., BPMN-D [19] or a combination of petri net and Declare modelling elements [20] have been proposed. Since these approaches only focus on control flow, organisational patterns are not yet part of the language specifications. Therefore, these languages do not need to be considered in our analysis.

3.1   Declare

Declare is a framework for modelling and executing rule-based process models. The framework allows for the definition of rule templates and languages. The most frequently used Declare languages are *ConDec* [16] and *DecSerFlow* [21]. In order to execute a model it has to be transformed to an interpretable formalism. Within Declare two formalisms have been used so far: *linear temporal logic (LTL)* and the *event calculus*. Therefore, for each rule template the formalized expression needs to be given. This way, process models can be translated into a validate and executable logical form. An example is the rule "in order to perform b, a must have been performed before" that is frequently captured by the macro *precedence(a, b)*. Additionally, Declare provides a graphical representation of rules. The *precedence* macro, e.g., is visualized by an arrow with a point. The transformation of the *precedence* macro to a LTL expression is given by $(\neg B)WA$. The symbol W, e.g., states that $\neg B$ has to hold until A occurs. For execution the LTL formula is transformed to an automaton [16]. The organisational perspective, however, is only rudimentary implemented in Declare. Independently of specific models the Declare system allows for the definition of simple organisational models, i.e., users and roles [16]. A definition of individual relations between organisational elements is not possible.

During the specification of concrete models the user can assign one or more roles to activities. At runtime, activities are then offered to users in the assigned roles for execution. Hence, Declare only allows for the definition of a direct or a role-based task allocation. More complex organisational patterns like, e.g., binding or separation of duties cannot be modelled and executed by Declare. Declare only constrains the starts of activities and interrelates them temporally. However, a rule as a whole may depend on arbitrary conditions including the data context. The rule *precedence(a, b)* with the condition $x < 3$ claims that a must have been performed before b can be started only if $x < 3$. However, a coherency like "before publication the document of a student must be reviewed by his supervisor" cannot be expressed in this way. Hence, Declare does not support cross-perspective modelling.

Figure 1 visualizes the example process in Declare. The control flow can easily be captured by a *precedence* rule between the activities "apply for trip" and "approve application". However, roles and resources are not part of the graphical notation but are defined in the Declare system. This way, "apply for trip" and "book flight" can be carried out by all the defined resources while "approve application" can only be performed by persons with role "administration". The binding of duties between application and booking cannot be modelled in Declare. Furthermore, it is not possible to combine the control flow and organisational circumstances, i.e., the fact that only students need to stick to a certain execution order cannot be modelled.

Fig. 1. Agile example process modelled in Declare

3.2   DCR-Graphs

Dynamic Condition Response-Graphs (DCR-Graphs) [17] is a declarative process modelling language similar to Declare. The graphical representation of events and rules relates to Declare. However, the number of rule templates in DCR graphs is considerably smaller than in Declare. Activities can only be connected by rules of the types *Condition, Response, Milestone, Inclusion* and *Exclusion*. Nevertheless, DCR graph models reach the same expressiveness as Declare. DCR graph models are not relying on a LTL formalism but are directly interpreted and executed based on a transformation to Buechi automatons. Like in Declare the organisational perspective in DCR graphs is limited to the definition and assignment of resources and roles [17]. Modeling of complex allocation rules is currently not possible. Since only the rule types mentioned above can be modelled between activities, cross-perspective relation are not supported, too.

Therefore, the influence of organisational coherencies on the control flow cannot be modelled in DCR graphs.

Figure 2 shows the example process in DCR graph notation. The temporal dependency between "apply for trip" and "approve application" can be modelled by a *Condition* rule that relates to a *precedence* rule in Declare. In contrast to Declare, role-based allocations are part of the graphical notation. Hence, the model shows that applications need to be approved by resources with role "administration". The binding of duties between the application and the booking as well as the cross-perspective temporal dependency between the approval and the booking cannot be modelled with DCR graphs.

Fig. 2. Agile example process modelled as DCR graph

3.3   Case Management Modeling and Notation (CMMN)

The *Case Management Model and Notation (CMMN)* [12] has been introduced by the Object Management Group (OMG) in 2013 and is based on the *Guard-Stage-Milestone (GSM)* model [22]. In CMMN a case is considered as an agile process. A case is structured into stages and contains Tasks, i.e., activities and CaseFileItems, i.e., data objects and documents. Rules are defined through so-called Sentries that form a tripel comprising an event, a condition and an action. If the specified event occurs and a certain condition is satisfied then the defined action is triggered. Here, events can refer to transitions of data objects as well as Tasks and Milestones. The condition of a Sentry, however, can only refer to data objects. CMMN neglects the organisational perspective. The potential performer of a human task can only be selected on the basis of a role and the perspective is completely missing in the graphical representation of CMMN models (diagrams). Therefore, only a direct and a role-based allocation pattern can be modelled in CMMN. Cross-perspective modelling is limited in CMMN, too. Rules may only depend on events of informational entities, i.e., case file items and activities and may only constrain the entry and exit of activities. They may not, e.g., depend on or constrain organisational aspects.

Figure 3 shows the example process in CMMN. The temporal dependency between "apply for trip" and "approve application" is modelled by a dashed arrow with a diamond (Sentry). Since CMMN only allows for the definition of roles. Hence, it can be defined that the task "approve application" must be performed by a person with role "administration". However, this is not visualized in the graphical notation. Furthermore, it is not possible to model the binding of duties. Since Sentries can only refer to Tasks and CaseFileItems, cross-perspective coherencies like the one between "apply for trip" and "book flight" cannot be modelled in CMMN.

Fig. 3. Agile example process modelled in CMMN

3.4   Declarative Process Intermediate Language (DPIL)

The textual *Declarative Process Intermediate Language (DPIL)* [11] is a multi-perspective rule-based modeling language. It allows representing several business process perspectives, namely, control flow, data and resources. The expressiveness of DPIL and its suitability for business process modelling have been evaluated [11] with respect to the Workflow Resource Patterns [13]. Some of the elements of a DPIL process model undergo a life cycle composed of events that is managed by the execution engine. A human task, e.g., can be started and completed while a data object can be read or written. Besides the static elements like human tasks and data objects, a process model may specify rules constraining that series of events. It may, e.g., claim that some data object may only be written after some task has been started. DPIL provides a textual notation based on the use of *macros* to define reusable rules. For instance, the *sequence* macro (*sequence*(a, b)) states that the existence of a *start event* of task b implies the previous occurrence of a *complete event* of task a.

In order to express organisational relations, DPIL builds upon a generic organisational meta model that has been described in [23] and is depicted in Fig. 4a. It comprises the following elements: *Identity* represents agents that can be directly assigned to activities, i.e., both human and non-human resources. *Group* represents abstract agents that may describe several identities as a whole, e.g., roles or groups. *Relation* represents the different relations (*RelationType*) that may exist between these elements. It is suitable to define, e.g., that an identity has a specific role, that a person is the boss of another person, or that a person belongs to a certain department. Figure 4b illustrates an exemplary organisational model of a university research group. It is composed of two roles (Professor, Student) assigned to three people (SJ, SS, BR) and several relations between them indicating who is supervised by whom. Based on the described organisational meta model, DPIL allows for modelling basic, i.e., direct and role-based allocation as well as more complex organisational patterns., i.e., separation and binding of duties as well as capability-based and organisational allocation patterns. Since in DPIL it is not possible to specify relations that relate

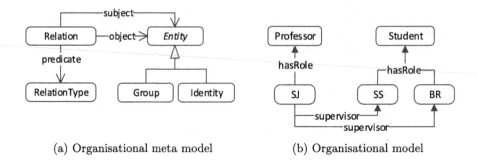

(a) Organisational meta model   (b) Organisational model

Fig. 4. Organisational meta model and example organisational model

to other process instances, the history-based allocation pattern cannot be modelled. Rules in DPIL can relate do different perspectives at the same time. Hence, cross-perspective modelling is unrestricted possible.

```
use group Administration
use group Student
use relationtype hasRole

sequence(a,b) iff start(of b at :t) implies complete(of a < t)
binding(a,b) iff start(of a by :p) and start(of b) implies start(of b by p)
role(t,r) iff start(of t by :p) implies
                relation(subject p predicate hasRole object r)
roleSequence(a,b,r) iff start(of b by :i at :t) and
                    relation(subject i predicate hasRole object r)
                    implies complete(of a at < t)

process Business Trip {
    task Apply for trip
    task Approve application
    task Book flight

    ensure sequence(Apply for trip, Approve application)
    ensure role(Approve application, Administration)
    ensure binding(Apply for trip, Book flight)
    ensure roleSequence(Approve application, Book flight, Student)
}
```

Fig. 5. Process for trip management modelled with DPIL

Figure 5 shows the example process modelled in DPIL. The first three lines refer to roles and relation types of the organisational model. In the following lines four different macros are defined, i.e., the macros *sequence*, *binding*, *role* and *roleSequence*. The *sequence* macro relates to the *precedence* template of Declare. The *role* macro defines a role-based task allocation. The *binding* macro defines the structure of a binding of duties pattern. The *roleSequence* finally depicts a cross-perspective rule template, i.e., the start of activity *b* by an actor in role *r* requires the completion of activity *a* before. The actual process model starts with the definition of the three tasks. The temporal dependency between application and approval is modelled by use of the *sequence* macro. The role-based task sequence is modelled by instantiating the *role* macro. Furthermore, the binding of duties between trip application and flight booking can be defined by the usage of the *binding* macro. The fact that only students have to stick to a certain execution order is modelled by using the *roleSequence* macro, i.e., booking a flight by a student implies the approval of the application before.

3.5   EM-BrA^{2}CE

The EM-BrA^{2}CE framework [18,24] supports declarative process modeling by relying on a vocabulary based on the OMG Semantics for Business Vocabulary and Business Rules (SBVR) specification. As the EM-BrA^{2}CE vocabulary extends the conceptual vocabularies of the SBVR, it supports the specification of highly expressive statements, concerning business concepts and rules of the organisation, the involved interacting agents and the events characterizing the execution of the systems. The SBVR specification defines a structured, english vocabulary for describing and verbalizing rules. For execution, the SBVR rules are translated to event-condition-action (ECA) rules using templates. Therefore, processes are effectively modelled using the ECA templates. The organisational perspective in EM-BrA^{2}CE implements the existing standard for Role-Based Access Control (RBAC) patterns, i.e., it is possible to model seperation and binding of duties as well as the case handling pattern. Since SBVR is used as an ontology language, agents can be described with arbitrary relations and attributes that rules can directly refer to [24]. Therefore, also capability-based and organisational allocation patterns can be expressed. Like in DPIL, modeling of history-based patterns is not possible in EM-BrA^{2}CE. The following SBVR rules depict the example process in EM-BrA^{2}CE notation:

An <u>approve application activity1</u> can only start after a <u>apply for trip activity2</u> has completed.
An <u>agent</u> that *has role* <u>administration</u> can perform <u>approve application activity</u>. It is necessary that an <u>agent</u> that *has been assigned* to an <u>apply for trip activity</u> performs a <u>book flight</u> activity.
An <u>agent</u> that *has role* <u>student</u> can only perform an <u>book flight activity1</u> after a <u>approve application activity2</u> has completed.

4   Discussion and Solution Approach

The results of the analysis are summarized in Table 1. The table highlights a considerable discrepancy between the expressiveness of graphical and textual

Table 1. Organisational patterns in declarative modelling languages

organisational Pattern	Declare	DCR	CMMN	DPIL	EM-BrA^{2}CE
Direct Allocation	✓	✓	✓	✓	✓
Role-based Allocation	✓	✓	✓	✓	✓
organisational Allocation	-	-	-	✓	✓
Separation of Duties	-	-	-	✓	✓
Case Handling	-	-	-	✓	✓
Binding of Duties	-	-	-	✓	✓
Capability-Based Allocation	-	-	-	✓	✓
Deferred Allocation	-	-	-	✓	✓
History-Based Allocation	-	-	-	-	-
Organisation-Based Control Flow (Cross-Perspective Rules)	-	-	-	✓	✓
Graphical Notation	✓	✓	✓	-	-

declarative process modelling languages. While the biggest part of organisational patterns cannot be expressed in current graphical notations, the analysed textual languages offer rich support for modelling both complex resource assignment patterns and cross-perspective coherencies. In DPIL and EM-BrA^{2}CE, only the instance spanning history-based allocation pattern cannot be expressed. However, the textual notations are generally more difficult to model and to understand. It is widely accepted that visual notations can be beneficial for system development [25]. Hence, a visual notation with well-defined semantics for declaratively modelling organisational aspects in an integrated way is convenient.

It is striking that the development of a new graphical notation is not essential. In order to bridge the gap, we propose to map an existing and well-evaluated visual notation to one of the analysed textual process modelling notations. Here, we consider the extended Compliance Rule Graphs (eCRG) [26] a appropriate candidate notation. eCRG is a visual language for modeling compliance rules that not only covers the control flow perspective, but provides integrated support for the resource perspective as well. Note, that eCRG is not an executable declarative process modelling language but represents process compliance rules. That is why the language is not considered in our analysis. In eCRG, however, it is possible to graphically model cross-perspective patterns.

Figure 6 shows the different organisational patterns of the example process depicted as a eCRG model. The binding of duties between trip application and flight booking as well as the role-based allocation for the approval task can be adequately modelled with eCRG and are visualized in Fig. 6a and b, respectively. The role-based task sequence is modelled as a eCRG model in Fig. 6c. The eCRG model states that whenever *Book flight* is performed by a *Student* then *Approve application* must have been performed before. The concrete mapping of eCRG to, e.g., DPIL should hence be up to future research.

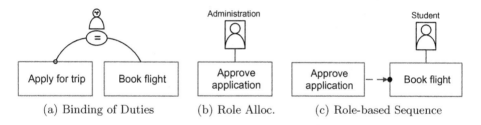

(a) Binding of Duties   (b) Role Alloc.   (c) Role-based Sequence

Fig. 6. Organisational patterns of the example process in eCRG

5   Conclusion

The work at hand presents an in-depth analysis of the support for the organisational perspective in existing declarative process modeling languages. We studied and outlined the capabilities and expressiveness of several well-known rule-based modeling languages and frameworks according to well-defined criteria and identified missing aspects. The results of our analysis show a considerable discrepancy between the capabilities of graphical and textual notations. While the biggest part of organisational patterns cannot be expressed in current graphical notations, the analysed textual languages offer rich support for modelling both complex resource assignment patterns and cross-perspective coherencies. With a language like, e.g., DPIL almost every organisational coherency can be modelled, however, it does not offer a graphical notation which is essential for a language to be adequately usable for end users. In order to close the gap, we propose to map an existing and well-evaluated visual notation to one of the analysed textual process modelling notations. Here, we consider the extended Compliance Rule Graphs (eCRG) notation as an adequate candidate. The concrete mapping of eCRG to, e.g., DPIL should hence be up to future research.

References

1. Dumas, M., Rosa, M.L., Mendling, J., Reijers, H.A.: Fundamentals of Business Process Management. Springer, Heidelberg (2013)
2. Jablonski, S.: MOBILE: A modular workflow model and architecture. In: Working Conference on Dynamic Modelling and Information Systems (1994)
3. van der Aalst, W., Pesic, M., Schonenberg, H.: Declarative workflows: Balancing between flexibility and support. Comput. Sci. Res. Dev. **23**(2), 99–113 (2009)
4. Pichler, P., Weber, B., Zugal, S., Pinggera, J., Mendling, J., Reijers, H.: Imperative versus declarative process modeling languages: An empirical investigation. Business Process Management Workshops, pp. 383–394 (2012)
5. Vaculín, R., Hull, R., Heath, T., Cochran, C., Nigam, A., Sukaviriya, P.: Declarative business artifact centric modeling of decision and knowledge intensive business processes. In: Enterprise Distributed Object Computing Conference (EDOC), no. Edoc, pp. 151–160 (2011)
6. Jablonski, S., Bussler, C.: Workflow management: modeling concepts. architecture and implementation (1996)

7. Cabanillas, C., Resinas, M., del Río-Ortega, A., Ruiz-Cortés, A.: Specification and automated design-time analysis of the business process human resource perspective. Inf. Syst. **52**, 55–82 (2015)
8. Van der Aalst, W.M., Ter Hofstede, A.H.: Yawl: yet another workflow language. Inf. Syst. **30**(4), 245–275 (2005)
9. Cabanillas, C., Knuplesch, D., Resinas, M., Reichert, M., Mendling, J., Ruiz-Cortés, A.: RALph: a graphical notation for resource assignments in business processes. In: Zdravkovic, J., Kirikova, M., Johannesson, P. (eds.) CAiSE 2015. LNCS, vol. 9097, pp. 53–68. Springer, Heidelberg (2015)
10. Van der Aalst, W.M., Weske, M., Grünbauer, D.: Case handling: a new paradigm for business process support. Data Knowl. Eng. **53**(2), 129–162 (2005)
11. Zeising, M., Schönig, S., Jablonski, S.: Towards a common platform for the support of routine and agile business processes. In: Collaborative Computing: Networking, Applications and Worksharing (2014)
12. Object Management Group (OMG). Case Management Model and Notation (CMMN), Version 1.0 (2014)
13. Russell, N., van der Aalst, W.M.P., ter Hofstede, A.H.M., Edmond, D.: Workflow resource patterns: identification, representation and tool support. In: Pastor, Ó., Falcão e Cunha, J. (eds.) CAiSE 2005. LNCS, vol. 3520, pp. 216–232. Springer, Heidelberg (2005)
14. Vaculin, R., Hull, R., Vukovic, M., Heath, T., Mills, N., Sun, Y.: Supporting collaborative decision processes. In: International Conference on Services Computing, pp. 651–658 (2013)
15. Schönig, S., Cabanillas, C., Jablonski, S., Mendling, J.: Mining the organisational perspective in agile business processes. In: Gaaloul, K., Schmidt, R., Nurcan, S., Guerreiro, S., Ma, Q. (eds.) BPMDS 2015 and EMMSAD 2015. LNBIP, vol. 214, pp. 37–52. Springer, Heidelberg (2015)
16. Pesic, M., van der Aalst, W.M.P.: A declarative approach for flexible business processes management. In: Eder, J., Dustdar, S. (eds.) BPM Workshops 2006. LNCS, vol. 4103, pp. 169–180. Springer, Heidelberg (2006)
17. Hildebrandt, T., Mukkamala, R.R., Slaats, T., Zanitti, F.: Contracts for cross-organizational workflows as timed dynamic condition response graphs. J. Logic Algebraic Program. **82**(5), 164–185 (2013)
18. Goedertier, S., Vanthienen, J.: Declarative process modeling with business vocabulary and business rules. In: Meersman, R., Tari, Z. (eds.) OTM-WS 2007, Part I. LNCS, vol. 4805, pp. 603–612. Springer, Heidelberg (2007)
19. De Giacomo, G., Dumas, M., Maggi, F.M., Montali, M.: Declarative process modeling in bpmn, In press (2015)
20. Westergaard, M., Slaats, T.: Mixing paradigms for more comprehensible models. In: Daniel, F., Wang, J., Weber, B. (eds.) BPM 2013. LNCS, vol. 8094, pp. 283–290. Springer, Heidelberg (2013)
21. van der Aalst, W.M.P., Pesic, M.: DecSerFlow: towards a truly declarative service flow language. In: Bravetti, M., Núñez, M., Zavattaro, G. (eds.) WS-FM 2006. LNCS, vol. 4184, pp. 1–23. Springer, Heidelberg (2006)
22. Hull, R., Damaggio, E., Fournier, F., Gupta, M., Heath III, F.T., Hobson, S., Linehan, M., Maradugu, S., Nigam, A., Sukaviriya, P., Vaculin, R.: Introducing the guard-stage-milestone approach for specifying business entity lifecycles. In: Bravetti, M. (ed.) WS-FM 2010. LNCS, vol. 6551, pp. 1–24. Springer, Heidelberg (2011)
23. Bussler, C.: Organisationsverwaltung in Workflow-Management-Systemen. Dt. Univ.-Verlag (1998)

24. Goedertier, S.: Declarative techniques for modeling and mining business processes. Ph.D. thesis, Katholieke Universiteit Leuven (2008)
25. Whittle, J., Hutchinson, J., Rouncefield, M.: The state of practice in model-driven engineering. Softw. IEEE **31**(3), 79–85 (2014)
26. Semmelrodt, F., Knuplesch, D., Reichert, M.: Modeling the resource perspective of business process compliance rules with the extended compliance rule graph. In: Bider, I., Gaaloul, K., Krogstie, J., Nurcan, S., Proper, H.A., Schmidt, R., Soffer, P. (eds.) BPMDS 2014 and EMMSAD 2014. LNBIP, vol. 175, pp. 48–63. Springer, Heidelberg (2014)

A Case Modelling Language for Process Variant Management in Case-Based Reasoning

Riccardo Cognini[2], Knut Hinkelmann[1,4], and Andreas Martin[1,3(✉)]

[1] School of Business, FHNW University of Applied Sciences
and Arts Northwestern Switzerland, Olten, Switzerland
{knut.hinkelmann,andreas.martin}@fhnw.ch
[2] Computer Science Department, School of Science and Technology,
University of Camerino, Camerino, Italy
riccardo.cognini@unicam.it
[3] School of Computing, University of South Africa,
Florida Park, Roodepoort, Johannesburg, South Africa
[4] Department of Informatics, University of Pretoria, Pretoria, South Africa

Abstract. Conventional business process management has been very successful for routine work but has deficiencies in dealing with the flexibility of knowledge workers' work, since the tasks are hard to determine and highly dependent on the current situation. For knowledge workers it is useful to structure the processes just in part as process variants, which can be adapted, modified and even newly created at runtime by them. This paper describes an application of a case-based reasoning approach and introduces a process variant modelling language that supports the manual generation and refinement of generalized process variants. This approach is demonstrated in a public administration scenario.

Keywords: Case modelling · Modelling language · Process flexibility · Knowledge work · Case-based reasoning · Adaptive Case Management

1   Introduction

Knowledge work cannot be represented sufficiently in traditional business process management, where the work is structured and described in advance. It is especially difficult to predict upcoming tasks because knowledge work can deal with different requirements at the same time. Type and scope of tasks are hard to determine in advance, while sequence of tasks and even the tasks themselves may vary due to already achieved results and unforeseeable events. Knowledge work is not routine work, and "[...] the sequence of actions depends so much upon the specifics of the situation [...] necessitating that part of doing the work is to make the plan itself" [1, p. 8]. It is not always possible to define the whole structure including all elements of a knowledge-intensive process at build-time or just before instantiation.

For knowledge work it seems useful to take approaches that structure the BP just in part as process fragments since no fully defined models can be easily

© Springer International Publishing Switzerland 2016
M. Reichert and H.A. Reijers (Eds.): BPM Workshops 2015, LNBIP 256, pp. 30–42, 2016.
DOI: 10.1007/978-3-319-42887-1_3

adapted/modified at runtime by the users [2]. "Process fragments are reflecting the partial and intermittent knowledge one modeller [or a knowledge worker] has at a certain time about a specific situation" [3, p. 399]. Knowledge workers are required to make decisions based on process fragments, which can only be made by the knowledge workers themselves, given the process elements that can only be executed by humans (see e.g., case management model and notation human tasks [4]). In the past, related work introduced sophisticated similarity and adaptation mechanisms, such as case-based reasoning (CBR), which provides huge reasoning power to support process flexibility. Unfortunately, no significant attention has been paid to knowledge workers' need to model process fragments, which require human decision, using CBR during run-time. *Therefore, a CBR vocabulary and case content representation (modelling language) are needed that support the manual planning, modelling, generation and refinement of process fragments during run-time.*

Case-based reasoning (CBR) is a technologically independent methodology that uses the knowledge of previously experienced situations and its solution, to propose a potential solution to a new situation (the current problem) [5]. CBR has been applied in business process contexts, e.g., for workflow retrieval, adaptation, construction and monitoring (see [6–8]). Existing work mainly focuses on the management of structured and predictable business processes. Some related work supports ad-hoc changes of workflows; several sophisticated similarity and adaptation mechanisms and frameworks were developed recently. CBR is originally designed to retrieve, reuse, revise and retain concrete cases for a specific situation [9]. Based on the original notion of CBR, some researchers investigated the generalization and abstraction of cases [10]. This can reduce the complexity of the cases, increase the flexibility and reduce the size of the case base to enhance the retrieval efficiency [9]. Abstraction differs from generalization. According to Mueller and Bergmann [8, p. 396], "[...] abstraction [...] would require reducing the overall granularity of workflows (e.g. less tasks and data items) [...]". This differentiation is particular important when implementing an automatic algorithm.

This work focuses on the man-made modelling of cases without a requirement of reducing the granularity of process fragments depending on the variety of the situation of the knowledge workers. *Therefore, this paper describes the application of a CBR approach and introduces a case-based process fragment modelling language named Business Process Feature Model (BPFM) that supports the manual generation and refinement of generalized cases.* This approach can be appropriately demonstrated in a specific application scenario. In the following we describe a process fragment modelling language that differs from existing work for representing the case content that is appropriate to variants.

2   Application Scenario

In this section we present an application scenario in order to show how to use BPFM as case content representation (modelling language).

The application scenario is the master study admission process of the FHNW. Figure 1 shows the process model in BPMN 2.0. The admission process starts when an application has arrived. In a first activity the study assistant prepares the eligibility check. He collects and prepares all the information in order to allow the dean of the programme to check the eligibility of the candidate. In the case the candidate is eligible, she/he is invited for an oral interview. Otherwise, a rejection letter is sent. If after the interview the candidate is accepted, the administration department determines the tuition fee. At the end an acceptance letter is sent to the candidates. If the candidate is not eligible, a rejection letter is sent.

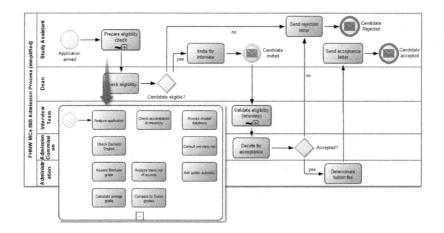

Fig. 1. Master study admission process including prepare eligibility check

Although this process looks like a structured process, the activity *Prepare eligibility check* is a complex knowledge intensive sub-process. In interviews with the stakeholder, the following activities are identified, which are modelled in Fig. 1 as sub-process: It is determined whether the bachelor degree qualifies for the master programme. Because candidates can come from different countries, there can be a huge variety of degrees and certificates. If the bachelor degree is unknown, the transcript of record is analysed. The university from which the candidate earned the bachelor degree is checked for accreditation. If the university is unknown to the study assistant, the study assistant can access a database called Anabin. Furthermore, many countries have a list of accredited universities on the Web. Access to them is provided via enic-naric.net. There are several other databases and online resources. The selection of the appropriate resource depends on the country. If the university cannot be found in any resource, the study assistant can ask a public authority for confirmation. The eligibility furthermore depends on the average grade of the bachelor degree, which must be at least "B". If the average grade is not mentioned in the transcript of records, it is calculated by the study assistant. For unknown grading systems one has to find out how it compares to Swiss grades.

It is not clear in advance which activities are required or in which order they are executed. By analysis of a number of cases of the application scenario, we derived research objectives for the CBR approach, especially (1) the modelling of the case content and (2) its characterization. In the terminology of CBR, the characterisation can be regarded as the problem description (of the situation) and the case content can be regarded as the solution or lesson [11], which consists of at least one knowledge item (e.g., documents, processes, etc.) [12].

Demanding Example for Current Modelling Languages. In the following we describe three possible instances of the activity *Prepare eligibility check*. They are real cases derived from the application scenario, pointing out specific aspects that challenge existing modelling approaches. The cases as shown in Figs. 2, 3 and 4 are different solutions to the problem involving a candidate coming from an unknown university.

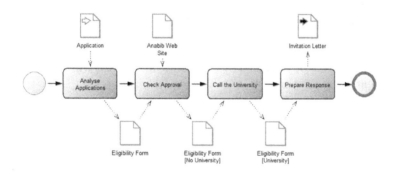

Fig. 2. Case A

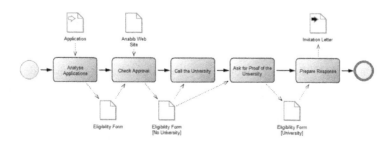

Fig. 3. Case B

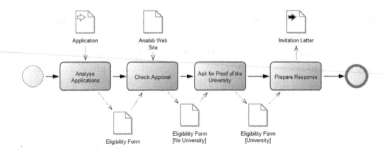

Fig. 4. Case C

In the first case (Fig. 2) the problem is solved by calling the university of the applicant student asking for some information. In the second case (Fig. 3) the university is called and then proof of the existence of the university. In the last case (Fig. 4) just the proof of the of existence of the university is requested.

The described cases are similar, and each one of them can be used to solve the problem. In all the cases there is some implicit knowledge missing. Even though the CBR case description (not shown in figures) can be considered, it is not possible, e.g., to recognize immediately the conditions that lead to a certain decision. To make decisions visible and to present alternative flows, a generalized case could potentially be modelled by the knowledge worker, which might be also abstracted at the same time.

3   Approach Comparison

From our experience BPMN or any other imperative or BPMN-like language seems to be unsuitable to represent cases in the CBR system. In [13], the author gives some motivations specifying why BPMN could not be used for BP modelling in Adaptive Case Management systems; this motivation is also valid in the CBR context.

The end users of a CBR system do not have enough knowledge and skills to model or update a BPMN model. Generally, end users are able to specify which activities should be performed, defining how one has to perform them, but they are not able to establish a temporal order of these activities since they are focused just on their own tasks. In addition, we also have to consider that modifying a BPMN diagram modelled by someone else can be a difficult task like modifying a software source code. Another issue of imperative languages in this context is that they are designed to express something that is fully defined including all the possible aspects of a BP.

In order to deal with BP that cannot be fully defined in recent years, the OMG designed the Case Management Model and Notation (CMMN) language [4]. In contrast to BPMN 2.0, CMMN is a declarative language designed to model no predefined, partially structured and no repeatable BPs. Mandatory and optional activities can be modelled without specifying an execution order or specifying the

Table 1. Comparison of modelling languages

	BPMN	CMMN	DECLARE	BPFM
For BP modelling	Yes	Yes	Yes	Yes
Language type	Imperative	Declarative	Declarative	Declarative
Defined activities flow	Full	In part	In part	In part
Complex constraints	Yes	No	No	Yes
Data representation	Yes	In part	No	Yes
Variants representation	No	No	No	Yes

situation in which an activity can be executed. In our opinion, the main issue of CMMN is that it is not possible to specify complex execution criteria. For instance, it is not possible to specify at least one of the activities in a set has to be executed. Constraints to specify such situation should be defined in order to model more detailed cases. Another issue of CMMN is that no complex data elements are provided; it implies that just little information about the type of data or document will be available to the performers during the execution of a case. This issue affect also other declarative languages [2] such as DECLARE [14], which is a notation designed to support loosely structured BPs.

To deal with these issues we propose the use of BPFM notation as a language for case representation in CBR. BPFM notation permits defining the BP activities that must or can be performed without including, or including only partially, an execution order of them considering complex constraints and different types of data objects. Furthermore, a BPFM model is a Configurable Process Model since it can encapsulate more than one BP variant. A BP variant can also be easily extracted via the process configuration step. Table 1 summarizes the comparison of BPFM with the other languages.

4 The Approach

4.1 Business Process Feature Model Notation

A Business Process Feature Model is constituted by a tree of related activities [15]. The root identifies the service under analysis as well as the family of the BPs behind of the service itself. Each internal (non-leaf) activity denotes a subprocess that can be further refined, and the external (leaf) activity represents an atomic task. To better specify how to execute tasks, BPFM allows one to type them using the same meaning and graphical representation given by BPMN 2.0. A BPFM model allows for the defining of constraints between activities in two adjacent levels of the tree. Constraints are used to express (i) if child activities can or have to be selected in the configuration to be included in the BP variant, and (ii) if they can or have to be included in each execution path of the BP variant, considering in this way the static and dynamic (run-time) inclusion of the activities. Depending on the type, each constraint has only one father activity, and it can have one (binary constraints) or more (multiple constraints) child activities. Constraints are described as follows.

- A *Mandatory Constraint* requires that the connected child activity be inserted in each BP variant, and it must also be included in each execution path (Fig. 5A).
- An *Optional Constraint* allows for the connected child activity to be inserted (or not) in each BP variant, and it could be included (or not) in each execution path (Fig. 5B).
- A *Domain Constraint* requires that the connected child activity be inserted in each BP variant, but it could be included (or not) in each execution path (Fig. 5C).
- A *Special Case Constraint* allows for the connected child activity to be inserted (or not) in each BP variant. When it is inserted it has to be included in each execution path (Fig. 5D).
- An *Inclusive Constraint* requires that at least one of the connected child activities be inserted in each BP variant, and at least one of them must be included in each execution path (Fig. 5E).
- A *One Optional Constraint* requires that exactly one of the connected child activities be inserted in each BP variant, and it could be included (or not) in each execution path (Fig. 5F).
- A *One Selection Constraint* requires that exactly one of the connected child activities be inserted in each BP variant, and it has to be included in each execution path (Fig. 5G).
- An *XOR Constraint* requires that all the connected child activities be inserted in each BP variant, and exactly one of them has to be included in each execution path (Fig. 5H).
- An *XOR Selection Constraint* requires that at least one of the connected child activities be inserted in each BP variant, and exactly one of them has to be included in each execution path (Fig. 5I).

Finally, *Include* and *Exclude* relationships between activities are also considered according to the base definition of FM (Fig. 5J and K).

(A) (B) (C) (D) (E) (F) (G) (H) (I) (J) (K)

Fig. 5. BPFM constraints

BPFM notation gives also the possibility to model Data Objects since each BP variant could include completely different sets of Data Objects [16]. BPFM manages all types of Data Objects introduced by BPMN 2.0 and uses the same graphical representation. As well as in BPMN 2.0, Data Objects can be connected as inputs and outputs to one or more activities (Fig. 6A). In modelling Data

Objects we also give the possibility to include information concerning the state. Therefore an activity can require or can generate a Data Object in a specific state. A Data Object cannot be in two different states at the same time (Fig. 6B).

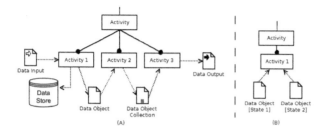

Fig. 6. Data object in BPFM.

4.2 BPFM in Case-Based Reasoning

In traditional CBR terminology, a case consists of a *problem* description that is used for describing a *solution* [11]. Based on Bergmann [11], we extended this CBR terminology in such a way that the solution is denoted as *case content*, which contains not only the solution itself but also information that is useful to find a solution. To describe the case content we are using the term *case characterisation* based on Bergmann [11, p. 50], which enriches the classical problem with additional information, e.g. "derived descriptions or properties that were not present in the problem solving situations from which the experience emerges".

Case Content Containing Process Knowledge. The introduced modelling language Business Process Feature Model (BPFM) provides the expressiveness to tackle the objectives for case content. In addition to the BPFM elements, the following case content elements are used to describe case inter-relationships:

- *ParentTask*: The parent task element is used to express a possible sub-task/case relationship.
- *ChildTask*: The child task element is the inverse of the parent task element.
- *RelatedTask*: This element is used to express that there exist related tasks.
- *ReusedTask*: The reused task element is used to list tasks, which have been (re)used in the adaptation phase of CBR.

Adapting Case Models. The BPFM modelling approach allows for a flexible adaptation of cases. Assume that during execution of the case model it turns out that the case model needs to be adapted. Standard CBR *revises* the case model and *retains* it as a new case. This new case is independent from all the other cases. The information that it is a variant of an already existing case is lost. Using BPFM this dependency could be made explicit. Instead of storing a new case, the user can adapt the current case model by adding a child/parent task, related task or reused task.

Case Characterisation Describing Process Knowledge. Figure 7 shows a partition of the case characterisation configuration including elements of the process and domain knowledge using the ontology-based, case-based reasoning (OBCBR) approach of Martin et al. [17].

In brief, the reused approach of Martin et al. [17] provides a wide range on similarity functions for *retrieval* and *adaptation*. As shown in Fig. 7, the *similarity configuration* is made in an RDFS ontology using specific concepts that are *attached to the properties*.

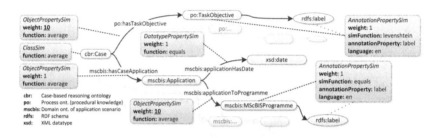

Fig. 7. Exemplary configuration of the case characterisation

The vocabulary for describing the cases is domain specific and therefore different from one application scenario to another. Considering the objectives from the application scenario and the results of the task management system KISSmir introduced by Martin and Brun [18] and Brander et al. [19], we could derive the following basic domain independent vocabulary elements:

- *TaskObjective*: The task objective element describes the goal of the task itself. This is similar to the name and/or description of an BPMN activity.
- *TaskRole*: The task role element is used to describe the role of the involved person of the task. Through the inclusion of an enterprise or domain ontology, it is possible to reuse an existing enterprise specific role/organisational model.
- *TaskUser*: The task user elements is used to indicate the person who described the case.

5   Demonstration and Evaluation

We represented all the cases of the application scenario described in Sect. 2 using BPFM. For the sake of space, in this paper we present only the two cases. In particular, Fig. 8A shows a case in which a student has all the hallmarks to be eligible but graduates (bachelor degree) in a foreign university that is not stored in the Anabib website (it is related to the cases represented in Sect. 2). Conversely, Fig. 8B shows a case in which a student cannot be eligible since he has just a three-year degree in commerce taken in South Africa. The activities of the example case in Fig. 8A are described as follows. *Analysis Applications* is a mandatory atomic activity in which the application is analysed by the study assistant. *Things to Check* is a mandatory composed activity in which some checks are done in order to approve or reject the application. In this case, it is composed by two sub-activities, which are:

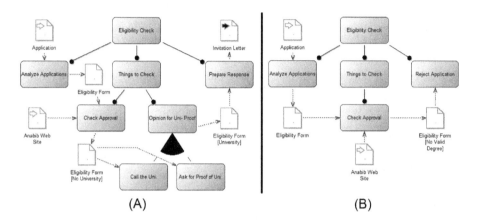

Fig. 8. BPFM model of cases related to the application scenario

- *Check Approval* is a mandatory atomic activity in which the study assistant checks if the final degree university is in the Anabin website and if it is acceptable. In this case, the university is not stored in the Anabib website.
- *Option for Uni. Proof* is a mandatory composed activity in which the study assistant has to have a proof of existence of the Final Degree University. It is composed by two sub-activities connected via an Inclusive Constraint, which means three possible solution variants can be applied. These sub-activities are: *Phone Call to University* in which the study assistant calls the university to be sure that it exists, and *Ask for Proof of University* in which the study assistant asks to the applicant student a proof of the existence of the university.

Prepare Response is a mandatory atomic activity in which the study assistant prepares the invitation letter for the meeting with the eligible student.

The activities of the example case in Fig. 8B are described as follows. *Analysis Applications* is a mandatory atomic activity in which the application is analysed by the study assistant. *Things to Check* is a mandatory composed activity in which some check are done in order to approve or reject the Application. In this case, it is composed by just one sub-activity:

- *Check Approval* as described above.

Reject Application is a mandatory atomic activity in which the study assistant rejects the application.

Since the described cases are similar, using the BPFM notation can be encapsulated in a single BPFM model including their commonalities and variabilities. To do that, we include all the activities and data objects that the two previous BPFM models include. This is shown in Fig. 9. As the reader can see, the activity *Option for Uni. Proof* is now connected to the father activity via a *Special Case Constraint* since it has to be available even if the university is not in the Anabin website (the case in Fig. 8A). In the figure, the activity *Response* and the related *One Selection Constraint* were added in order to distinguish the two different types of outcomes. In fact, if the candidate is eligible, the activity *Prepare Response* has to be available (the case in Fig. 8A), otherwise the activity *Reject Application* must be available (the case in Fig. 8B).

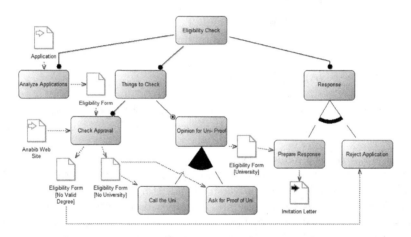

Fig. 9. Cases in Fig. 8 joined in a single BPFM model

The case characterisation contains the elements of the basic vocabulary as introduced in Sect. 4.2 and the domain specific elements of the application scenario ontology. In addition to the basic elements, the following domain specific concepts were used:

- *Person*: The person concept is used to identify the applicant and its *Role*. Apart from that it is linked to the following elements:
  - The *AcademicQualification* is divided into the *Degree* (e.g., Bachelor), *DegreeType* (e.g., Science), *DegreeSubject* (e.g., Information Systems) and the *FinalDegreeUniversity* (e.g., FHNW), where the degree has been awarded.

- The applicant has to show its *LanguageCompetence* and adequate *ProfessionalExperience*.
- Finally, the *Nationality* and *Residence* information is captured.
- *Application*: The application concept contains *AdditionalInformation* and the reference to the *Programme* where the applicant applies for.

6 Conclusion and Future Work

CBR case representation is an aspect that needs to be taken into account more in knowledge-intensive BPs. This paper presented an approach to model cases in knowledge-intensive BPs. The approach merges CBR with BPFM notation in order to represent cases. We applied the approach to a concrete case in a public administration scenario in order to show its suitability.

In the future, we will deal with the granularity of the BPFM case models. On one extreme, a manager could make only one bpFM model representing all the cases. In this case the BPFM is adapted, and then CBR is not needed. On the other hand, a manager could represent each case as a separate model. But, in this case, variants are not a need. To find the appropriate granularity we plan to make further evaluation in the application scenario and also test it in a new scenario.

References

1. Swenson, K.D., Palmer, N., Silver, B.: Taming the Unpredictable Real World Adaptive Case Management: Case Studies and Practical Guidance. Future Strategies Inc., New York (2011)
2. Reichert, M., Weber, B.: Enabling Flexibility in Process-Aware Information Systems: Challenges, Methods, Technologies. Springer, Heidelberg (2012)
3. Eberle, H., Unger, T., Leymann, F.: Process fragments. In: Meersman, R., Dillon, T., Herrero, P. (eds.) OTM 2009, Part I. LNCS, vol. 5870, pp. 398–405. Springer, Heidelberg (2009)
4. OMG: case management model and notation (CMMN), Version 1.0., May 2014
5. Aamodt, A., Plaza, E.: Case-based reasoning: foundational issues, methodological variations, and system approaches. AI Commun. **7**(1), 39–59 (1994)
6. Madhusudan, T., Zhao, J., Marshall, B.: A case-based reasoning framework for workflow model management. Data Knowl. Eng. **50**(1), 87–115 (2004)
7. Minor, M., Bergmann, R., Görg, S.: Case-based adaptation of workflows. Inf. Syst. **40**, 142–152 (2014)
8. Müller, G., Bergmann, R.: Generalization of workflows in process-oriented case-based reasoning. In: The 28th International FLAIRS Conference, At Hollywood, Florida, USA, pp. 391–396 (2015)
9. Bergmann, R., Wilke, W.: On the role of abstraction in case-based reasoning. In: Smith, I., Faltings, B.V. (eds.) EWCBR 1996. LNCS, vol. 1168, pp. 28–43. Springer, Heidelberg (1996)
10. Maximini, K., Maximini, R., Bergmann, R.: An investigation of generalized cases. In: Ashley, K.D., Bridge, D.G. (eds.) ICCBR 2003. LNCS, vol. 2689, pp. 261–275. Springer, Heidelberg (2003)

11. Bergmann, R.: Experience Management: Foundations, Development Methodology, and Internet-Based Applications. LNAI, vol. 2432. Springer, Heidelberg (2002)
12. Bergmann, R., Schaaf, M.: Structural case-based reasoning and ontology-based knowledge management: a perfect match? J. Univ. Comput. Sci. **9**(7), 608–626 (2003)
13. Swenson, K.D.: Position: BPMN is incompatible with ACM. In: La Rosa, M., Soffer, P. (eds.) BPM Workshops 2012. LNBIP, vol. 132, pp. 55–58. Springer, Heidelberg (2013)
14. Pesic, M., Schonenberg, H., Van der Aalst, W.M.: Declare: full support for loosely-structured processes. In: 11th IEEE International Enterprise Distributed Object Computing Conference (EDOC 2007), p. 287. IEEE (2007)
15. Cognini, R., Corradini, F., Polini, A., Re, B.: Extending feature models to express variability in business process models. In: Persson, A., Stirna, J. (eds.) CAiSE 2015 Workshops. LNBIP, vol. 215, pp. 245–256. Springer, Heidelberg (2015)
16. Cognini, R., Corradini, F., Polini, A., Re, B.: Using data-object flow relations to derive control flow variants in configurable business processes. In: Business Process Management Workshops - BPM 2014 International Workshops, Eindhoven, The Netherlands, September 7–8, 2014, Revised Papers, pp. 210–221 (2014)
17. Martin, A., Emmenegger, S., Wilke, G.: Integrating an enterprise architecture ontology in a case-based reasoning approach for project knowledge. In: Proceedings of the First International Conference on Enterprise Systems (ES 2013), pp. 1–12. IEEE, November 2013
18. Martin, A., Brun, R.: Agile process execution with KISSmir. In: 5th International Workshop on Semantic Business Process Management collocated with 7th Extended Semantic Web Conference, Heraklion, Greece (2010)
19. Brander, S., Hinkelmann, K., Hu, B., Martin, A., Riss, U.V., Thönssen, B., Witschel, H.F.: Refining process models through the analysis of informal work practice. In: Rinderle-Ma, S., Toumani, F., Wolf, K. (eds.) BPM 2011. LNCS, vol. 6896, pp. 116–131. Springer, Heidelberg (2011)

Embracing Process Compliance and Flexibility Through Behavioral Consistency Checking in ACM

A Repair Service Management Case

Thanh Tran Thi Kim[1]([✉]), Erhard Weiss[1], Christoph Ruhsam[1], Christoph Czepa[2], Huy Tran[2], and Uwe Zdun[2]

[1] ISIS Papyrus Europe AG, Maria Enzersdorf, Austria
{thanh.tran,erhard.weiss,christoph.ruhsam}@isis-papyrus.com
[2] Research Group Software Architecture, University of Vienna, Vienna, Austria
{christoph.czepa,huy.tran,uwe.zdun}@univie.ac.at

Abstract. Enabling flexibility in unpredictable situations with ad hoc actions decided at runtime by knowledge workers is the main focus of Adaptive Case Management (ACM) systems. However, ad hoc actions added during case execution and ACM templates prepared at design time need to be within the boundaries defined by business constraints, company regulations and legal systems. In this paper we report our experience in addressing this challenge by using model checking and runtime monitoring techniques for behavioral consistency checking that can handle both ACM aspects: support by means of predefined process templates and high flexibility by allowing ad hoc actions at runtime. Our study is conducted using a practical ACM system for repair service management handling different customer requirements under diverse compliance and law regulations.

Keywords: Adaptive Case Management · ISIS papyrus ACM solution · Consistency checking · Compliance checking · Business process management · Compliance rules

1 Introduction

A challenge of business process management (BPM) systems is to react on spontaneous or short time process adaptions due to changing business conditions. The rigidness of process definitions and the involved bureaucracy with change management cycles are hindering process innovation. Although many different approaches have been suggested to enhance the flexibility of BPM systems, most of them have not managed to escape from the restrictive nature of the approach [1, 2]. ACM is proposed in the context of knowledge intensive and content centric work. The ACM principle "design-by-doing" allows users acting as knowledge workers (KW) to evolve processes embracing both, support of predictable business scenarios by using well-defined sub-processes and unpredictable scenarios by allowing ad hoc actions and changes during runtime.

A rigid process configuration aims to ensure that business operation is under control and satisfies the compliance requirements related to law and regulations. Thus, process

© Springer International Publishing Switzerland 2016
M. Reichert and H.A. Reijers (Eds.): BPM Workshops 2015, LNBIP 256, pp. 43–54, 2016.
DOI: 10.1007/978-3-319-42887-1_4

validation needs to consider both, the process model (syntactical consistency) and the compliance requirements (semantic consistency) [3]. As a consequence of the evolving nature of ACM cases with ad hoc actions it is unclear how to ensure the process compliance within the constraints imposed on the business operation by compliance requirements. There are numerous techniques for checking and handling inconsistencies for well-defined business processes [4].

In our study, the compliance requirements are described using temporal logics, represented in terms of high-level specification patterns [5]. As the KWs involved in our studies found temporal logics unfamiliar to their domain of expertise, we devise a simple high-level domain-specific constraint language that is close to natural language to help the KWs in describing compliance requirements defined as compliance rules. These are automatically translated into temporal logics to be verified for any potential inconsistencies by powerful model checkers and runtime monitoring engines. We report in this paper the first attempt in applying well-known formal modeling and verification techniques to support KWs in ensuring business compliance in ACM. Our experience is based on applying consistency checking techniques to an ACM solution for repair service management (RSM) in the ISIS Papyrus ACM system [6]. In RSM, diverse requirements from a broad variety of customers have to comply with a vast range of different laws and regulations. The multiplicity of possible requirements, constraints and exceptions cannot be efficiently covered alone by predefined processes. Depending on particular cases, the repair service officer, i.e. the KW, decides on specific conditions and work lists corresponding to the requirements of the customer and the discovered circumstances. Still, the KW needs to act in compliance defined by company rules and laws because violations permanently jeopardize the business and its economical reputation. Since rules must be considered at runtime and design time, compliance checking must apply for ad hoc actions as well as templates.

Our work is related to existing studies in the domain of verification of business processes at design or runtime and to specification languages for the definition of business rules. Liu et al. propose a framework for model checking of business processes at design time that transforms process models into Finite State Machines (FSM) and translates constraints from a graphical specification language into LTL [7]. Namiri et al. translate temporal logic patterns to Event-Condition-Action rules and perform runtime verification [8]. An approach presented by Awad et al. aims at checking compliance of business process models using a visual query language BPMN-Q with recurring patterns like 'leads to' and 'precedes' to describe constraints and performing model checking to assure constraints are satisfied [9]. Van der Aalst et al. proposes an approach for checking LTL properties against an event log [10]. Complex Event Processing (CEP) is used for compliance monitoring in the context of service-oriented architectures (SOA) [11, 12]. The vast amount of existing studies in this field affirms the need for research and contributions, especially in the area of runtime verification [13]. We are neither aware of previous studies that proposed a unified checking approach based on model checking and CEP for the verification of ACM cases at runtime and design time nor of existing experience reports on handling business compliance in the context of ACM.

The remainder of our paper is organized as follows: Sect. 2 introduces our concept for consistency checking as applied to the ISIS Papyrus ACM system. The configuration

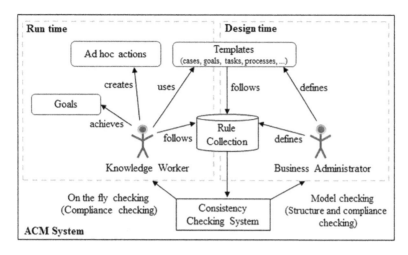

Fig. 1. The ISIS papyrus ACM environment with consistency checking

process for behavioral consistency checking is described in Sect. 3. Section 4 describes our experience of applying the checking in the RSM application. Finally, Sect. 5 discusses the lessons learned and concludes the paper.

2 Concepts of Consistency Checking in ACM

2.1 Overview of ACM

ACM cases are driven by goals which are in combination with tasks the core ACM elements. A significant feature of ACM systems is that the main actor, i.e. the KW, is empowered to handle events that are unpredictable or even never happened before. KWs use their implicit knowledge stemming from experience as well as from assessments and research of the current situation to react flexibly to new requirements in daily work within a permanently evolving business environment. To support KWs in such situations, ACM provides (a) automation of routine work by sub-processes which are predefined at design time and executed in the defined order and (b) flexibility by the free design of activities and their sequences through ad hoc goals and tasks which are added at runtime by the KW [14, 15]. Goals are achieved by completing its sub-processes and/or ad hoc tasks and a case closes when all its goals are reached.

2.2 Consistency Checking Applied to the ISIS Papyrus ACM System

Figure 1 shows an overview of the approach taken in this paper: The ISIS Papyrus ACM system is enhanced with a consistency checking system to ensure that the ACM case definition at design time and its evolution at runtime do not violate structural and/or behavioral consistency.

Consistency is regulated by a set of constraints formulated by compliance rules stored in a rule collection, which are expressed in natural language by business administrators. At design time, business administrators define goal and task templates, and link them with related compliance rules. Consistency checking is done in a twofold way: (a) The structural and behavioral consistency of templates is verified by using model checking alerting the administrator in case of violations. As model checking is computationally expensive and demands well-defined case models, it suits a design time approach. (b) The focus of this paper is on compliance checking at runtime, when KWs create ad hoc actions to reach a goal. These are verified by on-the-fly checking, which operates on the current execution trace of a running case instance and is based on CEP [16] providing real time feedback in case of constraint violations by alerting KWs performing ad hoc changes at runtime.

As shown in Fig. 2, compliance rules from different sources are imposed on the execution of ACM cases which are related to laws, contracts with business partners, general standards, best practices and company internal regulations. A usually underestimated source is coming from tacit business knowledge of the KWs [17].

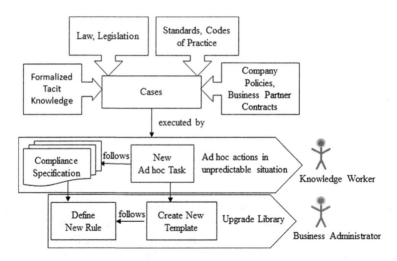

Fig. 2. Definition and maintenance of compliance rules in ACM systems

In real life, there are basically two scenarios where compliance rules have to influence the case execution:

1. Unpredictable situations: (1.1) In such cases, there are typically not yet suitable templates available. Thus, the KW creates ad hoc actions from generic templates and takes the responsibility that the ad hoc actions comply with constraints, that must be followed [18]. (1.2) Applying the best practice principle, business administrators and/or empowered KWs create new templates from case instances, which proofed that case goals where repeatedly satisfyingly reached. Additionally, new compliance rules, which were discovered in (1.1) will be added to the rule collection. This way,

knowledge is preserved in the system to support KWs the next time when such situations occur.

2. Predictable scenarios: Alternatively, new situations, which a company plans to deal with, can be analyzed and prepared in advance by business administrators. The necessary templates and associated compliance rules are added to the system similar to (1.2) above, before KWs will start to work on such cases.

In both (1.2) and (2) the business administrators benefit from compliance checking as they will receive alerts during design time if certain constraints are violated.

We have successfully applied a User Trained Agent [19] to suggest best next actions to KWs in ad hoc situations that are similar to previously handled cases. In the context of behavioral consistency checking it is important that the UTA builds its knowledge on compliant ad hoc actions. Thus, the definition of compliance rules is important in the maintenance of ACM systems.

3   Configuration Process for Behavioral Consistency Checking

Figure 3 shows a configuration process for applying the behavioral consistency checking in ACM. The process includes two phases: (a) translating the compliance specifications stemming from different sources from natural language into compliance rules expressed in a constraint language, (b) assigning compliance rules to templates.

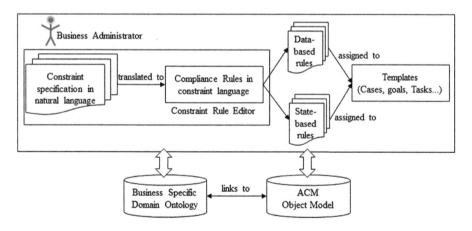

Fig. 3. Configuration process for behavioral consistency checking in ACM systems

Allowing business people to define such rules in natural language, a constraint rule editor is supplied, supporting business terms defined by business domain specific ontologies. It is built upon temporal logic patterns to support the definition of consistency requirements [5, 20]. The rules are linked to ACM elements which are mapped by business domain specific ontologies to the underlying ACM object model. This way, new templates (goals, tasks) being adjusted to new requirements are affected by existent compliance rules, as they are mapped with the associated ontology concepts. Depending on the scope of rules, they are stored in a rule collection for later reuse in several templates or embedded into specific cases. Compliance rules defined within our study are classified into two types which are created for different situations:

(a) State-based rules define the sequence of actions purely based on the state of tasks or goals. For example *TaskB* must start after completion of *TaskA*.

(b) Data-based rules explicitly involve data in the rule definition. An example is *TaskA.Attribute_n > value*. If a new rule relates to data that is already defined in the system, business administrators simply create a new data-based rule without support from database experts.

However, if the needed data (*Attribute_n* in the example above) are not yet modeled in the system, database experts would be needed for the implementation of the new data requirement with all agility hindering consequences of a product release management cycle. To overcome such situations, state-based rules in combination with voting tasks can be defined to enforce the necessary execution sequence. Voting tasks contain checklists (see Fig. 5a) that are suitable for checking conditions manually by users. Later it may be worthwhile to add such data from best practice cases explicitly to the data model and apply them in data-based rules.

A constraint is composed from business ontology elements which relate to the ACM core elements case, goal, task, data, and temporal patterns expressing the temporal dependency of them, e.g.:

Constraint C1 **for** CaseN{
    TaskA.*finished* **precedes** TaskB.*started*}

A constraint can be assigned to specific cases (*Constraint C1 for CaseN*) which will be triggered when the defined elements in that case are affected, or defined globally without the 'for'-part, which will be triggered if any of the defined elements are affected. The states of ACM elements, considered in the constraint definitions are for goals {initiated, reached, ongoing} and tasks {started, finished, running}.

To enable the definition of more detailed temporal patterns [5], we introduce the following constraint language expressions:

- Existence: *TaskA.finished* occurs
- Absence: *TaskA.finished* never occurs
- Response: *TaskA.finished* leads to *TaskB.started*. It means if *TaskA.finished* happens, *TaskB.started* must follow.
- Precedence: *TaskA.finished* precedes *TaskB.started*. It means if *TaskB.started* shall happen, *TaskA.finished* must happen first.

Additionally, each pattern of the aforementioned constraint language expressions can have a scope, which defines the temporal extent for constraint observation. For example, if the constraint *C1* shall apply only after *TaskA.started*, it is defined as

Constraint C1 **for** CaseN{
After TaskA.*started*
[TaskA.*finished* **precedes** TaskB.*started*]}

The scope *after* defines the execution after a given event. Particularly in this example, only after the event *TaskA.started* happened, the events *TaskA.finished precedes TaskB.started* must be executed. As shown in Fig. 4, there are five basic kinds of scopes: (1) Global: the entire execution; (2) Before: before the first occurrence of event R; (3) After: after the first occurrence of event R; (4) Between: between events Q and R; (5) After-Until: after event Q until event R.

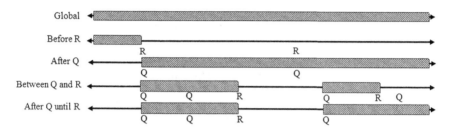

Fig. 4. Pattern scopes

4   Repair Service Management

ISIS Papyrus delivers business applications serving cross industry customer require-ments. The RSM application is based on the requirements of a customer from the managed services domain offering facility repair services to industrial and commercial customers. It was used as prototype for applying the consistency checking solution and validating its practicability. These services involve maintenance, cleaning and repairs performed by the enterprise's own employees as well as the engagement of subcontrac-tors. A broad variety of requirements from the customers and a large quantity of different laws and regulations must be considered.

From our experience we notice that several business domains are rather overre-gulated. Thus, compliance regulations imposed externally must be translated into internal directives being obeyed by processes and KWs and also support external audit requirements. Company internal standards are treated similarly although they may be executed more casually. If quantitative measures like time or money are defined, KWs frequently look for workarounds to reach their goals faster. If they are instructed to follow strictly predefined steps their knowledge from daily work is not considered. Thus, excluding their experience from process adaptions causes frustra-tion and poor customer experience.

The RSM case focuses on the on-the-fly checking as well as on the possibility to perform consistency checking on ACM templates prepared by business administrators. We focus on the compliance considerations implied by the United States Environmental Protection Agency's Lead Renovation, Repair and Painting Rule (RRP Rule) [21] and the consistency of the team selection process.

4.1 Compliance Definitions

A repair service officer, acting as KW of a company supplying repair services, receives an order for the replacement of several water pipes in a staff accommodation of the customer in the United States of America. According to the RRP Rule, the KW who is dealing with a new service request needs to check whether the repair service involves activities disturbing painted surfaces in a home or child-occupied facility built before 1978. Then, it requires a certified inspector or risk assessor to confirm the repair site to be free of lead-based paint or itemize and depict the surfaces covered with lead-based painting.

Following the scenario (1.1) from Sect. 2.2, the KW creates a new case for this repair service order and when facing RRP rules for the first time, adds one or more generic ad hoc tasks for the treatment of the RRP rule related examinations. He has to check, (a) whether painted surfaces will be disturbed; (b) whether the repair site is in a home or child-occupied facility; (c) whether the repair site is in a building built before 1978; (d) whether the repair site contains lead-based paint (i.e. whether the repair site has been inspected by a certified inspector or needs to be inspected for objects painted with lead-based paint); (e) whether a list of items and surfaces covered with lead-based paint exists or needs to be compiled and whether the repair activities will affect one of this items and surfaces.

Based on the outcome of the examinations, the KW continues with the case, executing ad hoc tasks selected from a list of specific or generic task templates. When the case handling was confirmed as best practice, an empowered KW or business administrator saves related tasks as templates and the business administrator builds specific task templates for the investigation tasks containing checklists (see Fig. 5a), composes the necessary compliance rules and references the rules to the repair service case template.

Fig. 5. *Task_RRP_Site* with checklist and constraint rule editor in ISIS ACM system

The checking result is implied through a voting by the KW: approved for *Yes* and deny for *No*. The *TaskRRP_Repair* contains a checklist proving whether painted surfaces will be disturbed by the repair activities or not. The *TaskRRP_Site* holds a checklist with the information whether the repair site is a home or a child-occupied facility and built before 1978. The *TaskRRP_Lead* contains a checklist informing on the inspection status of the repair site. The *TaskLead_Items* holds the information whether a list of items and surfaces covered with lead-based paint exists or needs to be compiled and whether the repair service affects one of those items and surfaces. These task templates are involved in the RRP rule which is described in the following compliance rules.

```
Constraint RRP_Compliance0 for RepairServiceCase {
  TaskRRP_Repair.started occurs exactly 1x}
Constraint RRP_Compliance1 for RepairServiceCase {
  TaskRRP_Repair.approved leads to TaskRRP_Site.started}
Constraint RRP_Compliance2 for RepairServiceCase {
  TaskRRP_Site.approved leads to TaskRRP_Lead.started}
Constraint RRP_Compliance3 for RepairServiceCase {
  TaskRRP_Lead.approved leads to TaskLead_Items.started}
```

Compliance rules are checked on the fly during the execution of ad hoc actions. For the definition of compliance rules in natural language, a constraint rule editor implemented in the ISIS Papyrus ACM system (see Fig. 5b) supports business administrators with terms used in their daily business work. These are concepts defined in a business domain specific ontology. The task templates *TaskRRP_Repair* and *TaskRRP_Site* are mapped to business language through the ontology concepts *Repair Impact* and *Site Categorization*, respectively.

4.2 On-the-Fly Consistency Checking

The next time such an RSM case is executed making use of the newly created templates, the first rule is triggered on case instantiation fulfilling *RRP_Compliance0*. This means, *TaskRRP_Repair* is part of the case and thus, cannot be skipped or added multiple times. The KW needs to check on the issue and fulfills the task by selecting a vote. If *TaskRRP_Repair* is approved, *TaskRRP_Site* is suggested to the clerk to end the temporary violation of constraint *RRP_Compliance1*. As soon as *TaskRRP_Site* is approved, *TaskRRP_Lead* is suggested to the clerk to end the temporary violation of constraint *RRP_Compliance2*, and so on.

Although the sequence of tasks is constrained in this case, other tasks can be executed in between which empowers the KW to react to the specific situation as needed. For example, after the completion of *TaskRRP_Repair*, the clerk could add the tasks *Order Material*, *Choose Workers*, and so on. At that stage of *TaskRRP_Repair* the constraint *RRS_Compliance1* is still temporarily violated as *TaskRRP_Site* is not started yet. The KW is notified of the violation by proposing it as next task. But he has the flexibility to perform any additional actions, which he assesses are necessary to fulfill the goal of the case. The proper point in time for the execution of the suggested *TaskRRP_Site* is determined by the KW.

Every action of the clerk triggers events monitored by the online checker. The online checker collates the information of the events with the constraints of the compliance rules. If rules are violated, the online checker produces notifications and suggestions. By creating state-based rules with the compliance rules editor and building related task templates with checklists and voting options, the business administrator is able to induce consistency checking without the involvement of IT development. This approach allows flexible and fast adaption of rapidly changing rules through KWs without unnecessarily restricting the adaptability of ACM due to changes of underlying data models by IT.

5   Lessons Learned and Conclusion

Our general finding in this study is that behavioral consistency checking of compliance rules has significantly enhanced the ACM solution by embracing flexibility and enforcing control of company regulations or laws where imposed. Adequate consistency checking has empowered business users in ad hoc situations by providing the necessary support, allowing them to focus on and engage actively in their work instead of being locked out due to the rigidness of process definitions.

To summarize, business users have been empowered to react ad hoc on individually assessed situations within the guardrails defined by compliance rules. This was achieved by the combination of: (i) predefined processes whose behavioral and structural consistency is checked by model checking techniques during design time, and (ii) flexibility, which is supported by on-the-fly checking during case execution of ad hoc added goals and tasks. Business users select ad hoc actions from a set of templates. When being added to the case, tasks were checked for overall behavioral consistency. Business users acknowledge the advantage of working goal-oriented allowing them to define the actually needed tasks and their execution sequences as they need within the guardrails of compliance rules defined in a business specific language. Our decision in introducing the aforementioned domain-specific constraint language supporting the business users' domain of expertise was well accepted. As the domain-specific ontology concepts can map the elements of the compliance rules with the underlying data models, the administrators were able to better relate high-level compliance requirements with technical elements such as cases, process fragments, data objects, etc. The possibility to define voting tasks with freely configurable check list items without IT involvement for data model extensions is also seen as an important factor for enabling flexibility in an agile business environment.

Compliance rules are centrally managed and associated with specific cases they shall apply to. The ACM stakeholders also perceived positively the categories of consistency rules. That is, two types of business rules have provided a responsive solution for ad hoc changes in ACM: stated-based and data-based. State-based rules are used by the business administrator or an empowered business clerk to define compliance rules without the support from IT staff. Data-based rules are applied when the available data models allow explicit access to data attributes in order to constrain the execution of goals and/or tasks of a case.

Our study is one of the first attempts in applying existing formal modeling and verification techniques to the domain of ACM and in a particular ACM system. Thus, there is room for future work. For instance, to address the organization of compliance rules and how to deal with compensation of acceptable compliance rule violations. Also how ontologies can be effectively applied to formulate domain specific business rules by business users (non-IT) needs further investigations. We also aim to expand our findings to other ACM applications and emerging standards. This will help to improve and strengthen our findings in a broader context, and underline the application of formal methods in highly flexible and knowledge intensive systems.

Acknowledgement. This work was supported by the FFG project CACAO, no. 843461 and the Wiener Wissenschafts-, Forschungs- und Technologiefonds (WWTF), Grant No. ICT12-001.

References

1. van der Aalst, W.M.P., Weske, M., Grünbauer, D.: Case handling: a new paradigm for business process support. Data Knowl. Eng. **53**(2), 129–162 (2005)
2. Reichert, M., Weber, B.: Enabling Flexibility in Process-Aware Information Systems: Challenges, Methods, Technologies. Springer, Heidelberg (2012)
3. Ly, L.T., Rinderle, S., Dadam, P.: Integration and verification of semantic constraints in adaptive process management systems. Data Knowl. Eng. **64**(1), 3–23 (2008)
4. Fellmann, M., Zasada, A.: State-of-the-art of business process compliance approaches: a survey. In: 22nd European Conference on Information Systems. Tel Aviv, Israel (2014)
5. Dwyer, M.B., Avrunin, G.S., Corbett, J.C.: Patterns in property specifications for finite-state verification. In: Proceedings of the 21st International Conference on Software Engineering, New York (1999)
6. ISIS papyrus: adaptive case management. http://www.isis-papyrus.com/e15/pages/business-apps/acm.html
7. Liu, Y., Müller, S., Xu, K.: A static compliance-checking framework for business process models. IBM Syst. J. **46**(2), 335–361 (2007)
8. Namiri, K., Stojanovic, N.: Pattern-based design and validation of business process compliance. In: Meersman, R., Tari, Z. (eds.) On the Move to Meaningful Internet Systems 2007: CoopIS, DOA, ODBASE, GADA, and IS, pp. 59–76. Springer, Heidelberg (2007)
9. Awad, A., Decker, G., Weske, M.: Efficient compliance checking using BPMN-Q and temporal logic. In: Dumas, M., Reichert, M., Shan, M.-C. (eds.) BPM 2008. LNCS, vol. 5240, pp. 326–341. Springer, Heidelberg (2008)
10. van der Aalst, W.M.P., de Beer, H.T., van Dongen, B.F.: Process mining and verification of properties: an approach based on temporal logic. In: Meersman, R., Tari, Z. (eds.) On the Move to Meaningful Internet Systems 2005: CoopIS, DOA, and ODBASE, pp. 130–147. Springer, Berlin (2005)
11. Birukou, A., D'Andrea, V., Leymann, F., Serafinski, J., Silveira, P., Strauch, S., Tluczek, M.: An integrated solution for runtime compliance governance in SOA. In: Maglio, P.P., Weske, M., Yang, J., Fantinato, M. (eds.) ICSOC 2010. LNCS, vol. 6470, pp. 122–136. Springer, Heidelberg (2010)
12. Holmes, T., Mulo, E., Zdun, U., Dustdar, S.: Model-aware monitoring of SOAs for compliance. In: Dustdar, S., Li, F. (eds.) Service Engineering, pp. 117–136. Springer, Berlin (2011)
13. Ly, L.T., Maggi, F.M., Montali, M., Rinderle-Ma, S., van der Aalst, W.M.P.: A framework for the systematic comparison and evaluation of compliance monitoring approaches. In: IEEE 17th International Enterprise Distributed Object Computing Conference (EDOC), pp. 7–16 (2013)
14. Swenson, K.: Case management: contrasting production vs. adaptive. In: Fischer, L. (ed.) How Knowledge Workers Get Things Done. Future Strategies Inc., Lighthouse Point (2012)

15. Tran, T.T.K., Pucher, M.J., Mendling, J., Ruhsam, C.: Setup and maintenance factors of ACM systems. In: Demey, Y.T., Panetto, H. (eds.) OTM 2013 Workshops 2013. LNCS, vol. 8186, pp. 172–177. Springer, Heidelberg (2013)
16. Espertech: complex event processing (CEP). http://www.espertech.com
17. Governatori, G., Rotolo, A.: Norm compliance in business process modeling. In: Dean, M., Hall, J., Rotolo, A., Tabet, S. (eds.) RuleML 2010. LNCS, vol. 6403, pp. 194–209. Springer, Heidelberg (2010)
18. Sem, H.F., Carlsen, S., Coll, G.J.: Combining compliance with flexibility. In: Fischer, L. (ed.) Thriving on Adaptability: Best Practices for Knowledge Workers, pp. 59–71. Future Strategies Inc., Lighthouse Point (2015)
19. Tran, T.T.K., Ruhsam, C., Pucher, M.J., Kobler, M., Mendling, J.: Towards a pattern recognition approach for transferring knowledge in ACM. In: IEEE 18th International Enterprise Distributed Object Computing Conference Workshops and Demonstrations (EDOCW), pp. 134–138 (2014)
20. van der Aalst, W.M., Pesic, M.: DecSerFlow: towards a truly declarative service flow language. In: Bravetti, M., Núñez, M., Zavattaro, G. (eds.) WS-FM 2006. LNCS, vol. 4184, pp. 1–23. Springer, Heidelberg (2006)
21. United States environmental protection agency: lead renovation, repair and painting program rules. http://www2.epa.gov/lead/lead-renovation-repair-and-painting-program-rules

Modeling Crisis Management Process from Goals to Scenarios

Elena Kushnareva$^{(\boxtimes)}$, Irina Rychkova,
Rébecca Deneckére, and Bénédicte Le Grand

University Paris 1 Panthéon-Sorbonne, 12, Place de Panthéon, 75005 Paris, France
`elena.kushnareva@malix.univ-paris1.fr`,
`{irina.rychkova,rebecca.deneckere,benedicte.le-grand}@univ-paris1.fr`
`http://www.univ-paris1.fr/`

Abstract. Process manager plays the central role in crisis management. In order to capture the intentions of the process manager, the process should be specified at a strategic level. In order to analyze how these intentions are fulfilled during the process execution, the process should be specified at an operational level. Whereas the variety of techniques for goal modeling and process modeling is presented in the market, possibility to design a process seamlessly, from intentions (process goals) to executable scenarios, remains a challenging task. In this paper, we introduce an approach for modeling and simulating a crisis management process from goals to scenarios. We consider an example of flood management process specified for floods on Oka River in the Moscow region in Russia. In order to specify the intentions behind the flood management process, we use MAP formalism. For representing the process at the operational level, we use Statecharts formalism. To align the strategic and operation process levels, we translate the MAP model of flood management process to statecharts. We simulate the flood management process, showing how the process goals defined on the strategic level can be achieved by various scenarios executed in the operational level.

Keywords: Statecharts · MAP · Process flexibility · Intentional modeling · State-based modeling

1 Introduction

Crisis management process is an example of a knowledge-intensive process (KiPs) [5]: it strongly depends on the situation (context) and tacit knowledge of human actors plays the central role in this process. On the other hand, crisis management has to comply with federal regulations such as the Emergency Management Guidelines. These characteristics make specification and implementation of crisis management solutions challenging.

In this paper, we consider the case of flood management process specified for floods on Oka River in the Moscow region in Russia. This process is implemented as a part of COS Operation Center (COSOC) - a smart city solution developed

© Springer International Publishing Switzerland 2016
M. Reichert and H.A. Reijers (Eds.): BPM Workshops 2015, LNBIP 256, pp. 55–64, 2016.
DOI: 10.1007/978-3-319-42887-1_5

by COS&HT [8]. The existing COSOC solution was designed following traditional workflow-based approach: the flood management process is specified as a sequence of activities that have to be executed according to the current conditions (i.e., water level and status of the flooded regions) and in compliance with the Emergency Management Guidelines defined by the Ministry of Emergency Situations (MES) in Russia.

The experience shows that execution of workflows proposed by COSOC can often be problematic due to unforeseen circumstances (e.g., lack of resources, disrupted traffic, etc.) Current system provides only limited support for process flexibility and in order to implement an alternative scenario, the process manager often switches to "off-line" mode.

To improve the process flexibility and adaptability:

(1) Process specification should capture its intentional perspective, or should answer a question "WHY do we carry out an activity/procedure?". Understanding intentions behind the guidelines will help to define alternative scenarios in the situations when the default scenario cannot be implemented [1, 16].

(2) Process specification should focus on WHAT has to be done instead of HOW it must be done [6]. In this case, only the process outcomes need to be fixed at design while concrete procedures or activities leading to these outcomes can be chosen by the process manager at run-time.

In this paper, we introduce an approach for modeling crisis management process from goals to executable scenarios. We use MAP to reason about intentions behind the flood management process (strategic level). MAP is a goal-oriented modeling language introduced by Rolland in [11, 12, 14].

We use statecharts formalism for representing the flood management process at the operational level. Statecharts is a state-oriented modeling formalism defined by Harel [7].

To align the strategic and operation process levels we translate the MAP model of flood management process to the statecharts.

Statecharts specifications are executable. We simulate the flood management process, showing how the process goals defined on the strategic level can be achieved by various scenarios executed in the operational level.

The remainder of the paper is organized as follows: in Sect. 2 we introduce the case study of a flood management process and specify this process on the operational level using statecharts; in Sect. 3 we specify a goal model for the flood management process; in Sect. 4 we translate MAP model to statecharts; in Sect. 5 we illustrate how the complete model of the flood management process - strategic and operational levels - can be simulated in YAKINDU Statecharts tool; in Sect. 6 we draw our conclusions.

2   Flood Management Process: Operational Level

In this section we briefly introduce our case study - the flood management process; we show how this process can be modeled with Statecharts formalism.

2.1   Flood Management Process

Floods on the Oka River in the Moscow region are seasonal events caused by an increase in the flow of the river, provoked by intensive snow melting during the spring months. Cities built along the Oka River are confronted to the risk of flooding and can expect important damages, affecting thousands of people. Floods on Oka also represent substantial risks for the critical infrastructure facilities situated in the area: a railway bridge, a pontoon road bridge, an electric power plant, etc.

Along with other types of crisis, the flood management process has to comply with the Emergency Management Guidelines [15] defined by MES. This document prescribes the activities that have to be carried before, during and after crisis situations by different public services and agencies of the city.

As specified in Sect. 1, the flood management process is implemented as a part of COSOC - a process-aware information system used by a government to manage the variety of cross-domain operations within the city.

The functions of COSOC can be roughly divided into three groups: (i) data collection and visualization, (ii) analysis of the situation and decision making and (iii) triggering response processes.

The COSOC process manager is a member of the city administration who is responsible for monitoring the situation and handling emerging issues. He/she can accept or decline the solution proposed by the system; when a workflow is triggered, he/she monitors its execution and intervenes when decision-making is required.

When the problematic situation is resolved, the process manager can provide feedback to the system: request for process improvement, modification of monitored parameters list, etc.

In our previous work [10], we examined the BPMN specification of the flood management process designed for COSOC and showed that the capacity of PAIS to support flexibility of the process is inherent to the underlying process modeling paradigm.

In order to provide the flexibility of the process, we design a state-oriented model of the flood management process in the YAKINDU Statechart Tool (SCT) using the formalism of statecharts.

2.2   Statecharts Model

The statecharts formalism specifies hierarchical state machines (HSM) and extends classical finite-state machines (FSM) by providing: *depth* (the possibility to model states at multiple hierarchical levels); *orthogonality* (the possibility to model concurrent or independent sub-machines within one state machine); *broadcast communication* (the possibility to synchronize multiple concurrent sub-machines via events).

The statecharts model (Fig. 1) describes the process with a set of states (e.g., *Alert, Emergency, Restoring Normal Functioning*, etc.) and transitions between them. Process execution starts at an initial state and terminates at a final state.

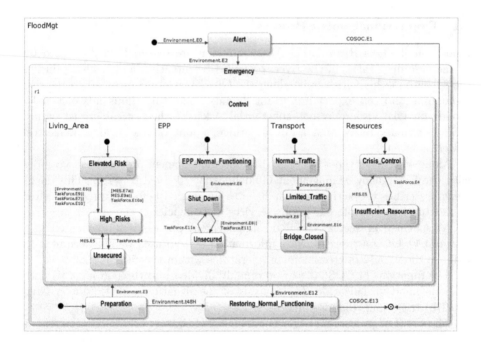

Fig. 1. Statechart model of a flood management process

The sequence of states and transitions that leads from the initial state to the final state can be seen as a process scenario.

In statecharts (unlike Petri Nets, where transitions are associated with the execution of an activity) each state transition can be triggered by a specific event or combination of events. For example, the event *E2: water level h > 10* cm *and keeps rising* triggers a transition from *Alert* to *Emergency*. The activities producing these events can be selected at run-time. We call this *deferred binding*.

As a result, a process specification is divided into two parts: the state-transition part, defined with a set of states and transitions between states and their triggering events, and the activity part, defined by a list of activities specified by their preconditions and outcomes. The process enactment can be seen as a dynamic selection of activities to produce some outcomes (events) that make the process progress towards its (desired) final state.

3   Flood Management Process: Strategic Level

In this section we explain our choice of modeling formalism, introduce the concept of MAP, illustrated on the flood management process example, and propose a procedure for transforming a MAP to a Statechart model.

3.1   Choosing the Formalism

Processes may be formalized in an intentional way in goal-modeling approaches to model the processes according to the purpose of the actors/organizations. We quote among them i* [17,18], KAOS [3] and MAP. We choose the MAP modeling language in our approach because it allows formalizing flexible processes with high level organizational intentions. It supports variability for the goals and offers the possibility to follow different strategies by focusing on the intentional aspect when enacting methodological processes [4]. i* has an operational semantic for the tasks but not for the goals and it is not used to model strategic goals; it is not designed to be a variable framework, therefore it does not afford a high level of flexibility. As for KAOS, it supports variability and have a well-structured semantic but is less involved in the intentional aspect of IS actors. Furthermore, KAOS has a rigid task-decomposition; modeling complex intentional processes is then difficult [13].

3.2   MAP Model

MAP specifies processes in a flexible way by focusing on the intentions and the different ways to fulfill them, according to the context of each actor. A MAP model is presented as a graph which nodes represent *intentions* and edges represent *strategies*. An edge is defined between two nodes where its related strategy can be used to achieve the intended target node. There may be several edges

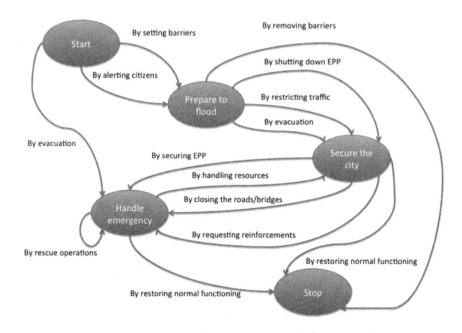

Fig. 2. MAP model of the flood management process

entering a node representing all the strategies to fulfill an intention. A *section* is a triplet <source intention, strategy, target intention>, which represents a particular process step to achieve an intention (the target intention) from a specific situation (the source intention) following a particular technique (the strategy). The MAP meta-model has been validated in several domains as IS engineering [14], requirement engineering [13], method engineering [9], enterprise knowledge development [2], etc.

The MAP corresponding to the flood management process is presented in Fig. 2.

There are three intentions specified on this level: *Prepare to flood, Secure the city* and *Handle emergency*. Each intention can be fulfilled by several strategies. For example, *Handle emergency* intention can be reached either from the initial intention (*Start*) - in case of need for emergency evacuation of the citizens before the preparations finished, or from the *Secure the city* intention - in case of lack of resources, or getting the 'Electric Power Plant (EPP) is flooded' alert. The final intention (Stop) corresponds to the process termination and can be attained either *By removing barriers*, or *By restoring normal functioning* of objects of the city infrastructure. The flood management MAP model also contains a recursive section *<Handle emergency, By rescue operations, Handle emergency>*, which represents the maintenance of a need in emergency handling while receiving the rescue operations requests.

All goal-oriented models share the same problem concerning the intentions operationalization. The MAP model highlights this problem by proposing several kind of guidelines to guide the user through the navigation in the map and to explain how a specific intention can be realised with a specific strategy (IAG: intention achievement guideline). This guideline can be described in several ways: in natural language, with an algorithm, through a workflow, etc. However, it is always difficult to offer an automatic way of operationalizing this guideline. Statecharts open an essential dimension to this problem by offering an automatic operationalization of the process contained in the IAG.

4   Statecharts Semantics for MAP

In this section we propose a procedure for transforming a MAP to a Statechart model by using the example of the flood management process, and discuss the advantages that can be gained by this transformation.

As introduced in Sect. 3, a MAP is specified as a set of *intentions* to be achieved, and *strategies* for achieving them. The *intentions* can be interpreted as sets of states a process manager desires to reach. However, reaching a state does not necessarily mean that the intention is achieved. Some goals may require a number of actions to be performed before being achieved. Furthermore, taking an action aimed at attaining the goal, does not necessarily end in achieving this goal, but should reach a state which is closer to that goal than the previous one. As a result, *intentions* in statechart representation have a "core", which is a set of states where some actions towards attaining the goal are performed. This is a statechart representation of *strategies*.

The MAP flood management model transformed in statecharts semantics is shown in Fig. 3.

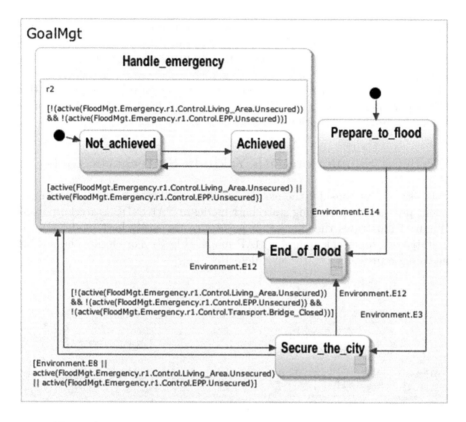

Fig. 3. Statechart representation of a MAP flood management model

For example, the condition that triggers the *Handle emergency* state is either water rises higher than 45 cm (which implies closing roads/bridges), or the *Living Area* or *EPP* sub-state becomes *Unsecured* (Fig. 1). Following the statechart model, the *Living Area* goes to *Unsecured* state when lack of resources is detected. The *EPP* sub-state, in its turn, can only reach the *Unsecured* state when the EPP is flooded and needs to be secured. Hence, lack of resources, need in closing roads/bridges or a flooded EPP force process manager to change his/her intention from *Secure the city* towards *Handle emergency*. In order to fulfill the goal and leave the state, the process manager has to request reinforcements, close roads/bridges or secure EPP. In other words, he/she has to make a decision, which *strategy* to use.

In our example of crisis, the decision-making process in statecharts can easily be operationalized.

Each state of the statechart is associated with the list of mandatory and optional activities that must/can be carried out upon entering, upon exiting and while in this state. With the state-oriented paradigm, the objective of the flood management process is as follows: the process participants (i.e., MES and Police Taskforce) should respond to the events that occur in the environment (e.g., rise of water, flooded EPP, etc.) by executing the operation procedures and producing the outcomes in order to maintain the secure functioning of the city in specified domains.

Thus, transforming a MAP representation to a Statechart representation enables operationalization of MAP and, therefore, linking them to the process scenarios for further simulation.

5   Process Simulation with Yakindu Statecharts Tools

In this section, we consider the executable level of scenarios of the flood management process by simulating statechart model in YAKINDU Statecharts tool.

Figure 4 illustrates the simulation process of the Statechart model (Fig. 1) and Statechart representation of a MAP model (Fig. 3). For clarity, the bottom right model represents a water level detector.

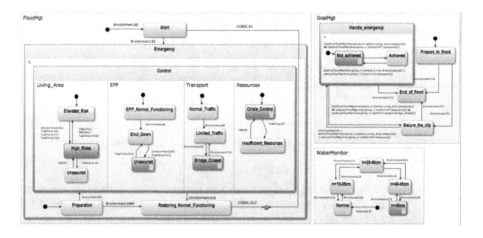

Fig. 4. Simulation of the flood management process in YAKINDU SCT (Color figure online)

The statecharts are executed concurrently. Current situation is described by the six active (red) states: the water level is above 45 cm; the active intention is *Handle emergency*, which is not yet achieved; extremely high water level triggers a set of procedures in *High risk* state in *Living Area*; the EPP is flooded and *Unsecured* at the moment; roads/bridges are closed; resources are under *Crisis Control*.

In order to fulfill the *Handle emergency* intention and return to *Secure the city*, a process manager needs to provide EPP with security, so that the *Unsecured* state would not be active.

The state-oriented paradigm allows for *deferred activity planning*: an activity can be defined at run time, based on the desired outcome and on the context (i.e., resources, etc.). In response to unforeseen conditions, the process manager can select the next best step from the list of available activities. Thanks to *deferred binding*, he/she can also define a new activity better adapted for a situation.

Thus, the state-oriented paradigm creates a recommendation system where the process manager plays the leading role in scenario definition.

6   Conclusion

Crisis management process is safety-critical its failure could result in loss of life, significant property or environment damage. To ensure safety and security, the activities performed during crisis management are highly regulated at federal level. However, crisis handling requires high agility and never follows the same scenario.

Our experience with COSOC processes shows that a concrete flood management process relies a lot on the experience and decisions of the process manager. Assessment of a situation, adaptive scenario planning and handling the unpredictable situations represent challenges for the supporting information system.

By combining the MAP and Statecharts we arrived at a formalism which defines how human intentions drive a process. The result is an intention-driven approach to process modeling that offers an intention operationalization and provides a process manager with guidelines from goals identification to scenarios execution.

In our future work, we intend to test this process modeling approach on other cases and implement it as a part of recommendation system within COSOC.

References

1. Amyot, D., Mussbacher, G.: URN: towards a new standard for the visual description of requirements. In: Proceedings of 3rd International WS on Telecommunications and beyond: the broader applicability of SDL and MSC (2002)
2. Barrios, J., Nurcan, S.: Model driven architectures for enterprise information systems. In: Persson, A., Stirna, J. (eds.) CAiSE 2004. LNCS, vol. 3084, pp. 3–19. Springer, Heidelberg (2004)
3. Dardenne, A., van Lamsweerde, A., Fickasu, S.: Goal-directed requirements acquisition. Sci. Comput. Program **20**, 3–50 (1993)
4. Deneckre, R., Rychkova, I., Nurcan, S.: Modeling the role variability in the map process model. In: Proceedings of Fifth International Conference on Research Challenges in Information Science (RCIS), pp. 1–9. IEEE (2011)
5. Di Ciccio, C., Marrella, A., Russo, A.: Knowledge-intensive processes: characteristics, requirements and analysis of contemporary approaches. Data Semant. **4**, 29–57 (2014)

6. Dietz, J.: Basic notions regarding business processes and supporting information systems. In: Proceedings of BPMDS 2004, CAiSE 2004 workshops proceedings, vol. 2, pp. 160–168. Springer (2004)
7. Harel, D.: Statecharts: a visual formalism for complex systems. Sci. Comput. Program. **8**, 231–274 (1987)
8. Helvas, A., Badanin, M., Pashkov, R., Kushnareva, E., Medovik, O.: COS operation center (2012). http://cosoc.ru/home
9. Kornyshova, E., Deneckére, R., Salinesi, C.: Method chunks selection by multicriteria techniques: an extension of the assembly-based approach. Situational Method Engineering: Fundamentals and Experiences. IFIP – The International Federation for Information Processing, pp. 64–78. Springer, Heidelberg (2007)
10. Kushnareva, E., Rychkova, I., Le Grand, B.: Modeling business processes for automated crisis management support: lessons learned. In: IEEE 9th International Conference on Research Challenges in Information Science (RCIS) (2015)
11. Rolland, C.: A comprehensive view of process engineering. In: Pernici, B., Thanos, C. (eds.) CAiSE 1998. LNCS, vol. 1413, pp. 1–24. Springer, Heidelberg (1998)
12. Rolland, C.: Capturing system intentionality with maps. In: Krogstie, J., Opdahl, A.L., Brinkkemper, S. (eds.) Conceptual Modelling in Information Systems Engineering, pp. 141–158. Springer, Heidelberg (2007)
13. Rolland, C., Prakash, N.: Systems design for requirements expressed as a map. In: The conference IRMA 2006 (2006)
14. Rolland, C., Prakash, N., Benjamen, A.: A multi-model view of process modelling. Requirements Eng. **4**, 169–187 (1999)
15. The ministry of the Russian Federation for civil defense and elimination of consequences of natural disasters. Emergency management guidelines (2013). http://www.mchs.gov.ru/
16. van Lamsweerde, A.: Reasoning about alternative requirements options. In: Borgida, A.T., Chaudhri, V.K., Giorgini, P., Yu, E.S. (eds.) Conceptual Modeling: Foundations and Applications. LNCS, vol. 5600, pp. 380–397. Springer, Heidelberg (2009)
17. Yu, E.: Modelling Strategic Relationships for Process Reengineering. University of Toronto, Department of Computer Science (1995)
18. Yu, E., Mylopoulos, J.: Using goals, rules, and methods to support reasoning in business process reengineering. Int. J. Intell. Syst. Account. Finance Manage. **5**(2), 1–13 (1996)

Supporting Adaptive Case Management Through Semantic Web Technologies

Marian Benner-Wickner[1], Wilhelm Koop[1(✉)], Matthias Book[2], and Volker Gruhn[1]

[1] paluno – The Ruhr Institute for Software Technology, University of Duisburg-Essen,
Essen, Germany
{marian.benner,wilhelm.koop,volker.gruhn}@uni-due.de
[2] Faculty of Industrial Engineering, Mechanical Engineering and Computer Science,
University of Iceland, Reykjavik, Iceland
book@hi.is

Abstract. In the rehabilitation management domain, we find many situations where actors have to manage complex cases. To facilitate patients' quick recovery from their individual conditions, case managers need a high degree of flexibility in organizing their tasks. Unfortunately, giving them complete flexibility is challenging for two reasons: Firstly, process owners may want to tame the flexibility to conform with compliance policies. Secondly, without complete information about the possible processes in the problem domain, software engineers are struggling to design information systems that can support these case management processes effectively. In this paper, we will therefore show how semantic web technologies can complement adaptive case management techniques in order to cope with the cases' flexibility. Following the ideas of linked data and the open-world assumption, these techniques facilitate (1) a data structure that is easily extendable, (2) data quality improvements, and (3) the definition and checking of business rules using domain concepts. As a proof of concept, we integrated the method into a case management tool and conducted a small case study using real-life examples from the rehabilitation domain.

Keywords: Adaptive case management · Semantic web · Agenda-driven case management · Business rules

1 Introduction

In the case management domain, business processes are less-structured and hence not automatable. Due to the high diversity between cases, there is no predefined process model that can be used by information systems to prepare the tasks for a case manager. Instead, case managers need a high degree of flexibility when organizing their tasks and gathering information from different sources. As a result, some researchers aim at making control flow process models more flexible. The case handling approach introduced by van der Aalst et al., for example, introduces the ability to skip or redo tasks in a model [1]. However, such models are usually still imperative (i.e. they only allow control flows that are explicitly defined). This is an issue in case management processes, because they cannot cope with sudden events forcing the case manager to redesign the

© Springer International Publishing Switzerland 2016
M. Reichert and H.A. Reijers (Eds.): BPM Workshops 2015, LNBIP 256, pp. 65–77, 2016.
DOI: 10.1007/978-3-319-42887-1_6

process with alternative steps. Based on the reasoning of Rychkova and Pesic [10, 14], we believe that allowing only actions defined in such models will never satisfy the degree of flexibility needed in case management. Instead, we suggest using declarative models, which allow everything that is not explicitly forbidden by defined constraints (e.g. derived from business rules of the given domain).

This paper is based on the hypothesis that this paradigm switch matches concepts of the semantic web and agenda-driven case management (adCM [2]) well. We therefore connect these concepts in order to find new opportunities for supporting case management processes. In this section, we will first describe how agenda-driven case management and semantic web concepts can each contribute to satisfying the need for flexibility resulting from the above-mentioned paradigm switch. In Sect. 2, we then discuss benefits that could be gained by connecting both fields, and which novel capabilities for case management support this would enable. In Sect. 3, we then show how such a connection can actually be implemented, and demonstrate some of the resulting features in a prototype of a "Semantic Case Management" tool. We compare the approach with the related work in Sect. 4 and finish with a conclusion in Sect. 5.

1.1 Agenda-Driven Case Management

In our previous work, we introduced adCM as a new approach to support case management. Due to the high diversity of such processes, the approach reflects the need for high flexibility in both the control flow perspective as well as the data perspective. It also provides the capability to record process knowledge during case execution. In this section, we will briefly introduce these concepts; details can be found in [3].

Agenda. The pivotal element of adCM is a hierarchically structured list containing all entities that a case manager considers important for the case's execution – the so-called agenda. Ideally, it is derived from common process knowledge discovered in past cases. However, the case manager is free to (re-)organize the agenda according to the particularities of each case instance, and may also start with a blank agenda. Due to this flexibility, each case manager can use agendas according to his preferences, which is in contrast to the traditional workflow management approach that tries to bind the process execution tightly to predefined control flow definitions. Consider, for example, the rehabilitation of a patient Mr. Smith. His case is managed by Mr. Fisher, who initially fills his agenda with common important process landmarks like "healing plan", "issue orders" and "care provider ranking" (Fig. 1). They could originate from a knowledge base containing common agenda items. The subordinate items, however, are specific to

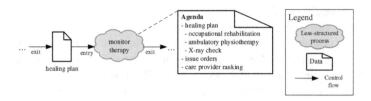

Fig. 1. Example agenda of a case from the rehabilitation management domain

the Mr. Smith's case instance and have been added by the case manager. According to the patient's symptoms, the healing plan contains individual indications (e.g. an ambulatory physiotherapy following an occupational rehabilitation).

Artifacts. One of the most frequently performed activities of a case manager is to search and explore information related to the case. For this purpose, the case manager will access multiple information sources, both internal and external to his organisation, some of which are structured, while others are not. We collectively call all information that the case manager gathers "artifacts". He can work with these by combining, evaluating, rating and relating the information they contain, and structure them by collecting related artifacts in individually defined workspaces. For example, Mr. Smith's healing plan is a key artifact in the rehabilitation domain. To organize the task's artifacts in the workspace, the case manager can include information and documents from heterogeneous sources. He can arbitrarily associate artifacts in his workspace with each other, and annotate these artifacts and associations with tags. In the course of the task completion, the case manager can dynamically re-arrange and relate the artifacts in his workspace. The adCM system architecture [3] is designed to store workspaces using a central knowledge base. This enables the adCM tool to perform data mining steps aiming to identify important artifacts.

1.2   Semantic Web Paradigms

Until recently, most of the information present on the Internet was meant to be used by humans, not machines. In the past decade, this was a challenge for those aiming to analyze web content automatically. Today, a set of technology standards focus on this issue, representing what is commonly known as the semantic web. We identified two main concepts of the semantic web that we believe are promising for case management support: linked data [4] and the open-world assumption [12].

Linked Data. Humans understand concepts by connecting them with terms already learned. When communicating, one can find out whether or not (most of) the concept's attributes match with those mentioned by another person, indicating that you are talking about the same term. In order to make terms comprehensible to machines, they need a capability to store and map terms with key attributes and other terms. In the semantic web, URIs are used to name things. They can be associated with each other using named relations, called properties. The corresponding graphs are stored using the resource description framework (RDF) [16]. The following listing shows an example of how to define a new class for healing plan artifacts using the turtle syntax [17]. It is organized using triples of subject-predicate-object order. The prefix adcm denotes that the term is a core adCM concept.

```
adcm:Artifact rdf:type :Class .
adcm:Document rdfs:subClassOf adcm:Artifact .
adcm:HealingPlan rdfs:subClassOf adcm:Document .
```

This way, machines managing their own graphs of connected information can compare, exchange, or verify their knowledge. Software systems called reasoners can also infer additional properties using first-order logic. Using the example above, a reasoner can infer transitive relations such as that any healing plan is also an artifact.

Open-World Assumption. When querying information systems, users assume them to be complete and accurate reflections of the world. That is, persons not listed in a phonebook database are assumed not to be reachable by phone. This closed-world assumption works well in well-known domains and processes with little uncertainty, as these systems can actually contain all the information they need. However, in some domains like healthcare, knowledge is rarely known to be complete, as the problem domain is not entirely explored. In this case, queries for information should be understood to return an incomplete, but steadily expanding body of knowledge. Consider, for example, a case manager searching for therapies that fit a given set of diagnoses. Assuming that the search fails, this does not imply that a therapy is impossible. Instead, it is not decidable whether or not a therapy exists (it may just not be explored yet). In the field of semantic web, this concept is called the open-world assumption.

2   Benefits of Semantic Web Technologies for adCM

In this section, we will show how the connection of agenda-driven case management with semantic web technologies facilitates (1) a flexible persistency layer for process knowledge base, (2) high data quality within the knowledge base, and (3) business rule definition using terms of the given domain.

2.1   Flexible Persistency

As described in Sect. 1.1, adCM's agenda lets the case manager organize any case-relevant activities flexibly, while the workspace enables him to organize any data sources as artifacts. Both concepts put considerable flexibility demands on the data model used to store agendas and artifacts. For example, the set of artifact types is specific to the domain or business process and will change in time. Based on our experience in the field, we assume that most of the artifacts will be documents, images, spreadsheets and web links. However, it is impossible to consider this set complete. Therefore, it has to be easy to integrate new types into the data model at runtime. When using relational databases, this would impose serious efforts in schema refactoring. We therefore propose to adapt the open-world assumption of the semantic web: Using description logic, we specify only an incomplete set of common types and rules on how they can be used. This set, representable as an RDF graph, can be appended at runtime by just adding further relations. The information about each specific case, containing its agenda with all associated agenda items and artifacts, can be represented as "individuals" in this graph. The graph then acts like a semantically connected knowledge base for the case management process. Section 3.2 will provide more details about the design of this solution approach, including examples.

2.2 Improving Data Quality and Analysis Outcome

Since names of agenda items, artifacts and their tags can be chosen freely by case managers, the names are subject to (conceptual) noise. A software system cannot understand that different terms or spellings may be synonyms, i.e. that they have the same meaning. This data quality issue is a challenge for data mining and hampers the effectivity of recommender systems. However, semantic web technologies are capable of addressing this issue. Following the idea of linked data, we can attach additional sources of knowledge such as lexical databases or domain ontologies to the common types. This way, synonyms can be identified within the knowledge base.

Moreover, linking domain ontologies does not only help to fix case data quality issues "a posteriori". It can also help to keep the quality level high by preventing the creation of synonyms "a priori". To achieve this, the concepts from the ontologies can be integrated into an unobtrusive auto-complete function when naming or tagging agenda items, for example. This way, a streamlined vocabulary can be established and noise and misspellings can be reduced without burdening the user with dialogs.

2.3 Business Rule Definition and Checking

Given that our approach entailed allowing everything that is not explicitly forbidden, we do not just need mechanisms for providing flexibility, but also for limiting the case manager's scope of action. For this purpose, business rules are useful. However, defining business rules is complicated if the modeling language does not employ domain-specific concepts. Let us assume, for example, that the process owner in Mr. Fisher's organization wants to ensure that a case can only be closed when a healing plan has been attached. Without using domain-specific concepts, such a definition is less expressive, resulting in a cumbersome rule like "When a case contains any agenda item containing an artifact with a name similar to 'healing plan', then the case can have a property named 'closed'." Using concepts defined in a domain-specific ontology, the rule could be more expressive: "When a case contains a healing plan, it can be closed." OWL, one of the key languages of the semantic web, enables the formal definition of such rules based on description logic. Given such rules, reasoning engines are capable of checking whether rules are violated in the case data. In Sect. 3.3, we will show how this approach can be used in more detail.

3 Semantic Case Management

In this section, we will show how the benefits discussed in Sect. 2 can be achieved by integrating the underlying semantic web technologies into the adCM approach. We will refer to this augmented approach as Semantic Case Management (SCM).

3.1   Flexible Persistency

To enable tool support that can be customized to the actual working environment of the case managers, domain experts need to be able to supply the adCM toolset with domain-specific information when adopting adCM in an organization. We therefore define a meta-model that describes the core concepts of adCM but is open for custom extensions. We chose to use a logic-based language (in this case OWL) for this purpose since the definition of business rules (described in Sect. 3.3) will require reasoning capability in the data model.

Since OWL is based on the open-world assumption, we can define the adCM concepts in the meta-model, but also allow the user to supplement additional semantics about the application domain. As described later, the user can define and reason about any information, as long as he does not violate adCM's pre-defined core rules.

For the meta-model, we first defined RDF classes for each existing concept, like a case, agenda item and artifact. Each class contains properties to describe required information of the concepts. A case, for example, has a Boolean property which describes if the case is closed, whereas artifacts contain a creation date, represented by a literal of type *xsd:DateTime*. In adCM, the concepts are related to each other in distinct ways: An agenda item can contain artifacts and multiple child agenda items, an agenda contains an ordered sequence of agenda items, and so on. We can describe the semantics of these relations by RDF properties. To describe, for example, that an agenda item can contain an artifact, we first have to define a property:

```
adcm:containsArtifact rdf:type owl:ObjectProperty
```

Without restricting its allowed subject (agenda item) and object type (artifact), the property could be used in violation of its intended semantic, causing invalid conclusions. Following the idea of a declarative model allowing everything that is not explicitly forbidden, we have to prevent such (accidental) misuse of adCM concepts. Therefore, we declare the allowed subject and object type using RDF Schema:

```
adcm:containsArtifact rdfs:domain adcm:AgendaItem .
adcm:containsArtifact rdfs:range adcm:Artifact
```

With this definition, the property *adcm:containsArtifact* can only be used to create a relation from instances of the type *adcm:AgendaItem* to instances of the type *Artifact*.

As a next step, we will show how domain experts can adapt this approach to augment the adCM meta model with additional concepts of the domain. A basic domain-specific extension to the meta model is the definition of specialized subclasses of adCM concepts. In rehabilitation management, for example, the healing plan as a central concept can be defined as a subclass of *adcm:Document*, as shown below. That way, it will be treated as an ordinary document by the adCM toolset, but could be specialized with properties and business rules from domain specialists (as described in Sect. 3.3). The prefix rehab denotes that the concept is neither an OWL concept, nor an adCM concept, but from rehabilitation management domain:

```
rehab:HealingPlan rdfs:subClassOf adcm:Document  .
```

A more advanced scenario for extending the meta-model with domain-specific concepts is the definition of custom properties. Consider, for example, that an extension should allow to add due dates to agenda items and artifacts. Regardless of its realization in the UI, changes in the data structure are minimal: We can define a new literal property *rehab:dueDate* which is of type *xsd:dateTime* and can be added to *adcm:AgendaItem* or *adcm:Artifact*. Due to the extensible meta-model, the additional information is stored in the same place and way as the existing data. Compared to relational data models, there is no need for expensive and risky schema migration [5].

3.2 Improving Data Quality and Analysis Outcome

As motivated in Sect. 2.2, a sound vocabulary is important for the success of data mining algorithms. Identifying common agenda items is difficult and error-prone if each case manager uses a different spelling or term for the same concept. The real frequency of common agenda items or artifacts can only be measured when resolving these naming issues. Also, when annotating agenda items and artifacts with tags, it is important to use a few distinct and well-known keywords. Unlike relational databases, graph structures used in the semantic web can cope with such issues. A lexical ontology like WordNet can be used to identify semantically similar agenda items by sets of synonyms ("synsets"). For example, if a colleague of Mr. Fisher uses the word "recuperation" instead of "healing", WordNet shows that both are in the synset of the other word. In addition, domain-specific ontologies such as ICD-10 (the international statistical classification of diseases and related health problems) can be used to identify different spellings. Consider for example another colleague of Mr. Fisher, who is using only ICD codes to denote diseases instead of human-readable labels (as shown in Fig. 2). Any algorithm that is not aware of these domain-specific terms would always handle codes and labels separately. As a result, it would underestimate the relevance of a common concept, just because its usage is fragmented.

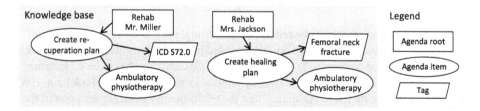

Fig. 2. Two similar cases containing different labels

We identified two different strategies for integrating such ontologies into an adCM implementation: Firstly, the ontology can be used as a lookup service. That is, a mining algorithm can use the ontology as an API providing synonyms for a given term. This strategy is recommended for big ontologies where the benefit of directly accessing linked information is eradicated by integration effort and strongly decreased reasoning performance.

This improves data quality and provides additional semantics, directly usable by all SCM tools and enhancements. Although this approach is closer to the linked-data design principle, this step should be executed before any case data is stored in the knowledge base. Otherwise, it would be time-consuming to connect all the existing terms with the vocabulary using properties like "same-as".

In our SCM prototype, we followed the first strategy and integrated an ontology as a lookup service, linking only analysis results in the knowledge base. This allows for easy change of the ontology in use when improving the analyzing algorithms or adding domain specific information. The service is employed by a synonym detection function of an algorithm identifying common agenda items. It preprocesses all agendas by replacing the agenda item names with IDs of their corresponding synsets. Frequent patterns within agendas are then calculated using the cluster synset IDs instead of natural language (which is also faster).

3.3   Business Rule Definition and Checking

As outlined in Sect. 2.3, business rule definitions are much more precise when using domain concepts. In this section, we will show how SCM supports process owners in defining and checking such business rules. We will do this using an example from rehabilitation management: At the beginning of each case, the rehabilitation manager has to classify the case using four groups (as shown by the decision tree in Fig. 3). The rule requires that each group involves a specific package of measures.

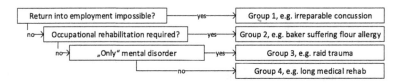

Fig. 3. Case classification decision tree (group numbers do not imply any order)

In this example, it would be beneficial if a SCM implementation could "understand" the classification and check, based on that knowledge, if the rehabilitation manager has applied the required measures. To achieve this, the classification has to be transformed into a formal language, so that a reasoning engine, as part of the SCM toolchain, can infer the classification itself. Assuming that the rehabilitation manager tags one of the pivotal agenda items or artifacts using keys like "employment impossible" or "reintegration impossible". This annotation is stored in the meta model using the *adcm:hasTag* property. Using the Apache Jena rule syntax, this example can be defined formally as follows:

```
(?x adcm:hasTag ?Tag)
(?Tag adcm:name "employment impossible")
-> (?x rdfs:subclassOf rehab:Group1)
```

Based on the standard RETE algorithm [6], the Jena reasoner can then classify the corresponding group by inference. Of course, the formal definition can be extended anytime, for example due to changes in the group definition. Based on this reasoning capability, the SCM implementation can query if the required package of measures has been applied (e.g. using the query language SPARQL).

Note that the first rule discussed above is a derivation rule according to the Semantics Of Business Vocabulary And Business Rules (SBVR) standard [9]. That is, it generates new information based on existing data. However, this only covers a subset of possible business rules. Another type of rules would be a static constraint like "A healing plan must contain a due date". To achieve this, the process owner has to define another formal rule. Given the due date example, we propose to use the violation property of Jena triggering an error message if the constraint is violated:

```
(?hp rdf:type rehab:HealingPlan)
noValue(?hp owl:onProperty rehab:dueDate)
-> (?hp rb:violation error('No due date!'))
```

3.4 Prototype Implementation

To conduct a small case study, we implemented the SCM approach in our adCM system prototype and defined the real life rules given above. Table 1 shows how we mapped the requirements with available (semantic) web technology:

Table 1. Requirements/Technology-Mapping

Requirements	Technology
Persistence Layer: Graph-based triple store	Apache Jena TDB
Data Access Layer: Interface for RDF data queries	Apache Jena Fuseki
Business Logic Layer: Manipulating RDF data	Apache Jena Ontology API
Presentation Layer: Business rule definition UI	Bootstrap
Operations: Application Server	WildFly (formerly JBoss)

When implementing the persistence and data access layer, one issue we had to address was bad performance, caused by our excessive use of reasoners to include domain knowledge and check business rules. The high expressiveness of OWL leads to reasoning algorithms with exponential time. Since the adCM approach aims at giving feedback in seconds, this is not acceptable. To address this problem, we optimized our system by replicating only case-specific data together with all rules locally on the client and synchronizing it with the complete case base on client shutdown. This solution scales very well as the small data sets are independent of each other and can benefit from load balancing and multiple processors or servers.

Another major issue when implementing SCM is usability. Defining classes and business rules using OWL syntax requires a significant amount of language expertise. Apart from the SPARQL interface provided by Fuseki, there is no distinct semantic web technology able to abstract from these languages. Therefore, we implemented a user interface (UI) for business rule definition and checking based on the Bootstrap framework. It provides both a dashboard for a compliance overview and a rule editor using a responsive design. Figure 4 shows the rule editor containing a business rule that corresponds with the case classification example. It uses a tree view to visualize the dependencies between predefined adCM meta model elements as well as domain-specific elements, if specified. If the pattern is found, the user-defined action is triggered. As long as the rules are not active, they are stored as Jena rule strings in a relational database. However, when becoming active, they are imported into the graph model and checked using the Jena reasoning engine.

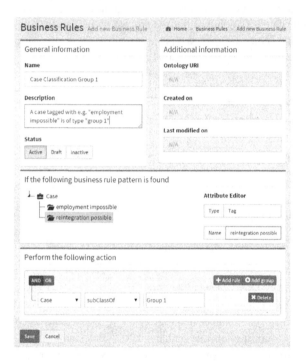

Fig. 4. SCM UI for developing business rules

As a case study, we defined the real life classification rules and the due date constraint rule and checked them against a model containing 30 artificial cases. Running on an Ubuntu server with an Intel Xeon L5640 CPU (2.27 GHz), the validation took only a few seconds. To demonstrate how the UI exposes violations, we manipulated two cases so that they do not comply with the due date constraint (i.e. they are "invalid"). Figure 5 shows a screenshot from the rule dashboard.

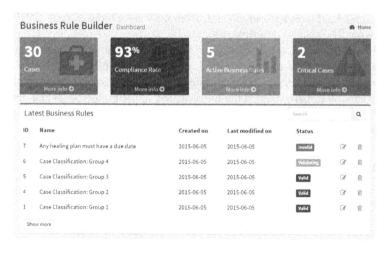

Fig. 5. SCM rule dashboard (Color figure online)

4   Related Work

In the field of ACM, only a few researchers explicitly use semantic web technologies. For example, Heil et al. use the linked data concept to apply social routing to ACM [7]. Ruiz et al. adapt semantic web technologies to knowledge work in general, with a clear focus on privacy policies in collaborative environments [13]. McGlothlin proposes how to connect domain-specific ontologies in healthcare [8].

There are also works discussing the application of declarative business logic, which is very similar to our approach. Pesic and van der Aalst [11] and Rychikova [14], for example, discuss how process models can be supplemented with declarative models. However, these approaches still focus on control flow constraints and neglect the data-centric notion of adaptive case management.

Voigt and Lehner introduce a flexible relational data model to cope with high mutability and variety in data [15]. Nevertheless, the approach lacks of the advantages that come with linked data (e.g. attaching custom ontologies using URIs).

5   Conclusion

In this paper, we discussed how semantic web paradigms and the underlying technologies can be utilized in the domain of adaptive case management (adCM). Linked data, for example, is a paradigm that can help to integrate domain-specific ontologies into the core adCM meta-model. Using languages like RDF and OWL, case data can be stored in graph structures according to formal semantics. This way, semantic reasoners can derive new facts or check the model against business rules defined by the process owner. In contrast to control-flow approaches, this approach follows the idea of a case management solution allowing sufficient flexibility for previously unknown process variations, but also providing process owners with the capability to define boundaries of the flexibility. This facilitates a paradigm shift from normative models, such as BPMN, to declarative models, such as description logics.

As a proof-of-concept, we integrated the semantic web technologies into our prototype case management system. Since the formal definition of business rules is quite difficult, we also implemented a business rule UI including a compliance dashboard for process owners. We plan to extend the functionality of the prototype so that new properties and classes can be added to the model, and additional types of business rules (according to SBVR) can be defined.

References

1. van der Aalst, W.M., Weske, M., Grünbauer, D.: Case handling: a new paradigm for business process support. DKE **53**(2), 129–162 (2005)
2. Benner, M., Book, M., Brückmann, T., Gruhn, V., Richter, T., Seyhan, S.: Managing and tracing the traversal of process clouds with templates, agendas and artifacts. In: Barros, A., Gal, A., Kindler, E. (eds.) BPM 2012. LNCS, vol. 7481, pp. 188–193. Springer, Heidelberg (2012)
3. Benner-Wickner, M., Book, M., Brückmann, T., Gruhn, V.: Execution support for agenda-driven case management. In: ACM 2014, pp. 1371–1377 (2014)
4. Berners-Lee, T.: Linked Data. W3C (2006). http://www.w3.org/DesignIssues/LinkedData.html
5. Curino, C., Moon, H.J., Tanca, L., Zaniolo, C.: Schema Evolution in Wikipedia - Toward a Web Information System Benchmark Enterprise Information Systems, 12–16 June 2008, Barcelona, Spain, vol. DISI, pp. 323–332 (2008)
6. Forgy, C.L.: Rete: a fast algorithm for the many pattern/many object pattern match problem. In: Raeth, P.G. (ed.) Expert Systems, pp. 324–341. IEEE Computer Society Press, Los Alamitos (1990)
7. Heil, S., Wild, S., Gaedke, M.: Collaborative adaptive case management with linked data. In: WWW 2014 Companion. International World Wide Web Conferences Steering Committee, Geneva, Switzerland, pp. 99–102 (2014)
8. McGlothlin, J.P., Khan, L.: Managing evolving code sets and integration of multiple data sources in health care analytics. In: DARE 2013, pp. 9–14 (2013)
9. OMG. Semantics of Business Vocabulary and Business Rules (SBVR), formal/2013–11-04 (2013). http://www.omg.org/spec/SBVR/1.2/PDF
10. Pesic, M.: Constraint-Based Workflow Management Systems: Shifting Control to Users, Eindhoven University of Technology (2008)
11. Pesic, M., van der Aalst, W.M.P.: A declarative approach for flexible business processes management. In: Eder, J., Dustdar, S. (eds.) BPM Workshops 2006. LNCS, vol. 4103, pp. 169–180. Springer, Heidelberg (2006)
12. Reiter, R.: On closed world data bases. In: Gallaire, H., Minker, J. (eds.) Logic and Data Bases, pp. 55–76. Springer, Boston (1978)
13. Ruiz, C., Álvaro, G., Gómez-Pérez, J.-M.: A framework and implementation for secure knowledge management in large communities. In: I-KNOW 2011, p. 1 (2011)
14. Rychkova, I.: Towards automated support for case management processes with declarative configurable specifications. In: La Rosa, M., Soffer, P. (eds.) BPM Workshops 2012. LNBIP, vol. 132, pp. 65–76. Springer, Heidelberg (2013)

15. Voigt, H., Lehner, W.: Flexible relational data model – a common ground for schema-flexible database systems. In: Manolopoulos, Y., Trajcevski, G., Kon-Popovska, M. (eds.) ADBIS 2014. LNCS, vol. 8716, pp. 25–38. Springer, Heidelberg (2014)
16. W3C. RDF 1.1 Concepts and Abstract Syntax (2014). Accessed 7 May 2015. http://www.w3.org/TR/rdf11-concepts/
17. W3C. RDF 1.1 Turtle: Terse RDF Triple Language (2014). Accessed 7 May 2015. http://www.w3.org/TR/turtle/

Supporting Knowledge Work by Speech-Act Based Templates for Micro Processes

Johannes Tenschert[(✉)] and Richard Lenz

Institute of Computer Science 6, University of Erlangen-Nuremberg,
Erlangen, Germany
{johannes.tenschert,richard.lenz}@fau.de

Abstract. Speech acts have been proposed to improve the design of interactive systems for decades. Nevertheless, they have not yet made their way to common practice in software engineering or even process modeling. Various types of workflow management systems have been successful to support or even automate mostly predictable schema based process patterns without the explicit use of speech acts as design primitives. Yet, todays work is increasingly characterized by unpredictable collaborative processes, called knowledge work. Some types of knowledge work are supported by case management tools which typically provide regulated access to case-related information. But communicative acts are not supported sufficiently. Since knowledge workers are well aware of the pragmatic dimension of their communicative acts, we believe that bringing this awareness of the nature of a speech act to a case management tool will allow for better support of unregulated knowledge intensive processes. In this paper we propose a speech-act-based approach to improve the effectivity of knowledge work. We thereby enhance case management systems by making them aware of speech acts. Speech act related micro processes can then be used to prevent misunderstandings, increase process transparency and make useful inferences.

Keywords: Adaptive case management · Speech Act Theory · Knowledge-intensive business process · Process template

1 Introduction

Today, around 50 % of the work in the US is knowledge work [19] and it is safe to assume a similar tendency in many other countries. Knowledge work is characterized by abstractly defined tasks opposite to the manual workers' clearly defined activities, flexible and expected application of knowledge, and the knowledge workers' responsibility for his own contribution in terms of quantity and quality [8]. The sequence of actions depends so much upon the specifics of the situation and therefore an important part of performing the work is to devise the plan on how to perform it [18]. Currently available techniques in process management do not sufficiently support this type of work.

© Springer International Publishing Switzerland 2016
M. Reichert and H.A. Reijers (Eds.): BPM Workshops 2015, LNBIP 256, pp. 78–89, 2016.
DOI: 10.1007/978-3-319-42887-1_7

Knowledge workers already reduce routine work by creating templates of documents and check lists for common tasks [17]. Typical systems for adaptive case management provide case folders that include stakeholders, documents, tasks and various other artifacts. The Object Management Group published the standard Case Management Model and Notation 1.0 (CMMN) [13] to create, use and exchange case models between different vendors' environments.

We use Speech Act Theory to classify communicative acts to gain process-specific advantages in case folders similar to deploying a Workflow Management System for routine work. In micro processes, the intentions of interactions are captured explicitly. No schema is necessary to document interactions. Storing the pragmatic intention of a document or some other artifact representing interaction already offers possibilities for inference, for example finding all promises that have been made. If a more detailed schema can be given, the possibilities for inference and support increase. For example, interactions can be supported by document templates using case data and annotations for the pragmatic intention. Currently, nearly half of all interactions between knowledge workers do not create the intended value because they have to hunt for information [4], which indicates that semantically enriching past interactions and making this information visible has a great potential to increase a knowledge workers' productivity.

The vision for micro processes and their potential environment is, that a knowledge worker creates and uses templates of interactions, which also include document templates. For every case, he or she decides whether the template resembles a suitable plan or interactions need to be documented and executed manually. A semantically rich overview of all interactions reduces the time to hunt for information and to make decisions. Using the stored pragmatic intention, contradictions and indicators for potential problems help to avoid errors or at least to reduce a problem's impact by discovering and solving it at an early stage. Checking off promised tasks or updating contact information of a case's stakeholder should also be possible with the knowledge workers' preferred tool, e.g. his or her mobile device or PIM software.

In the following sections, we briefly introduce Speech Act Theory and related work. Section 4 describes micro processes as well as coordination and production acts, and provides a speech act library for an attorneys' office. In Sect. 5, we model aspects of the work of an attorney with micro processes to document interactions and to automatically create preliminary or finished documents. We designed an architecture for the proposed approach and Sect. 6 describes the parts of it that we prototypically implemented. Section 7 discusses our approach and in Sect. 8 we conclude and describe further questions to be answered.

2   Speech Act Theory

Speech Act Theory was introduced by Austin [2] and further elaborated by Searle [15,16]. Austin acknowledged that saying something or in saying something we *do* something and classified the illocutionary force of utterances as well as potential infelicities. A speech act consists of its illocutionary force and its propositional content. Searle [16] distinguishes the following five categories of illocutionary forces, for which Table 1 shows some examples:

- **Assertive:** Commit the speaker to something being the case.
- **Commissive:** Commit the speaker to some future course of action.
- **Declarative:** Change the reality according to the propositional content.
- **Directive:** Attempt to cause the hearer to take some particular action.
- **Expressive:** Express the attitude or emotions of the speaker, for example thanking or apologizing.

In the $F(P)$ framework [15], with F as an illocutionary force and P as the propositional content, $F(P)$ can also be the propositional content of another illocutionary force. For example, $F_1(F_2(P))$ can stand for the promise (outer F_1), that one will inform someone (inner F_2) about P. There is no conceptual limit on how deep nesting can be, hence P in the example could be some speech act from the district court and an attorneys' statement on the phone like "Today, I will forward and comment on the letter from district court I got" could easily be documented using the framework while referencing already entered data.

3   Related Work

Auramäki et al. [1] already suggested a speech-act-based approach for office automation as early as 1988. Nowadays, office automation is well supported by workflow technology. Yet, the basic assumptions and principles are still valid and useful. They view offices as networks of commitments. Agents perform two types of acts: Speech acts and instrumental acts, e.g. creating or delivering goods. Their main focus is analyzing and modeling discourses containing both types of acts. Typical further acts are listed for each stage, for example a request is usually followed by an acceptance, counteroffer, clarification request or a rejection. These results can be applied on our approach: Potential further steps can be suggested to the user and deviations from the model can be detected in order to find and display candidates of communication problems so the user can decide if and how to resolve them. For knowledge work, we do not expect that every important discourse can be modeled a priori due to the costs and uncommonness.

Kimbrough and Moore [10] introduce a formal language for business communication in the context of an army office using Speech Act Theory. In the domain of an army office, paths of command and responsibility can easily be delineated and each dialog contains information on its implied force. A speech act is represented by speaker, hearer, illocutionary force, content and context. They apply inference on the propositional content and illocutionary force of documented speech acts, for example to find unfulfilled requests.

Hisarciklilar and Boujut [9] support design communication using Speech Act Theory and Semantic Web annotations. They add annotations to 3D instances of CAD models and other design artifacts describing their authors, intent, purpose, and free-form body text. The intent represents the illocutionary act and the body text is the locutionary act. The authors and purpose contain domain-specific information in the context of design communication, whereas the authors indicate domains of expertise and the purpose classifies annotations in groups, e.g. "Project requirement" or "Domain-specific constraint".

Schoop [14] analyzes communication problems in healthcare using Habermas' Theory of Communicative Action and Searle's Speech Act Theory. She classifies illocutionary forces in the medical domain and relates them to the appropriate roles. The paper argues that there is a clear need for a cooperative documentation system since it could offer many possibilities for information access, for example finding unfulfilled promises or particular propositional contents, and could help in avoiding communication breakdowns. We agree and intend micro processes to be one component of such a cooperative documentation system that not only documents speech acts but also offers mechanisms to make them transparent and to avoid misunderstandings.

Bider and Perjons [3] analyze a business process support system in regard to the users speech acts and classify typical communicative acts in business process cases. They conclude that the Language/Action perspective is an appropriate tool to analyze communication models of systems, which should also apply to the modeling of a speech act library.

Dietz [6,7] analyzes and models business processes and organizations taking Speech Act Theory into account. The main goal is to show the deep structure behind business processes invariant of the applied technology. Actors perform *coordination acts* and *production acts*. The effect of coordination acts are commitments between the performer and the addressee regarding the bringing about of production acts. Production acts are either material, e.g. creating goods, or immaterial, e.g. granting insurance claims. Since process models contain all acts and their dependencies, the detection of problems in a model can be easier than in models using BPMN. Micro processes also model speech acts and document performatives, but they are not restricted to standard processes, and they can be generic, reusable, and applied in different contexts as well as ad-hoc processes.

Van der Aalst et al. [20] introduce a framework for speech-act-based interacting workflow processes called *proclets*. The control flow of a process is divided into several proclets connected through channels following the principle of divide and conquer. The approach is based on petri nets. The communication between proclets is realized by exchanging performatives. A proclet class has a knowledge base to store and query previous performatives. However, interpreting the knowledge base of one proclet class as the knowledge base of a *case*, proclets do not fully satisfy their potential of assisting ad hoc processes. Our micro processes work on a shared case-level knowledge base and allow otherwise automated or manual input of performatives. We view proclets as a complementary approach aiming at more structured processes than micro processes. The focus on performatives allows to integrate both approaches in order to inference on documented speech acts and to apply business rules.

The Object Management Group recently published the standard *Case Management Model and Notation* (CMMN) [13]. It defines a meta-model to express a case, its contents and an interchange format for exchanging cases among tools of different vendors. The model does not focus on interactions, which currently need to be modeled with tasks and documents. The pragmatic intention of an interaction is not made explicit, but the model could be extended in that respect.

Neumann and Lenz [12] proposed a decentralized approach to support unregulated cooperative processes by sharing commonly used documents, so called α-Docs. We propose to extend this approach by annotating α-Docs with their pragmatic intentions. Storing a document in a case file is typically aimed at making the contents available to cooperating parties. This is important, but not the whole story: The document typically contains one or more illocutionary acts, i.e. the intentions that are connected with this document. The author of a document is typically well aware of his or her intentions, but the case file is not. If the case file knows that a file actually contains the information related to a promise, it can store a reference to this document in a to-do list. Classifying a document as a promise is just one click, but the case file can make inferences from this information. The approach is motivated by α-Flow, but the basic idea is actually independent from the decentralized case file provided by α-Flow. Sometimes an illocutionary act like a promise is connected with further information, e.g. a deadline or a priority level or other important conditions. By classifying a speech act properly, the system also knows that this information is still required, so it might ask for it. If the information is not available right now, the system can place reminders in a to-do list. The same kind of inference can be used for other types of illocutionary acts. Storing this speech act related information in a case file, which is aware of different types allows for more transparency. For example, it is now possible to trace back certain processes because the system *knows* that document x is the answer to document y, which is the fulfillment of a promise made by some cooperating agent.

4   Micro Processes

Micro processes contain two types of actions: Coordination acts (performatives) and production acts. Auramäki et al. [1] and Dietz [6] made a similar distinction. *Performatives* are annotated speech acts consisting of its `type`, e.g. whether it is a promise or an assertion, one `sender`, one or more `recipients`, the `medium`, a `timestamp`, the `content` and arbitrary `annotations`.

A production act is some non-coordinating action, for example to create a document or a physical product. Actually, the micro processes engine cannot definitely know whether a production act was performed unless it created the artifact itself. But it can know who *asserted* to the system that the production act was performed. Hence, production acts are documented by performatives and can be referenced in the propositional content of other performatives.

Micro processes are not speech acts themselves, but they are composed of speech acts and production acts. For example, a performative *promise* is related to a particular micro process *question* → *answer*. The prototypical implementation of this model is described in Sect. 6.

4.1   Coordination Acts

The propositional content of the speech act can be some free-form text, e.g. the utterance, a reference to some production act, a boolean expression, or an expression containing performatives. Since the goal is to support knowledge work, it is necessary to minimize the modeling effort. If no sender is stated, the user executing the current step is the sender. The timestamp is always set when executing. Appending the medium of a speech act is optional since it may be different from instance to instance and potentially the user does not know which medium was actually used, e.g. documenting a performative of a third party.

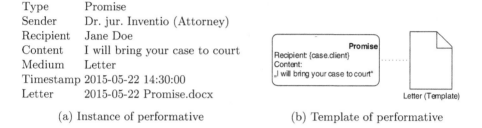

Type   Promise
Sender   Dr. jur. Inventio (Attorney)
Recipient Jane Doe
Content   I will bring your case to court
Medium   Letter
Timestamp 2015-05-22 14:30:00
Letter   2015-05-22 Promise.docx

(a) Instance of performative   (b) Template of performative

Fig. 1. Example instance and template of a common promise

Figure 1b shows the template of a promise with a generated letter attached. It uses some variables of the case file, e.g. `case.client` in the performative and his or her address in the document template. Figure 1a shows an actual instance of the template. The sender, recipient and timestamp are added automatically and the letter is generated by the system and altered by the attorney.

4.2 Production Acts

Hisarciklilar and Boujut [9] allow annotating several performatives to one design artifact. This is reasonable not only in the context of design, but generally for documents and arbitrary artifacts. Users should be able to discuss results, send them around, reference them, improve them and easily or implicitly document those interactions for later use. In order to increase user acceptance, a basic document templating system for Office Open XML (Microsoft Word) documents, plain text and HTML (for e-mail) was built to use the current context data of a case and micro process. Building a template for an interaction therefore can also include an actual letter to be sent which is already filled with relevant information. Figure 1b shows how document creation could be annotated to a performative.

Moreover, production acts could also represent calling web services or placing tasks in a to-do list. The content of a production act is the information necessary to initiate the act, for example the document template or the URL of a web service and the desired function name and parameters. The system can actually only know whether the production act was successful if some user or (document creation) system asserts that the act was performed and accepted. Hence, production acts primarily act as a referenceable object with various annotations and to make modeling more intuitive.

4.3   Speech Act Library

An important goal beyond the approach for micro processes is to have an extensible speech act library tailored to a particular domain. For example, the speech act library in a hospital [14] contains many different assertives and several expressives whereas the focus of the speech act library for army offices [10] focuses on a small set of seven common performatives within assertives, commissives, directives and declaratives. The broad classification of Searle [15] of illocutionary forces into assertives, commissives, declaratives, directives and expressives is applied in our approach. A performative of a particular domain is assigned to one category and its common and required annotations are specified.

Table 1 shows a possible speech act library for an attorney, which is used in the next section. A common annotation of an answer is the reference to the question being answered. The difference between *assure* and *inform* are the severity and certitude of the speaker, for example *informing* about an incoming letter and *assuring* the client that delivering some particular evidence is required to win the case. A *promise* usually contains a stated period. For *ask-user*, the system is sender, the current user is the recipient and the variable name to save the users answer to is a required annotation. *Ask* represents a question to any person and usually states no variable name. *Subscribe* and *unsubscribe* require to state the person receiving or not receiving correspondence of a particular kind.

If the speech acts of a domain are fanned out, the classification does not need to be flat. It should rather be a tree adhering to the Liskov substitution principle [11] in order to allow coarse-grained user input and to reduce complexity for inference and business rules.

5   Examples

The following example micro processes were created to support frequent similar tasks of an attorney. They are real processes that were examined and modeled in regard to speech acts and related micro processes. They use the speech act library depicted in Table 1. The models are vague in parts that vary between instances and strict where deviations are too rare to consider for automation.

Figure 2 shows a simple process that depicts the promising of creating some document. The main intention is to document and remind the attorney that he still has to create the promised document. Neither the recipient, medium, an optional deadline or a working title of the document are fixed, but all missing data is asked while running the micro process. If the promise was given per letter, the attorney *should* set a reference to it, but he is not required to. However, setting the recipient and a preliminary working title is mandatory. The attorney can be reminded to fulfill a promise by web interface, by e-mail, or by his smartphone.

Another typical task of an attorney is to forward documents he received from court. Usually, the paralegal scans the document, and the attorney reads and shortly comments the necessary actions if there are any. Figures 3 and 4 are two possible outcomes. Figure 3 asks the attorney, which document he wants to

Table 1. Speech act library for an attorneys' office

Illocutionary force	Performative
Assertive	Answer, assure, inform
Commissive	Promise
Declarative	Subscribe, unsubscribe, acknowledge, decline
Directive	Ask-user, ask, request, order
Expressive	Congratulate, excuse, thank

Fig. 2. Sample process: promising a document

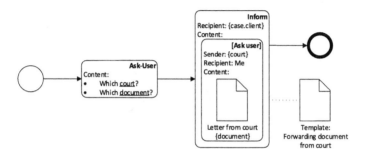

Fig. 3. Sample process: forwarding court documents

inform his client about and which court sent it. He is also asked of the type of the speech act the document represents, but of course he can add a pseudo-type to specify it later. The letter to his client is generated using case information (e.g. addresses) and potentially he only has to fill in missing comments.

Figure 4 expects incoming documents from an arbitrary sender. The received question is forwarded to the client along with some comments on the question and the promise to answer it. The attorney is first asked to fill in the sender and a reference to the incoming letter as well as to shortly summarize the question. The outgoing document describes two speech acts: informing the client, that a question was received and promising to write an answer. Hence, the next step after asking the attorney is to create the document and all speech acts are attached. The generated documents already contain all case data and entered answers, but still need the attorneys' commentary.

Figure 5 shows the request of adding another party to the list of recipients of letters to the client, e.g. legal guardians, parents, siblings or children. The request **Subscribe** has to be documented and the attorney has to decide whether

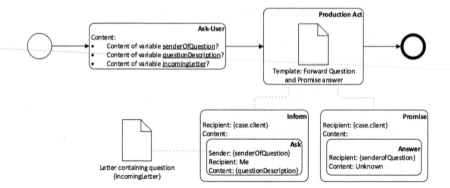

Fig. 4. Sample process: informing about questions and promise to answer

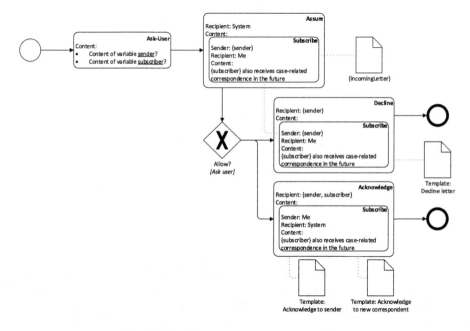

Fig. 5. Sample process: new correspondent

he acknowledges the request. If he acknowledges it, he informs the sender of the request and the new correspondent, that now he will send letters to the new correspondent, and uses one document template for each recipient. The `Subscribe` performative now contains him as a sender and the system as recipient in order to register the subscription. If he declines the request, the sender will receive a predefined decline letter and the attorney optionally fills in some legal reasons. Figure 5 does *not* require other process templates sending letters to the client to use a correspondent list. Since all performatives are documented, a business rules engine can detect new performatives with the client as recipient and prepare appropriate performatives and documents. For example, letters could be forwarded similar to Fig. 3, or a new task `Inform {correspondent} about {performative}` could be added to the attorneys' to-do list.

6   Implementation

The prototypical implementation consists of class representations of coordination and production acts, a document generation tool using case-related data, a simple representation of case-related data, and an engine to execute micro processes. Users interact with the system through a web interface. Coordination acts contain all attributes described in Sect. 4.1, arbitrary annotations as key-value pairs, and propositional content allows nested speech acts, connectors and free-form text to adhere to the $F(P)$ framework. The base class of production acts is a top-level representation providing standard attributes and arbitrary annotations. Subclasses can actually implement or initiate production acts.

Document generation is initiated by a production act or a document annotation for a coordination act. Templates are described adhering to an XML Schema definition that allows basic formatting and document headers for the word processing perspective, and conditional expressions using case data. Document templates are translated to Office Open XML (Microsoft Word), plain text and HTML. Plain text and HTML output are intended to later support e-mail communication. Case-related data is currently represented by key-value-pairs.

The workflow engine supports coordination and production acts as well as conditional branches with optional condition expressions on case-related data. At present, no modeling tool has been implemented yet and therefore elements of a micro process are either hard-coded instances of coordination and production acts or serialized XML files. It is planned to create a structured XML Schema definition for coordination and production acts and examining to what extent it could be based on CMMN [13] in order to leverage the infrastructure currently being built for it. The knowledge worker will create micro processes with a modeling tool in his or her browser.

7   Discussion

In order to document the progress of knowledge work, the focus on interactions instead of actions has several advantages. First of all, knowledge workers already try to automate their interactions using document templates and checklists, which clearly shows that support in this area *is* necessary. Sadly, those document templates currently do not contain any machine-recognizable information on the semantics of the interactions represented by a document. Creating a micro process of a template documents the semantics for later inferences by the user or a machine and offers to automatically insert case data. Finding out which promises are not yet fulfilled, what assertions had been given or whether all necessary stakeholders were informed about some important deadline may no longer require reading the whole history of a case.

Adding the semantic information to interactions only requires little to no additional effort for the user if he already has to document it somehow. Reports can be generated, which could already amortize the effort in some cases. Over a quarter of a typical knowledge workers' time is spent searching for information [5], and an index of interactions in which those information pieces often are buried therefore has a huge potential to increase the user's productivity.

Micro processes are intended to be created by domain experts themselves, since they know best what goals they want to achieve and how they intend to do that. Moreover, speech acts do not have to be supported solely by micro processes. They can be modeled and documented using another technique or manually. Furthermore, documented speech acts can be used to interact with structured processes similar to Proclets [20], to initiate other processes, to detect communication problems and for business rules. The user has the choice to use the technique that is in his view best suited for the case. Analysts can create business rules or invariants for compliance, which are applied to the knowledge base of cases including past performatives. Hence, the focus on interactions can bridge the gap between structured, semi-structured and ad-hoc processes.

Since performatives include semantics of an interaction, the engine can also infer how undoing it has to be performed, for example some compensatory interaction could be necessary or removing the documentation could probably suffice. The system may completely take care of it or at least create an item in a user's to-do list that describes what actions he has to perform to properly undo it.

8   Conclusion and Future Work

In this paper, we present micro processes, a speech-act-based approach to weakly structured processes that makes the pragmatic intention of interactions explicit. It enables knowledge workers to create templates of frequent interaction patterns in order to automate aspects of their work and to decrease the time spent on hunting for information. For example, finding unfulfilled promises and all related paperwork does no longer require the user to skim the whole case folder. Some types of speech acts are depicted exemplarily and we currently integrate more.

Still, there are many open questions. Integrating tasks, contacts, communication, documents and other artifacts of a case folder into the tools knowledge workers actually use or want to use to achieve their goals will decrease obstacles and scattering of information. For example, web standards like WebDAV, CardDAV and CalDAV enable additional user interfaces through their wide-spread support in mobile devices and groupware. Hence, it is planned to implement these standards and to evaluate the benefit for users. Finding out the actual pragmatic intention of actions on a mobile phone might prove to be difficult.

Inference on the speech act history is currently hard-coded and lacking a formal model as well as easy-to-use tools to analyze a case. It could enable automatically unveiling misunderstandings and potential future communication breakdowns in order to solve problems at an early stage. Micro processes are intended to be integrated with other techniques that tackle several aspects of process support. Interacting with structured processes modeled with Proclets [20] or BPMN will therefore be elaborated. Integrating speech-act-based business rules promises to for example properly inform all necessary stakeholders of a particular type of interaction or to unveil and warn about compliance breaches.

References

1. Auramäki, E., Lehtinen, E., Lyytinen, K.: A speech-act-based office modeling approach. ACM Trans. Inf. Syst. **6**(2), 126–152 (1988)
2. Austin, J.L.: How to Do Things with Words. Oxford University Press, Oxford (1975)
3. Bider, I., Perjons, E.: Reviving language/action perspective in the era of social software: research in progress. In: Short Paper Proceedings of the 5th IFIP WG 8.1 Working Conference on the Practice of Enterprise Modeling (2012)
4. Bisson, P., Stephenson, E., Viguerie, S.P.: The productivity imperative. McKinsey Q., June 2010
5. Davenport, T.H.: Rethinking knowledge work: a strategic approach. McKinsey Q. **1**(11), 88–99 (2011)
6. Dietz, J.L.G.: Enterprise Ontology: Theory and Methodology. Springer, Heidelberg (2006)
7. Dietz, J.L.G.: The deep structure of business processes. Commun. ACM **49**(5), 58–64 (2006)
8. Drucker, P.F.: Knowledge-worker productivity: the biggest challenge. Calif. Manag. Rev. **41**(2), 79–94 (1999)
9. Hisarciklilar, O., Boujut, J.F.: A speech act theory-based information model to support design communication through annotations. Comput. Ind. **60**(7), 510–519 (2009)
10. Kimbrough, S.O., Moore, S.A.: On automated message processing in electronic commerce and work support systems: speech act theory and expressive felicity. ACM Trans. Inf. Syst. **15**(4), 321–367 (1997)
11. Liskov, B.H., Wing, J.M.: A behavioral notion of subtyping. ACM Trans. Program. Lang. Syst. **16**(6), 1811–1841 (1994)
12. Neumann, C.P., Lenz, R.: The alpha-flow approach to inter-institutional process support in healthcare. Int. J. Knowl. Based Organ. (IJKBO) **2**(4), 52–68 (2012)
13. Object management group: case management model and notation (CMMN) (2014). http://www.omg.org/spec/CMMN/1.0
14. Schoop, M.: Habermas and searle in hospital: a description language for cooperative documentation systems in healthcare. In: Proceedings of the Second International Workshop on Communication Modeling - The Language/Action Perspective (1997)
15. Searle, J.R.: Speech Acts: An Essay in the Philosophy of Language. Cambridge University Press, Cambridge (1969)
16. Searle, J.R.: A classification of illocutionary acts. Lang. Soc. **5**, 1–23 (1976)
17. Swenson, K.D.: Workflow for the information worker. In: Fischer, F. (ed.) Workflow Handbook, pp. 39–49. Future Strategies, Lighthouse Point (2001)
18. Swenson, K.D.: The nature of knowledge work. In: Swenson, K.D. (ed.) Mastering the Unpredictable: How Adaptive Case Management Will Revolutionize the Way that Knowledge Workers Get Things Done. Meghan-Kiffer Press, Tampa (2010)
19. Swenson, K.D.: Robots don't innovate - innovation vs automation in BPM, May 2015
20. Van Der Aalst, W.M., Barthelmess, P., Ellis, C.A., Wainer, J.: Proclets: a framework for lightweight interacting workflow processes. Int. J. Coop. Inf. Syst. **10**(04), 443–481 (2001)

Towards Structural Consistency Checking in Adaptive Case Management

Christoph Czepa[1]($\boxtimes$), Huy Tran[1], Uwe Zdun[1], Thanh Tran Thi Kim[2], Erhard Weiss[2], and Christoph Ruhsam[2]

[1] Software Architecture Research Group, Faculty of Computer Science, University of Vienna, Währingerstraße 29, 1090 Vienna, Austria
{christoph.czepa,huy.tran,uwe.zdun}@univie.ac.at
[2] Isis Papyrus Europe AG, Alter Wienerweg 12, 2344 Maria Enzersdorf, Austria
{thanh.tran,erhard.weiss,christoph.ruhsam}@isis-papyrus.com

Abstract. This paper proposes structural consistency checking for Adaptive Case Management (ACM). Structures such as a hierarchical organization of business goals and dependencies among tasks are either created at design time or evolve over time while working on cases. In this paper, we identify structures specific to current ACM systems (as opposed to other BPM systems), discuss which inconsistencies can occur, and outline how to discover these issues through model checking and graph algorithms.

1 Introduction

In contrast to classical Business Process Management (BPM) which mainly utilizes predefined, rigid business processes, processes in knowledge-intensive domains (e.g., medical care, customer support, contract management) tend to be rather unpredictable and shall be handled in a more flexible manner. Flexibility and structuredness, however, do not necessarily contradict each other since structures can remain adaptable even at runtime. Adaptive Case Management (ACM) combines classical structural features such as process flows with new structures such as dependencies among tasks and business goal hierarchies [5,11]. A high degree of flexibility increases the chance for potential errors or inconsistencies. For example, a new goal could be in conflict with an existing goal or a new dependency among two tasks could result in contradicting pre- and postconditions of these tasks.

In this paper, we illustrate exemplary structures that can be found in today's ACM solutions. Our study is based on our work with ISIS Papyrus[1], a state-of-the-art commercial ACM solution, several customer applications realized in Papyrus, our analysis of other solutions, and the Case Management Model and Notation (CMMN) standard[2] [8]. We discuss potential inconsistencies that can occur in such structures. Verification of classical process definitions has been

---

[1] http://www.isis-papyrus.com.
[2] http://www.omg.org/spec/CMMN/1.0/PDF/.

© Springer International Publishing Switzerland 2016
M. Reichert and H.A. Reijers (Eds.): BPM Workshops 2015, LNBIP 256, pp. 90–95, 2016.
DOI: 10.1007/978-3-319-42887-1_8

discussed by a plethora of studies [1,3,4,6,7,9,10,13], but we are not aware of any prior study related to structural consistency checking in the domain of ACM. We are working towards bridging this research gap.

2   Identification of Structures and Discussion of Inconsistencies

In this section, we illustrate structures that can be found in today's ACM solutions and discuss which inconsistencies can possibly occur in these structures. For the sake of illustration, we make use of the open CMMN standard instead of proposing a new or using a vendor-specific proprietary notation for the discussion of recurring structures in ACM and their inconsistencies. Please note that the focus is clearly on the structural concepts of ACM, not on a specific notation.

2.1   Goal Hierarchies

A goal defines what a knowledge worker has to achieve and thus, is directly linked to operational business targets and strategic objectives. Goals of a case can be structured hierarchically [5,11]. On top of the hierarchy stands the main goal of a case which can be broken down into subgoals. Naturally, we would not want to pursue contradictory goals simultaneously. Therefore, consistency checks that reveal contradicting completion criteria of potentially simultaneously pursued goals would be helpful in the design of ACM cases.

Example 1. In the goal hierarchy depicted in Fig. 1, a knowledge worker can work towards *Subgoal 1* and *Subgoal 2* or *Subgoal 1.1* and *Subgoal 2* at the same time, so their completion criteria must not be contradictory.

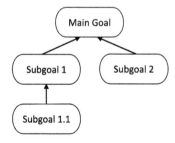

Fig. 1. Goal hierarchy example

2.2   Structures of Interdependent Criteria in the Case Structure

Starting to work on a case or the completion of a task usually leads to one or more other elements of the case to become accessed, depending on whether criteria along the way to such an element can be satisfied altogether. Every element of the case must be accessible. When an element is inaccessible due to an unsatisfiable combination of criteria, it is in any case an inconsistency that must be revealed. If an entry criterion is assigned to a goal, then it is also called a completion criterion. If an entry criterion (resp. exit criterion) is assigned to a task, then it is also called a precondition (resp. postcondition).

Example 2. Figure 2 extends the goal hierarchy presented in Fig. 1 with tasks, subprocesses and substructures. In the following, we analyze for each element what combination of criteria must be satisfiable for its accessibility.

The precondition of *Task S1.1* must not contradict the entry criterion of *Substructure 1* because *Task S1.1* is the only task that can be started directly after having gained access to the substructure. *Subgoal 1.1* is only accessible from *Task S1.1* if the postcondition of the task is not contradictory to the completion criterion of the goal. To complete *Subgoal 1*, its completion criterion must be consistent with both the postcondition of *Task SS1.1* and the completion criterion of *Subgoal 1.1*. *Subgoal 2* is accessible if the postcondition of *Task 1* does not contradict the completion criterion of Subgoal 2. The process of *Subprocess 1* can only be started properly if the preconditions of *Task P1.1* and *Task P1.2* are consistent because they are logically and-connected due to the parallel split

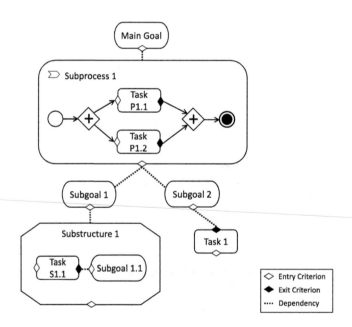

Fig. 2. Example case

gateway ('process start structure'). Additionally, the structure composed of the entry criterion of the subprocess and the access structures of both *Subgoal 1* and *Subgoal 2* must be satisfiable ('subprocess access structure'). Consequently, the process start and subprocess access structure of *Subprocess 1* must also not be contradictory. To be able to fulfill the *Main Goal* of the case, the process finish structure composed of the postconditions of *Task P1.1* and *Task P1.2* must be consistent with the completion criterion of the *Main Goal*.

2.3 Dependency Loops

Dependencies can be arranged so as to create loops. There must be a way to enter this dependency loop.

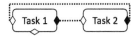

Fig. 3. Dependency loop example

Example 3. Figure 3 contains an example of a dependency loop. If we remove the second entry criterion of *Task 1* (which has no explicit dependency) the loop would lose its entry point and become inaccessible.

Please note that a dependency loop does not behave like a loop in flow-based business process language (e.g., BPMN) because a knowledge worker can decide whether or not to execute the next task and can, therefore, easily break out.

3   Outline of the Approach

In this section, we outline our approach for structural consistency checking of ACM case template. Our approach is based on model checking and graph algorithms. Model checking is used for the checking of goal hierarchies, structures of interdependent criteria and structured subprocesses. Graph algorithms are used for the discovery of loops and for expressing structures of interdependent criteria.

For the most part, structural consistency checking in ACM can be performed based on structures of interdependent criteria. This reduces the checking effort drastically because only parts of the model must be considered when checking for specific errors in the model. Flow-based subprocesses are the exception because the subprocess must also be verified as a whole.

EF p is a Computation Tree Logic operator, and its meaning is that p must be satisfiable on at least one subsequent path. Model checking of this formula can be described as nondeterministic changes of data values until a fitting solution is found or all possibilities are exhausted. The most atomic checkable item in ACM is a single criterion c which must meet the specification $EF(c)$, followed by two criteria c_d and c'_d that are related to the same dependency d which must meet the specification $EF(c_d \wedge c'_d)$.

```
VAR
Data#Person#First_Name#String : {Christoph, Christopher, Christian, Huy, Uwe, Thanh};

DEFINE Data#Person#First_Name#String#startsWith#Chr := (Data#Person#First_Name#String =
    Christoph) | (Data#Person#First_Name#String = Christian) | (Data#Person#First_Name#
    String = Christopher);

DEFINE Data#Person#First_Name#String#startsWith#T := (Data#Person#First_Name#String = Thanh);

CTLSPEC EF Data#Person#First_Name#String#startsWith#Chr & Data#Person#First_Name#String#
    startsWith#T
```

Listing 1.1. NuSMV code

Example 4. Let us assume that both c_d and c'_d are criteria which are related to a string function 'starts with', where c_d demands that the first name of a person must start with 'T' and c'_d requires the first name to start with 'Chr'. Listing 1.1 contains code for checking the consistency of these two criteria. When we input this code into the model checker NuSMV [2], it detects that the specification is not satisfiable, so these interdependent criteria are contradicting each other.

For the generation and representation of logical expression trees that represent structures of interdependent criteria which then can be verified by model checking (generalization of Example 4), graph algorithms are leveraged in accordance with the analysis outlined in Sect. 2.2. Dependency loops can be discovered as strongly connected components in a graph representation of the case by Tarjan's algorithm [12] in linear time.

4 Related Work

Kherbouche et al. use model checking to find structural errors in BPMN2 models [6]. Eshuis proposes a model checking approach for the verification of UML activity diagrams [4]. Van der Aalst created a mapping of EPCs to Petri nets to check whether there are structural errors such as gateway mismatches [1]. Sbai et al. also use model checking for the verification of workflow nets (Petri nets representing a workflow) [10]. Raedts et al. propose the transformation of models such as UML activity diagrams and BPMN2 models to Petri nets for verification with Petri net analyzers [9]. Xiao et al. transform XPDL structures to Petri nets [13]. Köhler et al. describe a process by means of an automaton and check this automaton by model checking [7]. El-Saber et al. provide a formalization of BPMN and propose a verification through model checker [3]. These approaches have been created for flow-based business processes. None of the existing approaches considers the structural features that are present in Adaptive Case Management.

5 Conclusion and Future Work

This paper discusses structural consistency checking in the domain of Adaptive Case Management and proposes the use of model checking and graph algorithms as a potential solution. We identify several structural features, discuss possible inconsistencies, and propose preliminary concepts for discovering inconsistencies. Our study is based on our work with checking cases in ISIS Papyrus, a state-of-the-art ACM commercial product, as well as our analysis of other solutions and the CMMN standard. In future work, we intend to elaborate and formalize our checking approach and evaluate its scalability and performance.

Acknowledgements. The research leading to these results has received funding from the FFG project CACAO, no. 843461 and the Wiener Wissenschafts-, Forschungs- und Technologiefonds (WWTF), Grant No. ICT12-001.

References

1. Van der Aalst, W.M.P.: Formalization and verification of event-driven process chains. Inf. Softw. Technol. **41**(10), 639–650 (1999)
2. Cimatti, A., Clarke, E., Giunchiglia, F., Roveri, M.: NUSMV: a new symbolic model verifier. In: Halbwachs, N., Peled, D.A. (eds.) CAV 1999. LNCS, vol. 1633, pp. 495–499. Springer, Heidelberg (1999)
3. El-Saber, N., Boronat, A.: BPMN formalization and verification using maude. In: 2014 Workshop on Behaviour Modelling-Foundations and Applications (BM-FA), pp. 1:1–1:12. ACM (2014)
4. Eshuis, R.: Symbolic model checking of UML activity diagrams. ACM Trans. Softw. Eng. Methodol. **15**(1), 1–38 (2006)
5. Greenwood, D.P.A.: Goal-oriented autonomic business process modeling and execution: engineering change management demonstration. In: Dumas, M., Reichert, M., Shan, M.-C. (eds.) BPM 2008. LNCS, vol. 5240, pp. 390–393. Springer, Heidelberg (2008)
6. Kherbouche, O., Ahmad, A., Basson, H.: Using model checking to control the structural errors in BPMN models. In: 7th International Conference on RCIS, pp. 1–12 (2013)
7. Koehler, J., Tirenni, G., Kumaran, S.: From business process model to consistent implementation: a case for formal verification methods. In: 6th International Conference on EDOC, pp. 96–106 (2002)
8. Kurz, M., Schmidt, W., Fleischmann, A., Lederer, M.: Leveraging CMMN for ACM: examining the applicability of a new OMG standard for adaptive case management. In: 7th International Conference on Subject-Oriented BPM. ACM, New York (2015). pp. 4:14:9
9. Raedts, I., Petković, M., Usenko, Y.S., van der Werf, J.M., Groote, J.F., Somers, L.: Transformation of BPMN models for behaviour analysis. In: MSVVEIS, pp. 126–137. INSTICC (2007)
10. Sbai, Z., Missaoui, A., Barkaoui, K., Ben Ayed, R.: On the verification of business processes by model checking techniques. In: 2nd International Conference on ICSTE, vol. 1, pp. 97–103, October 2010
11. Stavenko, Y., Kazantsev, N., Gromoff, A.: Business process model reasoning: from workflow to case management. Procedia Technol. **9**, 806–811 (2013)
12. Tarjan, R.: Depth first search and linear graph algorithms. SIAM J. Comput. **1**, 146–160 (1972)
13. Xiao, D., Zhang, Q.: The implementation of XPDL workflow verification service based on SaaS. In: International Conference on ICSS. pp. 154–158, May 2010

Towards Process Improvement for Case Management

An Outline Based on Viable System Model and an Example of Organizing Scientific Events

Ilia Bider[(⊠)]

Department of Computer and Systems Sciences (DSV),
Stockholm University, Stockholm, Sweden
ilia@dsv.su.se

Abstract. There are a number of methods for business process improvement that are used in practice and investigated in theory, such as Lean or Six Sigma. Most of these methods are activity based and they are aimed at optimizing the activities flow, and/or the usage of resources in the process. These methods suit well the workflow-based processes and thinking, but they are not easily adaptable to Case/Adaptive Case Management (CM/ACM) processes, the goal of improvement for which is improving the overall result from the knowledge workers cooperative work. Another distinctive feature of CM/ACM is that the process is guided not through which flow of activities to use in certain situations, but through a set of templates to use in these situations. This paper outlines a possible method of improving CM/ACM processes based on the Viable System Model (VSM). Though the usage of VSM for process improvement has been reported in the literature, it was not specifically applied to CM/ACM processes. The outline is based on the analysis of the process of organizing a series of scientific events, such as the *AdaptiveCM* workshop.

Keywords: Business process · Process improvement · Case management · Viable system model · VSM · ACM · BMP

1 Introduction

Process improvement is one of the main directions in Business Process Management (BPM). The traditional aim of process improvement is optimization of process flow and usage of resources engaged in the process. This, for example, can be achieved by removing operations/activities that do not produce value for the customer or substituting activities that result in waste of resources with more economical ones, automating where possible with the help of modern technology, designing optimal process logistics to ensure that expensive resources, such as experts, or equipment have the maximum of engagement. There are a number of methods recommended for systematic process improvement, based, for example, on Lean or Six Sigma ideas. These methods, however, are adjusted to the operational/workflow view on business processes, explicitly

© Springer International Publishing Switzerland 2016
M. Reichert and H.A. Reijers (Eds.): BPM Workshops 2015, LNBIP 256, pp. 96–107, 2016.
DOI: 10.1007/978-3-319-42887-1_9

dealing with operation/activities and resources needed for completing them, including, human and time resources.

As we proposed in [1], Case Management (CM) and Adaptive Case Management (ACM) processes are more appropriate to describe in terms of templates/forms that guide the knowledge workers in completing their work. Such a template may incorporate a mixture of goals to be attained, information to be obtained and, possibly, actions to be undertaken for attaining these goals. The knowledge workers are to pick an appropriate template and work with it according to the situation at hand. Though a CM/ACM system may impose some restrictions on what templates can/should be picked and in which order, the knowledge workers retain considerable freedom to do appropriate choices of templates, and which actions to complete when following a particular template. Considering improvement of CM/ACM business processes, the foremost goal here is improving the overall result from the knowledge workers cooperative work.

Due to the substantial difference between the workflow-based processes and CM/ACM processes, the existing process improvement methods developed for the former cannot be directly used in the latter without modification. The aim of improvement of CM/ACM processes could be defined as improving the templates used in these processes rather than optimizing the flow of activities and usage of resources. Therefore, adjusting the traditional methods of process improvement to CM/ACM processes means starting, more or less, from scratch. In this situation, other, less used, methods could be taken into consideration when deciding on the basis from which to develop process improvement methods suitable for CM/ACM processes. We believe that one of the promising approach to take is to utilize Viable System Model (VSM) of Beer [2] for designing the templates.

VSM is especially adjusted for modeling, analyzing and designing an organizational system that: (a) consists of semiautonomous units that work together for producing results, and (b) possesses the ability of adjusting itself to the changes in the environment without losing its identity. A CM/ACM process can be considered as such a system, where the individual knowledge workers function as semi-autonomous units when doing their parts of work. Though VSM is rarely used in the BPM world, there are some works where it is employed for process improvement. Mostly these are theoretical works related to the overall process architecture, see for example [3]. However, there exist some articles that use VSM for practical purposes, e.g. configuring a generic process to each specific unit in an organization [4]. As far as VSM in relation to improvement of CM/ACM processes is concerned, our search on Google Scholar has not produced any relevant results.

The goal of this paper is to outline an idea of how process improvement for CM/ACM processes based on VSM could be done. To explain the outline, we will be using an example of CM process related to organizing scientific events like the *AdaptiveCM* workshop [5]. The process has been chosen based on the following line of reason:

1. The flow of activities in this process - advertise, gather submissions, review, notify, etc. - is well known and there is but little chance that it can be improved.
2. The process is interesting from the point of view that it is completed by a virtual team of knowledge workers that might not know each other.

3. The author has experience of this type of processes in different capacities, chair, reviewer, submitter (customer).
4. The audience to which this paper is addressed has the knowledge of this process, at least from the submitter/customer perspective.

The rest of the paper is structured in the following matter. In Sect. 2, we give an overview of VSM and literature related to using VSM for process improvement. In Sect. 3, we give an outline of our idea. In Sect. 4, we discuss the details while demonstrating our suggestion on the process of arranging scientific events, such as *AdaptiveCM* [5]. In Sect. 5, we summarize the results achieved and draw plans for the future.

2 VSM and Its Usage for Process Improvement

Viable system model (VSM) has been developed by Beer [2] and his colleagues and follows, see for example [6]. It represents an organization as a system functioning in its environment and consisting of two parts: *Operation* and *Management*. In its own turn, *Operation* is split into a number of semiautonomous operational units, denoted as System 1, that have some communication mechanism to ensure their coordination. The latter is denoted as System 2. *Management*, in turn, is split in three parts, denoted as System 3, System 4, and system 5. Dependent on the author, these systems may be dubbed differently, see Table 1, but they have more or less the same meaning, see the last column of Table 1.

Table 1. Components of VSM

Identification	Naming	Function
System 1	Operations, Implementation, Delivery	Producing and delivering products and services for external customers, thus actively interacting with the environment
System 2	Coordination	Coordinate work of operational units included in System 1
System 3	Control, Delivery management, Cohesion [6], Homeostasis [7]	Managing operational units (System 1), and establishing/maintaining coordination mechanism (System 2). Making the semiautonomous units function well as a whole (cohesion) in the current business environment (homeostasis)
System 4	Intelligence [6], Future, Heterostasis [7]	Forward looking adaptation to possible future changes in the environment through identifying trends and preparing to changes or affecting the environment in the desired direction (intelligence). System 4 allows changing from one homeostasis (now) till possible

(Continued)

Table 1. (*Continued*)

Identification	Naming	Function
		homeostasis in the future thus allowing the system to function in a heterostatic environment. System 4 is considered as including development, marketing and research
System 5	Identity [7] (management), Policy [6] (management)	Solving conflicts between System 4 and System 3 [8]. Permitting System 4 to introduce changes despite the conservatism of System 3, and not allowing System 4 to change the identity of the whole system that exists via functioning of Systems 3, 2, 1. This is done through designing, maintaining and imposing policies that stay in place even when changes designed by System 4 are implemented in Systems 3, 2, 1

Note that components listed in Table 1 do not need to coincide with the organizational structure of a particular organization. Different components can be manned by the same people. This, for example, happens in a small enterprise where the same group of people does the job on all levels. The components in this case are differentiated not through who is doing the job, but through the nature of the job done, e.g. policy document writing belongs to System 5, while completing a customer order belongs to System 1.

The viability of the system with a structure like suggested by Beer is attained in two ways. Firstly, the viability is attained through each component being responsible for interacting with its own part of environment (though the parts that fall into responsibility of different components can partially intersect). This ensures fast (non-bureaucratic) response to fluctuations and changes. Secondly, it is attained through the recursive decomposition of components so that each of them has a structure of a viable system in respect to its own part of the total system environment (such decomposition concerns the units of System 1, in the first place).

The most common works on VSM in relation to business processes are the theoretical ones, a typical example of which is [3]. It discusses the needs for configuring/adjusting each generic process, e.g. inventory management, to the local environment that corresponds to the given operational unit of System 1. It also discusses the needs to review/update business processes at the rate that correspond to the dynamics of the environment of the operational unit in which these processes are enacted.

There are however, also works that try to envision a practical approach to using VSM for process improvement, as it is done in [4]. It shows how a generic purchase process can be configured (tuned) for each operational unit dependent on the environment in which the latter functions.

As we already mentioned in Sect. 1, the existing literature related to the usage of VSM for process improvement do not specifically takes the issues connected to CM/ACM processes. This paper is a try to fill this gap by finding relations between VSM and CM/ACM, and outlining an approach to CM/ACM business process improvement based on VSM.

3   An Outline for CM/ACM Processes Improvement

Our proposal is based on the following assumptions:

1. Templates used in running instances of a CM/ACM process are related to the goals connected to the process on one hand, and the external environment on the other hand. In addition, some templates need to be synchronized (aligned).
2. The relationships between the templates and the goals and environment could be revealed by building a VSM model of the organization that is responsible for the process and connecting the templates creation and usage to different components of the VSM system. In addition, positioning of the templates in the resulting model could help to understand which templates need to be synchronized.

Based on the above assumptions the improvement process can be defined as consisting of the following steps

1. Analyze the process at hand and identify templates used for running the process instances/cases.
2. Build a VSM model of an organization responsible for the process and relate templates to the components of the VSM model, thus establishing relationship between the templates and organizational goals and the environment.
3. Based on results of step 2, establish requirements on synchronization between the templates
4. Based on the results of steps 2&3, check whether the templates are aligned with goals, environment and with each other. Make changes where misalignment happens.

As can be seen from the above, the basis for the improvement consists of building an augmented VSM model – steps 1, 2 and 3. The details of this model are discussed in the next section, while we demonstrate its usage using a concrete practical example.

4   Demonstration on the Process of Organizing a Scientific Event

For discussing and demonstrating the details of the outline from the previous section, we will be using a process of organizing a series of scientific events in general, and running the *AdaptiveCM* workshop [5] in particular. The activity flow in such type of processes is well-known and looks like *Choose a conference to attached to → Submit a workshop proposal → Set up a website → Advertise the event → Set up a submission manage-ment system → Set up a PC → Gathering submission → Review → Make decision on submissions* → .... This sequence is more or less the same for anybody organizing a scientific event. Actually, the case of conference organization is quite often used in scientific papers devoted to business processes; see, for example [9]. So, the issue of organizing the flow of activities in this type of events is quite worked out. As despite the same flow of activities, some event series succeed better than the others, there are other (than workflow) factors that affect the success. We will demonstrate that these factors can be uncovered by following the steps from the outline in Sect. 3.

4.1 Analyzing the Process and Identifying Templates

The main actors of the process at hand can be divided in three categories:

1. Participants, who are both customers and value-creating agents. The participants create value for each other by presenting material to others and discussing the material of others at the event.
2. Program Committee (PC) that acts as Quality Assurance filtering the submissions and recommending improvements to be made in the materials to be presented.
3. Event chairs, responsible for each event running smoothly.

Note that there is no full separation between the categories. Many events series allow a chair to be a PC member and submit a paper, though some have stricter rules that exclude mixing the roles.

The main tools that are used to support running the process instances/cases are:

1. The event-web portal, like the one set for *AdaptiveCM* [5] in Fig. 1, and
2. A conference management system, like *EasyChair* [10], which is used for managing the workshop

Fig. 1. Web portal of *AdaptiveCM* 2015

The main templates used in managing the *AdaptiveCM* event are as follows:

1. *Topics* - list of topics to define the submissions of interest (Goal & Topics in Fig. 1)
2. *Categories* - submission categories to define the styles of papers acceptable for the event (*position paper, idea paper, experience report, research paper*)
3. *Guidelines* to explain the styles to the potential submitters
4. *Submission template* – see Fig. 2.
5. *Criteria* used in the reviewing to ensure consistent reviews independently of which members of the committee are completing them. Part of the reviewing template for *AdaptiveCM* is presented in Table 2.
6. *Channels* – a list of electronic channels through which to advertise the event, e.g. mailing lists, social media outlets, etc.

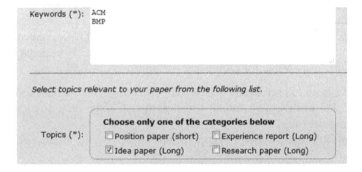

Fig. 2. Part of the submission template from *AdaptiveCM* 2015

Table 2. Reviewing criteria

#	Criterion	Values
1	**Relevance.** Assess the relevance of the paper to the goals and topics at http://acm2015.blogs.dsv.su.se/goal-topics/. If possible point out the topic number from this page when writing your comments	• Not relevant • Implicitly relevant • Explicitly relevant
2	**Categorization.** If you do not agree with the paper categorization by the authors, you can reclassify it. For instance, if an experience report does not follow the guidelines, you might want to reclassify it as a research or idea paper.	• The category is correct • Experience report • Idea paper • Research paper • Position paper
3	**Originality.** Assess the originality of the ideas and results and presence of: at least partial evaluation (FULL RESEARCH PAPER); interesting observations and lessons learned (EXPERIENCE REPORT); vision (IDEA PAPER); interesting question or position (POSITION PAPER)	• Nothing new or interesting presented • Some new or interesting material • Substantial amount of new or very interesting material

(*Continued*)

Table 2. (*Continued*)

#	Criterion	Values
4	**Discussability.** Rate the potential of the paper for raising useful and interesting discussion	• Low • Medium • High
5	**Style.** Is the style of the paper follows the recommendation given at http://acm2015.blogs.dsv.su.se/submission/ and guidelines given at http://acm2015.blogs.dsv.su.se/guidelines/	• No • Partly • Yes
6	**Language.** Evaluate the quality of the language used in, and the presentation of, the paper	• Unacceptable • Acceptable • Good
7	**Practicality.** Evaluate practical usefulness of the results and whether it was discussed or not in the paper	• Not useful • Uncertain, the practical usefulness has not been discussed • Could be useful • Definitely useful

4.2   VSM Model of Organizing a Scientific Event

A simple VSM model for organizing a scientific event in general, and *AdaptiveCM* in particular, is presented in Fig. 3, and described below.

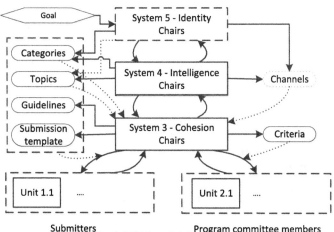

Fig. 3. A VSM model for *AdaptiveCM*

- System 1 consists of two types of units working relatively independent from each other: (a) authors that write and submit papers, and (b) members of PC who review the papers. The work of both types of units is controlled by a number of templates. Templates *categories, topics, guidelines, and submission template* regulate the work of submitters, while template *criteria* regulates the work of PC members. These two set of templates are synchronized via the criteria template referring to other templates, see Table 2, which serve as mechanism of *implicit* coordination between the operational units of two different types (System 2). There is no explicit coordination between the submitters, and little coordination between the PC members. However, communication between the PC members can happen when their opinions on the same submission differ. Both types of units have their local environment: area in which a particular research is being done by a submitter, and a wider area of research interests of a PC member. Naturally, these areas can intersect, but usually they do not coincide. The overlapping, but not coinciding local environments of operational units ensure a broader coverage of the scientific field of interest during the event, and makes the event interesting and appealing to the participants.

- System 3 (*Cohesion*), manned by Chairs, has responsibility for all System 1 units working in the same direction to produce an interesting event. It does this by preparing proper templates which regulate the outputs produced by the units, and by having one-, and two-ways communication with the units on the operational matters, such as deadlines, reminders, etc. For the latter, there are also templates but they are of lesser importance and are not considered here. System 3 interacts with the wider environment, the community of experts that are interested in the topics listed in the *topics* template, using channels from the *channels* template. It may also update the list of PC members, e.g. based on the new topics added by System 4 to *topics*.
- System 4 (*Intelligence*), also manned by chairs, is responsible for the event is on the frontier of the scientific field of interest. It looks at the trends and changes in the field and updates the *topics*, *categories*, and *channels*. It can also change the format of the event.
- System 5 (Identity), manned by chairs is responsible for changes made by system 4 not breaking the identity of the whole system. The desired identity, which is how the event is considered by observers, is identified in the goal set for the scientific events series. For *AdaptiveCM* it is set as "to bring together researchers and practitioners to discuss theoretical and practical problems and solutions in the area of non-workflow based approaches to BPM in general, and ACM (as a leading movement) in particular ..." [5]. The goal affects which categories and topics should be included and which channels are to be used. Therefore, System 5 can complete its task by ensuring that the *categories*, *topics* and *channels* templates are consistent with the goal. For *AdptiveCM* it means that: (a) *topics* appeal to both researchers and practitioners, (b) the submission categories are adjusted to the type of work both categories do, and (c) there are channels on the list to reach both categories.

4.3   Synchronizing the Templates Based on the VSM Model Built

As can be seen from the VSM model in the previous section, the system as a whole rely much on the templates in its functioning. These templates are not independent of each other, but require synchronization. The dependencies that exist and, thus, the needs for synchronization can be presented as a square matrix where both rows and columns represent the templates. The cross in the sell $<X,Y>$ means that the template of row X is dependent on the template of column Y. Beside the templates, a row and column that correspond to the goal of the process are included in the *dependencies matrix*. The dependencies matrix for *AdaptiveCM* is presented in Table 3.

Table 3. Templates dependencies in *AdptiveCM*

	Goal	Categories	Topics	Guidelines	Submission template	Criteria	Channels
Goal							
Categories	X		X				
Topics	X						
Guidelines		X					
Submission template		X					
Criteria	X	X	X	X			
Channels	X	X	X				

To demonstrate the importance of synchronization according to the dependencies, below, we present two examples of what happens if the dependencies between the templates are not implemented. We will use notation X → Y to denote that template Y depends on template X:

1. Consider dependency *topics → criteria*: if *topics* are not explicitly incorporated in *criteria*, there is a risk that a reviewer may reject the paper base on the *relevance* without realizing that the topic to which the paper belongs is explicitly mentioned in *topics*.
2. Consider dependencies *categories → submission template, submission template → criteria* and *categories → criteria*. Suppose a conference defines two categories of submissions: *research paper* and *experience-based paper* but does not introduce the categories in the submission template. There is a risk that a reviewer wrongly assigns the category to the paper, and rejects it in the end based on the mistaken categorization. Even greater risk of unappropriated rejection exists when *categories* are not incorporated in *criteria*.

The two examples above are not artificial. The first happened at one of early issues of *AdaptiveCM*, the second happened last year with our experienced-based paper [11] submitted first to *EDOC* (Enterprise Computing Conference) [12], then to *PoEM* (working conference on the Practice of Enterprise Modelling) [13], and then to *BPMDS* (working conference on Business Process Modeling, Development, and Support) [14].

All three conferences had a category of experience-based papers. For *EDOC*, the category was defined as "Industry experience reports or case studies". For *PoEM*, the category was defined as "Experience papers - present problems or challenges encountered in practice, relate success and failure stories, or report on industrial cases and practices". For *BPMDS*, the category was defined as "Experience reports, which should follow guidelines in <link>." As far as submission template is concerned, neither *EDOC*, nor *PoEM* listed submission categories, thus it was left up to the reviewer to decide to which category a particular paper belongs. *BPMDS* had a listing of categories in its submission template. What is more, neither *EDOC* nor *PoEM* had categories mentioned in the evaluation criteria, but *BPMDS* had special instructions of the same type as in Table 2.

As the result, the paper was rejected by both *EDOC* and *PoEM*. Though some reviewers' comments were valuable, others were clearly related to the reviewers evaluating the submission as a research paper, e.g. complaints that only one case has been described. The paper was finally accepted to *BPMDS* where it was evaluating according to its category and related to this category evaluation criteria. The lack of consistency in the templates in *EDOC* and *PoEM* results in the wrong evaluation of the experience-based papers. The consequence of this is the submitters getting impression that this category of papers is of no interest for these conferences. The latter affects the identity of these events, making them pure research events, independently of which categories of papers they list in their CFPs.

5   Discussion and Conclusion

The goal of this paper was to outline a possible approach to business process improvement for CM/ACM processes. The assumption for building such an approach was that a CM/ACM process can be improved via changing a set of templates used by knowledge workers when running the instances/cases of the given CM/ACM process. The approach is based on considering a process as a system for which a VSM model can be built, and a place for each template in it can be identified. The next step is to build a template dependency matrix, and adjust the templates to the process goals and the environment, while ensuring all templates being synchronized.

The approach has been demonstrated on the process of organizing scientific events, like conferences and workshops, having the *AdaptiveCM* workshop in view as an example. We also showed concrete examples of what happens when the templates become desynchronized. Though the approach seems working well on this particular type of processes, it is not clear how generic it is. The question whether it is possible to apply the approach to all CM/ACM processes, or only to a subclass of such processes remains open. To answer this question, more tests need to be completed, which is in our plans for the future.

A distinctive characteristic of the process chosen for the demonstration is that it is run by a virtual team the members of which work as autonomous units. If the area of applicability of the approach suggested needs to be limited, the processes completed by virtual teams could serve as a constraint to applicability of the approach.

It is also worthwhile to mention that to the best of our knowledge, the suggested approach is unique in respect it being solely directed at improving the process based on changing and synchronizing templates that guide the work of process participants.

An important issue that has not been discussed in this paper is how to measure the results of improvement. It is not clear whether there can be generic ways, but it seems reasonable to consider two types of measurements. One type is connected to the goal of the process. For our example, we can, for example, measure the ratio between practitioners and academics submitting/participating in the workshop, the number of submissions/participants, the number of re-participants, etc. The second type of measurements is connected to the template synchronizations, and can be expressed in the reducing the number of incidents/erroneous outcomes. In our example, it could be minimizing the number of rejections on the wrong ground.

Acknowledgements. The author is grateful to the reviewers and AdaptiveCM 2015 participants whose comments helped to improve the final version of this paper.

References

1. Bider, I., Jalali, A., Ohlsson, J.: Adaptive case management as a process of construction of and movement in a state space. In: Demey, Y.T., Panetto, H. (eds.) OTM 2013 Workshops 2013. LNCS, vol. 8186, pp. 155–165. Springer, Heidelberg (2013)
2. Beer, S.: The Heart of Enterprise. Wiley, Chichester (1979)
3. Vidgen, R., Wang, X.: From business process management to business process ecosystem. J. Inf. Technol. (JIT) **21**, 262–271 (2006)
4. Azadeh, A., Darivandi, K., Fathi, E.: Diagnosing, simulating and improving business process using cybernetic laws and the viable system model: the case of a purchasing process. Syst. Res. Behav. Sci. **29**(1), 66–86 (2012)
5. AdaptiveCM 2015: DSV, Stockholm University (2015). http://acm2015.blogs.dsv.su.se/. Accessed June 2015
6. Espejo, R., Reyes, A.: Organizational Systems: Managing Complexity with the Viable System Model. Springer, Heidelberg (2011)
7. Golnam, A., Regev, G., Wegmann, A.: On viable service systems: developing a modeling framework for analysis of viability in service systems. In: Snene, M., Ralyté, J., Morin, J.-H. (eds.) IESS 2011. LNBIP, vol. 82, pp. 30–41. Springer, Heidelberg (2011)
8. Hoebeke, L.: Identity: the paradoxical nature of organizational closure. Kybernetes **35**(1/2), 65–75 (2006)
9. Gao, S., Krogstie, J.: A combined framework for development of business process support systems. In: Persson, A., Stirna, J. (eds.) PoEM 2009. LNBIP, vol. 39, pp. 115–129. Springer, Heidelberg (2009)
10. EasyChair. http://www.easychair.org/. Accessed June 2015
11. Josefsson, M., Widman, K., Bider, I.: Using the process-assets framework for creating a holistic view over process documentation. In: Gaaloul, K., Schmidt, R., Nurcan, S., Guerreiro, S., Ma, Q. (eds.) BPMDS 2015 and EMMSAD 2015. LNBIP, vol. 214, pp. 169–183. Springer, Heidelberg (2015)
12. EDOC (2015). https://edoc2015.unisa.edu.au/. Accessed June 2015
13. PoEM (2015). http://www.pros.upv.es/es/home-poem2015. Accessed June 2015
14. BPMDS (2012). http://www.bpmds.org/. Accessed June 2015

BPI Workshop

Introduction to the 11th International Workshop on Business Process Intelligence (BPI 2015)

Boudewijn van Dongen[1], Diogo R. Ferreira[2], Jochen De Weerdt[3], and Andrea Burattin[4]

[1] Eindhoven University of Technology, Eindhoven, The Netherlands
[2] Instituto Superior Técnico, University of Lisbon, Lisboa, Portugal
[3] Faculty of Economics and Business, KU Leuven, Leuven, Belgium
[4] Institut für Informatik, Universität Innsbruck, Innsbruck, Austria

Business Process Intelligence (BPI) is a growing area both in industry and academia. BPI refers to the application of data- and process-mining techniques to the field of Business Process Management. In practice, BPI is embodied in tools for managing process execution by offering several features such as analysis, prediction, monitoring, control, and optimization.

The main goal of this workshop is to promote the use and development of new techniques to support the analysis of business processes based on run-time data about the past executions of such processes. We aim at bringing together practitioners and researchers from different communities, e.g. Business Process Management, Information Systems, Database Systems, Business Administration, Software Engineering, Artificial Intelligence, and Data Mining, who share an interest in the analysis and optimization of business processes and process-aware information systems. The workshop aims at discussing the current state of ongoing research and sharing practical experiences, exchanging ideas and setting up future research directions that better respond to real needs. In a nutshell, it serves as a forum for shaping the BPI area.

The 11th edition of this workshop attracted 28 international submissions. Each paper was reviewed by at least three members of the Program Committee. From these submissions, the top twelve were accepted as full papers for presentation at the workshop.

The papers presented at the workshop provide a mix of novel research ideas, evaluations of existing process mining techniques, as well as new tool support. *Mannhardt, de Leoni, Reijers*, and *van der Aalst* extend existing precision metrics to incorporate other perspectives such as data, resources, and time. *Lu, Fahland, van Den Biggelaar* and *van der Aalst* propose a novel approach to detect deviations on the event level by identifying frequent common behavior and uncommon behavior among executed cases. *Calvanese, Montali, Syamsiyah* and *van der Aalst* devise a novel framework to support domain experts in the extraction of XES event logs from relational databases, where the extraction is driven by an ontology-based representation. *Senderovich, Leemands, Harel, Gal, Mandelbaum* and *van der Aalst* focus on the discovery of resource queues, in particular on the problem of accurately discovering queue lengths. *Vogelgesang* and *Appelrath* introduce a data-warehouse approach for process mining based on multidimensional modeling of event logs. *Evermann, Thaler* and *Fettke* present a trace clustering method based on local alignment of sequences and k-means clustering. *Havur, Cabanillas, Mendling* and *Polleres* introduce an approach for automatically allocating resources to process activities by representing the problem in the framework of Answer Set Programming (ASP). *Leemans, Fahland* and *van der Aalst* investigate the automatic discovery of process models from event logs by taking into account activity life-cycle information. *Verenich, Dumas, La Rosa, Maggi* and *Di Francescomarino* address the prediction of the most likely outcome of an ongoing case based on a set of traces of historical cases. *Kundra, Juneja* and *Vidushi* present a parallel version of the Alpha Miner algorithm by using MATLAB built-in multi-threaded constructs for CPU- and GPU-based computation. *Bayomie, Helal, Awad, Ezat* and *Elbastawissi* propose a new approach to deduce the case ids for an unlabeled event log by leveraging knowledge about the process model. Finally, *Martin, Depaire* and *Caris* focus on modeling inter-arrival times (IAT) based on event log data, for the purpose of process simulation.

As with previous editions of the workshop, we hope that reader will find this selection of papers useful to keep track of the latest advances in the BPI area, and we are looking forward to keep bringing new advances in future editions of the BPI workshop.

November 2015

Program Committee

Alessandro Sperduti	University of Padua, Italy
Ana Karla de Medeiros	Centraal Beheer Achmea, The Netherlands
Andreas Rogge-Solti	Wirtschaftsuniversität Wien, Austria
Anna Kalenkova	Higher School of Economics (HSE), Russia
Anne Rozinat	Fluxicon, The Netherlands
Antonella Guzzo	University of Calabria, Italy
Artur Caetano	Universidade de Lisboa, Portugal
Daniela Grigori	Paris-Dauphine University, France
Domenico Saccà	University of Calabria, Italy
Eric Verbeek	Eindhoven University of Technology, The Netherlands
Gianluigi Greco	University of Calabria, Italy
Hans Weigand	University of Tilburg, The Netherlands
Jan Mendling	Wirtschaftsuniversität Wien, Austria
Jorge Munoz-Gama	Pontificia Universidad Católica de Chile, Chile
Manfred Reichert	University of Ulm, Germany
Michael Leyer	Frankfurt School of Finance and Management, Germany
Michael Rosemann	Queensland University of Technology, Australia
Phina Soffer	University of Haifa, Israel
Seppe vanden Broucke	KU Leuven, Belgium
Suriadi Suriadi	Massey University, New Zealand
Viara Popova	Tallinn University of Technology, Tallinn
Walid Gaaloul	Insitut Telecom France
Wil van der Aalst	Eindhoven University of Technology, The Netherlands

Measuring the Precision of Multi-perspective Process Models

Felix Mannhardt[1,2]([✉]), Massimiliano de Leoni[1], Hajo A. Reijers[1,3],
and Wil M.P. van der Aalst[1]

[1] Eindhoven University of Technology, Eindhoven, The Netherlands
{f.mannhardt,m.d.leoni,h.a.reijers,w.m.p.v.d.aalst}@tue.nl
[2] Lexmark Enterprise Software, Naarden, The Netherlands
[3] VU University Amsterdam, Amsterdam, The Netherlands

Abstract. Process models need to reflect the real behavior of an organization's processes to be beneficial for several use cases, such as process analysis, process documentation and process improvement. One quality criterion for a process model is that they should precise and not express more behavior than what is observed in logging data. Existing precision measures for process models purely focus on the control-flow dimension of a process model, thereby ignoring other perspectives, such as the *data objects* manipulated by the process, the *resources* executing process activities, and *time-related* aspects (e.g., activity deadlines). Focusing on the control-flow only, the results may be misleading. This paper extends existing precision measures to incorporate the other perspectives and, through an evaluation with a real-life process and corresponding logging data, demonstrates how the new measure matches our intuitive understanding of precision.

Keywords: Process mining · Process model quality · Precision · Multi-perspective process mining

1 Introduction

Process mining is a quickly developing field that aims to discover, monitor, and improve real processes by extracting knowledge from event logs readily available in today's information systems. For most use cases of BPM, the discovered process model needs to *adequately* reflect the real behavior of the process. An obvious question is then: How does one know if a model is adequate? Clearly, a process model should be able to explain the behavior of the process using the process model: The model should *recall* the observed behavior. In other words, using process-mining terminology, the model should *fit* [1] the real behavior observed in the event log. However, the model should also be *precise* [1]: It should not allow for more behavior than observed in the event log and, thus, allow for

---

M. Leoni—This work has received funding from the European Community's Seventh Framework Program FP7 under grant agreement num. 603993 (CORE).

M. Reichert and H.A. Reijers (Eds.): BPM Workshops 2015, LNBIP 256, pp. 113–125, 2016.
DOI: 10.1007/978-3-319-42887-1_10

behavior without empirical support. Therefore, the precision of a model is not an absolute value but it is relative to an event log. In other words, precision depends on what has been observed.

Multiple measures for *precision* have been proposed in the literature [2–7]. However, these approaches can only be used to measure precision of models that do not encompass data-, resource and time-related aspects. This is a serious limitation, since these aspects play an important role in real business processes. The importance of data in business processes is, for example, paramount as it is often data that drives the decisions that participants make [8]. In industrial practice, the modeling of additional perspectives is picking up, too. Consider, for example, that support for the standard *Decision Model And Notation* (DMN) was recently added to the process modeling tool of a major vendor[1].

Table 1. Event log $\mathcal{E}$ recorded by a fragment of a credit application process

Id	Case	Activity	Resource	Loan		Id	Case	Activity	Resource	Loan
					.. .. ..				..	..
1	1	Handle Request	Rory	750		13	4	Handle Request	Rory	1500
2	1	Simple Check	Rory	$\perp$		14	4	Simple Check	Rory	$\perp$
3	1	Call Customer	Amy	$\perp$		15	4	Call Customer	Amy	$\perp$
4	1	Decide	Amy	$\perp$		16	4	Decide	Amy	$\perp$
5	2	Handle Request	Rory	750		17	5	Handle Request	Rory	1500
6	2	Call Customer	Amy	$\perp$		18	5	Extensive Check	Rory	$\perp$
7	2	Simple Check	Rory	$\perp$		19	5	Call Customer	Amy	$\perp$
8	2	Decide	Rory	$\perp$		20	5	Decide	Rory	$\perp$
9	3	Handle Request	Rory	1250		21	6	Handle Request	Rory	5000
10	3	Simple Check	Rory	$\perp$		22	6	Extensive Check	Rory	$\perp$
11	3	Call Customer	Amy	$\perp$		23	6	Call Customer	Amy	$\perp$
12	3	Decide	Amy	$\perp$		24	6	Decide	Amy	$\perp$
..	..	..	..	..						

We wish to illustrate the problem of measuring precision while ignoring perspectives beyond control flow. Let us consider a fragment of a credit application process that generated the event log shown in Table 1. Figures 1 and 2 show BPMN models that describe the entire behavior of the process, i.e., the models are perfectly fitting with respect to the event log $\mathcal{E}$. When disregarding the data perspective, model M_1 (Fig. 1) can be seen as a precise representation of the observed behavior. The difference between models M_1 and M_2 (Fig. 2) is that the latter specifies additional rules: Depending on the requested loan amount either activity Simple Check or activity Extensive Check needs to be executed. For certain loan amounts between 1,000 and 2,000 the decision between Simple Check or Extensive Check is left to the process worker.[2] Moreover, in M_2, a separation-of-duty constraint is implemented between activities Call Customer and Handle Request: These must be performed by different resources.[3] Intuitively, these rules based on process data make the process model M_2 more

---

[1] http://www.signavio.com/news/managing-business-decisions-with-dmn-1-0/.

[2] We apply this non-standard BPMN semantics as simplification.

[3] We use an annotation as this rule cannot be expressed in BPMN.

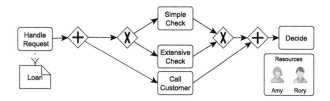

Fig. 1. BPMN model M_1 without rules and perfect fitness

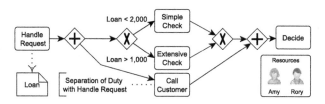

Fig. 2. BPMN model M_2 with data and resource rules and perfect fitness

precise than M_1: Their presence provides additional constraints that reduce the amount of allowed behavior. For example, model M_1 would allow to execute Simple Check for any amount, but Simple Check is only considered for an amount smaller than 2,000 in the event log. The major insight here is that *existing* approaches [2–7] would return the *same* precision score for both models.

The main contribution of this paper is a technique that generalizes the *precision* measure proposed in [6,9] to incorporate additional rules relating to multiple perspectives. More precisely, it supports multi-perspective rules that can be encoded as constraints over data attributes and directly influence the execution of the process. The approach in [6] returns, for both M_1 and M_2, the same precision score of 0.913, because it ignores the constraints of duty separation as well as those at decision points. By contrast, our approach, when applied to the shown process model and event log, returns a lower precision score 0.757 for process model M_1 and a higher precision score 0.848 for the process model M_2. Thus, the precision added by specifying data-driven rules for choices in process models is reflected in our measure. Note that the scores returned by our approach should not be compared directly to the scores returned by the approach in [6], since we compute the precision in a new, more generic manner that acknowledges the precision added by those rules and penalizes their absence. We implemented the multi-perspective precision measure as a plug-in in the ProM framework, and evaluated it in the context of a real-life process.

The remainder of the paper is organized as follows. In Sect. 2, we define the precision measure for multi-perspective process models, illustrate the measure using examples and describe its actual implementation. Section 3 evaluates the introduced measure using several process models created for a real-life event log. Finally, Sect. 4 concludes with a summary and sketches future work.

2   Precision of Multi-perspective Process Models

In this section, we define a precision measure for multi-perspective process models that determines the precision of process models in relation to event logs.

2.1   Event Log and Process Model

In Sect. 1 we informally introduced event log $\mathcal{E}$ by listing the recorded events in Table 1. Each of the recorded events refers to the execution of an activity in a process instance, therefore, each event is unique. In the remainder of our paper, we define an **event log** $\mathcal{E}$ as a collection of unique events: $\mathcal{E} = \{e_1, \ldots, e_n\}$ [1,9]. Each event is associated with a set of pairs (v, u) indicating that the event assigns value u to a process attribute v. In the remainder of the paper, we use V to define the set of attribute names that are relevant for the process in question and U to indicate the universe of possible values for attributes. Each event records some special attributes such as the case identifier `Case` and the activity name `Activity`. Each event and its location in the trace is uniquely identified through an `Id`. We denote with $A \subseteq U$ the set of recorded activity names. Given an event log $\mathcal{E}$, we also introduce the function $act \in \mathcal{E} \to A$ that extracts the name of the executed activity from an event.

Our approach to measure the precision of multi-perspective process models is independent of the formalism used to model the process, e.g., BPMN, EPCs or YAWL. To safeguard this independence, we use a transition-system notation to represent a process model. We use a transition system, which can be considered as a foundational formalism to capture processes:

Definition 1 (Process Model). *A process model defines a transition system* $\mathcal{P} = (S, s_0, S_F, F)$ *consisting of a set S of states, an initial state $s_0 \in S$, a set of final states $S_F \subseteq S$, and a transition function $F \in \left(S \times A \times (V \nrightarrow U) \right) \nrightarrow S$.*[4]

Here, we abstract from details on the *state* function to be configurable for different settings. For process models expressed as Petri nets, the reachability graph is an example of a possible transition-system representation. Several translations from BPMN models to transition systems are available. In the remainder of the paper, we assume the existence of a transition system having the following structure. Given a function f, we use $\mathsf{dom}(f)$ to denote the domain of that function. Given the set V of model attributes, the set U of potential values, and the set A of labels of BPMN activities, the transition system of BPMN models is a tuple $\mathcal{P} = (S, s_0, S_F, F)$ where

- $S \subseteq (A^* \times (V \nrightarrow U))$;
- the initial state is $s_0 = (\langle \rangle, ass_0)$ with ass_0 being the function with an empty domain (initially no model attributes take on values);
- the set of final states $S_F \subseteq S$ contains all activity sequences (with the latest value assignments to model attributes) that reach the final BPMN event;

---

[4] Symbol $\nrightarrow$ is used to indicate partial functions.

- from any state $(\sigma, ass) \in S$, a state transition $\delta = (a, w) \in A \times (V \nrightarrow U)$ is defined if the BPMN activity $a \in A$ together with the value assignments $w \in V \nrightarrow U$ can be executed in state (σ, ass);
- for each state $s = (\sigma, ass) \in S$, for each transition $\delta = (a, w) \in A \times (V \nrightarrow U)$ defined in that state, the state-transition function is defined as follows: $F((\sigma, ass), \delta) = (\sigma', ass')$ with $\sigma' = \sigma \oplus \langle a \rangle$ and:

$$ass'(v) = \begin{cases} w(v) & \text{if } v \in \text{dom}(w) \\ ass(v) & \text{otherwise.} \end{cases}$$

Events in the log can be related to a state of the transition system as follows:

Definition 2 (State Prior to the Occurrence of an Event). *Given an event log $\mathcal{E}$ and a process model $\mathcal{P} = (S, s_0, S_F, F)$, we define function $state_\mathcal{P} : \mathcal{E} \to S$ that, for each event, returns the state reached in the transition system just before the event happened.*

For the sake of simplicity, we assume that the event log fits the process model. Also, the names/labels of attributes and their values observed in the event log (including the activity labels as a special case) are matched with the ones in the process model. Moreover, if the process model contains unobservable routing activities (i.e., invisible transitions) or multiple activities sharing the same label (i.e., duplicate activities), then we assume that the event log contains information to uniquely identify all executed activities including unobservable ones. For any event log that does not meet these requirements, we can transform the log to the closest event log matching the requirements. This can be done, for example, by using alignment-based techniques for multi-perspective process models as [10], which "squeeze" any non-compliant log portion into a compliant one, adds events for required unobservable activities, and uniquely identifies every executed activities. In [6] it is reported that this alignment has little effect on the precision measurement even for event logs with major deviations.

2.2 Precision Measure

The *precision* of a process model in relation to an event log must take into account the extra behavior allowed by the model that is not seen in the event log. In Sect. 1, we mentioned that the *precision* of a process model is computed with respect to an event log that records executions of such a process. It is the ratio between the amount of observed behavior as recorded in the log and the amount of possible behavior as allowed by the model. All behavior that is allowed by the model yet never observed in the log makes a model less precise.

More precisely, we define *possible behavior* with respect to each event $e \in \mathcal{E}$. It consists of the possible activities that can be executed in the state prior to the occurrence of e according to the process model.

Definition 3 (Possible Behavior). *Let $\mathcal{P} = (S, s_0, S_F, F)$ the transition system of a process model. Let $\mathcal{E}$ be an event log. The possible behavior when event e occurs as allowed by a model can be represented as a function $pos_\mathcal{P} : \mathcal{E} \rightarrow 2^A$:*

$$pos_\mathcal{P}(e) = \{a \in A \mid \exists w \in V \nrightarrow U : \exists(state_\mathcal{P}(e), a, w) \in dom(F)\}.$$

In a similar way, we define the observed behavior prior to the occurrence of any event $e \in \mathcal{E}$ as the activities that can observed in the whole event log when being in the same state as prior to the occurrence of e:

Definition 4 (Observed Behavior). *Let $\mathcal{P} = (S, s_0, S_F, F)$ be the transition system of a process model. Let $\mathcal{E}$ be an event log, and $e \in \mathcal{E}$ an event. The observed behavior as seen in the event log can be represented as a function $obs_\mathcal{P}$: $\mathcal{E} \rightarrow 2^A$:*

$$obs_\mathcal{P}(e) = \{a \in A \mid \exists\, e' \in \mathcal{E} : state_\mathcal{P}(e) = state_\mathcal{P}(e') \wedge act(e') = a\}.$$

Using the definitions of possible and observed behavior in the context of an event, we define the precision of a multi-perspective process model $\mathcal{P}$ according to an event log $\mathcal{E}$ as follow.

Definition 5 (Precision of a Process Model wrt. an Event Log). *Let $\mathcal{P}$ be the transition system of a process model. Let $\mathcal{E}$ be an event log. The precision of $\mathcal{P}$ with regard to $\mathcal{E}$ is a function $precision : \mathcal{P} \times \mathcal{E} \rightarrow [0, 1]$:*

$$precision(\mathcal{P}, \mathcal{E}) = \frac{\sum_{e \in \mathcal{E}} |obs_\mathcal{P}(e)|}{\sum_{e \in \mathcal{E}} |pos_\mathcal{P}(e)|}.$$

Since for each event $e \in \mathcal{E}$, $|obs_\mathcal{P}(e)| \leq |pos_\mathcal{P}(e)|$, precision scores are always between 0 and 1. Note that the transition system is finite: a state s is only considered if there is an event $e \in \mathcal{E}$ such that $state_\mathcal{P}(e) = s$. Since the number of events is finite, the number of states to consider is also finite.

For each event $e \in \mathcal{E}$, computing $state_\mathcal{P}(e)$ is $O(|\mathcal{E}|)$, because, in the worst case, one needs to iterate over all events in $\mathcal{E}$ to reconstruct the state. Once $state_\mathcal{P}(e)$ is computed, computing $obs_\mathcal{P}(e)$ and $pos_\mathcal{P}(e)$ is linear in the number of activities: $O(|A|)$. Since these functions need to be computed for each $e \in \mathcal{E}$, the worst-case time complexity of computing precision is $O(|\mathcal{E}|(|A|+|\mathcal{E}|))$, which is $O(|\mathcal{E}|^2)$ as $|\mathcal{E}| \gg |A|$ (the number of events is way larger than the process activity).

2.3   Illustration of the Measure

We proceed to show that our definition is intuitive by discussing a series of illustrative examples. In this section activities and attribute names are abbreviated with their first letter; also, with abuse of notation, any model M_i also refers to its transition-system representation as defined in Sect. 2.1. We obtain the following sets of observed and possible behavior for the events listed in Table 1 and the initial model M_1:

$$pos_{M_1}(e_1) = \{\text{H}\}, \ pos_{M_1}(e_2) = \{\text{S}, \text{E}, \text{C}\}, \ pos_{M_1}(e_3) = \{\text{C}\}, \ pos_{M_1}(e_4) = \{\text{D}\}, \ldots$$
$$obs_{M_1}(e_1) = \{\text{H}\}, \ obs_{M_1}(e_2) = \{\text{S}, \text{C}\}, \quad obs_{M_1}(e_3) = \{\text{C}\}, \ obs_{M_1}(e_4) = \{\text{D}\}, \ldots$$

For example, the set of observed behavior for e_2 is $\{S, C\}$ because the execution of both activities Simple Check and Call Customer can be observed in those events that are carried out when the transition system is in the state prior to the occurrence of e_2: $state_{M_1}(e_2) = (\langle H \rangle, \{R := Rory, L := 750\})$. This state is reached when activity Handle Request has already been executed and the latest values assigned to the attributes Resource and Loan are $Rory$ and 750 respectively. By consulting Table 1, it becomes clear that events e_2 and e_6 contribute to the set of observed behavior for e_2. Please note that the e_2 and e_6 are events from different traces, i.e., the whole event log is considered when computing the observed behavior. Continuing in the same manner with the remaining events yields a precision of $precision(M_1, \mathcal{E}) = \frac{28}{37} \approx 0.76$. Applying the same measure on the process model M_2, we get:

$$pos_{M_2}(e_1) = \{H\}, \; pos_{M_2}(e_2) = \{S, C\}, \; pos_{M_2}(e_3) = \{C\}, \; pos_{M_2}(e_4) = \{D\}, \ldots$$
$$obs_{M_2}(e_1) = \{H\}, \; obs_{M_2}(e_2) = \{S, C\}, \; obs_{M_2}(e_3) = \{C\}, \; obs_{M_2}(e_4) = \{D\}, \ldots$$

and subsequently a value of $precision(M_2, \mathcal{E}) = \frac{28}{33} = 0.848$. It is easy to see that the added constraints regarding the attribute Loan limits the set of possible activities for event e_2 to Simple Check and Call Customer. The activity Extended Check cannot be executed anymore in the state prior to the occurrence of e_2, as the value of the attribute Loan would need to be higher than 1,000. This improves the precision of model M_2. Moreover, the observed parallelism of activities Simple Check and Call Customer for a Loan value of 750 is not seen as imprecision in either case, as reflected in the set of observed behavior $\{S, C\}$ for event e_2. Note that the assignment of data attributes needs to be *exactly* the same in order to detect parallelism in the model as a precise representation of the observed behavior. Otherwise, when parallelism is observed with different attribute values, it is seen as an imprecision because a more precise process model using the different attribute values for a data rule can be created.

Next to the two process models introduced in Figs. 1 and 2, we consider two additional, illustrative process models representing extreme cases. Figure 3 shows an example of a process model that is very imprecise in relation to event log $\mathcal{E}$. Always starting with Handle Request, model M_3 in Fig. 3 allows to execute the remaining activities any arbitrary number of times and, also, in any order. On the opposite side of the spectrum, model M_4 in Fig. 4 is very precise, as only exactly the observed behavior in $\mathcal{E}$ is possible. For instance, the order of the

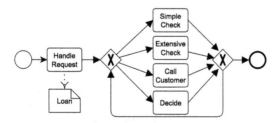

Fig. 3. BPMN model M_3 for log $\mathcal{E}$ with a precision of 0.359

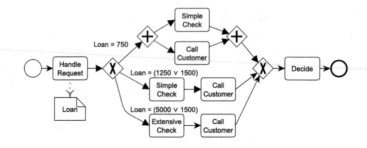

Fig. 4. BPMN model M_4 for log $\mathcal{E}$ with a precision of 1

activities `Simple Check` and `Call Customer` depends on the value of the data attribute `Loan`; if it has 750 as value both activities are carried out in any order, for the values 1,500 and 1,250 only the modeled order is observed.

For the process model M_3, we obtain $precision(M_3, \mathcal{E}) = \frac{28}{78} \approx 0.359$, which is less than half of the precision measure of M_1 in Fig. 2 (0.848). On the other end of the spectrum, model M_4 in Fig. 4 has a perfect precision: $precision(M_4, \mathcal{E}) = 1$, as only the behavior seen in the event log is allowed. These examples demonstrate that the computed values for *precision* behave intuitively, as model M_3 is the least precise, and model M_4 is the most precise of the presented examples.

The example above also shows that models scoring a very high precision value are not always the most preferable. In particular, model M_4 in Fig. 4 with a perfect precision score allows for exactly the behavior observed in the event log and nothing more. Given that event logs only contain example behavior as observed in a limited time frame, one cannot assume that all possible behavior has been observed. Hence, a process model should to some extent *generalize* and allow for more behavior than what has simply been observed, yet is potentially admissible. In other words, using data-mining terminology, model M_4 is probably *over-fitting* the event log. Therefore, when using the proposed precision measure to, e.g., rank the quality of discovered process models it should be balanced with other quality criteria [9], rather than aiming for a perfect precision score.

2.4   Implementation

This section shows the concrete implementation of the precision measure as a plug-in for the process mining framework ProM[5]. We use Data Petri Nets (DPN-nets) [10] as modeling language with simple and clear semantics.

A DPN-net is a Petri net [11] extended with variables (i.e., data attributes). Transitions update the values of variables through so-called *write operations* and can be associated with guards that further constrain when transitions are enabled to fire. A transition in a DPN-net can fire only if all its input places contain at least one token and the guard, if any, is satisfied. Guards can be formulated as an expression over the process variables. Figure 5 shows how the BPMN model M_2

---

[5] Available at http://www.promtools.org in the *DataAwareReplayer* package.

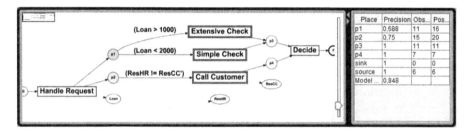

The following table appears within the figure:

Place	Precision	Obs...	Pos...
p1	0,688	11	16
p2	0,75	15	20
p3	1	11	11
p4	1	7	7
sink	1	0	0
source	1	6	6
Model ...	0,848		

Fig. 5. Screenshot of the implementation in ProM showing the precision visualization of M_2 and $\mathcal{E}$. The darker the color of a place in the DPN-net, the lower its precision

(Fig. 2) can be expressed using the DPN-net notation. For instance, transition (i.e., activity) Extensive Check is enabled if place $p1$ contains at least a token and the value of variable *Loan*, which has been written by transition Handle Request, is larger than 1,000. However, at times one may wish to constrain the values that a transition is allowed to write. In those cases, variables are post-fixed with a *prime* symbol, indicating the value assigned by the transition. For instance, the guard of transition Call Customer states that the resource executing the activity must differ from the resource who executed the Handle Request: in this way, we can enforce a separation of concerns. Readers are referred to [10] for more details. The behavior of a DPN-net can be represented as a transition system similarly as discussed in Sect. 2.1 for BPMN models.

To provide diagnostics on the precision measurement, we can compute a local precision score for each place by including only those events that correspond to DPN-net transitions that consume tokens from the place. A visualization of this diagnostics for model M_2 is shown in Fig. 5. Each place is colored according to its local precision score (darker colors correspond to lower precision). Additionally, the table on the right side provides an overview about the precision scores.

3   Evaluation

The evaluation is based on a real-life case study, which is concerned with the process of handling road-traffic fine by an Italian local police force [10]. Specifically, we employed a real-life event log[6] that records the execution of 11 different activities and contains 550,000 events grouped into 150,000 traces. In total there are 9 data attributes. All experiments were conducted with a memory limit of 2 GB, which is lower than what current-day, regular computers contain.

For this evaluation, we used five different models:

Model A, which is discovered using the Inductive Miner (IM) set to guarantee perfect fitness [12];

---

[6] http://dx.doi.org/10.4121/uuid:270fd440-1057-4fb9-89a9-b699b47990f5.

122   F. Mannhardt et al.

Table 2. Precision and fitness scores for the normative and discovered process models of a process managing road traffic fines enacted in an Italian municipality

Process model	Precision	Fitness
A: Inductive Miner	0.298	1
B: Inductive Miner with discovered rules	0.344	0.922
C: Normative Model without guards	0.639	0.997
D: Normative Model	0.694	0.972
E: Normative Model with discovered rules	0.801	0.981

Model B, which extends model A with guards as discovered by the decision-tree miner (DTM) [13]; *the minimal instances per decision-tree leaf* parameter was set to 125 to avoid over-fitting;

Model C, which is the normative model, shown in [10], but without any guards;

Model D, the normative model from [10] again, yet including all those guards that concern attributes available in the public event log;

Model E, which extends Model C with the guards discovered with the DTM (using the same as for model B).[7]

Table 2 shows the precision and fitness scores for the described process models. Intuitively, **Model A** should be the least precise process model. This model does not constrain the allowed behavior with any data rules. Also, the *IM*, set to guarantee perfect fitness, is unlikely to discover a precise model for this event log, which includes infrequent behavior. Indeed, Model A scores a low precision of 0.298. Model B (shown in Fig. 6) has the same control-flow as Model A, but additional guards based on discovered rules. As expected, the discovered rules in Model B result in an improved precision of 0.344 and a lower fitness. Figure 6 shows the precision measurement for **Model B** as it is returned by the ProM plug-in. The coloring of the places allows to locate the effect of the discovered rules on precision. It shows that the data rule added for *Send for Credit Collection* results in a perfect precision in that part of the model, i.e., the rule added to this transition is mutually exclusive with the rule added for the alternative transition τ_4. Still, Model B arguably allows for too much behavior. The normative model without data rules, **Model C**, is more precise than the models discovered with the IM; it precision is 0.639. As expected, adding the normative data rules shown in [10] to arrive at **Model D** will increase its precision to 0.694. However, adding those data rules has an impact on the fitness of model D (-0.025). As reported in [10], the event log shows that the rules are not always respected. Finally, we applied the DTM on the normative model, which resulted in **Model E**. It scores best on precision (0.801), and better on fitness than model D.

Completely in line with expectations, Model E scores better in fitness, because it discovers the as-is rules rather than the to-be rules. A cursory glance

---

[7] All models can be retrieved from http://purl.tue.nl/726309911741849.

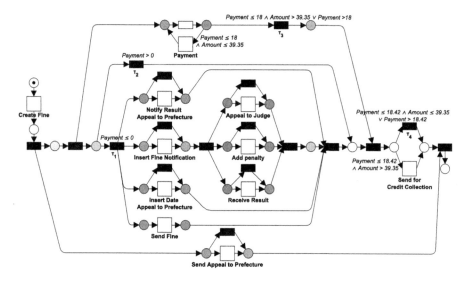

Fig. 6. The visualization in ProM provides a "helicopter view" of the precision measurement of Model B. Black rectangles depict invisible routing transitions. Write operations are omitted and the figure was redrawn to improve the readability on paper

on the results may invoke surprise that the precision of model E is higher than the precision of model D. However, this can be expected: The guards are discovered so as to maximize fitness and precision. Therefore, the rules added in model D only reflect constraints on the process from a compliance perspective, e.g. `Send of Credit Collection` should only be executed if the fine is not yet fully paid. By contrast, the DTM strives for discovery of mutually-exclusive rules that describe the real behavior as observed in the event log. Being based on the real process executions, these rules may violate the normative rules and provide logic that has no business relevance. This case study shows that our way of computing precision is applicable to evaluate the quality of multi-perspective process models and provides intuitive results.

4   Conclusion

In this paper, we proposed a new measure for the *precision* of multi-perspective process models in relation to behavior that is described in the form of an event log. Whereas process modeling languages commonly used in practice (e.g. BPMN) allows one to specify data-driven rules to model choices, existing approaches to measure the precision of a process model ignore data-related aspects. The precision of a process model can be seen as the fraction of the possible behavior allowed by the model in relation to what has actually been observed, as recorded in the event log. This paper reports on the *first proposal* to measure precision for multi-perspective process models.

As future work, we aim to put our technique to the test in several real-life case studies. In particular, we want to perform an end-user evaluation with business analysts to verify whether our notion of precision is in line with their expectations. Our preliminary results make us believe that will be the case. In particular, given an event log of a certain process and a number of models for the same process, we are able to determine which model scores higher on precision. For each model, the respective precision score can be combined with the fitness score, which, for instance, can be computed using the approach reported in [10]. In many cases, higher values of precision are associated with lower values of fitness, and vice versa. By finding the right trade-off between these two quantities, we can determine which model provides a better representation of the process in question. Last but not least, we aim to employ the precision measure to improve the discovery of guards. The approach proposed in [13] only allows for discovering mutually exclusive guards at decision points. Often, guards at decision points are not mutually exclusive: in the same process state, multiple alternatives need to be enabled. We want to allow for multiple alternatives (to increase fitness), but not for too many (which would reduce precision).

References

1. van der Aalst, W.M.P.: Process Mining - Discovery, Conformance and Enhancement of Business Processes. Springer, New York (2011)
2. Greco, G., Guzzo, A., Pontieri, L., Saccá, D.: Mining expressive process models by clustering workflow traces. In: Dai, H., Srikant, R., Zhang, C. (eds.) PAKDD 2004. LNCS (LNAI), vol. 3056, pp. 52–62. Springer, Heidelberg (2004)
3. de Medeiros, A.K.A., Weijters, A.J.M.M., van der Aalst, W.M.P.: Genetic process mining: an experimental evaluation. Data Min. Knowl. Discov. **14**(2), 245–304 (2007)
4. Rozinat, A., van der Aalst, W.M.P.: Conformance checking of processes based on monitoring real behavior. Inf. Syst. **33**(1), 64–95 (2008)
5. Munoz-Gama, J., Carmona, J.: A general framework for precision checking. Int. J. Innov. Comput. I **8**(7(B)) 5317–5339 (2012)
6. Adriansyah, A., Munoz-Gama, J., Carmona, J., van Dongen, B.F., van der Aalst, W.M.P.: Measuring precision of modeled behavior. Inf. Syst. E-Bus. Manage. **13**(1), 37–67 (2015)
7. van den Broucke, S., De Weerdt, J., Vanthienen, J., Baesens, B.: Determining process model precision and generalization with weighted artificial negative events. IEEE Trans. Knowl. Data Eng. **26**(8), 1877–1889 (2014)
8. Maggi, F.M., Dumas, M., García-Bañuelos, L., Montali, M.: Discovering data-aware declarative process models from event logs. In: Daniel, F., Wang, J., Weber, B. (eds.) BPM 2013. LNCS, vol. 8094, pp. 81–96. Springer, Heidelberg (2013)
9. van der Aalst, W.M.P., Adriansyah, A., van Dongen, B.F.: Replaying history on process models for conformance checking and performance analysis. Wiley Interdiscip. Rev. Data Min. Knowl. Discov. **2**(2), 182–192 (2012)
10. Mannhardt, F., de Leoni, M., Reijers, H.A., van der Aalst, W.M.P.: Balanced multi-perspective checking of process conformance. Computing **98**(4), 407–437 (2016)
11. Desel, J., Esparza, J.: Free Choice Petri Nets. Cambridge University Press, Cambridge (1995)

12. Leemans, S.J.J., Fahland, D., van der Aalst, W.M.P.: Discovering block-structured process models from event logs - a constructive approach. In: Colom, J.-M., Desel, J. (eds.) PETRI NETS 2013. LNCS, vol. 7927, pp. 311–329. Springer, Heidelberg (2013)
13. de Leoni, M., van der Aalst, W.M.P.: Data-aware process mining: discovering decisions in processes using alignments. In: SAC 2013, pp. 1454–1461. ACM (2013)

Detecting Deviating Behaviors Without Models

Xixi Lu[1](✉), Dirk Fahland[1], Frank J.H.M. van den Biggelaar[2],
and Wil M.P. van der Aalst[1]

[1] Eindhoven University of Technology, Eindhoven, The Netherlands
{x.lu,d.fahland,w.m.p.v.d.aalst}@tue.nl
[2] Maastricht University Medical Center, Maastricht, The Netherlands
f.vanden.biggelaar@mumc.nl

Abstract. *Deviation detection* is a set of techniques that identify deviations from normative processes in real process executions. These diagnostics are used to derive recommendations for improving business processes. Existing detection techniques identify deviations either only on the process instance level or rely on a normative process model to locate deviating behavior on the event level. However, when normative models are not available, these techniques detect deviations against a less accurate model discovered from the actual behavior, resulting in incorrect diagnostics. In this paper, we propose a novel approach to detect *deviation on the event level* by identifying *frequent common behavior* and *uncommon behavior* among executed process instances, without discovering any normative model. The approach is implemented in ProM and was evaluated in a controlled setting with artificial logs and real-life logs. We compare our approach to existing approaches to investigate its possibilities and limitations. We show that in some cases, it is possible to detect deviating events without a model as accurately as against a given precise normative model.

1 Introduction

Immense amounts of event data have been recorded across different application domains, reflecting executions of manifold business processes. The recorded data, also called *event logs* or *observed behavior*, show that real-life executions of process instances often deviate from normative processes [12]. Deviation detection, in the context of *conformance checking*, is a set of techniques that *check process conformance* of recorded executions against a normative process and identify where observed behavior does not fit in and thus deviates from the normative process model [1]. Accurately detecting deviating behavior at the event level is important for finding root causes and providing diagnostic information. The diagnosis can be used to derive recommendations for improving process compliance and performance [13].

Existing techniques for detecting deviations, such as alignment-based techniques [1], require a normative process in the form of a process model. However, normative models are often not available, especially in flexible environments. For instance, in healthcare, each patient often follows a unique path through

M. Reichert and H.A. Reijers (Eds.): BPM Workshops 2015, LNBIP 256, pp. 126–139, 2016.
DOI: 10.1007/978-3-319-42887-1_11

the process with one-of-a-kind deviations [11]. A solution is to discover a model from an event log. The discovered model is assumed to describe the normative behavior, and then conformance checking techniques discern where the log deviates. However, the quality of deviation detection depends heavily on the discovered model, which again depends on the discovery algorithm used and the design decisions made in the algorithm. When an event log shows high variety (for example, containing multiple process variants), discovering one normative process almost always results in underfitting models, rendering them useless for detecting deviations.

In this paper, we consider the problem of detecting deviations without discovering a normative process model. We limit our scope to only detecting *deviating events*; we define deviations as *additional* behavior observed in an event log but not allowed in the normative process; other deviations, such as steps of the normative process that are skipped, are not considered in this paper. We present a new technique to detect deviating events by computing *mappings* between events, which specify similar and dissimilar behavior between process instances. The more they that *agree* on a certain behavior, the less such a behavior is a deviation. We use this information to classify deviations.

The approach has been implemented as ProM plugin and was evaluated using artificial logs and real life logs. We compared our approach to existing approaches to investigate the possibility and the limitations of detecting deviations without a model. We show that the approach helps identify deviations without using a normative process model. In cases where dependencies between events can be discovered precisely, it is possible to detect deviating events as accurately as when using a given precise normative model. In other cases, when deviating events happen frequently and in patterns, it is more difficult to distinguish them from the conforming behavior without a normative model. We discuss ideas to overcome these problems in our approach.

In the remainder, we first discuss related work in Sect. 2, including input for our approach. Sections 3, 4 and 5 explain our method in more depth: in Sect. 3, we define and explain the relevant concepts, e.g. similar and dissimilar behavior, mapping, and cost function; Sect. 4 presents two algorithms to compute mappings; Sect. 5 discusses how to use mappings for detecting deviations. The evaluation results are presented in Sects. 6 and 7 discusses the limitations and concludes the paper.

2   Related Work

We consider an event log as input for our approach for detecting deviations. In addition, we discuss related work more in detail in this section.

Event Logs and Partial Orders. An *event log* is a collection of *traces*, each of which is *a sequence of events* describing the observed execution for a case. Most process mining techniques use an event log as input. Recently, research has been conducted to obtain partial orders over events, called partially ordered traces, and use them instead to improve process mining [6,9]. The work in [9] discussed various ways to convert sequential traces into partially ordered traces and has shown that such a conduct improves the quality of conformance checking when the as-is total ordering of events is unreliable. The approach proposed in this paper can handle partial orders as inputs, which we refer to as *execution graphs*. Two types of partial order [9] are used in this paper: data based partial order over events, i.e. two events are dependent if they access the same data attributes; and time based partial order over events, i.e. two events are dependent if they have different time stamps.

Outlier Detection and Deviance Mining. Existing outlier detection approaches have a different focus and are not applicable to our problem. These approaches first converting executions of cases to items of features and then using classification or clustering techniques [7]. However, they only identify deviating cases (thus items) and omit deviation on the event level (an analogy to classical data mining would be detecting a deviating value in a item for one feature) and are often unable to handle the situation in which a multitude of cases contain deviation. One different stream, known as *deviance mining*, classifies cases as normal or deviant, independent of their control-flow execution, but rather based on their performance (e.g. whether throughput time of a case is acceptable) [10]. Our approach is inspired by and similar to a log visualization technique known as *trace alignment* [3]. However, this visualization technique does not classify deviations but simply visualizes the mappings between traces to a user.

Conformance Checking. A state-of-art conformance checking technique is known as *(model-log) alignment* [1,9], which computes a most similar run of a given normative model with respect to each input trace. Events observed in traces that have no matching behavior in such a run are classified as deviating events, also known as log moves. However, the current cost function used by the approach is rather simple and static. For example, it is unable to distinguish consecutive events sharing the same event class. In addition, a precise model is required to identify deviations accurately, which might be unavailable and difficult to discover, whereas our approach does not require models.

Process Discovery and Trace Clustering. Process discovery algorithms aim to discover structured process models using an event log [4,8], but still face various difficulties [5]. When event logs are highly unstructured and contain deviating behavior, discovery algorithms often fail to find the underlying structure and return *spaghetti models* due to overfitting. Some discovery algorithms aim to be noise/deviation robust but often result in returning over-generalized or underfitted models. To discover better models, one may preprocess event logs using, for example, trace clustering. Syntactic-based trace clustering [5] is a set of techniques that focus on clustering traces in such a way that structured models can be discovered as different variant of the normative model. In our evaluation, we compare our approach to [1,2,5,8,9] more in depth.

3   Mappings - Similarities and Dissimilarities Between Executions

In this section, we introduce the key concepts used in this paper and explain how *similarity* and *dissimilarity* between executions of cases helps identify deviations.

Execution Graphs and Neighbors. For describing execution of a case, we use an *execution graph*. An execution graph is a directed acyclic graph $G = (E, R, l)$: the nodes E are the events recorded for the case, the edges R are the relations between the events, and the function l assigns to each event its event type. Each event is unique and has a set of attributes; one event belongs to one single execution graph. Figure 1 shows two execution graphs. On the right of Fig. 1, e_8, e_9, e_{10} are considered concurrent because, for example, they have the same timestamps [9]. Let e be an event in an execution graph. *k-predecessors* $N_k^p(e)$ denotes the set of events from which (1) there is a path in the execution graph to e and (2) the length of the path is at least 1 and at most k; similar for *k-successors* $N_k^s(e)$. In addition, we call the set of events for which there is no path to or from e the *concurrences* $N^c(e)$ of e. Moreover, for $e' \in N^c(e)$, we define the distance $dist_G(e, e') = 0$, in contrast to the traditional graph theory.

The *k-neighbors* $N_k(e)$ of e is a 3-tuple composed of the *k-predecessors*, the *concurrences* and the *k-successors* of e. For example, as shown in Fig. 1, $N_1(e_8) = (\{e_7\}, \{e_9, e_{10}\}, \{e_{11}\})$.

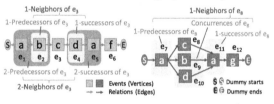

Fig. 1. Two examples of execution graphs. (Color figure online)

Deviations, Mappings and Similarity. We consider *deviations* as non-conforming behavior that consists of observed events in an execution graph. The assumption is that such deviating events occur much less frequently and occur in a highly dissimilar context, e.g. have dissimilar neighbors and locations, since they are not specified in the normative process. In addition, it would be difficult to find the events in other cases that are similar and comparable to these deviating events. Therefore, we compute similar behavior and dissimilar behavior between each two execution graphs as a *mapping*: the *similar behavior* is formed by all pairs of events that are mapped to each other, whereas events that are not mapped are *dissimilar behavior*. Formally, a *mapping* $\lambda_{(G,G')}$ between two execution graphs is a set of binary, symmetric relations between their events, in which each event is only mapped to one other event. Figure 2 exemplifies a mapping between the two execution graphs shown in Fig. 1. For instance, the mapping in Fig. 2 specifies that e_3 and e_8 are not mapped, and therefore, according to this particular mapping, they are dissimilar and show discrepancies between the two cases. We use $\overline{\lambda}$ to refer to the set of events that are not mapped, i.e. $\overline{\lambda}_{(G,G')} = \{e \in E \mid \neg \exists e' \in E' : (e, e') \in \lambda\} \cup \{e' \in E' \mid \neg \exists e \in E : (e, e') \in \lambda\}$[1].

---

[1] We omit G and G' for both λ and $\overline{\lambda}$ where the context is clear.

Based on a mapping, we also obtain *similar neighbors* and *dissimilar neighbors* surrounding two events and are able to compare the events more accurately. A pair of events are more similar, if they share more similar neighbors. For example, using a mapping, we can derive the similar predecessors and the dissimilar predecessors of two paired events (e, e'). We refer to the dissimilar predecessors as $DN_k^p(e, e', \lambda)$, where the k indicates the k-predecessors. The same applies to the set of *dissimilar successors* $DN_k^s(e, e', \lambda)$ and *dissimilar concurrences* $DN^c(e, e', \lambda)$. Figure 2 shows an example: because events e_5 and e_{11} have respectively $\{e_3, e_4\}$ and $\{e_7, e_8, e_9, e_{10}\}$ as their 2-*predecessors*, of which e_4 and e_{10} are paired, therefore $DN_2^p(e_5, e_{11}, \lambda) = \{e_3, e_7, e_8, e_9\}$. The pair (e_5, e_{11}) has two dissimilar successors e_6 and e_{12}, but no dissimilar concurrences as shown in Fig. 2. Hence, $DN_2^s(e_5, e_{11}, \lambda) = \{e_6, e_{12}\}$, and $DN^c(e_5, e_{11}, \lambda) = \emptyset$.

Cost Function and Cost Configurations. To evaluate a mapping, we define a *cost function* that assesses the similarity between paired events in the mapping. A mapping that captures more similar behavior is assigned with a lower cost. The mappings with the minimal cost are the *optimal mappings*. The cost function is shown in Eq. 1 and comprises three components $cost_{Matched}$, $cost_{Struc}$ and $cost_{NoMatch}$ that assess a mapping as follows. For each pair of events (mapped to each other) in a mapping, $cost_{Matched}$ and $cost_{Struc}$ assess their *local similarity* and *global similarity*, respectively. Moreover, $cost_{NoMatch}$ assigns a penalty to the mapping for each event that is classified to be dissimilar (i.e. not mapped). For each component, we assign a weight, i.e. w_M, w_S, w_N.

$$cost(G, G', \lambda) = w_M * cost_{Matched}(G, G', \lambda) + w_S * cost_{Struc}(G, G', \lambda)$$
$$+ w_N * cost_{NoMatch}(G, G', \lambda) \tag{1}$$

The function $cost_{Matched}$, defined in Eq. 2, helps to assess the similarity between two events regarding their properties and their local execution contexts (in this case their labels and their neighbors). The more similar, the lower the cost. Thus, a higher cost

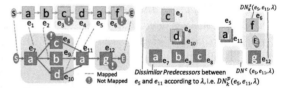

Fig. 2. An example of a mapping specifying similar and dissimilar behavior.

is assigned to prevent two locally dissimilar events being mapped to each other. In this paper, we only allow two events with the same label to be mapped to each other, i.e. $cost(l(e), l(e')) = 0$ if $l(e) = l(e')$, otherwise infinite.

$$cost_{Matched}(G, G', \lambda) = \sum_{(e,e') \in \lambda} cost(l(e), l(e'))$$
$$+ \mid DN_k^p(e, e', \lambda) \mid + \mid DN_k^s(e, e', \lambda) \mid + \mid DN^c(e, e', \lambda) \mid \tag{2}$$

In addition, the function $cost_{Struc}(G, G', \lambda) = \sum_{(p,p'),(e,e') \in \lambda} \frac{|dist_G(p,e) - dist_{G'}(p',e')|}{2}$ helps to assess how similar two events are with respect to their positions in the global context of execution graphs. The more similar their positions in the global context, the lower cost; the cost is high if they are in very different stages of execution graphs.

Futhermore, we define the function $cost_{NoMatch}(G, G', \lambda) = \sum_{e \in \bar{\lambda}} C_N + | N_k(e) |$, which assigns a cost to events that are not mapped and helps to asses when not to map an event. For example, a higher cost is assigned to a not-mapped event if it is *important* and should be mapped. We use the number of neighbors of an event to indicate the importance in addition to a basic cost C_N of not matching an event.

The final cost of a mapping depends on the k (defining the neighbors) and the four weights w_M, w_S, w_N and C_N. A 5-tuple composed of these five numbers is called a *cost configuration* of the cost function. The mappings with the minimal cost between two execution graphs according to a configured cost function are the *optimal mappings*.

4 Algorithms for Computing Mappings

For computing mappings between execution graphs, we propose two algorithms: one uses backtracking with a heuristic function and guarantees the return of the optimal mappings; the other provides no guarantees but runs in polynomial time.

Backtracking and Heuristic Function. The backtracking algorithm uses a *heuristic function* to prune our search space. The heuristic function is similar to the cost function and reuses $cost_{Matched}$, $cost_{Struc}$, and $cost_{NoMatch}$. The same *configuration* as the cost function is required to guarantee the lower bound property.

The algorithm starts with an empty mapping between two cases and then inductively computes the cost of the next decision, i.e. to consider two events similar or not, using the heuristic function. After making a decision to map two events, a part of the similar and dissimilar neighbors of the two events is known, according to the mapping so far, for which the

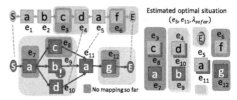

Fig. 3. An example of an incomplete mapping and the estimated lowerbound cost. (Color figure online)

heuristic function uses $cost_{Matched}$ to compute the cost. For the neighbors not yet mapped, the heuristic function estimates the cost by predicting an *optimal situation* of a future complete mapping. The optimal situation means that a maximal set of *possibly similar neighbors*, i.e. the neighbors that have the same label and are not mapped yet, becomes *similar neighbors*. Maximizing the set of *possibly similar neighbors* minimizes the set of possibly dissimilar neighbors (impossible to become similar neighbors in the future) and thus gives us a lower bound of the unknown part of the cost. Formally, we perform label multiset subtraction of not mapped neighbors to estimate the lower bound.

Figure 3 illustrates an incomplete mapping that states e_4 and e_{10} are similar and e_9 is dissimilar (i.e. $\lambda_{sofar} = \{e_4 \rightarrow e_{10}, e_9 \rightarrow \perp\}$). If we decide that e_5 and e_{11} are similar (thus mapping e_5 to e_{11}), we obtain their similar neighbors e_4 and e_{10} and dissimilar neighbor e_9 according to the mapping so far. We also identify the *possibly similar neighbors* e_3 and e_8 (both labeled with c and not mapped yet), and possibly dissimilar neighbors e_7, e_6 and e_{12}. Thus, the cost returned by $cost_{Matched}$ is 1 and the estimated additional future cost is 3. The cost of structure returns 2 because the distance from S to e_5 is 5, which differs from the distance of 3 between S and e_{11}.

The running time of the back tracking algorithm is $O(2^n)$, if each graph contains n events all with unique labels, because for each event, there is a choice between mapping the event or not. In the worst case when all events have the same label, the running time is $O((n+1)!)$.

Greedy Algorithm. The second algorithm we propose is greedy and runs in polynomial time. The greedy algorithm makes the current optimal choice to map two events or not. The quality of the algorithm depends heavily on the ordering of the choice that is made. The idea is to start with *finding the "most important and unique" event e (which has the least probability to be a deviating event or to be matched to another deviating event); then, select, for e, the current most similar event, if any.* As the mapping becomes more complete, the cost returned by the heuristic function resembles more accurately the cost returned by the cost function, which helps the algorithm to make more difficult choices later.

For formalizing this "importance and uniqueness", we introduce the concept of a *k-context* and its frequency as an example. A *k-context* $C_k(e)$ of an event e consists of the label of e, the labels of its k-predecessors, the labels of its concurrences, and the labels of its k-successors. Figure 4 shows three *3-contexts* with label a (on the right) based on the four execution graphs on the left. For example, $C_3(e_5) = C_3(e_{25}) = C_3(e_{35}) = (a, [b, c, d], [], [f, E])$. The *absolute frequency of a k-context* of an event e is the number of events that have the exact same k-context and is formally defined as follows. Let $\mathbb{G}$ denote a set of execution graphs. For each event e in E of $G \in \mathbb{G}$, the *absolute frequency of a k-context* is $Freq_\mathbb{G}(C_k(e)) = \sum_{G \in \mathbb{G}} |\{e' \in E \mid C_k(e) = C_k(e')\}|$. For example, in Fig. 4, we have $Freq(a, [b, c, d], [], [f, E]) = 3$. A context having a high absolute frequency indicates that there is a large set of events sharing the same context and can be mapped to each other.

To compute a *good* mapping between two given execution graphs, the greedy algorithm first sorts the nodes (i.e. events) based on the absolute frequencies of their context, and then simply starts with the "most important" node according to the ordering, and selects the best match for this node using the heuristic function introduced in the previous section. This process of making choices is repeated, and the algorithm simply works through the nodes linearly. Therefore, the running time of the greedy algorithm is quadratic in terms of the number of events.

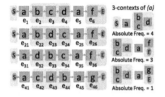

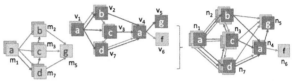

Fig. 4. 3-contexts and their absolute frequency.

Fig. 5. Fusion process: two *regs* fused into one *reg*

5   Deviation Detection Using Mappings

We use the mappings to compute *representative execution graphs (regs)* of cases and use them to locate uncommon behavior and identify deviations. A *reg* can be seen as an aggregation of a cluster of similar execution graphs and represents one variant of process execution. Each node of a *reg* represents a set of similar events; the number of events a node represent indicates the *commonness* of this behavior among cases of the *reg*. Similarly, each edge depicts a set of similar relations between the events. Figure 5 shows three *regs*. As can be seen, a *reg* resembles a directly follows graph with unfolded duplicated labels and shows executions of its cases, but the commonness of the nodes can also be used for detecting deviations and visualizing their positions.

Figure 5 also shows the process of aggregating execution graphs into a *reg* which we refer to as *fusion*. We compute *regs* of cases by fusing execution graphs *among which all mappings are consistent regarding all behavior*. In other words, the mappings between a set of execution graphs are consistent when all of them agree with each other about the similar behaviors. Formally, assuming a set of execution graphs is given, and Λ denotes the set of all mappings between them: Λ is *consistent* iff. Λ is transitive, i.e. for all $(e, e'), (e', e'') \in \Lambda \Rightarrow (e, e'') \in \Lambda$. The consistency of guarantees that the ordering of fusing a set of similar events (e.g. e, e', e'') is irrelevant (thus commutative and associative). Figure 5 illustrates a fusion of two *regs* representing four cases. The nodes m_1 and v_1 are fused into n_1, meaning that the mappings between them all agree that the four events are similar. The same holds for the rest of the nodes. Now, assume that, according to a mapping, one of the events of m_1 is actually similar to one of the events of v_4 instead of v_1, then the two *regs* will not be fused. We apply this principle incrementally by simply fusing the two most similar (groups of) cases indicated by the cost of their mappings. The algorithm returns a set of *regs* that can no further be fused.

Deviations are assumed to be uncommon behavior. If the number of events that a node n in a *reg* represents is low, it indicates that the behavior rarely occurs among the cases that are similar. If this number is below a certain threshold T relative to the maximum number of events represented by another node that has the same label in the same *reg*, we classify this node n to be uncommon and the events of n to be deviating. For example, assuming we have the *reg* on the right of Fig. 5 and T is 60 %, then the events of nodes n_5 and n_6 are classified as conforming since they represent the maximum number of events with respect to their labels g and f, respectively, whereas the one of n_4 is only 50 % of the maximum as 2 of 4 (represented by node n_1). Thus, the events of n_4 are classified as deviating. Another example, if the two *regs* shown on the left of Fig. 5 were not fused due to inconsistency and T is 60 %, then all events are classified as normal behavior; the same for any *reg* that only represents one execution graph.

6   Evaluation and Results

The proposed deviation detection approach is implemented in the process mining toolkit ProM[2]. We conducted controlled experiments to compare our approach to existing approaches and discuss the results in this section.

Experimental Setup. We compared our approach to other techniques on how accurately deviating events are detected as shown in Fig. 6. Given a log with each event labeled as deviant or conforming, our approach and existing approaches classify each of the events as deviating or conforming. Events correctly classified as deviations (based on the labels) are considered *true positives (TP)*. Similarly, *false positives (FP)* are conforming events that are incorrectly classified as deviations; *false negatives (FN)* are deviating events that are incorrectly classified as conforming events; *true negatives (TN)* are correctly classified as conforming events. Based on this, we compute the *accuracy* score (abbreviated to acc)[3], i.e. $acc = (TP+TN)/(TP+TN+FP+FN)$. For example, achieving an accuracy score of 0.9 after classifying 10 events means one of the events is incorrectly classified as deviating (FP) or conforming (FN).

We compared the accuracy of our approach to three existing methods shown in Fig. 6: (1) classify deviations by checking conformance [1] against the given normative model; (2) discover a normative model and then apply conformance checking using the discovered model; (3) first cluster traces to discover a more precise normative model for each process variant, and then check conformance for each cluster of traces against the corresponding variant model. For conformance checking, we use alignments [1,9]. The Inductive Miner (IMinf) [8] with filter (from 0.2 to 1.0[4]) is used for discovering models and the best result is chosen. For clustering, we used the ActiTraC (4 clusters) [5] and the Generic Edit Distance (GED with 4 and 10 clusters) [2] with standard settings.

We ran this experiment on 1 artificial and 2 real-life logs. In an artificial setting, an artificial normative model was used to generate a perfect log. For

---

[2] Both the plugins and the experiments can be found in the *TraceMatching* package of the ProM.

[3] In this paper, we only discuss the accuracy score. However, one may use the confusion matrix and compute the F1 score of event identification or swap the confusion matrix to compute the F1 score of deviation identification. We have computed all three, and they have shown similar results.

[4] Using filter from 0.0 to 0.2, IMinf returns a flower model which is the same as classifying all events as conforming.

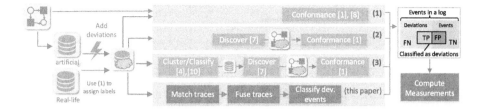

Fig. 6. Experiment design: comparing our approach to existing approaches

each trace in the perfect log, we then randomly add k_{dev} deviating events to derive a log with deviations labeled. The artificial hospital process model in [9] was used for generating event logs. The generated logs contain 1000 cases, 6590 events, and data-based relations between events which are used to derive the execution graphs.

For the two real-life logs, i.e. the MUMC and the Municipality (GOV) logs, we acquired their normative process model and used alignments to label deviating events (thus (1) achieves an accuracy of 1). The labeled real-life logs are then used to compare our approach to (2) and (3). The MUMC data set provided by Maastricht University Medical Center (a large academic hospital in the Netherlands) contains 2832 cases and 28163 events. The Municipality log[5] contains 1434 cases and 8577 events.

Results. In the following, we show results organized in the forms of experiments. *Experiment 1: How does our approach perform in comparison to (1), (2) and (3), and what is the effect of different configurations?* Figure 7 shows the accuracy scores (on the y-axis) of our algorithms along different configurations (on the x-axis)[6]. For other approaches, the accuracy scores remain constant (i.e. the horizontal lines) along our configurations. Interestingly, using the right configuration (highlighted by boxes), the backtracking algorithm is able to detect deviating events more accurately than sequential alignments (1) against the normative model. This is due to the situation in which two events of the same event type executed consecutively. From these two events, sequential alignments cannot find the deviating event, whereas our cost function uses the neighbors and their relative position in a global structure to distinguish them. Both backtracking and greedy have higher accuracies than (2) and (3). Another observation is that a configuration has a strong influence on the accuracy scores since the score fluctuates along the x-axis. We observe that no weight has a dominant effect on the accuracy. Some of the configurations that achieve the highest accuracies are the following: $k = 1, c_n = 3, w_M = w_N \geq w_S$, e.g. $w_S = w_M = w_N = 1$ (we write [k1M1N1C3S1] as a shorthand).

---

[5] http://dx.doi.org/10.4121/uuid:a07386a5-7be3-4367-9535-70bc9e77dbe6.
[6] For each case, we added one deviating event resulting in a log with 13.2 % deviating events. Repeating this five times, we show the average *acc* scores.

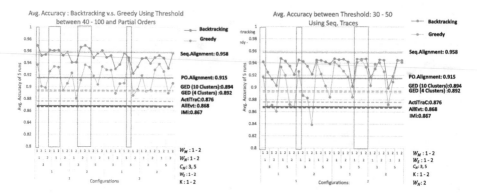

Fig. 7. Avg. *accuracy* scores using data and compared to existing approaches (Color figure online)

Fig. 8. Avg. *acc* scores using the sequential ordering (Color figure online)

Experiment 2: What is the effect of using sequential orders instead of partial orders on the scores? Figure 8 (similar to Fig. 7) shows the *acc* scores of our approach using sequential ordering. The *acc* scores in Fig. 8 show a decrease in backtracking if sequential ordering is used instead of data-based partial orders. However, we still observe that our approach can perform better than partially ordered alignments [9] and (2) and (3). Interestingly, the greedy approach shows that it is less sensitive for the input format; accuracy is, for some configurations, even higher when using sequential traces.

Experiment 3: What is the effect of different deviation levels? The effects of increasing the number of deviations from 13.2 % up to 43.1 % (by increasing k_{dev}) on the accuracy of identifying deviating events are shown in Fig. 9. For the backtracking and the greedy approach, we used configuration $[k1M1N1S1C3]$ and configuration $[k2M2N1S1C5]$ based on the previous results. As can be seen, backtracking $[k1M1N1S1C3]$ with $T = 100$ performs as well as (1) using sequential alignments. Also, as expected, using the same configuration but with a lower threshold $T = 40$, the approach classifies fewer events as deviating and therefore is less accurate when the level of deviation increases.

Experiment 4: Performance and Scalability. We compute the average running time of the approach of 5 runs while increasing the average number of events per trace from 6.59 to 10.59. The running time of the greedy algorithm increased only by 78 %, from 0.18 min (11.8 s) to 0.32 min (19.2 s), whereas the backtracking shows an exponential increase from 2.7 min to more than 3 h, which is more than 10000 %. The average running time of using ActiTraC together with discovery and alignments increased from 0.016 min to 0.172 min, showing an increase of 975 %. For GED, the average running time increased by 800 %, from about 0.010 min to 0.090 min.

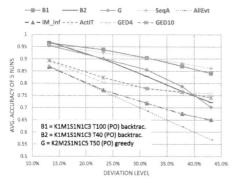

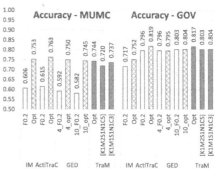

Fig. 9. Effect of deviation level on Backtrac. v.s. Greedy with selected settings (Color figure online)

Fig. 10. *Accuracy* of different approaches on real life logs (Color figure online)

Experiment 5: Different Models and Real-life Logs. For the two real-life logs, the results are shown in Fig. 10. For the MUMC data set, existing approaches perform better than our approach. ActiTraC achieves the best accuracy and is about 0.02 higher than our approach. Surprisingly, discovering an imprecise model that allows all activities to be executed in any order was better than applying our approach. For the GOV data set, our approach achieves the second best accuracy with 0.002 lower than the ActiTraC method. Most other approaches perform worse than when classifying all events as conforming behavior. This is due to an event class which occurs frequently in the log and all occurrences are deviations. Techniques (2) based on discovery only are unable to detect these deviations.

7   Discussion and Conclusion

In this paper, we investigated the problem of detecting deviating events in event logs. We compared existing techniques, which either use or construct a normative model to detect deviations via conformance checking, with a new technique that detects deviations from event logs only. The result of our evaluation shows four interesting observations.

Firstly, when the deviations are less structured and the dependencies between events are precise, we can detect deviations as accurately as performing conformance checking using a precise normative model. This indicates that our cost function is indeed able to distinguish individual events and accurately identify similar and dissimilar behavior. However, we also observe that the accuracy of our approach depends heavily on the way the cost function is configured. Some possible solutions to ease choosing a configuration could be: (1) normalizing the cost function (e.g. one divided by each components); (2) having predefined criteria or configurations such as "matching as many events as possible"; (3) showing

visual mappings between events, allowing the users to select the right ones, and
ranking configurations accordingly.

Another interesting observation is that, using the cost function, the backtracking algorithm performs worse than the greedy approach for sequential traces.
This may suggest that the current definition of neighbor and structure is too rigid
for sequential ordering of concurrent events. One may consider the union of predecessors, concurrences and successors as the neighbor of an event, instead of distinguishing them.

We also observer that when deviations are frequent and more structured,
our approach achieves slight lower accuracy than existing approaches. However,
all approaches performed rather poorly on the real life data sets. One way to
improve this is to conduct "cross checking" between different process variants
using the mappings between *regs* to find frequent deviations that occur in one
variant but not in others. Still, all current approaches have difficulty in detecting
very frequent deviations, when no normative model is available, as shown by the
results for GOV data sets.

A interesting challenge is to use mappings for detecting other deviations such
as missing events. Detecting some events are missing may be simple (e.g. frequent
but incomplete nodes in *regs*), whereas the deduction of the exact events that
are missing only from an event log appears to be much more difficult. In any
cases, it is possible to implement many other deviation classifiers using *regs*, or
to use the computed costs of mappings as a measure of similarity for clustering
traces and detecting deviating traces instead of events. Future research will be
aimed at investigating these possibilities, different cost functions, and the use of
regs for improving process discovery.

References

1. van der Aalst, W.M.P., Adriansyah, A., van Dongen, B.F.: Replaying history on
   process models for conformance checking and performance analysis. Wiley Interdisc. Rev. Data Min. Knowl. Disc. **2**(2), 182–192 (2012)
2. Bose, R., van der Aalst, W.M.P.: Context aware trace clustering: towards improving
   process mining results. In: Proceedings of the SIAM International Conference on
   Data Mining, SDM 2009, Sparks, Nevada, USA, 30 April–2 May, pp. 401–412
   (2009)
3. Bose, R.P.J.C., van der Aalst, W.M.P.: Process diagnostics using trace alignment:
   opportunities, issues, and challenges. Inf. Syst. **37**(2), 117–141 (2012)
4. Carmona, J., Cortadella, J.: Process discovery algorithms using numerical abstract
   domains. IEEE Trans. Knowl. Data Eng. **26**(12), 3064–3076 (2014)
5. De Weerdt, J., vanden Broucke, S.K.L.M., Vanthienen, J., Baesens, B.: Active trace
   clustering for improved process discovery. IEEE Trans. Knowl. Data Eng. **25**(12),
   2708–2720 (2013)
6. Fahland, D., van der Aalst, W.M.P.: Simplifying discovered process models in a
   controlled manner. Inf. Syst. **38**(4), 585–605 (2013)
7. Ghionna, L., Greco, G., Guzzo, A., Pontieri, L.: Outlier detection techniques for
   process mining applications. In: An, A., Matwin, S., Raś, Z.W., Ślęzak, D. (eds.)
   ISMIS 2008. LNCS (LNAI), vol. 4994, pp. 150–159. Springer, Heidelberg (2008)

8. Leemans, S.J.J., Fahland, D., van der Aalst, W.M.P.: Discovering block-structured process models from event logs containing infrequent behaviour. In: Lohmann, N., Song, M., Wohed, P. (eds.) BPM 2013 Workshops. LNBIP, vol. 171, pp. 66–78. Springer, Heidelberg (2014)
9. Lu, X., Fahland, D., van der Aalst, W.M.P.: Conformance checking based on partially ordered event data. In: Fournier, F., Mendling, J. (eds.) BPM 2014 Workshops. LNBIP, vol. 202, pp. 75–88. Springer, Heidelberg (2015)
10. Nguyen, H., Dumas, M., La Rosa, M., Maggi, F.M., Suriadi, S.: Mining business process deviance: a quest for accuracy. In: Meersman, R., Panetto, H., Dillon, T., Missikoff, M., Liu, L., Pastor, O., Cuzzocrea, A., Sellis, T. (eds.) OTM 2014. LNCS, vol. 8841, pp. 436–445. Springer, Heidelberg (2014)
11. Rebuge, A., Ferreira, D.: Business process analysis in healthcare environments: a methodology based on process mining. Inf. Syst. **37**(2), 99–116 (2012)
12. Suriadi, S., Wynn, M.T., Ouyang, C., ter Hofstede, A.H.M., van Dijk, N.J.: Understanding process behaviours in a large insurance company in Australia: a case study. In: Salinesi, C., Norrie, M.C., Pastor, Ó. (eds.) CAiSE 2013. LNCS, vol. 7908, pp. 449–464. Springer, Heidelberg (2013)
13. Yang, W., Hwang, S.: A process-mining framework for the detection of healthcare fraud and abuse. Expert Syst. Appl. **31**(1), 56–68 (2006)

Ontology-Driven Extraction of Event Logs from Relational Databases

Diego Calvanese[1], Marco Montali[1(✉)], Alifah Syamsiyah[1], and
Wil M.P. van der Aalst[2]

[1] Free University of Bozen-Bolzano, Bolzano, Italy
{calvanese,montali}@inf.unibz.it, alifah.syamsiyah@stud-inf.unibz.it
[2] Eindhoven University of Technology, Eindhoven, The Netherlands
w.m.p.v.d.aalst@tue.nl

Abstract. Process mining is an emerging discipline whose aim is to discover, monitor and improve real processes by extracting knowledge from event logs representing actual process executions in a given organizational setting. In this light, it can be applied only if faithful event logs, adhering to accepted standards (such as XES), are available. In many real-world settings, though, such event logs are not explicitly given, but are instead implicitly represented inside legacy information systems of organizations, which are typically managed through relational technology. In this work, we devise a novel framework that supports domain experts in the extraction of XES event log information from legacy relational databases, and consequently enables the application of standard process mining tools on such data. Differently from previous work, the extraction is driven by a conceptual representation of the domain of interest in terms of an ontology. On the one hand, this ontology is linked to the underlying legacy data leveraging the well-established ontology-based data access (OBDA) paradigm. On the other hand, our framework allows one to enrich the ontology through user-oriented *log extraction annotations*, which can be flexibly used to provide different log-oriented views over the data. Different data access modes are then devised so as to view the legacy data through the lens of XES.

Keywords: Multi-perspective process mining · Log extraction · Ontology-based data access · Event data

1 Introduction

Process mining aims to *discover, monitor and improve real processes by extracting knowledge from event logs* readily available in today's information systems [13]. Dozens (if not hundreds) of process-mining techniques are available and their value has been proven in various case studies [9]. Process mining techniques can be used to discover the real process, to detect deviations from

A. Syamsiyah—Supported by the European Master's Program in Computational Logic.

M. Reichert and H.A. Reijers (Eds.): BPM Workshops 2015, LNBIP 256, pp. 140–153, 2016.
DOI: 10.1007/978-3-319-42887-1_12

Table 1. A fragment of an event log: each line corresponds to an event

Case id	Timestamp	Activity	Resource	Cost
654423	30-04-2014:11.02	register request	John	300
654423	30-04-2014:11.06	check completeness of documents	Ann	400
655526	30-04-2014:16.10	register request	John	200
654423	30-04-2014:11.18	prepare decision	Pete	400
...	...	...	...	...

some normative process, to analyze bottlenecks and waste, and to predict flow times [13]. Normally, "flat" *event logs* serve as the starting point for process mining [13,14]. These logs are created with a particular process and a set of questions in mind. An event log can be viewed as a multiset of *traces*. Each trace describes the life-cycle of a particular *case* (i.e., a *process instance*) in terms of the *activities* executed. Often event logs store additional information about events. E.g., many process-mining techniques use extra information such as the *resource* (i.e., person or device) executing or initiating the activity, the *timestamp* of the event, or *data elements* recorded with the event (e.g., the size of an order). Table 1 shows a small fragment of a larger event log. Each row corresponds to an event. The events refer to two cases (654423 and 655526) and have additional properties, e.g., the registration for case 654423 was done by John at 11:02 on 30 April 2014 and the cost was 300€. An event may also contain transactional information, i.e., it may refer to an "assign", "start", "complete", "suspend", "resume", "abort", etc. action. For example, to measure the duration of an activity it is important to have a start event and a complete event. We refer to the *XES standard* [10] for more information on the data possibly available in event logs. See [14] for logging guidelines and details on getting event data from databases using redo logs.

It is apparent that a *condition sine qua non* for the application of process mining is the availability of faithful event logs, adhering to accepted standards (such as XES) and guaranteeing a certain quality level [15]. In many real-world settings, though, such event logs are not explicitly given, but are instead implicitly represented inside legacy information systems of organizations, which are typically managed through relational technology. This calls for the need of suitable methodologies, techniques and tools for *extracting event logs from relational databases*. This problem is extremely challenging, as pointed out in Chap. 4 of [13], which overviews the different problems encountered when extracting event data. On the one hand, this extraction process spans across several levels of abstractions: from the high-level, namely the domain-independent notions which are characterized at the conceptual level by the so-called *domain ontology*, and coming down to the concrete level at which data are effectively stored. On the other hand, there is no such a notion of "single" event log, but multiple event logs can be obtained by focusing on the dynamics of different domain entities. For example, in many applications there is not a single instance (case) notion. This is addressed in the context of *artifact-centric process mining* [5].[1] Various tools for event log extraction have been proposed, e.g., XESame [16] and ProMimport [8]. Moreover, commercial tools like Disco make it easy to convert a CSV or Excel file into a XES log. In [14] it is shown how event data can be extracted from the redo-logs of a database. However, none of the tools and approaches actually puts the domain ontology in the loop. As a result, the extraction is often ad-hoc, data is duplicated for different views, and the semantics of the resulting event log cannot be traced back. Furthermore, the extraction cannot be driven by experts of the domain who do not have any technical knowledge about the underlying information systems and concrete storage mechanisms. Some work has been done on *semantically annotated event logs* [4]. However, these approaches do not consider the extraction of event data. Their focus is on exploiting ontological information during analysis.

In this work, we overcome these issues by proposing a novel framework that supports domain experts in the extraction of XES event log information from legacy relational databases, and consequently enables the application of standard process mining tools on such data. Differently from previous work, the extraction is driven by a conceptual representation of the domain of interest in terms of an ontology. This ontology is linked to the underlying legacy data leveraging the well-established *ontology-based data access* (OBDA) paradigm [1,11]. In this way, domain experts can focus on the ontological level only, while the connection with the underlying data is automatically managed by the OBDA system. Notably, after more than a decade of foundational investigation [3], OBDA systems relying on lightweight description logics [1] are now subject to extensive implementation efforts [2,12], so as to make them able to manage huge amounts of data [7]. To leverage OBDA in the context of event log data extraction and access, our framework allows one to enrich the ontology through user-oriented *log extraction annotations*, which can be flexibly used to provide different log-oriented views over the data. Once these annotations are specified, we show how it is possible to automatically construct a direct link from the raw relational data sources to a general-purpose ontology that captures the XES standard. This, in turn, provides the basis for the process mining algorithms to extract this information either by materializing it explicitly, or by accessing it on-demand. The framework has been implemented in a prototype ProM[2] plug-in that relies on the state-of-the-art OBDA system Ontop[3]. The full code with a tutorial and examples, is available at http://tinyurl.com/op6y82s.

2   Problem Overview

To describe the problem we want to attack and introduce the main technical challenges towards its solution, we informally discuss a real-world example. John, the owner of a conference submission web portal, is interested in applying process mining techniques on the historical system data. His goal is to better

---

[1] Cf. also the EU ACSI Project: www.acsi-project.eu.

[2] http://www.processmining.org/prom/start.

[3] http://ontop.inf.unibz.it/.

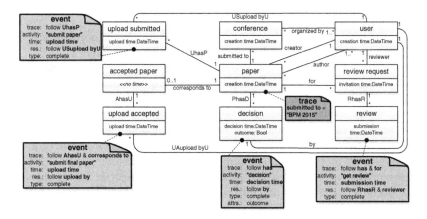

Fig. 1. Domain ontology of the conference submission portal in UML, with annotations to track the dynamics of BPM 2015 papers

LOGIN	
ID	User
5	Alifah
6	Marco
2	Diego
3	Wil

LOGINSTATS		
User	CT	LastAccess
5	15.10.14	15.03.15
6	17.10.14	20.03.15
2	18.10.14	20.03.15
3	18.10.14	18.03.15

PUB						
ID	Title	CT	User	Conf	Type	Status
151	Mining	09.11.14	5	5	FP	R01
127	Monitoring	10.02.15	3	32	SP	A03
945	OBDA	13.03.15	2	21	FP	S02
724	BPM	15.03.15	3	56	FM	A02

Fig. 2. Excerpt of a possible instance of the conference submission information system

understand how the different users of the system actually use it, and consequently take strategic decisions on how to restructure the portal and improve its functionalities.

As it is typical in contemporary organizations, the relevant knowledge used by John and the other members of his company to *understand* the application domain, is captured through a conceptual schema (such as a UML class diagram). We call such a schema a *domain ontology*. This ontology provides a high-level, shared conceptual view of the domain. In John's case, it contains the relevant concepts and relations that must be captured in order to manage a conference. A fragment of this knowledge is shown in Fig. 1 (for the moment, we ignore the colored annotations). However, the actual data are not maintained at this level of abstraction, but are instead stored inside an underlying relational information system. Figure 2 provides the excerpt of a possible relational database keeping track of papers and authors. At this level, data are hardly understandable by John. First, the vocabulary and the organization of the data radically depart from that of the domain ontology, due to design and implementation choices made by the IT staff of the company. Second, internal codes with an implicit semantics are employed, like in the *Status* column of the PUB table (which tracks whether a publication has been submitted, reviewed, accepted, . . .) or in the *Type* column of the same table (which tracks whether the publication is a full/short paper, a front matter, or other). This so-called *impedance mismatch* is a challenging problem that has been thoroughly investigated in the field of intelligent data access and integration [11].

When John wants to apply process mining techniques on this complex information system, he does not only face the impedance mismatch problem, but also the equally challenging problem of "process-orientation": the underlying data must be understood through a conceptual lens that is different from the domain ontology, and that focuses on the process-related notions of trace, event, resource, timestamp, and so on. In other words, John needs to extract an *event log* that explicitly represents the dynamics John wants to analyze. In this paper, we consider XES as the reference standard for representing event logs. This problem becomes even more difficult if one considers that, in general, a plethora of different event logs may be extracted from the same data, by changing perspective and by focusing on the evolution of different entities. For example, John could decide to analyze his data by following the submission and review of papers within or across conferences, or he could focus on users and the operations they execute to submit and review papers.

In this light, supporting John requires to solve three technical problems:1. How can John overcomes the impedance mismatch between the domain ontology and the underlying data? 2. How can John captures the connection of the domain ontology and the representation of an event log, depending on the dynamics he wants to track? 3. How can John finally obtains a view of the low-level data in terms of a corresponding event log? In this work, we tackle this overarching problem by resorting to a novel combination of techniques coming from intelligent data access and integration, extended and adapted to the case of process mining and flexible extraction of multi-dimensional event logs from raw relational data. To attack the first problem, we resort to the well-established OBDA framework, which allows one to link the raw data to the domain ontology and overcome the impedance mismatch [1,11]. To tackle the second challenge, we define an event log ontology that mirrors XES, and provide an annotation language to the user, which makes it possible

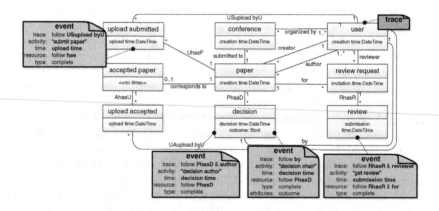

Fig. 3. Domain ontology annotations to track the dynamics of users

to capture semantic links between the constitutive (combinations of) elements in the domain ontology, and corresponding elements in XES. John could employ this annotation language to enrich the domain ontology of Fig. 1, ultimately producing the two schemas illustrated in Fig. 1 itself and in Fig. 3. In particular, Fig. 1 declares that each trace is related to the evolution of a single paper submitted to the BPM 2015 conference, and that meaningful events in a trace are paper submissions, reviews, final decisions, and upload of the camera-ready version. Figure 3 declares instead that each trace tracks the operations of a user, and that meaningful operations are paper submissions, reviews, and final decisions (to be listed both in the trace of the person chair who took the decision, and the paper creator who received it). The third problem is finally solved by automatically establishing a direct bridge from the low-level relational data to the event log ontology, in a way that is completely transparent to the user. The user can then access the event log with different modalities, and apply process mining without knowing how traces, events, and attributes are concretely stored in the underlying information system.

3   Preliminaries

We introduce some necessary background material, namely the description logic (DL) *DL-Lite$_\mathcal{A}$* and the ontology-based data access (OBDA) framework. To capture domain ontologies, we use the *DL-Lite$_\mathcal{A}$* language [1]. This allows for specifying *concepts*, representing sets of (abstract) objects, *roles*, representing binary relations between objects, and *attributes*, representing binary relations between objects and (domain) values. The syntax of *concept expressions* (B) and *role expressions* (R) in *DL-Lite$_\mathcal{A}$* is:

$$B \longrightarrow N \mid \exists R \mid \delta(U) \qquad R \longrightarrow P \mid P^-$$

Here, N, P, and U respectively denote a *concept name*, a *role name*, and an *attribute name*, and P^- denotes the *inverse* of role P. The concept $\exists R$, also called *unqualified existential restriction*, denotes the *domain* of a role R, i.e., the set of objects that R relates to some object. Notice that $\exists P^-$ actually denotes the *range* of role P. Similarly, the concept $\delta(U)$ denotes the *domain* of an attribute U.

A *DL-Lite$_\mathcal{A}$* ontology is a pair $(\mathcal{T}, A)$, where $\mathcal{T}$ is a TBox, i.e., a finite set of *TBox assertions*, and A is an Abox, i.e., a finite set of *ABox assertions*. *DL-Lite$_\mathcal{A}$* TBox assertions have the following form:

$B_1 \sqsubseteq B_2$	$R_1 \sqsubseteq R_2$	$U_1 \sqsubseteq U_2$	(funct R)
$B_1 \sqsubseteq \neg B_2$	$R_1 \sqsubseteq \neg R_2$	$U_1 \sqsubseteq \neg U_2$	(funct U)

In the first three columns, assertions of the first row denote *inclusions* between concepts, roles, and attributes, respectively; assertions of the second row denote *disjointness*. Assertions of the last column denote *functionality* on roles and attributes, i.e., that every object in the domain of R/U is related via R/U to at most one other object/value.

DL-Lite$_A$ ABox assertions are used to express extensional knowledge about specific objects and values in the domain of interest. They have the form $N(t)$, $P(t,t')$, or $U(t,v)$, where t and t' denote individual objects and v denotes a value.

The semantics of *DL-Lite$_A$* is given in [1]. Interestingly, *DL-Lite$_A$* TBoxes are suitable to formally capture the semantics of UML class diagrams (with the exception of *covering constraints* in a class hierarchy) [1]. Consequently, whenever we talk about a *DL-Lite$_A$* domain ontology, we can always imagine that the intensional knowledge of such an ontology can be modelled and graphically rendered in UML.

Example 1. Let *Paper* and *User* be *DL-Lite$_A$* concepts, *creator* and *author* roles, and *pCT* and *uCT* attributes (corresponding to the creation time of a paper and of a user respectively). The following *DL-Lite$_A$* TBox captures a portion of the UML domain ontology shown in Fig. 1:

$$\exists creator \sqsubseteq Paper \qquad \exists author \sqsubseteq Paper \qquad \delta(pCT) \sqsubseteq Paper$$
$$\exists creator^- \sqsubseteq User \qquad \exists author^- \sqsubseteq User \qquad Paper \sqsubseteq \delta(pCT)$$
$$Paper \sqsubseteq \exists creator \qquad Paper \sqsubseteq \exists author \qquad \delta(uCT) \sqsubseteq User$$
$$(\mathsf{funct}\ creator) \qquad\qquad\qquad\qquad\qquad User \sqsubseteq \delta(uCT)$$

The first column captures the semantics of the *creator* UML association, where the first two rows capture the typing of the association, the third row the fact that every paper must have a creator, and the fourth that every paper has at most one creator. Collectively, the last two assertions capture the 1 cardinality of the association from the perspective of the paper class. The second column captures the semantics of the *author* UML association. The third column instead deals with the creation time attributes for papers and users.   ∎

To interact with the domain ontology, we make use of *queries*. As typical in DLs, to *query* a *DL-Lite$_A$* ontology we make use of conjunctive queries (CQs) and union thereof (UCQs). CQs are first-order queries that corresponds to the well-known SPJ (select-project-join) queries in SQL. Syntactically, we specify UCQs using SPARQL, the standard ontology query language for the Semantic Web.

Ontology-Based Data Access. In an OBDA system, a relational database is connected to an ontology that represents the domain of interest by a mapping, which explicitly accounts for the impedance mismatch by relating database values with values and (abstract) objects in the ontology (c.f. [1]).

Technically, we consider a countably infinite set $\mathcal{V}$ of values and a set Λ of function symbols, each with an associated arity. Intuitively, function symbols are used to construct an abstract object in the ontology from a combination of values in the underlying database. We also define the set $\mathcal{C}$ of constants as the union of $\mathcal{V}$ and the set $\{f(d_1, \ldots, d_n) \mid f \in \Lambda$ and $d_1, \ldots, d_n \in \mathcal{V}\}$ of *object terms*.

Formally, an OBDA system is a structure $\mathcal{O} = \langle \mathcal{R}, \mathcal{T}, \mathcal{M} \rangle$, where: *(i)* $\mathcal{R} = \{R_1, \ldots, R_n\}$ is a database schema, constituted by a finite set of relation schemas; *(ii)* $\mathcal{T}$ is a *DL-Lite$_A$* TBox; *(iii)* $\mathcal{M}$ is a set of mapping assertions, each of the form $\Phi(\vec{x}) \rightsquigarrow \Psi(\vec{y}, \vec{t})$, where: (a) $\vec{x}$ is a non-empty set of variables, (b) $\vec{y} \subseteq \vec{x}$, (c) $\vec{t}$ is a set of object terms of the form $f(\vec{z})$, with $f \in \Lambda$ and $\vec{z} \subseteq \vec{x}$, (d) $\Phi(\vec{x})$ is an arbitrary SQL query over $\mathcal{R}$, with $\vec{x}$ as output variables, and (e) $\Psi(\vec{y}, \vec{t})$ is a set of atoms over the variables $\vec{y}$ and the object terms $\vec{t}$, whose predicate symbols are atomic concepts, atomic roles, and attributes of $\mathcal{T}$. Without loss of generality, we use the special symbol val/1 to map values from the relational layer to the range of attributes in the semantic layer.

Each mapping assertion creates a link between the database and the ontology, expressing how instances of the involved concepts/roles are obtained from the answers of queries posed over the database. We ground this definition to our running example.

Example 2. Consider an OBDA framework devised to link the database shown in Fig. 2 to the ontology in Fig. 1. Suitable mapping assertions must be devised so as to interconnect these two information layers. We consider the definition of *User* and *Paper*, with their creation times. One could argue that a paper can be extracted from the PUB table, by considering only those entries that have type FP or SP (respectively denoting full and short papers). This is captured by the following mapping assertion (p/1 constructs a publication object from its identifier in the database):

$$\text{SELECT } ID, CT \text{ FROM PUB WHERE } CT={'}\text{FP}{'}\text{OR } CT={'}\text{SP}{'}$$
$$\rightsquigarrow \{Paper(\mathsf{p}(ID)), pCT(\mathsf{p}(ID), \mathsf{val}(CT))\}$$

A user and his/her system creation time are extracted by joining LOGIN and LOGINSTATS tables:

$$\text{SELECT } L.User, S.CT \text{ FROM LOGIN } L, \text{ LOGINSTATS } S \text{ WHERE } L.ID{=}S.User$$
$$\rightsquigarrow \{User(\mathsf{u}(L.User)), pCT(\mathsf{u}(L.User), \mathsf{val}(S.CT))\}$$

where u/1 constructs a user object from its username in the database.   ∎

A UCQ q over an OBDA system $\mathcal{O} = \langle \mathcal{R}, \mathcal{T}, \mathcal{M} \rangle$ is simply a UCQ over $\mathcal{T}$. To compute the answers of q over $\mathcal{O}$ wrt a database instance D over $\mathcal{R}$, two approaches can be followed. In the first approach, which we call *materialization*, query answering consists of two steps. In the first step, an ABox is explicitly materialized starting from D and by applying the mapping assertions in a forward way. In particular, the ABox generated from D by a mapping assertion $m = \Phi(x) \rightsquigarrow \Psi(y, t)$ in $\mathcal{M}$ is $m(D) = \bigcup_{v \in eval(\Phi, D)} \Psi[x/v]$, where $eval(\Phi, D)$ denotes the evaluation of the SQL query Φ over D. Then, the ABox generated from D by the mapping $\mathcal{M}$ is $\mathcal{M}(D) = \bigcup_{m \in \mathcal{M}} m(D)$. In the second step, the query is posed directly over the domain ontology $\langle \mathcal{T}, \mathcal{M}(D) \rangle$.

In the second approach, which we call *on-demand*, the data are kept in D and no further information is explicitly materialized. Instead, the input query q is subject to a multi-step reformulation approach, which: *(i)* compiles away $\mathcal{T}$; *(ii)* unfolds the components of the obtained query by applying $\mathcal{M}$. This produces a corresponding SQL query that can be posed directly over the underlying database [11]. The answers are then computed and returned in the form of ontological objects. Notably, the two approaches yield the same answer, and can be therefore be interchangeably applied.

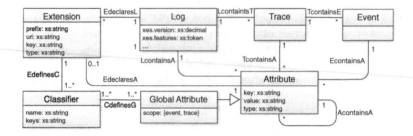

Fig. 4. General event ontology

4 Log Extraction Framework

Our log extraction process is organized in two phases:

1. the *design phase*, in which a domain expert specifies how to view the domain ontology using the lens of an event ontology for XES;
2. the *data access phase*, in which the result of the first phase is applied over actual data, so as to obtain a corresponding event log that is then accessed by domain experts or process mining algorithms.

In this section, we focus on the design phase. Data access is discussed in Sect. 5. The purpose of the design phase is to support a domain expert in the annotation of a domain TBox given as input, so as to properly link it to the event ontology that captures XES. Notice that the domain expert is not required, in this phase, to employ actual data, nor to have any specific knowledge about how such data are stored inside the company information system.

Specifically, we discuss how XES has been modeled as a *DL-Lite$_A$* TBox, and then focus on the language and modeling language to annotate the domain TBox, implicitly establishing a link with the XES TBox.

The XES Event Log TBox. We carefully analyzed the documentation of XES [10], and consequently derived the *DL-Lite$_A$* TBox $\mathcal{X}$, rendered in Fig. 4 as a UML class diagram. This TBox is fixed once and for all in our framework, and does not depend on the modeled domain. Beside the standard XES elements of *Trace*, *Event*, and *Attribute*, we also consider the following standard extensions: *(i) Concept* extension (to assign a name to events); *(ii) Time* extension (to assign a timestamp to events); *(iii) Lifecycle* extension (to link the event type to the XES transactional model); *(iv)* (optionally) *Organizational* extension (to link an event to its responsible resource).

Annotations. Annotations are defined by a domain expert to link a domain-specific *DL-Lite$_A$* TBox $\mathcal{T}$ to the generic XES TBox $\mathcal{X}$. Intuitively, they take the form reported in Figs. 1 and 3. Technically, a *log annotation* over $\mathcal{T}$, written $\mathcal{L}_{\mathcal{T}}$, is a pair $\langle \Phi_{tr}(t, l), \mathcal{E} \rangle$, where $\Phi_{tr}(t, l)$ is a *trace annotation*, i.e., a SPARQL query expressing how to extract traces (and their corresponding log) from $\mathcal{T}$, and $\mathcal{E}$ is a set of *event-attribute annotations*. Each event-attribute annotation is a tuple $\langle \Phi_{ev}(\vec{e}, t), \Phi_{ts}(ts, \vec{e}), \Phi_n(n, \vec{e}), [\Phi_a^1(v_1, a_1, c_1, \vec{e}), \ldots, \Phi_a^k(v_k, a_k, c_k, \vec{e})] \rangle$ of SPARQL queries over $\mathcal{T}$, where: *(i)* query $\Phi_{ev}(\vec{e}, t)$ is an *event annotation*, i.e., a SPARQL query extracting events from $\mathcal{T}$, together with the trace they belong to; *(ii)* queries $\Phi_{ts}(ts, \vec{e})$ and $\Phi_n(n, \vec{e})$ bind events to the two mandatory attributes of timestamp and activity name (and are consequently called *timestamp* and *name annotations*); *(iii)* each query $\Phi_a^i(v_i, a_i, c_i, \vec{e})$ (with $i \in \{1, \ldots, k\}$) is an *attribute annotation* that extracts the value(s) v_i of an attribute of type a_i and with key c_i, binding it/them to event $\vec{e}$. Attribute annotations are optional. Among all possible attributes, they can be used to extract the responsible resource for an event, or its transactional lifecycle type (cf. the XES *Organizational* and *Lifecycle* extensions). Obviously, different guidelines and constraints apply to the different queries in $\mathcal{L}_\mathcal{T}$. We discuss this issue in the following.

Note that each query in $\mathcal{L}_\mathcal{T}$ is centred around a concept/role/attribute of $\mathcal{T}$. Hence, it is straightforward to ideally "attach" an annotation to the corresponding element in $\mathcal{T}$.

Trace Annotations. A trace focuses on the evolution of an entity/object over time. In Fig. 1, the focus is on the evolution of papers, whereas in Fig. 3 it is on users. In general, a trace can be annotated only by selecting a concept in $\mathcal{T}$, possibly adding further conditions on which members of such concept give raise to a trace. Technically, this means that in $\Phi_{tr}(t, l)$, t must be bound to a concept of $\mathcal{T}$. For example, the trace annotation in Fig. 1 can be formalized as:

```
SELECT ?t "BPM15-papers-log"
WHERE {?t a:Paper; :submittedTo ?conf.
       ?conf a:Conference. FILTER regex(?conf,"BPM 2015","i").}
```

where `"BPM15-papers-log"` identifies the log l we are constructing.

Event Annotations. Event annotations differ from trace annotations in two respects. First of all, any element of $\mathcal{T}$ may be subject of an event annotation: not only concepts, but also relations and attributes. The arity of the corresponding SPARQL query then depends on which element is targeted: if it is a concept, than a single event variable will be used; it if is a relation or an attribute, two variables will be employed, matching with the involved subject and object. Second, to be a valid target, such an element must be "timed", i.e., either directly or undirectly univocally associated to exactly one timestamp attribute, and have a unique name. To check whether this property is guaranteed or not, one could pose its corresponding SPARQL query over the input OBDA system, and verify that, for each event, exactly one timestamp and one name is returned. By referring again to Fig. 1, the indication that a submission upload is an event is captured by:

```
SELECT ?e ?t WHERE {?e a:UploadSubmitted; :has? t. ?t a:Paper.}
```

Note that event annotations always have event and trace variables as distinguished variables, establishing a correspondence between the returned events and their traces. Also notice that a single variable is used for the event, since it is extracted from a concept.

Timestamp and Name Annotations. We consider two mandatory attributes: a timestamp and an activity name. Both of them are distinguished variables in the SPARQL query together with its event. As pointed out before, each event is required to be associated with exactly one timestamp and exactly one name. Obviously, in general many different possibilities exist. For example, in Fig. 1 it is apparent that the submission time associated to a submission upload may be the upload time of the upload itself, or the creation time borrowed either from *User* by navigating the *uploadBy* relation, or from *Paper* by navigating the *has* relation. As for the activity name, the most typical situation is the one in which the name is directly bound to an explicitly specified string. However, in general one could construct such a name by navigating through $\mathcal{T}$ and even composing the name by concatenating together strings and query results. As for the timestamp, three annotation patterns typically emerge. We discuss each of them.

1. Concept with single timestamp. The timestamp attests that the concept is directly timed, and therefore the concept itself is marked as an event. This is the case, e.g., for the submission upload in Fig. 1.

2. Concept with pre-defined multiple timestamps. This pattern emerges whenever there are objects that flow through different "phases" over time. For example, a cart may be associated to a pre-defined set of timestamps, such as the creation time, the finalization time, and the payment time. Each of such timestamps represent a specific phase transition, and some of such timestamps may be null (this is the case, e.g., for a cart that has been created but not finalized). Each phase transition could be singled out as a relevant event, by annotating the corresponding timestamp attribute.

3. Variable CRUD timestamps. This situation arises whenever a certain concept/relation is subject to many different operations over time, whose number is not known a priori. For example, objects may have *create*, *read*, *update*, *delete* actions related to them, and there can be any number of actions related to the same object, e.g., multiple updates. Similarly, there may also be *create* and *delete* actions for relations. If we imagine to have an "operation table", containing the different operation types and the corresponding object identifiers (each denoting the object over which an operation is applied), then such a table will be annotated as an event, whose name depends on the operation type.

Optional Attribute Annotations. Optional attributes are annotated by using specific SPARQL queries having, as distinguished variables: *(i)* the attribute type, *(ii)* its key, *(iii)* its value, *(iv)* the variables of the corresponding event.

5   XES Log Extraction and Access

In Sect. 4, we have shown how a domain expert can annotate a domain *DL-Lite$_A$* TBox so as to express how to conceptually identify traces, events and their attributes starting from the domain concepts, relations and attributes. We now show how such annotations can be employed so as to make the framework operational. We assume to have, as input, not only a domain TBox, but also an entire OBDA system, previously prepared to link the domain TBox with the corresponding underlying relational database. This process is completely independent from process mining-related interests. Hence, the overall input for our log extraction framework is an OBDA system $\mathcal{O} = \langle \mathcal{R}, \mathcal{T}, \mathcal{M} \rangle$. After the design phase, we also have a log annotation $\mathcal{L}_\mathcal{T}$ for $\mathcal{T}$. To make the framework operational and effectively get the data contained in a concrete instance D of the company database $\mathcal{R}$, we proceed in two steps: *(i)* The annotations are used to automatically create a new OBDA system that links the company database $\mathcal{R}$ to the XES TBox $\mathcal{X}$, according to the semantics of annotations in $\mathcal{L}_\mathcal{T}$. *(ii)* This OBDA system is exploited to access the concrete data in D through the conceptual lens of $\mathcal{X}$, following the materialization or the on-demand paradigm (cf. Sect. 3 (Ontology-Based Data Access)). We focus on both aspects, discussing how they have been implemented using ProM as process mining infrastructure, OpenXES as reference implementation for XES, and Ontop for OBDA.

Automatic Generation of Schema-to-XES Mapping Assertions. Given an OBDA system $\mathcal{O} = \langle \mathcal{R}, \mathcal{T}, \mathcal{M} \rangle$ and a log annotation $\mathcal{L}_\mathcal{T}$ for $\mathcal{T}$, we automatically construct a new OBDA system $\mathcal{O}_{log} = \langle \mathcal{R}, \mathcal{X}, \mathcal{M}_{log} \rangle$ that directly links schema $\mathcal{R}$ to the XES TBox $\mathcal{X}$. This is done by iterating through the annotations present in $\mathcal{L}_\mathcal{T}$, and by transforming each annotation into a corresponding mapping assertion in $\mathcal{M}_{log}$. Intuitively, this is done as follow. Let $\Phi(\vec{x})$ be the SPARQL query associated to one of the annotations in $\mathcal{L}_\mathcal{T}$. We first reformulate $\Phi(\vec{x})$ as a corresponding SQL query $Q(\vec{x})$ directly posed over $\mathcal{R}$. We then construct a mapping assertion of the form $Q(\vec{x}) \rightsquigarrow \Psi(\vec{y}, \vec{t})$, where Ψ is a set of atoms over $\mathcal{X}$, built according to the semantics of the annotation. Since we have 5 kinds of annotations (for trace, event, event timestamp, event activity name, event attributes), 5 corresponding translation rules must be provided do as to generate such mapping assertions. As an example, we consider the case of the trace annotation $\Phi_{tr}(t, l)$ in $\mathcal{L}_\mathcal{T}$. The corresponding mapping assertion to be inserted in $\mathcal{M}_{log}$ is:

$$Q(t,l) \rightsquigarrow \left\{ \begin{array}{l} LcontainsT(\log(l), \mathsf{tr}(t)), \ TcontainsA(\mathsf{tr}(t), \mathsf{attr}(t)), \\ key_{Attribute}(\mathsf{attr}(t), \texttt{"concept:name"}), \\ value_{Attribute}(\mathsf{attr}(t), t), \ type_{Attribute}(\mathsf{attr}(t), \texttt{"literal"}) \end{array} \right\}$$

where $Q(t,l)$ is the SQL query corresponding to $\Phi_{tr}(t,l)$, and specific unary function symbols are used to construct the abstract objects of log, trace, and attribute, out from the flat values for t and l. The first line defines the relationships between the log $\log(l)$ and the trace $\mathsf{tr}(t)$, as well as between $\mathsf{tr}(t)$ and an attribute generated for it. Note that there is no need to explicitly assert the concepts to which these three objects belong, as all relations are typed in $\mathcal{X}$. The features of the trace attribute are fixed in the second and third line, which model that value t is a literal that constitutes the name of $\mathsf{tr}(t)$.

Data Access. Once the OBDA system $\langle \mathcal{R}, \mathcal{X}, \mathcal{M}_{log} \rangle$ has been obtained, the data contained in $\mathcal{R}$ (D henceforth) can be "viewed" and accessed through the lens of the XES ontology $\mathcal{X}$ thanks to $\mathcal{M}_{log}$. We support in particular two access modes, which have been effectively implemented. The first mode is the *XES log materialization* mode, and consists in concretely materializing the actual event log in the form of the ABox $\mathcal{M}_{log}(D)$, using Ontology-Based Data Access procedure. This ABox is then automatically serialized into an XML file that is fully compliant with the XES standard. Multiple XES logs can be seamlessly obtained by just changing the annotations. This mode has been implemented as a ProM 6 plug-in. It currently supports only a textual specification of the ontology and the annotations, but we are working on a GUI that exposes the domain TBox as a UML class diagram, and allows the user to visually annotate it.

The second mode is the *on-demand access*. With this approach, do not use $\mathcal{M}_{log}$ to concretely materialize the log, but we maintain the data in D, and reformulate queries posed over $\mathcal{X}$ as SQL queries directly posed over D. In this light, the XES log only "virtually" exists: no redundant copy of the data is created, and log-related information is directly fetched from D. Since the caller does not perceive any difference when adopting this strategy or the other one, process mining algorithms can seamlessly exploit both techniques without changing a line of code. This mode has been realized by providing a new implementation of the OpenXES interface, used to access XES logs from JAVA. The implementation combines the on-demand OBDA approach with the well known design pattern of *lazy loading* [6], which intutively indicates to defer the initialization of an object to when it is needed. In particular, the JAVA side does not really maintain in memory the whole log, but when a portion of the log is needed by the requester, it is lazily constructed by issuing a query to the underlying database.

6   Conclusions

We have proposed a novel methodology and technology to flexibly extract event logs from legacy, relational data sources, by leveraging the ontology-based data access paradigm. This is especially useful for multi-perspective process mining, since event logs reflecting different views of the same data can be obtained by just changing the ontology annotations. Our framework enables the materialization of event logs from legacy data, or the possibility of maintaining logs virtual and fetch log-related information on-demand. We are currently following three lines of research: *(i)* application of the framework to real-world case studies; *(ii)* improvement of the framework with visuali interfaces; *(iii)* benchmarking of the different data access strategies.

References

1. Calvanese, D., De Giacomo, G., Lembo, D., Lenzerini, M., Poggi, A., Rodriguez-Muro, M., Rosati, R.: Ontologies and databases: the *DL-Lite* approach. In: Tessaris, S., Franconi, E., Eiter, T., Gutierrez, C., Handschuh, S., Rousset, M.-C., Schmidt, R.A. (eds.) Reasoning Web. LNCS, vol. 5689, pp. 255–356. Springer, Heidelberg (2009)
2. Calvanese, D., De Giacomo, G., Lembo, D., Lenzerini, M., Poggi, A., Rodriguez-Muro, M., Rosati, R., Ruzzi, M., Savo, D.F.: The Mastro system for ontology-based data access. Semantic Web J. **2**(1), 43–53 (2011)
3. Calvanese, D., De Giacomo, G., Lembo, D., Lenzerini, M., Rosati, R.: DL-Lite: tractable description logics for ontologies. In: Proceedings of AAAI (2005)
4. Alves de Medeiros, A.K., van der Aalst, W.M.P., Pedrinaci, C.: Semantic process mining tools: core building blocks. In: Proceedings of ECIS (2008)

 5. Fahland, D., De Leoni, M., van Dongen, B., van der Aalst, W.M.P.: Many-to-many: some observations on interactions in artifact choreographies. In: Proceedings of ZEUS (2011)
 6. Fowler, M.: Patterns of Enterprise Application Architecture. Addison-Wesley (2003)
 7. Giese, M., et al.: Scalable end-user access to big data. In: Rajendra, A. (ed.) Big Data Computing. CRC (2013)
 8. Günther, C.W., van der Aalst, W.M.P.: A generic import framework for process event logs. In: Eder, J., Dustdar, S. (eds.) BPM Workshops 2006. LNCS, vol. 4103, pp. 81–92. Springer, Heidelberg (2006)
 9. IEEE Task Force on Process Mining. Process mining case studies (2013). http://tinyurl.com/ovedwx4
10. IEEE Task Force on Process Mining. XES standard definition (2013). http://www.xes-standard.org/
11. Poggi, A., Lembo, D., Calvanese, D., De Giacomo, G., Lenzerini, M., Rosati, R.: Linking data to ontologies. In: Spaccapietra, S. (ed.) Journal on Data Semantics X. LNCS, vol. 4900, pp. 133–173. Springer, Heidelberg (2008)
12. Rodríguez-Muro, M., Kontchakov, R., Zakharyaschev, M.: Ontology-based data access: Ontop of databases. In: Alani, H., et al. (eds.) ISWC 2013, Part I. LNCS, vol. 8218, pp. 558–573. Springer, Heidelberg (2013)
13. van der Aalst, W.M.P.: Process Mining: Discovery, Conformance and Enhancement of Business Processes. Springer, Heidelberg (2011)
14. van der Aalst, W.M.P.: Extracting event data from databases to unleash process mining. In: Proceedings of BPM. Springer (2015)
15. van der Aalst, W.M.P., et al.: Process mining manifesto. In: Daniel, F., Barkaoui, K., Dustdar, S. (eds.) BPM Workshops 2011, Part I. LNBIP, vol. 99, pp. 169–194. Springer, Heidelberg (2012)
16. Verbeek, H.M.W., Buijs, J.C.A.M., van Dongen, B.F., van der Aalst, W.M.P.: XES, XESame, and ProM 6. In: Soffer, P., Proper, E. (eds.) CAiSE Forum 2010. LNBIP, vol. 72, pp. 60–75. Springer, Heidelberg (2011)

Discovering Queues from Event Logs with Varying Levels of Information

Arik Senderovich[2(✉)], Sander J.J. Leemans[1], Shahar Harel[2], Avigdor Gal[2],
Avishai Mandelbaum[2], and Wil M.P. van der Aalst[1]

[1] Eindhoven University of Technology, Eindhoven, The Netherlands
[2] Technion, Haifa, Israel
sariks@tx.technion.ac.il

Abstract. Detecting and measuring resource queues is central to business process optimization. Queue mining techniques allow for the identification of bottlenecks and other process inefficiencies, based on event data. This work focuses on the discovery of resource queues. In particular, we investigate the impact of available information in an event log on the ability to accurately discover queue lengths, i.e. the number of cases waiting for an activity. Full queueing information, i.e. timestamps of enqueueing and exiting the queue, makes queue discovery trivial. However, often we see only the completions of activities. Therefore, we focus our analysis on logs with partial information, such as missing enqueueing times or missing both enqueueing and service start times. The proposed discovery algorithms handle concurrency and make use of statistical methods for discovering queues under this uncertainty. We evaluate the techniques using real-life event logs. A thorough analysis of the empirical results provides insights into the influence of information levels in the log on the accuracy of the measurements.

1 Introduction

Detecting and measuring resource queues is central to business processes. Resource queues reveal bottlenecks and violations of service-level agreements. Moreover, sojourn times and delays are basic Key Performance Indicators (KPI) that cannot be accurately calculated without queueing measurements. Process mining is a research field which aims to extract such performance information from event logs [1]. Queue mining can be seen as a particular class of process mining techniques focusing on the use of queueing theory to characterize queues from data and facilitate performance analytics [2]. Existing queue mining approaches consider event logs in which full queueing-related information is readily available. Such information includes timestamps of enqueue and service start events. However, for real-life processes, queueing information is often unavailable in the event log. Thus, previous work on the analysis of resource behavior discovered queueing information from logs with missing start timestamps, with the use of extensive resource information [3]. Moreover, both [2,3] did not consider complex process models with parallelism, but rather worked at the perfectly-ordered log level.

M. Reichert and H.A. Reijers (Eds.): BPM Workshops 2015, LNBIP 256, pp. 154–166, 2016.
DOI: 10.1007/978-3-319-42887-1_13

And in [4], missing timestamps were imputed by using a class of stochastic Petri nets. However, they consider a single timestamp per activity, without differentiating activity times from queues.

In this paper, we explore the influence of available information in the log on the accuracy of the aforementioned queue mining techniques. The event logs that we consider are general and accommodate a life cycle of three stages per activity: (1) in transition, (2) in queue, and (3) in service. To measure queues, even in case of missing timestamps for enqueueing/service start information, we assume that a process model containing the control flow of the process is given. Such a model can be discovered from the event log using a process discovery algorithm, e.g. in the form of a process tree [5] and subsequently extend the control-flow perspective with queueing measurements. The discovered model enables the extraction of a queue log, which (ideally) contains activity instances with the corresponding enqueue, start, and end timestamps.

Our methodology for measuring queue lengths, i.e. the number of work items in queue at a given point in time, starts with a queue log. First, we cluster the log according to durations (e.g. sojourn time), and get clusters with similar durations, and therefore loads. Then, we use these loads to fit a phase type distribution to life cycle durations with the use of Bayesian inference. For the evaluation of our proposed approach we applied our techniques to three real-life event logs: two call center logs and a hospital log. The results show that the queue length can be estimated using only partial information from the event log. Furthermore, the accuracy of our techniques depends on the amount of available information, and on the parameters of our techniques.

The remainder of this paper is organized as follows. Section 2 defines the event log, the role of process models in queue discovery, and the levels of available information that we assume on our event logs. Moreover, the section states the main problem that we solve in this paper. Section 3 presents our methodology for queue length discovery. Section 4 presents our experiments and discusses their results. Section 5 concludes the paper.

2 Information Levels in Event Logs and Process Models

In this section we define event logs and an activity life-cycle model. We then offer a classification of the levels of information that we consider in the event logs, and state the main problem that we solve in this paper.

2.1 Event Logs

An *event log L* is a multi-set of traces, where a *trace* represents a single case, *e.g.*, a customer or a patient visiting a hospital. A trace consists of several *activity instances*, which represent pieces of work performed for the trace. Consider the process model presented in Fig. 1. A trace for a patient in this process may include blood draw and doctor examination:

$$\langle \dots \text{blood draw}_{start}^{11:27}, \text{blood draw}_{complete}^{11:29}, \text{exam}_{enqueue}^{11:45}, \text{exam}_{start}^{12:02}, \text{exam}_{complete}^{12:15} \dots \rangle.$$

Each of the above *events* contains a timestamp at which the event occurred, and the life-cycle transition, which denotes a change of state for the activity instance. The life-cycle transitions of the last three events, belonging to the activity instance 'exam' is as follows: the patient reports at the waiting room and enters a queue (*enqueue*); after a while she is invited into the examination room (*start*); and finally her examination finishes (*complete*). At the bottom of Fig. 1 the activity life-cycle is illustrated. We assume that the transition *initiate* is not available explicitly in the event log, but that it coincides with the last completed activity instance. In our example, at 11:29, after blood draw completion, the examination was initiated and the patient started transit (she walked towards the examination room). In this paper, we aim to estimate performance measures if not all timestamps are present.

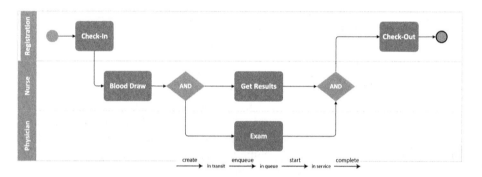

Fig. 1. An examination process in an outpatient hospital; activity life-cycle

2.2   Process Models

To infer the initiate life-cycle transition, we assume it coincides with the last completed activity instance. However, this is not necessarily the activity instance of which the completion time is the closest. For instance, in our example, a lab test is processed for results in parallel with the examination activity. This would obviously have no influence on the transit time of the patient, as she has to walk from the laboratory to the examination room. Even though the lab results are ready before she reaches the room, it does not imply that she started walking later. Therefore, knowledge of the control-flow of the process is required, i.e. the initiation time of an activity is the *last completed non-parallel activity instance*. In our experiments, we used process trees [6] because there are powerful discovery techniques available for this class of models, and the models are guaranteed to be deadlock and livelock free. Process trees provide information whether activities are parallel by their structure. Other formalisms such as Petri nets and BPMN might provide this information as well.

Our approach assumes the presence of a process model to infer initiation events, to identify activity instances and to deal with deviations [7]. We do not assume that the event log describes activity instances. Therefore, in Sect. 3.1, we introduce a method to obtain activity instances from an event log and a process model, and show how we handle with process deviations.

2.3 Levels of Information

Not all event logs encountered in practice contain timestamps for all life-cycle transitions. Throughout the paper, we investigate the ability to measure queues lengths, as a function of the available information. More formally, let $\mathcal{I} = \{e, s, c\}$ be the event types that an event log may contain with e, s, c corresponding to enqueue, start and complete events, respectively. The level of information that is available in a given event log can be described by $I \subseteq \mathcal{I}$. We consider the following three levels of information:

- $\{c\}$ Activities and completion timestamps; e.g., $\langle a_{complete}^{11:38} \rangle$.
- $\{s,c\}$ Activities, start and completion timestamps; e.g., $\langle a_{start}^{11:35}, a_{complete}^{11:38} \rangle$.
- $\{e,s,c\}$ Activities, enqueue, start, and completion timestamps; e.g., $\langle a_{enqueue}^{11:30}, a_{start}^{11:35}, a_{complete}^{11:38} \rangle$.

For the latter level of information ($\{e, s, c\}$), queues in front of activities can simply be computed when a suitable process model is at hand. In the remainder of the section we state the main problem that we solve in the paper.

2.4 Problem Statement

In business processes, cases queue waiting for resources rather than for activities. However, in this work, we assume not to have enough data to describe the resource perspective completely. Therefore, we aim at measuring queues in front of activities, which is, in a sense, a more informative view than the one that would be provided by the resource perspective, since we also incorporate the notion of control-flow.

Let M be a process model with $\mathcal{A}_M$ being the set of activities present in the model and the log. Denote L_I the event log with information level I, and let $[0, T]$ be the time interval such that 0 is set to be the time of the first measured activity in the log and T being the time of the last measured activity (we use a continuous notation for simplicity). For simplicity we shall assume that the exogenous arrival time of each case is known. The *queue measurement - activities* (QMA) problem receives a model M, and a log, L_I. The solution to the problem is a quantifier for queue lengths (exact or approximated) for each activity in the model at any point in time, namely $\tilde{Q}_A(t)$, $A \in \mathcal{A}_M$, $t \in [0, T]$. For example, in [2], this problem is solved by trivially deriving the queue length from a full information log ($\{e, s, c\}$).

3   Methodology and Algorithms

This section describes our methodology and algorithms for solving the QMA problem. The approach is shown in Fig. 2: the first step in the methodology is to extract a queue log per activity, containing the execution information for that activity. The queue log then serves as an input to a clustering step, which in turn is used both for load inference, and for a first-attempt measurement of the queue length. The result of the clustering algorithm is the input for our statistical method, namely, the phase type fitting method, which fits a stochastic model to the event log via Bayesian inference. Below, we present the technique for extraction of a queue log, define queueing quantification, and present our techniques for measuring queue lengths.

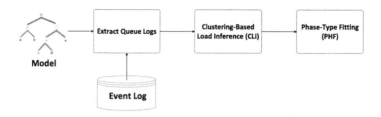

Fig. 2. A methodology for queue measurement in logs with partial information

3.1   Extracting Queue Logs

The first step is to split the event log, L_I, into several activity queue logs, L_A, one for each activity, $A \in \mathcal{A}_M$. An activity queue log describes the execution information for all activity instances of that activity, namely for each execution of A in the event log, a queue log contains all activity instances of A that were recorded in the event log [2]. For simplicity, we assume that each activity is performed by a single resource type, and the resource type performs a single activity. Therefore, we may consider a queue log per each activity separately.

Obtaining queue logs requires a few steps. First, deviations between the event log, L_I, and model, M, should be removed. Then, activity instances should be derived from the events in L_I. This step yields the timestamps of *enqueue*, *start* and *complete*. Subsequently, activity instances are be mapped to activities, according to M. Last, the *initiate* timestamps should be derived from the activity instances and M. In this step, knowledge of concurrent activities is necessary. We perform the first three steps by computing an optimal alignment, cf. [7]. The last step is performed by inspection of M, and detection of parallel activities. Note that the relation between traces and activity instances does not exist in the resulting queue log, and therefore we regard each activity instance as an independent queueing entity.

3.2   Notation and Queue Quantification

In this part, we present notation that we use when describing our methods and algorithms. Then, we provide a quantification framework for $\tilde{Q}_A(t)$, which is the log-based solution to the QMA problem.

Let $\mathcal{T}_j^A$ be a random function that maps activity instances from log L_A to timestamps of the jth element of the life-cycle denoted $j \in \{init, enqu, start, comp\}$. When a timestamp for element j is available, the random functions becomes deterministic, denoted $\tau_j^A : L_A \to \mathbb{TS}$. Note that for the considered information levels, τ_{comp} is assumed to be know, while τ_{init} is obtained during the extraction of the queue log.

We denote $X_n^A(t), t \in [0, T]$ the stochastic process that corresponds to the cumulative time that the nth activity instance spends in A at time t, namely $X_n^A(t) = t - \mathcal{T}_{init}^A(n)$. The realization of $X_n^A(t)$, denoted $x_n^A(t)$, can be obtained by the value $t - \tau_{init}^A(n)$, i.e. the time spent between initiation and t.

An activity instance n is in queue for A at time t whenever the following probabilistic event holds: $q_n^A(t) = \{\mathcal{T}_{enqu}^A(n) \leq t \leq \mathcal{T}_{start}^A(n)\}$. Denote $\mathbb{1}_{q_n^A(t)}|X_n^A(t) > x_n^A(t)$, the random variable that indicates whether activity instance n is enqueued in A at time t, conditioned on a cumulative length of stay of $x_n^A(t)$. Clearly, when the log contains the enqueue timestamp the indicator is constant (either zero or one), since the values of $\tau_{enqu}^A(n), \tau_{start}^A(n)$ are known.

For the general case, of various levels of information, we define the following quantity to measure queue-lengths:

$$\tilde{Q}_A(t) = \sum_{n \in L_A} \mathbb{E}[\mathbb{1}_{q_n^A(t)}|X_n^A(t) > x_n^A(t)], \tag{1}$$

for every activity and time in the log, with $\mathbb{E}$ being the expectation of a random variable. In other words, we quantify the queue length in-front of activity as the sum of expected values of the indicator. The quantifier for queue length, $\tilde{Q}_A(t)$, can be written as follows:

$$\mathbb{E}[\mathbb{1}_{q_n^A(t)}|X_n^A(t) > x_n^A(t)] = P(q_n^A(t)|X_n^A(t) > x_n^A(t)). \tag{2}$$

For each $n \in L_A$, the right-hand side part of Eq. (2) is quantified in the techniques that follow.

3.3   Clustering-Based Load Inference

The idea behind the clustering step is to categorize each trace of the activity queue log, L_A, according to the observed total durations, i.e. $\tau_{comp}^A(n) - \tau_{init}^A(n)$, $\forall n \in L_A$. For the completes only information level ($\{c\}$) total durations are sojourn times, while for the $\{s, c\}$ the total durations are time in transit and in queue. The main assumption of this method is that one of the resulting clusters contains traces of L_A for which queue size in-front of activity A was 0. In other words, we assume that the resources are not working 100 % of the time for the entire time period recorded in the queue log. All other clusters are expected to contain traces that were enqueued during their stay.

We are now ready to present our Clustering-based Load Inference (CLI) algorithm, with clustering being performed on the feature: observed total durations. Denote $1, ..., K$ the cluster indexes with K being a predefined number of clusters. As a first step, a K-Means algorithm runs to partition the traces in the log, L_A, into sub-logs L_A^k (see [8] for references on clustering techniques). Following the aforementioned assumption, L_A^1 contains only non-queueing cases. Other clusters, $k = 2, ..., K$, are assumed to contain traces that were enqueued, with time in queue increasing as k approaches K. The clusters represent K variants of system load, which we then pass on to the next two methods of Fig. 2. Note that the selection of K is process dependent, e.g. in call centers, the load is often partitioned into 4 clusters: no load, typical load, moderate load, heavy load [2].

The result of clustering can already be used to construct a first-attempt quantifier for the queue length. Specifically, we obtain the probability for an activity instance to be in queue by applying Bayes' Theorem to Eq. (2):

$$P(q_n^A(t) \mid X_n^A(t) > x_n^A(t)) = \frac{(1 - \pi(n \in L_A^1)) \, P(X_n^A(t) > x_n^A(t) \mid q_n^A(t))}{P(X_n^A(t) > x_n^A(t))},$$
(3)

with $\pi(n \in L_A^1)$ being the prior probability of a case belonging to the non-queueing cluster, $P(X_n^A(t) > x_n^A(t) \mid q_n^A(t))$ being the probability for the current time in activity being longer than $x_n^A(t)$ given that an activity instance, n, is in queue, and $P(X_n^A(t) > x_n^A(t))$ being the probability for total time being longer than $x_n^A(t)$). The three components of Eq. (3) can be easily estimated by using the corresponding Maximum Likelihood Estimates (MLE). The results serve an input to the next phase of our methodology, namely the phase type fitting algorithm.

3.4   Phase Type Fitting

In this part, we assume that each step of the activity life-cycle has an exponential duration, with a rate that changes per each cluster (depends on system load). Moreover, we assume that the times a case spends in each step are independent. The assumption that the time in transit and in service is exponential is quite common in queueing literature [10, 11]. However, waiting times in queue were shown to be exponential only for several specific queueing models; e.g., the time in queue for $M/M/n$ queues, conditioned that a case waits, is exponential. Another example in which waiting times are exponentially distributed is for queues in heavy-traffic [12]. Nevertheless, since we allow the rate of the exponential distribution per each component of the life-cycle to vary among clusters, we assume, as an approximation, that the time in queue is indeed exponential.

Under these assumptions, the suitable model for our life-cycle is that of a continuous-time Markov-chain (CTMC) that has $S = 3$ states in sequence. The chain absorbs after going through the three stages (transit, queue, service) when the activity terminates. The total time that it takes for a case to go through the life-cycle (i.e. the sojourn time) has a phase type distribution [9]. The phase type distribution is characterized by two parameters: (1) a vector of initial states, η, of size S (e.g. for the $\{c\}$ level of information all traces start in the first phase, and thus $\eta = (1, 0, 0)$), and (2) a transition-rate matrix G that describes the rates with which the CTMC moves between states.

Several techniques were suggested to fit a phase type distribution to data, when the available measurements include total time in process [13]. In our work, we use a Bayesian approach that relies on a Markov-Chain Monte-Carlo method, which we refer to as K-Phase Type Fitting (K-PHF) [14]. The K in the algorithm comes from the number of clusters that it receives from CLI. The algorithm is based on the structure of the phase type process, the initial state η, and prior distributions for the transition rates. The output is the matrix $\hat{G}$, estimated based on the data. In this work, we used priors that assume that the total time is uniformly divided among the stages of the life-cycle. For example, consider the completes only information level ($\{c\}$), a case spends $1/3$ of the total time in each of the stages: transit, queue, and service. Thus, $1/3$ serves as the prior to our K-PHF method.

The output of the K-PHF algorithm is used to estimate the probability from Eq. 2, for each trace individually. It is well-known that the probability for the phase type process to be in state s with $i = 1, ..., S$, given that the elapsed time in process is x is given by $\eta \exp(xG)_s$. The expression $\exp(xG)_s$ is the s column of the matrix exponential for the original transition-rate matrix, G, multiplied by x. Thus, for every point in time $t \in [0, T]$:

$$P(q_n^A(t) \mid X_n^A(t) > x_n^A(t)) = \eta \ \exp(x_n^A(t)G)_s, \tag{4}$$

with the right-hand side expression easily obtained from the K-PHF algorithm. We fit a phase type distribution to each of the clusters, namely $k = 1, ..., K$, and consequently get a corresponding transition matrix G^k per cluster. Last, we use the latter to calculate the expression in Eq. (4).

4   Evaluation

Finally, in order to evaluate our approach and illustrate the influence of different log information levels, we perform experiments using three real-life event logs with full information ($\{e, s, c\}$). We removed events from these logs (resulting in $\{s, c\}$ and $\{c\}$) to test how close the techniques described in this paper come to the actual queue length. The first two logs (L_1 and L_2) originate from a call center of an Israeli bank, while the third log (L_3) comes from an outpatient hospital.

4.1   Datasets

Logs L_1 and L_2 both contain a process in which customers call the bank and are initially answered by a computer system, namely the Voice Response

Unit (VRU), which is designed to handle basic questions and requests. If the customer requires further service beyond the VRU, she can choose to join the queue. Customers can abandon at any moment while they are in queue, and can also leave the VRU without reaching the queue. However, we filter these customers out of the original log, since they do not match our assumption on activity life-cycle Sect. 2. None of our techniques directly uses the dependency between the customers in queue, and therefore this filtering does not reduce the validity of our experiments. The queue that we measure in this paper is the queue in-front of the human agents. The entire time in VRU is considered transit. Log L_2 is derived from L_1 by setting the transit time to 0.

To highlight the parallelism-handling capabilities of our approach, log L_3 originates from a process that contains parallelism: patients being examined and undergo several concurrent procedures. Of this process, the activity 'exam' was selected for queue measurement, as it is the most constrained activity in the process.

4.2 Experimental Setup

We start with one of the event logs, L_1, L_2 or L_3, and derive the corresponding queue log L_A of each activity A by using the method described in Sect. 3.1. Then, a model is discovered by Inductive Miner - infrequent [15] using default settings. Subsequently, we apply CLI and K-PHF to L_A in order to quantify $\tilde{Q}_A(t)$ (using a milisecond resolution). Similarly, the real queue length, $Q_A(t)$, is computed, using the enqueue and start timestamps. To evaluate the accuracy of the techniques, we consider the root mean squared error and the bias. First, the root mean squared error (RMSE) is computed per activity:

$$\sqrt{\frac{1}{T} \cdot \sum_{t \in [0,T]} (\tilde{Q}_A(t) - Q_A(t))^2}.$$

As a second measure, we consider the bias, which can indicate systemic error in our techniques:

$$\frac{1}{T} \cdot \sum_{t \in [0,T]} (\tilde{Q}_A(t) - Q_A(t)).$$

This procedure is applied to all methods that we described in Sect. 3, all levels of information, and the three event logs. In addition, we provide two baselines for comparison. First, we added the Busy Periods method (BP), which is based on [3,10]. For time $t \in [0,T]$, BP simply counts the number of cases that are currently in the activity. BP assumes the following: (1) full knowledge of busy periods, namely times in which all resources are busy, (2) the number of resources are constant and known, and (3) in busy periods, resources are work-conserving (non-idling). We provide the algorithm with an approximation to busy periods per activity $A \in \mathcal{A}_M$, since we consider times in which $Q_A(t) > 0$ (a busy period can start with an empty queue, and all resources busy).

As a second baseline, we considered the Uniform Prior method (UP), which divides the number of cases in the activity at timestamp t by the number of unknown time intervals. For example, if the log contains the initiate and completion timestamps, UP divides the total time spent in the activity by 3, similarly to the prior that we consider for K-PHF. In case that all information is known ($\{e, s, c\}$), UP counts the precise number of cases in queue.

For our clustering-based methods that we present in Sect. 3, i.e. CLI and K-PHF, we have selected K to be 4, which is a standard selection for call center data [2]. For K-PHF we also consider $K = 1$, to test the impact of load knowledge on the goodness-of-fit for the phase type distribution. To investigate the influence of K on the clustering-based methods, the procedure was repeated for CLI with various values of K.

4.3   Results and Discussion

Table 1 shows the results for different combinations of event logs, information levels and techniques. Figure 3 shows the influence of K on CLI, tested on L_1. Last, Fig. 4 shows the queue length obtained by 1-PHF, and 4-PHF (best algorithm for complete only information) as function of time, compared to the real queue length.

Table 1. Queue length evaluation.

		BP		UP		1-PHF		CLI		4-PHF	
		RMSE	bias	RMSE	bias	RMSE	bias	RMSE	bias	RMSE	bias
L_1	$\{c\}$	21.18	11.91	8.11	-5.12	10.68	-7.76	25.96	-21.34	6.20	-1.63
	$\{s, c\}$	”	”	4.63	0.83	8.08	4.04	4.22	-3.17	8.45	4.81
L_2	$\{c\}$	13.05	6.18	5.99	-2.40	13.85	8.97	20.98	-16.99	6.53	1.56
	$\{s, c\}$	”	”	7.34	4.87	9.23	5.77	2.63	2.00	11.93	7.96
L_3	$\{c\}$	21.38	-17.51	4.08	1.20	6.84	5.32	10.69	7.25	8.58	6.98
	$\{s, c\}$	”	”	4.86	3.22	10.37	8.62	10.80	8.31	12.48	10.47

Considering log L_2, our experiments show the sensitivity of BP in case assumptions (2) and (3) do not hold: for L_2, with no transit time and known busy periods, BP overestimates the log considerably (L_2 RMSE 13.05; bias 6.18). This is hardly surprising when considering resource dynamics in real-life settings: resources go on breaks, and start/end their shifts during the day. Surprisingly, UP is superior in all $\{c\}$ scenarios, except for 4-PHF.

We notice that CLI performs poorly for the $\{c\}$ level of information. A sensitivity analysis revealed that indeed $K = 4$ is not optimal for CLI with completes only, and it can be improved by selecting $K = 2$ (Fig. 3). However, for the $\{s, c\}$ scenarios and the two call center logs (L_1, L_2), the results are superior to all methods.

Across our experiments, 1-PHF performs mediocre on performance, since it neglects differences in system load. When changes in the load are considered,

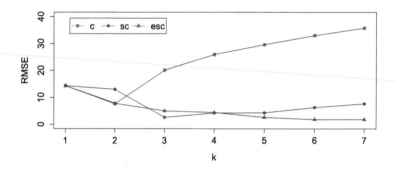

Fig. 3. Influence of K on CLI with L_1.

we indeed see an improvement, and 4-PHF is indeed the superior algorithm across the $\{c\}$ information level. Intuitively, one would expect that methods perform better when given more information. However, 4-PHF performs best when given only completion timestamps; when given more information, i.e. start events, 4-PHF performs worse. We suspect that our choice of K in CLI might be of influence here.

Inspecting only averaged results can be misleading. Thus, we turn our attention to Fig. 4, and observe the behavior of queue lengths of two methods: 1-PHF and 4-PHF, under knowledge of completion timestamps. We observe that 1-PHF is able to capture the first peak of the day. However, it misses the remainder of the day by overestimating the queue length, especially for the peak period. In contrast, 4-PHF captures much of the behavior, except for sudden changes in queue lengths.

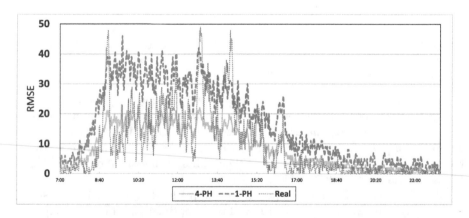

Fig. 4. Queue length for 1-PHF, 4-PHF and real with L_1; the x-axis represents time (one day).

5   Conclusion

In this paper, we showed how to discover queue lengths for activities in operational processes. Specifically, queue lengths were quantified for event logs with varying levels of information. In particular, we proposed a comprehensive approach, which includes the use of a process model and recorded event data to derive a queue log. The queue log then feeds a sequence of two techniques for measuring the queue length. The first technique is based on K-Means clustering, while the second technique is based on phase type fitting. We performed a thorough evaluation of our methods against baselines and presented the deviations from the real measurements. We tested the methodology on three real-life logs: two call centers logs, and one log of an outpatient hospital. The results show that our methods are able to discover queue lengths with various levels of accuracy. This accuracy is sensitive to the level of information, and to the K of the clustering algorithm.

In future work, we intend to take the resource perspective into account, since cases wait for resources and not for activities. We aim at utilizing the information on the matching between activities and the corresponding resources that is often available in event logs to improve the accuracy of our methods. Furthermore, we aim to consider the dependencies between queued cases in a more rigor way, by discovering queueing models that correspond to the resources involved.

References

1. van der Aalst, W.M.P.: Process Mining: Discovery, Conformance and Enhancement of Business Processes. Springer, Heidelberg (2011)
2. Senderovich, A., Weidlich, M., Gal, A., Mandelbaum, A.: Queue mining for delay prediction in multi-class service processes. Technical report (2014)
3. Nakatumba, J.: Resource-aware business process management: analysis and support. Ph.D. thesis, Eindhoven University of Technology (2013)
4. Rogge-Solti, A., Mans, R.S., van der Aalst, W.M.P., Weske, M.: Repairing event logs using timed process models. In: Demey, Y.T., Panetto, H. (eds.) OTM 2013 Workshops 2013. LNCS, vol. 8186, pp. 705–708. Springer, Heidelberg (2013)
5. Leemans, S.J.J., Fahland, D., van der Aalst, W.M.P.: Discovering block-structured process models from event logs - a constructive approach. In: Colom, J.-M., Desel, J. (eds.) PETRI NETS 2013. LNCS, vol. 7927, pp. 311–329. Springer, Heidelberg (2013)
6. Buijs, J., van Dongen, B., van der Aalst, W.M.P.: A genetic algorithm for discovering process trees. In: IEEE Congress on Evolutionary Computation, pp. 1–8. IEEE (2012)
7. Adriansyah, A.: Aligning observed and modeled behavior. Ph.D. thesis, Eindhoven University of Technology (2014)
8. Hastie, T., Tibshirani, R., Friedman, J.: The Elements of Statistical Learning. Springer Series in Statistics. Springer New York Inc., New York (2001)
9. Neuts, M.F.: Renewal processes of phase type. Nav. Res. Logistics Q. **25**(3), 445–454 (1978)
10. Mandelbaum, A., Zeltyn, S.: Estimating characteristics of queueing networks using transactional data. Queueing systems **29**(1), 75–127 (1998)

11. Mandelbaum, A., Zeltyn, S.: Service engineering in action: the Palm/Erlang-A queue, with applications to call centers. In: Advances in Services Innovations, pp. 17–45. Springer, Heidelberg (2007)
12. Kingman, J.: On queues in heavy traffic. J. Roy. Stat. Soc. Ser. B (Methodol.) **24**, 383–392 (1962)
13. Asmussen, S.: Phase-type distributions and related point processes: fitting and recent advances. In: International Conference on Matrix-Analytic Methods in Stochastic Models, pp. 137–149 (1996)
14. Aslett, L.J., Wilson, S.P.: Markov chain monte carlo for inference on phasetype models. ISI (2011)
15. Leemans, S.J.J., Fahland, D., van der Aalst, W.M.P.: Discovering block-structured process models from event logs containing infrequent behaviour. In: Lohmann, N., Song, M., Wohed, P. (eds.) BPM 2013 Workshops. LNBIP, vol. 171, pp. 66–78. Springer, Heidelberg (2014)

PMCube: A Data-Warehouse-Based Approach for Multidimensional Process Mining

Thomas Vogelgesang$^{(\boxtimes)}$ and Hans-Jürgen Appelrath

Department of Computer Science, University of Oldenburg, Oldenburg, Germany
thomas.vogelgesang@uni-oldenburg.de

Abstract. Process mining provides a set of techniques to discover process models from recorded event data or to analyze and improve given process models. Typically, these techniques give a single point of view on the process. However, some domains need to differentiate the process according to the characteristic features of their cases. The healthcare domain, for example, needs to distinguish between different groups of patients, defined by the patients' properties like age or gender, to get more precise insights into the treatment process. The emerging concept of *multidimensional process mining* aims to overcome this gap by the notion of data cubes that can be used to spread data over multiple cells. This paper introduces *PMCube*, a novel approach for multidimensional process mining based on the multidimensional modeling of event logs that can be queried by OLAP operators to mine sophisticated process models. An optional step of consolidation allows to reduce the complexity of results to ease its interpretation. We implemented this approach in a prototype and applied it in a case study to analyze the perioperative processes in a large German hospital.

Keywords: Data warehousing · OLAP · Multidimensional process mining · Comparative process mining

1 Introduction

Process mining comprises a set of techniques for the automatic analysis of business processes. It is based on *events* which are recorded during process execution and collected in an *event log.* Figure 1 illustrates the typical structure of an event log. Inside the event log, the events are grouped by their process instance or *case.* The ordered sequence of events belonging to a case is called *trace.* Both, events and cases, may have arbitrary attributes holding additional information about the observed events or process instances.

Generally, the field of process mining can be classified into three kinds: (1) *process discovery* generates a process model describing the behavior recorded in the event log, (2) *conformance checking* compares an event log to a model in order to measure the quality of the model, and (3) *process enhancement* maps additional information stored in the events attribute (e.g., timestamps) to the process model to enrich it with new perspectives (e.g., execution times).

© Springer International Publishing Switzerland 2016
M. Reichert and H.A. Reijers (Eds.): BPM Workshops 2015, LNBIP 256, pp. 167–178, 2016.
DOI: 10.1007/978-3-319-42887-1_14

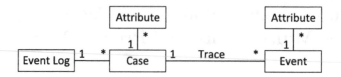

Fig. 1. General structure of an event log

Process mining can be applied to healthcare processes. In contrast to traditional business processes, healthcare processes are typically unstructured and very complex, due to the individuality of patients. The treatment has to be adjusted to the individual situation of the patient considering age, sex, comorbidity, and so on. Institutional characteristics, like available resources or the experience of the medical staff, may influence the treatment process as well. For the analysis of such processes, it is desirable to minimize the influence of these features on the mined process model by grouping patients with similar features and to create a separated process model for each group. Otherwise, the variation of features would result in very complex models (so-called spaghetti models), also blurring the influence of particular features.

Traditional process mining techniques, however, consider the entire event log. Filtering operations can be used to restrict the event log to a particular group of patients. However, this requires high effort if multiple groups should be analyzed and compared to each other. Such a scenario requires an approach that allows the dynamic and flexible partitioning of event logs into groups of cases with similar features. Then, these groups can be mined separately and compared to each other.

This can be achieved by the notion of *multidimensional process mining* (MPM). It considers the attributes of the event log, which describe the variable features of patients and their treatment, as dimensions of a multidimensional data space. This is similar to the concept of data cubes from the data warehouse (DWH) domain. The cells of the cube contain *sublogs*, which are subsets of the original event log. The data cube can be manipulated using OLAP operators to define different views on the data.

In this paper, we present a novel approach for MPM called *PMCube* which is based on a DWH. Section 2 introduces the main idea of this approach. In Sect. 3, we introduce the underlying multidimensional data model. Section 4 focuses on the OLAP queries and the mining of data cells. In Sect. 5, we introduce sophisticated concepts, like the consolidation of process models, for supporting the analyst during result interpretation. The implementation of PMCube and its application in a case study is presented in Sect. 6. Section 7 discusses related work. Finally, we summarize the paper in Sect. 8.

2   Basic Concept of PMCube

Figure 2 illustrates the basic concept of PMCube: Starting-point of an analysis is the *multidimensional event log* (MEL; step 1). It adapts the traditional event log structure (cf. Fig. 1) to a multidimensional representation forming a data cube. It relies on well-established DWH techniques and serves as an all-encompassing event store providing an integrated view on the available data. The MEL is discussed in more detail in Sect. 3.

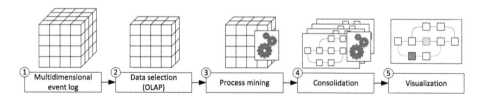

Fig. 2. Basic concept of PMCube

By using OLAP operators (step 2), it is possible to filter (slice) the MEL or to change its level of aggregation (roll-up or drill-down). This allows to create flexible views on the event data. The query result consists of cells, each containing a subset of the event data (*sublog*) from the MEL. The extracted sublogs are independently mined (step 3) to create a process model for each cell. Every model captures the behavior of the event data described by its cell. Besides process discovery, it is also possible to enhance the discovered model with additional perspectives or to verify its quality with conformance checking techniques. Details on the OLAP queries and the mining of cells are presented in Sect. 4.

Depending on the OLAP query, a high number of cells could be extracted from the MEL resulting in an unmanageable amount of process models. In order to reduce the complexity of the result, a subset of potentially interesting process models can be selected by an optional step of consolidation (step 4). This is required as MPM tends to create many process models, which makes a pairwise comparison challenging, especially if the models are big, or unstructured. The consolidation aims to simplify the result interpretation by offering a focus on the results to the analyst. Finally, the process models have to be visualized for the analyst to interpret them (step 5). As MPM strongly benefits from comparing the different process models, it is not sufficient to visualize each model on its own, so more sophisticated visualization techniques are required. The main idea behind the consolidation and different consolidation approaches, as well as some advanced approaches for process model visualization, are elaborated in Sect. 5.

3 Multidimensional Event Logs

The MEL forms the multidimensional data model of PMCube by mapping the structure of event logs to data cubes commonly used for data warehouses. In contrast to traditional data warehousing, the cells of the MEL do not contain numerical values as facts, but a set of cases. The attributes of the cases form the dimensions of the cube. Each combination of attribute values determines a cell of the MEL. Each case is implicitly mapped to a cell by its individual attribute values. However, it does not make sense to create a dimension from each attribute. For example, some attributes like the name of a patient might represent highly individual properties of a case. Using such attributes as a dimension does not add any benefit to the multidimensional analysis as they lead to cubes with high sparsity. Otherwise, these attributes might be necessary during analysis to identify individual cases or to draw conclusions from them. Therefore, ignoring them is not a solution. Instead, they are directly attached to the cases as *simple attributes*.

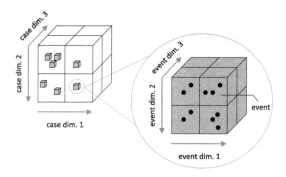

Fig. 3. Nested cubes

The MEL also contains all events which are stored together with their respective case. The event attributes can be interpreted as dimensions as well, forming a multidimensional space on their own. To avoid the aggregation of events (cf. Sect. 4) from different, independent cases, the event attributes constitute a separated data space for each case. This can be considered as *nested cubes* as shown in Fig. 3. Each cell of a nested cube contains a set of events described by the values of the cubes dimensions. Similar to cases, cubes on the event level may have simple attributes, too, which are directly attached to the event. All dimensions, both on the case and event level, may be hierarchically structured with an arbitrary number of levels.

The MEL serves as a global, all-encompassing data store and is modeled as a relational-based DWH. Figure 4 shows its generic database schema as an entity-relationship model. The schema extends the traditional snowflake-schema, a widely-used modeling approach for data warehouses.

Similar to the traditional snowflake-schema, there is a *fact* table for storing the cells of the data cube. Each cell is identified by a unique combination of foreign keys referencing the cells dimension values. These values are stored in normalized dimension tables (e.g., $D_1.K_0$ to $D_1.K_m$ for a dimension D_1) to avoid redundancy. In contrast to the traditional snowflake-schema, the fact table does not directly store the cells value, but a unique *id*. The data content of the cells, namely the cases, is normalized and stored in the *case table*, which also stores

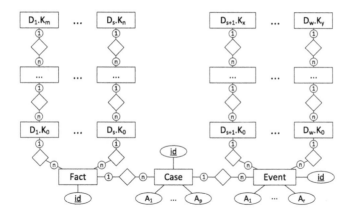

Fig. 4. Generic database schema of the MEL

the simple attributes (A_1 to A_p) of the cases. The corresponding cell of a case is referenced by the *fact id*. The events are normalized in an analogous manner and stored in the *event* table, which also holds the simple attributes of the event. Events can also have dimension attributes, which are stored in dimension tables similar to the case dimensions. However, the event table directly references the dimension tables, as dimension values might differ for events of the same case.

4   OLAP and Cell Mining

The sublogs are extracted from the MEL by a set of base operators. Due to different semantics, the definition of the operators might vary between case and event level. Figure 5 illustrates this using the example of the *aggregation* operator. Aggregating cells on the case level creates the union of all the cells cases. For example, aggregating the cube on the left-hand of Fig. 5 along the dimensions *sex* and *age* results in a single cell containing all cases for both women and men of all age for a specific year.

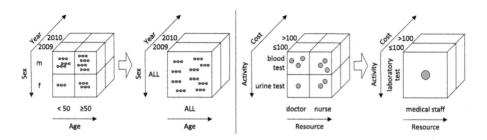

Fig. 5. Aggregation of cases (left) and events (right)

On the contrary, aggregating cells on the event level merges all events into a single, more abstract event. This is demonstrated on the right-hand of Fig. 5, showing the aggregation of events along the dimensions *activity* and *resource*. Previously, various events are spread across different cells, each representing different kinds of activities performed by either doctors or nurses. The aggregation abstracts from the original events and replaces them by a merged event. This style of aggregation can be useful if the analyst is only interested if a laboratory test was performed or not, regardless of which kind of test or how many tests were performed. Reducing the number of events may simplify the mined process model by reducing its number of nodes.

The MEL can be filtered by *selection* operators on both the case and the event level. All cases respectively events that do not match the selection predicate are discarded from the query result. For filtering the event level, the selection predicate contains only event attributes (dimensions, as well as simple attributes). This allows, for example, to remove all events representing non-medical activities to focus on the medical treatment process. On the case level, the MEL can be filtered by both case and event attributes. However, a quantifier ($\exists$ or $\forall$) must be specified for each event attribute of the selection predicate. This allows to specify whether the condition must hold for at least one event or for all events of a case. Alternatively, an aggregation function (*min*, *max*, *avg*, *sum*, or *count*) can be specified, e.g. to select only cases exceeding a maximum cost limit.

The *projection* operator discards all attributes that are not required during analysis from the query result to reduce the data volume. For instance, the attributes can be limited to the *Activity* attribute if the analyst is interested in the control-flow perspective only. The traditional OLAP operators like *slice*, *dice*, *roll-up*, and *drill-down* can be derived from the base operators by defining them in relation to the previous query result instead of in relation to the data base.

As the MEL is based on a relational database, the OLAP query is mapped to SQL. In contrast to traditional relational-based DWH, PMCube creates a single SQL query for each cell which returns all the events of the cell. This way, a sublog can be mined immediately after loading without waiting for all other sublogs. The concurrent execution of loading and mining can improve performance if the cells' sublogs contain big amounts of event data.

The OLAP query results in a set of cells, which contain disjoint subsets of the MEL's data. Each of this sublogs is mined independently from the others using process mining techniques. While executing the SQL query, the multidimensional event data is implicitly flattened to a result table, that can be easily mapped to the commonly used event log structure (cf. Fig. 1). This way, arbitrary process discovery algorithms can be used to analyze the sublogs without adapting them to the multidimensional data model. The result is a process model for each cell representing its individual behavior.

In addition to process discovery, PMCube also supports conformance checking. To measure the quality of the mined process models, the fitness of each model is calculated in relation to its sublog. The fitness can be also calculated in relation to an external model to measure the deviations of a sublog from a predefined reference model. Furthermore, the process models can be enhanced with additional perspectives by projecting additional attributes onto the model. E.g., one can map *timestamp* attributes from the sublog to the activity nodes to calculate waiting times and identify bottlenecks in the process.

5   Analysis Support: Consolidation and Visualization

PMCube creates an individual process model for each cell extracted from the MEL. Depending on the query, this may result in a high number of process models. Consequently, it is more difficult to get an overview of the results compared to traditional OLAP results, which typically consist of a numeric value per cell. The process models can also be very complex, which makes it even more difficult to understand and interpret the query results.

The consolidation tackles this problem by an automatic, heuristic preselection of process models that might by potentially more interesting to the analyst than others. By selecting a subset of the mined process models, it aims to significantly reduce the number of models, so the analyst can focus on the most relevant results. One approach for such a consolidation is to cluster process models with similar behavior and select a representative from each cluster. It assumes that analysts are interested in the fundamental differences between the process models while marginal differences are less relevant.

The clustering approach of PMCube uses density-based clustering algorithms, namely DBSCAN [5], to identify process models belonging together. Partitional clustering algorithms (like k-means [1]), however, cannot be used, because the number of clusters is not known in advance. Besides, DBSCAN is able to find clusters of any shape and to identify outliers, which is important to identify cells with strong deviating process models. Like almost all clustering algorithms, density-based algorithms require a *distance metric* to quantify the differences between to objects. Though there are no distance metrics for process models in literature, a broad range of *similarity metrics* for process models exist, which can be easily converted to distance metrics. We use *causal behavioral profiles* (CBP) [14] for calculating distances between process models. It is a behavioral similarity metric and compares the behavior described by the process models instead of their structure. Additionally, a CBP is easy and fast to calculate, while it provides relatively good results [4].

Although the optional step of consolidation discards process models that are considered as less relevant, it is important to note that this is only a heuristic that should support the analyst by providing a first idea to get a starting-point for analysis. This does not mean that the neglected process models are irrelevant. Even the discarded process models can reveal valuable insights into the process.

After the step of consolidation, the process models must be visualized for interpretation. This can be done by different approaches. If the analyst, e.g., wants to explore the process models for distinctive features without any hypothesis, the process models can be visualized simultaneously in a matrix. This allows the analyst to get an overview of the mining results and identify conspicuous process models that should be inspected in more detail.

If the analyst, on the contrary, wants to compare two particular models to find deviations between them, this can be supported by a *difference view*. First, the differences between the models are automatically calculated by a differencing algorithm. Both models are integrated into a common model, where similar process model elements are merged. The previously identified differences are visually highlighted in the model, e.g., by variations in color. This makes the variations between process models more obvious to the analyst. The difference visualization approach of PMCube is presented in more detail in [3].

6   Prototype and Case Study

We implemented our approach as a prototype, called *PMCube Explorer*, using Microsoft .NET and C#. It provides a graphical user interface to query the MEL, which is externally stored in a relational database like Oracle or Microsoft SQL Server. The extracted sublogs can be mined with different process discovery algorithms which are integrated by plug-ins. It currently supports the Inductive Miner – infrequent [7], Fuzzy Miner [6], and Flexible Heuristics Miner [15]. The process models are represented in variable modeling languages, depending on the used discovery algorithm. They can be visualized in a single model view, a matrix view, and a difference view. Besides some simple consolidation strategies, e.g., filtering for model properties, PMCube Explorer provides a clustering consolidation. Additionally, sublogs can be replayed on their cells' process model or on an external reference model to measure the model's fitness. Futhermore, PMCube Explorer allows to enhance the process models with time information.

We started the evaluation study after the approval of the ethical committee of the Justus Liebig University (ethical review committee of the Faculty of Human Medicine at the Justus Liebig University Gießen, chairman Prof. Dr. Tillmanns, vote number 261/14) with an anonymized data set. We applied PMCube Explorer to a healthcare process of a university hospital as a center of maximum care in Germany. During that case study, we focused on the perioperative process, which comprises all activities in the periphery of surgical interventions, especially activities related to anesthesia. The event data was extracted from the several clinical information systems and anonymized by the hospital IT, before we integrated it into the multidimensional structure of the MEL. The analyzed data covers a random sample of 16280 surgical interventions of four medical departments in 2012 and 2013 with a total of 388395 events.

The data included several attributes like gender and age of the patient, diagnoses, main operation procedure, the state of admittance (ambulant or inpatient), the priority of operation (planned surgical intervention or emergency), date of surgical intervention and the responsible medical department, the outcome (did the patient die during hospital stay?), and the reason for discharging the patient from hospital. We modeled these attributes as case dimensions of the MEL to provide multiple options for filtering and aggregation. Additionally, the data contains the hours of artificial respiration for each patient, which is stored as a simple case attribute. On the event level, we modeled the activity and event specific attributes (like the target ward for patient transfers) as dimensions. In our case study, we considered each surgical intervention as a single case.

We analyzed the data by applying multiple OLAP queries in an explorative way to the MEL to get various points of view on the process. We discussed the discovered models with a medical expert, who is familiar with the perioperative processes of that hospital. The case study focused on the influence of different features on the department-specific processes. Due to the unstructured characteristic of the process, we mainly used the Fuzzy Miner to discover the models from the cell's sublogs, which turned out to provide the best balance between fitness and precision.

As an example, we analyzed the influence of the urgency on the department-specific processes. We selected the medical department and the urgency as the dimensions of the data cube, which resulted in 12 cells. Additionally, we applied a roll-up on the event dimension *activity* to aggregate the events. This was necessary, because – compared to other event classes – the high number of laboratory events lead to a heavy bias on the metrics calculation of the Fuzzy Miner, resulting in too highly abstracted process models for some cells. Figure 6 shows an example of the difference view, comparing the planned surgical interventions to the emergencies for a medical discipline with minor surgery. The dashed edges are only contained in the model for the planned surgical interventions, while the dotted edges only exist in the model for the emergencies. The medical expert confirmed the identified differences to be the major differences in the process, that can be explained by a high time pressure in case of an emergency.

The case study showed that MPM allows to analyze processes from different angles in a dynamic and flexible way. Queries can be easily adjusted, which allows the explorative analysis of the processes. However, PMCube preliminarily requires a relatively high initial effort for integrating the data into the MEL. Additionally, the case study revealed that MPM can become quite complex and confusing, especially when comparing many process models. Although the consolidation and the different visualization techniques showed to be a helpful tool during analysis, they need to be improved and complemented by more sophisticated techniques to deal with the high complexity of results. For example, fine-tuning the clustering algorithm parameters turned out to be very challenging during the case study. E.g., too strict settings tend to classify all models as outliers, while too relaxed settings lead to a single cluster comprising all models. However, the matrix of calculated CBP distances gives a good overview of the similarity of process models. The clustering consolidation and the distance matrix proved to be useful to confirm observations from the matrix view. Furthermore, the visualization of process model differences has to be improved, especially for process models enhanced by additional perspectives like time information. The case study also revealed, that the aggregation of events is able to improve the quality of the resulting model, i.e. if the event frequency per case does not correlate with its importance to the process. However, a

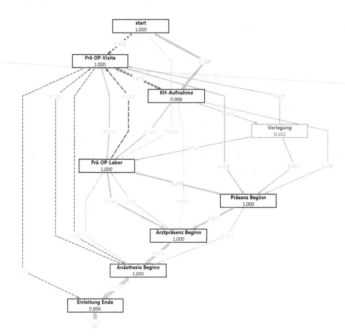

Fig. 6. Excerpt of a difference model highlighting the differences between planned surgical interventions and emergencies for a medical discipline with minor surgery

major decrease in model fitness turned out to be a possible drawback of this way of event aggregation.

7 Related Work

The process mining manifesto [13] gives an overview of the field of process mining. For a comprehensive introduction to this topic, we refer to [11]. Event cubes [10] are a first approach for MPM. In contrast to our approach, it is not based on a multidimensional modeling of the event log. It uses information retrieval techniques to create an index over a traditionally structured event log and derives a data cube from it. In contrast to our approach, the cells of an event cube contain precomputed dependency measures instead of raw event data. From this dependency measures a single process model is generated on-the-fly where each value of the considered dimensions are mapped to different paths in the model.

Process cubes [12] are another approach for MPM. Similar to our approach, it uses OLAP operators to partition the event data into sublogs. However, process cubes do not distinguish between the case and event level and combine all dimensions in a common data space. The cells of the cube consequently contain sets of events instead of sets of cases. In contrast to our approach, process cubes do not allow to filter full cases by event attributes and do not support the aggregation of events into a new high-level event. Its implementation Process Mining Cube

[2] provides the visualization of multiple process models which is similar to our matrix view. However, process cubes do not provide more advanced concepts to ease the result interpretation like the difference view or the consolidation of process models.

Besides, there are several approaches for special DWH for storing process data (e.g. [8,9]). These *process warehouses* (PWH) aim to analyze the underlying processes to identify problems in process execution. In contrast to our approach, they do not store complete event logs, but measures for process performance (e.g. execution times), where events and cases form the dimensions of the cube. The analysis is performed by aggregating the measures along the dimensions. However, these approaches generally do not support process mining.

8   Conclusion

Traditional process mining techniques typically create a single process model describing the behavior seen in the event log. However, in domains like healthcare, it is desirable to get multiple points of view on the process according to different features of the data. MPM uses the notion of data cubes to provide such points of view on the process in a flexible and dynamic way.

In this paper, we presented PMCube, a DWH-based approach for MPM. The underlying MEL can be queried by OLAP operators to extract sublogs. From each sublog, an independent process model is discovered. Different techniques for consolidation and visualization are provide to decrease the complexity of results in order to support the analyst during the interpretation.

The case study showed, that PMCube, and MPM in general, are applicable to real world healthcare processes and enable the analyst to easily take different points of view on a process. The consolidation of process models, as well as the difference view, turned out to be useful tools during the analysis. However, the case study also revealed a number of limitations that should be tackled by further research. For example, the support for the analyst to handle complex results, should be improved.

Acknowledgments. The authors would like to thank Rainer Röhrig, Lena Niehoff, Raphael W. Majeed, and Christian Katzer for their support during the case study.

References

1. Aggarwal, C.C., Reddy, C.K. (eds.): Data Clustering: Algorithms and Applications. Data Mining and Knowledge Discovery. Chapman & Hall/CRC, Boca Raton (2013)
2. Bolt, A., van der Aalst, W.M.P.: Multidimensional process mining using process cubes. In: Gaaloul, K., Schmidt, R., Nurcan, S., Guerreiro, S., Ma, Q. (eds.) BPMDS 2015 and EMMSAD 2015. LNBIP, vol. 214, pp. 102–116. Springer, Heidelberg (2015)

3. Cordes, C., Vogelgesang, T., Appelrath, H.-J.: A generic approach for calculating and visualizing differences between process models in multidimensional process mining. In: Fournier, F., Mendling, J. (eds.) BPM 2014 Workshops. LNBIP, vol. 202, pp. 383–394. Springer, Heidelberg (2015)
4. Dijkman, R., Dumas, M., van Dongen, B.F., Käärik, R., Mendling, J.: Similarity of business process models: metrics and evaluation. Inf. Syst. 36(2), 498–516 (2011)
5. Ester, M., Kriegel, H.-P., Sander, J., Xiaowei, X.: A density-based algorithm for discovering clusters in large spatial databases with noise. In: Simoudis, E., Han, J., Fayyad, U.M., (eds.) Proceedings of the Second International Conference on Knowledge Discovery and Data Mining (KDD 1996), Portland, Oregon, USA, pp. 226–231. AAAI Press (1996)
6. Günther, C.W., van der Aalst, W.M.P.: Fuzzy mining – adaptive process simplification based on multi-perspective metrics. In: Alonso, G., Dadam, P., Rosemann, M. (eds.) BPM 2007. LNCS, vol. 4714, pp. 328–343. Springer, Heidelberg (2007)
7. Leemans, S.J.J., Fahland, D., van der Aalst, W.M.P.: Discovering block-structured process models from event logs containing infrequent behaviour. In: Lohmann, N., Song, M., Wohed, P. (eds.) BPM 2013 Workshops. LNBIP, vol. 171, pp. 66–78. Springer, Heidelberg (2014)
8. Neumuth, T., Mansmann, S., Scholl, M.H., Burgert, O.: Data warehousing technology for surgical workflow analysis. In: Proceedings of the 2008 21st IEEE International Symposium on Computer-Based Medical Systems, CBMS 2008, Washington, DC, USA, pp. 230–235. IEEE Computer Society (2008)
9. Niedrite, L., Solodovnikova, D., Treimanis, M., Niedritis, A.: Goal-driven design of a data warehouse-based business process analysis system. In: Proceedings of the 6th Conference on 6th WSEAS International Conference on Artificial Intelligence, Knowledge Engineering and Data Bases, AIKED 2007, vol. 6, pp. 243–249, Stevens Point, Wisconsin, USA. World Scientific and Engineering Academy and Society (WSEAS) (2007)
10. Ribeiro, J.T.S., Weijters, A.J.M.M.: Event cube: another perspective on business processes. In: Meersman, R., Dillon, T., Herrero, P., Kumar, A., Reichert, M., Qing, L., Ooi, B.-C., Damiani, E., Schmidt, D.C., White, J., Hauswirth, M., Hitzler, P., Mohania, M. (eds.) OTM 2011, Part I. LNCS, vol. 7044, pp. 274–283. Springer, Heidelberg (2011)
11. van der Aalst, W.M.P.: Process Mining: Discovery, Conformance and Enhancement of Business Processes. Springer, Heidelberg (2011)
12. van der Aalst, W.M.P.: Process cubes: slicing, dicing, rolling up and drilling down event data for process mining. In: Song, M., Wynn, M.T., Liu, J. (eds.) AP-BPM 2013. LNBIP, vol. 159, pp. 1–22. Springer, Heidelberg (2013)
13. van der Aalst, W., et al.: Process mining manifesto. In: Daniel, F., Barkaoui, K., Dustdar, S. (eds.) BPM Workshops 2011, Part I. LNBIP, vol. 99, pp. 169–194. Springer, Heidelberg (2012)
14. Weidlich, M., Polyvyanyy, A., Mendling, J., Weske, M.: Causal behavioural profiles - efficient computation, applications, and evaluation. Fundam. Inf. 113(3–4), 399–435 (2011)
15. Weijters, A., Ribeiro, J.T.S.: Flexible heuristics miner (FHM). Technical report, Technische Universiteit Eindhoven (2011)

Clustering Traces Using Sequence Alignment

Joerg Evermann[1]([✉]), Tom Thaler[2,3], and Peter Fettke[2,3]

[1] Memorial University of Newfoundland, St. John's, Canada
jevermann@mun.ca
[2] Deutsches Forschungszentrum für Künstliche Intelligenz, Saarbrücken, Germany
[3] Universität des Saarlandes, Saarbrücken, Germany

Abstract. Process mining discovers process models from event logs. Logs containing heterogeneous sets of traces can lead to complex process models that try to account for very different behaviour in a single model. Trace clustering identifies homogeneous sets of traces within a heterogeneous log and allows for the discovery of multiple, simpler process models. In this paper, we present a trace clustering method based on local alignment of sequences, subsequent multidimensional scaling, and k-means clustering. We describe its implementation and show that its performance compares favourably to state-of-the-art clustering approaches on two evaluation problems.

Keywords: Process mining · Process discovery · Trace clustering · Sequence alignment

1 Introduction

Process discovery is that field of process mining that deals with the discovery/mining of process models from event logs. An event log is a set of sequences of events (traces of process instances). Logs may contain traces that differ widely in the sequences of events within them. Mining such heterogeneous event log leads to complicated process models as the mining algorithm constructs models that account for a large proportion of the observed behaviour. Trace clustering addresses this issue by identifying clusters of homogeneous traces within such a heterogeneous log. Constructing a set of process models from sets of homogeneous traces is likely to lead to simpler models.

Most existing trace clustering techniques are based on fairly generic methods for clustering in multivariate settings [1]. These methods operate either by locating individuals in a feature space (e.g. k-means clustering), or directly on a distance[1] matrix between individuals (e.g. k-median clustering) [2].

The main challenge in trace clustering, when using such generic clustering techniques, is the gap between clustering and evaluation [3]. In most existing

---

[1] We use the terms distance and dissimilarity matrix interchangeably, and also use the term similarity matrix synonymously, as one can cluster equally well by maximal similarity or minimal distance.

© Springer International Publishing Switzerland 2016
M. Reichert and H.A. Reijers (Eds.): BPM Workshops 2015, LNBIP 256, pp. 179–190, 2016.
DOI: 10.1007/978-3-319-42887-1_15

approaches, the evaluation of process model quality is performed only after clustering is complete. Clustering decisions, e.g. which cluster contains a particular trace, which clusters to split or to combine in hierarchical clustering, are based purely on statistical criteria, i.e. distances in feature space and the inter- and intra-cluster variance, or statistics derived from these. However, depending on how feature space or distance metric are defined, this information is not necessarily a good indicator of the quality of the final process model for each cluster.

There are two ways to address this gap between clustering and evaluation. First, and ideally, mining the model and evaluating its quality should happen during, not after, clustering [3]. However, process model mining and log replay for computing model quality characteristics is computationally expensive. Performing these computations at every step of an iterative clustering algorithm, such as proposed in [3], may be prohibitive for large logs.

Second, one may focus on the definition of an appropriate feature space or distance metric so that it provides the right information for the clustering algorithm to cluster traces that are similar in the sense of being describable by the same simple yet high quality process model. We consider this second issue one of the key challenges in trace clustering. As noted by [2, p. 506], "specifying an appropriate dissimilarity measure is far more important ... than choice of clustering algorithm. This aspect of the problem is emphasized less in the clustering literature ... since it depends on domain knowledge specifics ...."

In this paper we propose a trace clustering method, called *AlignCluster*, that explicitly takes into account information about the sequences of events in a trace. Specifically, our method uses the Smith-Waterman-Gotoh algorithm for sequence alignment to compute dissimilarity or distances between traces, applies multidimensional scaling to construct a feature space, and then applies k-means clustering. We evaluate our cluster solutions by discovering process models using the flexible heuristics miner (FHM) [4]. The quality of resulting models is typically considered in terms of replay fitness, precision, generalizability and simplicity [5] although information retrieval based measures also exist [6].

The remainder of the paper first introduces our method and then briefly describe its implementation. We then present an evaluation of our method and comparison to state-of-the-art in two evaluation scenarios. Our work is then situated in prior research and the subsequent discussion comprises a brief presentation of future work and some general comments on trace clustering.

2   Trace Clustering Using Sequence Alignment

Our approach consists of four steps, from preprocessing the log to clustering, described in the following paragraphs.

Step 1: Preprocessing. We remove duplicate traces while reading the log. This greatly reduces the size of the clustering problem but gives equal "weight" to each unique trace during clustering.

Step 2: Sequence Alignment. To compare traces, we adopt methods developed in the bio-informatics discipline, which has developed algorithms for optimal alignment sequences of DNA and protein building blocks. An alignment is a sequence of pairs, either of elements of the two sequences, or of an element of the first and a "gap" in the second sequence, or of a gap in the first and an element of the second sequence. The notion of gaps is similar to "move log" and "move model" operations in log replay techniques for conformance checking [5]. For example, the sequences GCATGCA and GATTACA may be aligned as ('-' represents a gap):

```
GCATG-CA
G-ATTACA
```

An alignment may be optimal by some scoring system, which consists of the similarity matrix between sequence elements and the gap scoring scheme. For example, a simple scoring system might assign a score of +1 for all exact matches, and a score of −1 for mismatches and gaps. In general, the similarity matrix between elements depends on the application area and should be defined with substantive knowledge about the sequence elements, i.e. the workflow events.

An early algorithm for optimal alignment was developed by [7] and is a type of *global alignment* algorithm. A variation on this [8] was improved by [9] and is a type of *local alignment* algorithm. The latter type of algorithm identifies multiple regions of smaller optimal alignments and is appropriate when the sequences are of different lengths, as is typically the case with process event logs.

We rely on the Smith-Waterman-Gotoh (SWG) local alignment algorithm [8,9] for local alignment. Our scoring schema assigns a value of 1 for exact matches and a fixed penalty otherwise (parameter *mismatchPenaltyRelative*, (mmP)). Our gap scoring scheme defines a penalty for beginning a gap (parameter *gapOpenCostRelative* (gOC)) and another for extending a gap by one position (parameter *gapExtendCostRelative* (gOE)). These parameters are relative to the value for an exact match.

This step of our method is a critical place to apply substantive business knowledge. For example, the events "customer query processed" and "support request completed" may be highly similar in a particular organization and process, despite the fact that they bear little superficial similarity. While one could try to devise automated comparison of event names, perhaps even based on domain ontologies or WordNet lookup, this can never be a full substitute for application-specific knowledge of the processes that produced the event log.

The SWG algorithm provides two results. The first is the similarity between the aligned sequences as a count of the number of exact matches. The second result is the alignment cost as the sum of penalties for opening and extending gaps in either sequence. Our implementation can use either result to construct the trace similarity or distance matrix. The choice is parametrized using the boolean parameter *useSim*, which, when true, uses the similarity metric, otherwise the cost-based metric is used.

Step 3: Multi-dimensional Scaling. Clustering algorithms operate either on features of instances or on a distance matrix. The feature set spans an n-dimensional space in which instances can be located and on which a distance metric can be defined. Using this metric, computing distances from features is straightforward. Many distance metrics have been defined for numerical characteristics (e.g. euclidean distance, Manhattan distance) but also for character-valued characteristics (e.g. string-edit distances). On the other hand, when only a distance matrix is available, one can use multi-dimensional scaling (MDS) [10] to span a space of arbitrary dimensions and locate the instances in that space. MDS can be considered as an optimization problem:

$$\min_{x_1,\ldots,x_I} \sum_{i<j} (||x_i - x_j|| - \delta_{i,j})^2$$

Here, $|| \ldots ||$ is the distance metric to be used for the spanned space, x_i, x_j are vectors locating instances i and j in the space, and δ is the distance between cases i and j.

One of the key choices in MDS is the dimensionality of the space. A higher dimensionality allows for a better separation of clusters in the following clustering step. However, when the space gets too sparse, it may be difficult to identify clusters at all. On the other hand, once the space gets too dense because of too few dimensions, clusters may not cleanly separate. Moreover, because the dimensionality of the space is the maximum number of clusters, the dimensionality should not be too small. In our work, the dimensionality of the space is a function of the number of unique traces, e.g. $\sqrt{n}$ and $\log_e n$.

Step 4: Clustering. One of the key decisions in clustering is the number of clusters to choose. Different approaches to characterizing the quality of a clustering solution and for identifying the optimal number of clusters have been proposed in the literature. However, in the context of trace clustering, these approaches lack a direct connection to the final outcome of the process mining step, i.e. the quality of the resulting process models. This has been termed the clustering versus evaluation bias by [3]. Thus, considerations of within cluster and between cluster sums-of-squares and derived statistics are only of limited value in the context of trace clustering. Hence, rather than investigate the performance of different heuristics for choosing the optimal number of clusters, we defer to the process analyst to evaluate the resulting process models and to make informed decisions about the optimal number of clusters. We use k-means clustering for this research.

3   Implementation

We have implemented our approach as a Java application. The application reads a log in CSV format and creates a distance matrix using the SWG algorithm, using the `jaligner` implementation of the SWG algorithm[2]. It then writes the distance matrix and a script for the R statistical system [11] to file and calls the R system to execute the script. MDS and clustering are performed using R and it is easy to substitute different options and parameters at this stage. Our work uses the `cmdscale` function for MDS and the `kmeans` function for clustering. The R script writes a set of files with cluster assignments, which is then read back and used to create logs in XES format.

For evaluation purposes, our application then creates a script for the ProM process mining framework [12] and calls ProM to execute it. ProM reads each XES log and applies the FHM [4] with default parameters. FHM is used in other trace clustering methods as well, specifically the DWS and ActiTraC methods [3,13] and we found it to be very robust. The heuristics net is then converted to a Petri Net. We then use the log replay technique [14], as implemented in the *PNetReplayer* plugin [15] to compute fitness, and the *PNetAlignmentAnalysis* plugin [16] to compute precision and generalizability.

This scripting approach allows us to automate as much of the process as possible in order to experiment with different values for important parameters, such as the sequence element similarities and gap costs for the SWG algorithm, the dimensionality of the space created by MDS, the number of clusters to identify, and the clustering algorithm. Our implementation is available from the first author's website[3].

4   Evaluation

We have evaluated our approach and compared its performance to earlier methods. Specifically, we compared our method to the same set of algorithms as in [1], i.e. Sequence Clustering (SC) [17], Trace Clustering (TC) [18], ActiTraC (AT) [3] and DWS [13]. Implementations for these are provided in the ProM framework [12]. We evaluated our approach in two scenarios, taken from [1].

4.1   Evaluation Scenario 1

We constructed a log comprised of 500 traces each from three different logs so that a correct clustering solution exists. Logs from the incident management process at RaboBank Group ICT [19], the loan application process at a Dutch financial institute [20], and the translation process at Leginda.de [21] were randomly extracted and aggregated. Results for the state-of-the-art clustering implementations on separating the three processes in the log, reported by [1], show that only AT was able to cleanly separate the log.

We used the simple scoring scheme described in Sect. 2. As noted earlier, this is the place in our algorithm where substantive business knowledge about the similarity of different activities could be applied. In this artificial problem the number of clusters is known to be 3. The parameter settings in Table 1 are those with which our method was able to cleanly separate the three component logs.

---

[2] http://jaligner.sf.net.
[3] http://joerg.evermann.ca/software.html.

Table 1. Parameters, their descriptions, and settings for evaluation scenario 1

$mismatchPenaltyRelative$	mmp	Penalty for an alignment mismatch, relative to an exact match	-1.0
$costGapOpenRelative$	cGO	Cost to open a gap, relative to an exact match	0.0
$costGapExtendRelative$	cGE	Cost to extend a gap, relative to the cost of opening a gap	0.5
$useSim$		Use similarity, rather than alignment cost	$false$
$numDimensions$	dim	Function to compute number of dimensions for MDS from number of traces	$sqrt$
$numClusters$	c	Number of clusters to identify	3

4.2   Evaluation Scenario 2

The second scenario is a more realistic case, using a log of 1,500 traces from the above mentioned loan application process [20], available from the first author's website. We evaluated the four quality dimensions of fitness, precision, generalization using existing ProM plugins [15,16], as described above. For assessing simplicity we refer to [22] and use three different metrics. The cyclomatic number CN is defined as $CN = |A| - |N| + 1$ where $|A|$ is the number of arcs and $|N|$ is the number of nodes in the Petri net. The coefficient of connectivity CNC is defined as $CNC = \frac{|A|}{|N|}$ and the density Δ is defined as $\Delta = \frac{|A|}{|N|*(|N|-1)}$. We aggregated the quality metrics across clusters using the weighted mean, weighted by the number of traces in each cluster.

Many trace clustering methods are extensively parametrized, as is our own. For our comparison to the state-of-the-art, it is impractical to systematically explore the different parameter settings for existing approaches. We followed [1] and limited the number of configurations. ActiTraC was applied in three configurations (3 clusters; 6 clusters; 6 clusters with ICS set to 0.95). DWS was applied in two configurations (default settings; max clusters per split = max feature length = max splits = 5 and max number of features = 10). Trace clustering was applied in five configurations (default; width 1, height 3; width 2 height 3; width 3, height 3; width 4, height 3). Sequence clustering was applied in five configurations (number of clusters 3, 6, 9, 12, 15). Table 2 shows the performance of the state-of-the-art systems on the different quality dimensions with the best values highlighted.

We conducted an experiment that systematically varied the parameters for our method. Table 3 shows the parameter values we applied, yielding 720 experimental conditions. From these we identified the configuration that yields the optimum outcome for each quality characteristic, shown in the bottom part of Table 2 and plotted in Fig. 1. The complete set of 720 results is available from the first author's website.

On this evaluation scenario the optimal configurations were fairly close in performance, even though optimized for different quality criteria (Table 2). For example, generalizability was close to 1 for all configurations, precision close to 0.6 for all but one configuration, and fitness was high at approx. 0.85 even for conditions optimized for simplicity (minCNC, minCN). Examining the parame-

Table 2. Performance of the state-of-the-art and different AlignCluster configurations on evaluation scenario 2, best values for each quality criterion shaded, worst values italicized

Conf	CNC	CN	Delta	Fit	Prec	Gen	mmP	cGO	cGE	useSim	dim	c
AT-3	1.1670	33.7120	0.0240	0.7000	0.4737	0.7322						
AT-6	1.1198	26.1960	*0.0326*	*0.6670*	0.5663	0.6011						
AT-6-ICS95	1.1709	27.3087	0.0072	0.8529	0.3751	0.9661						
DWS-Std	1.2275	30.8013	0.0103	0.8783	*0.3219*	0.9586						
DWS-55510	1.1579	17.3960	0.0208	0.7721	0.5459	0.9581						
TC	1.1773	31.6533	0.0270	0.7823	0.4062	0.7419						
TC-W1-H3	*1.2434*	*46.1867*	0.0129	0.8213	0.3232	0.8937						
TC-W2-H3	1.1792	35.1787	0.0217	0.7235	0.4413	0.8037						
TC-W3-H3	1.1542	31.6587	0.0279	0.6991	0.4686	*0.7309*						
TC-W4-H3	1.1542	31.6587	0.0279	0.6991	0.4840	0.7332						
SC-3	1.1976	32.9653	0.0071	0.8475	0.3631	0.9598						
SC-6	1.1346	20.5973	0.0071	0.8644	0.5103	0.9905						
SC-9	1.1273	17.7667	0.0078	0.8623	0.5408	0.9335						
SC-12	1.1048	13.6540	0.0083	0.8607	0.5502	0.9628						
SC-15	1.0974	12.0793	0.0104	0.8919	0.5760	0.9793						
maxPrec	1.1201	15.0000	0.0094	0.8036	0.5992	0.9957	-0.5	0.5	1.0	false	log	9
maxGen	1.1507	22.0000	0.0073	0.7775	0.5158	0.9988	-0.5	1.0	0.5	false	log	3
maxFit	1.1209	14.0000	0.0104	0.8540	0.5679	0.9965	-0.5	1	0.5	false	log	9
minCNC	1.1164	13.0000	0.0108	0.8502	0.5872	0.9969	-1	1	1	false	log	9
minCN	1.1164	13.0000	0.0108	0.8502	0.5872	0.9969	-1	1	1	false	log	9
minDelta	1.1840	30.0000	0.0072	0.7888	0.4767	0.9941	-0.5	0.5	0.5	false	sqrt	3

Table 3. Parameters and settings for evaluation scenario 2

mismatchPenaltyRelative	*mmP*	0.0, −0.5, −1.0, −2.0
costGapOpenRelative	*cGO*	0.0, 0.5, 1.0
costGapExtendRelative	*cGE*	0.0, 0.5, 1.0
useSim		*false, true*
numDimensions	*dim*	*sqrt, log*
numClusters	*c*	3, 6, 9

ter values of the configurations shows that while moving from 9 to 3 clusters may have optimized generalizability or minimized Δ, the trade-off on other quality characteristics was significant. The configuration minimizing CNC and CN also performs well on the other quality characteristics. Consequently, we recommend this configuration for logs similar to this log. As this log is similar to others we have encountered, *we recommend this as the default configuration.*

Comparing this default configuration to the performance of existing methods in Table 2 shows that the our method performs comparably to ActiTraC but providing somewhat simpler models with somewhat better precision and generalizability, and comparable trace fitness. It performs comparably to DWS in its standard configuration but with better precision. Our method outperforms Trace Clustering in all its configurations, yielding simpler models with better fitness, precision, and generalizability. Finally, our method performs similar to Sequence Clustering with 9 or more clusters, but has a slight advantage in terms of precision and generalizability.

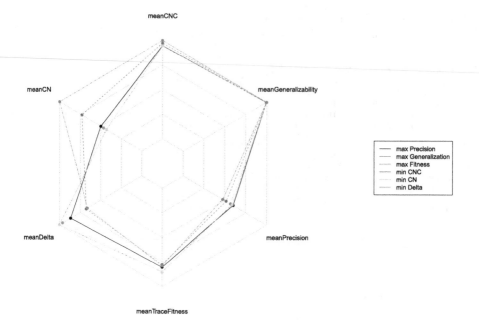

Fig. 1. Radarplot of AlignCluster performance on evaluation scenario 2 (Color figure online)

5 Related Work

Sequence alignment and related techniques have been used in process mining before. Most similar to our work is the work on trace alignment by [23,24]. Also inspired by bio-informatics research, it uses the Needleman-Wunsch algorithm [7] for *global* alignment, rather then *local* alignment as we do. Their work is implemented in the *Trace Alignment* plugin for ProM. However, clustering is not their primary goal and is used only to construct the "guide tree" which guides the selection of sequences for alignment. Clustering in [23,24] is not based on sequence alignment but is an agglomerative method on a feature space spanned by maximal repeat features [25].

The approach in [26] uses the edit distance between sequences for clustering. While not based on a local or global sequence alignment, as in this paper, string edit distance also accounts for sequence characteristics of traces and is known to be equivalent to sequence alignment approaches [27]. As in our work, models are not mined or evaluated until clustering is completed and the gap between clustering and evaluation is addressed indirectly through the choice of trace similarity metric.

The model-based approach by [17,28] represents each cluster by a Markov chain that can generate the behaviour of sequences in that cluster. Traces are assigned to clusters by maximizing the probability that traces are produced by their cluster's Markov chain. An implementation based on commercial tools is described in [28]; an implementation in the *Sequence Clustering* ProM plugin is presented by [17]. This method address the gap between clustering and evaluation directly by using a notion analogous to replay fitness in the clustering algorithm. However, the estimation of Markov Chain parameters is computationally expensive. Our own approach achieves similar, and even slightly better performance, using a less computationally demanding method.

ActiTraC [3] also addresses the gap between clustering and evaluation directly by repeatedly mining and evaluating process models during clustering. It uses maximal repeat features [25] to select candidate traces for assignment to clusters, which are then evaluated using the FHM and replay fitness. Both ActiTraC and Sequence Clustering are computationally intensive. Because it mines process models during clustering, ActiTraC provides not only clusters as a result, but also the generated model, which we have not used in our evaluation. However, as these are also based on the FHM algorithm they are likely to be similar to the ones post-hoc generated in our evaluation.

Other log clustering methods account for sequence information in a more limited way. The *Trace Clustering* method and ProM plugin [18] is based on a feature space of which the "follows" relation between events is the only sequence-related dimension. Additionally, data attributes for cases, event, and performance characteristics are used to span the feature space. A variety of distance metrics and standard clustering methods can then be applied.

DWS [13] is a divisive hierarchical clustering method and ProM plugin that is based on a vector space spanned by frequent features. A frequent feature is a subsequence and a task such that the feature is frequent in the log, but the sequence and appended task are not. By using such sequence frequency information, DWS attempts to include the notion of soundness, which is somewhat analogous to the notion of fitness in that it indicates how well the model explains the traces, into the clustering algorithm.

The method in [29] is based on the number of repeating features (subsequences) in a trace. This accounts for some sequence information, but then abstracts by creating a feature space based on the number of occurrences of subsequences and using these to locate traces in the space for clustering.

6   Discussion

The key challenge in trace clustering, bridging the gap between clustering and evaluation, can be addressed in two ways. The direct, but computationally expensive way, exemplified by the ActiTraC [3] and Sequence Clustering [17] methods, incorporates process mining and model evaluation into the clustering method. We have chosen the less direct, but computationally less demanding way of focusing on the definition of a distance metric and feature space that allows the application of generic multivariate clustering methods. Our experiments, albeit limited in scope to two evaluation scenarios, show that this less direct way is able to yield results as good as those obtained by the more direct approaches.

Despite our initial results, many open questions remain. For example, there is a lack of agreed upon quality characteristics for *sets* of process models. In this paper, we have followed [1] in using simple weighted averages over the clusters, but this is surely a naive view and a better approach rooted in considerations of the process models is required. Consider the optimal results highlighted in Table 2. As the number of clusters increases, the models tend to improve in quality. This reduction in model size, and improvement in fitness and precision is expected as it is the main reason for performing clustering in the first place. Hence, what is required is either a "correction" or "adjustment" for the number of clusters (models) or a restriction to clustering solutions with the same number of clusters.

Second, there may be possible interactions between the clustering method and the mining method. For example, a particular mining algorithm might yield better results when operating on clusters from one clustering method than from another clustering method. For example, a mining algorithm geared towards discovering parallelism requires clusters that separate choices, while an algorithm that favors choice requires clusters with sequential parallel behaviour[4]. Despite some concerns about the use of heuristics and the lack of semantic preserving translation from heursistic models to Petri nets, in this work we have used only the FHM as it is also used by other approaches and yields sensible models in many situations. Exploring this potential inter-dependency remains a challenge for future research.

There are many possible extensions to the method presented here. First, the elimination of duplicate traces in the log greatly reduces the size of the problem, but may bias the resulting quality metrics, computed by replaying each trace against a model. Consequently, a variation of our method may choose to not remove the duplicate traces and opt for worse runtime performance instead.

We use a *local* alignment method, whereas [23,24] use a *global* alignment method. The latter is better suited to sequences that are similar in length. It may be worthwhile to compare the performance of these types of alignment methods and choose based on log characteristics.

An optimal alignment offers a range of possible similarity or distance measures beyond the simple match/mismatch and gap-cost-based ones explored here. One possibility is to use a weighted mean of the two measures we have presented. Another possibility is to not simply count the matches and mismatches, but to weight these by the similarity of the trace events that are aligned.

Finally, a variation of k-means clustering is k-median clustering. This uses the distance matrix for clustering and removes the need to use MDS. In k-median clustering the cluster center is represented by a specific individual. Given the typically large number of traces in trace clustering applications, we expect differences to k-mean clustering to be minimal, as there is likely to be an individual very close to the k-mean cluster center.

In conclusion, this initial application of sequence alignment to trace clustering shows promising results and improves on the existing state-of-the-art, but much future research remains in this area.

---

[4] We thank one of the anonymous reviewers for this specific example.

References

1. Thaler, T., Ternis, S.F., Fettke, P., Loos, P.: A comparative analysis of process instance cluster techniques. In: Thomas, O., Teuteberg, F., (eds.) Smart Enterprise Engineering: 12. Internationale Tagung Wirtschaftsinformatik, WI 2015, Osnabrück, Germany, 4–6 March 2015, pp. 423–437 (2015)
2. Hastie, T., Tibshirani, R., Friedman, J.: The Elements of Statistical Learning. Springer, New York (2009)
3. De Weerdt, J., Vanthienen, J., Baesens, B., et al.: Active trace clustering for improved process discovery. IEEE Trans. Knowl. Data Eng. **25**(12), 2708–2720 (2013)
4. Weijters, A., Ribeiro, J.: Flexible heuristics miner (FHM). In: Proceedings of the IEEE Symposium on Computational Intelligence and Data Mining CIDM 2011, Paris, France (2011)
5. van der Aalst, W.M.P.: Process Mining: Discovery, Conformance and Enhancement of Business Processes. Springer, Heidelberg (2011)
6. De Weerdt, J., De Backer, M., Vanthienen, J., Baesens, B.: A robust f-measure for evaluating discovered process models. In: Proceedings of the IEEE Symposium on Computational Intelligence and Data Mining, CIDM 2011, Part of the IEEE Symposium Series on Computational Intelligence 11–15 2011, Paris, France, pp. 148–155. IEEE (2011)
7. Needleman, S.B., Wunsch, C.D.: A general method applicable to the search for similarities in the amino acid sequence of two proteins. J. Mol. Biol. **48**(3), 443–453 (1970)
8. Smith, T.F., Waterman, M.S.: Identification of common molecular subsequences. J. Mol. Biol. **147**(1), 195–197 (1981)
9. Gotoh, O.: An improved algorithm for matching biological sequences. J. Mol. Biol. **162**(3), 705–708 (1982)
10. Cox, T.F., Cox, M.A.: Multidimensional Scaling. CRC Press, Boca Raton (2000)
11. R Core Team: R: A Language and Environment for Statistical Computing. R Foundation for Statistical Computing, Vienna, Austria (2014)
12. van Dongen, B.F., de Medeiros, A.K.A., Verbeek, H.M.W.E., Weijters, A.J.M.M.T., van der Aalst, W.M.P.: The ProM framework: a new era in process mining tool support. In: Ciardo, G., Darondeau, P. (eds.) ICATPN 2005. LNCS, vol. 3536, pp. 444–454. Springer, Heidelberg (2005)
13. de Medeiros, A.K.A., Guzzo, A., Greco, G., van der Aalst, W.M.P., Weijters, A.J.M.M.T., van Dongen, B.F., Saccà, D.: Process mining based on clustering: a quest for precision. In: Hofstede, A.H.M., Benatallah, B., Paik, H.-Y. (eds.) BPM Workshops 2007. LNCS, vol. 4928, pp. 17–29. Springer, Heidelberg (2008)
14. Rozinat, A., van der Aalst, W.M.: Conformance checking of processes based on monitoring real behavior. Inf. Syst. **33**(1), 64–95 (2008)
15. van der Aalst, W.M.P., Adriansyah, A., van Dongen, B.F.: Replaying history on process models for conformance checking and performance analysis. Wiley Interdisc. Rev.: Data Min. Knowl. Discovery **2**(2), 182–192 (2012)
16. Adriansyah, A., Munoz-Gama, J., Carmona, J., van Dongen, B.F., van der Aalst, W.M.P.: Alignment based precision checking. In: La Rosa, M., Soffer, P. (eds.) BPM Workshops 2012. LNBIP, vol. 132, pp. 137–149. Springer, Heidelberg (2013)
17. Veiga, G.M., Ferreira, D.R.: Understanding spaghetti models with sequence clustering for ProM. In: Rinderle-Ma, S., Sadiq, S., Leymann, F. (eds.) BPM 2009. LNBIP, vol. 43, pp. 92–103. Springer, Heidelberg (2010)

18. Song, M., Günther, C.W., van der Aalst, W.M.P.: Trace clustering in process mining. In: Ardagna, D., Mecella, M., Yang, J. (eds.) Business Process Management Workshops. LNBIP, vol. 17, pp. 109–120. Springer, Heidelberg (2009)
19. Van Dongen, B., Weber, B., Ferreira, D., De Weerdt, J.: Business process intelligence challenge (BPIC 2014) (2014)
20. Van Dongen, B., Weber, B., Ferreira, D.: Business process intelligence challenge (BPIC 2012) (2012)
21. Thaler, T., Fettke, P., Loos, P.: Process mining - Fallstudie leginda.de. HMD Praxis der Wirtschaftsinformatik **293**, 56–66 (2013)
22. Melcher, J.: Process Measurement in Business Process Management- Theoretical Framework and Analysis of Several Aspects. KIT Scientific Publishing, Karlsruhe, Germany (2012)
23. Bose, R.P.J.C., van der Aalst, W.M.P.: Process diagnostics using trace alignment: opportunities, issues, and challenges. Inf. Syst. **37**(2), 117–141 (2012)
24. Bose, R.P.J.C., van der Aalst, W.M.P.: Trace alignment in process mining: opportunities for process diagnostics. In: Hull, R., Mendling, J., Tai, S. (eds.) BPM 2010. LNCS, vol. 6336, pp. 227–242. Springer, Heidelberg (2010)
25. Bose, R.P.J.C., van der Aalst, W.M.P.: Trace clustering based on conserved patterns: towards achieving better process models. In: Rinderle-Ma, S., Sadiq, S., Leymann, F. (eds.) BPM 2009. LNBIP, vol. 43, pp. 170–181. Springer, Heidelberg (2010)
26. Bose, R.P.J.C., van der Aalst, W.M.P.: Context aware trace clustering: towards improving process mining results. In: Proceedings of the SIAM International Conference on Data Mining, SDM 2009, 30 April–2 May 2009, Sparks, Nevada, USA, pp. 401–412. SIAM (2009)
27. Sellers, P.H.: On the theory and computation of evolutionary distances. SIAM J. Appl. Math. **26**(4), 787–793 (1974)
28. Ferreira, D.R.: Applied sequence clustering techniques for process mining. In: Cardoso, J., van der Aalst, W. (eds.) Handbook of Research on Business Process Modeling, pp. 481–502. Information Science Reference, Hershey, PA (2009)
29. Bose, R.P.J.C., van der Aalst, W.M.P.: Trace clustering based on conserved patterns: towards achieving better process models. In: Rinderle-Ma, S., Sadiq, S., Leymann, F. (eds.) BPM 2009. LNBIP, vol. 43, pp. 170–181. Springer, Heidelberg (2010)

Automated Resource Allocation in Business Processes with Answer Set Programming

Giray Havur$^{(\boxtimes)}$, Cristina Cabanillas, Jan Mendling, and Axel Polleres

Vienna University of Economics and Business, Vienna, Austria
{giray.havur,cristina.cabanillas,jan.mendling,axel.polleres}@wu.ac.at

Abstract. Human resources are of central importance for executing and supervising business processes. An optimal resource allocation can dramatically improve undesirable consequences of resource shortages. However, existing approaches for resource allocation have some limitations, e.g., they do not consider concurrent process instances or loops in business processes, which may greatly alter resource requirements. This paper introduces a novel approach for automatically allocating resources to process activities in a time optimal way that is designed to tackle the aforementioned shortcomings. We achieve this by representing the resource allocation problem in Answer Set Programming (ASP), which allows us to model the problem in an extensible, modular, and thus maintainable way, and which is supported by various efficient solvers.

Keywords: Answer set programming · Business process management · Resource allocation · Timed Petri net · Work scheduling

1 Introduction

Human resources[1] are crucial in business process management (BPM) as they are responsible for process execution or supervision. A lack of resources or a suboptimal work schedule may produce delayed work, potentially leading to a reduced quality and higher costs.

In this paper, we address the problem of allocating the resources available in a company to the activities in the running process instances in a time optimal way, i.e., such that process instances are completed in the minimum amount of time. Our approach lifts limitations of prior research pursuing similar goals, which assumes simplified non-cyclic processes and does not necessarily search for an optimal resource allocation [1,2]. To this end, we rely on Answer Set Programming (ASP) [3], a declarative knowledge representation and reasoning formalism that is supported by a wide range of efficient solvers. ASP has been successfully used to address planning and configuration problems in other domains [4].

Our solution is divided into three layers: The core layer represents process models in ASP. The second layer adds all the information related to time, such

---

Funded by the Austrian Research Promotion Agency (FFG), grant 845638 (SHAPE).
[1] From now on *resources* for the sake of brevity.

© Springer International Publishing Switzerland 2016
M. Reichert and H.A. Reijers (Eds.): BPM Workshops 2015, LNBIP 256, pp. 191–203, 2016.
DOI: 10.1007/978-3-319-42887-1_16

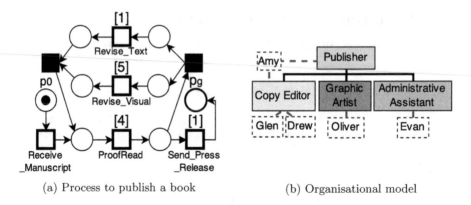

(a) Process to publish a book   (b) Organisational model

Fig. 1. Running example

as the estimated activity durations. Finally, resource-related information including, among others, the characteristics of the resources available according to an organisational model as well as the conditions that must be fulfilled to assign resources to activities (e.g., to have a specific organisational role), is encoded on top of these two layers. An ASP solver can use all this data to compute possible optimal solutions for the resource allocation problem. We have evaluated our approach with a proof-of-concept implementation and we have measured its performance with non-trivial scenarios that contain loops and concurrent process instances.[2]

Our modular encodings in ASP provide flexibility and extensibility so that, e.g., additional instances of pre-defined processes can be added. In addition, the declarative nature of the encodings of constraints enables an executable specification of the problem.

The paper is structured as follows: Sect. 2 presents a scenario that motivates this work as well as related work. Section 3 defines technical background required to understand our approach. Section 4 describes our modular approach for resource allocation in business processes with ASP. Section 5 presents the evaluations performed and Sect. 6 concludes and outlines future work.

2   Background

In the following, we describe an example scenario that motivates this work and shows the problems to be addressed, and then we outline related work.

2.1   Running Example

In this paper we rely on (timed) Petri nets [5] for business process modelling, commonly used for this purpose due to their well defined semantics and their

---

[2] Our encoding and the problem instances are provided at http://goo.gl/lzf1St.

analysis capabilities. Nonetheless, any process modelling notation can be used with our approach as long as it can be mapped to Petri nets, for which several transformations have already been defined [6]. Figure 1a depicts a model representing the process of publishing a book from the point of view of a publishing entity. In particular, when the publishing entity receives a new textbook manuscript from an author, it must be proofread. If changes are required, the modifications suggested must be applied on text and figures, which can be done in parallel. This review-and-improvement procedure is repeated until there are no more changes to apply, and the improved manuscript is then sent back to the author for double-checking. In Fig. 1a, the numbers above the activities indicate their (default maximum) duration in generic time units (TU)[3].

The organisational model depicted in Fig. 1b shows the hierarchy of roles of a publishing entity. Specifically, it has four roles and five resources assigned to them. The following relation specifies how long it takes to each role and resource to complete the process activities: $(Role \cup Resource) \times Activity \times TU \supset \{$(Copy Editor, Proofread, 2), (Glen, Proofread, 5), (Drew, Proofread, 2), (Drew, Revise Text, 2)$\}$. For resource allocation purposes, the duration associated with a specific resource is used in first place followed by the duration associated with roles and finally, the duration of activities (cf. Fig. 1a). Resources are assigned to activities according to their roles. In particular, the relation activity-role in this case is as follows: $Role \times Activity \supset \{$(Publisher, Receive Manuscript), (Copy Editor, Proofread), (Copy Editor, Revise Text), (Graphic Artist, Revise Visual), (Admin. Asst., Send Press Release)$\}$.

For the purpose of planning the allocation of resources to process activities in an optimal way, the following aspects must be taken into consideration: (i) several process instances can be running at the same time; (ii) the review-and-improvement procedure is a loop and hence, it may be repeated several times in a single process instance. Since one cannot know beforehand the number of repetitions that will be required for each process instance, assumptions must be made about it. Optimality is reached when the activities in all instances of a business process are assigned resources so that the overall execution of all instances takes as little time as possible.

2.2   Related Work

The existing work on resource allocation in business processes has mostly relied on Petri nets. In fact, the goal we pursue is doable at the Petri net level with some shortcomings and limitations. van der Aalst [1] introduced a Petri net based scheduling approach to show that the Petri net formalism can be used to model activities, resources and temporal constraints with non-cyclic processes. However, modelling this information for multiple process instances leads to very large Petri nets. Moreover, other algorithms for resource allocation proved to perform better than that approach [7]. Rozinat and Mans [2] used Coloured Petri nets (CPNs) to overcome the problems encountered in traditional Petri nets. In

---

[3] Please, note that events are instantaneous, and hence, they take zero time units.

CPNs, classes and guards can be specified to define any kind of constraints. However, the approach proposed is greedy such that resources are allocated to activities as soon as they are available, overlooking the goal of finding an optimal solution. This may make the allocation problem unsatisfiable.

Several attempts have also been done to implement the problem as a constraint satisfaction problem. For instance, Senkul and Toroslu [8] developed an architecture to specify resource allocation constraints and a Constraint Programming (CP) approach to schedule a workflow according to the constraints defined for the tasks. However, they aimed at obtaining a feasible rather than an optimal solution and the approach does not support the schedule of concurrent workflows. Besides, Heinz and Beck [9] demonstrated that models such as Constraint Integer Programming (CIP) outperform the standard CP formulations. In addition, loops are disregarded in these approaches.

Resource allocation in projects has been widely investigated [10,11]. However, projects differ from business processes in that they are typically defined to be executed only once and decision points are missing. Therefore, the problem is approached in a different way. The agent community has also studied how to distribute a number of resources among multiple agents [12,13]. Further research is necessary to adapt those results to resource allocation in business processes [14].

3   Preliminaries

Timed Petri Nets. [15] associate durations with transitions: a *timed Petri net* is a 5-tuple $N_T = \langle P, T, F, c, M_0 \rangle$ such that P is a finite set of *places*, T is a finite set of *transitions*, with $P \cap T = \emptyset$, $F \subset (P \times T) \cup (T \times P)$ describes a bipartite graph, M_0 is the *initial marking*. and $c : T \to \mathbb{N}$ is a function that assigns firing delays to every transition $t \in T$. Here, a *marking*(state) $M : P \to \mathbb{Z}^+$ assigns to each place a non-negative integer, denoting number of tokens in places. For each $t \in T$ the *input place set* $\bullet t = \{p \in P \mid (p,t) \in F\}$. The output place set $t\bullet$, and analogously input $\bullet p$ (and output $p\bullet$, resp.) transition sets of a place $p \in P$ can be defined analogously. A transition may *fire*, written $\xrightarrow{t}$, when all $p \in \bullet t$ have tokens: all tokens in $\bullet t$ are consumed and tokens produced in each $p \in t\bullet$.

A Fig. 1a shows an example of a timed Petri net: circles represent places, squares represent transitions, and numbers in brackets on transitions denote firing delays. Filled squares denote "silent" transitions that have no firing delays, i.e., $c(t) = 0$. However, note that also normal transitions that correspond to activities can have no delay, e.g., t_m in Fig. 1a.

A marking M_k is *reachable* from M_{k-1} in *one step* if $M_{k-1} \xrightarrow{t_{k-1}} M_k$. A firing sequence of transitions $\overrightarrow{\sigma} = \langle t_1 t_2 ... t_n \rangle$ changes the state of the Petri net at each firing: $M_0 \xrightarrow{t_1} M_1 \xrightarrow{t_2} M_2 \xrightarrow{....} M_n$. In this paper we use *1-safe Petri nets*, i.e., each place contains at most one token in any state. N_T is called *sound* if from every reachable state, a proper final state can be reached in N. N_T is called *free-choice* if every for transitions t_1 and t_2, $\bullet t_1 \cap \bullet t_2 \neq \emptyset$ implies $\bullet t_1 = \bullet t_2$.

Answer Set Programming (ASP). [3,16] is a declarative (logic-programming-style) paradigm for solving combinatorial search problems

An *ASP program* Π is a finite set of rules of the form

$$A_0 :\text{-} A_1, \ldots, A_m, \; not \; A_{m+1}, \ldots, \; not \; A_n. \tag{1}$$

where $n \geq m \geq 0$ and each $A_i \in \sigma$ are (function-free first-order) atoms; if A_0 is empty in a rule r, we call r a constraint, and if $n = m = 0$ we call r a fact. Whenever A_i is a first-order predicate with variables within a rule of the form (1), this rule is considered as a shortcut for its "grounding" $ground(r)$, i.e., the set of its ground instantiations obtained by replacing the variables with all possible constants occurring in Π. Likewise, we denote by $ground(\Pi)$ the set of rules obtained from grounding all rules in Π.

Sets of rules are evaluated in ASP under the so-called stable-model semantics, which allows several models (so called "answer sets"), that is subset-minimal Herbrand models, we again refer to [16] and references therein for details.

ASP Solvers typically first compute (a subset of $ground(\Pi)$, and then use a DPLL-like branch and bound algorithm is used to find answer sets for this ground program. There are various solvers [17,18] for ASP problem specifications, we use *clasp* [3] for our experiments herein (cf. Sect. 5), as one of the most efficient implementations available.

As syntactic extension, in place of atoms, *clasp* allows set-like *choice expressions* of the form $E = \{A_1, \ldots, A_k\}$ which are true for any subset of E; that is, when used in heads of rules, E generates many answer sets, and such rules are often referred to as *choice rules*. For instance, $\Pi_4 = \{lights\_on.\{shop\_open, door\_locked\} :\text{-} lights\_on.\}$ has both answer sets of Π_3 plus the answer set $\{lights\_on\}$. Note that in the presence of choice rules, answer sets are not necessarily subset-minimal, we refer to [3] for details.

Another extension supported in *clasp* are optimisation statements [3] to indicate preferences between possible answer sets:

$$\#minimize \; \{A_1 : Body_1 = w_1, \ldots, A_m : Body_m = w_m\}$$

associates integer weights (defaulting to 1) with atoms A_i (conditional to $Body_i$ being true), where such a statement expresses that we want to find only answer sets with the smallest aggregated weight sum; again, variables in $A_i : Body_i = w_i$ are replaced at grounding w.r.t. all possible instantiations.

Finally, many problems conveniently modelled in ASP require a boundary parameter k that reflects the size of the solution. However, often in problems like planning or model checking this boundary (e.g., the plan length) is not known upfront, and therefore such problems are addressed by considering one problem instance after another while gradually increasing this parameter k. However, re-processing repeatedly the entire problem is a redundant approach, which is why incremental ASP (iASP) [3] natively supports incremental computation of answer sets; the intuition is rooted in treating programs in program slices (extensions). In each incremental step, a successive extension of the program is considered where previous computations are re-used as far as possible.

An iASP program is a triple $(B, A[k], Q[k])$, where B describes *static* knowledge, and $A[k]$ and $Q[k]$ are ASP programs parameterized by the incremental parameter $k \in \mathbb{N}^+$. In the iterative answer set computation of iASP, while the knowledge derived from the rules in $A[k]$ accumulates as k increases, the knowledge obtained from $Q[k]$ is only considered for the latest value of k. $A[k]$ and $Q[k]$ are called *cumulative* knowledge and *volatile* knowledge, resp. More formally, an iASP solver computes in each iteration i

$$\Pi[i] = B \cup \bigcup_{1 \leq j \leq i} A[k/j] \cup Q[k/i]$$

until an answer set for some (minimum) integer $i \geq 1$ is found. We will demonstrate next, how iASP can be successfully used to model and solve various variants of resource allocation problems in business process management.

4   Resource Allocation with iASP

For tackling the problem of resource allocation in business processes, we have developed a modular iASP program consisting of three layers. The bottom layer is the generic iASP encoding Π_N for finding a firing sequence between initial and goal markings of a 1-safe Petri net N. This provides a marking of N at each value of parameter k. On a second layer we extend Π_N towards Π_T to encode timed Petri Nets, i.e., we support business processes encoded as timed Petri nets whose activities can have a duration. Consequently, this encoding cannot only compute possible markings, but also the overall duration for a firing sequence. In other words, now we also know about the value of the overall time spent time at a firing sequence of length k. In the upper layer Π_R, we include rules and constraints about resources in order to encode an iASP program that allocates activities to available resources for a certain period of time.

Please, note some general assumptions that we make about the structure of a resource allocation problem: (i) no resource may process more than one activity at a time; (ii) each resource is continuously available for processing; (iii) no pre-emption, i.e., each activity, once started, must be completed without interruptions; and (iv) the processing times are independent of the schedule, and they are known in advance. These assumptions are common in related approaches [1].

4.1 Π_N: A Generic Formulation of 1-safe Petri Nets

Based on the notions introduced in Sect. 3, we formalise the firing dynamics of 1-safe Petri net $N = \langle P, T, F, M_0 \rangle$ in an iASP program $(B_N, A_N[k], Q_N[k])$. Given a goal state M_k, which for the sake of simplicity we assume to be defined in terms of a single goal place p_g, the aim is to find a shortest possible firing sequence $\overrightarrow{\sigma} = \langle t_1 t_2 ... t_k \rangle$ that does not violate the constraints, from M_0 to M_k. B_N: $N = \langle P, T, F, M_0 \rangle$ is represented using predicates $\texttt{inPlace}_N(\texttt{p}, \texttt{t})$ and $\texttt{outPlace}_N(\texttt{p}, \texttt{t})$ that encode F. We encode different instances i of N by the predicate $\mathtt{instance}_N$, which allows us to run the allocation problem against different instances of the same process; initial markings of instance M_{0i} are defined via predicate $\mathtt{tokenAt}_N(\mathtt{P_0,k_0,i})$ where for each $p \in P_0$, $M_0(p) = 1$.[4]

$\boldsymbol{A_N[k]}$: is shown in Fig. 2. Rule (2) guesses all subsets of possible firing actions for each instance of N. Constraint (3) ensures that any transition $t \in \mathbf{T}$ is fired only if all input places in $\bullet t$ have tokens. Rule (4) models the effect of the action fire on output places by assigning a token to each output place in the step following the firing. Constraint (5) prohibits concurrent firings of transitions $t \in p\bullet$. Rules (6) and (7) preserve tokens at place p in successive steps if none of the transitions $t \in p\bullet$ fires.

$A_N[k]$:

$$\{\mathtt{fire(T,k,I) : inPlace(P,T), instance(I)}\}. \tag{2}$$

$$\mathtt{{:}{-}fire(T,k,I), instance(I), inPlace(P,T), not\ tokenAt(P,k,I)}. \tag{3}$$

$$\mathtt{tokenAt(P,k,I){:}{-}fire(T,k-1,I), outPlace(P,T), instance(I)}. \tag{4}$$

$$\mathtt{{:}{-}inPlace(P,T1), inPlace(P,T2), T1! = T2, fire(T1,k,I), fire(T2,k,I),} \tag{5}$$
$$\mathtt{instance(I)}.$$

$$\mathtt{consumeToken(P,k,I){:}{-}inPlace(P,T), fire(T,k,I), instance(I)}. \tag{6}$$

$$\mathtt{tokenAt(P,k,I){:}{-}tokenAt(P,k-1,I), not\ consumeToken(P,k-1,I)}. \tag{7}$$

$Q_N[k]$:

$$\mathtt{{:}{-}not\ tokenAt(p_g,k,I), instance(I)}. \tag{8}$$

Fig. 2. 1-safe Petri net formulation in iASP

$\boldsymbol{Q_N[k]}$: Finally, constraint (8) in Fig. 2 enforces a token to reach the goal place p_g (for all instances $i \in I$). The computation ends as soon as this constraint is not violated in an iteration of the iASP program, i.e., it computes the minimally necessary number of iterations k to reach the goal state.

4.2 Π_T: Activity Scheduling using Timed Petri Net

In order to model activity durations, we extend the above iASP encoding towards Timed Petri nets: that is, Π_N is enhanced with the notion of time in Π_T. By doing so, $\Pi_N \cup \Pi_T$ becomes capable of scheduling activities in instances of a timed Petri net N_T.

$\boldsymbol{B_T}$: We expand the input of Π_N with facts related to time and with the rules that are independent from the parameter k. For each fact $\mathtt{tokenAt(p_0,k_0,i)}$ previously defined we add in B_T a fact $\mathtt{timeAt(p_0,c_0,k_0,i)}$ where c_0 is the initial time at p_0. In order to distinguish activity transitions and ("silent") non-activity transitions[5], we add facts $\mathtt{activity(t)}$ for all activities. Durations of activities

---

[4] Since in the following we only consider instances of the same Petri Net, we will drop the subscript N in the predicates.

[5] Recall: in Petri nets representing business processes, activity transitions are empty squares while silent transitions are represented in filled squares (cf. Fig. 1a).

are specified with facts `timeActivity(t,c)` where t is an activity and $c \in \mathbb{Z}^+$. The remainder of B_T is given by rules (9, 10) in Fig. 3: rule (9) defines firing delays of each transition in N and rule (10) assigns duration zero to activity transitions per default, where the delay is not otherwise specified.

B_T :

```
firingDelay(T,C):-timeActivity(T,C).                              (9)
firingDelay(T,0):-not timeActivity(T,_),activity(T).              (10)
```

$A_T[k]$:

```
greTimeInPlace(P1,T,k,I):-inPlace(P1,T),inPlace(P2,T),fire(T,k,I),   (11)
                timeAt(P1,C1,k,I),timeAt(P2,C2,k,I),P1!=P2,
                C1<C2,instance(I).
maxTimeInPlace(P,T,k,I):-inPlace(P,T),not greTimePlace(P,T,k,I),     (12)
                fire(T,k,I),instance(I).
timeAt(P2,C,k,I):-not activity(T),fire(T,k-1,I),outPlace(P2,T),      (13)
                maxTimeInPlace(P,T,k-1,I),timeAt(P,C,k-1,I),
                instance(I).
timeAt(P2,C1,k,I):-activity(T),fire(T,k-1,I),outPlace(P2,T),         (14)
                maxTimeInPlace(P,T,k-1,I),timeAt(P,C,k-1,I),
                firingDelay(T,D),C1=C+D,instance(I).
timeAt(P,C,k,I) :-not consumeToken(P,k-1,I),inPlace(P,T),            (15)
                timeAt(P,C,k-1,I),instance(I).
```

$Q_T[k]'$:

```
#minimize{timeAt(pg,C,k,I) : instance(I)=C}                         (16)
```

Fig. 3. Scheduling extension

$\boldsymbol{A_T[k]}$: Rule (13) defines the effect of action `fire` on `timeAt` for all output places $t\bullet$ where t is a *non-activity* transition. In this case, the maximum time among the input places, which is computed by rules (11, 12), is propagated over all output places. As opposed to (13), rule (14) defines the effect of action `fire` on `timeAt` for *activity* transitions. Time value derived in rule (14) for the next step is the sum of the maximum time value at the input places and the value of the activity duration. Rule (15) conserves the time value of a place in the succeeding step k in case the transition does not fire at step $k - 1$.

$\boldsymbol{Q_T[k]}$: On top of $Q_N[k]$, an optimization statement (16) is added for computing answer sets with the minimum time cost.

4.3 Π_R: Resource Allocation

In the last layer of our iASP program, Π_R, we additionally formalise resources and related concepts. $\Pi_N \cup \Pi_T \cup \Pi_R$ allow allocating resources to activities for a time optimal execution of all defined instances of N_T.

B_R: The facts related to resources and organisational models are defined in the input of Π_T. An example organisational model is shown in Fig. 1b. Facts hasRole(r,l) relates a resource r to a role l. Activities are related to a role via facts of the form canExecute(l,t), which means that a role l is allowed to performing an activity t. An optional estimated duration for a resource to execute an activity can be defined by timeActivityResource(t,r,c). Similarly an optional estimated duration for a role per activity can be defined by timeActivityRole(t,l,c). Both can override the default timeActivity(t,c). In particular, the order ($>$) preferred in resource-time allocation is timeActivityResource $>$ timeActivityRole $>$ timeActivity. This is especially useful when a resource or a role is known to execute a particular activity in a particular amount of time, which can be different from the default duration of the activity. In our program (cf. Fig. 4) this preference computation is encoded in rules (17–21). Rules (17, 18) are projections of optionally defined activity execution durations. Rules (19–21) derive correct execution duration for resource-activity pairs considering both mandatory and optional durations.

$A_R[k]$: In the iterative part, rule (22) allocates a resource r to an activity t from time c to time $c2$. Note that, for handling optional execution durations, rule (14) from Fig. 3 is replaced by rule (14)*. Rule (23) along with constraint (24) prohibits any firing of an activity transition that is not allocated to a resource. Constraint (25) ensures that an activity cannot be assigned to more than one resource. Constraints (26–28) guarantee that only one resource is assigned to one activity at a time. Constraints (29, 30) prevents a busy resource to be reassigned.

Time Relaxation. In case a resource is busy at the time when s/he is required for another activity, our program would be unsatisfiable as it is. We add rules (31) and (32) (cf. Fig. 5) into $A_T[k]$ for allowing the demanding activity to wait until the required resource is available again.

5   Evaluation

We demonstrate the applicability and effectiveness of the proposed computational method for resource allocation in business processes by using it with a specific process. In order to measure performance and scalability, we conduct a batch experiment using generated examples of timed Petri nets of different sizes.

5.1   Example Scenario

We apply our method to a business process model that specifies the process of publishing a book as described in Sect. 2.1. The input of the program encoded in ASP following the explanations in Sect. 4 is: (i) three different instances $i1$, $i2$, $i3$ of the timed Petri net depicted in Fig. 1a, whose starting times are defined as $t_{0i1} = 0$, $t_{0i2} = 6$ and $t_{0i3} = 11$, respectively; (ii) the organisational model and optional activity times for resources and roles as shown in Fig. 1b, (iii)

B_R :

```
existsTimeActivityResource(T,R):-timeActivityResource(T,R,C).                    (17)
existsTimeActivityRole(T,L):-timeActivityRole(T,L,C),hasRole(R,L).               (18)
takesTime(T,R,C):-timeActivityResource(T,R,C).                                    (19)
takesTime(T,R,C):-timeActivityRole(T,L,C),hasRole(R,L),canExecute(L,T),          (20)
            not existsTimeResource(T,R).
takesTime(T,R,C):-firingDelay(T,C),hasRole(R,L),canExecute(L,T),                 (21)
            not existsTimeActivityResource(T,R),
            not existsTimeActivityRole(T,L).
```

$A_R[k]$:

```
{assign(R,T,C,C2,k,I) : takesTime(T,R,C),C2 = C+D}:-inPlace(P1,T),               (22)
            timeAt(P1,C,k,I),activity(T),instance(I).
timeAt(P2,C2,k,I):-activity(T),assign(R,T,C1,C2,k−1,I),                          (14)*
            fire(T,k−1,I),outPlace(P2,T),instance(I).
assigned(T,k,I):-assign(R,T,C1,C2,k,I).                                          (23)
:-not assigned(T,k,I),fire(T,k,I),activity(T),instance(I).                       (24)
:-assign(R,T,C1,C2,K,I),assign(R1,T,C3,C4,K,I),R! = R1.                          (25)
:-assign(R,T1,C1,C2,K1,I1),assign(R,T2,C1,C2,K2,I2),C1! = C2,T1! = T2.           (26)
:-assign(R,T,C1,C2,K1,I1),assign(R,T,C1,C2,K2,I2),C1! = C2,I1! = I2.             (27)
:-assign(R,T1,C1,C2,K1,I1),assign(R,T2,C1,C2,K2,I2),                             (28)
   C1! = C2,I1! = I2,T1! = T2.
:-assign(R,T,B1,B2,K1,I),assign(R,T2,A1,A2,K2,I2),A1 > B1,A1 < B2.               (29)
:-assign(R,T,B1,B2,K1,I),assign(R,T2,A1,A2,K2,I2),A2 < B2,A2 > B1.               (30)
```

Fig. 4. Allocation extension

role-activity relation defined in Sect. 2. We also add additional constraints for enforcing the firing sequence to go through the loop present in the process two, three and one times for $i1$, $i2$ and $i3$, respectively.

The computed optimal resource allocation is visualised in Fig. 6. The allocation periods are depicted as coloured rectangles with a tag on it. Each tag has three parts: an initial with the initials of a resource, a short version of the allocated activity name and a subscript representing the instance ID. For example, $D : PR_1$ means that *Drew* is allocated to activity *Proofreading*. The colours of

$A_T[k]'$:

```
relaxationAt(P,C+1,k,I):-timeAt(P,C,k−1,I),inPlace(P,T),activity(T),            (31)
            not consumeToken(P,k−1,I),instance(I).
timeAt(P,C,k,I):-relaxationAt(P,C,k,I).                                          (32)
```

Fig. 5. Time relaxation for optimality

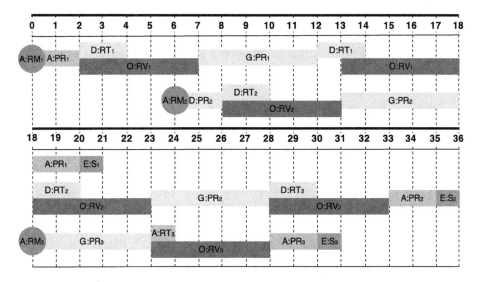

Fig. 6. Instance I - 2 loop repetitions / instance II - 3 loop repetitions / instance III - 1 loop repetition (Color figure online)

these rectangles correspond to the colours used for the roles depicted in Fig. 1b. Note that *Amy* has more than one roles in the organisation.

The longest process instance *i2* finishes in 36 time units. Several solutions were found for that global minimum time. In Fig. 6, instances 1 and 2 finish without interruptions. However, instance 3 waits 7 time units for the availability of *Glen* to start performing activity *Proofread*, since he is busy performing that activity for process instance 2 until time unit 23. All-in-all, this computation optimises the use of resource *Oliver*, who is the only *Graphic Artist* and is required in all the process instances. Please, note that, e.g., in instance 2 *Drew* is selected to perform activity *Proofread* because it takes him only 2 time units (cf. Fig. 1b), half of the default duration associated with the activity (cf. Fig. 1a). This responds to the preference order described in Sect. 4.3.

5.2 Performance

For our experimental evaluation, we generated a set of sound choice-free timed Petri nets (cf. Sect. 3). We varied the number of existing loops in these Petri nets and the number of parallel process instances. We use the same organisational model for all of the generated Petri nets, specifically the one depicted in Fig. 1b. We performed these experiments on a Linux server (4 CPU cores/2.4 GHz/32 GB RAM). *clasp* was used as ASP solver with the multi-threading mode enabled.

The results are shown in Table 1 in two parts. In the programs on the left hand side (1–9), no transitions in the loops are enforced to be fired. In the programs on the right hand side (10–18), each loop in the Petri net is constrained to be followed at least one time. The columns of the table are as follows: *id* is the identifier of a generated program, $|I|$ is the number of parallel instances, $|L|$ is the number of loops, $|f(T)|$ is the number of fired transitions from initial to goal state, k is the final value of that parameter, s is the time in seconds to find the answer set of the program, and m is the maximum memory usage in megabytes.

Table 1. Experiments: (1–9) Loops not enforced, (10–18) Loops enforced

id	$|I|$	$|L|$	$|f(T)|$	k	s	m	id	$|I|$	$|L|$	$|f(T)|$	k	s	m
1	1	1	10	8	1.13	10.2	10	1	1	24	4	15.02	101.6
2	2	1	20	21	7.38	72.2	11	2	1	48	25	90.87	419
3	3	1	38	9	176.45	432.1	12	3	1	72	33	193.72	372.9
4	1	2	10	3	0.57	0	13	1	2	28	29	33.96	186.2
5	2	2	20	21	83.03	459.4	14	2	2	60	7	1314.73	2877.2
6	3	2	42	31	199.46	756.8	15	3	2	n/a	n/a	10800	5744.1
7	1	3	10	11	1.27	17.9	16	1	3	24	25	17.5	83.9
8	2	3	20	16	28.57	229	17	2	3	48	28	161.15	496.5
9	3	3	38	21	85.73	475.1	18	3	3	96	4	2366.24	4473.9

For instance, it takes the solver 1.13 s to find an answer set for a Petri net with one loop that is not enforced at run time, and 15.02 s for a similar Petri net in which the loop is executed. This is satisfactory for many planning scenarios with large processes, as they can be scheduled in a few seconds/minutes and executed for a long period of time.

6   Conclusions and Future Work

We have introduced an approach for automated resource allocation in business processes that relies on ASP to find an optimal solution. The result is a work distribution (i.e., an activity allocation) that ensures that all the process activities can finish in the minimum amount of time given a set of resources. Unlike similar approaches, it is capable of dealing with cyclic processes and concurrent process instances as our encoding in ASP is flexible and extensible. Note that extensions like constraints enforcing separation and binding of duties [19] can be easily added in our formalism, which we omitted due to space restrictions.

We plan to conduct further performance measurements and compare them to other formalisms, e.g., constraint solvers. We are confident that there is room for optimisations (e.g., symmetry breaking [4] or similar techniques) that have been successfully applied in ASP.

References

1. van der Aalst, W.M.P.: Petri net based scheduling. Oper. Res. Spektr. **18**(4), 219–229 (1996)
2. Rozinat, A., Mans, R.S.: Mining CPN models: discovering process models with data from event logs. In: Workshop and Tutorial on Practical Use of Coloured Petri Nets and the CPN, pp. 57–76 (2006)
3. Gebser, M., Kaminski, R., Kaufmann, B., Schaub, T.: Answer Set Solving in Practice. Synthesis Lectures on Artificial Intelligence and Machine Learning. Morgan & Claypool Publishers, San Rafael (2012)
4. Falkner, A.A., Schenner, G., Friedrich, G., Ryabokon, A.: Testing object-oriented configurators with ASP. In: Workshop on Configuration at ECAI 2012, pp. 21–26 (2012)
5. Murata, T.: Petri nets: properties, analysis and applications. IEEE **77**(4), 541–580 (1989)
6. Lohmann, N., Verbeek, E., Dijkman, R.: Petri net transformations for business processes – a survey. In: Jensen, K., van der Aalst, W.M.P. (eds.) Transactions on Petri Nets and Other Models of Concurrency II. LNCS, vol. 5460, pp. 46–63. Springer, Heidelberg (2009)
7. Carlier, J., Pinson, E.: An algorithm for solving the job-shop problem. Manage. Sci. **35**(2), 164–176 (1989)
8. Senkul, P., Toroslu, I.H.: An architecture for workow scheduling under resource allocation constraints. Inf. Syst. **30**(5), 399–422 (2005)
9. Heinz, S., Beck, C.: Solving resource allocation/scheduling problems with constraint integer programming. In: COPLAS 2011, pp. 23–30 (2011)
10. Weglarz, J.: Project scheduling with continuously-divisible, doubly constrained resources. Manage. Sci. **27**(9), 1040–1053 (1981)
11. Hendriks, M.H.A., Voeten, B., Kroep, L.: Human resource allocation in a multi-project R&D environment: resource capacity allocation and project portfolio planning in practice. Int. J. Project Manage. **17**(3), 181–188 (1999)
12. Chevaleyre, Y., Dunne, P.E., Endriss, U., Lang, J., Lematre, M., Maudet, N., Padget, J., Phelps, S., Rodrguez-aguilar, J.A., Sousa, P.: Issues in multiagent resource allocation. Informatica **30**, 3–31 (2006)
13. Zhang, C., Lesser, V., Shenoy, P.: A multi-agent learning approach to online distributed resource allocation. In: International Joint Conference on Artificial Intelligence (IJCAI 2009), vol. 1, pp. 361–366 (2009)
14. Yuhong Yan, Z., Maamar, W.S.: Integration of workflow and agent technology for business process management. In: Computer Supported Cooperative Work in Design, pp. 420–426 (2001)
15. Popova-Zeugmann, L.: Time Petri Nets. Springer, Heidelberg (2013)
16. Brewka, G., Eiter, T., Truszczyński, M.: Answer set programming at a glance. Commun. ACM **54**(12), 92–103 (2011)
17. Calimeri, F., Gebser, M., Maratea, M., Ricca, F.: The Design of the Fifth Answer Set Programming Competition. CoRR (2014.)
18. Heule, M.J., Schaub, T.: What's hot in the SAT and ASP competitions. In: AAAI (2015)
19. Leitner, M., Rinderle-Ma, S.: A systematic review on security in Process-Aware Information Systems Constitution, challenges, and future directions. Information and Software Technology **56**(3), 273–293 (2014)

Using Life Cycle Information
in Process Discovery

Sander J.J. Leemans$^{(\boxtimes)}$, Dirk Fahland, and Wil M.P. van der Aalst

Eindhoven University of Technology, Eindhoven, The Netherlands
{s.j.j.leemans,d.fahland,w.m.p.v.d.aalst}@tue.nl

Abstract. Understanding the performance of business processes is an important part of any business process intelligence project. From historical information recorded in event logs, performance can be measured and visualized on a discovered process model. Thereby the accuracy of the measured performance, e.g., waiting time, greatly depends on (1) the availability of start and completion events for activities in the event log, i.e. transactional information, and (2) the ability to differentiate between subtle control flow aspects, e.g. concurrent and interleaved execution. Current process discovery algorithms either do not use activity life cycle information in a systematic way or cannot distinguish subtle control-flow aspects, leading to less accurate performance measurements. In this paper, we investigate the automatic discovery of process models from event logs, such that performance can be measured more accurately. We discuss ways of systematically treating life cycle information in process discovery and their implications. We introduce a process discovery technique that is able to handle life cycle data and that distinguishes concurrency and interleaving. Finally, we show that it can discover models and reliable performance information from event logs only.

Keywords: Process mining · Process discovery · Performance measurement · Rediscoverability · Concurrency

1 Introduction

One of the central tasks in business process intelligence is to understand the actual performance of a process and the impact of resource behaviour and process elements on overall performance. Event data logged by Business Process Management (BPM) systems or Enterprise Resource Planning (ERP) systems typically contains time stamped *transactional events* (start, completion, etc.) for each activity execution. Process mining allows to analyse this transactional data for performance. Typically, first a model of the process is discovered, which is then annotated with performance information.

Performance information might consist of several measures, for example service time (the time a resource is busy with a task), waiting time (the time between an activity becoming enabled and a resource starting to execute it),

© Springer International Publishing Switzerland 2016
M. Reichert and H.A. Reijers (Eds.): BPM Workshops 2015, LNBIP 256, pp. 204–217, 2016.
DOI: 10.1007/978-3-319-42887-1_17

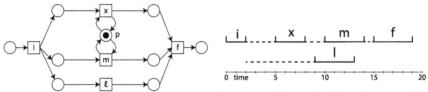

(a) A Petri net modeling a process.

(b) A trace. The dashed lines denote waiting time. The solid lines denote service time.

Fig. 1. A process with concurrency and interleaving and a trace.

sojourn time (the sum of both) and synchronisation time (for concurrent activities, the time between completion of the first and completion of the last).

Figure 1a shows an example process in some imaginary hospital: after an *initial examination* (i), tissue samples are investigated in a *laboratory* (*l*). Meanwhile, the patient undergoes two tests: an *x-ray* (x) and an *mri* (m) test. When all tests are completed, the patient meets the doctor for a *final* time (f). Figure 1b shows a patient (a *trace*) of this process where each activity is logged as an interval of a *start* (s) event and a *complete* (c) event; the dashed lines denote waiting time. The patient cannot perform the *x* and *m* tests at the same time, i.e. they are *interleaved* (due to place *p*), thus the waiting time before *m* starts after the completion of *x*. In contrast, the lab test *l* can be executed independently of the *x* and *m* tests, i.e. they are *concurrent*, so the waiting time before *l* starts at the completion of *i* (waiting time starts at the last time *i* became enabled). Without knowledge of the model, the waiting time of *l* cannot be positioned properly and thus waiting, sojourn and synchronisation times will be measured incorrectly: The waiting time is $9 - 2 = 7$ time units rather than $9 - 8 = 1$ unit. Therefore, in order to reliably compute performance measures, a process model is required to provide information on concurrency and interleaving.

The difficulty in discovering concurrency lies in the event logs: Most process discovery algorithms [2, 14–16, 19] assume that the event log contains events representing atomic executions of activities. On atomic task executions, concurrency and interleaving cannot be distinguished, and more information is required. In this paper, we assume that the event log contains examples of non-atomic executions of activities, i.e. for each activity instance the start and the completion time is known. The XES standard [8] is often used as an input format for event logs and supports this with the *lifecycle:transition* extension. Several process discovery techniques exist that take transactional data into account, such as Tsinghua-α (Tα) [20], Process Miner (PM) [17]. and several other approaches [4, 9]. Unfortunately, none of these distinguishes concurrency and interleaving, and most [4, 9, 20] do not guarantee to return sound models, i.e. without deadlocks or other anomalies; both of which are prerequisites for reliable computation of performance measures.

In the remainder of this paper, we first study the impact of transactional data on event logs and models. Second, we elaborate on the problem of incomplete/inconsistent transactional data in event logs and give a way to repair such event logs (Sect. 3). and we introduce an abstraction (collapsed process models) that enables reasoning about such data (Sect. 4). Third, we introduce a new process discovery algorithm based on the Inductive Miner (IM) framework [12] that uses this information to discover collapsed process models (Sect. 5). The new algorithm faces two challenges: first, the transactional data must be handled correctly; and second, it should distinguish concurrency from interleaving. In Sect. 6, we illustrate its functioning, study of the implications of this abstraction on any process discovery algorithm and on existing model quality measures, and discuss related work; Sect. 7 concludes the paper.

2   Transactional Information in Event Logs

A *trace* is a sequence of *events*, denoting for a case, e.g. a customer, what process steps (*activities*) were executed for that case. Events may carry additional attributes, such as timestamps and a *transaction type*. The latter indicates whether the activity started, completed, etc. An *activity instance* is the execution of an activity in a trace, and may consist of a start event and a completion event, as well as events of other transaction types. For instance, $t = \langle a_s^{11:50}, a_c^{11:53}, b_s^{12:03}, b_c^{12:50} \rangle$ denotes a trace of 4 events: first, an instance of activity a was started, second, an instance of a completed, after which an instance of activity b started and an instance of activity b completed. The timestamps in superscript denote the times at which the events occurred; we will omit timestamps if they are not relevant. An *event log* is a multiset of traces.

In trace t, it makes sense to assume that a_s and a_c are events of the same activity instance. However, this information is usually not recorded in the event log, and the techniques introduced in this paper neither need nor try to infer this information. In the following sections, we assume presence of at least start and completion events; the techniques describe in this paper will ignore other transaction types.

Consider the trace $t = \langle a_s \rangle$. As an activity instance of a was started but never completed, there is either an a_c event missing, or the a_s event should not have been recorded. Similar problems could have occurred when unmatched completion events appear. This raises the notion of a *consistent trace*, similar to [4]:

Definition 1. *A trace is consistent if and only if each start event has a corresponding completion event and vice versa.*

3   Preparing the Input

In real-life data sets, it is possible that some traces in an event log do not adhere to Definition 1. A trace can be checked for consistency easily with a single pass over the trace and some bookkeeping. Nevertheless, our approach requires consistent traces, so any inconsistency need to be dealt with.

We illustrate the decisions that have to be made using an example trace $t = \langle a_s^{11:30}, a_s^{12:40}, a_c^{13:50} \rangle$. Clearly, this trace is not consistent, as there are two start events of activity a and only one complete event. There are several ways to make t consistent:

- $\langle \rangle$
- $\langle a_s^{11:30} a_c^{13:50} \rangle$
- $\langle a_s^{12:40}, a_c^{13:50} \rangle$
- $\langle a_s^{11:30}, a_c, a_s^{12:40}, a_c^{13:50} \rangle$
- $\langle a_s^{11:30}, a_s^{12:40}, a_c, a_c^{13:50} \rangle$
- $\langle a_s^{11:30}, a_s^{12:40}, a_c^{13:50}, a_c \rangle$

Without further information, we cannot decide on the trace that matches reality in the best way possible. Additional information in the event log could be used, such as the *concept:instance* extension of the XES standard [8], which links start and complete events of activity instances. If this extension would indicate that events $a_s^{12:40}$ and $a_c^{12:40}$ form an activity instance, it makes sense to opt for $\langle a_s^{12:40}, a_c^{13:50} \rangle$ or $\langle a_s^{11:30}, a_c, a_s^{12:40}, a_c^{13:50} \rangle$. For our experiments, we choose option $\langle a_s^{11:30}, a_c, a_s^{12:40}, a_c^{13:50} \rangle$, i.e. each completion event is matched with the last occurring start event, and completion events are inserted right after unmatched start events. Completion events are handled symmetrically. Please note that by considering unmatched completion events as atomic, we can handle logs that contain only completion events using the same approach.

The pre-processing step ignores all events that contain other life cycle annotations than start or completion (see e.g. the *lifecycle:transition* extension of the XES 2.0 standard [8]). In the remainder of this paper, we only consider event logs consisting of consistent traces.

4   Transactional Information in Process Models

In standard Petri nets, a transition is considered atomic, i.e. when firing a transition its start is indistinguishable from its completion. This poses a problem for performance measurements if we map activities onto transitions, as a transition cannot take time.

A solution could be to use separate transitions for the start and completion of activities, such that their execution can be distinguished. This poses a new challenge to process models: if the start and completion transitions do not match, the model might allow for inconsistent traces, such as two starts followed by one completion. This may severely jeopardise the accuracy of performance measurements. Moreover, in order to measure performance, it must be known which combinations of start and completion transitions correspond to an activity.

A common solution to these issues is to expand each transition (a, Fig. 2a) in two transitions, connected with a place: one transition denotes the start (a_s), the other transition denotes the completion (a_c) of the transition (Fig. 2b) [3]. The connection between the two newly created transitions is kept, and therefore the

(a) Collapsed.   (b) Expanded.

Fig. 2. Excerpt of a collapsed and its expanded workflow net.

model does not allow inconsistent traces. We refer to this existing technique as
expanding a process model; the un-expanded process model is a *collapsed* model.
   Process Trees. Process trees are abstract representations of block-structured
workflow nets [2]. Process trees are particularly suitable for process discovery,
as they are by definition free of deadlocks and other anomalies (*sound* [1]).
A process tree describes a language, and it consists of a hierarchy of operators being the nodes of the tree, and activities being the leaves of the
tree. An activity describes the singleton language of that activity, while
an operator describes how the languages of its children are to be com-
bined. In [12], the four operators sequence ($\rightarrow$), exclusive choice ($\times$), concurrency ($\wedge$) and loop ($\circlearrowleft$) are considered. For example, the process tree
$\rightarrow(a, \times(\wedge(b,c), \circlearrowleft(d,e)), f)$ has, among other things, the following traces
$\langle a,b,c,f\rangle$, $\langle a,c,b,f\rangle$, $\langle a,d,f\rangle$, $\langle a,d,e,d,e,d,f\rangle$. We use $\mathcal{L}(T)$ to denote the language of process tree T.
   Collapsed Process Trees. Process trees can be mapped onto Petri nets using
the translation presented in [12]. Hence, they face the problem of atomicity as
well. Therefore, we lift the expanding technique to process trees by introducing a
variant that keeps the link between starts and completes: *collapsed process trees*.
A collapsed process tree can be expanded into a normal process tree, e.g. $\times(a,b)$
expands to $\times(\rightarrow(a_s, a_c), \rightarrow(b_s, b_c))$.

Definition 2. *A collapsed process tree is a process tree in which each activity
-a- denotes the process tree* $\rightarrow(a_s, a_c)$.

5   Inductive Miner - Life Cycle

In this section, we introduce an algorithm (Inductive Miner - life cycle (IMLC))
that is able to handle life cycle data and distinguishes concurrency and interleaving. In this section, we first recall principles of recursive process discovery with
IM. Second, we describe how transactional data is dealt with in this framework
(Sect. 5.2), and introduce a way to distinguish interleaving from concurrency
(Sect. 5.3). Finally, we give an example (Sect. 5.4) and we describe the implementation (Sect. 5.5).

5.1   Inductive Miner

The divide-and-conquer framework Inductive Miner [12] (IM) recursively applies
four steps. (1) Select a *cut*: a division of activities in the event log and a process

tree operator, e.g. $(\wedge, \{a, b\}, \{c\})$. (2) Split the log into smaller sub-logs according to this cut. (3) Recurse on each sub-log. The recursion ends when a base case, e.g. a log containing only a single activity, is left. (4) If no cut can be selected, a *fall through* is returned. We will make use of this conceptual framework. However, in its current form, IM simply treats each event as a separate activity instance.

In order to select a cut, IM considers the directly-follows graph, which contains which activities were directly followed by other activities. Each of the process tree operators leaves a specific footprint in the directly-follows graph. Thus, IM detects cuts by identifying these footprints. Figure 3 shows the footprints of the process tree operators (ignoring the dashed box); [12] provides details and log splitting procedures.

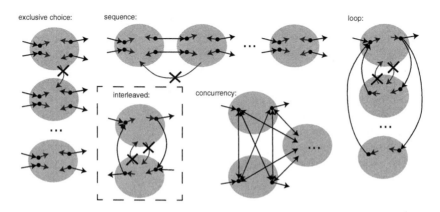

Fig. 3. Cut footprints in the directly-follows graph, see [12].

IMLC uses the IM framework and needs to adapt all four steps to cope with transactional events and to detect interleaving. We first introduce how IMLC handles transactional events, after which we introduce how it detects interleaving.

5.2 Transactional Events

In order to handle transactional events, changes are required in three of the four steps of IM; log splitting requires no changes. As base case detection involves little changes to cope with transactional events, it will not be discussed in this paper.

Cut Detection. Most parts of cut detection remain roughly as in previous works [12], however cut detection in IM relies on directly-follows graphs, which are constructed differently in case of transactional events. The method presented here is based on ideas used in e.g. Tα and PM, but differs in details. (Collapsed) activity a follows (collapsed) activity b directly, if in the

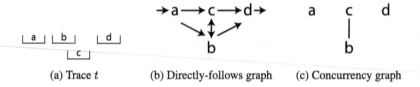

| (a) Trace t | (b) Directly-follows graph | (c) Concurrency graph |

Fig. 4. Trace t and its corresponding graphs.

event log an (expanded) event of a follows an (expanded) event of b without both a start and completion event of the same activity between them. For instance, consider trace $t = \langle a_s, a_c, b_s, c_s, b_c, c_c, d_s, d_c \rangle$; visualised in Fig. 4a. In t, consider the event c_s. Obviously, c_s follows b_s directly, so in Fig. 4b, c directly follows b. Moreover, c_s follows event a_c directly, as there is only a completion event of b in between them, which is not a full activity instance. In contrast, between a_c and d_s there are two full activity instances (b and c), thus a is not directly followed by d in t.

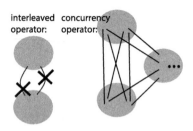

Fig. 5. Cut footprints in the concurrency graph.

Any activity instance of which the start event is not preceded by the completion event of another activity instance is called a *start activity*. In t, a is the only start activity; b, c and d are not, as there occurs an a_c event before them. Similarly, d is the only end activity of t. In Fig. 4b, these start and end activities are denoted by incoming and outgoing edges.

Fall Throughs. If no cut can be found, a fall through is to be selected. IMLC contains several fall throughs, of which the last one is a model that expresses all behaviour in the event log, and therefore guarantees fitness. For non-collapsed process trees, the flower model $\circlearrowleft(\tau, a, b, c, \ldots)$ serves this purpose, as it allows for any behaviour of the included activities a b c .... For collapsed process trees, a model allowing for all behaviour may not exist, as in a collapsed process tree, no activity can be concurrent with itself (see Sect. 6.3). Hence, IMLC counts the maximum number of times an activity is concurrent with itself in the event log, and constructs a model accordingly. For instance, in the event log $\{\langle a_s, a_s, a_c, b_s, a_c, b_c \rangle\}$, at most 2 a's and 1 b are concurrent with themselves. Then, the fall through collapsed model that IMLC chooses is $\wedge(\circlearrowleft(\tau, a), \circlearrowleft(\tau, a), \circlearrowleft(\tau, b))$. This model can produce any behaviour of two a's and one b all concurrent to each other.

5.3   Interleaving

Besides handling transactional data, IMLC is able to detect interleaving. We first introduce the corresponding process tree operator, then describe how to

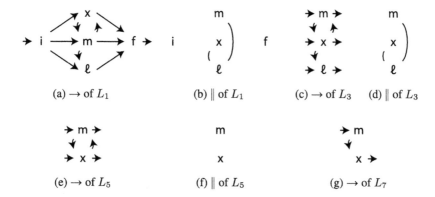

(a) → of L_1 (b) ‖ of L_1 (c) → of L_3 (d) ‖ of L_3

(e) → of L_5 (f) ‖ of L_5 (g) → of L_7

Fig. 6. The directly-follows ↦ and concurrency ‖ graphs for a few (sub-)logs.

detect it. The interleaving operator ↔ takes any number of subtrees ($\geqslant 2$) and combines their languages.

Definition 3. *Let* $T_1 \ldots T_n$ *be process trees. Let* $p(n)$ *be the set of all permutations of the numbers* $\{1 \ldots n\}$. *Then* $\mathcal{L}(\leftrightarrow(T_1, \ldots, T_n)) = \bigcup_{(i_1 \ldots i_n) \in p(n)} \mathcal{L}(\rightarrow(T_{i1} \ldots T_{in}))$.

Note that the union can also be expressed as an exclusive choice over each sequence $\rightarrow(T_{i1} \ldots T_{in})$.

Detection Strategy. This structure is exploited in the detection of ↔, and IMLC applies a three-stage strategy: (1) An interleaving cut is detected using the footprint of ↔ (see Fig. 3). However, detection of this footprint is insufficient to conclude interleaving, as e.g. the footprint does not guarantee that each child is executed at most once. Therefore, we denote the detection with an additional operator (*maybe-interleaved* (⇿)), e.g. the cut (↔, {a}, {b}) is detected but (⇿, {a}, {b}) is reported. (2) Using the ⇿ cut, the event log is split and recursion continues as usual. (3) After recursion, interleaving is derived from the structure of the process tree, e.g. each occurrence of ⇿(→(T_1, T_2), →(T_2, T_1)) is replaced by ↔(T_1, T_2).

(1) Detection of ↔. To detect interleaving, IMLC uses the footprint of the ↔ operator in the directly-follows graph. This footprint is shown in Fig. 3: from each end activity, an edge must be present to all start activities of all other circles, and vice versa. Other directly-follows edges between circles are not allowed.

Notice that if the start and end activities overlap, this footprint might overlap with the concurrency footprint, e.g. ↔(a, b) has the same footprint as ∧(a, b). Therefore, IMLC also considers the *concurrency graph*. As shown in [20], transactional data allows for direct detection of concurrency: whenever two activity instances overlap in time (such as b and c in Fig. 4a), their activities are concurrent. Figure 4c shows the concurrency graph of our example. For this step, it suffices to keep track of the number of started-but-not-yet-completed activity instances. Interleaving and concurrency have clearly different footprints in the concurrency graph (see Fig. 5).

(2) Log Splitting for ⇸. For ⇸, the log is split by dividing traces based on the activities with which they start. For instance, consider the event log $L = \{\langle x_s, x_c, m_s, m_c \rangle, \langle m_s, m_c, x_s, x_c \rangle\}$ and the cut $(⇸, \{x\}, \{m\})$. Based on this cut, L is split into the sub-logs $\{\langle x_s, x_c, m_s, m_c \rangle\}$ and $\{\langle m_s, m_c, x_s, x_c \rangle\}$.

(3) From ⇸ to ↔. Intuitively, log splitting 'unravels' the interleaved execution: the sub-trees of $\{x\}$ and $\{m\}$ can be executed in any order; for each such ordering, a different sub-log is returned. After unraveling the order, recursion continues and, by the interleaving semantics, we expect → operators to appear in both branches. Therefore, after recursion, each occurrence of the pattern $⇸(\rightarrow(T_1, T_2), \rightarrow(T_2, T_1))$ (or an n-ary generalisation thereof) is replaced with $↔(T_1, T_2)$. In case further recursion shows that interleaving was not present, i.e. the pattern does not show up, any remaining ⇸ operator is replaced with an × operator; the subtrees remain untouched. Effectively, this allows a single activity label to occur in multiple branches of the model.

5.4   Example

We illustrate IMLC using an example, derived from Fig. 1a. Consider log $L_1 = \{\langle i_s, i_c, m_s, m_c, x_s, l_s, x_c, l_c, f_s, f_c \rangle, \langle i_s, i_c, l_s, x_s, x_c, m_s, l_c, m_c, f_s, f_c \rangle\}$. The directly-follows and concurrency graphs of L_1 are shown in Figs. 6a and b. Cut detection will find the cut $(\rightarrow, \{i\}, \{x, m, l\}, \{f\})$, after which L_1 is split into $L_2 = \{\langle i_s, i_c \rangle\}$, $L_3 = \{\langle m_s, m_c, x_s, l_s, x_c, l_c \rangle, \langle l_s, x_s, x_c, m_s, l_c, m_c \rangle\}$ and $L_4 = \{\langle f_s, f_c \rangle\}$. The partial result up till this point is $\rightarrow(\text{IMLC}(L_2), \text{IMLC}(L_3), \text{IMLC}(L_4))$. Next, IMLC recurses on the first and last branch, both of which result in a base case, after which the partial result becomes $\rightarrow(i, \text{IMLC}(L_3), f)$. Next, IMLC recurses on L_3; Figs. 6c and d show the corresponding graphs. Based on the concurrency graph, IMLC selects the cut $(\wedge, \{m, x\}, \{l\})$. Using this cut, L_3 is split into $L_5 = \{\langle m_s, m_c, x_s, x_c \rangle, \langle x_s, x_c, m_s, m_c \rangle\}$ and $L_6 = \{\langle l_s, l_c \rangle, \langle l_s, l_c \rangle\}$. A recursion on the base case L_6 yields the partial result $\rightarrow(i, \wedge(\text{IMLC}(L_5), l), f)$. Next, IMLC recurses on L_5; Figs. 6e and f show its graphs. As the directly-follows graph shows interconnected activities m and x that are not concurrent according to the concurrency graph, IMLC selects $(⇸, \{m\}, \{x\})$. Log L_5 is split into $L_7 = \{\langle m_s, m_c, x_s, x_c \rangle\}$ and $L_8 = \{x_s, x_c, m_s, m_c\}$. The partial result becomes $\rightarrow(i, \wedge(⇸(\text{IMLC}(L_7), \text{IMLC}(L_8)), l), f)$. As IMLC recurses on L_7, using the directly-follows graph of Fig. 6g, the cut $(\rightarrow, \{m\}, \{x\})$ is selected, and by log splitting, two recursions and two base cases, the intermediate result becomes $\rightarrow(i, \wedge(⇸(\rightarrow(m, x), \text{IMLC}(L_8)), l), f)$. A similar recursion on L_8 yields the result $\rightarrow(i, \wedge(⇸(\rightarrow(m, x), \rightarrow(x, m)), l), f)$. Finally, the post-processing step transforms this result into $\rightarrow(i, \wedge(↔(m, x), l), f)$, which corresponds to Fig. 1a.

5.5   Implementation

IMLC and the pre-processing step described in Sect. 3 are available as plug-ins of the ProM framework [7]. To guarantee compatibility with existing plug-ins, IMLC returns models being collapsed trees, i.e. the leaves are activities (for instance $\wedge(a,b)$). A separate plug-in ("expand collapsed process tree") is available to expand these trees according to Definition 2.

6   Discussion

In this section, we first study some guarantees offered by IMLC and illustrate some results using real-life data. Second, we discuss the theoretical limits of any process discovery algorithm that uses the abstraction of Sect. 4.

6.1   Guarantees

As IMLC uses process trees, any model returned by it is guaranteed to be sound. Furthermore, by the collapsed/expanding concept, all traces that such a model can produce are consistent.

Fitness and termination are guaranteed by the Inductive Miner framework for consistent traces: Theorem 3 of [12] holds because Definition 1 of [12] holds: case distinction on the patterns of Fig. 3 ensures that we add an $\leftrightarrow$ node in the model as a short-hand for the $\leftrightarrow(\rightarrow(\ldots),\rightarrow(\ldots))$ construct (which enumerates all interleaved sequences) only when partitioning the log into several sublogs based on the start activity (preserves fitness to each interleaving); each sublog is strictly smaller (termination).

Rediscoverability, i.e. whether IMLC is able to rediscover the language of a system underlying the event log, is still guaranteed for systems consisting of $\times$, $\rightarrow$, $\wedge$

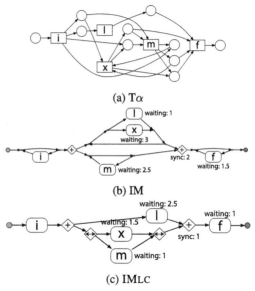

(a) Tα

(b) IM

(c) IMLC

Fig. 7. Results on PN of Fig. 1a.

and $\circlearrowleft$. Under which assumptions rediscoverability holds for $\leftrightarrow$ requires further research.

6.2   Illustrative Results

We applied IMLC, IM, and Tα to the event log of Fig. 1a and Sect. 5.4, enriched with time stamps: $L_1 = \{\langle i_s^1, i_c^2, m_s^3, m_c^4, x_s^5, l_c^6, x_c^7, l_c^8, f_s^9, f_c^{10}\rangle, \langle i_s^2, i_c^3, l_s^4, x_s^5, x_c^6, m_s^7, l_c^8, m_c^9, f_s^{10}, f_c^{11}\rangle\}$; Fig. 7 shows the results. IM misses the concurrency relation between m and l and does restrict the number of times each activity

214   S.J.J. Leemans et al.

can be executed. The model produced by Tα can only fire i (it is not sound), so no performance measure can be computed.

For the two other models, we measured waiting and synchronisation time by first removing the deviations using an alignment [3], after which we obtained average synchronisation and waiting times by considering the last completed non-concurrent activity instance, as described in [21]. Even on such a small log, the measured waiting and synchronisation times differ wildly, illustrating the need for reliable performance measures. In case x and m are indeed interleaved instead of concurrent, we argue that the measured times on the model returned by IMLC are correct.

As a second experiment, we created a secondary algorithm that applies infrequent-behaviour filtering, similar to IMi [11]. This algorithm, *Inductive Miner - infrequent & life cycle* (IMilc) was applied to the BPI challenge log of 2012 [6], filtered to contain a subset of activities (starting with A and W), and only the cases denoted as 'successful' in the log. This event log describes a mortgage application process in a Dutch financial institution. Figure 8 shows an exerpt of the results obtained by IMilc and IMi, enriched with average waiting and sojourn times. The model obtained by applying tα is unsound and therefore, performance could not be computed. Waiting time can be computed deterministically only for *W_completeren aanvraag*, as that is the only activity in the event log having start events. In the model by IMi, *W_Completeren aanvraag* has a waiting time of 16 and a sojourn time of 13. This is inconsistent, as sojourn time = waiting time + service time. Manual inspection reveals that this activity overlaps with the A activities in this excerpt, which is correctly captured by concurrency. IMi (Fig. 8a) did not detect the concurrency, and therefore some sojourn times are measured with respect to completion events of different activities, making the results unreliable.

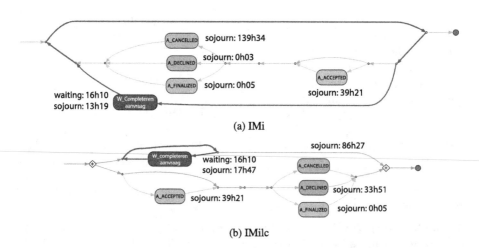

Fig. 8. Excerpts of models obtained from BPIC12.

6.3 Limitations of Collapsed Models

The idea of collapsed tasks implies some representational bias on several process formalisms; we identified three main restrictions. First, as the start and complete transitions acts as a transactional envelope for an activity, no restrictions can be posed on start and completion transitions themselves. For instance, take the partial workflow net

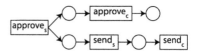

Fig. 9. A partial workflow net in which *approve_s* happens before *send*.

shown in Fig. 9, in which *approve_s* must happen before *send* starts. This restriction is not expressible in collapsed process models, as it inherently involves targeting the 'hidden' start in a collapsed activity, regardless of the formalism used.

Second, unbounded concurrency cannot be expressed in most formalisms. Consider the infinite set of traces $\mathcal{L} = \{\langle a_s, a_s, \ldots a_c, a_c \rangle\}$, i.e. a can be parallel with itself arbitrarily often. The YAWL [10] language supports unbounded concurrency by means of 'multiple-instance activities'. However, correctly handling multi-instance activities requires an emptiness test [13] which is expressible in neither process trees nor regular Petri nets. This restriction also implies that a flower model that produces only consistent traces cannot exist.

Third, the language of any collapsed process model can obviously only contain consistent traces (Definition 2). Even though, as shown in Sect. 3, inconsistent traces show inherent ambiguity, input traces might be inconsistent and therefore, traditional perfect fitness might be unachievable. e.g. there is no collapsed process model to represent $\langle a_s, a_s \rangle$. We argue that fitness measures should be robust against such ambiguities, but adapting measures is outside the scope of this paper.

6.4 Related Work

Several process discovery techniques take transactional data into account, e.g. [4,9,17,20]: transactional data is used to aid in directly-follows relation construction. For instance, transactional data enables explicit concurrency detection in low information settings [20]. IMLC uses a similar idea, but slightly differs in details, e.g. in IMLC, two activity instances can be both directly-following as well as concurrent. However, none of the other approaches distinguishes concurrency and interleaving, and most [4,9,20] do not guarantee to return sound models. Unsound models, as shown in Sect. 6.2, cannot be used to measure performance in some cases.

Of the mentioned approaches, only PM [17] guarantees to return sound models: it constructs structured models similar to process trees based on the directly-follows relation over transactional data. However, the particular approach does not generalise the behaviour of the log [17], is not robust to noise [5], and does not distinguish concurrency and interleaving.

7   Conclusion

We investigated an aspect of measuring business process performance by discovering process models with performance information from event logs with transactional data, i.e., start and complete events that are recorded for each activity instance. We have shown that performance information depends on whether activities have been executed truly concurrently or interleaved. All existing process discovery algorithms assume no difference between concurrency and interleaving and thus may yield inaccurate performance results.

We presented a first process discovery technique that can distinguish concurrency and interleaving in the presence of transactional data, i.e. start and completion events, using the Inductive Miner [12] framework. The algorithm guarantees soundness and fitness; a first evaluation showed that it can return more accurate performance information than the state of the art.

An open question remaining is under which assumptions rediscoverability holds for IMlc, and how discovery can benefit from other life cycle transitions, e.g. assign, reassign, schedule, suspend etc. For instance, an *enqueue* event [18] might reveal when queueing commenced and hence provide even more information about dependencies with other activities. Another point of future research is how expanding and collapsing influences the existing model/log evaluation criteria fitness, precision and generalisation.

References

1. van der Aalst, W.M.P., van Hee, K.M., ter Hofstede, A.H.M., Sidorova, N., Verbeek, H.M.W., Voorhoeve, M., Wynn, M.T.: Soundness of workflow nets: classification, decidability, and analysis. Formal Asp. Comput. **23**(3), 333–363 (2011)
2. van der Aalst, W., Weijters, A., Maruster, L.: Workflow mining: discovering process models from event logs. IEEE Trans. Knowl. Data Eng. **16**(9), 1128–1142 (2004)
3. Adriansyah, A.: Aligning Observed and Modeled Behavior. Ph.D. thesis, Eindhoven University of Technology (2014)
4. Burattin, A., Sperduti, A.: Heuristics miner for time intervals. In: ESANN (2010)
5. De Weerdt, J., De Backer, M., Vanthienen, J., Baesens, B.: A multi-dimensional quality assessment of state-of-the-art process discovery algorithms using real-life event logs. Inf. Syst. **37**, 654–676 (2012)
6. van Dongen, B.: BPI Challenge 2012 Dataset (2012). http://dx.org/10.4121/uuid: 3926db30-f712-4394-aebc-75976070e91f
7. van Dongen, B.F., de Medeiros, A.K.A., Verbeek, H.M.W., Weijters, A.J.M.M., van der Aalst, W.M.P.: The ProM framework: a new era in process mining tool support. In: Ciardo, G., Darondeau, P. (eds.) ICATPN 2005. LNCS, vol. 3536, pp. 444–454. Springer, Heidelberg (2005)
8. Günther, C., Verbeek, H.: XES v2.0 (2014). http://www.xes-standard.org/
9. Günther, C., Rozinat, A.: Disco: discover your processes. In: CEUR Workshop Proceedings, vol. 940, pp. 40–44. CEUR-WS.org (2012)
10. ter Hofstede, A.H.M., van der Aalst, W.M.P., Adams, M., Russell, N.: Modern Business Process Automation - YAWL and its Support Environment. Springer, Heidelberg (2010)

11. Leemans, S.J.J., Fahland, D., van der Aalst, W.M.P.: Discovering block-structured process models from event logs containing infrequent behaviour. In: Lohmann, N., Song, M., Wohed, P. (eds.) BPM 2013 Workshops. LNBIP, vol. 171, pp. 66–78. Springer, Heidelberg (2014)

12. Leemans, S.J.J., Fahland, D., van der Aalst, W.M.P.: Discovering block-structured process models from event logs - a constructive approach. In: Colom, J.-M., Desel, J. (eds.) PETRI NETS 2013. LNCS, vol. 7927, pp. 311–329. Springer, Heidelberg (2013)

13. Linz, P.: An Introduction to Formal Languages and Automata. Jones & Bartlett Learning, Burlington (2011)

14. Redlich, D., Molka, T., Gilani, W., Blair, G., Rashid, A.: Constructs competition miner: process control-flow discovery of BP-domain constructs. In: Sadiq, S., Soffer, P., Völzer, H. (eds.) BPM 2014. LNCS, vol. 8659, pp. 134–150. Springer, Heidelberg (2014)

15. Redlich, D., Molka, T., Gilani, W., Blair, G.S., Rashid, A.: Scalable dynamic business process discovery with the constructs competition miner. In: CEUR-WP, vol. 1293, 91–107 (2014)

16. Schimm, G.: Process miner - a tool for mining process schemes from event-based data. In: Flesca, S., Greco, S., Leone, N., Ianni, G. (eds.) JELIA 2002. LNCS (LNAI), vol. 2424, pp. 525–528. Springer, Heidelberg (2002)

17. Schimm, G.: Mining exact models of concurrent workflows. Comput. Ind. **53**(3), 265–281 (2004)

18. Senderovich, A., Leemans, S., Harel, S., Gal, A., Mandelbaum, A., van der Aalst, W.: Discovering queues from event logs with varying levels of information. BPI (2015, accepted)

19. Solé, M., Carmona, J.: Process mining from a basis of state regions. In: Lilius, J., Penczek, W. (eds.) PETRI NETS 2010. LNCS, vol. 6128, pp. 226–245. Springer, Heidelberg (2010)

20. Wen, L., Wang, J., van der Aalst, W., Huang, B., Sun, J.: A novel approach for process mining based on event types. JIIS **32**(2), 163–190 (2009)

21. Wolffensperger, R.: Static and Dynamic Visualization of Quality and Performance Dimensions on Process Trees. Master's thesis, Eindhoven University of Technology (2015)

Complex Symbolic Sequence Clustering and Multiple Classifiers for Predictive Process Monitoring

Ilya Verenich[1,2]([✉]), Marlon Dumas[2], Marcello La Rosa[1],
Fabrizio Maria Maggi[2], and Chiara Di Francescomarino[3]

[1] Information Systems School, Queensland University of Technology,
Brisbane, Australia
{ilya.verenich,m.larosa}@qut.edu.au
[2] Institute of Computer Science, University of Tartu, Tartu, Estonia
{marlon.dumas,f.m.maggi}@ut.ee
[3] FBK-IRST, Trento, Italy
dfmchiara@fbk.eu

Abstract. This paper addresses the following predictive business process monitoring problem: Given the execution trace of an ongoing case, and given a set of traces of historical (completed) cases, predict the most likely outcome of the ongoing case. In this context, a trace refers to a sequence of events with corresponding payloads, where a payload consists of a set of attribute-value pairs. Meanwhile, an outcome refers to a label associated to completed cases, like, for example, a label indicating that a given case completed "on time" (with respect to a given desired duration) or "late", or a label indicating that a given case led to a customer complaint or not. The paper tackles this problem via a two-phased approach. In the first phase, prefixes of historical cases are encoded using complex symbolic sequences and clustered. In the second phase, a classifier is built for each of the clusters. To predict the outcome of an ongoing case at runtime given its (uncompleted) trace, we select the closest cluster(s) to the trace in question and apply the respective classifier(s), taking into account the Euclidean distance of the trace from the center of the clusters. We consider two families of clustering algorithms – hierarchical clustering and k-medoids – and use random forests for classification. The approach was evaluated on four real-life datasets.

Keywords: Process mining · Predictive process monitoring · Complex symbolic sequence · Clustering · Ensemble methods

1 Introduction

Modern business processes are supported by information systems that record data about each individual execution of a process, also referred to as a case. These data can be structured in the form of event logs consisting of traces, each

© Springer International Publishing Switzerland 2016
M. Reichert and H.A. Reijers (Eds.): BPM Workshops 2015, LNBIP 256, pp. 218–229, 2016.
DOI: 10.1007/978-3-319-42887-1_18

capturing the events produced in the context of one case. Such event logs can be used for various business process analytics tasks [21].

Predictive process monitoring [14] is concerned with exploiting such event logs to predict how running (uncompleted) cases will unfold up to their completion. One particular type of predictive process monitoring is that of estimating the probability that an ongoing case will lead to a certain outcome among a set of possible outcomes. In this context, an outcome could be, for example, the timely completion of the case with respect to a deadline (versus late completion), or the fulfillment of a desired business goal (e.g., a sales process leading to an order, or an issue handling process leading to successful resolution).

Given that event logs consist of sequences of event records (each possibly associated to a corresponding payload), the above predictive monitoring problem can be seen as the one of early sequence classification [27], that is a problem of assigning a "label" (outcome) to a sequence based on: (i) a prefix thereof; and (ii) a set of labeled completed sequences (the "history"). A direct approach to this problem is to extract features from prefixes of historical sequences and use them to train a classifier. This classifier is then used at runtime in order to assign a label to the incomplete trace of an ongoing case.

This paper investigates an alternative cluster-and-classify approach to this predictive monitoring problem. The proposed approach proceeds in two phases. First, prefixes of previous traces are clustered. Secondly, a classifier is built for each cluster to discriminate between different outcomes (e.g., "normal" versus "deviant" cases). At runtime, a prediction is made on a running case by mapping it to one or multiple clusters and applying the corresponding classifier(s).

The paper explores multiple variants of the proposed approach based on two clustering techniques (k-medoids and hierarchical) as well as a single-classifier approach versus a multiple-classifier (ensemble) approach. These variants are experimentally compared using as baseline a plain classication-only approach.

The paper is organized as follows. In Sect. 2, we provide a brief survey of previous work on the predictive process monitoring. Section 3 presents the proposed method for predictive process monitoring. The validation is discussed in Sect. 4. Finally, Sect. 5 draws conclusions and outlines possible future work.

2   Background and Related Work

This section provides a review of existing predictive business process monitoring approaches. Most of these approaches are based on sequence classification methods.

Many previous works deal with the problem of identifying and eliminating process-related risks. For example, Pika et al. [17] make predictions about time-related process risks, by identifying and exploiting indicators observable in event logs that affect the likelihood of violating specified deadlines. Conforti et al. [3] propose a technique to reduce possible process risks by supporting the process participants in making risk-informed decisions. Risks are predicted by traversing decision trees generated from the logs of past process executions. Suriadi et al. [20] present an approach for Root Cause Analysis through classification algorithms. Decision trees are used to retrieve the causes of overtime faults on a log enriched with information about delays, resources and workload. Metzger et al. [15] present a technique for predicting "late show" events in transportation processes. Specifically, they apply standard statistical techniques to find correlations between "late show" events and external variables related to weather conditions or road traffic. Grigori et al. [8] present an approach and a tool suite for real-time exception analysis, prediction, and prevention.

Another group of works deals with the time perspective. In [25], van Dongen et al. develop an approach for predicting the remaining cycle time of a case by using non-parametric regression with case-related data as predictor variables. In [22,23], van der Aalst et al. present a set of approaches in which annotated transition systems, containing time information extracted from event logs, are used to check time conformance while cases are being executed, predict the remaining processing time of incomplete cases, and recommend appropriate activities to end users working on these cases. Rogge-Solti and Weske [18] use stochastic Petri nets to predict the remaining execution time of a process, taking into account the time passed since the last observed process event. Folino et al. [6] develop a predictive clustering approach, where various context-related execution scenarios are discovered and modeled via distinct state-aware performance predictors. A predictive model is obtained eventually that can make performance forecasts for any new running test case.

Zeng et al. [29] adopt the ARIMA forecasting method to predict performance criteria for event sequences. The approach is applied for aggregated key performance indicators (KPI) rather than single instances. Then classification is applied to separate cases that meet KPIs from those that violate them. Kang et al. [9] propose an approach for predicting abnormal termination of business processes. They apply a fault detection technique based on k-nearest neighbor algorithm to estimate the probability that a fault occurs. Alarms are generated for an early notification of probable abnormal terminations. Lakshmanan et al. [11] develop a technique to estimate the probability of execution of any potential future task in an ongoing process instance using extended Markov chain. Xing et al. [26] mine a set of sequential classification rules as a classifier. An evaluation was conducted based on simple DNA sequence datasets and the method was demonstrated to be very accurate. Greco et al. [7] approach the issue of classifying a process instance using frequent itemset detection.

Closely related to predictive monitoring is deviance mining [5]. While predictive monitoring deals with predicting the impact of actions and decisions of process participants on the outcomes of ongoing process executions, deviance mining deals with the offline analysis of process execution logs in order to detect common abnormal executions and to explain deviance that leads to increased or decreased performance [19]. Together, these two techniques provide evidence-based management of business processes, which enables process participants to receive guidance to achieve required process outcomes and performance [5].

Most of the above mentioned works rely either on the control-flow or on the data perspective for making predictions at runtime, but they do not take both perspectives into consideration. The two perspectives have been considered together only by Maggi et al. [14], where a framework was proposed to predict whether or not an ongoing case will fulfill a given predicate upon its completion based on: (i) the sequence of activities executed in a given case; and (ii) the values of data attributes after each execution of an activity in a case. This framework has been shown to be relatively accurate, but at the expense of high runtime overhead, since the classifiers used by the model are constructed at runtime. Thus this framework is not applicable in settings with high throughput or when instantaneous response times are required to help users make rapid decisions.

In order to overcome this problem, the framework has been extended in [4] by introducing a clustering pre-processing phase which allows for the pre-computation of the classification models. This allows for a drastic reduction of the prediction time and for facing high throughput loads. Nevertheless, a limitation of this approach is that only the payload of the last executed event is taken into account, while neglecting the evolution of data values throughout the execution traces. In [13], this limitation is addressed by treating execution traces as complex symbolic sequences and processing them as such. Our research extends the approach presented in [4] through the use of a multiple classifier method and the combination of the clustered-based approach with the approach based on complex symbolic sequences introduced in [13].

3   Approach

We propose a two-phased approach for predictive process monitoring. In the first phase, from a log of historical (i.e., completed) cases, we extract prefixes of a fixed length n and encode them using complex symbolic sequences. In particular, we use the index-based encoding presented in [13]. Thus, we obtain feature vectors that can be clustered. In the second phase, we use the sequences contained in each cluster to train a classifier. In this work, we apply random forest. Random forest is a powerful classifier that has been already applied for similar problems [16,24]. To predict the outcome of an ongoing case at runtime given its (uncompleted) trace, we select the closest cluster(s) to the trace in question (taking into account the Euclidean distance of the trace from the center of the clusters) and apply the respective classifier(s).

3.1   Sequence Encoding

In the proposed approach, an execution trace is treated as a complex symbolic sequence, i.e., a sequence of events each carrying a data payload consisting of event attributes. In order to apply the clustering approach, trace prefixes need to be encoded in terms of a feature vector. Complex sequences can be encoded as feature vectors in several ways. In this paper, we use an encoding based on indexes as proposed by Leontjeva et al. in [13], which has been shown to yield a relatively high accuracy. In particular, index-based encoding specifies for each position in a trace, the event occurring in that position and the value of each data attribute in that position.

3.2   Clustering

Clustering is a type of unsupervised learning technique in which a structure has to be devised on top of unlabeled data. The main idea behind clustering is organizing a dataset into groups (clusters), so that elements within a cluster are more similar to each other than elements belonging to different clusters. Many clustering algorithms have been proposed in the literature, as well as a number of possible dimensions for their classification. In this work, we apply two clustering approaches – hierarchical clustering and k-medoids.

Hierarchical Agglomerative Clustering. Hierarchical agglomerative clustering (HAC) belongs to a family of clustering algorithms that measure the distance between clusters based on the distances between pairs of elements (e.g., maximum or minimum distance between two elements of the clusters) [28]. In particular, hierarchical agglomerative clustering groups data elements into a tree of clusters (dendrogram), building it in a bottom-up fashion. It starts by placing each individual data element in its own cluster and then merges these atomic clusters into larger clusters. This process continues until all data elements are gathered in a single cluster or certain termination conditions are satisfied.

In hierarchical clustering, clusters are defined as branches of a cluster tree. The constant height branch cut, a commonly used method to identify branches of a cluster tree, is not ideal for cluster identification in complicated dendrograms. In this work, we use *adaptive* hierarchical clustering as defined by Langfeldera et al. [12]. They describe a new dynamic branch cutting approach for detecting clusters in a cluster tree based on their shape.

K-Medoids Clustering. In k-medoids clustering (KM), clusters are represented by the so-called medoid element and, hence, the distance between clusters is based on the distance between their medoid elements. The k-medoids algorithm selects first k data elements, which become the medoids elements. The algorithm then assigns each of the remaining data elements to the clusters, based on the distance between the element and the cluster medoid. Then, a new medoid for each cluster is computed. This process iterates until convergence has been reached. The k-medoids algorithm is closely related to the k-means algorithm.

3.3   Classification

Random Forest. The random forest is an ensemble classifier that consists of a large number of randomly trained decision trees. To classify a case, each tree outputs its prediction, or "vote", and the final decision is determined by majority voting [1].

The performance of the random forest is linked to the level of correlation between any two trees in the forest. The lower the correlation is, the higher the overall performance of the entire forest is [2].

Multiple Classifier Method. For classifying an ongoing case at runtime, generally, we select the closest cluster, run the classifier that has been trained for that cluster and output the probability of a case belonging to class "normal" or class "deviant". The closest cluster is chosen based on the smallest distance of the point representing the case from each center. However, it is often the case that the point is almost equally distant from two or more centers. To accommodate this situation, we take the output of each classifier with a weight that is inversely proportional to the distance from the point to the center of the cluster. For example, if we have two clusters, and a point is equally distant from the center of each cluster, then, we take the output of each classifier with weight 0.5.

4   Evaluation

4.1   Setup and Datasets

We conducted the experiments on four real-life datasets. Table 1 summarizes the characteristics of the logs (number of normal and deviant cases, average case length, total number of events, and total number of event classes).

Table 1. Case study datasets.

Dataset	Normal cases	Deviant cases	Total cases	Median trace length	Num of events	Event classes
$BPIC_{\varphi_1}$	743	172	915	44	120,036	623
$BPIC_{\varphi_2}$	232	683	915	44	120,036	623
Hospital	448	363	811	18	14,825	26
Insurance	788	277	1065	12	16,869	9

The first dataset (BPI) is taken from the BPI 2011 challenge and contains events related to treatment and diagnosis steps for patients diagnosed with cancer in a Dutch Academic Hospital. Specifically, each case refers to the treatment of a particular patient. The event log contains domain specific attributes that are both case attributes and event attributes. For example, *Age*, *Diagnosis*, *Diagnosis code*, and *Treatment code* are case attributes, whereas *Activity code*, *Number of executions*, *Specialism code*, and *Group* are event attributes. From this log, we define a deviance as a violation of a compliance rule. In particular, we use the following linear temporal logic rules [14]:

- $\varphi_1 = \mathbf{G}(\text{"}CEA-tumor\ marker\ using\ meia\text{"} \to \mathbf{F}(\text{"}squamous\ cell\ carcinoma\ using\ eia\text{"}))$
- $\varphi_2 = \mathbf{F}(\text{"}historical\ examination - big\ resectiep\text{"})$

where $\mathbf{F}\varphi$ indicates that φ is true sometimes in the future and $\mathbf{G}\varphi$ means that φ is true always in the future. The rule φ_1 states, hence, that every time "CEA-tumor marker using meia" occurs, then "squamous cell carcinoma using eia" has to occur eventually, while rule φ_2 states that "historical examination - big resectiep" has to occur eventually at least once.

The second log we used (Hospital) refers to the treatment of patients with chest pain in an emergency department of an Australian hospital. To classify the cases in this log, we used a temporal deviance criterion. In particular, we labeled as quick those cases that complete within 180 min and as slow those cases that need more than 180 min to complete. We considered the slow cases as deviant. With this definition, the dataset is nearly balanced w.r.t. the class labels – 448 normal cases and 363 deviant cases (Table 1).

The third log (Insurance) is taken from a large Australian insurance company and records an extract of the instances of a commercial insurance claim handling process. In this log, we also used a temporal deviance criterion for classification, marking cases quick if they complete within 30 days, and slow, i.e., deviant otherwise.

It should be noted that cases in the datasets have very different lengths and the values in Table 1 only indicate the median length. Moreover, normal and deviant cases typically have different lengths. Figure 1 shows the distribution of lengths of normal and deviant cases in each dataset.

4.2   Evaluation Metrics

Most classifiers are capable of outputting not only class labels, but also class probabilities, i.e., probabilities that a data sample belongs to a particular class. In this case, predictive ranking ability can be measured with the *receiver operating characteristic* (ROC) curve. A ROC curve represents *ranked* accuracy. The horizontal axis is the proportion of false positives (FPR), that is negative cases that were incorrectly identified as positives, and the vertical one is the corresponding proportion of true positives (TPR), that is actual positive cases that were correctly identified [10]. For a well-performing classifier this curve would be as closer to the top left corner as possible, thus minimizing FPR, and maximizing TPR. For a random guessing this curve would be diagonal.

The area under a ROC curve (AUC) represents the probability that the binary classifier will score a randomly drawn positive sample higher than a randomly drawn negative sample [10]. A value of AUC equal to 1 indicates a perfect ranking, where any positive sample is ranked higher than any negative sample. A value of AUC equal to 0.5 indicates the worst possible classifier that is not better than random guessing. Finally, a value of AUC equal to 0 indicates a reserved perfect classifier, where all positive samples get the lowest ranks.

4.3   Results

We evaluated 5 different variants obtained by applying the only random forest classification (No clustering) or by combining clustering techniques (*KM* and *HAC*) with classification techniques (single and multiple classifiers).

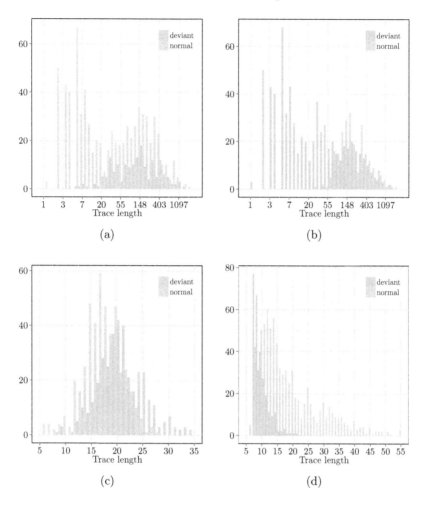

Fig. 1. Distribution of case lengths for the $BPIC_{\varphi_1}$ (a), $BPIC_{\varphi_2}$ (b), *hospital* (c) and *insurance* (d) datasets. (Color figure online)

We split each log into training set (80 %) and test set (20 %). To classify an ongoing case of length n, we select the set of pre-built (offline) clusters containing prefixes of length n.[1] Then, we determine cluster that is the closest to the ongoing case. Through the associated classifier, we estimate the probability for the case to end up normally. Considering that in the logs we have full information about the completion of cases also in the test set, we can compare predicted and actual labels and calculate AUC. Figure 2 shows the average AUC for various prefix lengths, i.e., n varying from 2 to 20. Additionally, Table 2 reports the average AUC values across various prefix lengths.

---

[1] except for the "No clustering" approach.

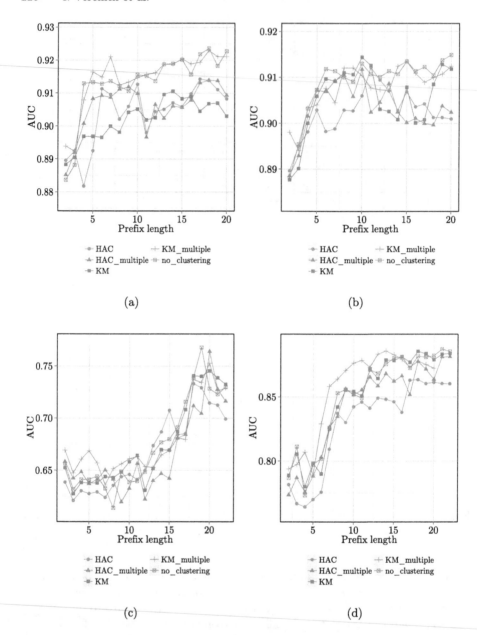

Fig. 2. Mean AUC values using prefixes of different lengths for the $BPIC_{\varphi_1}$ (a), $BPIC_{\varphi_2}$ (b), *hospital* (c) and *insurance* (d) datasets. (Color figure online)

Looking at the plots and at the table, we can notice that the multiple-classifiers k-medoids approach outperforms by a small margin other methods, including random forest without clustering which corresponds to the approach

Table 2. Mean AUC values across various prefix sizes. Best method for each dataset is highlighted.

Method	Prefix sizes 2 to 5				Prefix sizes 2 to 20			
	$BPIC_{\varphi_1}$	$BPIC_{\varphi_2}$	Hospital	Insurance	$BPIC_{\varphi_1}$	$BPIC_{\varphi_2}$	Hospital	Insurance
No clustering	0.899	0.898	0.643	0.792	0.913	**0.908**	0.674	0.847
KM	0.893	0.896	0.639	0.793	0.902	0.905	0.675	0.847
KM, multiple cl.	**0.903**	**0.900**	**0.662**	**0.797**	**0.915**	**0.908**	**0.679**	**0.856**
HAC	0.889	0.896	0.629	0.771	0.904	0.902	0.667	0.826
HAC, multiple cl.	0.897	0.898	0.647	0.781	0.906	0.903	0.665	0.839

implemented in [13]. Interestingly, for smaller prefix sizes ($2 < n < 10$) its advantage is more evident, but with the increase of n it becomes much less visible.

On the other hand, almost all methods were able to achieve AUC > 0.9 on the *BPIC* datasets with prefix sizes $n \geq 5$, which is about the 10 % of the median case length. For the *Insurance* dataset, we achieved AUC > 0.8 for $n \geq 7$, which is about half of the median case length. The result for the *Hospital* dataset was lower (average AUC never exceeded 0.68), probably due to the fact that this dataset includes mostly *case* attributes that do not change over a case, rather than *event* attributes.

For real-time prediction, it is also important to be able to output the results as fast as possible. Thus, we also measured the time needed to classify test cases. The experiments were conducted using GNU R version 3.2.0 on a computer with a 2.4 GHz Intel Core i5 quad core processor and 8 Gb of RAM. We found that the average time needed to classify a test case using random forest without clustering is around 0.2 milliseconds for the maximum prefix size $n = 20$. For clustering with multiple classifiers, the prediction time ranges from 20 to 50 milliseconds per case. Therefore, we can conclude that the proposed approach allows for low run-time overhead predictions. Additionally, the time needed to cluster training cases and build offline classifiers for each cluster never exceeds 60 seconds for $n = 20$.

5 Conclusion

The paper has presented a cluster-and-classify approach to address the problem of predicting the outcome of individual cases of a business process. We have explored the design space by considering two clustering techniques (*HAC* and *KM*) and by considering the case where an ongoing case is matched against one single classifier (associated to one cluster) or against multiple classifiers (associated to multiple clusters). The evaluation on real-life datasets has shown that the multiple-classifiers k-medoids variant outperforms others (including a pure classification-based approach) in the context of early prediction, i.e., predictions based on short prefixes of a case.

The presented work has several limitations. First, the observations are based on a rather reduced number of datasets, representing two application domains (hospital healthcare and insurance). A broader evaluation is warranted to back the initial observations. Second, the advantages of the cluster-and-classify approach relative to a pure classification approach, while consistent, are relatively minor. Designing further optimizations of the proposed methods to achieve higher accuracy is a direction for future work. Finally, deeper comparison with alternative methods such as methods based on generative models, e.g., Hidden Markov Models (HMMs) or Conditional Random Fields, could be considered. A systematic comparative evaluation covering this latter technique, the proposed cluster-and-classify method, and other alternative methods is another avenue for future work.

References

1. Breiman, L., Friedman, J., Olshen, R., Stone, C.: Classification and Regression Trees. Wadsworth and Brooks, Monterey, CA (1984)
2. Breiman, L.: Random forests. Mach. Learn. **45**, 5–32 (2001)
3. Conforti, R., de Leoni, M., La Rosa, M., van der Aalst, W.M.P., ter Hofstede, A.H.M.: A recommendation system for predicting risks across multiple business process instances. Decis. Support Syst. **69**, 1–19 (2015)
4. Francescomarino, C.D., Dumas, M., Maggi, F.M., Teinemaa, I.: Clustering-Based Predictive Process Monitoring. ArXiv e-prints, June 2015
5. Dumas, M., Maggi, F.M.: Enabling process innovation via deviance mining and predictive monitoring. In: vom Brocke, J., Schmiedel, T. (eds.) BPM - Driving Innovation in a Digital World. Management for Professionals, pp. 145–154. Springer, Heidelberg (2015)
6. Folino, F., Guarascio, M., Pontieri, L.: Discovering context-aware models for predicting business process performances. In: Meersman, R., et al. (eds.) OTM 2012, Part I. LNCS, vol. 7565, pp. 287–304. Springer, Heidelberg (2012)
7. Greco, G., Guzzo, A., Manco, G., Sacca, D.: Mining unconnected patterns in workflows. Inf. Syst. **32**(5), 685–712 (2007)
8. Grigori, D., Casati, F., Dayal, U., Shan, M.-C.: Improving business process quality through exception understanding, prediction, and prevention. In: Proceedings of the 27th International Conference on Very Large Data Bases, VLDB 2001, pp. 159–168. San Francisco, CA, USA (2001). Morgan Kaufmann Publishers Inc
9. Kang, B., Kim, D., Kang, S.-H.: Real-time business process monitoring method for prediction of abnormal termination using knni-based lof prediction. Expert Syst. Appl. **39**(5), 6061–6068 (2012)
10. Kononenko, I., Kukar, M.: Machine Learning and Data Mining. Elsevier Science, New York (2007)
11. Lakshmanan, G.T., Shamsi, D., Doganata, Y.N., Unuvar, M., Khalaf, R.: A markov prediction model for data-driven semi-structured business processes. Knowl. Inf. Syst. **42**(1), 97–126 (2015)
12. Langfeldera, P., Zhangb, B., Horvatha, S.: Dynamic tree cut: in-depth description, tests and applications, November 22, 2007
13. Leontjeva, A., Conforti, R., Francescomarino, C.D., Dumas, M., Maggi, F.M.: Complex symbolic sequence encodings for predictive monitoring of business processes. In: Motahari-Nezhad, H.R., Recker, J., Weidlich, M. (eds.) Business Process Management. LNCS, vol. 9253, pp. 297–313. Springer, Heidelberg (2015)

14. Maggi, F.M., Di Francescomarino, C., Dumas, M., Ghidini, C.: Predictive monitoring of business processes. In: Jarke, M., Mylopoulos, J., Quix, C., Rolland, C., Manolopoulos, Y., Mouratidis, H., Horkoff, J. (eds.) CAiSE 2014. LNCS, vol. 8484, pp. 457–472. Springer, Heidelberg (2014)
15. Metzger, A., Franklin, R., Engel, Y.: Predictive monitoring of heterogeneous service-oriented business networks: The transport and logistics case. In: SRII Global Conference (SRII), 2012 Annual, pp. 313–322. IEEE (2012)
16. Nguyen, H., Dumas, M., La Rosa, M., Maggi, F.M., Suriadi, S.: Mining business process deviance: a quest for accuracy. In: Meersman, R., Panetto, H., Dillon, T., Missikoff, M., Liu, L., Pastor, O., Cuzzocrea, A., Sellis, T. (eds.) OTM 2014. LNCS, vol. 8841, pp. 436–445. Springer, Heidelberg (2014)
17. Pika, A., van der Aalst, W.M.P., Fidge, C.J., ter Hofstede, A.H.M., Wynn, M.T.: Predicting deadline transgressions using event logs. In: La Rosa, M., Soffer, P. (eds.) BPM Workshops 2012. LNBIP, vol. 132, pp. 211–216. Springer, Heidelberg (2013)
18. Rogge-Solti, A., Weske, M.: Prediction of remaining service execution time using stochastic petri nets with arbitrary firing delays. In: Basu, S., Pautasso, C., Zhang, L., Fu, X. (eds.) ICSOC 2013. LNCS, vol. 8274, pp. 389–403. Springer, Heidelberg (2013)
19. Setiawan, M.A., Sadiq, S.: A methodology for improving business process performance through positive deviance. Int. J. Inf. Syst. Model. Des. (IJISMD) $4(2)$, 1–22 (2013)
20. Suriadi, S., Ouyang, C., van der Aalst, W.M.P., ter Hofstede, A.H.M.: Root cause analysis with enriched process logs. In: La Rosa, M., Soffer, P. (eds.) BPM Workshops 2012. LNBIP, vol. 132, pp. 174–186. Springer, Heidelberg (2013)
21. van der Aalst, W.M.P.: Process Mining: Discovery, Conformance and Enhancement of Business Processes. Springer, Heidelberg (2011). http://link.springer.com/book/10.1007%2F978-3-642-19345-3
22. van der Aalst, W.M.P., Pesic, M., Song, M.: Beyond process mining: from the past to present and future. In: Pernici, B. (ed.) CAiSE 2010. LNCS, vol. 6051, pp. 38–52. Springer, Heidelberg (2010)
23. Van der Aalst, W.M.P., Schonenberg, M.H., Song, M.: Time prediction based on process mining. Inf. Syst. $36(2)$, 450–475 (2011)
24. van der Spoel, S., van Keulen, M., Amrit, C.: Process prediction in noisy data sets: a case study in a dutch hospital. In: Cudre-Mauroux, P., Ceravolo, P., Gašević, D. (eds.) SIMPDA 2012. LNBIP, vol. 162, pp. 60–83. Springer, Heidelberg (2013)
25. van Dongen, B.F., Crooy, R.A., van der Aalst, W.M.P.: Cycle time prediction: when will this case finally be finished? In: Meersman, R., Tari, Z. (eds.) OTM 2008, Part I. LNCS, vol. 5331, pp. 319–336. Springer, Heidelberg (2008)
26. Xing, Z., Pei, J., Dong, G., Philip, S.Y.: Mining sequence classifiers for early prediction. In: SDM, pp. 644–655. SIAM (2008)
27. Xing, Z., Pei, J., Keogh, E.: A brief survey on sequence classification. ACM SIGKDD Explor. Newsl. $12(1)$, 40–48 (2010)
28. Xu, R., Wunsch, D.: Clustering. IEEE Press Series on Computational Intelligence. Wiley, New York (2008)
29. Zeng, L., Lingenfelder, C., Lei, H., Chang, H.: Event-driven quality of service prediction. In: Bouguettaya, A., Krueger, I., Margaria, T. (eds.) ICSOC 2008. LNCS, vol. 5364, pp. 147–161. Springer, Heidelberg (2008)

Vidushi: Parallel Implementation of Alpha Miner Algorithm and Performance Analysis on CPU and GPU Architecture

Divya Kundra[1], Prerna Juneja[1], and Ashish Sureka[2(✉)]

[1] Indraprastha Institute of Information Technology, Delhi (IIITD), New Delhi, India
[2] Software Analytics Research Lab (SARL), New Delhi, India
ashish@iiitd.ac.in
http://www.iiitd.ac.in/
http://www.software-analytics.in/

Abstract. Process Aware Information Systems (PAIS) are IT systems which support business processes and generate event-logs as a result of execution of the supported business processes. Alpha Miner is a popular algorithm within Process Mining which consists of discovering a process model from the event-logs. Discovering process models from large volumes of event-logs is a computationally intensive and a time consuming task. In this paper, we investigate the application of parallelization on Alpha Miner algorithm. We apply implicit multithreading parallelism and explicit parallelism through **parfor** on it offered by MATLAB (Matrix Laboratory) for multi-core Central Processing Unit (CPU). We measure performance gain with respect to serial implementation. Further, we use Graphics Processor Unit (GPU) to run computationally intensive parts of Alpha Miner algorithm in parallel. We achieve highest speedup on GPU reaching till $39.3\times$ from the same program run over multi-core CPU. We conduct experiments on real world and synthetic datasets.

Keywords: Alpha miner algorithm · GPU · MATLAB · Multi-core CPU · Parallel Computing Toolbox (PCT) · Parallel programming · PAIS

1 Research Motivation and Aim

Process Mining consists of analyzing event-logs generated by PAIS for the purpose of discovering run-time process models, checking conformance between design-time and run-time process maps, analyzing the process from control flow and organizational perspective for the purpose of process improvement and enhancement [1]. Performance improvement of computationally intensive Process Mining algorithms is an important issue due to the need to efficiently process the exponentially increasing amount of event-logs data generated by PAIS. Distributed and Grid computing, parallel execution on multi-core processors and

© Springer International Publishing Switzerland 2016
M. Reichert and H.A. Reijers (Eds.): BPM Workshops 2015, LNBIP 256, pp. 230–241, 2016.
DOI: 10.1007/978-3-319-42887-1_19

using hardware accelerators such as GPU are well-known solution approaches for speeding-up the performance of data mining algorithms.

Alpha Miner algorithm is one of the fundamental algorithms in Process Mining for discovering a process model (reconstructing causality and workflow between activities) from event-logs consisting of process instances or traces [2]. Our analysis of the Alpha Miner algorithm reveals that the algorithm contains independent tasks which can be split among different workers or threads and thus we believe that the algorithm has the ability or property of paralleliza-tion. The work presented in this paper is motivated by the need to reduce the execution time of Alpha Miner algorithm on multi-core CPU and GPU based hardware accelerators. The research aim of the work presented in this paper is as follows:

1. To propose a parallel approach for Alpha Miner algorithm by designing a decomposition strategy for partitioning the workload across multiple cores on CPU through implicit and explicit parallelism provided by MATLAB.
2. To perform parallelization of Alpha Miner algorithm on a GPU and examine the extent of speedup due to the hardware accelerator.
3. To investigate the efficiency and performance gain of different types of par-allelisms (implicit, explicit, GPU) on Alpha Miner algorithm by conducting a series of experiments on both real world and synthetic datasets.

2   Related Work and Research Contributions

Implementation of data mining algorithms on multi-core CPU and GPU proces-sors is an area that has attracted several researchers attention. Ahmadzadeh et al. [3] present a parallel method for implementing k-NN (k-nearest neighbor) algorithm in multi-core platform and tested their approach on five multi-core platforms demonstrating best speedup of 616×. Arour et al. [4] present two FP-growth (Frequent Pattern) implementations that takes advantage of multi-core processors and utilize new generation GPUs. Lu et al. [12] develop a method which adopts the GPU as a hardware accelerator to speed up the sequence alignment process. Ligowski et al. [11] uses CUDA programming environment on Nvidia GPUs and ATI Stream Computing environment on ATI GPUs to speed up the Smith Waterman sequence alignment algorithm. Their implemen-tation strategy achieves a 3.5× higher per core performance than the previous implementations of this algorithm on GPU [11]. In context to existing work and to the best of our knowledge, the study presented in this paper makes the following novel contributions:

1. A parallel implementation of Alpha Miner algorithm and an in-depth study (with several real and synthetic dataset) on improving the execution perfor-mance by using multi-core CPU.
2. A focused study on accelerating Alpha Miner algorithm through parallelism on GPU and testing the approach on various real and synthetic datasets.

3   Research Framework and Solution Approach

In sequential programming, there is an ordered relationship of execution of instructions where only a single instruction executes at a particular instance of time. On the contrary, parallel programming lets execution of multiple tasks at the same instance of time by distributing work to different processors which run in parallel [10]. The Alpha Miner algorithm [2] starts with finding the direct succession relation by scanning the event-logs. For activities 'x' and 'y' if activity 'y' occurs immediately after activity 'x' in log trace direct succession relation holds on 'xy'. Causal (direct succession holds on 'xy' but not on 'yx'), parallel (direct succession holds both on 'xy' and 'yx') and unrelated relations (direct succession holds neither on 'xy' nor on 'yx') are determined through direct succession relation between every two activities and stored in a footprint matrix. All pair of sets (A,B) (A and B are sets containing distinct activities) are found such that all activities within set A and B are unrelated to each other whereas every activity in set A has causal relation with every activity of set B. All activities in A are connected to arcs directed to a place (represented by circle which symbolises conditions) and from the place arcs are directed to all activities in set B. Pair of sets (A,B) that connect maximum activities through a single place are only retained as maximal set pairs. Set of initial and final activities which are detected for connecting to a initial and final place respectively along with pair of maximal sets connected through a place represent the Petri Net [7] output of Alpha Miner. The algorithm can be broken into discrete and independent tasks which can be solved concurrently. We implement parallelization on single-threaded version of Alpha Miner algorithm by 3 kinds of parallelism supported by MATLAB. For all the implementations, we encode activity names in the input event-log by unique positive integers.

3.1   Sequential Single Threading on CPU

A single-threaded program runs sequentially. Serial implementation done on a single thread provides a base for evaluating comparisons from other implementations (multi-threaded, `parfor`). To prevent the trigger of implicit multi-threading by MATLAB, we enable only a single thread in the program by using `maxNumCompThreads(1)`. We use none of the inbuilt multi-threaded functions[1] available in MATLAB for single-threaded implementation. As shown in Fig. 1(a) the main functionalities in Alpha Miner algorithm like determining all the direct succession relations by scanning the entire event- log, building the footprint matrix and determining the maximal set pairs are implemented through `for` loop. Use of `for` loops makes the program work sequentially and slower. At each iteration of `for` loop conditions are checked and branching occurs adding to more overheads and affecting the code performance.

---

[1] http://www.mathworks.com/matlabcentral/answers/95958-which-matlab-functions-benefit-from-multithreaded-computation.

```
for  i=1:traces                      parfor  i=1:traces
%Find  DirectSuccession              %Find  DirectSuccession
end                                  end


for  i=1:activities                  parfor  i=1:activities
%Build  Footprint                    %Build  Footprint
end                                  end


for  i=1:activities                  parfor  i=1:activities
%Find  Maximal  Set  Pairs           %Find  Maximal  Set  Pairs
end                                  end
```

(a) Single-threaded   (b) parfor implementation.
   implementation.

```
[m n]=size(InputFile);
ShiftedFile=InputFile(1:m,2:n);
DirectSuccession=arrayfun(@CantorPairing,InputFile,ShiftedFile);
```

(c) Multi-threaded implementation.

Fig. 1. Fragments of alpha miner algorithm implementation in MATLAB Code showing programming constructs for Multi-core CPU and GPU implementations.

3.2   Explicit Parallelism on CPU

MATLAB has Parallel Computing Toolbox (PCT)[2] for applying external parallelism over set of independent tasks. parfor[3] in PCT allows execution of the loop iterations in parallel on workers. Workers are threads that are executed on processor cores. Using parfor, a separate process is created for each worker having its own memory and CPU usage. There are communication overheads associated with setting the workers and copying the data to each of them.

When parfor is executed, the MATLAB client coordinates with the MATLAB workers which form a parallel pool. The code within the parfor loop is distributed to workers executing in parallel in the pool and the results from all the workers are collected back by the client[4]. The body of the parfor is an iteration which is executed in no particular order by the workers. Thus the loop iterations are needed to be independent of each other. If number of iterations equals the number of workers in the parallel loop, each iteration is executed by one worker else a single worker may receive multiple iterations at once to reduce the communication overhead[5]. To start a pool of workers parpool (profilename, poolsize)[6] is used where name of the parallel pool forming a cluster is to be specified in the 'profilename' and size of the cluster in the 'poolsize' argument.

---

[2] http://in.mathworks.com/products/parallel-computing/.
[3] http://in.mathworks.com/help/distcomp/parfor.html.
[4] http://cn.mathworks.com/help/pdf_doc/distcomp/distcomp.pdf.
[5] http://in.mathworks.com/help/distcomp/introduction-to-parfor.html.
[6] http://in.mathworks.com/help/distcomp/parpool.html?refresh=true.

We identify following 3 `for` loops (amongst several `for` loops within the algorithm) executing the main functionalities of the algorithm and also containing the code body that is independent at each iteration (a condition for parallel execution) enabling us to apply `parfor`:

1. **Determining direct succession relation**: The task of discovering the pair of activities having direct succession relation can be distributed to different workers with first worker calculating the direct succession relations from one trace, second worker from some other trace and so on. As shown in Fig. 1(b), first `parfor` loop distributes the total 'traces' present in input file among various workers. Results can be gathered from each worker, redundancies can be removed and unique pair of activities having direct succession between them can be deduced.

2. **Building up the footprint matrix**: The process of creating the footprint can be broken into independent work of finding all different relations (causal, paralllel, unrelated) of an activity with the rest of the activities by a worker. In second `parfor` loop of Fig. 1(b), each worker upon receiving a activity from total unique 'activities' computes all relations of the received activity with the remaining activities.

3. **Forming maximal set pairs**: The function to discover maximal set pairs can also be broken into smaller independent tasks of determining all the maximal set pairs (A,B) by a worker that can be formed by including a particular activity in set A. In third `parfor` loop of Fig. 1(b) a worker on receiving an activity from total unique 'activities', computes all the possible maximal set pairs (A,B) that can be formed by including the received activity in set A. With each worker doing the same simultaneously, we can gather the results faster and after removing redundancies we can get distinct maximal set pairs.

Through experiments we observe that both the footprint matrix building and maximal set pair generation do not consume much time (less than 1% of program's execution time) in single-threaded implementation. Whereas calculating direct succession incurs about 90% of program's execution time. The majority of the program's execution time incurred towards computing direct succession is because in most real world datasets the count of activities is less than the number of traces to be scanned for determining direct succession by several orders of magnitude. Thus, calculating direct succession is the bottleneck for the program and bringing the benefits of parallelization to it can help in attaining a good speedup.

3.3   Multithreading Parallelism on CPU

In MATLAB by default implicit multithreading[7] is provided for functions and expressions that are combinations of element wise operations. In this type of parallelism, multiple instruction streams are generated by one instance of MATLAB

---

[7] http://www.mathworks.com/matlabcentral/answers/95958-which-matlab-functions-benefit-from-multi-threaded-computation.

session that are accessed by multiple cores[8]. To achieve implicit multithreading each element wise operation should be independent of each other. Size of data should be big enough so that speedup achieved by the concurrent execution exceeds the time required for partitioning and managing different threads. To fulfil these requirements and thus implicit parallelism, vectorization[9] of independent and big tasks is essential. Vectorization is one of the most efficient ways of writing the code in MATLAB [8]. It performs operations on large matrices through a single command at once instead of performing each operations one by one inside the `for` loop. An effective way of applying vectorization is replacing `for` loops by vector operations. Code using vectorization uses optimised multi-threaded linear algebra libraries and thus generally run faster than its counterpart `for` loop [8]. The determination of the bottleneck direct succession relation can be vectorized using `arrayfun`[10]. MATLAB uses implicit multithreading using commands such as- `arrayfun`. We use `arrayfun` for performing element wise operations on input matrices. `arrayfun`(func,A1,...,An) applies the function specified in function handle 'func' to each element of equal sized input arrays. The order of execution of function on the elements is not specific, thus tasks should be independent of each other. Figure 1(c) shows the implementation of `arrayfun` in the algorithm in which the 'ShiftedFile' argument to `arrayfun` is the input event-log file ('InputFile') shifted to left by 1. Each cell of the 'ShiftedFile' contains the immediate succeeding activity of the activity present in the corresponding cell of 'InputFile'. Thus direct succession relation holds between corresponding cells of the 'InputFile' and 'ShiftedFile'. We apply Cantor pairing function[11] [5,6] in 'func' as shown in Fig. 1(c) on each two corresponding elements of the input matrices by which pair of activities having direct succession relation are uniquely encoded and stored.

3.4 Parallelism on GPU

While a CPU has a handful number of cores, GPU has a large number of cores along with dedicated high speed memory [9]. GPUs perform poor when given a piece of code that involves logical branching. They are meant for doing simple scalar arithmetic (addition, subtraction, multiplication, division) tasks by hundreds of threads running in parallel [13]. GPU can be accessed by MATLAB through Parallel Computing Toolbox[12]. We can offload discovering of direct succession relation which consumes major part in the running time of the algorithm as discussed in Sect. 3.2 to GPU. Computation of direct succession does not involve much of branching across its code, can be transformed into element wise operations and its computation time far exceeds the transfer time to and from

---

[8] http://in.mathworks.com/company/newsletters/articles/
parallel-matlab-multiple-processors-and-multiple-cores.html.
[9] http://in.mathworks.com/help/matlab/matlab_prog/vectorization.html.
[10] http://in.mathworks.com/help/matlab/ref/arrayfun.html.
[11] http://en.wikipedia.org/wiki/Pairing_function.
[12] http://in.mathworks.com/discovery/matlab-gpu.html.

GPU. GPU works with numbers (signed and unsigned integers, single-precision and double-precision floating point) only thus we convert activities across input file to distinct positive integers. We make use of `arrayfun` which is also available for GPU to do element wise operations on two large arrays. The call to `arrayfun` on GPU is massively parallelized [13]. Using `arrayfun` one call is made to parallel GPU operation that performs the entire calculation instead of making separate calls for each pair of elements. Also the data transfer overheads are incurred just once instead on each individual operation. GPU implementation is same as CPU multi-threaded implementation with the difference of one of the arguments of `arrayfun` already on GPU (with `gpuArray`) to compute direct succession on GPU. The results are brought back to CPU through `gather`.

4   Experimental Dataset

We conduct experiments on 2 real world datasets – Business Process Intelligence 2013 (BPI 2013)[13] and Business Process Intelligence 2014 (BPI 2014)[14]. BPI 2013 dataset contains logs of VINST incident and problem management system. We consider two attributes from VINST case incidents log dataset namely, Problem Number to map as Case ID and Sub-status to map as Activity. The dataset contains 13 unique activities, 7554 traces and 65533 events. BPI 2014 contains Rabobank Group ICT data. We map attribute Incident ID as the Case ID and IncidentActivity_Type as Activity in the Detail Incident Activity log. It consists of 39 unique activities, 46616 traces and 466737 events.

We create synthetic dataset due to lack of availability of very large real world data for research purposes (much larger and diverse than the BPI 2013 and BPI 2014 dataset). We first randomly define relations (causal, parallel, unrelated) between all the activities. We then use a half normal distribution with a mean and standard deviation to randomly generate the length of each trace. We create dataset A with 20 activities, standard deviation 10, mean 20 and dataset B with 50 activities, standard deviation 25, mean 50. To gain insights into the performance of parallelization strategies with different dataset sizes, each dataset is recorded for increasing trace counts. For CPU, datasets A and B are generated with trace counts 500, 2000, 8000, 32000 and 128000. Since GPUs are designed to work with large computationally intensive data [13], we generate larger dataset A and B with trace counts 10000, 50000, 250000, 1250000 and 6250000. We make our programs (MATLAB code) and synthetic data generation code publicly available[15] so that our experiments can be replicated and used for benchmarking and comparison.

5   Experimental Settings and Results

Table 1 displays the hardware and software configuration of the computer use for testing. We perform the experiments after closing the background applications

---

[13] doi:10.4121/500573e6-accc-4b0c-9576-aa5468b10cee.

[14] doi:10.4121/uuid:c3e5d162-0cfd-4bb0-bd82-af5268819c35.

[15] http://bit.ly/1LFJqyM.

that can affect the execution time of the MATLAB programs. We measure execution time using two MATLAB functions, namely `tic` which starts stopwatch timer and `toc` that displays the elapsed time. For all the implementations, we record time that includes both the computations involved and data transfers to and from workers or GPU. Implicit multithreading in MATLAB uses all the available cores accessible to MATLAB. We run the program using `parfor` after it is connected to specific number of workers, thus not recording time to start the parallel pool. Implicit multithreading in MATLAB uses threads equal to number of logical processor when hyperthreading[16] is enabled or uses threads equal to number of physical cores when there is no hyperthreading. The CPU that we use for performing experiments has hyperthreading enabled leading to access of 20 threads by MATLAB. `parfor` construct by default access only physical cores. Thus, in the experiments we access upto 10 workers. We calculate the speedup as S $=T_{old}/T_{new}$ where T_{old} is old execution time and T_{new} is the new execution time with improvement[17]. We set the speedup value to $1\times$ for implementations whose execution time is considered as T_{old}.

Table 1. Machine hardware and software configuration used for experiments

Parameter	Value
CPU	Intel (R) Xeon(R) CPU E5-2670v2 @ 2.50GHz
Physical Cores	10
Logical Cores	20
Available Memory	66 GB
Operating System	Linux, 64 bit
Graphics Card	NVIDIA Tesla K40c
GPU Cores	2880
GPU Memory	12 GB
MATLAB Version	R2014b

Figures 2 and 3 shows the speedup achieved due to `parfor` and multi-threaded parallelism on Alpha Miner algorithm over CPU with T_{old} being time taken by single-threaded implementation. In Fig. 2 speedup is shown at highest trace count 128000 for dataset A and B. As shown in Fig. 2, using 2 workers good speedup values are obtained with increase in datasize, ranging from $1.55\times$ in the smallest dataset (BPI 2013) to $6.04\times$ in the largest dataset (dataset B). We observe with 2 workers performance improves with increase in datasize. We expect the performance to double using 4 workers but it ranges from minimum value of $2.19\times$ (BPI 2013) to maximum of $8.60\times$ (dataset B). Similar effect is

---

[16] http://www.intel.in/content/www/in/en/architecture-and-technology/ hyper-threading/hyper-threading-technology.html.

[17] http://en.wikipedia.org/wiki/Speedup.

observed with further increase in workers with speedup values increasing marginally. Marginal increase in performance happens as adding more workers leads to more communication overheads eventually reducing the gains of parallelism[18]. In fact, over the largest dataset B, performance degrades with increase in number of workers. Although due to largest size, dataset B involves maximum computations, overheads of calling workers and data transfers will also be maximum in dataset B. We observe constant drop in speedup values after adding more than 4 workers on dataset B due to large communication overheads associated with workers on it.

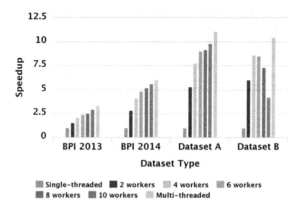

Fig. 2. Speedup gain by `parfor` and Multi-threaded Parellelism on CPU across various datasets.

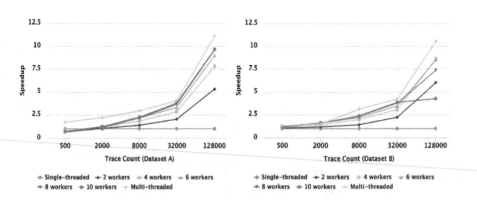

Fig. 3. Speedup gain by `parfor` and Multi-threaded Parallelism on CPU with varying dataset size.

---

[18] http://in.mathworks.com/company/newsletters/articles/
improving-optimization-performance-with-parallel-computing.html.

Communication overheads also outweighs benefits of parallelism when computations are too less i.e. while working with smaller dataset. Figure 3 reveals that speedup value comes to be less than 1× for smallest trace count (500) in dataset A for 10 workers. In Fig. 3, speedup values increases with increase in both trace count and worker within dataset A and dataset B till the time computation time outweighs communication overheads with workers. We observe that with 20 logical cores available on machine, CPU utilisation grows approximately by 10 % with each increase in two workers on the use of `parfor`. As observed from Figs. 2 and 3, highest speedup is always achieved through multi-threaded parallelism. This can be attributed to the fact that mulithreading does not incur the cost of creating separate processes for each worker. Use of shared memory by multi-cores saves the communication and data transfer costs.

We further accelerate the algorithm on GPU after optimising it on multi-core CPU. We choose the CPU multi-threaded implementation that is implemented in the same manner as the GPU implementation for making comparisons to GPU. In Figs. 4 and 5 speedup gained by GPU is calculated with T_{old} being the exeution time of multi-threaded CPU implementation. Speedup values achieved are shown in Fig. 4 which comes out to be significant in every dataset going as far as 39.3×. Figure 5 reveals that within a given dataset with increase in trace count, GPU performance improves. The penalty of overheads associated with data transfers to and from GPU decreases with increase in datasize, hence speedup value improves with increase in trace count. Based on our experimental analysis and insights, we believe that the performance will further increase with increase in trace count. At trace count 6250000 in dataset B, the size of 'InputFile' transferred on GPU exceeds the memory limit of GPU. Thus 'InputFile' is broken into two parts and direct succession computed separately for each part. Hence we infer that GPU memory limits should be taken into account while working with GPU. The line chart in Fig. 5 reveals that performance on dataset B grows relatively slower than on dataset A. Alpha Miner on dataset B

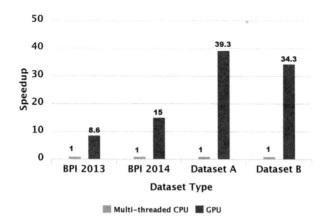

Fig. 4. Speedup gain by GPU across various datasets.

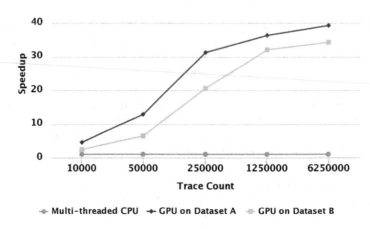

Fig. 5. Speedup gain by GPU with varying dataset size

containing larger number of activities (50) will have more of its time spend on doing activity intensive tasks like building footprint matrix, maximal set pairs generation etc. than on dataset A (20 activities). Thus on dataset A there will be larger part for doing direct succession than on dataset B. Also dataset B spends more time in transfer of data to and from GPU than dataset A due to bigger data size. Thus for every trace count point speedup on dataset B comes to be lower than on dataset A.

6   Conclusion

We conduct a series of experiments on synthetic and real world dataset which involves running computationally intensive and independent tasks of Alpha Miner algorithm in parallel on a single machine. We use MATLAB Parallel Computing Toolbox for using `parfor` to distribute computations across multiple-cores and for accessing GPU. On multi-core CPU, implicit multithreading shows higher speedup than explicit parallelism done through `parfor`. The communication overheads associated in `parfor` for creating different processes for each worker and copying data to them is significantly larger leading to reduction in parallelism benefits with addition of each worker. Alpha Miner algorithm runs with minimum execution time on GPU, showing promising speedups of as far as 39.3×.

References

1. van der Aalst, W.: Process mining: Making knowledge discovery process centric. SIGKDD Explor. Newsl. **13**(2), 45–49 (2012)
2. van der Aalst, W., Weijters, T., Maruster, L.: Workflow mining: Discovering process models from event-logs. Knowl. Data Eng. IEEE Trans. **16**(9), 1128–1142 (2004)
3. Ahmadzadeh, A., Mirzaei, R., Madani, H., Shobeiri, M., Sadeghi, M., Gavahi, M., Jafari, K., Aznaveh, M.M., Gorgin, S.: Cost-efficient implementation of k-NN algorithm on multi-core processors. In: 2014 Twelfth ACM/IEEE International Conference on Formal Methods and Models for Codesign (MEMOCODE), pp. 205–208. IEEE (2014)
4. Arour, K., Belkahla, A.: Frequent pattern-growth algorithm on multi-core CPU and GPU processors. CIT **22**(3), 159–169 (2014). http://cit.srce.unizg.hr/index.php/CIT/article/view/2361
5. Cantor, G.: Ein beitrag zur mannigfaltigkeitslehre. J. fr die reine und angewandte Mathematik **84**, 242–258 (1877). http://eudml.org/doc/148353
6. Cantor, G.: Contributions to the Founding of the Theory of Transfinite Numbers. Dover, New York (1955). http://www.archive.org/details/contributionstot003626mbp
7. Desel, J., Reisig, W., Rozenberg, G. (eds.): Lectures on Concurrency and Petri Nets, Advances in Petri Nets. LNCS, vol. 3098. Springer, Heidelberg (2003). This tutorial volume originates from the 4th Advanced Course on Petri Nets, ACPN 2003, held in Eichstätt, Germany in September 2003. In addition to lectures given at ACPN 2003, additional chapters have been commissioned
8. Higham, D.J., Higham, N.J.: MATLAB Guide. Society for Industrial and Applied Mathematics, Philadelphia, PA, USA (2005)
9. Hwu, W.M.W.: GPU Computing Gems Emerald Edition, 1st edn. Morgan Kaufmann Publishers Inc., San Francisco, CA, USA (2011)
10. Kumar, V.: Introduction to Parallel Computing, 2nd edn. Addison-Wesley Longman Publishing Co., Inc, Boston, MA, USA (2002)
11. Ligowski, L., Rudnicki, W.: An efficient implementation of Smith Waterman algorithm on GPU using CUDA, for massively parallel scanning of sequence databases. In: IEEE International Symposium on Parallel and Distributed Processing, IPDPS 2009, pp. 1–8. IEEE (2009)
12. Lu, M., Tan, Y., Bai, G., Luo, Q.: High-performance short sequence alignment with GPU Acceleration. Distrib. Parallel Databases **30**(5–6), 385–399 (2012). http://dx.doi.org/10.1007/s10619-012-7099-x
13. Suh, J.W., Kim, Y.: Accelerating MATLAB with GPU Computing: A Primer with Examples, 1st edn. Morgan Kaufmann Publishers Inc., San Francisco, CA, USA (2013)

Deducing Case IDs for Unlabeled Event Logs

Dina Bayomie$^{(\boxtimes)}$, Iman M.A. Helal$^{(\boxtimes)}$,
Ahmed Awad, Ehab Ezat, and Ali ElBastawissi

Faculty of Computers and Information, Information Systems Department,
Cairo University, Giza, Egypt
{dina.sayed,i.helal,a.gaafar,e.ezat,alibasta}@fci-cu.edu.eg

Abstract. Event logs are invaluable sources of knowledge about the *actual* execution of processes. A large number of techniques to mine, check conformance and analyze performance have been developed based on logs. All these techniques require at least case ID, activity ID and the timestamp to be in the log. If one of those is missing, these techniques cannot be applied. Real life logs are rarely originating from a centrally orchestrated process execution. Thus, *case ID* might be missing, known as *unlabeled* log. This requires a manual preprocessing of the log to assign case ID to events in the log.

In this paper, we propose a new approach to *deduce* case ID for the unlabeled event log depending on the knowledge about the process model. We provide a set of labeled logs instead of a single labeled log with different rankings. We evaluate our prototypical implementation against similar approaches.

Keywords: Unlabeled event log · Missing data · Event correlation · Decision trees · Process mining · Unmanaged business process

1 Introduction

Most of information systems produce event logs as an evidence of the activities that have been executed. An *event log* consists of a set of events. Each event represents an executed *activity* in a business process. Events have specific *timestamps* and might be associated with other *context* data such as the human resources who participated to the completion of the activity, input and output data etc.

Postmortem analysis techniques of an event log, e.g., process discovery [2], conformance checking or process performance analysis assume the existence of *case identifier* associated with each event. A case identifier is important to correlate the different events recorded in a log. However, case identifiers only exist in execution logs of centrally orchestrated process instance, so called *labeled* event log.

Logs with automatically assigned case identifiers are classified as ($\star\star\star\star$) or higher level of maturity of event logs [2], also classified as level-5 of logging information as in [6]. On the other hand, when the process is executed in an unmanaged environment, logs extracted from the different information systems do not have case identifier, so called *unlabeled* event logs. There are many reasons why business processes may produce event logs with missing information and errors [6,8], such as: some events are

© Springer International Publishing Switzerland 2016
M. Reichert and H.A. Reijers (Eds.): BPM Workshops 2015, LNBIP 256, pp. 242–254, 2016.
DOI: 10.1007/978-3-319-42887-1_20

collected and recorded by humans, as well as the lack of central systems that are aware of the process model. The latter case is the most common case in real life and represents the middle level of the event logs categories [2], as well as level-4 or lower of logging information as in [6]. This calls for a preprocessing step of a fresh *unlabeled* log to assign a case identifier for the different events before any of the log analysis techniques can be applied.

The problem of *labeling* unlabeled logs has received little attention in the community of business process management [1]. The work in [6,7,18] has addressed the issue in the form of directly mining process models from unlabeled event logs. The approach presented in [7] turns an *unlabeled* log into a *labeled* log. However, there might be uncertainty in deducing case ID for an unlabeled event, which means that there are several possible ways to label such a log.

In this paper, we address one of process mining challenges which is *"Finding, Merging, and Cleaning Event Data"* [2]. This challenge is concerned with extracting and preparing event logs for analysis. We are concerned with the subproblem of the preprocessing needed to prepare the unlabeled event logs for any further usages. We propose an approach to *automate* this preprocessing step by deducing the case identifiers (DCI) for the unlabeled event logs. In addition to the execution log, DCI requires as input the executed process model and heuristic information about the execution time of the different activities within the process. The output is a set of labeled event logs, each with a ranking score indicating the degree of trust in the labeling of events within each log.

The remainder of this paper is organized as follows: an overview of the approach along with foundational concepts and techniques are discussed in Sect. 2. In Sect. 3, we present the details of DCI. Implementation details and comparison with related approaches are discussed in Sect. 4. Related work is discussed in Sect. 5. Finally, we conclude the paper in Sect. 6 with a critical discussion and an outlook on future work.

2   Approach Overview

The DCI approach overview is described in Fig. 1. It has three main inputs: the unlabeled event log, the heuristic data, and the process model. Also, it has an optional input: the ranking-score threshold, to display the results based on the user-specified value (by default: display all results). DCI produces a set of labeled event logs due to the inherent uncertainty, as a single unlabeled event might be assigned to more than one case with different probabilities.

There is a preprocessing step to produce an relation matrix between activities of the process model, so called the behavioral profile [21] of the process model. The generated behavioral profile is an *adapted* version of the original in [21], we elaborate more on this shortly.

The case ID *deducing* process starts with the "Build Case Decision Tree" step. It uses the unlabeled event log to construct a decision tree. It benefits from the behavioral profile and the heuristics data to filter for permissible labelings while building the tree. The "Build Event Logs" step generates the different compatible combinations of cases and writes each combination into a different labeled event log along with its ranking

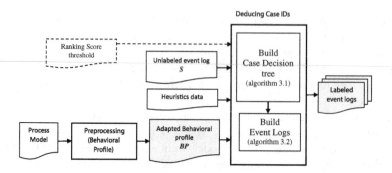

Fig. 1. Approach overview

score. The resulted logs provides variety of choices to enhance quality for post analysis and mining techniques. Details about how DCI works are presented in Sect. 3. The rest of this section provides the background concepts needed to help understand how DCI works in addition to discussing the running example.

2.1 Decision Tree

In general, a decision tree represents the different decisions and their possible course of actions. Each node has a set of properties that describe its conditional probability to its parent and how it contributes to decisions in the tree. In the context of this paper, a decision tree is used to represent the different *possible* labelings of each input *unlabeled* event. Each unlabeled event may be represented by more than one node in the tree.

Definition 1 (Case Decision Tree).
CTree = ⟨*Node, F, root, Leaves*⟩

- *Node is the set of nodes within a tree. Each node is further attributed by the caseId, timestamp, activity, and a probability,*
- *F ⊆ Node × Node is the relationship between nodes,*
- *root ∈ Node is the root node of the tree, defined with caseId = 0*
- *Leaves ⊂ Node is the set of leaf nodes in the tree.*

A branch(n_i) σ in the tree is the sequence of nodes visited when traversing the tree from the node n_i to the root. $\sigma = n_i, n_{i-1}, ...n_1, root|(root, n_1) \in F \wedge \forall_{i=2}^{j}(n_{i-1}, n_i) \in F$.

Definition 1 describes the structure of the decision tree used in deducing case IDs. Each child of the *root* is a start of a new case, i.e. increments the case ID. Each node carries its conditional probability w.r.t its parent node. This will help calculate the ranking score for the generated labeled log. We elaborate more on that in Sect. 2.3.

2.2 Behavioral Profile

A Behavioral profile (BP) [20,21] describes a business process model (BPM) in terms of abstract relations between activities of the model.

Definition 2 (Behavioral Profile). *Let A be the set of activities within a process model BPM. The behavioral profile is a function BP* $: A \times A \rightarrow \{\perp, \leadsto, +, \|\}$ *that for any pair of activities defines the behavioral relation as none* $\perp$*, sequence* $\leadsto$*, exclusive* $+$ *or parallel* $\|$*.*

A behavioral profile returns one of the relationships $\leadsto, +, \|, or \looparrowleft$ for any pair of activities (a, b) that belong to the process model under investigation [21]. However, as per Definition 2, we have restricted the relationships to be defined among adjacent activities only. This is needed for the calculations in the deduction algorithms.

2.3 Additional Information

In Fig. 1, one of the required inputs is *heuristic* data about the execution time of the individual activities within the process model.

Activity Heuristics. Each activity in a business process model has some properties. Such properties could be (timestamp, case ID, data, resource, ...). However, there is some other information related to the expected execution duration of each activity. The execution duration could be in the range $[avg - SD, avg + SD]$, where (avg) is the average execution time, and (SD) is an user-defined standard deviation for execution time. This information is very useful in filtering the case decision tree.

Definition 3 (Execution Heuristics). *Let A be the set of all activities within a process model. Execution Heuristics is a function defined using* $h_{avg} : A \longrightarrow \mathbb{R}$*; is the average execution time of an activity.* $h_{SD} : A \longrightarrow \mathbb{R}$*; is user defined standard deviation execution time of an activity, aka acceptable error.* $h_{range} : [h_{avg} - h_{SD}, h_{avg} + h_{SD}]$*; is Heuristic range.*

Node Probability. As we will be *guessing* about the likelihood of membership of an *event*, in the log, within a specific case, we employ probabilities to assign events as nodes in the decision tree. In general the probability of an activity within an event log is fairly distributed and calculated as:

$$p(activity) = \frac{k}{n} \qquad (1)$$

where k is the number of occurrences of an activity in a sample space of size n. In our case the sample space is the unlabeled event log.

Based on Definition 1, each node has a conditional probability that describes the existence of *node* given its *parent*. Equation 2 describes how a node satisfying h_{avg} will be prioritized than other nodes. Equation 3 describes how to calculate the probability of a node in heuristic range.

$$p(h_{avg}) = \frac{m+1}{m^2}; \forall h_{avg} \in H_{avg} \qquad (2)$$

$$p(h_{range}) = \frac{m - \frac{|H_{avg}|}{|H_{range}|}}{m^2} ; \forall h_{range} \in H_{range} \qquad (3)$$

In the above formulas, m is the number of possible parent nodes for the event that will be classified, H_{avg} is the set of nodes satisfying average heuristics, H_{range} is the set of nodes satisfying other parents in heuristic range.

Ranking Score Function. Deducing case IDs for an unlabeled event log will generate different possible labeled event logs. Each of these labeled logs should have a score that reflects the degree to which DCI trusts that events should be correlated that way. Scoring uses the *Rule of Elimination* [19] to describe the probability of an event log, i.e. selected branches for each case, w.r.t the included nodes. The resulting value is divided by the number of the extracted cases from the *unlabeled* event log. Equation 4 shows the scoring function we use.

$$RS(W) = \frac{\sum_{i=1}^{k} p(node|parentNode_i)p(activity)}{number\ of\ cases\ per\ log} \qquad (4)$$

where W represents a labeled event log, k is the number of total nodes, i.e. represent the events in the selected branch of the case, in W, $p(activity)$ is calculated based on Eq. 1, and $p(node|parentNode_i)$ represents the conditional probability of *node* w.r.t its *parentNode_i* calculated based on Eqs. 2 and 3.

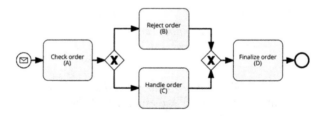

Fig. 2. Simple order handling process

2.4 Running Example

Considering the order business process model in Fig. 2, our approach as described in Fig. 1 needs the following inputs:

(1) The behavioral profile. This is represented as the matrix M for the process model in Fig. 2. The matrix is shown in Fig. 3a.
M is presenting the adapted behavioral profile matrix based on Definition 2. For example, in the model presented in Fig. 2, $BP(A, C)$ is $\rightsquigarrow$, while $BP(A, D)$ is $\perp$, as there is no direct relation between them.

(2) The unlabeled event log S with activity and timestamp pairs, where case ID is unknown. A sample unlabeled log is shown in Fig. 3b.

(3) The activities heuristics h, cf. Definition 3, data about the execution of each activity, i.e. avg, SD, which will affect the filtering process on the case decision tree from the unlabeled log S. Example values of these heuristics for activities of the process in Fig. 2 are shown in Fig. 3c.

(4) The threshold ranking-score (optional) will eliminate some of the generated labeled event log.

	A	B	C	D
A	+	⇝	⇝	⊥
B	⊥	+	+	⇝
C	⊥	+	+	⇝
D	⊥	⊥	⊥	+

(a) BP Matrix

Case ID	Activity	Timestamp
-	A	2015-01-01 01:00:00
-	A	2015-01-01 02:00:00
-	B	2015-01-01 08:00:00
-	C	2015-01-01 09:00:00
-	D	2015-01-01 13:00:00
-	D	2015-01-01 17:00:00

(b) Unlabeled Event Log (S)

Activity	Avg	SD
A	5	3
B	5	5
C	7	2
D	7	2

(c) Heuristic Data

Fig. 3. Required input for example in Fig. 2

There are some *assumptions* that are considered while deducing case IDs for events in the unlabeled event log S. First, each event in S has a timestamp that represents the *completion* time of an activity and the start time of the next activity. Second, the process model is an acyclic model. Third, the process model has a single start so we can identify the new case.

The result of DCI is a set of labeled logs that are categorized into either complete or noisy event logs. Complete logs include all events recorded in S. Whereas noisy logs contain inconsistent events with the model, its behavioral profile, or the heuristic data.

3 Deducing Case IDs

In this section, we explain in details how DCI works (cf. Fig. 1). Section 3.1 shows the steps to build the *CTree* from the unlabeled log S. It describes the *filtering* process to avoid incorrect combinations based on the input model and the heuristics data. Section 3.2 illustrates the process of generating the set of *labeled* event logs from the *CTree* with their ranking scores.

3.1 Building Case Decision Tree

The first step in generating labeled event logs is deducing case identifier (*caseId*) for each event in the unlabeled log (S) while building Case Decision Tree (*CTree*).

Algorithm 3.1 builds the *CTree*, cf. Definition 1. It uses the unlabeled event log S, the behavioral profile BP and the heuristic data *Heur*. By processing unlabeled events with their appearance order in S, based on the time stamp, the *CTree* is built by finding

Algorithm 3.1. Building Case Decision Tree

Input: S	//the unlabeled event log (Fig. 3b)
Input: BP	//the behavioral profile (Fig. 3a)
Input: $Heur$	//the heuristics about activity executions (Fig. 3c)
Output: $Tree$	// case decision tree $CTree$ in Definition 1

```
 1: Tree = new CTree()
 2: labelCaseId = 1
 3: for all (s ∈ S) do
 4:       Parents = modelBasedParentFiltering(s, BP, Tree)                    //using Definition 2
 5:       heurDic = heuristicsBasedParentFiltering(s, Heur, BP, Tree, Parents)  //using Definition 3
 6:       Parents = heurDic[avg] ∪ heurDic[otherRange]   //list of possible parents
 7:       for all (n ∈ Parents) do
 8:             caseId = n.caseId
 9:             if (caseId == 0) then        //n represents root
10:                   caseId = labelCaseId      //defines a new case
11:                   labelCaseId+ = 1
12:             end if
13:             node = new Node()              // in Definition 1
14:             node.setProbability(heurDic)   //calculated using (Eq: 2, 3)
15:             node.setTimestamp(timestamp),  node.setActivity(activity),  node.setCaseID(caseId),  node.setParent(n)
16:             Tree.addNode(node);
17:       end for
18: end for
```

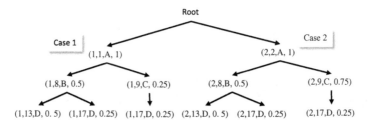

Fig. 4. Case decision tree

the different possible parents of event $s \in S$. The candidate parents are identified based on model and heuristic data (cf. Definitions 2 and 3). For candidate parents that pass the filtering steps, a new node, representing the labeled version of s, is added as a child of the candidate parent respectively with a probability computed based on (Eqs. 2 and 3). Due to space limitations, we excluded the details of model- and heuristic-based filtering, these details can be found in [3].

Figure 4 presents the decision tree generated by Algorithm 3.1 for the inputs in Fig. 3. The tuple (id, ts, a, p) with each node defines the deduced case ID, the time stamp, the activity name and node *probability* respectively. Timestamps are abstracted to hours from the original timestamps in Fig. 3b. In Fig. 4, event $(9; C)$ is represented in $Tree$ by two nodes, case 1 includes one node with probability 0.25 for this event and the same for case 2 but with probability 0.75 based on Eqs. 2 and 3. In order to assign node $(9; C)$, it is checked w.r.t. its heuristics $avg = 7, SD = 2$ for its set of possible parents, i.e. $(1, 1, A, 1), (2, 2, A, 1)$. Hence, children nodes for node $(2, 2, A, 1)$ are calculated using Eq. 2, while children nodes for node $(1, 1, A, 1)$ are calculated using Eq. 3. Also note that the event $(17; D)$ is represented by four nodes, in case 1 it has two nodes with different parents and the same for case 2.

3.2   Generating Labeled Event Logs

Algorithm 3.2 uses the *CTree* built by Algorithm 3.1 to generate a set of *labeled* event logs associated with their ranking score. The generation process avoids any unnecessary event logs, to prevent both *redundant cases* and *duplicated events* in the same labeled event log.

Algorithm 3.2. Generate Labeled Event Log(s)

Input: *Tree*   // *CTree* built in algorithm 3.1
Input: *rsThresold*   // user-defined Ranking Score threshold
Output: $Ws = \{completeEls, NoisyEls\}$ // set of labeled event logs contains both complete and noisy event logs sets
1: $ELDic = newDict()$ // {ID:Branches} where *branch* represents one of possible execution of the *case*
2: $EventLogId = 1$
3: $numOfCases = count(Tree['root'].children)$
4: $completeELs = \{\}$ //set of generated complete event log(s)
5: $noisyELs = \{\}$ // set of generated noisy event log(s)
6: **for all** $(b \in Tree.Branches)$ **do**
7:      $tempIDs = getELsIDs(ELDic, caseId - 1)$ //set of ids for each log in *ELDic* includes the previous case$(caseId - 1)$
8:      **for all** $(el_{id} \in tempIDs)$ **do**
9:          $conflictSet = \{branch\ for\ branch\ in\ ELDic[el_{id}]\ where\ b.caseId = branch.caseId\}$
10:         $conflictSet = conflictSet \cup \{branch\ for\ branch\ in\ ELDic[el_{id}]\ where\ b.events \cap branch.events\}$
11:         **if** $(conflictSet == \phi)$ **then**
12:             $ELDic[el_{id}] = ELDic[el_{id}] \cup \{b\}$
13:         **else**
14:             $ELDic[EventLogId] = ELDic[el_{id}] - conflictSet$
15:             $ELDic[EventLogId] = ELDic[el_{id}] \cup \{b\}$
16:             $EventLogId+ = 1$
17:         **end if**
18:     **end for**
19: **end for**
20: $validLogs = getELsValues(ELDic, numOfCases)$ //set of event logs from *ELDic* which contain last case
21: **for all** $(el \in validLogs)$ **do**
22:     $rs = RS(el)$ //based on Eq. 4
23:     **if** $(length(el) == length(S)\ \&\ rs \geq rsThresold)$ **then**
24:         $completeELs = completeELs \cup \{el\}$
25:     **else**
26:         $noisyELs = noisyELss \cup \{el\}$
27:     **end if**
28: **end for**
29: $Ws = \{completeELs, noisyELs\}$

Algorithm 3.2 considers the combination C_r^b, where b is the number of branches in *CTree* and r is the number of cases. Ordering of the branches by *caseId* is used to avoid unnecessary event logs. For example, a branch with leaf node (2:13:D), with *caseId* = 2, checks only the event logs containing branch with *caseId* = 1, cf. Fig. 4. The output categorizes the labeled event logs into *completeELs* and *noisyELs* event logs, based on the given threshold and the number of events in the generated labeled event log.

```
1 Ranking Score : 0.229175
1:1:A 2:2:A 1:8:B 2:9:C 1:13:D 2:20:D
------------------------------
2 Ranking Score : 0.1875
1:1:A 2:2:A 2:8:B 1:9:C 2:13:D 1:20:D
```

Fig. 5. All possible event logs for example in Fig. 2

Figure 5 is the output for the given inputs, cf. Fig. 3, after applying Algorithms 3.1 and 3.2 respectively.

4   Evaluation

In this section, we explain the evaluation setup of our approach. We discuss our prototype in Sect. 4.1. Section 4.2 shows the evaluation procedure and results.

4.1   DCI Implementation

We implemented a prototype[1] for the *DCI* using Python. As a preprocessing of the input, we modified the implementation of the behavioral profile [12] presented in Java as defined in Definition 2. The implementation of DCI is divided into two subprocesses, cf. Fig. 1:

- *Building Case Decision tree* (Algorithm 3.1): Its performance is affected by both the length of the unlabeled event log S and the number of branches in $CTree$. The time complexity of this part is defined as in Eq. 5.

$$O(nm) = n(km + p) \qquad (5)$$

  where n is the number of events in S, m is the number of *leaf* nodes in $CTree$, k is the number of activities in the process model, p is the number of nodes in the tree.
- *Generating Labeled Event Log* (Algorithm 3.2): Its performance is affected by the number of generated combinations between $CTree$ branches, where the complexity of bCr increases exponentially with the growth of the number of branches b. Hence, avoiding incorrect combinations, while building labeled event logs, overcomes this problem. The time complexity is defined as in Eq. 6.

$$O(u(m + 1)) = km.bu + u \qquad (6)$$

  where u is the number of generated labeled event logs, m is the number of *leaf* nodes in $CTree$, k is the number of activities in the process model, b is the number of branches within the event log, i.e. maximum number of cases in S.

4.2   Evaluation Procedure

Figure 6 shows the evaluation steps of DCI with both synthetic and real life logs. To generate synthetic logs, we use the ProM [16] plug-in: "Perform a simple simulation of a (stochastic) Petri net". Then the simulated log is updated to reflect the heuristic data. For real life logs, we used the ProM [16] plug-in: "Mine Petri net with Inductive Miner" for inductive mining technique [10] to obtain the process model. Then we extract heuristic information from the real life log using a tool we built. In either case,

---

[1] Complete implementation in https://github.com/DinaBayomie/DeducingCaseId.

we remove *caseId* from the labeled log to produce an unlabeled log. Also we build the behavioral profile for the process model.

We evaluate DCI against the Expectation-Maximization approach (*E-Max*) [7]. E-Max is a greedy algorithm that mines the unlabeled event log. Table 1 compares between DCI and E-Max. DCI produces multiple labeled event logs. E-Max generates a single log. As a consequence, E-Max is sensitive to overlapping cases [7], which is irrelevant for DCI. Moreover, E-Max partially supports *parallelism*, while DCI fully supports. Neither DCI nor E-max support *Loops*.

Table 1. Comparison between DCI and E-Max [7] features

	Inputs	Event logs	Effect of overlapping cases	Parallelism	Loop
E-Max	Unlabeled log	1	+	+/−	−
DCI	Unlabeled log + Model + Heuristics	m	−	+	−

Table 2 shows that execution time of E-Max approach is usually smaller than DCI, since E-Max is a greedy algorithm that generates one labeled log. However, the real log (CoSeLoG project) has many default paths in the original model that affects the breadth of the decision tree in DCI exponentially. Regarding the number of generated cases, DCI is more accurate in determining the instances executed in the event log than E-Max, which is a consequence of considering the process model. From mining the generated event logs, DCI-based models are closer to the original model than E-Max-based model. More details about models and results could be found in https://github.com/DinaBayomie/DeducingCaseId.

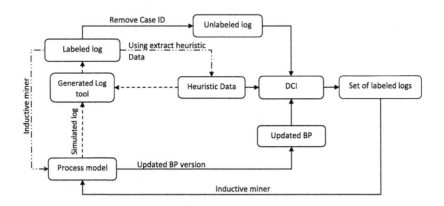

Fig. 6. Evaluation steps

Table 2. Comparison between DCI and E-Max execution

Original model	Log size	Criteria	DCI	E-Max
CoSeLoG project[2]	521 events	Execution time Number of cases	$\approx$ 36000 s 100	$\approx$3.58 s 100
Synthetic log 1	651 events	Execution time Number of cases	18.428 s 100	0.907 s 104
Synthetic log 2	498 events	Execution time Number of cases	10.773 s 100	2.2612 s 149

Receipt phase of an environmental permit application process (WABO), CoSeLoG project http://data.3tu.nl/repository/uuid:a07386a5-7be3-4367-9535-70bc9e77dbe6

5   Related Work

In [4,5], a business provenance graph data model was used to generate an automated auditing report. One of the main challenges was to create internal controls to deal with incomplete data. Moreover [11] has presented a method of modeling the uncertainty associated with the raw information and deducing relationships within the provenance model [9]. The main deduced item is the timestamp of an activity, and its level of confidence and accuracy. In [13,14], a stochastic process model is used to repair missing events in the log. It uses path probabilities to determine which are the most likely missing events. We can see that work in [4,5,9,11,13,14] is complementary to our work, where we deduce the missing case identifier, whereas the other work deduces or predicts the timestamp.

There are several process mining techniques that discover and conform the model from event logs. Most of these techniques need a labeled event log to proceed [1]. Also there are different performance analysis techniques that use labeled event logs to extract process performance indicators [15]. We see our work as intermediate step between low quality logs, according to [2], and those mining and analysis approaches.

In [6], authors discuss how to discover web service workflows and the difficulty of finding a rich log with specific information. The execution of web services has missing workflow and case identifiers in order to analyze workflow execution log. They also discuss the need of extra information regarding execution time heuristics.

Moreover, the work in [17,18] discusses the problem from a different point of view. Instead of generating labeled log, it provides a sequence partitioning approach to produce a set partitions that represents the minimum cover of the unlabeled log. The main limitations of the approach are handling loops and also the representation of parallelism as it will represent the execution of concurrent parts of the process into different patterns as if they are not related. We share the same limitation with respect to loops. However, our approach can handle concurrency.

6   Conclusion and Future Work

In this paper, we have introduced an approach to deduce case IDs for unlabeled event logs, DCI. We use as input, in addition to the unlabeled event log, process behavioral profiles and heuristic data about activity execution in order to generate a set of labeled event logs with ranking scores.

DCI handles *noise* in event log as defined in [1]. The *noisy* unlabeled event log might contain a different behavior other than the presented in the process model. Another type of noise is based on *inaccurate* heuristic data with the actual process model execution. Also, DCI handles *incompleteness* of event log [1], i.e. a snapshot from a process execution which violates the process model.

As a limitation, DCI does not support cyclic models. Cyclic models is a problem in most of process mining techniques. Also, the performance of our algorithm is affected by the number of concurrent branches within the process as the number of combinations grows exponentially. Finally, if the heuristic data are inaccurate this will also affect the the number of possible labelings of the event log.

As a future work, we intend to address labeling event logs of cyclic process models. Also, we intend to consider the availability of additional contextual data in the log.

References

1. der Aalst, W.V.: Process Mining: Discovery, Conformance and Enhancement of Business Processes. Springer, Heidelberg (2011)
2. van der Aalst, W.M.P., et al.: Process mining manifesto. In: Daniel, F., Barkaoui, K., Dustdar, S. (eds.) BPM Workshops 2011, Part I. LNBIP, vol. 99, pp. 169–194. Springer, Heidelberg (2012)
3. Bayomie, D., Helal, I.M.A., Awad, A., Ezat, E., ElBastawissi, A.: Deducing Case IDs for unlabeled Event Logs. Technical report, Cairo University. http://scholar.cu.edu.eg/?q=ahmedawad/files/bplabellingeventlog.pdf
4. Doganata, Y.N.: Designing internal control points in partially managed processes by using business vocabulary. In: ICDE Workshops. pp. 267–272. IEEE (2011)
5. Doganata, Y., Curbera, F.: Effect of using automated auditing tools on detecting compliance failures in unmanaged processes. In: Dayal, U., Eder, J., Koehler, J., Reijers, H.A. (eds.) BPM 2009. LNCS, vol. 5701, pp. 310–326. Springer, Heidelberg (2009)
6. Dustdar, S., Gombotz, R.: Discovering web service workflows using web services interaction mining. Int. J. Bus. Process Integr. Manag. 1(4), 256 (2006)
7. Ferreira, D.R., Gillblad, D.: Discovering process models from unlabelled event logs. In: Dayal, U., Eder, J., Koehler, J., Reijers, H.A. (eds.) BPM 2009. LNCS, vol. 5701, pp. 143–158. Springer, Heidelberg (2009)
8. Herzberg, N., Kunze, M., Rogge-Solti, A.: Towards process evaluation in non-automated process execution environments. In: ZEUS. CEUR Workshop Proceedings, vol. 847, pp. 97–103 (2012). www.CEUR-WS.org
9. Idika, N.C., Varia, M., Phan, H.: The probabilistic provenance graph. In: IEEE Symposium on Security and Privacy Workshops. pp. 34–41. IEEE Computer Society (2013)
10. Leemans, S.J.J., Fahland, D., van der Aalst, W.M.P.: Discovering block-structured process models from event logs containing infrequent behaviour. In: Lohmann, N., Song, M., Wohed, P. (eds.) Business Process Management Workshops. LNBIP, vol. 171, pp. 66–78. Springer, Heidelberg (2014)
11. Mukhi, N.K.: Monitoring unmanaged business processes. In: Meersman, R., Dillon, T.S., Herrero, P. (eds.) OTM 2010. LNCS, vol. 6426, pp. 44–59. Springer, Heidelberg (2010)
12. Polyvyanyy, A., Weidlich, M.: Towards a compendium of process technologies - the jBPT library for process model analysis. In: CEUR Workshop Proceedings onCAiSE 2013 Forum, vol. 998, pp. 106–113 (2013). www.CEUR-WS.org
13. Rogge-Solti, A.: Probabilistic Estimation of Unobserved Process Events. University of Potsdam, Ph.D. (2014)

14. Rogge-Solti, A., Mans, R.S., van der Aalst, W.M.P., Weske, M.: Repairing event logs using timed process models. In: Demey, Y.T., Panetto, H. (eds.) OTM 2013 Workshops 2013. LNCS, vol. 8186, pp. 705–708. Springer, Heidelberg (2013)

15. Suriadi, S., Ouyang, C., van der Aalst, W.M., ter Hofstede, A.H.: Event Gap Analysis: Understanding Why Processes Take Time. Technical report QUT: ePrints (2014)

16. Van Der Aalst, W.M.P., Van Dongen, B.F., Günther, C., Rozinat, A., Verbeek, H.M.W., Weijters, A.: Prom: the process mining toolkit. In: CEUR Workshop Proceedings, vol. 489 (2009)

17. Walicki, M., Ferreira, D.R.: Mining sequences for patterns with non-repeating symbols. In: IEEE Congress on Evolutionary Computation, CEC. pp. 1–8. IEEE (2010)

18. Walicki, M., Ferreira, D.R.: Sequence partitioning for process mining with unlabeled event logs. Data Knowl. Eng. **70**(10), 821–841 (2011)

19. Walpole, E.R., Myers, R.H., Myers, S.L., Ye, K.E.: Probability and Statistics for Engineers and Scientists, 9th edn. Pearson, London (2011)

20. Weidlich, M.: Behavioral profiles - a relational approach to behaviour consistency. Ph.D. thesis, University of Potsdam (2011)

21. Weidlich, M., Polyvyanyy, A., Mendling, J., Weske, M.: Causal behavioural profiles - efficient computation, applications, and evaluation. Fundamenta Informaticae **113**, 399–435 (2011)

Using Event Logs to Model Interarrival Times in Business Process Simulation

Niels Martin[1(✉)], Benoît Depaire[1], and An Caris[1,2]

[1] Hasselt University, Agoralaan – Building D, 3590 Diepenbeek, Belgium
{niels.martin,benoit.depaire,an.caris}@uhasselt.be
[2] Research Foundation Flanders (FWO), Egmontstraat 5, 1000 Brussels, Belgium

Abstract. The construction of a business process simulation (BPS) model requires significant modeling efforts. This paper focuses on modeling the inter-arrival time (IAT) of entities, i.e. the time between the arrival of consecutive entities. Accurately modeling entity arrival is crucial as it influences process performance metrics such as the average waiting time. In this respect, the analysis of event logs can be useful. Given the limited process mining support for this BPS modeling task, the contribution of this paper is twofold. Firstly, an IAT input model taxonomy for process mining is introduced, describing event log use depending on process and event log characteristics. Secondly, ARPRA is introduced and operationalized for gamma distributed IATs. This novel approach to mine an IAT input model is the first to explicitly integrate the notion of queues. ARPRA is shown to significantly outperform a benchmark approach which ignores queue formation.

Keywords: Business process simulation · Process mining · Interarrival time modelling

1 Introduction

Business process simulation (BPS) refers to the imitation of business process behavior through the use of a simulation model. By mimicking the real system, simulation can identify the effects of operational changes prior to implementation and contribute to the analysis and improvement of business processes [7].

A BPS model is composed of several building blocks such as entities, activities and resources [6]. This work is related to entities, which are dynamic objects that flow through the system and on which activities are executed [2], e.g. passengers when modelling an airline's check-in process. As for each BPS model building block, several modelling tasks are related to entities [6]. This paper focuses on the entity arrival rate, i.e. the pattern according to which entities arrive in the process.

Accurately modelling entity arrival is crucial as it has a major influence on process performance metrics such as the average waiting time or the flow time, i.e. the total time spent in the system. To identify an interarrival time (IAT) input model, i.e. a parameterized probability distribution [3] for the time between the arrival of consecutive entities, inputs can be gathered by e.g. observing the process. However, as process

© Springer International Publishing Switzerland 2016
M. Reichert and H.A. Reijers (Eds.): BPM Workshops 2015, LNBIP 256, pp. 255–267, 2016.
DOI: 10.1007/978-3-319-42887-1_21

observations are rather time-consuming, the presence of more readily available information sources should be investigated. In this respect, process execution information stored in event logs can be useful. Such files, originating from process-aware information systems (PAIS) such as CRM-systems, contain events associated to a case, e.g. the start of a passenger's check-in, where a case is the event log equivalent for an entity. For each event, information is recorded such as the associated activity and a timestamp [12]. This work focuses on the use of process mining, i.e. the analysis of event logs, to support IAT input model specification.

Despite the potential value of event log analysis to model the entity arrival rate, research efforts on the topic are limited. Moreover, they implicitly assume that the first recorded timestamp is the actual arrival of a case, which is not necessarily true. To this end, this paper presents an IAT input model taxonomy for process mining, demonstrating that the latter assumption is only appropriate under particular conditions. When these do not hold, entity arrival times can no longer be directly retrieved from a log as queues are formed for the first activity. Hence, novel modelling methods are required. In this respect, this work presents a new algorithm, called ARPRA, which is the first to integrate the notion of queues when mining an IAT input model.

The remainder of this paper is structured as follows. The following section illustrates the importance of accurate IAT modelling and discusses the scarce related work. The third section presents the aforementioned IAT input model taxonomy. The new algorithm, APRRA, is discussed and evaluated in the fourth and fifth section, respectively. The paper ends with a conclusion.

2 Preliminaries

2.1 Running Example and Problem Statement

Throughout this paper, the check-in process of a fictitious small airline will serve as a running example. The process model is visualized in Fig. 1.

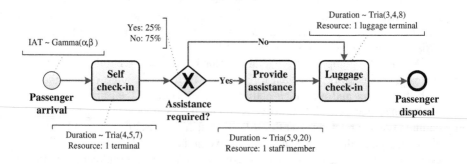

Fig. 1. Running example

A small airline recently started operations at a local airport. To limit staff requirements, the airline installed a self check-in terminal. Arriving passengers follow the terminal's check-in procedure. When assistance is required, they can proceed to the airline's assistance desk. The final process step is the luggage check-in at the luggage terminal. Based on limited process observations, the company assumes that activity durations follow a triangular distribution and assistance is required for 25 % of the passengers. All assumed parameters are annotated in Fig. 1, with minutes as the time unit. Resource capacities are constant throughout the day.

The running example can be used to show the importance of accurate arrival rate modelling. Suppose passenger IATs are gamma distributed, a more generic distribution than the popular exponential distribution [5], with 1.50 and 5.80 as its shape and scale parameters. Table 1 presents some process performance metrics for alternative parameter values. Note that the process will reach a steady state for each parameter set as the utilization factor ρ is smaller than one for each activity in each scenario [4]. After 30 replications of 12 h, results show that deviations from the assumed IAT input model parameters can have disproportionate effects on performance metrics. E.g. a 10% underestimation of the distribution parameters leads to an overestimation of the average flow time and average waiting time for self check-in of 13.34 % and 70.80 %, respectively. When the simulation study is used to e.g. evaluate the necessity of adding a second self check-in terminal, a flawed IAT input model can lead to inappropriate decisions. This shows the need for accurate entity arrival rate modelling.

Table 1. Effect of inaccurate IAT modelling

Gamma distr. parameter (shape/ scale)	Average flow time	Average waiting time for self check-in	Utilization self check-in terminal
1.50/5.80 (assumed)	18.06	2.74	0.64
1.65/6.38 (+10 %)	15.80 (−12.51 %)	1.39 (−49.27 %)	0.53 (−17.19 %)
1.80/6.96 (+20 %)	14.78 (−18.16 %)	0.76 (−72.26 %)	0.45 (−29.69 %)
1.35/5.22 (−10 %)	20.47 (+13.34 %)	4.68 (+70.80 %)	0.73 (+14.06 %)
1.20/4.64 (−20 %)	32.82 (+81.73 %)	15.81 (+477.00 %)	0.90 (+40.63 %)

2.2 Related Work

Despite the importance of an accurate IAT input model and the fact that event logs typically contain vast amounts of process execution information, thorough research on how to use this information to support entity arrival rate modeling is lacking.

A dotted chart, representing the events of all cases by dots [11] can provide preliminary insight in the arrival rate. However, a mere visual inspection of a dotted chart is insufficient to determine an appropriate IAT input model. The only reference on process mining in a BPS context that briefly mentions arrival rate modelling is Rozinat et al. [9]. These authors calculate IATs as the difference between the first recorded timestamp of two consecutive cases. Afterwards, an a priori assumed exponential distribution is fitted on these IATs.

Both dotted charts and the approach of Rozinat et al. [9] implicitly assume that a case arrives at its first recorded timestamp, which is not necessarily the case. As will be shown in Sect. 3, queues for the first activity can cause entities to have arrived earlier than their first registered timestamp. Despite the fact that queue formation is a common situation in real-life, research which takes this observation into account when mining an IAT input model is lacking. When an entity's entrance in the first activity's queue is recorded, as is the case in the recently introduced notion of Q-logs [10], this event's timestamp corresponds to entity arrival. However, hypothesizing the presence of a Q-log is a strong assumption. de Smet [1] takes this into account by representing the process as a set of queues based on an event log without queue-related events. However, entity arrival in a particular queue is still equated to the start event timestamp. Consequently, retrieving an IAT input model from a log without queue-related events remains an open challenge, stressing the relevance of this work.

3   IAT Input Model Taxonomy for Process Mining

Defining an IAT input model requires insights in the entity arrival time. This entity arrival time might or might not be directly observable in an event log, depending on the process structure and logging characteristics. When arrival times are directly retrievable, IATs can be calculated from the log and a probability distribution can be fitted. Other-wise, more advanced techniques are required.

To structure the use of process mining in IAT input modeling, Fig. 2 introduces a novel taxonomy. It takes into account four dimensions influencing the IAT modeling approach that should be used: (i) the number of first activities in the process, (ii) whether the first activity involves processing, (iii) whether resource limitations are present and (iv) the logged event types. For the sake of clarity, the numerical references in Fig. 2 will also be used in the discussion below.

When focusing on processes with a single start activity (1), as is the case in the running example, entity arrival times are directly available in the event log in two taxonomy situations. Firstly, the entity arrival timestamp corresponds to the first activity start timestamp when this activity involves no processing (1.1). Moreover, both the start and end timestamp coincide in the absence of processing. Secondly, even when the first activity requires processing, the modeler can proceed to direct IAT calculation when the associated resources have an unlimited capacity and start events are recorded (1.2.1.1, 1.2.1.2). In both aforementioned situations, the implicit assumption made in dotted chart analysis and by Rozinat et al. [9] outlined above is suitable.

In contrast, other taxonomy entries inhibit the exact determination of an entity's arrival time from an event log. Firstly, this is the case when unlimited resources are available, but only end events are recorded (1.2.1.3). The discrepancy between entity arrival and the first recorded timestamp corresponds to the first activity duration. Dealing with this issue is beyond the scope of this work. Secondly, when the first activity requires processing and the associated resources are limited (1.2.2), entities might have arrived earlier than their first recorded timestamp as queues can be formed. In these cases, assuming a correspondence between entity arrival and the first recorded timestamp falsely ignores this notion of queues. Consequently, new methods are required to deter-mine an IAT input model without exactly knowing the moment at which entities arrive, taking into account queue formation. ARPRA, outlined in Sect. 4, is developed in this context.

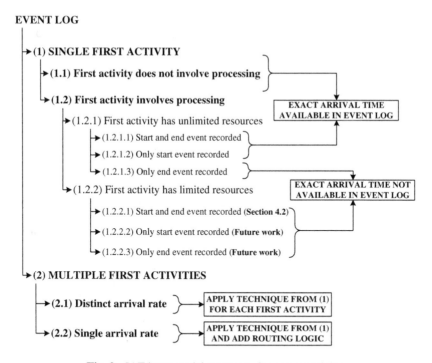

Fig. 2. IAT input model taxonomy for process mining

The prior discussion focuses on processes with a single first activity. In reality, multiple activities can instigate the process (2). Consider e.g. that the airline also develops an online check-in platform as an alternative for the self check-in terminal. Regarding arrival rate modeling, a distinct arrival rate might be specified for each of these first activities or a single IAT input model might need to be defined. When every first activity has its proper arrival rate (2.1), the appropriate technique from the single first activity situation is applied for each of them. Conversely, suppose the modeler wishes to create a simulation model that meets the workflow net requirements, only a single source place and hence IAT input model is allowed [14]. In this case, no distinction is made between the first activities and the appropriate method from case (1) is applied. The single source place should be followed by a decision point determining the first activity for a particular entity.

4   Overview of ARPRA

This section introduces ARPRA, an Arrival Rate Parameter Retrieval Algorithm, which is the first algorithm integrating the queue notion when mining an IAT input model. Queue formation for the first activity renders it impossible to calculate IATs directly from the log as exact arrival times are unknown. This has to be taken into account to avoid a bias in the IAT input model, which stresses ARPRA's contribution.

The first subsection presents the general principles of ARPRA, which are widely applicable as it is e.g. defined independent of the used IAT probability distribution. The second subsection operationalizes the algorithm for gamma distributed IATs.

4.1   Outline of ARPRA

The logic behind ARPRA, as visualized in Fig. 3, can be summarized as follows. Its main input is the proportion of entities that queued upon arrival in the event log (q). Given this percentage, the algorithm iteratively adjusts the parameter set (Ψ) of a particular IAT probability distribution ($\tilde{f}$) until the queue proportion in a simulated log ($\tilde{q}$) matches the queue proportion from the original event log (q). After a pre-specified number of matches (r) is obtained, an aggregated parameter set estimate ($\Psi_{selected}$) is returned.

The remainder of this subsection will outline ARPRA in more detail. Consider a PAIS-supported real-life process with an unknown probability distribution $f(\Psi_{real})$ for the IATs and $g(\theta_{real})$ for the first activity duration (FAD). This process generates an event log, from which three ARPRA inputs are retrieved: the percentage of entities that queued upon arrival (q), knowledge on the first activity duration ($\widetilde{(g(\theta))}$) and an initial estimate for the IAT distribution parameter set (ψ_0). Executable definitions will be provided in Sect. 4.2.

Besides the event log inputs, global parameters are required to use ARPRA. An IAT probability distribution ($\tilde{f}$) needs to be put forward, which will determine the size of the parameter set (Ψ). Other global parameters that need to be specified are the tolerated deviation from the queue proportion in the log (δ), the size of the simulated log in each iteration ($\tilde{n}$), the number of tolerable estimates required to end the algorithm (r) and the number of additional iterations to verify the stability of the queue proportion associated to the recorded tolerable estimates (v).

Based on the above event log inputs and global parameters, ARPRA can mine the IAT input model. In Fig. 3, the rectangle representing ARPRA is subdivided in two parts by a dashed line. The upper part refers to the identification of a series of candidate parameter sets, the lower part reflects final output selection.

Given the IAT probability distribution ($\tilde{f}$) and initial parameter set (ψ_0), an initial IAT input model is obtained. The process is simulated and the queue proportion ($\tilde{q}$) is calculated from a simulated log. When $\tilde{q}$ is outside a tolerance margin δ from the original event log queue proportion (q), the parameter set is adjusted and a new iteration starts. Conversely, when $\tilde{q}$ is between $q - \delta$ and $q + \delta$, the solution of the current iteration is recorded in Φ and iteration continues. Iteration ends when a pre-specified number of parameter set estimates are recorded, i.e. when $|\Phi| = r$.

When r candidate parameter sets are recorded, the lower part of the rectangle in Fig. 3 will select the final output. For each of the r candidate parameter sets, v additional $\tilde{q}$ values are determined and recorded in $\tilde{q}_{list}$ to verify if the initially recorded $\tilde{q}_i$ is representative for parameter set Ψ_i. Given the fact that each simulated log is based on random IAT draws from $\tilde{f}(\Psi)$, different $\tilde{q}$ values can be obtained for the same parameter set Ψ. This can be illustrated using the running example, assuming that passenger IATs follow

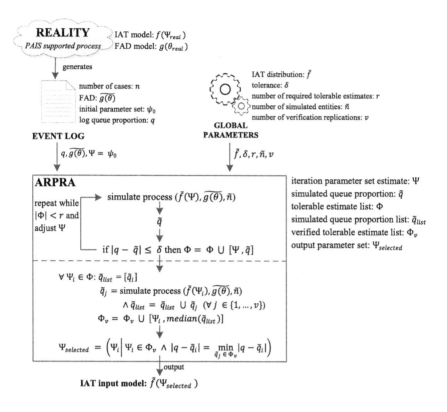

Fig. 3. Overview of ARPRA

a gamma distribution with $\alpha = 1.5$ and $\beta = 5.80$. After generating 2000 simulated logs with the same first activity durations, the obtained $\tilde{q}$ values for these logs range from 39.50 % to 64.25 % with a first and third quartile of 49.69 % and 54.50 %, respectively. This shows the necessity to verify the representativeness of the queue proportion associated to the candidate parameter sets. A verified tolerable estimate list Φ_v is created in which each parameter set from Φ is recorded, together with the median value from its associated $\tilde{q}_{list}$.

From Φ_v, the final output of ARPRA is retrieved, which is the recorded parameter set Ψ that leads to the closest approximation of q. In case of ties, an aggregated parameter set is returned by e.g. calculating the mean.

4.2 ARPRA Operationalization

To evaluate the performance of ARPRA, this subsection outlines an operationalization for situation 1.2.2.1 in the taxonomy presented in Fig. 2. For the sake of clarity, this subsection focuses on the key implementation concepts.

4.2.1 Event Log Inputs

ARPRA requires three key event log inputs, which need to be operationalized to obtain an executable algorithm. Firstly, the main input of ARPRA, the proportion of entities that queued upon arrival (q), is mined by studying the first activity start timestamp of consecutive entities. An entity had to wait when the execution of the first activity started immediately after the first activity is completed for the previous entity. When this is the case, e.g. for passenger 3 in Table 2, the value True is assigned to a boolean *Queue*. Otherwise, this variable is set to False. Once the *Queue* value is determined, q can be determined by dividing the number of cases for which *Queue* equals True by the total number of cases.

Table 2. Illustration of *Queue*-value assignment

Passenger	Self check-in start	Self check-in end	Queue
1	26/05/2015 11:04:28	26/05/2015 11:09:07	False
2	26/05/2015 11:14:55	26/05/2015 11:20:04	False
3	26/05/2015 11:20:04	26/05/2015 11:25:40	True
4	26/05/2015 11:27:42	26/05/2015 11:30:51	False
...	...	...	...

Secondly, initial parameter estimates ψ_0 are determined by fitting probability distribution $\tilde{f}$ on known IAT values in the original event log. IATs are exactly known when two consecutive entities did not queue upon arrival, i.e. have *Queue* = False.

Finally, a trace-driven approach is used regarding first activity durations [8], which refers to the direct use of event log durations when simulated logs are created in ARPRA's iterations. This approach is selected because queue formation is influenced by the interaction between entity arrival and activity duration. As a consequence, ARPRA will use the first activity durations in the same order as observed in reality. When the number of simulated entities ($\tilde{n}$) exceeds the number of entities described in the event log (n), the observed FAD sequence is repeated.

4.2.2 Global Parameters

Values also need to be assigned to ARPRA's global parameters. IAT distribution $\tilde{f}$ is equated to a gamma distribution: a two-parameter distribution with shape parameter α and scale parameter β. When $\alpha = 1$, a gamma distribution corresponds to an exponential distribution [5], which is commonly cited in simulation literature for IAT modeling purposes [2, 5, 8, 13]. The gamma distribution is purposefully selected because it is more generic, but still allows for the popular exponential IAT distribution. Hence, $\Psi = \{\alpha, \beta\}$.

Besides $\tilde{f}$, several other global parameters need to be specified. In the operationalization, the queue proportion tolerance margin $\delta = 0.01$, the size of the simulated log created in each iteration $\tilde{n} = n = 400$ and the required number of tolerable parameter sets (r) and the number of verification replications (v) are both set equal to 10.

4.2.3   Parameter Adjustment Method

A final key operationalization effort involves specifying a method to adjust Ψ across iterations. To this end, the observation that the mean of a gamma distribution μ equals $\alpha\beta$ is used [5]. The mean IAT fixes the relationship between both parameters. Hence, given the mean IAT, adjustments in one parameter automatically generates changes in the other parameter. The mean IAT is mined from the original event log by considering the time between the start timestamps of the first and last entity. Dividing the length of this time frame by the number of arrivals in this period renders an approximation of μ. Given μ, the adjustment of Ψ can be brought down to varying $\tilde{\alpha}$ and changing the value of $\tilde{\beta}$ according to the relationship $\tilde{\beta} = \mu/\tilde{\alpha}$. The adjustment of $\tilde{\alpha}$ across iterations occurs as follows:

- When $\tilde{q} > q + \delta$ in the current iteration, too many entities have been queueing in the simulated log. As a consequence, $\tilde{\alpha}$ is increased for the following iteration as this increases the mean IAT for a given scale parameter. The adjustment size is determined by applying a percentage increase to $\tilde{\alpha}$ corresponding to the percent point deviation between $\tilde{q}$ and q. However, as there is no linear relationship between $\tilde{\alpha}$ and $\tilde{q}$, this value is smoothed downward to avoid too large adjustments. More specifically, it is rounded down to the nearest negative power of 10, e.g. a calculated adjustment of 0.03 results in an actual increase in $\tilde{\alpha}$ of 10^{-2} or 0.01.

- When $\tilde{q} > q - \delta$ in the current iteration, too few entities have queued upon arrival. Consequently, $\tilde{\alpha}$ is decreased as this reduces the mean IAT for a given scale parameter. The size of the parameter decrease is determined analogously to the previous situation.

- When $q - t \leq \tilde{q} \leq q + t$, $\{\tilde{\alpha}, \tilde{\beta}\}$ is recorded in Φ. In order to explore the entire range of parameter values that lead to tolerable queue percentages, a large adjustment occurs to push $\tilde{q}$ outside the tolerance limits in the next iteration. The direction of this adjustment is determined by the value of $\tilde{q}$ for the current and two prior iterations compared to q. If $\tilde{q} > q$ in the current iteration, $\tilde{\alpha}$ is doubled for the next iteration to reduce $\tilde{q}$, unless for the two prior iterations $\tilde{q} < q$. In the latter case, $\tilde{\alpha}$ is halved to explore another parameter region. The inverse holds when $\tilde{q} < q$ in the current iteration. When $\tilde{q} = q$ for the current iteration, the three prior iterations are taken into consideration, where the third lag serves as a tie-breaker.

5   Evaluation

5.1   Experimental Design

The performance of ARPRA is evaluated using the operationalization outlined in Sect. 4.2. As the presented algorithm aims to provide an improved method to mine an IAT input model, its performance should be compared to a benchmark approach representing the state-of-the-art on the topic. Given ARPRA's central premise that queue formation cannot be ignored, the selected benchmark approach does not include the notion of queues by assuming that entities arrive at their first recorded timestamp. Hence, a gamma distribution can directly be fitted on IATs calculated from the event log, based on the first recorded timestamp of each case.

To compare ARPRA's performance to the benchmark approach, the airline example introduced in Sect. 2.1 is used. Given this setting, values for α and β are selected to represent the real arrival process, which forms the basis to generate an event log. Solely using this event log, parameter estimates are obtained using both the benchmark approach and ARPRA. When ARPRA outperforms the benchmark technique, the former's output should correspond more closely to the real parameter values than the latter's. This experiment is repeated for 500 real IAT distribution parameters, where α is randomly drawn from a uniform distribution between 1 and 2 and β from a uniform distribution between 5.5 and 7. These boundaries are purposefully selected such that the lower bound of the distribution mean $\alpha\beta$ still leads to a steady state situation, as the utilization factor ρ is smaller than one for each activity [4].

5.2   Evaluation Results

As indicated in Sect. 5.1, ARPRA's evaluation consists of approximating real parameters of the IAT distribution using both the benchmark approach and ARPRA. The random draws for α and β from the aforementioned uniform distributions to create an event log are visualized in Fig. 4a and b. These show that the drawn values are to a large extent evenly spread and span the entire range of possible values. The queue proportion in the event log, a guiding concept for ARPRA, is represented in Fig. 4c. The mean q equals 49.17 %, with minimum and maximum values of 18.25 % and 93.00 %, respectively.

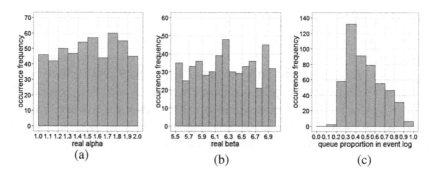

Fig. 4. Occurrence of (a) real, (b) real and (c) real queue proportion

For each of the 500 experiments, the deviation between the estimated parameters and its real value is recorded. ARPRA outperforms the benchmark approach in 498 experiments because ARPRA provides a better approximation of both the real α and β. For the remaining 2 experiments, results are mixed, i.e. one parameter is better approximated by the benchmark approach and the other one by ARPRA. As a consequence, the benchmark approach never outperforms ARPRA. Moreover, the t-test in Table 3 shows that, at a 5% significance level, ARPRA delivers an unbiased estimator for the real parameter values, i.e. no consistent over- or underestimation is observed. In contrast, the benchmark approach renders biased estimates for both α and β.

Table 3. Results t-test on deviation between real parameters and ARPRA output

Parameter	t-value	p-value	95% confidence interval
Shape parameter α	1.07	0.2869	[−0.006; 0.021]
Scale parameter β	1.94	0.0533	[−0.001; 0.029]

Regarding the magnitude of the performance difference, key results are reported in Table 4. To put the observed deviations into perspective, Table 4 considers the percentage deviation from the real value. The results confirm that ARPRA renders more accurate approximations of the real parameters than the benchmark approach. For instance: the mean deviation from the real shape parameter equals 184.70 % for the benchmark approach and only 0.74 % for ARPRA. For the sake of completeness, the statistical significance of the performance difference is verified using a paired t-test. The null hypothesis is tested that the mean absolute value of the percentage deviation is the same for the benchmark approach and ARPRA. Table 5 shows highly significant differences and, hence, the null hypothesis can be rejected at a 5 % significance level. The benchmark approach leads to much larger deviations than ARPRA.

Table 4. Percentage deviation between real parameters and obtained estimates

Key figure	Benchmark approach	ARPRA
Shape parameter α		
Mean deviation	184.70 %	0.74 %
Quartile 1 / Quartile 3	70.66 % / 205.00 %	−8.40 % / 8.66 %
Standard deviation	211.47 % points	15.51 % points
Scale parameter β		
Mean deviation	−54.79 %	1.42 %
Quartile 1 / Quartile 3	−66.90 % / −41.10 %	−8.46 % / 8.73 %
Standard deviation	17.17 % points	16.39 % points

Table 5. Paired t-test of absolute value of percentage deviation from real α and β

Parameter	t-value	p-value	95% confidence interval
Shape parameter α	28.69	$< 2.2 \cdot 10^{-16}$	[155.08; 191.51]
Scale parameter β	57.31	$< 2.2 \cdot 10^{-16}$	[41.36; 44.30]

It can be concluded that ARPRA presents an important improvement over the benchmark approach. Consequently, it is shown that queue formation has to be taken into account when mining an IAT input model. Given the implications of inaccurate IAT input models, illustrated in Sect. 2.1, BPS model construction can benefit from ARPRA when an IAT input model needs to be mined from an event log.

6   Conclusion

This paper focused on process mining support for IAT modelling when constructing a simulation model. The main contribution of this work is twofold. Firstly, an IAT input model taxonomy for process mining is developed, showing that the current approach in literature is only appropriate when no queues are formed for the start activity. Secondly, ARPRA is introduced, which is the first to explicitly take the notion of queues into account when mining an IAT input model. When the algorithm is operationalized for gamma distributed IATs, the conducted experiments show that: (i) ARPRA provides an unbiased estimator for both distribution parameters and (ii) ARPRA significantly outperforms a benchmark approach ignoring queue formation.

Future work will focus on the development of a more advanced parameter search strategy, taking into account the non-linear relationship between the distribution parameters and the queue proportion. Moreover, a sensitivity analysis will be performed to investigate ARPRA's sensitivity to the queue proportion in the original log, the size of the original log, etc. Finally, ARPRA can be extended to mine an IAT input model when (i) no a priori distribution is assumed, (ii) input model distributions and/or parameters vary over time, (iii) only start or end events are recorded and (iv) more complex resource behavior such as batch processing is present in the process under consideration.

References

1. de Smet, L.: Queue mining: combining process mining and queuing analysis to understand bottlenecks, to predict delays, and suggest process improvements. Master thesis, Eindhoven University of Technology (2014)
2. Kelton, W.D., Sadowski, R.P., Zupick, N.B.: Simulation with Arena. McGraw-Hill, New York (2015)
3. Henderson, S.G.: Input modeling uncertainty: why do we care and what should we do about it. In: Proceedings of the 2003 Winter Simulation Conference, pp. 90–100 (2003)
4. Hillier, F.S., Lieberman, G.J.: Introduction to Operations Research. McGraw-Hill, New York (2010)
5. Law, A.M.: Simulation Modeling and Analysis. McGraw-Hill, New York (2007)
6. Martin, N., Depaire, B., Caris, A.: The use of process mining in a business process simulation context: overview and challenges. In: Proceedings of the 2014 IEEE Symposium on Computational Intelligence and Data Mining, pp. 381–388 (2014)
7. Melão, N., Pidd, M.: Use of business process simulation: a survey of practitioners. J. Oper. Res. Soc. **54**(1), 2–10 (2003)
8. Robinson, S.: Simulation: the Practice of Model Development and Use. Wiley, Chichester (2004)
9. Rozinat, A., Mans, R.S., Song, M., van der Aalst, W.M.P.: Discovering simulation models. Inform. Syst. **34**(3), 305–327 (2009)

10. Senderovich, A., Weidlich, M., Gal, A., Mandelbaum, A.: Queue mining – predicting delays in service processes. In: Jarke, M., Mylopoulos, J., Quix, C., Rolland, C., Manolopoulos, Y., Mouratidis, H., Horkoff, J. (eds.) CAiSE 2014. LNCS, vol. 8484, pp. 42–57. Springer, Heidelberg (2014)
11. Song, M., van der Aalst, W.M.P.: Supporting process mining by showing events at a glance. In: Proceedings of the 17th Annual Workshop on Information Technologies and Systems, pp. 139–145 (2007)
12. van der Aalst, W.M.P.: Process Mining: Discovery, Conformance and Enhancement of Business Processes. Springer, Heidelberg (2011)
13. van der Aalst, W.M.P.: Business process simulation survival guide. BPM Center Reports no. BPM-13-11 (2013)
14. van der Aalst, W.M.P., van Hee, K.M., ter Hofstede, A.H.M., Sidorova, N., Verbeek, H.M.W., Voorhoeve, M., Wynn, M.T.: Soundness of workflow nets: classification, desirability and analysis. Form. Asp. Comput. **23**, 333–363 (2011)

BPMS2 Workshop

Introduction to the 8th Workshop on Social and Human Aspects of Business Process Management (BPMS2 2015)

Rainer Schmidt[1] and Selmin Nurcan[2,3]

[1] Faculty of Computer Science and Mathematics,
Munich University of Applied Sciences,
Lothstrasse 64 80335 Munich, Germany
Rainer.Schmidt@hm.edu
[2] Sorbonne School of Management, Paris, France
[3] CRI, University Paris 1 Panthéon-Sorbonne, Paris, France

Introduction

Social software [1, 2] is a new paradigm that is spreading quickly in society, organizations and economics. It enables social business that has created a multitude of success stories. More and more enterprises use social software to improve their business processes and create new business models. Social software is used both in internal and external business processes. Using social software, the communication with the customer is increasingly bi-directional. E.g. companies integrate customers into product development to capture ideas for new products and features. Social software also creates new possibilities to enhance internal business processes by improving the exchange of knowledge and information, to speed up decisions, etc. Social software is based on four principles: weak ties, social production, egalitarianism and mutual service provisioning.

Enterprises use social software to improve their business processes and create new business models. Social software is used both in internal and external business processes. Using social software, the communication with the customer is increasingly bi-directional. E.g. companies integrate customers into product development to capture ideas for new products and features. Social software also creates new possibilities to enhance internal business processes by improving the exchange of knowledge and information, to speed up decisions, etc.

In parallel to the fact that more and more enterprises are using business process management also the individual is involved in a multitude of business processes. This creates a number of new challenges. Individuals have to cope with multiple process contexts and thus have to administer data appropriately. Furthermore, individuals have to integrate the external business processes into their own work environment or even to couple several external business processes. Human aspects in business process management relate to the individual who creates a process model, to the communication among people, during and after the process execution, and to the social process of collaborative modeling. Human aspects also relate to the interaction/collaboration/ coordination/cooperation that should be implemented in the business process or to specific human-related aspects of the business process itself and their representations in models.

Up to now, the interaction of social and human aspects with business processes has not been investigated in depth. Therefore, the objective of the workshop is to explore how social software interacts with business process management, how business process management has to change to comply with weak ties, social production, egalitarianism and mutual service, and how business processes may profit from these principles.

The workshop discussed the three topics below.

1. **Social Business Process Management (SBPM),** i.e. the use of social software to support one or multiple phases of the business process lifecycle
2. **Social Business: Social software supporting business processes**
3. **Human Aspects of Business Process Management**

Based on the successful BPMS2 series of workshops since 2008, the goal of the 8th BPMS2 workshop is to promote the integration of business process management with social software and to enlarge the community pursuing the theme.

Six papers have been accepted for presentation:

The paper with the title "Discovering Intentions and Desires within Knowledge Intensive Processes" from João Carlos De A. R. Gonçalves, Fernanda Araujo Baiao, Flavia Santoro and Kate Revoredo introduces a method to extract intentions and desires from participants of knowledge intensive processes. It uses techniques from neuro-linguistic programming and integrated social media content. A case study using Twitter shows the approach in practice.

Serge Delafontaine, Florian Evequoz and Christiane Jungius present in their paper "Opportunities and Challenges of Process Sharing Platforms in E-Government" a process sharing platform for the Swiss E-Government BPM community. The platform is open to public administrations, private BPM practitioners, and academics. Four domains are identified, in which the platform can greatly improve the efficiency of BPM projects and the general BPM uptake: planning, process modeling, comparative analysis and systemic analysis.

The paper "Job construals – Conceptualizing and measuring process participant's perception of process embeddedness" from Janina Kettenbohrer, Daniel Beimborn and Ina Siebert draws on the change supportive attitude by the affected employees in business processes. The paper develops a theoretical concept named 'job construals'. To measure the construct, a valid measurement scale is developed using a card sorting approach with BPM experts to assess the validity of the measure.

Barbara Keller, Rainer Schmidt, Michael Möhring, Ralf Haerting, and Alfred Zimmermann conceptualize in their paper called "Enabling Social-Data Driven Sales Processes in Local Clothing Retail Stores" a data-driven sales process. The latter uses data from social software in order to increase revenue. Furthermore, it identifies and tracks the customer using RFIDs in customer loyalty cards. Social data is used in all phases of the purchase and individual product suggestions and offerings can be tailored. In this way, local retailers are able to catch up with online retailers in their cross- and upselling revenues.

Michael Möhring, Rainer Schmidt, Ralf Haerting and Christopher Reichstein investigated on "Can Coffee Consumption Influence Business Process Modeling Behavior?" in order to develop a general and accepted metrics to measure modeling performance. The paper strives to create a foundation for such a metrics, by measuring the influence of caffeine on the modeling performance. A research model is developed and the result of a pre-study are discussed.

In Considering Effects of Business Process Change: from a Viewpoint of Business Flow Notation Structure the authors "Kayo Iizuka, Yasuki Iizuka and Chihiro Suematsu" analyze the manner in which business process modeling (BPM) impacts the business process change such as business process reengineering (BPR) or business process improvement. The paper takes into account the Japanese style of business process change and analyzes the results of a survey that the authors had conducted on BPM methods and the effect of business process change.

We wish to thank all authors for having shared their work with us, as well as the members of the BPMS2'2015 Program committee and the workshop organizers of BPM'2015 for their help with the organization of the workshop.

References

1. Schmidt, R., Nurcan, S.: BPM and Social Software. In: Ardagna, D., Mecella, M., Yang, J., Aalst, W., Mylopoulos, J., Rosemann, M., Shaw, M.J., Szyperski, C. (eds.) Business Process Management Workshops, pp. 649–658. Springer, Berlin (2009)
2. Bruno, G., Dengler, F., Jennings, B., Khalaf, R., Nurcan, S., Prilla, M., Sarini, M., Schmidt, R., Silva, R.: Key challenges for enabling agile BPM with social software. J. Softw. Maintenance Evol. Res. Pract. **23**, 297–326 (2011)

Discovering Intentions and Desires Within Knowledge Intensive Processes

João Carlos de A.R. Gonçalves[✉], Fernanda Baião, Flávia Maria Santoro,
and Kate Revoredo

Departamento de Informática Aplicada,
Universidade Federal do Estado do Rio de Janeiro (UNIRIO), Rio de Janeiro, Brazil
{joao.goncalves,fernanda.baiao,flavia.santoro,
katerevoredo}@uniriotec.br

Abstract. Traditional approaches for process modeling usually comprise the control flow of well-structured activities that an organization performs in order to achieve its objectives. However, many processes involving decision-making and creativity do not follow a well-structured flow of activities, having rather a more ad-hoc nature at each instance. Knowledge Intensive Processes (KIP) is an example of this kind of process. It is difficult to gather information about a KIP and create a representative model, since it might vary from instance to instance due to decisions made by its participants. The contextual information of each activity - as well as the desires and intentions of the participants - are vital to the complete understanding of the process itself. In this paper, we propose a method to extract intentions and desires from KIP participants using NLP Techniques and social media content, as well as exploring its possibilities on a real case study using Twitter.

1 Introduction

Traditional approaches for process modeling usually depict a process focusing on the control flow of well-structured activities that an organization performs in order to achieve its objectives. However, not all processes present a well-characterized control flow; in fact, business processes may be classified according to their complexity and structure. In [4], four attributes to be considered when evaluating the degree of complexity of a business process are suggested: process steps, stakeholders, process dynamics and interdependencies.

In [12] business processes are classified in structured, semi-structured or unstructured. Structured processes are completely pre-defined, easily modeled using a specific language such as Business Process Model and Notation (BPMN), and repetitive, having a fixed sequence of activities. Examples of structured processes are: attendance orders, deliveries, inventory control, and payroll. Distinct from them, semi-structured processes share unstructured and structured parts. For these processes, the next step is not pre-defined for all activities, but only for some of them. Unstructured (or ad hoc) processes, however, is a kind of process that frequently changes from instance to instance, with an unpredictable flow of activities, being difficult to model with a traditional method or notation such as BPMN. They contain activities that typically involve a great level of

M. Reichert and H.A. Reijers (Eds.): BPM Workshops 2015, LNBIP 256, pp. 273–285, 2016.
DOI: 10.1007/978-3-319-42887-1_22

tacit knowledge in their execution and usually several steps of the flow are decided by the process executor after the completion of the previous activity and the analysis of its results. This kind of process is also called a Knowledge Intensive Process (KIP), and is defined as a process in which value can only be created through the fulfillment of the knowledge requirements of the process participants [12]. KIPs can only be partially mapped in a process model using traditional approaches, due to unpredictable decisions or tasks guided by creativity. However, this hindrance in modeling a KIP becomes critical as knowledge flows and knowledge exchanges between media and persons are necessary to achieve a successful process completion [9].

Apart from the difficulty in modeling, KIPs usually involve decision making, innovation or creative tasks, bringing the issue of collaboration as another dimension to be treated by the analysis. Nurcan et al. [19] addressed this issue by focusing on the representation of the work within collaborative processes based on the idea of plan context, providing advice for users on the ordering of component activities as well as giving support on the decision making during the execution of each activity.

Given that a KIP contains Knowledge Intensive Activities, part of the background for the knowledge intensive activity being performed is the "intent" or "desire" from stakeholders or process participants. They are considered mainly as a rationale for the activity execution and for the decision-making that guides the ad-hoc flow of a KIP and the "sequence" of activities at each instance of the process. These particular elements are also a key factor, for example, as a statement of opinion or desire of a process participant to another, becoming a means for collaboration and knowledge exchange, or even an explicit rationale for its actions within the scope of the process.

The perceptions, intentions and desires of people are vital to the correct representation of a KIP, as decision-making is a major part of the process itself. [23] reinforces this notion by pointing out that the profile of a process participant in a decision-making scenario suffered an important change nowadays, as decisions are not taken based solely on intuition and past experience but also on information extracted from web sources and, especially, from social networks. Acquiring shared knowledge between participants of a KIP during process execution remains a key challenge [29] and is related to the usage of social networks by users expressing not only their actions but also the contextual information such as opinions and feelings about an specific activity or goal to be achieved during the process execution.

The acquisition of subtle elements such as intentions and desires is a difficult task even for a human analyst, due to sheer amount of data to be considered at social networks. Among the automatic and semi-automatic methods to be considered, wish detection is a Natural Language Processing (NLP) [15] application that defines a wish as "a desire or hope for something to happen" [7]. Usually, wish detection aims to acquire the consumption intention of possible customers on websites, based on their commentaries or evaluations of past purchases. It frequently comprises mining social network media - such as Facebook and Twitter - for possible clients for an organizations services and products, based on the contents of its posts and profile [11].

The usage of social network data and sources characterized as Big Data copes with a limitation of the past, when the information sources for opinions on a specific subject were restricted to organizational reports, interviews or meeting notes as sources of interesting data [20]. Using massive data from social networks broadens the possibilities of applying mining techniques due to the huge available amount of real-time data about people's perception, desires and other forms of contextual information [3].

This paper proposes applying wish detection and related NLP techniques in order to acquire intentions and desires of KIP participants. The proposal was preliminarily evaluated in a real scenario using data acquired from Twitter.

The paper is organized as follows: Sect. 2 describes the Intent Analysis field, the NLP area used for the acquisition of the contextual KIP elements, and describes a formal model to guide its implementation; Sect. 3 describes the Knowledge Intensive Process Ontology, used as a metamodel to guide the extraction process; Sect. 4 describes the technical details of the extraction method; Sect. 5 performs an exploratory study of the method and discuss its results and Sect. 6 concludes the paper and presents some future works.

2 Intent Analysis and Related Areas

Textual information can be broadly classified into two main categories, facts and opinions [16]. Facts are objective statements about entities and events in the world and Opinions reflect people's sentiments or perceptions about the entities and events. Much of the existing research on text information processing has been almost exclusively focused on mining and retrieval of factual information, e.g., information retrieval, Web search, and many other text mining and NLP tasks.

Important subtypes of textual information, closely related to opinions, are intentions and desires. Both are representational states, expressing a possible attitude towards a current state of affairs, occupying however different places in path that leads towards action: An intention is the result of a reflection process, pondering through different desires and perspectives, being a step closer to real action than a desire [17]. Analyzing intent is orthogonal to sentiment analysis as well as opinion mining [14] and provides a different perspective about the human goals and desires. Strohmaier and Kröll [25, 27] propose a novel NLP application called Intent Analysis, focusing on the extraction of goals and intentions present in textual context. Intent Analysis is similar to Sentiment Analysis; the main difference is while the former focuses on topic categorization by labeling them "positive" or "negative", the latter aims to classify text by the presence or not of an intent on its contents. Opinions, beliefs, desires and intentions comprise subjective statements that are more difficult to acquire than facts and events in an automatic or semi-automatic manner, using Text Mining and Natural Language Processing techniques [20]. However, they are generally critical forms of knowledge whenever a stakeholder or process participant needs to make a decision. This is not only true for individuals but also for groups and organizations. They also provide information about the context where an event or act occur, being part of the rationale of an event.

Finally, for our approach, we have chosen KIPO (Knowledge Intensive Process Ontology) as a meta-model for the knowledge extraction process. Its main advantage is the capacity of describing concepts involved in knowledge-intensive process, aiming at providing a common understanding of any KIP environment, as well as being domain independent [5]. The ontology and its elements are described in the next section.

3   Knowledge Intensive Process Ontology (KIPO)

Ontologies can be defined as an explicit and formal representation of a shared conceptualization [10]. KIPO ontology [6] was developed for the domain of Knowledge Intensive Processes from different and complementary perspectives: (i) Business Process, containing elements such as Activities, Flows and Data Objects; (ii) Collaboration, depicting concepts common to the knowledge exchange and collaboration between process participants; (iii) Decision-Making Rationale, representing the "why" and "how" decisions were made by the people involved in the process; (iv) Business Rules, since KIPs are typically more declarative than procedural by nature, being affected by organizational norms and usually described by business rules.

As the main scope of this work is the Intention and Desire elements of KIPs, our focus is on the Knowledge Intensive Process Core Ontology (KIPCO). The ontology deals mainly with Agents, the Knowledge Intensive Activities they perform and the contextual elements involved on the Knowledge Intensive Activity. The relationship among those elements is described as: "An Agent is the one who intentionally commits to reach a Goal by executing a Knowledge-Intensive Activity. The Agent is motivated by his Desire and acts according to his Beliefs. An Agent of a KIP may play the role of an Innovation Agent or of an Impact Agent. An Agent may experience many Feelings, and each one of those Feelings may be motivated by many of his Beliefs or Evidences." [5].

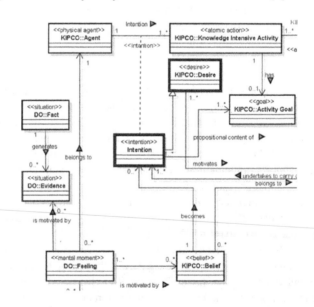

Fig. 1. KIPCO elements extracted from text (highlighted in bold black retangles)

Our approach focuses on two elements from KIPCO: Desire and Intention. Figure 1 depicts KIPCO and those two elements highlighted in bold black rectangles.

The two elements that our proposal aims to acquire are "KIPCO:Desire" and "KIPCO:Intention", and besides how they relate to KIPs in general. First, there is a direct relationship between one or more Intentions with the Activity Goal and the Knowledge Intensive Activity. Also, there "KIPCO:Intention" is a type of "KIPCO:Desire", and both are indirectly related to the Agent through the relationship with the corresponding Knowledge Intensive Activity.

Another part of KIPO, Decision Ontology (KIPO:DO) gives more evidence of the relationship between Agent, its corresponding Knowledge Intensive Activity and the Intentions and Desires involved, as depicted at Fig. 2.

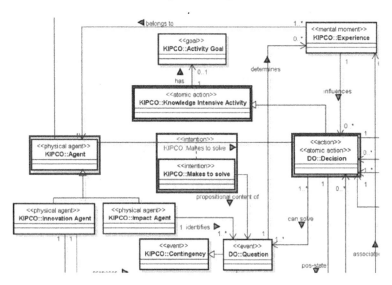

Fig. 2. Decision Ontology elements related to Intention (highlighted in bold black rectangles)

As shown in Fig. 2, an Intention is made to perform a Decision to solve a question regarding a certain activity or the flow of activities at the process by the Agent. The Decision is a Knowledge Intensive Activity itself, performed by an Agent; it can be compared to the Actor and Activity of a typical Business Process Model.

In the next section, we describe our method to apply Intent Analysis for the extraction of desires and intentions related to an activity of a Knowledge Intensive Process.

4   A Method for Intention and Desire Acquisition Within Knowledge Intensive Processes

The extraction of Knowledge Intensive Process elements is a difficult task, much more than the acquisition of typical business process elements such as activities and actors, due to diversity of activities and flow at each instance. The StoryMining method [8] was proposed for extraction of business process elements using Natural Language Processing and Text Mining techniques was proposed. We argue it is a promising approach in the case of Knowledge Intensive Processes, especially taking the vast amount of data sources about opinions, feelings, desires and other more subtle elements, being expressed at social networks throughout the web. Thus, we propose a novel method for the extraction of Desires and Intention of a KIP using social networks as data sources and NLP techniques, extending the Story Mining method. Figure 3 depicts the method and its main phases.

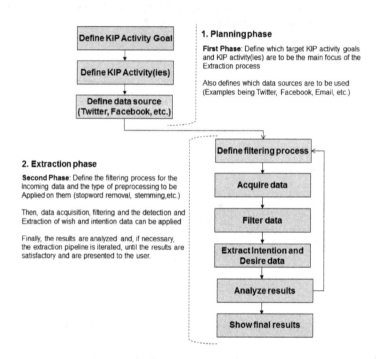

Fig. 3. Method for acquiring desires and intentions for knowledge intensive processes

The first phase is the Planning phase, where the KIP Activity Goal and KIP activities are defined, being the main focus for our extraction method. Also, the data sources for the method are defined, the possible sources being Twitter, Facebook or any other social network. The second phase is the Extraction phase, including criteria for searching string and patterns usually dependent on which social network was chosen as well as the preprocessing stages typical of Text Mining such as Tokenization, Stopword removal, stemming, among others. After the filtering process is defined, the data is acquired, either by streaming or by populating a specific dataset; filtered using the criteria specified previously; and the extraction of Intention and Desire is applied at the raw data. Finally, results will be analyzed and if, necessary, iterations of the same process will be executed, possibly with a variation of either the filtering process, data acquisition or modifying the intention and desire extraction method. At the last activity, the final results are formatted to a human-understandable format for the user to be analyzed and interpreted.

The method described will be detailed in the next subsection, especially the "Extract Intention and Desire data" and the "Acquire Data" phases.

5   Exploratory Case Study: "Black Friday"

The case study scenario was the Black Friday event. The term Black Friday is known to shoppers and retailers in the USA as both the day after the Thanks giving holiday and as one of the busiest shopping days of the year [26]. Moreover, millions of users wish for the best prices of desired products and make decisions on purchases during an entire day. The decision-making activity involved many factors, including the decision of purchase or not, the pondering about which products will be acquired and at which shop the prospective purchase will take place. Moreover, considerations regarding the traffic, crowds and other elements involved in such a scenario bring a dimension of knowledge intensity, both in terms of collaboration and knowledge exchange between participants (i.e. people pondering about the same decision to make) that characterizes a Knowledge Intensive Activity of a KIP. Thus, for our exploratory case study, our goal was to acquire the intentions and desires of members of a social network during this decision-making activity, that we consider a single Knowledge Intensive Activity, within a larger Knowledge Intensive "Product purchase" process. We perceive how the intention analysis proposed method works in a real world scenario of such a big scale of incoming high volume of data of as the Black Friday event.

Figure 4 depicts a simple product purchase process with the usual buying and selling activities and the decision-making activity of purchasing or not a specific product. The Community actor represents the role of the social network and other knowledge sources (such as newspaper feeds, internet advertising and other forms of collaborative software available to be consulted by a prospective buyer). This part of the process involves several activities: "Register desires for products" involves posting of desired products on social networks; "Provide insight about purchase", when the community provides insight through social network to help the buyer to make a decision; the last activity "Register decision and rationale", in which the community registers the context and

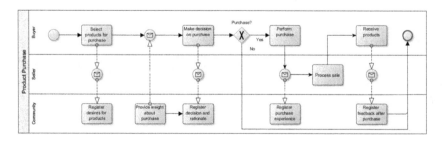

Fig. 4. Product purchase process in BPMN, including the role of community

rationale of why the product was purchased or not; "Register purchase experience", involving registering how the purchase experience with the seller occurred and finally, "Register feedback after purchase", in which the buyer communicates how satisfactory the product experience and the delivery process was. Every incoming message for "Community" will serve as basis to provide insight for the next prospective buyers, during future instances of the same process.

We can expand this decision-making design of the process using a specific notation, the Knowledge Intensive Notation (KIPN) proposed by [18]. Figure 5 depicts a simplified Decision Diagram in this notation regarding the decision-making activity of the process. Although the complete KIPN notation cannot be described in this paper due to space constraints, Fig. 5 shows the central diamond figure as decision to be performed, the circle with an interrogation mark above represents the main question involved and the negative and positive squares with a "V" and an "X" represent respectively the possible decisions to be made. Above and below each of them are the squares advantages and disadvantages of each choice, considered by the participants involved during the decision-making activity. Also, the black hand symbol depicts a restriction associated with this decision ("Perform the decision until the end of Black Friday") and the exclamation mark symbol describes the facts involved in the decision-making process ("The users' input about Black Friday and products").

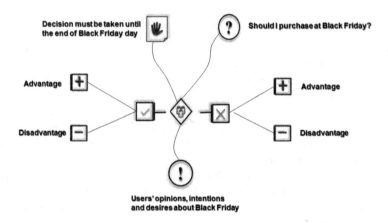

Fig. 5. KIPN decision diagram for the Black Friday purchase decision process

5.1 Planning Phase

The first step of the method is defining the KIP process and the main elements for the extraction process. As stated in Fig. 3, we have defined the Activity Goal, KIP Activities and Agents as follows:

Activity Goal:
  Making a decision of purchasing or not at Black Friday and which
  product(s)
Knowledge Intensive Activity:
Decision making on buying at Black Friday
Data Source:
Twitter
Agent:
User deciding whether or not to purchase products at Black Friday

The next step was defining the filtering criteria for the next phase: data source was collected from Twitter and a specific language filter being defined for the English language. Finally, we created a simple additional filter with the words "black Friday" for our application.

5.2   Acquisition of Data from Twitter

Twitter was chosen as source of data for our study, due to its limited scope of words on each post and its usage in the literature for event detection and other NLP application such as earthquake detection [24] and breaking news extraction [13].

We focused on the decision making process of purchasing a product during the Black Friday, converging to the participants (defined as possible customers using twitter) and their intentions and desires expressed at the social network. Following this idea, a dataset was acquired from Twitter at November 27th, 2014, just the day before the traditional Black Friday sale at the U.S. and many other places in the world.

Using the tweepy python component for Twitter extraction, we have acquired tweets that fulfilled two distinct conditions: (i) contained the words "black Friday" and (ii) were classified as being of the English language by Twitter itself. We run the collector for some hours, until we reached the optimal size of 100,000 tweets on a space of 3 h. This amount of tweets was chosen due to being the average rate of tweets in a single minute [22], thus being appropriate to represent a rich dataset in terms of content to be explored.

5.3   Method Application and Discussion

The traditional technique used for feature detection is the Naive Bayes Classifier, due to its simplicity (assuming each feature is independent given class) and its proven effectiveness in a variety of practical applications such as text classification [21], making it an adequate choice for our exploratory study. Our training configuration was using the Wish Corpus [7] as training data and using NLTk 3.0 on Python 2.7.1 as the framework for the implementation of the Naive Bayes algorithm.

A second classifier was implemented, using a list of words that depict "wishes" on text proposed by [28] that was expanded to a set of 13 feature words to be used as a information extraction template.

Those words can be compared as Intention Indicative Words in our template, due to their semantics. The list of words is specified below:

Feature_Words = *['may', 'can', 'might', 'could', 'would', 'will', 'should', 'need', 'wish', 'hope', 'hopefully', 'want', 'desire']*

The classifiers were applied, resulting on two result sets of sentences labeled as "wish" and "non-wish" for each classifier. Afterwards, the wish sentences of each result set were tokenized, cleaned of stopwords and the word frequency was calculated. The top frequency words in both result set were "shopping" and "deals", which is not surprising, due to the scope of our dataset being the search string "Black Friday". Among the words used to implement the WordList classifier, four of them ("wanna", "hope", "want", "wish") can be found in the NaiveBayes result set, which points out that they are indeed representative of wish phrases, being present in about 40 % of the wish phrases found on the first result set. Both these evidences point out to the necessity of a method combining both approaches, with possible lemmatization and POS-tagging functionalities as well, in order to contemplate the broader amount of Intention Statements as possible.

A qualitative analysis of the results was performed and more evidence, pointing to the richness of desires and intentions contained on the result set, was found. Most of the desires and intentions concerning going to purchase or not at Black Friday, as our data collection was started prior to the Black Friday day itself and reasons about whether to go or not was stated clearly such as *"Giving this black friday thing a shot"*.

Other tweets could be classified as output of each activity at the Community lane of the BPMN process at Fig. 4, as seen below:

(1) Register desires for products: *"Y'all think they got black friday deals on iPhone 5 chargers?", I want an iphone from black friday ugh"*
(2) Provide insight about purchase: *"When do the prices for Black Friday go live on the sight?", "The first thing I hope to see on sale for Black Friday is tuition."*
(3) Register decision and rationale: *"Going black friday shopping wish me luck", "Missing out on Black Friday cause I have zero money #thestruggle"*
(4) Register purchase experience: *"Black Friday sales start Thursday and this mall is really crowded", "Wow I'm currently in queue on a website because of high demand for Black Friday deals"*
(5) Register feedback after purchase: *"I just got 2 pairs of boots for 43 dollars at kohls. Thank the lord for black Friday", "I just got the four harry potter movies i didn't own yet for $2 each"*

Other statements contained other unexpected elements of contextual information such as opinions and criticisms regarding the Black Friday event itself, representing desires of what Black Friday could be or feeling about the decision making itself: "I wish Black Friday was not a thing. "How do we justify spending a day of thankfulness followed by a day of want and greed?" and "Supposed to go to the mall for black friday shopping tomorrow but i'm terrified". Also, many tweets were from retailers and other process participants, on the broader "Seller" lane of the BPMN Process, expressing desires such as "So I'm working black Friday tonight from 8 pm–8 am…wish me luck.", "If you're going out for Black Friday pls be respectful to the retail workers!!".

These unexpected elements show that, although the aim of the case study was focused on the intention and desire elements regarding the decision making activity, there were also contextual elements regarding the the whole KIP itself, as well as expressions of feeling and belief about the process.

6   Conclusions

We have proposed a method for acquisition of Intentions and Desires from a decision-making activity at a Knowledge Intensive Process applying NLP techniques from the field of Intent Analysis as well as using the KIPO Ontology for the extraction process. Our case study points out that it is feasible to apply the method at data sources described as Big Data, using real data being generated at a KIP such as the Black Friday product purchase process. The rich amount of information that can be extracted shows that using social networks for extracting information such as intention and desires regarding a knowledge intensive activity seems promising to be further explored in our research. However, while the case study´s scenario illustrates the proposal application and its results, there are limitations to this exploratory study due to its limited scope, in terms of being a simpler purchase process with a single decision making activity.

The desires and intentions discovered by our method can evolve to a broader method that can collect a sufficient number of instances of a KIP, together with its intentions, desires, decisions made by participants as well as its results, enabling managers and modelers to understand the flow of activities of a KIPs and its inner workings. For future work, we plan to perform a broader case study, applying analytics techniques focusing on the input of selected participants of the process, in order to analyze the patterns of knowledge acquired and cross-reference them with other related KIPO elements such as Belief and Feeling.

We also plan to explore the combination of both the Wordlist and Naive Bayes classifier in a NLP pipeline to maximize the results of the sentence extraction and also explore the different patterns in text for each of the distinct KIP elements to be discovered.

Acknowlegments.   This work was partially funded by FAPERJ (project number E-26/110.477/2014 and E-26/010.000738/2015). Fernanda Baião is partially funded by the CNPq brazilian research council, under the project 309069/2013-0.

References

1. Brants, T., Ashok, P., Xu, P., Och, F., Dean, J.: Large language models in machine translation. In: Proceedings of the Joint Conference on Empirical Methods in Natural Language Processing and Computational Natural Language Learning, pp. 858–867 (2007)
2. Deneckère, R., Hug, C., Khodabandelou, G., Salinesi, C.: Intentional process mining: discovering and modeling the goals behind processes using supervised learning. In: International Journal of Information System Modeling and Design, Research Challenges in Information Science (RCIS 2013), vol. 5 (4), pp. 22–47 (2014)
3. Dong, L., Wei, F., Duan, Y., Liu, X., Zhou, M., Xu, K.: The automated acquisition of suggestions from Tweets. In: Proceedings of the Twenty-Seventh AAAI Conference on Artificial Intelligence, pp. 239–245 (2013)

4. Eppler, M.J., Seifried, P.M., Ropnack, A.: Improving knowledge intensive processes through an enterprise knowledge medium. In: ACM Special Interest Group on Computer Personnel Research (1999)

5. França, J., Santoro, F., Baiao, F.: Towards characterizing knowledge intensive processes. In: IEEE International Conference on Computer Supported Cooperative Work in Design (CSCWD 2012) (2012)

6. França, J., Netto, J., Carvalho, J., Santoro, F., Baião, F., Pimentel, M.: KIPO: the knowledge intensive process ontology. Softw. Syst. Model. **14**(3), 1127–1157 (2014). Springer

7. Goldberg, A.B., Fillmore, N., Andrzejewski, D., Xu, Z., Gibson, B., Zhu, X.: May all your wishes come true: a study of wishes and how to recognize them. In: Proceeding of The Human Language Technologies: The 2009 Annual Conference of the North American Chapter of the ACL, pp. 263–271 (2009)

8. Gonçalves, J.C., Santoro, F.M., Baião, F.A.: Let me tell you a story – on how to build process models. J. Univ. Comput. Sci. **17**, 276–295 (2011)

9. Gronau, N., Weber, E.: Management of knowledge intensive business processes. In: Desel, J., Pernici, B., Weske, M. (eds.) BPM 2004. LNCS, vol. 3080, pp. 163–178. Springer, Heidelberg (2004)

10. Guarino, N.: Formal ontology, conceptual analysis and knowledge representation. Int. J. Hum. Comput. Stud. **43**(5/6), 625–640 (1995)

11. Gupta, V., Varshney, D., Jhamtani, H., Kedia, D., Karwa, S.: Identifying purchase intent from social posts. In: Proceedings of the Eighth International AAAI Conference on Weblogs and Social Media (2014)

12. Hagen, C.R., Ratz, D., Povalej, R.: Towards self-organizing knowledge intensive processes. J. Univ. Knowl. Manage. **2**, 148–169 (2005)

13. Hu, M. Liu, S. Wei, F., Wu, Y., Stasko, J., Ma, K-L.: Breaking news on twitter. In: CHI 2012, pp. 2751–2754 (2012)

14. Hollerit, B., Kröll, M., Strohmaier, M.: Towards linking buyers and sellers: detecting commercial Intent on twitter. In: Proceedings of the 22nd international conference on World Wide Web companion, pp. 629–632 (2013)

15. Jurafsky, D., Martin, J.H.: Speech and Language Processing, 2nd edn (2009)

16. Liu, B.: Sentiment Analysis and Opinion Mining. Morgan and Claypool (2012)

17. Malle, B.F., Moses, L.J., Baldwin, D.A.: Intentions and Intentionality. MIT Press, Cambridge (2001)

18. Netto, J.M., Santoro, F.M., Baião, F.A.: Evaluating KIPN for modeling KIP. In: Lohmann, N., Song, M., Wohed, P. (eds.) BPM 2013 Workshops. LNBIP, vol. 171, pp. 549–561. Springer, Heidelberg (2014)

19. Nurcan, S., Rolland, C.: Meta-modelling for cooperative processes. In: The 7th European-Japanese Conference on Information Modelling and Knowledge Bases, 27–30 May 1997, Toulouse, pp. 361–377 (1997)

20. Pang, B., Lee, L.: Opinion mining and sentiment analysis. Found. Trends Inf. Retrieval **2**, 1–135 (2008)

21. Rish, I.: An empirical study of the Naïve Bayes classifier. In: IJCAI-2001 Workshop on Empirical Methods in AI (2001)

22. Roy, S.D., Zeng, W.: Social Multimedia Signals: A Signal Processing Approach to Social Network Phenomena. Springer, Heidelberg (2014)

23. Sadovykh, V., Sundaram, D., Piramuthu, S.: Do online social networks support decision-making? Decis. Support Syst. **70**, 15–30 (2015)

24. Sakaki, T., Okazaki, M., Matsuo, Y.: Earthquake shakes twitter users: real-time event detection by social sensors. In: WWW 2010, pp, 851–860 (2010)

25. Strohmaier, M., Kröll, M.: Acquiring knowledge about human goals from Search Query Logs. Inf. Process. Manage. **48**(1), 63–82 (2012)
26. Thomas, J.B., Peters, C.: An exploratory investigation of Black Friday consumption rituals. Int. J. Retail Distrib. Manage. **39**(7), 522–537 (2011)
27. Kroll, M., Strohmaier, M.: Analyzing human intentions in natural language text. In: Proceedings of the Fifth International Conference on Knowledge Capture. pp. 197–198 (2009)
28. Wu, X., He, Z.: identifying wish sentence in product reviews. J. Comput. Inf. Syst. **7**(5), 1607–1613 (2011)
29. Erol, S., Granitzer, M., Happ, S., Jantunen, S., Jennings, B., Koschmider, A., Nurcan, S., Rossi, D., Schmidt, R., Johannesson, P.: Combining BPM and social software: contradiction or chance? J. Softw. Maintenance Evol. Res. Practice **22**, 449–476 (2010)

Opportunities and Challenges of Process Sharing Platforms in E-Government

Position Paper

Serge Delafontaine[✉], Christiane Jungius, and Florian Evequoz

Institut d'Informatique de Gestion (IIG),
HES-SO Valais – Wallis, Sierre, Switzerland
serge.delafontaine@hevs.ch

Abstract. A process sharing platform will be launched in 2015 for the Swiss E-Government BPM community. The platform will be open to public administrations, private BPM practitioners, and academics. We reflect in this paper on the general opportunities and challenges of such a platform. We have identified four domains in which it can greatly improve the efficiency of BPM projects and the general BPM uptake in public administrations: planning, process modeling, comparative analysis and systemic analysis. Despite all the potential of such a platform, we believe that there is also a risk that the users might not engage sufficiently in the community for the platform to be successful. We believe the communication on and about the platform should be given particular attention, by the use of professional marketing tools and methods. We also advise that a step-by-step BPM methodology serving as a general guideline for the public administration should be published on the platform and maintained by the community. This methodology could not only help in rising the success rate of BPM projects in the administration, but could also improve the perception of added value of the platform amongst practitioners and decision-makers by raising their understanding of BPM to the required level.

1 Introduction

In 2012, an E-Government priority project was launched in Switzerland to create a web platform where business process models could be shared between public administrations. The platform will be officially released in Fall 2015 under the ownership of the association E-Gov Schweiz. The platform will allow the users to:

- find process models in a process repository
- supply process models in the process repository
- have access to the BPM standards in Swiss E-Government (eCH standards)
- ask questions and obtain answers from specialists (community building) participate in discussions about process models, BPMN, and BPM in general

Based on the experience acquired in developing this platform, we reflect in this article about the general opportunities and challenges of process sharing platforms at the government level.

M. Reichert and H.A. Reijers (Eds.): BPM Workshops 2015, LNBIP 256, pp. 286–292, 2016.
DOI: 10.1007/978-3-319-42887-1_23

2 Related Work

Recent work discusses opportunities and challenges of process sharing. Several opportunities are identified: saving resources (Eid-Sabbagh et al. 2012, p. 1), allowing the re-use of process execution instances (Dijkman 2011, p. 5), helping to identify optimization opportunities (Arhend et al. 2014, p. 2), designing a common system (Pardo et al. 2006, p. 304), or aiding to provide high-quality government services (Kim and Lee 2006, p. 370).

Challenges of process sharing, and ways to cope with them are presented in Arhend et al. (2014, p. 8) who point out the "Inadequate adaptation of the BPM approach to public authority" and propose education and training in BPM to tackle the problem. Arhend (2014, p. 63) also states: "The main challenge […] is to increase the interlocking of business and IT." Eid-Sabbagh et al. (2012, p. 30) deem it necessary to offer incentives for the sharing of knowledge. Arhend et al. (2014, p. 9) share this view but warn that money incentives can have an opposite effect.

In this paper, we describe additional original opportunities and challenges of process sharing platforms, and formulate recommendations, based on our experience with developing the Swiss process-sharing platform. The work by Ahrend (2014) is similarly inspired by the experience acquired with the German Process Sharing Platform (Nationale Prozessbibliothek NPB).

3 Opportunities of Sharing Process Models

A process sharing platform provides access to already established process models, to BPM standards as well as a more direct access to BPM specialists. In this context, we have identified four key elements of our BPM methodology (Delafontaine 2015), derived from Weske (2007), which are subject to possible improvement:

1. Planning the BPM project
2. Preparation of process modeling through the concept of "sketching"
3. Analysis of processes through comparative analysis (benchmarking)
4. Analysis of processes through systemic analysis (i.e. analysis of the connections of processes between each other and the systemic impact of their components)

   We describe next how process models sharing can improve each of those elements.

3.1 Improving the Planning

The first element improved by a process sharing platform is the planning phase of any BPM project thanks to the access to BPM standards and guidelines, and to BPM specialists.

As the BPM maturity in the public administration is usually low (Ahrend et al. 2014, p. 8), BPM projects in E-Government put the public administration in a position where it has very little idea about how to integrate a BPM project into an improvement strategy or into other improvement approaches, like risk analysis, user-centric design, etc. Indeed, Schlatter (2014) notes that 74% of the communes participating in their survey have no BPM strategy (p. 7) and reports comments from communes like "Where do we begin, how do we proceed, does it bring us something or is it too big for our commune's size?" In order to achieve the goal of improving the planning, we advocate that precise guidelines, appealing to both beginners and advanced practitioners, be provided on the platform. Moreover, a question-answer module (similar to e.g. http://stackexchange. com/) should be provided, in order to accelerate the learnability of BPM in general and BPM project management in particular. We believe this would allow administrations to better understand the capacities and limitations of BPM, to take control of their BPM projects and therefore improve the chances of success.

3.2   Improving Process Modeling

Secondly, a process sharing platform provides an aid for the modeling of processes through the access to similar processes from other administrations.

The modeling of a process is usually done through the interviewing of stakeholders to obtain an "as is" view. With access to process models from other organizations, it becomes possible to analyze similar processes before the interviews take place. This allows the interviewer to sketch *a priori* versions of process models beforehand, and identify relevant questions, as well as optimization opportunities (Ahrend et al. 2014, p. 2). It therefore increases the relevance of the data obtained during the interviews, and the quality of the process models produced.

3.3   Improving Process Analysis – Benchmark

Thirdly, a process sharing platform enables comparative analysis of processes, thanks to the access to similar process models from other similar organizations.

With the process sharing platform, the collaboration between administrations extends the dynamics of continuous improvement from within a single administration to every administration in a global effort to find the best process to offer a service. Explicit tools that encourage such collaborative efforts, e.g. by automatically high-lighting differences between process models, are yet to be developed.

3.4   Improving Process Analysis – Connections

Fourthly, the process sharing platform enables the systemic analysis of processes and in particular of inter-organizational processes by the public administration,

What one person does in a process can have impacts on someone else's activity. This also applies in governments, especially in federal governments with multiple actors. Having access to the process models of other administrations involved in the processes can help understand the impacts of a modification onto the entire system.

Machine-readable process models could enable the automation of systemic analysis, thus helping to achieve this goal. The augmentation of process models with semantic metadata can be a promising step in that direction, as shown by Liu et al. (2013). Identifying and analyzing chains of processes as Jurisch et al. 2014 propose, is also relevant.

4   Challenges and Risks

Despite all those opportunities, the risks of failure for a government-wide process sharing platform are considerable. Indeed the German federal process sharing platform "Nationale Prozessbibliothek" (NPB 2015) has been closed at the end of June 2015, due to a lack of financing. Indeed, operating such a platform and managing the community around it requires sufficient sustainable funding. We believe this funding should come from both the public hand (e.g. in the form of time invested by public servants) and private investors (e.g. sponsors). However, both will invest only if they see opportunities and benefits. We describe next the main challenges that process sharing platforms should address in order to improve opportunities and benefits for their potential investors.

4.1   Engagement of Platform Users

The threat of a lack of participation has already been identified in Dargan and Evequoz (2015) who says: "However, actively sharing process descriptions and template business process, participation and contribution in the community, requires motivation and engagement in the part of public servants. A key factor in the success of the platform will be its ability to create, retain and expand a critical users' base." Gamification and user centric design, Dargan says, can help retain a users' base by creating a positive experience. We do believe, however, that the problem runs deeper than the overall ergonomy of the system. By introducing the example of the dancing bear, Cooper (2004) indeed states that a good ergonomic design gives a competitive advantage, but also that people will use a badly designed system if they can perceive an added value.

Our opinion is that the capacity of the process sharing platform to create a critical users' base will depend on its capacity to help potential users perceive the benefit they will obtain from the platform, i.e. that they can understand and experience the added value of sharing process models and knowledge in BPM.

4.2   Perception of Added Value and Social Marketing

The fact that BPM specialists can understand the benefit that can be obtained using the platform doesn't mean public servants and political decision-makers can, too. We believe the way the platform will be "sold" to the public servants will be a critical factor in the creation of the community. The same tools used in marketing can and should in our opinion be used for the launch of the platform. Ahrend (2014) already stated it for the German Nationale Prozessbibliothek: "First, it is necessary to analyze the target customers or groups […]". The personas created in the study by Dargan and Evequoz (2015) can serve as a basis for segmentation and targeting.

This relates to communication *about* the platform. But certain communication measures *on* the platform are also necessary:

- Participation in the community should not be limited due to technical constraints. It is very important that all potential users will be able to participate regardless of their IT environment and specifically their modeling software. This requirement is met by using the BPMN standard, which allows the exchange of processes across platforms and tools.
- Participants need to be able to obtain advice and guidance from specialists. Contacting specialists and asking questions should be easy and effective (e.g. questions-answers module). Access to field reports, information concerning positive experience or hints on where considerable improvement can be made using a manageable effort will motivate newcomers to join. This should be supported e.g. by a blog.
- Added value can also be supplied to those who make their processes available on the repository or participate by providing answers or advice. They can gradually develop a knowledge profile and receive feedback on their know-how.

In order to supply and maintain a high quality standard for the supplied information, there needs to be an editorial team in charge. This team will have to be open to participants of the platform.

Having a reflection on the message that will be sent to future users and overall preparing a true marketing strategy seems necessary. Once the added value will be perceived by the potential user, they will participate, no matter how basic or badly designed the tool could be, as Cooper's dancing bear metaphor shows.

4.3   Low Maturity Level of BPM in E-Government and ECH Standards

Ahrend et al. (2014, p. 8) describe the "Inadequate adaptation of the BPM approach to public authority" to be " not surprising due to the generally low BPM maturity level of public authority" In his study, Schlatter (2014, p. 9) also notes that 79% of the communes have modeled none to only a few of their processes, with only 12% modeled in BPMN. Therefore, it might happen that too few administrations in Switzerland have modeled their processes. If that is the case, few processes would be uploaded on the platform and the promise of large-scale process models sharing could be put in peril.

The actual state of the eCH standards (eCH 2015) doesn't give neophyte public servants the clear guidelines they would need to understand and launch a BPM project. The standards are mainly meant for BPM specialists and are therefore very hard to decipher for beginners, whereas most administrations have a low BPM maturity level.

One of the biggest expectations we perceive from public servants is guidance (what to do and how to do it) in a BPM project. Therefore we believe that an easy-to-use, step-by-step BPM methodology should be created and provided on the platform. It will help public servants understand the importance of process sharing and, in turn, help maintaining the community on the platform and ensuring its success in the long run.

5 Conclusion

We showed four areas of opportunity where process sharing platforms can greatly improve the efficiency of E-Government BPM projects. A lack of participation from the community, however, would present the main threat. We stated that in our opinion the cause of a lack of participation would be that potential users fail to perceive the added value of the platform. We also highlighted possible options to communicate this added value for different user groups. We proposed to create a step-by-step methodology to help the users understand the opportunities at their disposal and put them in practice. We proposed also to use marketing tools to communicate the benefits of the platform to the users.

Overall, we believe that even if the platform is operated and moderated by specialists, it must be targeted also, if not priorily, at beginners. The whole communication should be adapted to the actual state of BPM maturity of the targeted public and should not assume that they are also specialists who will immediately perceive the complete potential of the tool they are given.

References

Ahrend, N.: Opportunities and limitations of BPM initiatives in public administrations across levels and institutions. Dissertation zur Erlangung des akademischen Grades doctor rerum politicarum (Doktor der Wirtschaftswissenschaft), Wirtschaftswissenschaftilichen Fakultät der Humboldt-Universität zu Berlin (2014)

Ahrend, N., Pittke, F., Leopold, H.: Barriers and strategies of process knowledge sharing in public sector organizations. In: Multikonferenz Wirtschaftsinformatik (2014)

Cooper, A.: The Inmates Are Running the Asylum Why High-Tech Products Drive Us Crazy and How to Restore the Sanity. Sams Publishing, Indianapolis (2004)

Dargan, T., Evequoz, F.: Designing engaging e-government services by combining user-centered design and gamification: a use-case. To appear at ECEG 2015, Portsmouth, June 2015

Delafontaine, S.: Méthodologie d'application du BPM dans le cadre de projets informatiques. To be published, Institut d'Informatique de Gestion, HES-SO Valais – Wallis (2015)

Dijkman, R., La Rosa, M., Reijers, H.A.: Managing large collections of business process models - current techniques and challenges. In: Computers in Industry, 28 November 2011

eCH, E-Government Standards (2015). http://www.ech.ch/. Accessed 14 July 2015

Eid-Sabbagh, R.-H., Kunze, M., Weske, M.: An open process model library. In: Daniel, F., Barkaoui, K., Dustdar, S. (eds.) BPM Workshops 2011, Part II. LNBIP, vol. 100, pp. 26–38. Springer, Heidelberg (2012)

Jurisch, M., et al.: Entwicklung eines Domänenmodells zur Identifikation und Analyse von Prozessketten (2014). http://www.researchgate.net/publication/267705955. (Accessed 02 July 2015)

Kim, S., Lee, H.: The impact of organizational context and information technology on employee knowledge-sharing capabilities. Publ. Adm. Rev. 66(3), 370–385 (2006)

Liu, Z., Le Calvé, A., Cretton, F., Evéquoz, F., Mugellini, E.: A framework for semantic business process management in e-government. In: IADIS International Conference on WWW/Internet, Fort Worth, Texas, USA, pp. 259–267. International Association for Development of the Information Society (2013)

NPB, Nationale Prozessbibliothek (2015). http://www.prozessbibliothek.de/. Accessed 14 July 2015

Pardo, T.A., Cresswell, A.M., Thompson, F., Zhang, J.: Knowledge sharing in cross-boundary information system development in the public sector1. Inf. Technol. Manag. **7**, 293–313 (2006)

Schlatter, U.: Prozessmanagement in den Gemeinden der deutsch- und rätoromanisch- sprachigen Schweiz Umfragerresultate, ZHAW School of Management and Law, Institut für Wirtschaftsinformatik (2014)

Weske, M.: Business Process Management Concepts, Languages, Architectures. Springer, Berlin (2007)

Job Construals – Conceptualizing and Measuring Process Participants' Perception of Process Embeddedness

Janina Kettenbohrer[1]([✉]), Daniel Beimborn[2], and Ina Siebert[3]

[1] Department of Information Systems and Services,
University of Bamberg, Bamberg, Germany
janina.kettenbohrer@uni-bamberg.de
[2] Management Department, Frankfurt School of Finance and Management,
Frankfurt am Main, Germany
d.beimborn@fs.de
[3] Harz University of Applied Sciences, Wernigerode, Germany
i.siebert.90@googlemail.com

Abstract. Business Process Standardization (BPS) is an important instrument to enhance an organizations' competitiveness. A crucial element to achieve BPS is the change-supportive attitude by the affected employees. Previous studies have drawn attention on various determinants of attitude such as the employee's motivation and culture but also on the broader process and work environment and on an employee's perception of the embeddedness of their tasks. In this paper, we draw on the latter and on the theoretical concepts of self-construal and task interdependence to develop a theoretical concept named 'job construals'. To measure the construct, we develop a valid measurement scale. Therefore, we use a card sorting approach with BPM experts to assess the validity of the measure. The contribution of our work lies in understanding the drivers of BPS acceptance and consequently the successful implementation of process standardization initiatives.

Keywords: Business process standardization · Business process management · Job characteristics · Job construals

1 Introduction

Business Process Standardization (BPS) is one of the major topics within Business Process Management (BPM) [1]. To be successful, standardized processes need to be accepted by those involved in these processes. BPS can induce a lot of changes (e.g. changes with respect to technology or governance), which affect employees' work tremendously and are perceived as threatening by the employees. Consequently, employees' attitude towards BPS is often bearish or even negative [2]. As previous research [3] shows, a lack of change-supportive attitude by the employees is often one of the reasons why process improvement initiatives fail. To foster BPS acceptance, first studies have drawn attention on its determinants such as employee motivation and process culture [4–6]. Besides these factors, the broader environment and employees'

© Springer International Publishing Switzerland 2016
M. Reichert and H.A. Reijers (Eds.): BPM Workshops 2015, LNBIP 256, pp. 293–304, 2016.
DOI: 10.1007/978-3-319-42887-1_24

perception of the embeddedness of their tasks are supposedly playing an important role [2]. Because of this, we aim to develop a construct which draws on the broader process environment and the employees' perception of their tasks within this environment. Thus, our paper is guided by the following research question:

How can task embeddedness, as perceived by the individuals executing the task, be conceptualized and measured in order to serve as an explanatory factor in BPS acceptance research?

We draw on the theoretical concept of self-construals and job characteristics theory (introduced in the next section) in order to derive a new construct named 'job construals' (Sect. 3.1). Then we will develop a measurement instrument and qualify its content validity by applying a multi-stage card sorting approach with process management experts. Finally, the paper concludes with a discussion and an outlook on how this measure can be used to expand our understanding of the drivers or inhibitors of BPS acceptance and thus successful business process standardization projects.

2 Theoretical Background

2.1 Self-construals

Individuals have different perceptions of the self, of others, and of the interdependence between themselves and their fellow people, which are called 'self-construals' [7]. These different perceptions can influence the individual's experiences, cognitions, emotions, and motivation [7–9]. For example, people of collectivistic cultures, e.g. India or Japan, are more likely to see themselves *"as interdependent with close others and as defined by important roles and situations"* [10, p. 791]. In contrast, people of Western cultures, e.g. United States, *"tend to think of themselves as independent of relationships and as autonomous or separated from others"* [10, p. 791].

The independent self-construal is based on individualism, personal rights, and the autonomy of the individual [7]. The underlying assumption is the separation of an individual from the others [10]. In contrast, the interdependent self-construal is shaped by the assumption that *"the person is connected to others, so that the self is defined, at least in part, by important roles, group memberships, or relationships"* [10, p. 791]. The different forms of self-construals influence various self-related processes, e.g. cognitive processes, motivational processes or even relationships. So, acting in accordance with the self and subconscious goals are one of the key drivers for motivation [11]. Individuals with an independent self-construal perceive self-esteem and positive views on themselves by standing out, competing with others or defining themselves [10, 12]. Persons with an interdependent self-construal perceive positive feelings in the relationships with others [10].

2.2 Task Interdependence

Task interdependence is considered as one of the most important variables to influence team performance [13]. It is defined as *"the degree to which the interaction and coordination of team members are required to complete tasks"* [14, p. 514].

According to the job characteristics theory of Hackman and Oldham [15], five core job characteristics (skill variety, task identity, task significance, autonomy, and feedback) increase positive behavioral outcomes (e.g. job performance) and attitudinal outcomes (e.g. job satisfaction) and decrease negative behavioral outcomes (e.g. turnover) [15]. Kiggundu [16] extends this set of core job characteristics by developing a new construct named 'task interdependence'. He identifies two types of task interdependence: initiated and received. Initiated task interdependence is defined as *"the degree to which work flows from a particular job to one or more jobs. A person in a job characterized by high initiated task interdependence directly affects the jobs of others"* [16, p. 501], while received task interdependence refers to *"the extent to which a person in a particular job is affected by the workflow from one or more other jobs"* [16, p. 501]. According to Kiggundu [16], initiated task interdependence influences a person's experienced responsibility for work [17, 18]. In contrast to the positive effect of initiated task interdependence, received task interdependence is supposed to have a negative effect on experienced responsibility [16].

3   Construct Development

The goal of this paper is to expand the understanding of how the broader process environment and the employees' perception of their tasks influence their acceptance of business process standardization initiatives. In the following, we use the aforementioned theoretical concepts to derive the construct of 'job construals' and to propose its impact on individual BPS acceptance.

3.1   Definition of the Job Construal Construct

Business process standardization is defined as *"the unification of variants of a given business process by aligning the variants against an archetype process"* [19, p. 31]. Accordingly, BPS acceptance refers to a worker's acceptance of different BPS-caused changes of his or her work. These changes can involve changes in tasks, workflows, working conditions, technology, and governance. For example, new tasks have to be executed or existing workflows are changed because the process becomes more regulated. In addition, standardization can lead to changes in used technology, such as software applications or other tools. And modified governance structures can affect the employee by, for example, working for a new manager [20].

We propose that employees' BPS acceptance is largely determined by how they perceive their work embedded within the process. To capture this perception we draw on the two concepts of self-construals and task interdependence and define 'job construals' as an employee's self-perception of the embeddedness of his/her job in the overall work or process environment. As such, job construals refer to the interdependence respectively independence which the employee perceives to exist between his/her work and the work of his/her colleagues.

Accordingly, job construals are described on a continuum within two extremes: interdependence and independence. In the following, we will explain these two extremes in detail. The degree of employees' self-perception of the embeddedness of their job in the overall work or process environment is highly related to the degree of process orientation of the company [21]. A process-oriented organization is a company, which highlights the importance of processes as opposed to hierarchies at all levels by specially emphasizing outcomes and customer satisfaction [22]. Business process management is seen as a comprehensive approach to achieve process orientation because it combines several elements of other approaches, for example, total quality management or continuous process improvement [23]. As one prerequisite for process management success, employee empowerment and training receive increasingly attention [6, 24–26]. Škrinjar and Trkman [23] show that one important practice in employee empowerment is *"that employees begin to understand the entire process and the inter-process linkages and not just their individual activities"* [23, p. 55]. Interestingly, Škrinjar and Trkman [23] can also show that employees do not necessarily need new skills to be able to successfully execute tasks in the process environment. They rather need a new way of thinking [23]. For example, this new way of thinking can be created by employees getting involved in defining the new process, which in turn leads to commitment, ownership and less resistance against the BPS induced changes [6]. In addition, it creates a feeling of *"being part of a bigger picture"* [6, p. 11].

We assume that this new way of thinking and the acceptance of BPS induced changes are highly influenced by an employee's self-perception regarding his/her task in the overall process. Thus, we argue that employees who see their tasks highly interdependent to other tasks within the process and regard their tasks embedded in the overall process (exhibiting an interdependent job construal) perceive their job as cog in the wheel. Consequently, they are more likely to have the overall process in mind and put the process and its objectives over their single tasks.

According to task interdependence, the job construals extreme of interdependence is two folded. Employees can perceive initiated interdependence (initiated interdependent job construal) or received interdependence (received interdependent job construal) regarding their jobs in the process.

As initiated task interdependence influences a person's experienced responsibility for his/her work, it is positively related to employees' work motivation and work performance [16]. Several studies in psychological research show the motivational potential of initiated task interdependence. Kahn et al. [27] discuss that interdependence creates *"some pressure that arouses in the focal person a psychological force of some magnitude and direction"* [16, p. 504]. Lawler et al. [28] find that managers responded more positively for self-initiated interactions than for other-initiated interactions. In addition, the managers perceived self-initiated interactions as more satisfying, valuable, and interesting [28]. Some works state that these relationships may be attenuated by organizational stress [27, 29]. In the context of process management, employees who perceive high initiated interdependent job construals perceive their task in the process as important and very influencing on others' work. Thus, stress will arise, because the expected quality of task execution is often not clear for all involved participants. Without being certain of what is expected from them, they still know that the result of their work highly influences others' work.

In contrast to the motivational effect of initiated task interdependence, received task interdependence has a negative effect. Thompson [30] states that increased received task interdependence leads to a decrease in autonomy, which indirectly reduces motivation and work satisfaction. This finding is supported by Trist and Bamforth who show that workers executing a role of high received task interdependence feel, for example, less responsible for production and show more absenteeism and turnover than others [31]. Process employees who execute a task of high received interdependent job construal are highly dependent from tasks executed by their colleagues. If it is not clear who delivers what input in which time, it leads to irritation for the employees. Consequently, these employees will not take over responsibility for the results of their process tasks.

In contrast to an interdependent job construal, employees who exhibit an independent job construal perceive their job as self-contained, intellectual and/or artistic. They do not feel committed to and involved in the overall process. Due to the self- and task-oriented view, they do not give the overall process and its objectives as much importance as employees with interdependent job construals.

3.2   Operationalization of the Job Construals Construct

A construct can be seen as an abstract representation of a phenomenon of interest to researchers [32, 33]; it needs to be operationalized to be captured in empirical research. To operationalize our new construct, we followed the methodology by Churchill [34]. According to him, there are three stages for construct development: In stage 1 the domain of the construct is defined; In stage 2 the construct is operationalized by proposing and developing a measurement scale, e.g. creating survey items; In stage 3, data received by using the measurement instrument are statistically analyzed to prove the construct's reliability and validity [34]. Since this is a conceptual paper, we only focus on the first two stages which will be described in detail in the following sections.

Core goal of stage 2, the generation of a measure, is ensuring content validity, i.e., ensuring that the measure does adequately measure and empirically reflect the theoretical construct [33].

To derive a relevant measurement scale for job construals and to ensure content validity of our measures, we designed the items by adapting multi-item measures from existing psychology and management research on self-construals and task interdependence. In addition, we added self-developed items. Existing measurement scales were not blindly adapted but their appropriateness was tested by discussions with experts. We asked 17 BPM experts who work in a global service company in the aviation industry. The company uses a role-based, process-oriented management system to document its processes and organizational structures. All 17 experts work in the process management department and it is their daily business to work in and with processes (e.g., as process modeler, process owner or process participant).

In the following, we discuss the development of a new multi-item measurement scale for job construals whereby we followed established guidelines [35]. Table 1 lists the relevant literature screened for the item development.

We rephrased the items depending on their origin: items originally measuring self-construal were changed from self-perception to job-perception. For example, we adapted the item *"To what extent does the individual depend on his/her colleagues for*

Table 1. Literature sources for adapted multi-item measures for job construals

Construct	References
Self-construal	Cross (1995) [36]; Cross et al. (2000) [10];
	Jenkins et al. (1975) [37]; Singelis and Sharkley (1995) [38]
Task interdependence	Aiken and Hage (1968) [39]; Billings et al. 1977 [40];
	Lynch (1974) [41]; Mohr (1971) [42];
	Overton et al. (1977) [43]; Thomas (1957) [17]

doing his/her job?" [37, p. 177] to *"My task within the process highly depends on tasks of other colleagues"*. Items derived from task interdependence were changed from an objective view to an individual perceptual view. Table 3 shows the adaptation of the items.

To evaluate the content validity of the derived items, we applied a card sorting procedure: Experts needed to assign the items to the new construct of job construals. In the first round, we discussed each of the 58 items with six BPM experts.

Table 2 summarizes the number of experts involved in each round as well as their work experience and their expertise in terms of BPM.

Table 2. Expert qualification for each round

	1st round			2nd round			Overall		
	Average (years)	Minimum (years)	Maximum (years)	Average (years)	Minimum (years)	Maximum (years)	Average (years)	Minimum (years)	Maximum (years)
Company affiliation	10.4	1	30	11	1.5	19	10.8	1	30
Work experience	13.7	2	30	15.5	4	26	14.8	2	30
Experience in BPM	7.7	2	15	9.5	1.5	25	8.9	1.5	25
Number of experts		6			11			17	

Furthermore, we discussed the construct definition with the experts so that they had the opportunity to report on poor wording or potential misunderstandings. To guarantee construct validity of potential items and to identify poorly worded or ambiguous terms, we asked the experts to sort the items to three different construct categories (job construal, autonomy, and 'others'). To also check for 'discriminant' content validity, the 58 items included four items for measuring 'autonomy' [44], a construct that is strongly related to task independence, in the card sorting procedure. In the job characteristics model by Hackman and Oldham [45], autonomy is defined as *"the degree to which the [design of the] job provides substantial freedom, independence, and discretion to the individual in scheduling the work and in determining the procedures to be used in carrying it out"* [45, p. 258]. All six experts sorted these four items to the category 'autonomy', which indicates high content-wise differentiation among the two constructs. We also added the category 'others' to provide a kind of container category for all items which the experts seemed to be neither suitable for job construals nor for autonomy. As a result of the first round, eleven out of the 58 items showed high values of substantive validity (listed in Tables 3 and 4). Besides, we checked whether there are unclear or poorly formulated items. In such cases, we reworded the items according to the answers of the participants and started round two.

Table 3. Adaptation and assignment of items

Item	Original construct	Original item	Reference	Adapted item
JC1	Self-construal	When I think of myself, I often think of my close friends or family also	[10]	It is also part of my job to know the tasks of my colleagues
JC2		To what extent does the individual depend on his/her colleagues for doing his/her job?	[37]	My task within the process highly depends on tasks of other colleagues
JC3	Task interdependence	I have to talk to other workers to get my job done	[40]	I need to communicate with my colleagues to carry out my work
JC4		I must wait for someone to finish their job before I can do my job	[40]	I need to wait until others have finished their task so that I can start with my work
JC5	Self-developed items	My job is of great importance for my company/organization		
JC6		My task is a step in a longer process chain, a small step to fulfill a bigger task (to work on the assembly line)		
JC7		Tasks of others directly depend on mine		
JC8		Work activities highly depend on the work of other people		
JC9		The completion of my work depends on the work of many other people		
JC10		The successful fulfillment of my task highly depends on intensive consultation with my colleagues		
JC11		If others do not finish their job, I cannot get my job done		

In the second round, we repeated the sorting task: We asked 11 other BPM experts in face-to-face conversations to sort the 58 items into the three constructs (job construals, autonomy, and others). To ensure comprehensibility, the experts categorized the items and also reported on problems with wording of the single items. This round, seven (JC1, JC2, JC3, JC6, JC7 JC9, and JC11) out of 58 items were chosen (listed in Tables 3 and 4). To predict the measure's performance, we used a pre-test assessment of the measure's substantive validities proposed by Anderson and Gerbing [46]. A measure's substantive validity is a major prerequisite for construct validity.

In addition, the small-sample nature of substantive validity assessments is appropriate for pre-tests. To assess substantive validity, card-sorting is necessary. As described above, the experts sorted the single items to the constructs they thought the item fits the best. To analyze the assignments of the experts, Anderson and Gerbing [46] propose two indices: proportion of substantive agreement (P_{SA}) and substantive validity coefficient (C_{SV}). The proportion of substantive agreement is defined as *"the extent to which an item reflects its intended construct. [But it] does not indicate the extent to which an item might also be tapping other, unintended constructs"* [46, p. 734]. Therefore, the substantive validity coefficient is applied. The C_{SV} index *"reflects the extent to which respondents assign an item to its posited construct more than to any other construct"* [46, p. 734]. The values for P_{SA} range from 0.0 to 1.0 and for C_{SV} from -1.0 to 1.0. A higher value indicates a greater substantive validity for both indices, with 0.5 being the recommended threshold for sufficient substantive validity [46].

Table 4. Substantive validity pre-test per item

Item	1st round		2round	
	P_{SA}	C_{SV}	P_{SA}	C_{SV}
JC1	1.00	1.00	0.91	0.91
JC2	0.83	0.67	0.82	0.73
JC3	0.83	0.67	0.82	0.73
JC4	0.83	0.67	0.64	0.45
JC5	1.00	1.00	0.64	0.36
JC6	1.00	1.00	0.82	0.73
JC7	0.83	0.67	0.73	0.55
JC8	0.83	0.67	0.55	0.27
JC9	0.83	0.67	0.82	0.73
JC10	0.67	0.50	0.64	0.45
JC11	0.67	0.50	0.73	0.64

4　Implications, Limitations, and Conclusion

Since a construct is an abstract representation of a phenomenon of interest to researchers, it needs to be operationalized to be captured in empirical research. To operationalize job construals, we followed the methodology by Churchill [34]. We defined the domain of the construct (stage 1) and we operationalized the construct by proposing and developing a measurement scale (stage 2). Therefore, we applied the card-sorting method to derive adequate items. After adapting existing items from literature and discussing them with 17 BPM experts, seven items (after round two; JC1, JC2, JC3, JC6, JC7, JC9, and JC11) remained, which indicate high values of substantive validity of job construal. As Churchill [34] proposes, data received by using the measurement instrument have to be statistically analyzed to prove the construct's reliability and validity (stage 3).

The success of process standardization initiatives is highly dependent on employees executing single process-related tasks. Earlier research has drawn attention to them by considering employee motivation and process culture [4–6]. In addition, the broader environment and employees' perception of the embeddedness of their tasks have to be taken into account [2]. The construct derived and discussed in this paper is an important step towards a more employee-oriented view of process standardization. We argue that the higher employees perceive their tasks embedded in the overall process, the more likely they will accept process standardization induced changes. The development of the job construals construct as well as the corresponding measurement scale can be seen as a promising step towards an instrument allowing process managers to assess the perceived task embeddedness of their employees. We are convinced that this will help mangers to make the right decisions to increase process orientation of their employees. For instance, if managers find out that their process employees do not perceive their tasks embedded in the overall process, managers could organize trainings for them to enhance process orientation and process thinking [26]. Consequently, they will be more likely to accept changes induced by BPS.

Overall, with this new construct and its operationalization, we offer several contributions. First, we provide a conceptualization that explains the impact of process environment and employees' perception of the embeddedness of their tasks on process standardization acceptance. This is a major benefit for both, researchers and practitioners. It is important for BPM research to focus on the employees working in the processes [6] in the same extent as on e.g. modelling tools. Our newly developed construct is promising because it combines and enhances several research fields such as psychology, organizational management and business process management. We transferred the two constructs of self-construals [e.g., 7–9] and task interdependence [16, 47] into the context of BPM and BPS. Thus, we managed to develop a new construct, which stresses the importance of the broader process environment for process standardization acceptance, with which we will be able to support managers by planning and implementing process standardization initiatives.

So far, our research has several limitations. First, we only talked with experts within one company, which limits generalizability and could cause bias. To cure that, further interviews with individuals of different backgrounds could be held. Second, the measurement scale's development process described in this paper is not finished yet. Due to missing quantitative research, only the first steps of validation (i.e., content validity) were achieved so far. Therefore, we will test our construct empirically on a larger scale and evaluate it via an SEM-based approach.

However, although our construct is at its current state only conceptual, researchers and practitioners may benefit from our insights on how process standardization initiatives could be implemented successfully by considering the broader process environment as well the employees' perception of their tasks within a process.

References

1. Brucker-Kley, E., Kykalová, D., Pedron, C., Luternauer, T., Keller, T.: Business Process Management 2014 - Status quo und Perspektiven eines ganzheitlichen Geschäftsprozessmanagements (Business Process Management 2014 - Status quo and perspectives for comprehensive Business Process Management). vdf Hochschulverl, Zürich (2014)
2. Kettenbohrer, J., Eckhardt, A., Beimborn, D.: A theoretical perspective on meaningfulness of work and the success of business process standardization initiatives. In: 12th Internationale Tagung Wirtschaftsinformatik, Osnabrück, Germany (2015)
3. Tenner, A.R., deToro, I.J.: Process Redesign: The Implementation Guide for Managers. Prentice-Hall, Upper Saddle River (2000)
4. Tumbas, S., Schmiedel, T.: Developing an organizational culture supportive of business process management. In: 11th International Conference on Wirtschaftsinformatik, Leipzig, Germany (2013)
5. Schmiedel, T., vom Brocke, J., Recker, J.: Which cultural values matter to business process management? Bus. Process Manag. J. **19**, 292–317 (2013)
6. vom Brocke, J., Schmiedel, T., Recker, J., Trkman, P., Mertens, W., Viaene, S.: Ten principles of good business process management. Bus. Process Manag. J. **20**, 530–548 (2014)
7. Markus, H.R., Kitayama, S.: Culture and the self: implications for cognition, emotion, and motivation. Psychol. Rev. **98**, 224–253 (1991)
8. Triandis, H.C.: The self and social behavior in differing cultural contexts. Psychol. Rev. **96**, 506–520 (1989)
9. Shweder, R.A., Bourne, E.J.: Does the concept of the person vary cross-culturally? In: Shweder, R.A., LeVine, R.A. (eds.) Culture Theory: Essays on Mind, Self, and Emotion, pp. 158–199. Cambridge University Press, Cambridge (1984)
10. Cross, S.E., Bacon, P.L., Morris, M.L.: The relational-interdependent self-construal and relationships. J. Pers. Soc. Psychol. **78**, 791–808 (2000)
11. Barrick, M.R., Mount, M.K.: The theory of purposeful work behavior. The role of personality, higher-order goals, and job characteristics. Acad. Manag. Rev. **38**, 132–153 (2013)
12. Blaine, B., Crocker, J.: Self-esteem and self-serving biases in reactions to positive and negative events: an integrative review. In: Baumeister, R.F. (ed.) Self-esteem: The Puzzle of Low Self-Regard, pp. 55–85. Plenum Press, New York (1993)
13. Saavedra, R.P., Earley, P.C., van Dyne, L.: Complex interdepedence in task-performing groups. J. Appl. Psychol. **78**, 61–72 (1993)
14. Langfred, C.W.: Autonomy and performance in teams: the multilevel moderating effect of task interdependence. J. Manag. **31**, 513–529 (2005)
15. Hackman, J.R., Oldham, G.R.: Development of the job diagnostic survey. J. Appl. Psychol. **60**, 159–170 (1975)
16. Kiggundu, M.N.: Task interdependence and the theory of job design. Acad. Manag. Rev. **6**, 499–508 (1981)
17. Thomas, E.J.: Effects of facilitative role interdependence on group functioning. Hum. Relat. **10**, 347–366 (1957)
18. Turner, A.N., Lawrence, P.R.: Individual jobs and the worker. Harvard University, Graduate School of Business Administration, Boston (1965)

19. Münstermann, B., Eckhardt, A., Weitzel, T.: The performance impact of business process standardization: an empirical evaluation of the recruitment process. Bus. Process Manag. J. **16**, 29–56 (2010)
20. Borgen, W.A., Butterfield, L.D., Amundson, N.E.: The experience of change and its impact on workers who self-identify as doing well with change that affects their work. J. Employ. Couns. **47**, 2–11 (2010)
21. Hammer, M.: What is business process management? In: vom Brocke, J., Rosemann, M. (eds.) Handbook of Business Process Management 1, pp. 3–16. Springer, Heidelberg (2010)
22. McCormack, K.: Business Process Maturity: Theory and Application. BookSurge Publishing, Charleston (2007)
23. Škrinjar, R., Trkman, P.: Increasing process orientation with business process management: critical practices'. Int. J. Inf. Manage. **33**, 48–60 (2013)
24. Pritchard, J., Armistead, C.: Business process management - lessons from european business. Bus. Process Manag. J. **5**, 10–35 (1999)
25. Indulska, M., Recker, J., Rosemann, M., Green, P.: Business process modelling: current issuess and future challenge. In: Hutchison, D.E.A. (ed.) Advanced Information Systems Engineering, pp. 501–514. Springer, Heidelberg (2009)
26. Kohlbacher, M., Gruenwald, S.: Process orientation: conceptualization and measurement. Bus. Process Manag. J. **17**, 267–283 (2011)
27. Kahn, R.L., Wolfe, D.M., Quinn, R.P., Snoek, J.D., Rosenthal, R.A.: Organizational Stress: Studies in Conflict and Ambiguity. Wiley, New York (1964)
28. Lawler, E.E., Porter, L.W., Tannenbaum, A.: Managers' attitudes towards interaction episodes. J. Appl. Psychol. **52**, 432–439 (1968)
29. Kiggundu, M.N., Cook, W.: Testing for the double moderating effects of growth need strength in the Hackman-Oldham theory of job design. In: Alutto, J.A., Wahba, M.A. (eds.) Management and Organizations: Current perspectives (1978)
30. Thompson, J.D.: Organizations in Action. McGraw-Hill, New York (1967)
31. Trist, E.L., Bamforth, K.W.: Some social and psychological consequences of the longwall method of coal getting. Hum. Relat. **4**, 3–38 (1951)
32. Byrd, T.A., Turner, D.E.: Measuring the flexibility of information technology infrastructure: exploratory analysis of a construct. J. Manag. Inf. Syst. **17**, 167–208 (2000)
33. Lewis, B.R., Snyder, C.A., Rainer, R.K.J.: An empirical assessment of the information resource management construct. J. Manag. Inf. Syst. **12**, 199–223 (1995)
34. Churchill, G.A.: A paradigm for developing better measures of marketing constructs. J. Mark. Res. **16**, 64–73 (1979)
35. Moore, G., Benbasat, I.: Development of an instrument to measure the perceptions of adopting an information technology information. Inf. Syst. Res. **2**, 192–222 (1991)
36. Cross, S.E.: Self-construals, coping, and stress in cross-cultural adaptation. J. Cross Cult. Psychol. **26**, 673–697 (1995)
37. Jenkins, G.D.J., Lawler III, E.E., Nadler, D.A., Cammann, C.: Standardized observations: an approach to measuring the nature of of jobs. J. Appl. Psychol. **60**, 171–181 (1975)
38. Singelis, T.M., Sharkley, W.F.: Culture, self-construal, and embrrassability. J. Cross Cult. Psychol. **26**, 622–644 (1995)
39. Aiken, M., Hage, J.: Organizational interdependence and intra-organizational structure. Am. Sociol. Rev. **33**, 912–930 (1968)
40. Billings, R.S., Klimoski, R.J., Breaugh, J.A.: The impact of a change in technology on job characteristics. Adm. Sci. Q. **22**, 318–339 (1977)
41. Lynch, B.P.: An empirical assessment of perrow's technology construct. Adm. Sci. Q. **19**, 338–356 (1974)

42. Mohr, L.B.: Organization technology and organization structure. Adm. Sci. Q. **16**, 444–459 (1971)
43. Overton, P., Schneck, R.E., Hazlett, C.B.: An empirical study of the technology of nursing units. Adm. Sci. Q. **22**, 203–219 (1977)
44. Morgeson, F.P., Humphrey, S.E.: The work design questionnaire (WDQ): developing and validating a comprehensive measure for assessing job design and the nature of work. J. Appl. Psychol. **91**, 1321–1339 (2006)
45. Hackman, J.R., Oldham, G.R.: Motivation through the degin of work. test of a theory. Organ. Behav. Hum. Perform. **16**, 250–279 (1976)
46. Anderson, J.C., Gerbing, D.W.: Predicting the performance of measures in a confirmatory factor analysis with a pretest assessment of their substantive validities. J. Appl. Psychol. **76**, 732–740 (1991)
47. Kiggundu, M.N.: Task interdependence and job design: test of a theory. Organ. Behav. Hum. Perform. **31**, 145–172 (1983)

Social-Data Driven Sales Processes in Local Clothing Retail Stores

Barbara Keller[2(✉)], Rainer Schmidt[1], Michael Möhring[2],
Ralf-Christian Härting[2], and Alfred Zimmermann[3]

[1] Hochschule München, Lothstr. 64, 80335 Munich, Germany
Rainer.Schmidt@hm.edu
[2] Hochschule Aalen, Beethovenstr. 1, 73430 Aalen, Germany
{Barbara.Keller,Michael.Moehring,
Ralf.Haerting}@hs-aalen.de
[3] Reutlingen University, Alteburgstr. 150, 72762 Reutlingen, Germany
Alfred.Zimmermann@uni-reutlingen.de

Abstract. Local clothing retailers compete with online retailers but have difficulties to increase cross-selling revenues. Therefore, a data-driven sales process is conceptualized that uses data from social software in order to increase revenue. It identifies and tracks the customer using RFIDs in customer loyalty cards. By these means, social data can be used in all phases of the purchase and both for major and minor purchases. Individual product suggestions and offerings can be tailored. Local retailers are able to catch up with online retailers in their cross- and upselling revenues. In consequence, local retailers are able to stay competitive.

Keywords: Social BPM · Retail · Data driven · Local retailers · Social software · Social data · Sales processes · Clothing retail store

1 Introduction

The clothing retail sector is an important part of the German economy with revenues of 59 billion euro [Hand13] and grows continuously. In particular buyers of higher priced clothes, appreciate competent advice in a specialist shop and therefore usually avoid online retailers [Derh00, KeHa06]. Furthermore, consumer spending for clothing is constantly increasing, which affects positively the clothing industry as a whole [Dest13]. Local retailers compete more and more with online retailers like Amazon, Zappos or Rakuten. On the one hand, local retailers have not to cope with expensive product returns [WMKS14] as online retailers. On the other hand, retailers with classic branches have difficulties to increase cross-selling revenues unlike established online retailers such as Amazon.de, Zalando or the Otto Group. This is associated with shrinking revenues and decreasing customer contacts. The reason is that consumers and their interests often cannot be analyzed (in contrast to online shops with purchases and search history). This phenomenon is similar for local retailers outside Germany. Local retailers should implement more customer-oriented sales processes and focus on their individual core competencies like product guidance and mentoring as well as (after sales) service.

© Springer International Publishing Switzerland 2016
M. Reichert and H.A. Reijers (Eds.): BPM Workshops 2015, LNBIP 256, pp. 305–315, 2016.
DOI: 10.1007/978-3-319-42887-1_25

Therefore, this paper addresses the research question: how local retailers can improve sales business processes using social BPM. The paper is structured as follows. First, the basic paradigms of social BPM are discussed. Then the effects of Big Data and RFID are analyzed. We then introduce a data-driven sales architecture for local retailers. Based on it, we show how social BPM is leveraged for improving sales processes. Finally, we discuss related work and give an outlook on future work.

2   Fundamentals of Social BPM

Although Business Process Management introduced a customer-oriented perspective, it still contains many tayloristic [Tayl11] concepts. Therefore, it does not surprise, that a plenty of approaches tries to develop support for cooperation beyond strictly structured business processes (e.g. WFMS's, BPMS, case management). However, these approaches are not as successful as expected [BDJK11]. One of the reasons is that these early approaches limited the participation of stakeholders. For instance, although classical groupware abstained from pre-defining a strict control flow, specific access rights to documents had been assigned. Thus, the group of possible contributors had been limited. In this way, an apriori-decision had been made deciding who may contribute and who may not. Some stakeholders were not able to contribute.

Social software [ScNu09] is defined as software that uses three governing paradigms: social production [Benk06], weak ties [Gran83] and collective decisions [TaWi06]. It opposes to tayloristic [Tayl11], hierarchic and elitist models of the firm [ScNu09]. Social production organizes production by combining the decisions of a multitude of stakeholders instead of a plan created by management. Social software follows an a-posteriori approach. Everybody may contribute but only the contributions considered valuable pass through the later cooperative editing by all stakeholders. Social production enables value co-creation, the inclusion of the consumer into value creation.

Weak ties [Gran83] are relationships between individuals that are cross-cutting organizational boundaries. They are defined by competencies and experiences. Weak ties are created by incident or by deliberate search of the individual, but not in a top-down manner by management. The collaboration initiated by weak ties does not necessarily have to happen in software. Collective decisions [TaWi06] decorrelate errors by overlaying a large number of independent judgements.

Important types of social software are social media and social networks [Schm12]. Social media combines the concepts of social production and weak ties. Social networks establish weak ties [Gran83] and allow collective decisions [TaWi06].

3   Big Data and RFID

Big Data receives a great deal of attention in industry and research [LLSH11]. The largest benefits of Big Data can be leveraged by companies engaged in the business areas of IT and technology development and marketing [SMMP14]. Big Data is not a specific technology or technology platform such as Hadoop [Whit12], but embraces a series of technological advances creating a significant expansion of the analytical capabilities. The decision support in business was based for a long time primarily on structured data from internal sources. These structured data originate from commercial transactions and are typically managed by ERP systems. The structured data were transferred by extraction, loading and transformation in a data warehouse [ChDa97]. Analytic functions in the context of business analytics [Dave10] or Business Intelligence [KeBL13] are available. Typically, they use a descriptive, backward-looking perspective.

Because of the high costs and the long lead times, strategic decision-making processes were supported in the first place. However, this classical approach is often overwhelmed because of the centralized architecture. These limitations become even more evident when processing of semi-structured and unstructured data. Typically, customer comments from a web-site do not stick to predefined structures. Therefore, to process semi- and unstructured data a number of technologies have been developed such as Hadoop and NoSQL [FHBB11]. They are characterized by a significant deviation from the classical system architectures, such as a centralized database approach and the use of relational schemas [Codd72] (Fig. 1).

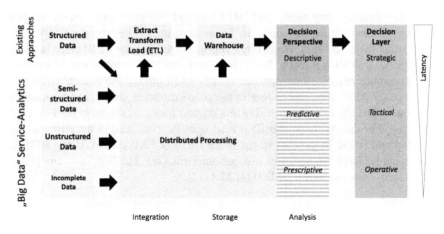

Fig. 1. Big Data to support decision making in business based on [SMZH14]

Using a parallel architecture, the processing of very large amounts of data is possible [SMMP14]. The considerably higher speed and lower costs of analysis creation allows it to be used for tactical and operational decision-making processes, too [SMMP14]. Therefore, Big Data is used for doing analyses to address the customer individually and enable an individualized pricing. It is also used to support classic customer loyalty programs [Mcbr11].

RFID [Fink02] is a technology for the identification and localization of objects with the aid of electromagnetic waves. There are the RFID tags attached to the products and a reader device installed inside the shop etc. The reader emits an alternating electromagnetic field. The RFID tag is activated by this electromagnetic field. The electromagnetic waves provide the power for the RFID tag. The chip decodes the commands transmitted by the reader and "broadcasts" information such as its identification number, et cetera. Thus, this technology allows contactless identify objects and forms the basis for new data-driven business processes. Legal basis and framework are already being discussed in various operational situations in the retail [Müll04, KnHa05] and depending on the allowed conditions and configurations.

RFID detection in clothing retail stores is carried out mainly by stitching tags into clothing [Wieh00, Lang05, Robe06]. In this way, RFID is used in the clothing sector for the overall optimization of the supply chain [KoPe07]. Companies such as Gerry Weber [Wieh00] use RFID in support of logistic business processes. By the use of RFID stitched into clothing, customer identification is theoretically possible. However, in practice there are some limitations. The customer would have to wear at least one known by RFID garment branches. Furthermore, the chip can be damaged by washing and similar processes.

4   Data-Driven Sales Architecture for Local Retailers

Previous work recommends to implement data driven sales business processes for local retailers to be more competitive [SMZH14, Mcbr11]. In contrast to online retailers, local retailers cannot track the consumer behavior in their stores the same way online retailers using their web-sites. However, it is possible to integrate RFID chips in loyalty cards [Stoc07, BaYY10, Robe06, Mcbr11]. In this way, the customer can be identified by a far-reaching readers (long distance reader) when joining the branch [SMZH14]. Through many RFID antennas ceiling in the shop customers are tracked by means of the customer card. As a result, each stay in a product range, as shown in the Fig. 2, can be recorded. For this, his customer ID is read from the contained in the customer card RFID chip and linked to the data stored in the CRM or ERP system. Using RFIDs in customer cards, local retailers can use customer tracking and Big Data analytics to improve their sales processes [SMZH14, Mcbr11].

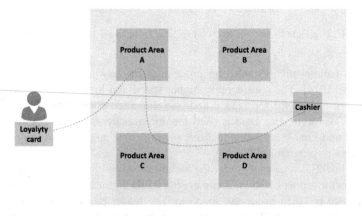

Fig. 2. Customer identification and tracking via RFID, based on [SMZH14]

Based on this tracking results combined with master data of the customer loyalty card (e.g. customer id, name, gender) and transaction data of previous purchases different sales processes can be improved [SMZH14]. For instance, category management can be improved as well as cross-selling by recommending the customer similar articles (e.g. calculated via basked analysis) during the shop stay through local shop assistants. Furthermore, after-sales processes can be improved by sending the customer special offers e.g. via SMS, Email after the visit in the store.

5 Social BPM for Improving Sales Processes

Social BPM can be used to improve the value of each customer (CLV) by influencing sales processes at different purchase phases and purchase types under support of the general information systems architecture (Fig. 3):

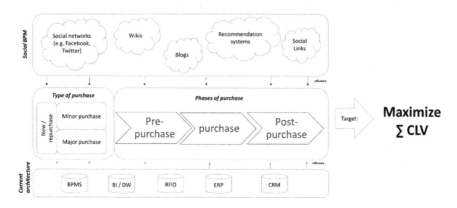

Fig. 3. Use of social BPM for sales processes

Social BPM can improve different sales processes in local retail stores. In general sales processes are influenced by other processes in the retail business [BeKR03]. Furthermore the purchase decisions can be differentiated through the type of purchase according to [Mada09] (Table 1).

Table 1. Type of purchases according to [Mada09, p. 78].

Type of purchase	Minor purchase	Major purchase
New purchase	Limited information search	Extensive information search
	Limited decision making (impulse buying)	Extensive decision making
Repurchase	Low information search	Limited search
	High frequency of purchase	Low frequency of purchase

In general, social BPM can improve sales processes at each type of purchase. Based on the identification of the customers via RFID in the local stores [SMZH14] and analysis of current buying behavior of each customer sales processes can be improved. The most important potential of use social BPM is to improve sales processes for new purchase decisions of the customer. Because in this type of purchase the online retailer must satisfy the customer's needs. Otherwise, the customer do not buy the product and the turnover will be decreased

For instance, recommender systems [Hung05] can help customers for a more structured and faster information search for a new minor purchase. Product recommendation sites are e.g. ciao.com or through large online stores like Amazon.

For new major purchases, Wikis and Blogs or (Facebook) Groups can be a good source for a more detailed perspective of each product. Furthermore, the customer can get in contact to other customers and discuss the design and performance of the product for personal evaluation. Additional to that, recommender systems can be also used as a first step. There are a lot of different domain-specific Blogs and Wikis. For instance, blogs like ZDNet can be used for the information technology sector.

In addition to the different purchase types, social BPM can improve sales processes at the different phases. The purchase process can be defined by different purchase phases: pre-purchase, purchase, post purchase [StSi10, SiSM09, ChBH06].

The Table 2 summarizes the possibilities of social software for improving sales processes:

Table 2. Social BPM support for different purchase phases.

Pre-Purchase Phase	Purchase Phase (in store)	Post-Purchase Phase
- **Customer acquisition** *(e.g. through social networks, corporate blogs, etc.)* - **Improved category management** *(e.g. through trend recognition via social networks etc.)*	- **Better product presentation** *(e.g. for presenting the interesting or demand products at the right time and at the right place)* - **Better customer guidance** *(through individual needs e.g. extracted from social networks and past purchases)* - **Improved cross-selling** *(through individual and peer-group preferences e.g. extracted from social networks and past purchases)*	- **Improved post purchase** - **Improved customer loyalty**

First, in the pre-purchase phase social software can help retailers to get in touch with the customers and improve the category management as well as the product presentation [AsHu10, GGKN05]. That could generate an advantage like following. Whenever people use social media they show their preferences in an unbiased manner while talking to friends, following tweets or liking comments or posts. This information can be collected via social software and use to develop product or customize the assortment [AsHu10, GGKN05].

In the purchase phase, the data generated by the social software could be established to influence consumers' behavior and the purchase decision at the point of sale. The knowledge about customers' needs and preferences offers the retailer a lot of possibilities to improve business and increase sales. For this reason customers could be satisfied customer, which leads to a raising sales quantity [Oliv80, Oliv93]. For example, if a fashion retailer knows that a certain color is often discussed and hip at the moment the products can be placed at the right time and at the right place. To do so it is possible to exhibit clothes in the trendy color in the shopping window. This could stimulate customers to visit the store, which implicates a rise of the purchase intention. Another positive aspect is the possibility to give further information to the product at the point of sale. If the analysis showed that for example people have problems with the handling again and again, an information sheet, which is placed next to the product in the store could be a good and easy appropriate action to fulfill customers' needs.

After purchase the knowledge can be used to intensify customer relation [ChPo03]. Knowledge about products or services customers are interested in enables the retailer to build detailed peer-groups in a very efficient manner [KoLe69]. Based on this information, offers and advertising can be placed along individual preferences. This could have and positive influence on customers' attitude. On the other hand the customer will be informed about products that fit the own needs so that a purchase intention can develop [Oliv80, Oliv93]. Furthermore, getting individual offers and information could be interpreted by customers as an interest of the retailer in the own person [Berr95]. This could have a positive influence on the purchase behavior. In the hard competitive markets with strong online competitors such a would-be personal relationship between the entities could help to increase sales and save the market position.

In general, all activities of data-driven sales processes through social BPM should improve the value of the customer for the retailer and be reach the break even. One method to evaluate the value of the customer is the CLV method (customer lifetime value) [JaSi02]. The customer lifetime value is e.g. calculated as the new present value (NPV) of each past, current and future revenues, and costs for each customer discounted by the given interest rate per time (i):

Customer Lifetime Value $[JaSi02]$:

$$CLV = \sum_{i=1}^{n} \frac{(revenue_i - costs_i)}{(1 + interest\ rate)^i} \tag{1}$$

The use of social software implies different new costs (e.g. costs for implementation, use, maintenance, etc.) [Fish09, Nega04]. This cost increases the cost term of each customer (in the Eq. 1). Therefore, the revenues through better sales processes through social software must also increase. Otherwise, the use of social software is not economically. Summarized, the following decision rule obtains:

Decision rule:

$$\sum CLV_{without\ social\ BPM\ use} \leq \sum CLV_{with\ social\ BPM\ use} \tag{2}$$

6 Related Work

The fundamentals of combining BPM and social software are shown in [BDJK11, EGHJ10, ScNu09] in more detail. General aspects of sales processes are defined by reference models for retail enterprises [BeKR03, BeSc04]. How retailers can implement data driven processes through RFID is described e.g. in [SMZH14, Mcbr11]. There are a number of further aspects of social software and retail processes. Context data of business process (like data from social software) can be used [MSHB14, SMHZ15]. How decision making can be supported via social software is described e.g. in [SZMJ14] and the influence as well as use of social data for marketing and customer relations is shown in [Schm13] A framework for Value Co-creation by software is defined in [Schm12]. Supply-chain oriented research of related business processes is shown e.g. in [Holm98, ChBH06] as well as forecasting oriented approaches e.g. for fashion retailers are discussed in [AuCY08]. Performance measuring for retailing are also discussed in research [MaKO02]. Beside the implementation via RFID and the aspects mentioned in this paper the technical opportunities of beacons can be seen as an interesting approach [Dano00]. This application is already used by well-known companies for e.g. like Apple to improve their customer-service and orientation in the U.S. market [Ibea00]. Furthermore, aspects like the use of Cloud Computing for implementing a competitive customer relationship management are discussed e.g. in [HMSR00].

7 Conclusion

In the clothing retail business, local retailers compete with more and more online retailers like Amazon, Zappos or Rakuten. However, retailers with classic branches have difficulties to increase cross-selling revenues using web-analytics as their online counterparts. Therefore, the integration of RFID chips in loyalty cards is proposed to identify the customer and their individual preferences, needs and interests when entering the shop and tracking him. Using the data collected, it is possible to create a Data-driven sales process that leverages further data from social software. By these means, local retailers are able to stay competitive (e.g. with online stores). Our paper shows that social software can support and improve sales processes. We contribute to the current literature by presenting why and in which way social software can change sales processes for local retailers. Therefore, research in the field of information systems as well as general management (e.g. in the field of retail and marketing management) can benefit from our results and can adopt current approaches. Local retailers can benefit from our results by choosing the best fit of social software support for their business case. Thus, sales business processes can be improved. Furthermore, local retailers can be more competitive to other retailers (e.g. online retailers). Limitations of our work can be e.g. found in the missing empirical validation as well as industry or category specific adoptions. Our work should be empirically validated in the future e.g. through laboratory or field experiments. Furthermore, category differences of the local retailers should be observed in the future.

References

[AsHu10]   Asur, S., Huberman, B.A.: Predicting the future with social media. In: 2010 IEEE/WIC/ACM International Conference on Web Intelligence and Intelligent Agent Technology (WI-IAT), pp. 492–499. IEEE (2010)

[AuCY08]   Au, K.-F., et al.: Fashion retail forecasting by evolutionary neural networks. Int. J. Prod. Econ. **114**(2), 615–630 (2008)

[BaYY10]   Bayraktar, A., et al.: Implementation of RFID technology for the differentiation of loyalty programs. J. Relat. Mark. **9**(1), 30–42 (2010)

[BDJK11]   Bruno, G., et al.: Key challenges for enabling agile BPM with social software. J. Softw. Maintenance Evol. Res. Pract. **23**(4), 297–326 (2011)

[BeKR03]   Becker, J., et al.: Process Management: a guide for the design of business processes: with 83 figures and 34 tables. Springer Science & Business Media (2003)

[Benk06]   Benkler, Y.: The Wealth of Networks: How Social Production Transforms Markets and Freedom. Yale University Press, New Haven (2006)

[Berr95]   Berry, L.L.: Relationship marketing of services—growing interest, emerging perspectives. J. Acad. Mark. Sci. **23**(4), 236–245 (1995)

[BeSc04]   Becker, J., Schütte, R.: Handelsinformationssysteme. MI Wirtschaftsbuch (2004)

[ChBH06]   Chae, M.-H., et al.: Pre-purchase and post-purchase satisfaction and fashion involvement of female tennis wear consumers. Int. J. Consum. Stud. **30**(1), 25–33 (2006)

[ChDa97]   Chaudhuri, S., Dayal, U.: An overview of data warehousing and OLAP technology. ACM Sigmod Rec. **26**(1), 65–74 (1997)

[ChPo03]   Chen, I.J., Popovich, K.: Understanding customer relationship management (CRM) People, process and technology. Bus. Process Manage. J. **9**(5), 672–688 (2003)

[Codd72]   Codd, E.F.: Relational completeness of data base sublanguages. IBM Corporation (1972)

[Dano00]   Danova, T.: BEACONS: What They Are, How They Work, And Why Apple's iBeacon Technology is Ahead of the Pack. http://uk.businessinsider.com/beacons-and-ibeacons-create-a-new-market-2013-12

[Dave10]   Davenport, T.: The New World of "Business Analytics." International Institute for Analytics (2010)

[Derh00]   derhandel.de: Textilhandel: P&C überzeugt Testkäufer - Der Handel. http://www.derhandel.de/news/unternehmen/pages/Textilhandel-P%26C-ueberzeugt-Testkaeufer-1280.html

[Dest13]   Destatis: Volkswirtschaftliche Gesamtrechnungen Private Konsumausgaben und Verfügbares Einkommen (2013)

[EGHJ10]   Erol, S., et al.: Combining BPM and social software: contradiction or chance? J. Softw. Maintenance Evol. Res. Pract. **22**(6–7), 449–476 (2010)

[FHBB11]   Friedland, A., et al.: NoSQL: Einstieg in die Welt nichtrelationaler Web 2.0 Datenbanken. Carl Hanser Verlag GmbH & CO. KG (2011)

[Fink02]   Finkenzeller, K.: RFID-handbuch. Hanser München (2002)

[Fish09]   Fisher, T.: ROI in social media: a look at the arguments. J. Database Mark. Customer Strategy Manage. **16**(3), 189–195 (2009)

[GGKN05]   Gruhl, D., et al.: The predictive power of online chatter. In: Proceedings of the Eleventh ACM SIGKDD International Conference on Knowledge Discovery in Data Mining, pp. 78–87. ACM (2005)

[Gran83]   Granovetter, M.: The strength of weak ties: A network theory revisited. Sociol. Theory **1**(1), 201–233 (1983)

[Hand13]   Handelsdaten.de: Aktuelle Statistiken zum Textileinzelhandel in Deutschland. Handelsdaten.de (2013)

[HMSR00]   Härting, R.-C., et al.: What drives users to use CRM in a Public Cloud environment? – Insights from European Experts. In: Proceedings of the 49th Hawaii International Conference on System Sciences (HICSS). IEEE, Kauai (forthcoming)

[Holm98]   Holmström, J.: Business process innovation in the supply chain–a case study of implementing vendor managed inventory. Eur. J. Purchasing Supply Manage. **4**(2), 127–131 (1998)

[Hung05]   Hung, L.: A personalized recommendation system based on product taxonomy for one-to-one marketing online. Expert Syst. Appl. **29**(2), 383–392 (2005)

[Ibea00]   ibeaconinsider: What is iBeacon? A Guide to iBeacons. http://www.ibeacon.com/what-is-ibeacon-a-guide-to-beacons/

[JaSi02]   Jain, D., Singh, S.S.: Customer lifetime value research in marketing: A review and future directions. J. Interact. Mark. **16**(2), 34–46 (2002)

[KeBL13]   Kemper, H.-G., et al.: An Integrated Business Intelligence Framework. In: Rausch, P., et al. (eds.) Business Intelligence and Performance Management, pp. 13–26. Springer, London (2013)

[KeHa06]   Keck, M., Hahn, M.: Integration der Vertriebswege: Herausforderung im dynamischen Retail Banking. Springer DE (2006)

[KnHa05]   Knyrim, R., Haidinger, V.: RFID-Chips und Datenschutz. Österreichisches Recht der Wirtschaft. **23**(1), 2–6 (2005)

[KoLe69]   Kotler, P., Levy, S.J.: Broadening the concept of marketing. J. Mark. **33**, 10–15 (1969)

[KoPe07]   Kolbe, H., Peseschk, S.: Wirtschaftlichkeitsanalyse des RFID-Einsatzes in einem Handelsunternehmen der Bekleidungsbranche. GI Jahrestagung (1), 99–102 (2007)

[Lang05]   Langheinrich, M.: Die Privatsphäre im Ubiquitous Computing— Datenschutzaspekte der RFID-Technologie. In: Fleisch, E., Mattern, F. (eds.) Das Internet der Dinge, pp. 329–362. Springer, Heidelberg (2005)

[LLSH11]   LaValle, S., et al.: Big data, analytics and the path from insights to value. MIT Sloan Manage. Rev. **52**(2), 21–32 (2011)

[Mada09]   Madaan, K.V.S.: Fundamentals of Retailing. Tata McGraw-Hill Education, New Delhi (2009)

[MaKO02]   Mattila, H., et al.: Retail performance measures for seasonal fashion. J. Fashion Mark. Manage. Int. J. **6**(4), 340–351 (2002)

[Mcbr11]   McBrearty, R.: The Future of Retail Customer Loyalty RFID Enables Breakthrough Shopping Experiences. Cisco Systems (2011)

[MSHB14]   Möhring, M., Schmidt, R., Härting, R.-C., Bär, F., Zimmermann, A.: Classification framework for context data from business processes. In: Fournier, F., Mendling, J. (eds.) BPM 2014 Workshops. LNBIP, vol. 202, pp. 440–445. Springer, Heidelberg (2015)

[Müll04]   Müller, J.: Ist das Auslesen von RFID-Tags zulässig. Datenschutz und Datensicherheit (DuD) **28**(5), 215 (2004)

[Nega04]   Negash, S.: Business intelligence. Commun. Assoc. Inf. Syst. **13**(1), 54 (2004)

[Oliv80]   Oliver, R.L.: A cognitive model of the antecedents and consequences of satisfaction decisions. J. Mark. Res. **17**, 460–469 (1980)

[Oliv93]   Oliver, R.L.: Cognitive, affective, and attribute bases of the satisfaction response. J. Consum. Res. **20**, 418–430 (1993)

[Robe06]   Roberts, C.M.: Radio frequency identification (RFID). Comput. Secur. **25**(1), 18–26 (2006)

[Schm12]   Schmidt, R.: A Framework for the Support of Value Co-creation by Social Software. In: Daniel, F., et al. (eds.) Business Process Management Workshops, pp. 242–252. Springer, Berlin Heidelberg (2012)

[Schm13]   Schmidt, R.: Social data for product innovation, marketing and customer relations. In: La Rosa, M., Soffer, P. (eds.) BPM Workshops 2012. LNBIP, vol. 132, pp. 234–245. Springer, Heidelberg (2013)

[ScNu09]   Schmidt, R., Nurcan, S.: BPM and social software. In: Ardagna, D., et al. (eds.) Business Process Management Workshops, pp. 649–658. Springer, Berlin Heidelberg (2009)

[SiSM09]   Silberer, G., et al.: Contacts between Retailers and Customers as a Basis for Customer Segmentation in Electronic Retail. Universitätsverlag Göttingen, 127 (2009)

[SMHZ15]   Schmidt, R., et al.: Leveraging textual information for improving decision-making in the business process lifecycle. In: Neves-Silva, R., et al. (eds.) Intelligent Decision Technologies, Sorrent (2015)

[SMMP14]   Schmidt, R., Möhring, M., Maier, S., Pietsch, J., Härting, R.-C.: Big data as strategic enabler - insights from central european enterprises. In: Abramowicz, W., Kokkinaki, A. (eds.) BIS 2014. LNBIP, vol. 176, pp. 50–60. Springer, Heidelberg (2014)

[SMZH14]   Schmidt,   R.,   et   al.:   Datenzentrierte   Unternehmensarchitekturen   im Bekleidungseinzelhandel. INFORMATIK 2014: Big Data - Komplexität meistern 44. Jahrestagung der Gesellschaft für Informatik. p. (im Druck), Stuttgart (2014)

[Stoc07]   Stockton, M.L.: Using radio frequency identification with customer loyalty cards to detect and/or prevent theft and shoplifting. Google Patents (2007)

[StSi10]   Steinmann, S., Silberer, G.: Clustering Customer Contact Sequences-Results of a Customer Survey in Retailing. European Retail Research, pp. 97–120. Springer (2010)

[SZMJ14]   Schmidt, R., Zimmermann, A., Möhring, M., Jugel, D., Bär, F., Schweda, C.M.: Social-software-based support for enterprise architecture management processes. In: Fournier, F., Mendling, J. (eds.) BPM 2014 Workshops. LNBIP, vol. 202, pp. 452–462. Springer, Heidelberg (2015)

[TaWi06]   Tapscott, D., Williams, A.: Wikinomics: How Mass Collaboration Changes Everything (2006)

[Tayl11]   Taylor, F.W.: The Principles of Scientific Management, vol. 202. Harper, New York (1911)

[Whit12]   White, T.: Hadoop: The definitive guide. O'Reilly Media (2012)

[Wieh00]   Wiehr, H.: Gerry Weber rollt RFID aus: Ab 2010 ein RFID-Chip in jedem Kleidungsstück - CIO.de. http://www.cio.de/retailit/bestpractice/2216267/

[WMKS14]   Walsh, G., et al.: Preventive product returns management systems-a review and model. In: Proceedings of the 21st European Conference on Information Systems (ECIS), Tel Aviv, Israel (2014)

Can Coffee Consumption Influence Business Process Modeling Behavior?

Michael Möhring[2]([⊠]), Rainer Schmidt[2], Ralf-Christian Härting[1],
and Christopher Reichstein[1]

[1] Hochschule Aalen, Beethovenstr. 1, 73430 Aalen, Germany
{Ralf.Haerting,Christopher.Reichstein}@hs-aalen.de
[2] Hochschule München, Lothstrasse 64, 80335 Munich, Germany
{michael.moehring,Rainer.Schmidt}@hm.edu

Abstract. Improving the quality and efficiency of modeling is an important goal of many research approaches. A number of influence factors outside the modeling environment are investigated. To measure the influence objective measures are necessary. Therefore, this paper strives to create a foundation for such a measures, by measuring the influence of caffeine on the modeling performance. Choosing caffeine has the important advantage to provide an unbiased setting. The possible path of influence of caffeine on the modeling performance is analyzed. A research model is developed and the result of a pre-study are discussed.

Keywords: Human centric · BPM · Coffee consumption · Modeling · Influence factor · Process modeling · Modeling behavior · Outside normal modeling environment · Neuro IS

1 Introduction

Modeling is very important to business process design and implementation as well as for operating and maintaining information systems [Wesk07]. Business processes can be modeled through different notations like BPMN, EPC, UML, Petrinets, etc. [ChTr12, Sche00, Wesk07] e.g. in the design phase of the business process lifecycle [Wesk07].

In general, business processes are modeled by human modelers [FrMP11, SMHZ15]. Therefore, the question arises, whether and how the performance of human modelers can be influenced. There are a number of approaches that strive to improve modeling performance by applying change patterns, etc. (e.g. [ATWR13]). All of these approaches focus on influence factors not outside of the normal modeling environment. However, a measure to evaluate such approaches has still to be found.

The problem is that the developer of a modeling approach will always be biased when selecting a measure for measuring modeling performance. Therefore, to pave the way for a generally accepted measure of modeling performance, a scenario has to be chosen that avoids bias as far as possible. We have chosen the influence of caffeine on modeling performance. Coffee is one of the most widely used drinks and often part of consumption at meetings and through the whole day [Harv00]. Furthermore, coffee consumption is associated with different positive states like health, wakefulness,

© Springer International Publishing Switzerland 2016
M. Reichert and H.A. Reijers (Eds.): BPM Workshops 2015, LNBIP 256, pp. 316–322, 2016.
DOI: 10.1007/978-3-319-42887-1_26

vitality [AA15, Fabr92, Mand02]. Nowadays, it is unclear whether coffee consumption before business process modeling can influence the modeling behavior.

Therefore, we address a human centric BPM research question in this *"idea paper"*: *How can coffee consumption influence business process modeling behavior?*. Coffee consumption can be seen as one example of modeling influences trough the modeling environment (and can be changed to any other influence factor outside the normal modeling environment). In this paper, we want to give a short intro how caffeine influences human behavior and how it might influence modeling behavior. In the next step, we want to check, if these theoretical assumptions can explored in practice. Therefore, we implement a small pre-study. Finally, we give a study overview and future research directions.

2 Coffee-Consumption and Business Process Modeling: A Research Model

Coffee consumption is an integral part in the daily business of many different human modelers [Harv00, Flow00]. People in the US drink 2–4 cups of coffee per day with a daily ingestion of caffeine of 4 mg per kg of body weight [Mand02]. Coffee is a primary source of caffeine and can be prepared in different ways (like instant, espresso, boiling, etc.) [Mand02]. Furthermore, coffee can be differentiated through the degree of roasting, amount of coffee beans, fineness of grinding and the amount of used water [Mand02]. After oral ingesting coffee, caffeine is absorbed and can interact with receptors [Mand02]. Caffeine is absorbed approximately half an hour (peak plasma level between 30–75 min.) after consumption [Mand02]. Normally, a low doses of caffeine "involves antagonism of adenosine receptors which are present in brain, blood vessels, kidneys, heart, the GI tract and the respiratory tree [Mand02, p. 1233]" [ChBe94]. Caffeine affects brain functions like sleep, learning, cognition, memory, etc. [RiSe10].

Based on these facts, how can caffeine (via coffee consumption) influence business process modeling behavior? Therefore, we can define some core influence factors.

According to the influence of the brain behavior [Mand02]: Does coffee consumption influence the quality of modeled business processes? Are people with consumption before modeling better? In addition to the three general core project indicators "quality", "time", "cost" [Atki99], we want to design our model: *Does a coffee consumption before modeling influence the time of business process modeling?; Does a coffee consumption before modeling influence the quality of business process modeling?; Does a coffee consumption before modeling influence the cost of business process modeling?*.

In this context, the main question to solve is: are there any differences between the human modelers? Past research argues that there are differences between the modeling experience of the modeler in terms of cost [NPTM13]. However, it is not well known whether age or gender aspects have an influence in this field. In connection with other studies in the field of social science, age and gender differences matter (e.g. [EWHB93]). Furthermore, a higher consumption of coffee before and after work might have some different affects [Mand02]. Therefore, we added the following moderators to our model: Gender, Business process modeling experience, age, daily coffee consumption.

Our research model is summarized in Fig. 1. In the next section, we want to pre-test parts of our research model, if it is practicable and to prepare further studies as well as generate first empirical insights. In general, a pre-test generates a small sample with mostly no significant results [ZiBa05]. First impressions of the design of the study and model can be evaluated and used to prepare further (main) studies.

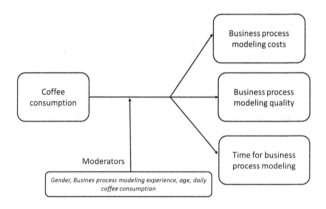

Fig. 1. Research Model

3   Pre-study

To explore if coffee consumption can influence business process modeling behavior (as one possible influence factor outside the modeling environment), we started to implement a pre-study with undergraduate business administration students (n = 54) from a small university in southern Germany. This study took place in a bachelor course about business information systems in January 2015. As a research method, we choose a laboratory experiment setting [ZiBa05]. Through this setting the researcher has the chance to a more systematically control of the experiment, but the observed persons know about the research process (in contrast to field experiments). All observed students had only business process modeling experience through this course (verify criteria: homogenous group). Because of the fact that 7 students did not want to drink coffee, we had to reduce the sample by 7 persons (all 7 students were placed in the experimental group; final sample n = 47). However, we want to clarify the following hypothesis as sample questions of our research model (cf. Sect. 2) in a pre-test study:

> *H1: Business process modelers with coffee consumption before modeling are faster as modelers without; H2: Business process modelers with coffee consumption before modeling design better business processes as modelers without.*

According to a general laboratory setting [ZiBa05], we split the homogenous student group randomly in two groups in different rooms (O1: experimental group; O2: control group). Each student of the experimental group is supposed to have a coffee consumption before modeling. After coffee consumption each student has to wait 30 min before starting modeling because of the caffeine absorption process [Mand02]. We choose the

Nespresso system because each coffee has the same water and coffee quantity [Nesp00]. Regarding the coffee type of the Nespresso coffee system, we chose the strong "Ristretto Intenso" with 6 gramm coffee/espresso [Nesp00]. It has to be noted that the students of the control group had no coffee consumption before modeling. All students got the same modeling case seen in the following Table 1 (translated from German) [SMHZ15]:

Table 1. Sample process important– interview text [SMHZ15, pp. 567–568]

"An important credit application is received by Mr. Right and he creates the credit data set in the creditIS system based on the document credit application. Then the creditIS system checks if the integrity of the data set is okay. If it is, the credit agreement and a credit agreement document are made by Ms. Wilson based on the data in the creditIS system. If the integrity check is not okay, Ms. Luck updates the data set in the creditIS."

The pre-defined modeling notation was the EPC notation [ScNü00]. For each student, the time of the modeling process was measured and the quality of process modeling recorded. The modeling quality were collected in two dimensions. First dimension was the syntactical quality (in relation to the notation guidelines [ScNü00]) and second dimension was imaged by the content of correctness (e.g. congruence of the process to the process interview text [SMHZ15]). The two dimensions were ranked on a one to five Likert scale [Alba97] (0: very poor → 5: very good) based on their individual process models and notation guidelines [ScNü00] of the course lecturer. The results of the experiments are shown in the following Table 2:

Table 2. Results of pre-study

	Experimental group (O1)	Control group (O2)
Sample size (n)	20	27
Average of syntactical quality	3.47	3.07
Average of content correctness	4.09	3.88
Mean modeling time (in minutes (mm:ss))	12:51	11:33
Mean age (in years)	21.15	21.00

According to the results, it can be assumed that there are differences through process modeling with coffee consumption. First, the syntactical quality and the content correctness is better through coffee consumption before modeling. In contrast to this, the modeling time is slower than the time of the control group. All students had no modeling experience before the course and were randomly separated. Because of the small sample, which is the general case of a pre-study, the results are not on a high significant level or rather not significant (Significance: syntactical quality: 0.14; content correctness: 0.2372; modeling time: 0.11; calculated with one-side T-Test) [ZiBa05]. Therefore, we cannot confirm our hypotheses (H1 and H2) via this pre-study. But the averages show interesting insights and possibilities for research (with a larger sample). Future research should now investigate the influence of coffee consumption in a broader sense.

4 Related Work

Although research on quality in business process modeling is well-established theme of research [Wesk07, ScNü00], it surprises that obvious factors for business process modeling such as nutrition have been neglected so far. General discussions on the impact of caffeine is discussed in [Mand02, ChBe94, RiSe10]. A study how factors can influence the understandable of process models is discovered in [ReMe11]. Human influence on BPM via social software is described in several publications like [ScNu09, EGHJ10].

5 Conclusion and Future Directions

The growing number of research approaches striving to improve process modeling creates an urgent need for a neutral, non-biased measure. We want to introduce to evaluate and improve business process modeling with influence factors outside of the general modeling environment. We have chosen the influence of coffee as scenario. Coffee consumption can be seen as one example of modeling influences trough the modeling environment. There might by further influence factors in the modeling environment (e.g. modeling location, temperature, stress level). Our research shows how human centric business process modeling might be influenced through coffee consumption. First, we give an overview of the possibilities of the coffee consumption and its influences. Second, we pre-test some important facts to get a better understanding if research can show modeling differences and how research can be designed. Based on our pre-test, there might be differences of the business process modeling behavior.

Our pre-test was not on a high significant level (not significant), which is very general for pre-test studies. Our study shows interesting differences between people who drink coffee before modeling compared to people without coffee consumption. Therefore, research can start in this new interesting human centric business process modeling area. There are also practical as well as research implications. Research about coffee consumption can help the scientific community to clarify which substances can influence the modeling behavior of a human process modeler. Based on our research we argue, that coffee consumption (maybe) can have an impact on intellectual abilities in general and on modeling as well as business process modeling in detail. Managers can use this results to decide if they want to support coffee consumption in their projects to reach the project goals.

Future research should start in this very interesting and practical topic. Research should investigate the influence of caffeine on the modeling behavior and enlarge the sample size as well as research methods (e.g. field experiments; qualitative study). Furthermore, a deeper understanding of the impact of factors out of the modeling process (e.g. caffeine) on elements and aspects of the modeling quality would be very good. We hope, that by applying our research, the comparison of different research approaches will be possible on an objective basis.

Acknowledgement. We thank Franziska Blum, Lisa Sobottka as well as the undergraduate students of the experiment for supporting our work!

References

[AA15]   Business Insider. Modest coffee consumption good for the heart: study (2015). http://www.businessinsider.com/afp-modest-coffee-consumption-good-for-the-heart-study-2015-3

[Alba97]   Albaum, G.: The Likert scale revisited. J. Market Res. Soc. **39**, 331–348 (1997)

[Atki99]   Atkinson, R.: Project management: cost, time and quality, two best guesses and a phenomenon, its time to accept other success criteria. Int. J. Project Manage. **17**(6), 337–342 (1999)

[ATWR13]   Ayora, C., Torres, V., Weber, B., Reichert, M., Pelechano, V.: Enhancing modeling and change support for process families through change patterns. In: Nurcan, S., Proper, H.A., Soffer, P., Krogstie, J., Schmidt, R., Halpin, T., Bider, I. (eds.) BPMDS 2013 and EMMSAD 2013. LNBIP, vol. 147, pp. 246–260. Springer, Heidelberg (2013)

[ChBe94]   Chou, T.M., Benowitz, N.L.: Caffeine and coffee: effects on health and cardiovascular disease. Comp. Biochem. Physiol. C: Pharmacol. Toxicol. Endocrinol. **109**(2), 173–189 (1994)

[ChTr12]   Chinosi, M., Trombetta, A.: BPMN: an introduction to the standard. Comput. Stand. Interfaces **34**(1), 124–134 (2012)

[EGHJ10]   Erol, S., et al.: Combining BPM and social software: contradiction or chance? J. Softw. Maintenance Evol. Res. Pract. **22**, 6-7, 449–476 (2010)

[EWHB93]   Eccles, J., Wigfield, A., Harold, R.D., Blumenfeld, P.: Ageand gender differences in children's self-and task perceptions during elementary school. Child Dev. **64**(3), 830–847 (1993)

[Fabr92]   Fabricant, F.: Americans Wake Up and Smell the Coffee (1992). http://www.nytimes.com/1992/09/02/garden/americans-wake-up-and-smell-the-coffee.html

[Flow00]   Flowcentric: coffee Archives - FlowCentric Business Process Management Solutions. http://www.flowcentric.com/tag/coffee/

[FrMP11]   Friedrich, F., Mendling, J., Puhlmann, F.: Process model generation from natural language text. In: Mouratidis, H., Rolland, C. (eds.) CAiSE 2011. LNCS, vol. 6741, pp. 482–496. Springer, Heidelberg (2011)

[Harv00]   Harvard: Coffee by the Numbers | News | Harvard T.H. Chan School of Public Health. http://www.hsph.harvard.edu/news/multimedia-article/facts/

[Mand02]   Mandel, H.G.: Update on caffeine consumption, disposition and action. Food Chem. Toxicol. **40**(9), 1231–1234 (2002)

[Nesp00]   Nespresso: Ristretto. https://www.nespresso.com/pro/de/de/products/coffee/ristretto-50-capsule-box-6885481.html

[NPTM13]   Nissen, V. et al.: A Cost Calculation Model for Determining the Cost of Business Process Modelling Projects. Universitätsbibliothek Ilmenau (2013)

[ReMe11]   Reijers, H., Mendling, J.: A study into the factors that influence the understandability of business process models. IEEE Trans. Syst. Man Cybern. Part A: Syst. Hum. **41**(3), 449–462 (2011)

[RiSe10]   Ribeiro, J.A., Sebastiao, A.M.: Caffeine and adenosine. J. Alzheimer's Dis. **20**, 3–15 (2010)

[Sche00]   Scheer, A.W.: ARIS-Business Process Modeling. Springer, Heidelberg (2000)

[ScNü00]   Scheer, A.-W., Nüttgens, M.: ARIS architecture and reference models for business process management. In: van der Aalst, W.M., Desel, J., Oberweis, A. (eds.) Business Process Management. LNCS, vol. 1806, pp. 376–389. Springer, Heidelberg (2000)

[ScNu09]   Schmidt, R., Nurcan, S.: BPM and social software. In: Ardagna, D., Mecella, M., Yang, J. (eds.) BPM 2008 Workshop. LNBIP, vol. 17, pp. 649–658. Springer, Heidelberg (2009)

[SMHZ15]   Schmidt, R., Möhring, M., Härting, R.C., Zimmermann, A., Heitmann, J., Blum, F.: Leveraging textual information for improving decision-making in the business process lifecycle. In: Neves-Silva, R., Jain, L.C., Howlett, R.J. (eds.) Intelligent Decision Technologies. Smart Innovation, Systems and Technologies. Springer, Switzerland (2015)

[Wesk07]   Weske, M.: Business Process Management: Concepts, Languages, Architectures. Springer, Heidelberg (2007)

[ZiBa05]   Zikmund, W.G., Babin, B.J.: Exploring Marketing Research. South Western Educ Pub, Mason (2005)

Consideration of the Business Process Re-Engineering Effect: Business Flow Notation Structure and the Management Perspective

Kayo Iizuka[1(✉)], Yasuki Iizuka[2], and Chihiro Suematsu[3]

[1] School of Network and Information, Senshu University, Kawasaki, Kanagawa, Japan
iizuka@isc.senshu-u.ac.jp
[2] School of Science, Tokai University, Hiratsuka, Kanagawa, Japan
iizuka@tokai-u.jp
[3] Graduate School of Management, Kyoto University, Kyoto, Japan
suematsu@econ.kyoto-u.ac.jp

Abstract. This study considers the manner in which business process modeling (BPM) effect the business process change such as business process reengineering (BPR) or business process improvement. The expectations of top management regarding information technology (IT) are considered to be increasing, therefore BPM with IT implementation is becoming increasingly important. Although Japanese firms tend to spend much more on improving business operational efficiency compared with firms in Western countries, however, the results do not seem to be effective enough [1]. One of the reasons for this situation is considered to be the Japanese style of business process change. The authors analyzed this issue by the results of a survey that the authors had conducted on BPM methods and the effect of business process change.

Keywords: Business process change · Business flow notation structure · Hierarchical business process modeling methods · Non-hierarchical business process modeling methods · Business process adjustment

1 Introduction

Numerous firms are in highly competitive business environment these days, and the expectations of top management regarding information technology (IT) are said to be increasing. Improving business process efficiency thorough business process change is an important issues as well as creating new business by enabling IT. "Process modeling becomes more and more an important task not only for the purpose of software engineering, but also for many other purposes besides the development of software" [2]. However, although Japanese firms tend to spend much more on improving business operational efficiency (as a percentage) compared with the firms in Western countries, the results do not seem to be effective enough [1]. One of the reason for this situation is considered to be the Japanese style of business process change. For instance, most Japanese firms adapt the bottom-up approach for decisionmaking, while most Western firms adopt the top-down approach. Japanese firms have been making business process change

© Springer International Publishing Switzerland 2016
M. Reichert and H.A. Reijers (Eds.): BPM Workshops 2015, LNBIP 256, pp. 323–333, 2016.
DOI: 10.1007/978-3-319-42887-1_27

based on their employee suggestions [3]. Furthermore, the BPM methods typically adopted in Japan can be considered as one of the reasons why Japanese firms tend to use custom software and drive forward with As-is based business process improvements. This means that Japanese firms tend to spend more for a small level change of their business processes. In this study, the authors focused on the BPM methods, especially from a business flow notation structure (hierarchical methods, non- hierarchical methods) perspective.

2 Related Studies

2.1 Business Process Change

Related studies concerning the effect of business process engineering (BPR) or business process improvement induced by IT implementation or IT operation can be classified into certain categories. Based on the BPR theory presented by Hammer and Champy [4], researchers have conducted studies from various perspectives. Grover [5] focused on the implementation problem, Earl [6] analyzed the relationship between BPR and strategic planning, and Attaran [7] explored the relationship between IT and BPR based on the capabilities and the barriers to effective implementation. Kadono [8] focused on the mechanism of how IT creates business value, particularly from an IT management perspective.

2.2 Business Process Modeling and Effectiveness

Studies related to BPM can be classified into several groups: BPM methodologies [9, 10], BPM tools [11, 12], the effectiveness of BPM [13, 14], etc. Sedera et al. modeled the success factors of BPM [13]. Critical success factors (CSF) in this model are

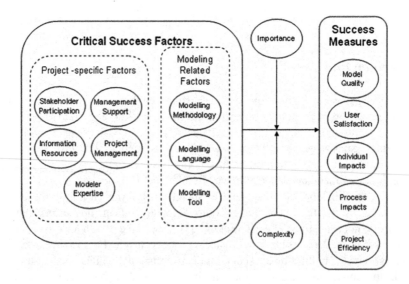

Fig. 1. Process modeling success model (Source: Sedera et al., 2004) [13]

classified into project-specific factors and modeling related factors (Fig. 1). For years, project-specific factors such as management support or project-management have been discussed in research areas such as project management and business process re-engineering, for the years. However, modeling-related factors such as modeling methodology or modeling language have seldom been discussed using success measures such as user satisfaction.

2.3 Business Process Modeling Methods

Business modeling methods can classified into hierarchical business process modeling methods, non-hierarchical business process modeling methods, and so on [15].

- Hierarchical Business Process Modeling Methods
  Some business process modeling methods have hierarchical layers and components. The authors call this type of modeling method the hierarchical business process modeling method. For instance, IDEF0 is a method that was brought out by the Integrated Computer Aided Manufacturing (ICAM) project of the United States Air Force in the 1970s. Its purpose was to increase the effectiveness of the purchase and manufacturing process of aircraft and their fitments by using an information system [16]. One of the features of IDEF0 is its hierarchical expression of processes, and an individual processes can be broken down to a detailed level if required. Many business process flow definition methods are contained in structured business process frameworks such as CIMOSA [17], GERAM [18], and contain hierarchical business process modeling methods.
- Non-hierarchical (End-User Focused) Business Process Modeling Methods
  Many business process modeling methods that are used popularly in Japanese companies belong to the non-hierarchical business process modeling method group. In these methods, people can trace a flow from its starting point to its end point using a finger, and it is easy to share information when discussing face-to-face, and thus it is suitable for a bottom-up style organizations. By using this tracing feature, Japanese firms had realized effective bottom-up based business process improvement. However, it is not always easy to manage business processes effectively because components cannot be not structurally organized, which causes difficulty in standardization of the business processes. Some Japanese firms or companies have used widely spread business flow charts even A0 size papers on which their business processes are scattered without hierarchical layers. They prefer to determine not to use top-down layered business processes modeling methods. Non-hierarchical modeling methods such as the Sanno-dai shiki flowchart [19], the JMA flow chart and the NOMA flowchart are major business process modeling methods in Japan.
- Semi-hierarchical Business Process Modeling Methods
  BPMN was developed by Business Process Management Initiative (BPMI) for the purpose of providing intuitively understandable notation to business users and technical developers [20]. (BPMI.org and Object Management Group™ (OMG™) merged their business process management activities in 2006). BPMN is applicable to only business processes, but not to organizational structures and resources, functional breakdowns, nor business rules. This means that other types of modeling done

by organizations for business purposes are beyond the scope of BPMN (e.g. organizational structures and resources, functional breakdowns, business Rules) [20]. Processes are described from left to right in swim lanes as in the Sanno-dai shiki flowchart or JMA flowchart. BPMN can be considered as a semi-hierarchical business process modeling method in the sense that it is able to handle sub-processes. However, it is different from hierarchical business process modeling methods that can deal with multiple layers, and it is also different from non-hierarchical business process modeling methods. BPMN is becoming a de facto standard, and much effort is currently being put into overcoming the challenges it have faced [21, 22].

- Business Process Modeling Methods with Special Purposes
  There are some methodologies with special purposes. For example, Design and Engineering Methodology for Organizations (DEMO) is a methodology for modeling, (re)designing, (re)engineering methodology for organizations (DEMO is an acronym that has had several long form in the course of time, starting with "Dynamic Essential MOdeling.") [23, 24], and there are case studies based on this methodology such as in [25].

Iizuka et al. described BPM issues and requirements in Japan, from the viewpoints of characteristics of traditional business process improvement and decision-making processes in Japan, as well as the environmental changes and issues facing Japanese firms [15]. The bottom-up culture and decision-making system have effectively worked at Japanese firms. Quality control (QC) circle is an example. Such labor participation in management has attracted attention from Western companies because it has been the foundation of international competitiveness for Japanese manufacturing firms or companies [26]. Therefore some Western companies tried to implement the Japanese-style QC circle, but they were not successful due to opposition by labors and labor unions [26]. However, since integrated efficiency and total optimization are becoming increasingly important with the globalization of Japanese companies, partial optimization come from the bottom-up approach. Under these conditions, to know about how the BPM methods affect business process change or BPR would become significant.

In this study, the authors present the results of an analysis of the relationship between the effects and BPM modeling method in Japan, and discuss the way to improve the effectiveness of business processes using IT.

3   Survey on the Effectiveness of Business Process Change and Business Process Notation Structure

The authors conducted a survey in February, 2015 to consider the effectiveness of BPR from the viewpoint of business process notation structure (and the types of BPM methods). The data were collected through an Internet survey service.

The keywords "manager in a company", "employee in a company (administration, sales)", "employee in a company (engineers)", and 'who had the experience of being engaged in business process re-engineering or business process improvement' were used to extract 4,000 potential respondents from 345,245 monitors. Ninety respondents answered during the February survey period.

3.1   Satisfaction About Business Process Improvement / Re-Engineering Effect

Figure 2 shows the survey results of satisfaction with business process improvements/re-engineering effects, summarized by the different business process notation structures that are in use at each company. Figure 3 shows the survey results of satisfaction with the business process enterprise system used by the respondents' companies. From these results, the companies using non-hierarchical BPM methods seem to be more effective than those using other types of BPM methods.

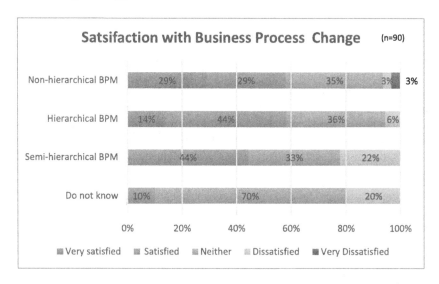

Fig. 2.   Satisfaction with business process change effect (Color figure online)

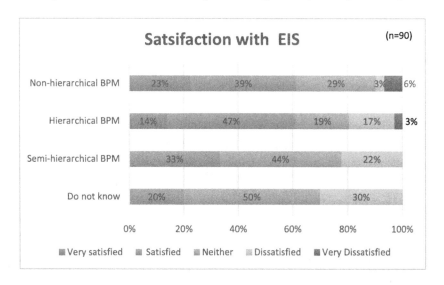

Fig. 3.   Satisfaction with enterprise information system (EIS) (Color figure online)

However, by looking at Fig. 4, which shows the scope of information standardization of the companies, we find that it is smaller for the companies using non-hierarchical BPM methods than it is for the other groups (approximately half of the respondents whose companies use non-hierarchical BPM answered 'not standardized' or only 'by division'). The reason why satisfaction with BPR for the companies using nonhierarchical BPM methods tends to be higher is considered to be the small range of scope of BPR. Decision making in Japan uses the bottom-up approach which is one of the unique features of the Japanese-style management [3, 15]. The reason why the scope of BPR projects tends to be smaller in Japan compared with Western countries may originate with the bottom-up decision-making style. In Japan, it is considered that every employee, even on production lines, tries to make efforts to be productive or efficient. However, this is only possible within the area that each employee can overlook. Traditional (post-1950s) Japanese-style management and Japanese-style BPM methods have worked well and proved their effectiveness. However, the business environment faced by Japanese companies has drastically changed. For example, a decrease in sales due to shrinking domestic markets requires companies to make an effort to reduce costs to maintain profits. Some companies have had to transfer production overseas to reduce labor costs. Because of such changes in the environment, companies have had to adapt in various ways, such as

- Changing business processes to realize enhancements in cost efficiency
- Changing business processes to realize integrated business processes corresponding to corporate marriages or enterprise integration at the domestic or global levels
- Improving information system operation efficiency (using packaged software is one option)
- Improving system maintenance efficiency

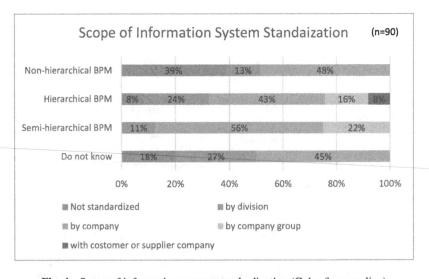

Fig. 4. Scope of information system standardization (Color figure online)

- Enhancing information systems to enable the analysis of business data to support management decision making
- Increasing agility in responding to environmental changes

3.2 Difficulties of Adjusting New Business Flow

In this section, the authors present survey results on the difficulties of adjusting to a new business flow. Respondents were asked to answer the questions on what makes adjusting to a new business flow difficult. The degree of difficulty was asked for the items of "difficulty of estimating total effect", "difficulty of estimating total workload", "difficulty of estimating effects at each division", "difficulty of estimating workload at each division" and "difficulty of consensus-building between divisions" (Fig. 5). Companies using non-hierarchical BPM methods seem to experience some difficulty, especially for the item "difficulty of consensus-building between divisions", compared with other companies. To cope with the changing environment mentioned in Sect. 3.1, consensus-building between divisions will become an important issue.

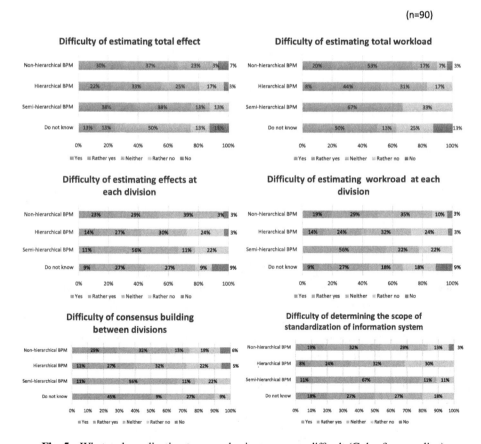

Fig. 5. What makes adjusting to a new business process difficult (Color figure online)

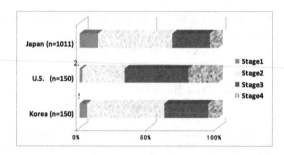

Fig. 6. Utilization Status (METI), 2010 [27]

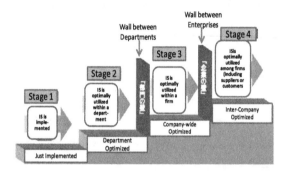

Fig. 7. IT Utilization Stage Stage (METI), 2010 [23]

3.3 Discussion

From the survey results, companies using non-hierarchical BPM methods are increasing effectiveness by focusing on the total optimization and standardization of their business and information systems. The scope of information system standardization for companies using non-hierarchical BPM tends to be small, as shown in Fig. 4. Although firms using non-hierarchical BPM tend to indicate low satisfaction levels, both in the business process improvement/re-engineering effect and their information systems compared to other firms (Figs. 2 and 3), those with high satisfaction levels are only realized on a smaller scale. For several years, many Japanese companies have been conducting as-is processes-based improvements. In addition, according to survey data by the authors, 72.9 % of the respondents (managers of information systems, business planning or internal audit divisions) stated that the policy of their BPR was 'drastic BPR', but only 28.4 % had attained it [15] (Fig. 8). It is still unclear why companies with a small scope of information system standardization tend to choose non-hierarchical BPM or vice versa. Future studies should focus on this issue.

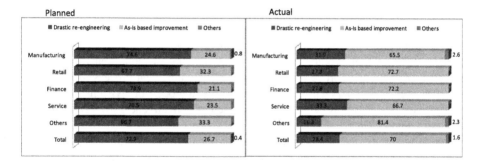

Fig. 8. Policy of business process change (Planned and actual) (Source: Business Strategy and IT Research Project, Senshu University, 2008 [15])

There is some data indicating the tendencies regarding the standardization of information systems compared to the United States and Korea, especially in terms of a smaller scope (Fig. 6). However, the environment that companies are facing are changing, such as the globalization of companies and the shift of plant activities overseas, and thus they have to seek ways to realize optimization and standardization over broader range, not losing advantage of Japanese business process quality which had built by employees' viewpoint.

As mentioned earlier, companies using non-hierarchical BPM methods are achieving effectiveness by focusing on a smaller scope for both the optimization and standardization of their business and information systems, which, in turn, will cause difficulties under environmental changes. Firms using non-hierarchical BPM methods should focus on 'estimating total effect' or the difficulties surrounding "consensus building between divisions" to correspond to the issues presented in Fig. 5 (*i.e.* what makes adjusting a new business process difficult?).

From the alignment perspective, companies using non-hierarchical BPM methods are aligned in the sense of scope, information system standardization and BPM methods. However, they may not be aligned in the sense of globalization strategies. Thus, it can be stated that the BPM methods and information system standardization strategies are not aligned for companies using hierarchical BPM methods with a small scope of information system standardization (Fig. 7).

Finally, most management styles of Japanese companies do not follow the topdown approach; however, adjustments among the divisions' when determining new business flow is extremely important. Therefore, case studies that thoroughly examine adjustment processes would be effective.

4   Conclusion and Future Research

In this study, the authors presented survey results showing the effectiveness of BPR from the viewpoint of business process notation structure. Companies using nonhierarchical BPM methods were aware of some difficulties in adjusting to new business processes between divisions within the company, which will become more important for achieving effectiveness in the future. An effective adjustment method, with respect to issues for Japanese companies, would facilitate business process improvement. In response to this issue, the authors proposed a modelling tool to support inter-organizational process flow adjustment. This tool would satisfy the requirements of both management and employees as well as improve the interorganization adjustment process of BPM. For future research, the authors will analyze the adjustment process of divisions when determining a new business flow to help companies achieve effectiveness from BPR through successful adjustment.

For future study, the authors are planning to analyze the alignment level and the reasons for business flow notation style and their strategy. Furthermore, we are planning to thoroughly analyze the adjusting processes of determining new business flow and to simulate them using multi-agent simulation.

Acknowledgments. This work was supported in part by the research grant of Senshu University. We really appreciate the companies who cooperated in the questionnaire and interviews.

References

1. Higano, T.: IT ni Yoru Work Wtyle Henkaku (Work Style Innovation, in Japanese). IT Solution Frontier, pp. 16–19 (2009)
2. Becker, J., Rosemann, M., von Uthmann, C.: Guidelines of business process modeling. In: Aalst, W.M., Desel, J., Oberweis, A. (eds.) Business Process Management. LNCS, vol. 1806, pp. 30–49. Springer, Heidelberg (2000)
3. Okui, N.: Nihongata management no shoraizo - gijutu hencho ga seisansei wo sogai. Kaizen no gokui wo seizogho ni manabe (future vision of Japanese style management: should systems developers learn kaizen from manufacturers in order to avoid technoid waning productivity, in Japanese). Nikkei IT Professional May 2005, p. 114 (2005)
4. Hammer, M., Champy, J.: Re-engineering the Corporation: A Manifesto for Business Revolution. Harper business, New York (1993)
5. Grover, V., Jeong, S.R., Kettinger, W.J., Teng, J.T.C.: The implementation of business process re-engineering. J. Manag. Inf. Syst. 12(1), 109–144 (1995)
6. Earl, M.J., Sampler, J.L., Short, J.E.: Strategies for business process re-engineering: evidence from field studies. J. Manag. Inf. Syst. 12(1), 31–56 (1995)
7. Attaran, M.: Exploring the relationship between information technology and business process re-engineering. Inf. Manag. 41(5), 585–596 (2004)
8. Kadono, Y., Tsubaki, H.: Development of IT management effectiveness and analysis. J. Jpn. Soc. Manag. 14(4), 69–83 (2006)
9. Giaglis, G.M.: A taxonomy of business process modeling and information systems modeling techniques. Int. J. Flex. Manuf. Syst. 13(2), 209–228 (2001). Springer
10. Lu, R., Sadiq, W.: A survey of comparative business process modeling approaches. In: Abramowicz, W. (ed.) BIS 2007. LNCS, vol. 4439, pp. 82–94. Springer, Heidelberg (2007)
11. Hall, C., Harmon, P.: The 2007 Enterprise Architecture, Process Modeling, and Simulation, Tools Report, BPTrends.com (2007)
12. Bosilj-Vuksic, V., Giaglis, G.M., Hlupic, V.: IDEF diagrams and petri nets for business process modeling: suitability, efficacy, and complementary use. In: Sharp, B., Filipe, J., Cordeiro, J. (eds.) Enterprise Information Systems II, pp. 143–148. Springer, Heidelberg (2001)

13. Sedera, S., Gable, G, Rosemann, M, Smyth, R.: A success model for business process modeling: findings from a multiple case study. In: Proceedings Eighth Pacific Asia Conference on Information Systems, pp. 485–498 (2004)
14. Kock, N., Verville, J., Danesh-Pajou, A., DeLuca, D.: Communication flow orientation in business process modeling and its effect on redesign success: results from a field study. Decis. Support Syst. **46**, 562–575 (2009)
15. Iizuka, K., Okawada, T., Tsubone, M., Iizuka, Y., Suematsu, C.: Issues about inter-organizational process flow adjustment in business process modeling. In: Barjis, J., Gupta, A., Meshkat, A. (eds.) EOMAS 2013. LNBIP, vol. 153, pp. 24–41. Springer, Heidelberg (2013)
16. IDEF (2010). http://www.idef.com/
17. Kosanke, K.: CIMOSA - overview and status original research article. Comput. Ind. **27**(2), 101–109 (1995)
18. IFIP-IFAC Task Force: GERAM - Generalized Enterprise Reference Architecture and Methodology, Version 1.6.2 (1998)
19. Eguchi, M., Gouhara, M., Takahara, M.: System bunseki, kaizen no tameno gyoumu flowchart no kakikata (the way of drawing flowchart for system analysis and improvement, in Japanese). Sannno Institute of Man(2006)agemnet Publication Department (2007)
20. Object Management Group (OMG): Business Process Modeling Notation, V1.1 - OMG Available Specification (2013). http://www.omg.org/spec/BPMN/2.0/PDF/
21. Recker, J.: Opportunities and constraints: the current struggle with BPMN. Bus. Process Manag. J. **16**(1), 181–201 (2008)
22. Wohed, P., van der Aalst, W.M., Dumas, M., ter Hofstede, A.H., Russell, N.: On the suitability of BPMN for business process modelling. In: Dustdar, S., Fiadeiro, J.L., Sheth, A.P. (eds.) BPM 2006. LNCS, vol. 4102, pp. 161–176. Springer, Heidelberg (2006)
23. Dietz, J.: Understanding and modeling business processes with demo, advances in conceptual modeling (ER 1999). In: Workshops on Evolution and Change in Data Management, Reverse Engineering in Information Systems, and the World Wide Web and Conceptual Modeling, November, 1999, pp. 188–202 (1999)
24. Dietz, J.: Enterprise Ontology - Theory and Methodology. Springer, Heidelberg (2006)
25. Barjis, J.: A business process modeling and simulation method using DEMO. In: Filipe, J., Cordeiro, J., Cardoso, J. (eds.) Enterprise Information Systems. LNBIP, vol. 12, pp. 254–265. Springer, Heidelberg (2009)
26. Moriya, T.: Gendai eikoku kigyo no roshi kankei – gorika to rodo kumiai (modern British companies and labor-management relations - rationalization and labor union, in Japanese). Zeimu Keiri Kyokai Co. Ltd (1997)
27. METI (Ministry of Economy, Trade and Industry): IT Keieiryoku Sihyo wo Mochiita IT no Rikatuyou ni Kansuru Genjou Chousa (Current Status Survey on IT Utilization Stage Evaluated by IT managerial Capability Index, in Japanese) (2010)

DAB Workshop

Introduction to the 4th International Workshop on Data- and Artifact-Centric BPM (DAB 2015)

Rik Eshuis[1], Fabiana Fournier[2], and Marco Montali[3]

[1] Eindhoven University of Technology, Eindhoven, The Netherlands
h.eshuis@tue.nl
[2] IBM Research - Haifa, Haifa University Campus, Haifa, Israel
fabiana@il.ibm.com
[3] Free University of Bozen-Bolzano, Bolzano, Italy
montali@inf.unibz.it

Two key perspectives on business processes are control ow and data. Traditionally, these two perspectives have been treated in isolation: control ow is typically managed by a business process management system while data is managed by a database management system. Each of the two perspectives has attracted wide interest both in academia and industry over the past years, resulting in an abundance of methods and tools that have been designed to assist with the management of processes and data. Yet, approaches that address both process and data management in a holistic way are lacking.

In recent years, we have witnessed the emergence of new paradigms that aim to blend control ow and data perspectives. New approaches are being developed that can naturally and seamlessly unify the two perspectives in order to better streamline the overall complexity in BPM. Contemporary examples include Artifact-Centric BPM and Case Management.

The Data and Artifact-Centric Business Process Management (DAB) workshop series aims to bring together researchers and practitioners whose common interest and experience are in the study and development of new foundations, models, methods, and technologies that are intended to uniformly and holistically align data and control ow for business processes.

In line with these aims, the 2015 edition of this workshop attracted ten submissions on these topics, out of which four submissions were accepted by the international Programme Committee. The accepted papers were presented at the DAB2015 workshop on August 31, 2015, together with two keynote presentations by Prof. Rod Franklin from Kühne Logistics University, Germany, and Dr. María Teresa Gómez López from the University of Seville, Spain. In his talk, Prof. Rod Franklin analyzed the problem of Supply Chain Orchestration from the perspective of data-centric information systems. Dr. Gómez López discussed in her talk how to diagnose the correctness of data in business processes. Included in these proceedings is a paper from Dr. Gómez López that summarizes her talk.

We thank both keynote speakers for their inspiring talks. We also wish to thank all authors for their hiqh-quality papers and talks and the Programme Committee members for their constructive reviews. We also acknowledge the support from the local organization and the BPM 2015 workshop chairs.

As with previous editions of DAB, we hope this selection of papers gives an inspiring impression of the current state of the art in this exciting field of research.

Organizers

Rik Eshuis	Eindhoven University of Technology, The Netherlands
Fabiana Fournier	IBM Research - Haifa, Haifa University Campus, Israel
Marco Montali	KRDB, Free University of Bozen-Bolzano, Italy

Programme Committee

Francesco Belardinelli	Université d'Evry, France
Dirk Fahland	Eindhoven University of Technology, The Netherlands
Dragan Gasevic	University of Edinburgh, UK
Thomas Hildebrandt	University of Copenhagen, Denmark
Lior Limonad	IBM Research - Haifa, Israel
Alessio Lomuscio	Imperial College London, UK
Fabrizio Maria	Maggi University of Tartu, Estonia
Fabio Patrizi	KRDB, Free University of Bozen-Bolzano, Italy
Zhe Shan	University of Cincinnati, USA
Ernest Teniente	Universitat Politcnica de Catalunya, Spain
Farouk Toumani	B. Pascal University, Clermont-Ferrand, France
Roman Vaculín	IBM Research, USA
Mathias Weske	HPI, University of Potsdam, Germany
Sira Yongchareon	Unitec Institute of Technology, New Zealand

Validation, Diagnosis and Decision-Making Support of Data in Business Processes

María Teresa Gómez-López$^{(\boxtimes)}$

Departamento de Lenguajes y Sistemas Informáticos,
Universidad de Sevilla, Seville, Spain
maytegomez@us.es
http://www.idea.us.es

Abstract. Business processes involve data that can be modified and updated by various activities at any time. The data involved in a business process can be associated with flow elements or stored data. This data must satisfy the business compliance rules associated with the process, where business compliance rules are policies or statements that govern the behaviour of a company. To validate the correctness of a business process, it is necessary to validate the managed data before and during the process instantiation, since none of the activities of a process can work correctly using incorrect data. The analysis of the correctness of the business process is typically related to the activity executed according to the value of a data variable in each case, that verifies whether the model and the log conform to each other. The incorporation of the study of the correctness of the semantic of data value (called Business Data Constraints) is also consider essential. The execution of the correct activity according to the data is fundamental: it is no less important, however, to validate the correctness of the input data of a business process, and whether it affects the workflow and the compliance of the policies. In this paper, every special characteristic for the analysis of the correctness of data in a business process is studied, as is how the classic techniques can be improved for the validation, diagnosis and decision-making support concerning data in Business Processes.

Keywords: Business data constraints · Data validation · Data diagnosis · Decision-making data support

1 Introduction

Many companies have adopted Process-aware Information Systems (PAISs) to support their business processes in some form [1]. PAIS is a software system that manages and executes operational processes involving people, applications, and/or information sources on the basis of process models. It provides a way to manage data stored in a repository layer. The business process description includes a workflow model, a set of business rules or policies, and the data exchanged during the execution. The correctness of the business process implies

© Springer International Publishing Switzerland 2016
M. Reichert and H.A. Reijers (Eds.): BPM Workshops 2015, LNBIP 256, pp. 339–351, 2016.
DOI: 10.1007/978-3-319-42887-1_28

the correctness of these three aspects. The analysis of the correctness of business processes is typically related to the activity executed according to the value of a data variable in each case, by verifying whether the model and the log conform to each other [2]. The use of relational databases as a repository where the changed data is stored instead of log events is considered in [3], and papers such as [4] highlight the importance to validate the correctness of data in PAISs, although it remains a challenge as to how to find a fault in data instead of in a decision related to data. Therefore conformance checking analysis on log events is insufficient [5] to claim correctness in a business process.

We also consider it essential to incorporate the study of the correctness of the semantic of data values, especially in PAISs. The execution of the correct activity according to the data is fundamental: it is no less important, however, to verify the correctness of the input data of a process, and whether it affects the workflow and the compliance of the policies. It is crucial to validate the managed data before and during process instantiation, since none of the activities of a process can work correctly using incorrect data.

Although log events can include data information, the natural place to store data is in a database. Data must satisfy business process policies in terms of their possible values and relations during the process execution, and for every instance. The study of the evolution and change of data produced by a system has been addressed in various domains by using model-based diagnosis [6], although it cannot be applied directly in a business process since a BP has special characteristics that need to be analysed in order to adapt the classic techniques. These techniques must be improved to provide for the validation, diagnosis and decision-making support of data. The analysis of correctness of data in business processes holds a special complexity, since the data used is not always produced by the business process itself, the fault can be intermittent, and the data can be aggregated and used in different instances.

The study of data correctness according to the process implies several decisions, such as:

– **When should the problem be studied?: At design time, runtime or post-mortem time?** The data model correctness is essential to ascertain whether the data model is correct [7]. Furthermore, since, in business processes data is continuously created, updated or eliminated, a validation analysis is necessary to preserve high data quality at runtime. It is especially important in systems where there is a high degree of exchanged data, since it is necessary to maintain aspects such completeness and correctness according to the business goals.
– **What analysis is needed?: Validation, diagnosis or decision-making?** Depending on the aim of the data analysis, different parts of the model and data are necessary. The validation of an instant implies to analyse the current data, while the diagnosis include to study the data evaluation in the past, and the decision-making support provokes a reasoning of the possible paths that an instance can execute in the future.

- **What is the objective of the analysis?: Data, activities, compliance rules or a combination of a number of objectives?** Depending on the type of business process and the latency of change that a BP supports, the possible causes responsible for a malfunction can differ. For example, for very a mature process, the cause of a malfunction is typically the introduced data, although if the policies are very changeable, they can be a source of the problem, or if the process has a high level of human interaction, it is more likely that the input data is the responsible for a malfunction.

The rest of the paper is organised as follows: Sect. 2 depicts the components of a business process model where the stored data and compliance rules are analysed. Section 3 explains the various characteristics that need to be adapted from classic model-based diagnosis to the business process area. Section 4 explains the differences between the various types of analysis (validation, diagnosis and decision-making support). Section 5 details how the above-mentioned objectives are performed. Finally, conclusions are drawn and open issues are explained in Sect. 6.

2 Modelling the Business Processes for Correctness Analysis of Data

In order to compare the expected behaviour of the system with the real behaviour, it is necessary to design the process and to extract the observations produced. This implies to consideration of a pair $\{SD, OBS\}$, where SD is the system description and OBS is a set of values of the observable variables. The process model is formed of a workflow, a set of business rules that describe the semantic of the data values, and a relational database schema. In the following subsections, these parts of the model are given in detailed, together with the observational model extraction.

2.1 Process Model Workflow

The elements that can conform a process model to support data validation or a diagnosis process are:

- SE, one start event to initialize the process.
- EE, a set of end events, with at least one element.
- A, a set of activities that defines the model of the process.
- CF, a set of control flow patterns (AND, OR, XOR) that describes the possible branches to execute.
- $Cond$, a set of conditions associated with the control flows OR and XOR, that describes the paths that the process can take depending on the values of the variables in the dataflow. These conditions are evaluated at runtime, when the values of the variables are known.

2.2 What Are Business Data Constraints?

The compliance rules which represent the semantic relation between the data values are called Business Data Constraints. BDCs are used to describe the possible correct data values that are introduced, read and modified during the business process instances [8]. BDCs are a fundamental part of the model to be validated or diagnosed, since they describe the correct value relations between the involved data. BDCs are presented as Numerical Constraints that involve stored information and dataflow, and can be expressed as a Boolean combination of arithmetic constraints for Natural, Integer and Float domains, following the grammar introduced in [9], where it is important to highlight that the variables participating in the constraints can come from the database or from the dataflow.

Regarding to how the rules are integrated in a framework to complement the business process model, in [10] there is an in-depth analysis concerning the integration of rules and process modelling and the shortcomings of existing solutions. The BDCs can be defined as either an invariant of the process, and therefore associated to the whole process, or as a contract (pre- or post-condition) for an activity or a set of activities. To support the storage, extraction and query of these constraints, the Constraint Database LORCDB is used [11,12]. The example shown in Fig. 1 presents a process example where BDCs are associated as pre-conditions, post-conditions, and invariants of the model.

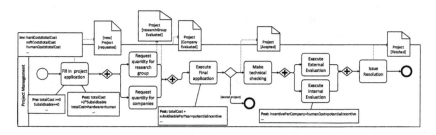

Fig. 1. Example of a process with Business Data Constraints and Data State Objects

2.3 Relational Database Model

A Relational Database is a collection of predicates over a finite set of variables described by means of a set of relations. A relation R is a data structure which consists of a heading and an unordered set of tuples which share the same type, where A_1, A_2, ..., A_n are attributes of the domains D_1, D_2, ..., D_n.

The set $\{A_1{:}D_1, A_2{:}D_2, ..., A_n{:}D_n\}$ is a relational-schema. A relation R defined over a relational-schema S is a set of assignments for each attribute for each domain. Therefore, the relation R is a set of n-tuples:

$\{A_1{:}d_1, A_2{:}d_2, ..., A_n{:}d_n\}$, where $d_1 \in D_1, d_2 \in D_2, ..., d_n \in D_n$.

2.4   Observational Model

The most important data changes in a business process are made persistent in a relational database. For this reason, the observational model contains the tuples of the database that refer to the variables included in the BDC. Depending on how these variables are introduced into the process models and hence into the database (such as input variables, triggered in the database, or derived by an activity), they play different roles in the diagnosis processes. These roles include:

- **Input Variable.** Variable whose value is introduced by the user in one of the activities of the business process model. It is a possible origin of problems if the data is incorrect.
- **Derived Variable.** Variable whose value depends on the value of other variables (input or derived variables). This means that its value is not introduced as an input, but it is calculated/created from other values. Therefore a derived variable cannot be responsible for a malfunction itself, although it can be involved in an incorrect BDC or it can be produced from incorrect input variables.
- **Key variables.** Set of variables that differentiate one tuple from another. They correspond to the primary key attributes of the relational model. These variables form a very important part in the diagnosis process since they enable one tuple to be isolated from another, but can seldom be determined as the origin of a problem.
- **Query variables.** Set of input variables and subset of key variables used to describe the set of tuples introduced and/or modified in an activity. These variables depend on the activity, and on the moment when the validation/diagnosis analysis is executed. These variables can be transferred through the activities as dataflow while they do not change in a process instance.

A tuple is a set of attributes $\{A_1, A_2, \ldots, A_n\}$, Input Variables (IV), Derived Variables (DV), Key Variables (KV) and Query Variables (QV), and the properties of these sets of variables are:

- $\{A_1, A_2, \ldots, A_n\} = \text{IV} \cup \text{DV} \cup \text{KV} \cup \text{QV}$
- $\text{QV} \subseteq \text{KV}$
- $\text{QV} \subseteq \text{IV}$
- $\text{IV} \cap \text{DV} = \emptyset$

3   Special Characteristics of Data Management Problems

Although business process analysis fortunately does not consider component degradation or deterioration as physical systems, it does contain other complexities and special characteristics, the most important of which are listed in the following subsections.

3.1   High Level of Human Interaction and Intermittence of Faults

None of the activities of a process can work correctly using incorrect data. Although activities may work correctly, the people that interact with them can work incorrectly and introduce incorrect values. This is especially important when there is a high level of human interaction, since humans can introduce intermittent faults in the system. The intermittence of faults makes the detection and the diagnosis of faults difficult, since an inconsistence detected during the execution of an activity does not imply a malfunction in the activity, or that this fault may appear in the future.

Some typical examples where intermittent faults in data can be found are:

– Financial applications, where several items of data are introduced by hand from application forms.
– Medical applications that use data introduced by different types of medical staff and places, for example data concerning blood test results.
– Electronic equipments, which produce a major quantity of data, that can cause intermittent faults, such as loose or corroded wire wraps, cracked solder joints and broken wires.

3.2   High Use of Stored Data

As mentioned before, data involved in the diagnosis is not strictly limited to that flowing in the process, some data is also stored in databases. This implies that the quantity of data involved in an instance can be very large, and problems of poor data quality must be detected and determined.

Some of the attributes of a relation can be described as *Primary Key Attributes* which means that "two tuples of a relation cannot have the same values for their primary key attributes". The relation between two tables is described by referential integrity. Two tables can be related by means of their *Primary* and *Foreign Key Attributes*, described in the literature as the relational model. Referential integrity is a database concept which ensures that relationships between tables remain consistent. When one table has a foreign key to another table, the concept of referential integrity states that a record may not be added to the table that contains the foreign key unless there is a corresponding record added to the linked table. The division of the related data into several tables helps in data integrity but makes the validation of the relation of the data values more difficult, since they are disseminated in various tables. The data involved in a BDC can therefore be found in various tables, and it is necessary to *denormalize* the information using the primary and foreign keys.

Moreover, the relational model is very detailed and is therefore difficult to understand and query by non-expert users, because it is isolated from how the data objects are modified during the process execution. BPMN 2.0 [13] and further improvements of its capacity to describe the data stored states give the capacity to enrich the model [14,15]. Thanks to these proposals, instead of a relational model, the Conceptual Model and Object-Relational Mapping (ORM) are used to facilitate the description and management of the stored business data objects, as shown in Fig. 1.

3.3   Combination of Business Rules and Data

Data is not the only aspect that can be modified during a business process execution. The compliance rules that describe the policies and the goals of the process also tend to be modified and updated to represent the necessities of the companies. The changeability of the policies makes the process adaptable to new conditions at runtime. For this scenario, the question becomes What type of element of the model can be held responsible for a malfunction? Only activities, only data, only business rules, or a combination of data and business rules?

Suppose that there are three different possible diagnoses, such as: 15 input data; 3 BDCs; or 2 BDCs and 5 input data at the same time. It is not possible to ascertain which is the most probable fault, since this can depend on:

- **The number of introduced items of data.** For example, if 16 items of data are introduced from the last validation or diagnosis, it is high improbable that 15 values are incorrect, but it is less improbable when $10,000$ items of data have been introduced.
- **Are the rules tested sufficient?** When a business rule has just been included in a model, it is likely that is has been insufficiently tested, and therefore it is more probable that other rules are incorrect.
- **Who has introduced the data?** Not all people in a company are equally reliable, and therefore this is an important factor when deciding between two possible diagnoses.
- **Who has introduced the rules?** A similar thing occurs with the rules, since different users can be more trustworthy when introducing rules.
- **The complexity of typing the data or rules.** Regardless of the person who introduces the process information, not every item of data or rule has the same complexity to be introduced, for example it is easier to introduce a fault into a number of 20 digits than into a number of 2 digits.

3.4   Data Shared Between Cases

The data of an instance is not independent from the data of other instances, since the same relational database is shared. This implies that the same data and rules can be involved in different validation or diagnosis processes for different instances. This implies that the final diagnosis needs to consider that the explanation of a malfunction in a case must also explain the good or wrong behaviour in the others.

For this reason, in a diagnosis process, it is necessary to incorporate every items of data involved in the independent-variable cluster. An independent-variable cluster is a set of BDCs whose variables are not involved directly or indirectly in another independent-variable cluster, thereby assuring that every variable involved is taken into account in the problem. A formal definition is:

Definition: Cluster of BDCs with Independent Variables. Let BC represent all the BDCs of a process, let B be a set of BDCs where $B \subseteq BC$, and let $V(B)$ be the set of variables involved in B. Therefore B is a Cluster of BDCs with Independent Variables iff $V(B) \cap V(BC{-}B) = \emptyset$, and B is minimal, which implies that $\nexists/B' \subset B \mid B'$ is a Cluster of BDCs with Independent Variables.

3.5   Data Uncertainty and Exoneration Principle

In the tables that form the database, it is usual to find unknown values during a process instantiation (*null* information in the database). This means that this data has not yet been introduced, because the instance has not finished or the data is not always necessary. This uncertainty needs to be included in the model to be validated or diagnosed, and this complicates the process since the exoneration principle, typically used in classic diagnosis, cannot be taken into account. The exoneration principle determines that a satisfiable BDC cannot contain incorrect variables and be correct itself at the same time. For business processes, this principle is not applicable since variables can be uninstantiated (*null* values), and the BDCs do not always determine strong relations between the variables (such as equal relations), since they can use soft data variable relations, such as $<$. For this reason, it is only possible to deduce incorrectness of BDCs for the tuples, but not correctness of BDCs applied to specific data.

4   Past, Present and Future of the Data in a Process Instance

The model described in Sect. 2 can be used for various purposes: the analysis of the validation of the model according to the data stored and data life-cycle (Subsect. 4.1); the diagnosis of the cause responsible for a found malfunction (Subsect. 4.2); or aid in the data introduction in the process to prevent future errors (Subsect. 4.3).

4.1   Data Validation

It is extremely complicated to determine how companies can adequately integrate their business objects stored in databases into a process model. Furthermore, it is possible to find non-conformances between the data model and the evolution of the states included in the workflow model [15]. The importance of data life-cycle validation has been the focus of several papers, where the data evolution during the business execution has been modelled as artifacts [7,16,17]. Artifact-centric proposals permit verification of the data model correctness according to their pre- and post-conditions, and the study of the possible data evolution. Artifact-centric solutions are especially focused on complex data models, such as those for the $n : m$ relation between objects [18].

In order to ascertain whether the data model and the stored data are consistent with the business process model, a systematic analysis is necessary on what activity modifies the state of the data, and which is the state of the stored data. It implies determining the relation between the data objects stored in the database and the activities that compose the business process model that modifies their states. However it is not only important to analyse the business data life-cycle, since the states of the objects are modified for activities of the model, and therefore the data life-cycle needs to be consistent with respect to the workflow. The possible states that an object can satisfy, and where it is read or written must be analysed. Certain analyses must assure that every object is in at least one state, or prevent that an object from satisfying two incompatible states.

4.2 Diagnosis to Find the Origin of the Problem

Not only is it crucial to ascertain that something is wrong, it is also essential to diagnose where the problem is in order to solve it and for it to be prevented in the future. Another major issue in diagnosis is to find the minimal diagnosis: the minimal possible number of conflicts that explain a malfunction in an efficient way. Minimal explanation of the problem is desirable, since model-based diagnosis is based on the parsimony principle [19]. It states that, among competing hypotheses, that with the fewest assumptions should be selected. A malfunction is visible when a discrepancy between the expected behaviour and the observed model is found. The objective is to determine what minimal part can explain the problem.

In relation to the persistence layer and dataflow, relational databases have been used in the business process, for example in [20] which presents a solution where data is audited and stored on a relational database. However, no validation of the semantics is performed for this persistence layer and the business rules. In papers such as [21], the necessity to resolve a fault after detection is identified, unfortunately the data aspect is not included. In previous papers, the possibility of finding incorrectness in input data is introduced [9, 22], although many challenges related to this problem are ready to be resolved as mentioned in the section future work.

4.3 From Data-Based Decisions to Decision-Making About Data

Several research studies have been published to improve the decision-making support during a business process execution. These decisions tend to be related to the execution of an activity analysing the values of the data involved in the process [23–25]. But when the goal of a process is oriented towards the decision-making support about data, instead of concerning the decision based on the data value of a process instance, we are faced with a completely different problem. The decision-making support about data is especially important when the information that flows between the activities can be introduced by the users. The user has sometimes to decide on which value to introduce while taking into account the potential actions in order to make the process instance correct [26], or for process outcome optimization [27]. In the business process scenario, this implies the analysis of all the possible branches that can be executed, and the

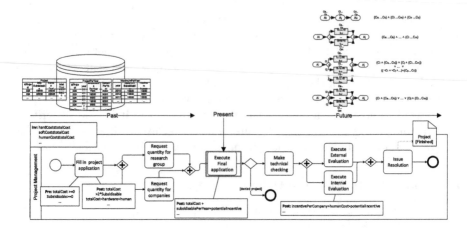

Fig. 2. Diagnosis, Validation and Decision-making in BP

decisions that can be taken in the future. If the decision made is incorrect, it will affect other decisions in the future, or it may even make it impossible to finish the instance correctly. The requirement for decision support always arises when decisions have to be made in complex, uncertain, and/or dynamic environments. From the point of view of input data values, the correctness of a business process is based on the correctness of the compliance rules that describe the policy of the company. For this reason, we propose a solution where the decision-making support for input data can be integrated into the business process instances, to inform the user about the possible values of the input variables, thereby rendering the instance of the business process consistent.

Figure 2 graphically depicts what parts of the model are used in accordance with the Validation analysis (Present), Diagnosis (Past including stored data), and Decision-making about data (analysing every possible paths that an instance can take in the future). In the three contexts, business data constraints are needed, and are incorporated into the analysed model.

5   Solving the Challenges

In order to transfer the capacity to manage data as a fundamental part of the business process enactment, it is necessary to propose a methodology that supports the solution of the problems introduced. The steps that are followed to extract the necessary part of the model (Fig. 3), and the observational model include: (1) Building a referential integrity graph that relates the data involved in the database to ascertain the independent cluster variables; (2) Extracting the BDCs involved in each case; (3) Creating the observational model joining the tuples in accordance with the stored data and the BDCs; and (4) Creating and solving using Constraint Programming Techniques [28] and a Max-CSP to find the minimal-conflict sets [9], or creating a CSP to validate the current process

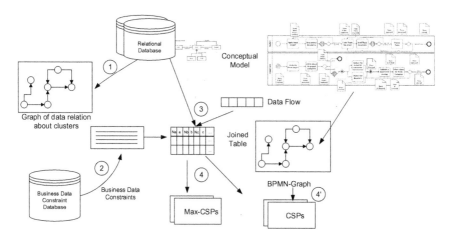

Fig. 3. Steps to evaluate the stored data

state. If decision-making support is performed, in Step 4′, a BPMN-Graph [29] needs to be included to ascertain the possible paths of the instance in the future.

6   Conclusions and Future Work

This paper emphasises the importance of changing the point of view in business processes: from data-based decisions to decisions about data. It implies the validation, diagnosis and decision-making in business processes where the aim of the analysis is data-centric, especially when there is a database with a great quantity of shared information. For this reason, the required composition of the model (workflow, database schema, BDCs and data states) it is detailed, and the observational model is extracted from the relational database. The special characteristics of data management for validation and diagnosis have been listed, and the steps to perform the different scenarios are presented. Several open issues have also been included in the paper, such as: the possibility of combining data and compliance rules at the same time as making a minimal diagnosis; the necessity to validate the data model of the stored information and the workflow; the uncertainty related to the unknown variables produced by the *null* values; or the challenge that supposes the incorporation of the trustworthiness of the users into the model.

The difficulties of stored data management have been applied to local relational databases, but obviously the complexity increase exponentially with big data, that implies volume, variety, velocity, and veracity of data sources.

Acknowledgement. This work has been partially funded by the Ministry of Science and Technology of Spain (TIN2015-63502-C3-2-R) and the European Regional Development Fund (ERDF/FEDER).

References

1. Weber, B., Sadiq, S.W., Reichert, M.: Beyond rigidity - dynamic process lifecycle support. Comput. Sci. R&D **23**(2), 47–65 (2009)
2. van der Aalst, W., Adriansyah, A., van Dongen, B.: Replaying history on process models for conformance checking and performance analysis. Wiley Int. Rev. Data Min. and Knowl. Disc. **2**(2), 182–192 (2012)
3. van der Aalst, W.M.P.: Extracting event data from databases to unleash process mining. In: Brocke, J.V., Schmiedel, T. (eds.) BPM - Driving Innovation in a Digital World. Management for Professionals, pp. 105–128. Springer, Heidelberg (2015)
4. Ly, L.T., Rinderle-Ma, S., Dadam, P.: Design and verification of instantiable compliance rule graphs in process-aware information systems. In: Pernici, B. (ed.) CAiSE 2010. LNCS, vol. 6051, pp. 9–23. Springer, Heidelberg (2010)
5. Rozinat, A., van der Aalst, W.M.P.: Conformance checking of processes based on monitoring real behavior. Inf. Syst. **33**(1), 64–95 (2008)
6. Ceballos, R., Gómez-López, M.T., Gasca, R.M., Del Carmelo, V.: A compiled model for faults diagnosis based on different techniques. AI Commun. **20**(1), 7–16 (2007)
7. Borrego, D., Eshuis, R., Gómez-López, M.T., Gasca, R.M.: Diagnosing correctness of semantic workflow models. Data Knowl. Eng. **87**, 167–184 (2013)
8. Gómez-López, M.T., Gasca, R.M.: Run-time monitoring and auditing for business processes data using contraints. In: International Workshop on Business Process Intelligence, BPI 2010, pp. 15–25. Springer, Heidelberg (2010)
9. Gómez-López, M.T., Gasca, R.M., Pérez-Álvarez, J.M.: Compliance validation and diagnosis of business data constraints in business processes at runtime. Inf. Syst. **48**, 26–43 (2015)
10. Muehlen, M.Z., Indulska, M.: Indulska.: Modeling languages for business processes and business rules: A representational analysis. Inf. Syst. **35**(4), 379–390 (2010)
11. Gómez-López, M.T., Gasca, R.M.: Using constraint programming in selection operators for constraint databases. Expert Syst. Appl. **41**(15), 6773–6785 (2014)
12. Gómez-López, M.T., Ceballos, R., Gasca, R.M., Del Valle, C.: Developing a labelled object-relational constraint database architecture for the projection operator. Data Knowl. Eng. **68**(1), 146–172 (2009)
13. OMG. Object Management Group, Business Process Model and Notation (BPMN) Version 2.0. OMG Standard (2011)
14. Meyer, A., Pufahl, L., Fahland, D., Weske, M.: Modeling and enacting complex data dependencies in business processes. In: Daniel, F., Wang, J., Weber, B. (eds.) BPM 2013. LNCS, vol. 8094, pp. 171–186. Springer, Heidelberg (2013)
15. Gómez-López, M.T., Borrego, D., Gasca, R.M.: Data state description for the migration to activity-centric business process model maintaining legacy databases. In: Abramowicz, W., Kokkinaki, A. (eds.) BIS 2014. LNBIP, vol. 176, pp. 86–97. Springer, Heidelberg (2014)
16. Hull, R.: Artifact-centric business process models: brief survey of research results and challenges. In: Tari, Z., Meersman, R. (eds.) OTM 2008, Part II. LNCS, vol. 5332, pp. 1152–1163. Springer, Heidelberg (2008)
17. Eshuis, R., Kumar, A.: Kumar.: An integer programming based approach for verification and diagnosis of workflows. Data Knowl. Eng. **69**(8), 816–835 (2010)
18. Borrego, D., Gasca, R.M., Gómez López, M.T.: Automating correctness verification of artifact-centric business process models. Inf. Softw. Technol. **62**, 187–197 (2015)

19. Peng, Y., Reggia, J.A.: Abductive Inference Models for Diagnostic Problem-solving. Symbolic computation. Springer, Heidelberg (1990)
20. van der Wil, M.P., van der Aalst, W.M.P., van Hee, K.M., van der Werf, J.M.E.M., Kumar, A., Verdonk, M.: Conceptual model for online auditing. Decis. Support Syst. **50**(3), 636–647 (2011)
21. Awad, A., Smirnov, S., Weske, M.: Towards resolving compliance violations in business process models. In: Proceedings of the 2nd International Workshop on Governance, Risk and Compliance - Applications in Information Systems, Amsterdam, The Netherlands, June 2009
22. Gómez-López, M.T., Gasca, R.M.: Fault diagnosis in databases for business processes. In: 21th International Workshop on Principles of Diagnosis, pp. 1–8 (2010)
23. Conforti, R., de Leoni, M., La Rosa, M., van der Aalst, W.M.P., ter Hofstede, A.H.M.: A recommendation system for predicting risks across multiple business process instances. Decis. Support Syst. **69**, 1–19 (2015)
24. van der Aa, H., Leopold, H., Batoulis, K., Weske, M., Reijers, H.A.: Integrated process and decision modeling for data-driven processes. In: 3th International Workshop on Decision Mining & Modeling for Business Processes, DeMiMo, pp. 15–25. Springer, Heidelberg (2015)
25. Bazhenova, E., Weske, M.: A data-centric approach for business process improvement based on decision theory. In: Bider, I., Gaaloul, K., Krogstie, J., Nurcan, S., Proper, H.A., Schmidt, R., Soffer, P. (eds.) BPMDS 2014 and EMMSAD 2014. LNBIP, vol. 175, pp. 242–256. Springer, Heidelberg (2014)
26. Gómez-López, M.T., Gasca, R.M., Pérez-Álvarez, J.M.: Decision-making support for the correctness of input data at runtime in business processes. Int. J. Coop. Info. Syst. **23**(2), 29 (2014)
27. Parody, L., Gasca, R.M., López, M.T.G.: Hybrid business process modelling for the optimization of outcome data. Inf. Softw. Technol. **70**, 68–70 (2015)
28. Rossi, F., van Beek, P., Walsh, T.: Handbook of Constraint Programming. Elsevier, New York (2006)
29. Weber, I., Hoffmann, J., Mendling, J.: Semantic business process validation. In: 3rd international workshop on Semantic Business Process Management (2008)

Integrating Activity- and Goal-Based Workflows: A Data Model Based Design Method

António Rito Silva[1][(✉)] and Vicente García-Díaz[2]

[1] ESW - INESC-ID, IST, University of Lisbon, Lisbon, Portugal
`rito.silva@tecnico.ulisboa.pt`
[2] Department of Computer Science, University of Oviedo, Oviedo, Spain
`garciavicente@uniovi.es`

Abstract. Data-centric approaches are very promising. The inference of business processes from the structure of data provides more flexibility than the activity-based approaches which enforce a specific flow of behavior. However, the price for this flexibility is the lack of a standard organizational behavior. Actually, there is a tension between the standardization of workers' behavior and allowing them to deal with unexpected situations by using their own tacit knowledge. The blended workflow approach [1] integrates activity-based with goal-based representations of a workflow to balance these two aspects. In this paper we describe how to design two workflow models, an activity-based and a goal-based, from a common data-model. The overall approach consists on a stepwise generation of models departing from an annotated data model where an intermediate state model is used to define the set of conditions that both workflow models, activity and goal, have to support.

Keywords: Activity-based workflow · Goal-based workflow · Data-centric BPM · Flexible workflow

1 Introduction

Blended workflow supports a novel approach [1] to workflow management systems that provides end users with two views of the same workflow instance, a "classical" workflow view based on an explicit process model [2,3] and a view which shows goals and their relationships [4,5]. By executing the workflow instance according to the former view, end users' work is guided by a definition of what is the standard behavior, specified by explicit organizational rules, whereas the latter view empowers end users to use their tacit domain knowledge to handle unexpected situations, while conforming to the business goals.

The two views are supported by two different specifications, one activity-based and the other goal-based. Both specifications share a common data model. As a workflow instance progresses toward its completion via consecutive instantiations of its data model, the two specifications describe a prescriptive and a descriptive way of instantiating the data model.

M. Reichert and H.A. Reijers (Eds.): BPM Workshops 2015, LNBIP 256, pp. 352–363, 2016.
DOI: 10.1007/978-3-319-42887-1_29

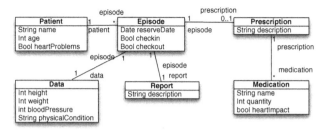

Fig. 1. Doctor Appointment Example - Data Model

The two specifications are equivalent from a semantic point of view: any workflow instance that is executing according to one of the specifications can continue executing according to the other. Therefore each view presents the current state of the workflow instance to end users, who can switch between them without having to redo any of the work they have done while using the other view.

Figure 1 presents the data model for a Doctor Appointment workflow specification. The creation of a workflow instance corresponds to the creation of an *Episode* instance and its association to an existing *Patient* instance. The workflow instance progresses by creating instances of the other entities. Eventually a *MedicalReport* will be written and the patient checked out. The data model can be enriched with additional contraints. For instance, the invariant rule below states that it is not possible to prescribe drugs that may adversely have impact on patients with heart problems.

```
RUL(NOT(DEF(Medication.heartImpact)) OR NOT(Medication.heartImpact) OR
    NOT(Medication.medicalPrescription.episode.patient.heartProblems))
```

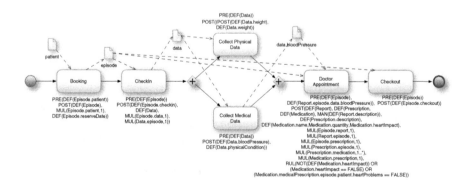

Fig. 2. Doctor Appointment Example - Activity Specification

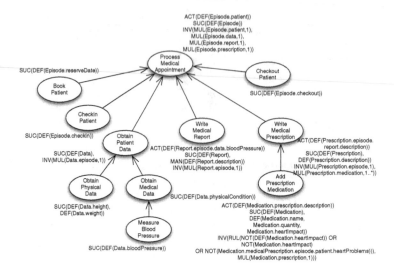

Fig. 3. Doctor Appointment Example - Goals Specification

Figure 2 presents the activity-based specification of the Doctor Appointment example. The specification follows a typical BPMN[1]-like activity-based specification enriched with pre- and post-conditions, denoted respectively by *PRE* and *POST*. For each activity, its pre- and post-conditions describe what should be the data model state immediately, respectively, before and after the execution of the activity.

The specification shows that the *Booking* activity creates an instance of *Episode* and sets its *reserveDate* attribute, post-conditions *DEF(Episode)* and *DEF(Episode.reserveDate)*. Note that the creation of an *Episode* instance requires a *Patient*, *MUL(Episode.patient,*1), and the relation between the pre-condition, *DEF(Episode.patient)* and the activity input value. As another example, note that the execution of *Checkout* only requires an instance of *Episode*, as is expressed in its pre-condition, which means that the patient can pay immediately after he books the appointment. However, the activity model adds additional organizational restrictions, flow-control restrictions. Therefore, in this case, the activity model defines a standard behavior where the checkout should be the last activity.

Figure 3 presents the goal-based specification that adapts the structure of goals from [6]. Therefore a goal can have an activation condition, *ACT*, a success condition, *SUC*, and an invariant condition, *INV*. Goals are specified in a tree of goals. To execute a goal its activation condition should hold true. After the execution of goal its success condition should hold true. A goal is accomplished when all its subgoals are accomplished and its invariant conditions hold true.

The success condition of goal `Write Medical Report` creates a `Report` entity, *SUC(DEF(Report))*, associating it with an episode instance, *INV(MUL(Report.episode,*1)), and produces a report description,

---

[1] http://www.bpmn.org/.

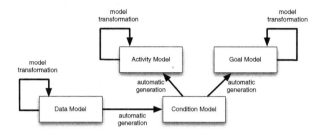

Fig. 4. Design Process

$MAN(DEF(Report.description))$, which is mandatory because it should be produced even in the non-standard execution of the workflow. In order to execute the goal, it is necessary a value for the patient's blood pressure, $ACT(DEF(Report.episode.data.bloodPressure))$. Note that the goal model, contrarily to the activity model, does not require a standard behavior, for instance the execution of this goal does not require that a checkin has previously occurred, only the blood pressure is required.

The blended workflow is implemented [7] and the prototype was already demonstrated using the Doctor Appointment case [8]. However, the design of these models is a challenging task. How can we create an activity and a goal model from a given data model?

In this paper we present a design method to build activity and goal models from a data model. The overall approach is described in Fig. 4.

The design of the activity and goal models is based on a data model which is designed through several model tranformations. From the data model a state model is automatically generated. This model describes the conditions that need to hold when the data model contains all the required data. The state model is the source of the next two other generations. The generation strategy is to preserve the state model in the generated models in order to guarantee their equivalence. After the generation, the designers can apply a set of transformations to the models in order to support end user requirements, like the rearrangement of the tree of goals. This paper addresses the automartic generation of models.

Several data and artifact centric approaches propose the generation of a workflow model from a data model [9,10], however they do not address the coexistence of activity and artifact-centric models. The recent work by Meyer and Weske [11] shows how to transform an artifact-centric process model to an activity-centric one and vice versa. The algorithms presented in this paper describe how to generate activity and goal models that allows the synchronized execution of a blended workflow instance.

2 Construction

2.1 Data and State Models

Blended workflow uses a UML-like data model, represented by D, which is composed of a set of entities, represented by E, their attributes, represented by ATT, and the binary relationships, represented by R, between such entities. Therefore, given an entity $e \in E$ and an attribute $att \in ATT$, $e.att$ denotes the attribute att of e. The set of attributes of an entity e is represented by $ATT(e) \in \mathcal{P}(ATT)$. The binary relationship $r((e1, r1, m1), (e2, r2, m2)) \in R$ represents a relationship between entities $e1, e2 \in E$, $r1(r2)$ is the role name associated with entity $e1(e2)$, and $m1(m2)$ its multiplicity, such that $e1.r2$ represents the set of entities $e2$ associated with $e1$ in the context of relationship r, and the cardinality of $e1.r2$ is constraint by $m2$.

From the data model D we define a set of conditions, represented by C, that are classified as either achieve or invariant conditions. Achieved conditions describe which data has to be created during the workflow execution whereas invariant conditions define constraints on the attribute values.

There are two kinds of achieve conditions: attribute and entity, represented by $ACH_{ATT}(C)$ and $ACH_{ENT}(C)$, respectively. Given an entity $e \in E$ and an attribute $att \in ATT(e)$, $DEF(e)$ and $DEF(e.att)$ represent their entity and attribute achieve conditions, respectively. These conditions hold when their entities and attributes are defined: a particular instance of an entity exists and an attribute has a value, respectively. An attribute achieve condition can refer to one or more attributes of the same entity. Given $aac \in ACH_{ATT}(C)$, $ENT(aac) \in E$ denotes the entity the attributes belong to, and $ATT(acc)$ denotes the set of attributes in acc. For instance, $ENT(Data.weight)$ denotes $Data$ and $ATT(Data.weight)$ denotes $\{Data.weight\}$. Obviously, for $DEF(e) \in ACH_{ENT}(C)$, $ATT(DEF(e)) = \emptyset$ and $ENT(DEF(e)) = e$.

It is possible to indicate that an attribute achieve condition is mandatory, which means that to have a successful completion of the workflow execution all its mandatory attribute achieve conditions must hold. The attribute achieve conditions are represented by $MAN(DEF(e.att))$. Given an attribute achieve condition $aac \in ACH_{ATT}(C)$, $MAN(ac)$ is true if the achieve condition is mandatory, false otherwise.

There is also a set of invariant conditions, represented by $INV(C)$, which comprises entity and attribute invariants, represented by $INV_{ENT}(C)$ and $INV_{ATT}(C)$, respectively.

The attribute invariant conditions are rules that state dependencies between the values of attributes and are represented as $RUL(Condition)$. Moreover, it is possible to combine any number of conditions with the logical operators NOT, AND, and OR. On the other hand, entity invariant conditions define the allowed number of instances in a given relation between entities and are represented as $MUL(e.rn, m)$ where $e \in E$, rn is a role name, and m is a valid multiplicity, e.g.,"1" or "1..*". Given $MUL(e.rn, m) \in INV_{ENT}(C)$, $ENT(MUL(e.rn, m))$ denotes the entity e but $ENT(e.rn)$ denotes the entity e refers through role name rn. For instance $ENT(MUL(Episode.patient, 1))$ represents $Episode$ and $ENT(Episode.patient)$ denotes $Patient$. Given $aic \in INV_{ATT}(C)$, $ATT(aic)$ denotes the set of attributes the invariant refers, for instance $ATT(RUL(E.att1 \geq E.rn1.att1))$ represents $\{E.att1, ENT(E.rn1).att1\}$.

Additionally, it is possible to express dependence conditions among different attributes, represented by $DEP_{ATT}(C)$. The dependence $DEP(DEF(e.att1), DEF(e.rn.att2))$ denotes that attribute $att1 \in ATT(e)$ depends on the attribute $att2 \in ATT(ENT(e.rn))$, which means that the latter should be defined first. On the other hand, it is possible to define entity dependencies, represented by $DEP_{ENT}(C)$, where $DEP(DEF(e), DEF(e.rn))$ means that $DEF(e.rn)$ should hold before $DEF(e)$. Note that we are extending the DEF operator to any path in the data model. The set of all dependencies in C is $DEP(C) = DEP_{ENT}(C) \cup DEP_{ATT}(C)$. Thus, we can say that the complete definition of the state model of D comprises the set of conditions $C = ACH_{ENT}(C) \cup ACH_{ATT}(C) \cup INV_{ENT}(C) \cup INV_{ATT}(C) \cup DEP_{ENT}(C) \cup DEP_{ATT}(C)$.

Below is presented the state model that is automatically generated from the data model. Note that it is possible to aggregate several attributes into a single attribute achieve condition, in the example the attributes of the Medication entity, but a constraint has to be enforced: the same attribute cannot be used in two different achieve attribute conditions. The aggregation of attributes, together with adding dependences and invariant rules, are examples of designer's operations on the data model. The workflow manages the doctor appointment process and assumes that the *Patient* entities already exist.

```
ENTITY ACHIEVE CONDITIONS
  EXISTS(DEF(Patient))
  DEF(Episode)
  DEF(Data)
  DEF(Report)
  DEF(Prescription)
  DEF(Medication)

ENTITY INVARIANT CONDITIONS
  MUL(Episode.patient,1)
  MUL(Episode.data,1)
  MUL(Episode.report,1)
  MUL(Episode.prescription,1)
  MUL(Data.episode,1)
  MUL(Report.episode,1)
  MUL(Prescription.episode,1)
  MUL(Prescription.medication,1..*)
  MUL(Medication.prescription,1)

ATTRIBUTE ACHIEVE CONDITIONS
  DEF(Episode.reserveDate)
  DEF(Episode.checkin)
  DEF(Episode.checkout)
  DEF(Data.height)
  DEF(Data.weight)
  DEF(Data.bloodPressure)
  DEF(Data.physicalCondition)

MAN(DEF(Report.description))
DEF(Prescription.description)
DEF(Medication.name,
    Medication.quantity,
    Medication.heartImpact)

ATTRIBUTE INVARIANT CONDITIONS
RUL(NOT(
        DEF(Medication.heartImpact))
    OR NOT(Medication.heartImpact)
    OR NOT(Medication.
        medicalPrescription.
        episode.patient.
        heartProblems))

DEPENDENCIES
  DEP(DEF(Report.description),
      DEF(Report.episode.data.
          bloodPressure))
  DEP(DEF(Prescription.description),
      DEF(Prescription.episode
          .report.description))
  DEP(DEF(Medication.name,
          Medication.quantity,
          Medication.heartImpact),
      DEF(Medication.prescription
          .description))
```

2.2 Goal Model

The set of goals of a blended workflow model, represented by G, are structured in a hierarchy: $PAR_{all}(g)$, where $g \in G$, represents the set of all parent goals of g; $SUB_{all}(g)$ represents the set of all its subgoals. If $g \in G$ is the root goal, represented by $root(G)$, then $PAR_{all}(g) = \emptyset$. Additionally, $SUB(g)$ represents the immediate subgoals of goal g.

Each goal $g \in G$ contains a success achieve condition, represented by $SUC(g)$, where $SUC(g) \subset (ACH_{ENT}(C) \cup ACH_{ATT}(C))$, an activation condition, represented by $ACT(g)$, where $ACT(g) \subset (ACH_{ENT}(C) \cup ACH_{ATT}(C))$ and a set of invariant conditions, represented by $INV(g)$, where $INV(g) \subset (INV_{ENT}(C) \cup INV_{ATT}(C))$.

The execution of a goal $g \in G$ corresponds to the change to a state where its $SUC(g)$ condition holds. Additionally, to be executed a goal has to be activated, its $ACT(g)$ condition holds.

A goal $g \in G$ is achieved, represented by $ACH(g)$, when the three following conditions are true, $SUC(g)$ and $ACT(g)$ and $INV(g)$, and all its subgoals are achieved. the execution of a goal workflow model terminates when all its goals are achieved, which corresponds to $ACH(root(G))$.

The goal model G is generated from the state model C according to Algorithm 1.

Algorithm 1. Goal Model Generation algorithm

1: **procedure**
2:     create a goal $g0$: $SUC(g0) = \emptyset$, $ACT(g0) = \emptyset$, $INV(g0) = \emptyset$, $SUB(g0) = \emptyset$
3:     **for** each $eac \in ACH_{ENT}(C)$ **do**
4:         create a goal g: $SUC(g) = \{eac\}$, $ACT(g) = \emptyset$, $INV(g) = \emptyset$, $SUB(g0) = SUB(g0) \cup \{g\}$
5:     **end for**
6:     **for** each $aac \in ACH_{ATT}(C)$ **do**
7:         create a goal g: $SUC(g) = \{aac\}$, $ACT(g) = \emptyset$, $INV(g) = \emptyset$, $SUB(ENT(acc)) = SUB(ENT(acc)) \cup \{g\}$
8:     **end for**
9:     **for** each $DEP(c1, c2) \in DEP(C)$ **do**
10:        $ACT(g) = ACT(g) \cup \{c2\}$ where $c1 == SUC(g)$
11:    **end for**
12:    **for** each $eic \in INV_{ENT}(C)$ **do**
13:        INV(g) = INV(g) $\cup$ {eic} where $DEF(ENT(eic)) == SUC(g)$
14:    **end for**
15:    **for** each $aic \in INV_{ATT}(C)$ **do**
16:        **for** each $g : ATT(SUC(g)) \cap ATT(aic) \neq \emptyset$ **do**
17:            INV(g) = INV(g) $\cup$ {aic}
18:        **end for**
19:    **end for**
20: **end procedure**

By applying the algorithm to the Doctor Appointment case we obtain the following set of goals.

```
g0:    SUC(∅), SUB(g1,g2,g3,g4,g5)
g1:    ACT(DEF(Episode.patient)), SUC(DEF(Episode)), SUB(g6,g7,g8)
       INV(MUL(Episode.patient,1), MUL(Episode.data,1),
           MUL(Episode.report,1), MUL(Episode.prescription,1))
g2:    SUC(DEF(Data)), SUB(g9,g10,g11,g12), INV(MUL(Data.episode,1))
g3:    SUC(DEF(Report)), SUB(g13), INV(MUL(Report.episode,1))
g4:    SUC(DEF(Prescription)), SUB(g14),
       INV(MUL(Prescription.episode,1), MUL(Prescription.medication,1..*))
g5:    SUC(DEF(Medication)), SUB(g15), INV(MUL(Medication.prescription,1))
g6:    SUC(DEF(Episode.reserveDate))
g7:    SUC(DEF(Episode.checkin))
g8:    SUC(DEF(Episode.checkout))
g9:    SUC(DEF(Data.height))
g10:   SUC(DEF(Data.weight))
g11:   SUC(DEF(Data.bloodPressure))
g12:   SUC(DEF(Data.physicalCondition))
g13:   ACT(DEF(Report.episode.data.bloodPressure)),
       SUC(MAN(DEF(Report.description))
g14:   ACT(DEF(Prescription.episode.report.description)),
       SUC(DEF(Prescription.description))
g15:   ACT(DEF(Medication.prescription.description)),
       SUC(DEF(Medication.name, Medication.quantity,
           Medication.heartImpact)),
       INV(RUL(NOT(DEF(Medication.heartImpact)) OR
           NOT(Medication.heartImpact) OR
           NOT(Medication.medicalPrescription.episode.
               patient.heartProblems)))
```

It is possible to apply a set of model transformations to the automatically generated goal model to get a model similar to the one in Fig. 3, while preserving its semantics. For instance goal $g0$ can be removed and $g1$ can be made super goal of $g2$, $g3$, and $g4$ because the creation of instances of *Data*, *Report*, and *Prescription* requires an instance of *Episode* due to the multiplicity invariants. Similarly, goal $g5$ can be made subgoal of $g4$. Note that after the algorithm is applied $\forall_{g \in G}$ **card**$(SUC(g)) == 1$ but the model transformations can make **card**$(SUC(g)) > 1$ for some for the goals.

2.3   Activity Model

The activity model, which set of activities is represented by A, have associated pre and post-conditions, represented by $PRE(a)$ and $POST(a)$, where $a \in A$, $PRE : A \rightarrow P(ACH(C))$ and $POST : A \rightarrow P(ACH(C) \cup INV(C))$. Additionally, an activity model has a control flow that defines a partial order of execution among its activities, which is defined by $PREC : A \rightarrow P(A)$, where $PREC(a)$ represents the set of activities that have to be executed before a.

We say that an activity $a \in A$ is flow-enabled for execution if for all $b \in PREC(a)$, b is executed before a. We say that an activity a is fully-enabled for execution if it is flow-enabled and $PRE(a)$ holds true before a executes. In a

Blended Workflow specification, if an activity is flow-enabled then it is fully-enabled due to the way a blended-workflow activity model is generated.

The algorithm that generates an activity-based workflow from the set of conditions C contains two parts: a first part where the activities are defined together with their pre- and post-conditions, whereas in the second part the precedence relationship is created. The second part of the algorithm is not described in this paper but it has to guarantee that control-flow preserves the pre- and post-conditions dependencies, such that if an activity is enabled by control flow then its pre-condition holds.

Algorithm 2 describes the activities's generation. The generated model depends on the set of achieve conditions that are chosen during each step (line 8), which may allow an assisted generation. The current implementation is completely automated, the algorithm uses a single achieve condition in each step. Afterwards the designer can transform the model by joining and splitting activities.

When we apply Algorithm 2 to the Doctor Appointment case we can obtain, depending on the choices in line 8, the following set of activities.

```
A1(Booking): PRE(DEF(Episode.patient)),
   POST(DEF(Episode.reserveDate), DEF(Episode), MUL(Episode.patient,1))
A2(Checkin): PRE(DEF(Episode)),
   POST(DEF(Episode.checkin), DEF(Data),
       MUL(Episode.data,1), MUL(Data.episode,1))
A3(Checkout): PRE(DEF(Episode)),
   POST(DEF(Episode.checkout))
A4(Collect Physical Data): PRE(DEF(Data)),
   POST(DEF(Data.height), DEF(Data.weight))
A5(Collect Medical Data): PRE(DEF(Data)),
   POST(DEF(Data.bloodPressure), DEF(Data.physicalCondition))
A6(Doctor Appointment):
  PRE(DEF(Episode), DEF(Report.episode.data.bloodPressure)),
  POST(DEF(Report), DEF(Prescription), DEF(Medication),
      MAN(DEF(Report.description)), DEF(Prescription.description),
      DEF(Medication.name,Medication.quantity,Medication.heartImpact),
      MUL(Episode.report,1), MUL(Report.episode,1),
      MUL(Episode.prescription,1), MUL(Prescription.episode,1),
      MUL(Prescription.medication,1..*), MUL(Medication.prescription,1),
      RUL(NOT(DEF(Medication.heartImpact)) OR NOT(Medication.heartImpact)
          OR NOT(Medication.medicalPrescription.
                 episode.patient.heartProblems)))
```

A brief explanation of the steps involved to assign all the achieve conditions to activities is described below.

- First iteration (A1). Two achieve conditions are selected (line 8) and a multiplicity invariant is added (lines 21–22) since both, $DEF(Episode.patient)$ and $DEF(Episode)$ are not in the $ACH \setminus POST(A1)$. Note that instances of patient already exist, they are not created in the context of this workflow. $DEF(Episode.patient)$ is in $PRE(A1)$ because of the $MUL(Episode.patient, 1)$ (lines 26–28).

Algorithm 2. Activities Generation algorithm

```
 1: procedure
 2:     A = ∅ // the set of activities to be created
 3:     ACH = ACH_ENT(C) ∪ ACH_ATT(C) //set of all achieve conditions
 4:     MUL = INV_ENT(C) //set of all entity invariants
 5:     RUL = INV_ATT(C) //set of all attribute invariants
 6:     while ACH ≠ ∅ do
 7:         a = newA(); A = A ∪ {a}
 8:         select SUB ≠ ∅ : SUB ⊆ ACH
 9:         POST(a) = SUB
10:         for each d1 ∈ SUB : DEP(d1, d2) ∈ DEP(C) do
11:             if d2 ∉ POST(a) then
12:                 PRE(a) = PRE(a) ∪ {d2}
13:             end if
14:         end for
15:         for each DEF(Entity.attribute) ∈ POST(a) do
16:             if DEF(Entity) ∉ POST(a) then
17:                 PRE(a) = PRE(a) ∪ {DEF(Entity)}
18:             end if
19:         end for
20:         for MUL(Entity.role, m) ∈ MUL do
21:             if     DEF(Entity)     ∉     (ACH  \  POST(a)))     AND
         DEF(ENT(Entity.role)) ∉ (ACH \ POST(a)) then
22:                 POST(a) = POST(a) ∪ {MUL(Entity.role, m)}
23:                 if DEF(Entity) ∉ POST(a) then
24:                     PRE(a) = PRE(a) ∪ {DEF(Entity)}
25:                 end if
26:                 if DEF(ENT(Entity.role)) ∉ POST(a) then
27:                     PRE(a) = PRE(a) ∪ {DEF(ENT(Entity.role))}
28:                 end if
29:                 MUL = MUL \ {MUL(Entity.role, m)}
30:             end if
31:         end for
32:         for rule ∈ RUL do
33:             if ∀_{att∈ATT(rule)} : DEF(att) ∉ (ACH \ POST(a)) then
34:                 POST(a) = POST(a) ∪ {rule}
35:                 for each att ∈ ATT(rule) do
36:                     if DEF(att) ∉ POST(a) then
37:                         PRE(a) = PRE(a) ∪ {DEF(att)}
38:                     end if
39:                 end for
40:                 RUL = RUL \ {rule}
41:             end if
42:         end for
43:         ACH = ACH \ POST(a) //equal to SUB
44:     end while
45: end procedure
```

- Second iteration (A2). Again, two achieve conditions are chosen and the two multiplicity invariants are added (lines 21–22). In addition, *Episode* had to be placed as a pre-condition (lines 23–28) to ensure that the invariants can be evaluated.
- Third iteration (A3). A single achieve condition is chosen, and $DEF(Episode)$ is added to the post-condition (lines 15–19).
- Fourth iteration (A4). In this case, two achieve conditions are chosen, requiring to have $PRE(Data)$ as a pre-condition (lines 15–19).
- Fifth iteration (A5). This is similar to the previous case, but addressing the other attributes of *Data*.
- Sixth iteration (A6). In this case, all the remaining achieve conditions are chosen. Thus, $DEF(Report.episode.data.bloodPressure)$ had to be chosen as a pre-condition (lines 10–14) since there is a dependency and that attribute is not defined in the post-condition part of the activity. The remaining multiplicity and rule conditions were also added (lines 20–31 and 32–42).

A particular $PREC$ is shown next, which fulfills the condition that control-flow preserves the pre- and post-conditions dependencies. The generated model has the order of execution in Fig. 2

```
PREC(Booking) = ∅
PREC(Checkin) = {Booking}
PREC(Collect Physical Data) = {Booking, Checkin}
PREC(Collect Medical Data) = {Booking, Checkin}
PREC(Doctor Appointment) = {Booking, Checkin, Collect Physical Data,
                            Collect Medical Data}
PREC(Checkout) = {Booking, Checkin, Collect Physical Data,
                  Collect Medical Data, Doctor Appointment}
```

3   Conclusions

In this paper we describe how to generate a activity model and a goal model from a data model. A domain specific language was defined to ease the model definition and the generation of a first version of the activity and goal models. The implementation uses Xtext[2] and is publicly available in the BlendedWorkflow repository[3]. In the next steps of the project we intend to define the model transformation operations to allow the designer to do consistent transformations for each one of the models, and address the cases where there are circular dependences between the activities' pre-conditions.

Acknowledgement. This work was supported by national funds through Fundação para a Ciência e a Tecnologia (FCT) with reference UID/CEC/50021/2013 and Ibero-America Santander Grant for Young Lecturers and Researchers 2015.

---

[2] http://eclipse.org/Xtext/.
[3] http://github.com/socialsoftware/blended-workflow.

References

1. Silva, A.R.: A blended workflow approach. In: Daniel, F., Barkaoui, K., Dustdar, S. (eds.) BPM Workshops 2011, Part I. LNBIP, vol. 99, pp. 25–36. Springer, Heidelberg (2012)
2. Russell, N., ter Hofstede, A., van der Aalst, W.: newyawl: Designing a workflow system using coloured petri nets. In: Proceedings of the International Workshop on Petri Nets and Distributed Systems (PNDS 2008) (2008)
3. OMG: Business process modelling notation (2015). http://www.bpmn.org/
4. Kueng, P., Kawalek, P.: Goal-based business process models: creation and evaluation. Bus. Process Manage. J. 3(1), 17–38 (1997)
5. Lapouchnian, A., Yu, Y., Mylopoulos, J.: Requirements-driven design and configuration management of business processes. In: Alonso, G., Dadam, P., Rosemann, M. (eds.) BPM 2007. LNCS, vol. 4714, pp. 246–261. Springer, Heidelberg (2007)
6. Van Lamsweerde, A.: Goal-oriented requirements engineering: A guided tour. In: Proceedings of the Fifth IEEE International Symposium on Requirements Engineering, 2001, pp. 249–262. IEEE (2001)
7. Pinto, B.O., Silva, A.R.: An architecture for a blended workflow engine. In: Daniel, F., Barkaoui, K., Dustdar, S. (eds.) BPM Workshops 2011, Part II. LNBIP, vol. 100, pp. 382–393. Springer, Heidelberg (2012)
8. Passinhas, D., Adams, M., Pinto, B.O., Costa, R., Silva, A.R., ter Hofstede, A.H.M.: Supporting blended workflows. In: Proceedings of the Demonstration Track of the 10th International Conference on Business Process Management (BPM 2012), Tallinn, Estonia, September 4, 2012, pp. 23–28 (2012)
9. Reijers, H.A., Limam, S., Van Der Aalst, W.M.P.: Product-based workflow design. J. Manage. Inf. Syst. 20(1), 229–262 (2003)
10. Künzle, V., Reichert, M.: Philharmonicflows: towards a framework for object-aware process management. J. Softw. Maintenance Evol.: Res. Pract. 23(4), 205–244 (2011)
11. Meyer, A., Weske, M.: Activity-centric and artifact-centric process model roundtrip. In: Lohmann, N., Song, M., Wohed, P. (eds.) BPM 2013 Workshops. LNBIP, vol. 171, pp. 167–182. Springer, Heidelberg (2014)

Towards Ontology Guided Translation of Activity-Centric Processes to GSM

Julius Köpke[1,2]([envelope]) and Jianwen Su[1]

[1] Department of Computer Science, UC Santa Barbara, Santa Barbara, USA
julius.koepke@aau.at, su@cs.ucsb.edu
[2] Alpen-Adria Universität, Klagenfurt, Austria

Abstract. There exist two major modeling paradigms for business process modeling: The predominant activity centric one and the artifact centric paradigm. Both are suitable for modeling and for executing business processes. However, process models are typically designed from different perspectives. Current translation methods operate on the syntactic level, preserving the point of view of the source process. The results of such translations are not particularly useful, understandable and insightful for stakeholders. In this paper we motivate the need for ontology-guided translations by comparing the results of a purely syntactic translation with a manual translation. We discuss shortcomings of the generated solutions and propose an ontology-based framework and sketch corresponding translation method for the generation of semantic translations, which allow to incorporate the point of view of the target modeling paradigm.

Keywords: Process translation · Artifact centric BPM · Guard Stage Milestone · GSM · Semantic process abstraction

1 Introduction

In business process modeling, traditionally the activity- or control-flow perspective achieved the major attention, while the data perspective was addressed in a much lesser degree. This resulted in the predominant activity-centric modeling paradigm, where the data perspective is treated as an implementation issue rather than a modeling concern.

Data-centric approaches in general and the artifact-centric modeling paradigm in particular have emerged and gained an increasing momentum in the last decade. The essence is an integrated modeling method for both perspectives. As a result both competing paradigms are attracting users. When interorganizational cooperations are concerned it is likely going to happen that interorganizational processes between companies that use activity-centric and the ones using artifact-centric modeling methods need to be established. Process

---

Research conducted while visiting UC SB and supported by the Austrian Science Fund (FWF) under grant J-3609.

M. Reichert and H.A. Reijers (Eds.): BPM Workshops 2015, LNBIP 256, pp. 364–375, 2016.
DOI: 10.1007/978-3-319-42887-1_30

views [6, 7, 14] have proven their usefulness to support activity-centric inter-organizational processes. Naturally, a new kind of "translating views" that allow the seamless interoperation of activity-centric and artifact-centric processes to allow cross organizational interoperability is worth exploring.

In this paper we consider a particular sub-problem, namely "meaningful" translation between activity-centric and artifact-centric processes. We argue that in an inter-organizational and therefore heterogeneous setting existing translation approaches [8, 15, 21] are not desirable since they only address the syntactic aspect rather than taking into consideration domain knowledge. Therefore, we aim for a "good" artifact-centric representation of some activity-centric source process, where "good" means using the modeling capabilities of the target language and, since we are in an inter-organizational setting, agreed terms of the application domain.

In this paper we initiate the study by focusing on the translation from executable activity-centric processes to declarative Guard Stage Milestone [12] (GSM) models. In this scenario the activity-centric representation (e.g. BPEL) also specifies the data perspective for the execution of the process. However, the activity-centric process does not define any explicit relation between process variables and relevant data entities of the business domain, nor there is any information about relevant stages of business objects. As a consequence, a simple syntactic translation approach results in an executable target process that does not relate to real-world business entities and their states. Additionally, the target process is not taking advantage of GSM's capability of stage hierarchies.

The core idea of our approach to overcome these limitations is to make relevant domain knowledge accessible to the translation process by using *ontologies* and *semantic annotations*. Since ontologies are gaining popularity in the business world (e.g. in the tourism sector the open travel alliance ontology or in the insurance industry, the ACORD ontology to name only two), we think that the required additional effort to provide these descriptions is reasonable. As a consequence the translation of a business process remains automatic, while we can generate meaningful translations that refer to agreed terms of the domain regarding both, the activity- and the data-perspective including suitable abstractions thereof.

The contributions of this paper are the following. We present a novel syntactic translation approach for block-structured processes with data that produces hierarchic GSM models based on the hierarchy of the input process in Sect. 2.3. Then we discuss the weaknesses of syntactic translations in Sect. 2.4. We introduce a framework for the definitions of relevant semantics based on semantic annotations and a reference ontology in Sect. 3. A corresponding novel semantic translation method is sketched in Sect. 4. Finally, Sect. 5 discusses related work and Sect. 6 concludes the paper.

2 Motivations

We illustrate the need for domain knowledge to achieve meaningful translations by examining the output of a syntactic translation approach in comparison to a translation that could be provided by a domain expert.

2.1 Activity-Centric Process Model

We base our activity-centric source process model on the essentials of BPEL and inter-organizational view approaches [6,7,14], following block-structured processes which can be represented as trees. Supporting the typical control-flow constructs sequence (SEQ), parallel (PAR), loop ($LOOP$) and decision nodes (XOR). In the usual graph based representation PAR, $LOOP$, XOR-blocks are represented by corresponding $split-$ and $join-$ nodes. See examples on the left of Fig. 1. To enforce the block-structure in the graph representation, each split node must have its corresponding join node. Activities are executed by activity-steps, which may occur as leaf nodes in the tree-representation. The data perspective is modeled by declaring process variables (literal or XML-Type) and by specifying, which activity-step reads and writes to what variables and by defining conditions of XOR- or LOOP blocks in form of boolean expressions over process variables. For example the XOR-split node in Fig. 1 may have the Boolean condition $\$a > 10$ *or* $\$b = 1$, where $\$a$ and $\$b$ are variables of the process. The activity step A may be defined to read $\$b$ and write to $\$a$.

2.2 Guard Stage Milestone (GSM)

We briefly discuss the essentials of Guard Stage Milestone (GSM) relevant for this work here and refer the reader to [4,12] for all details. A process is modeled in form of artifacts, where each artifact has a data schema holding data attributes and state attributes, and a life-cycle definition. GSM life-cycles are based on guards, stages and milestones. In the graphical representation (see Fig. 1), guards are depicted as diamonds, stages as rounded boxes with optional labels and milestone are depicted as circles. Guards, define when a particular stage becomes active, milestones define, when a stage is completed. Stages can be nested, where stages at leaf-level contain service calls for task execution. Guards and milestones may have labels and are specified by sentries. Sentries are defined in form of Event Condition (over the data schema) Action (ECA) Rules of the form *"on event if condition"*, *"on event"* or *"if condition"*. Events may be internal (such as achieving of a guard or a milestone) or external such as the completion event of a service call. Achieving events of sentries are denoted by the prefix + and their invalidation by the prefix −, respectively.

2.3 A Syntactic Translation Approach

Given a block structured activity centric process model as input, our syntactic translation is based on a set of transformation rules that transform each block-type to its GSM representation as shown in Fig. 1.

Translation Rules. A *sequence* $< A, B >$ is transformed to two stages A' and B', where the guard of B' gets activated after the milestone of A' is reached ($B'.Guard = on + A'.Milestone$). If A refers to an activity-step, then A' contains

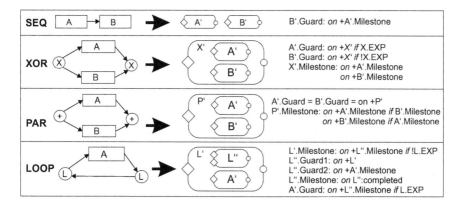

Fig. 1. Syntactic transformation rules

a service call and the milestone of A' is reached on the completion event of the service in A. Otherwise, the milestone of A' is reached after achieving the milestone of the nested stage.

A XOR node with the sub-blocks A and B is translated to an anonymous stage X' with two sub stages A' and B', where the guards of A' and B' are defined over the opening event of X' and the xor-expression of the input block. The guard of A' refers to the xor expression, the one of B' to its negation. The milestone of X' is achieved, when either the milestone of A' or B' are achieved.

Parallel Blocks with the sub-blocks A and B are translated to an anonymous stage P' with the sub stages A' and B'. The guards of A' and B' are open as soon as the guard of P' becomes active. The milestone of P' is achieved when the milestones of A' and B' are both achieved.

A Loop-Block L with the sub-block A is translated to an anonymous stage L', containing the sub stages A' and L''. The stage L'' is used to determine if the loop needs to be executed or repeated, while A' holds the loop body. L'' is activated, when L' becomes active or when the milestone of A'' is achieved. The milestone of L' is reached if the milestone of L'' is achieved and the loop condition $L.EXP$ is *false*. In order to comply with the flip-once [4] restriction of GSM, the milestone of L'' is defined over the task completion event of the dummy task in L''. The same approach is used, if an XOR-block contains empty branches.

2.4   Weaknesses of Syntactic Translations

We will now discuss the properties of the translation approach based on the partly simplified example process for order processing shown in Fig. 2. Part (a) of the example shows the activity-centric input process. Part (b) shows the translation of (a) based on the proposed syntactic translation algorithm. Part (c) shows a GSM version of (a) potentially created by a domain expert from scratch. Our syntactic translation shown in (b) has a number of disadvantages in comparison to (c):

1. Milestones and guards are defined on a solely technical level not relating to any agreed real-world states of data objects. For example the milestone for *Pay* in Fig. 2(b) is defined by the completion of the *Pay* task. In contrast, the domain expert has modeled a stage *PayInvoice* with the milestone *paid* in Fig. 2(c), where *paid* is a well-known state of order objects in the domain and *PayInvoice* is a defined activity in the domain.

2. While existing translation approaches produce completely flat GSM models [8,20,21], our algorithm faithfully preserves the structure of the input process regarding LOOP, PAR and XOR-Blocks. However, this still leads to a mostly flat output process in (b). In contrast, the domain expert makes use of nested stages in *GSM*, which allows to structure the process based on abstract state transitions that are well-known in the domain. As a consequence, (c) is much better understandable than (b). It encloses the activity stages in the upper-level stages *Shop*, *Checkout* and *ProcessOrder*. In addition, the stages are described by meaningful labels for stages, guards and milestones referring to agreed terms of the domain.

3. Our translation approach generates exactly one artifact for each activity centric process. This contradicts with the aim of GSM to identify and model key artifacts, where a process is possibly composed by the interplay of multiple different artifacts (e.g. *Order*, *Invoice*, *Payment*).

Only the last critics (3) is solved by other translation approaches [8,15,21]. No existing approaches are capable to address critics one and two. All other approaches generate flat GSM models and they either follow similar ideas for encoding control-flow into stages and guards as our approach or they assume to get the state of business objects as an input. Our aim is to automatically or semi-automatically generate models like (c) from models like (a). From a more generic perspective, we argue that the quality [9,18] of solution (c) is superior to the quality of solution (b). The reason is the different expressiveness of the activity-centric model and the GSM model, leading to partial triangle mappings between the real world, process (a) and process (c).

3 Towards Semantic Translations

As motivated in Sect. 2.4 a meaningful translation from an activity-centric process to a GSM process requires domain knowledge, which may only exist informally. We now present a framework that explicitly provides this knowledge by using a reference ontology defining relevant business objects and their states and a taxonomy of actions. The provided information is supposed to be generic for a specific domain and can therefore be reused for all activity-centric process models of that domain. The activity-centric processes are linked to the reference ontology by semantic annotations [13].

3.1 Ontology of Business Objects and States

The reference ontology (RO) is encoded using the DL fragment of OWL [19] and defines concepts for each relevant business entity such as *order* or *invoice*

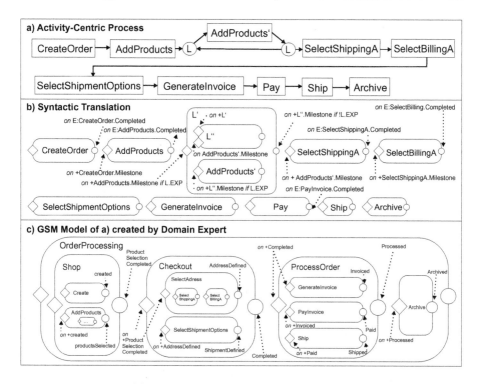

Fig. 2. Input process (a), Syntactic translation (b), GSM process of domain expert (c)

in our example. It also describes what attributes (data-type properties) and what relations to other entities (object properties) the different business entities have. Besides the conceptualization of business entities, the ontology also defines their valid states. States are described as defined OWL classes, which allow to derive a state hierarchy automatically and to classify instance data. For example the state *paid* of an *order* is defined as an *order* for which there exists an invoice and for that invoice there exists a payment. This can be expressed as following *DL* expression: *"invoice ⊓ ∃ hasInvoice.(Invoice ⊓ ∃has.payment)"*. In order to allow reasoning over states and matching of states against pre- and post-conditions of tasks, we propose to use such general definitions, rather than defining the states based on status attributes (e.g. an order is paid, if some attribute has the value *paid*). A fragment of an ontology for our *order* example is shown in Fig. 3. For simplicity, we depict no hierarchy of states.

3.2   Semantic Annotations

The concepts in the ontology are linked to the activity-centric process by semantic annotations [3,13,22]. We propose to use annotation paths [13] for annotating variable declarations of the activity centric process with the reference ontology. Following the annotation path method, we can for example anno-

Reference Ontology Classes	Example Class Definitions

BusinessEntity
    Order
    Invoice
    Payment
    BillingAddress
    ShippingAddress
    ...
States
    Order.State
        Empty
        ProductsSelected
        ProductSelectionCompleted
        BillingAddressSelected
        ShippingAddressSelected
        AddressDefined
        ShipmentDefined
        Completed
        Invoiced
        Paid
        Shipped
        Processed
        Archived
    ...
	$BillingAddressSelected \equiv$
	$Order.State \sqcap \exists\, hasBillingAddress.Address$
	$ShippingAddressSelected \equiv$
	$Order.State \sqcap \exists\, hasShippingAddress.Address$
	$AddressDefined \equiv$
	$BillingAddressSelected \sqcap ShippingAddressSelected$
	$ShipmentDefined \equiv$
	$Order.State \sqcap \exists\, hasShippingOption$
	$Invoiced \equiv$
	$Order.State \sqcap \exists\, has.Invoice$
	$Paid \equiv$
	$Order.State \sqcap \exists\, has.(Invoice \sqcap \exists\, has.Payment)$
	$Completed \equiv$
	$AddressDefined \sqcap ShipmentDefined$
	$Shipped \equiv Order.State \sqcap \exists\, hasShippingStatus.'shipped'$
	$Processed \equiv$
	$Invoiced \sqcap Paid \sqcap Shipped$
	    ...

Fig. 3. Fragment of the example ontology

tate a process variable, used to store an *ordernumber* with the annotation path*/order/has/orderNumber*, where *order* is a concept, *has* an object property and *orderNumber* a concept in the reference ontology. If the variable stores some complex XML-Type, then the XML-Type itself can be annotated using the annotation path method [13]. The annotations of variable declarations also implicitly maps read and write declarations of activities to the corresponding ontology concepts. This already allows to (heuristically) map pre- and post-conditions of activities to states in the ontology. For example, we can derive that the post condition of the task *pay* refers to the *paid* concept ($Order.State$ $\sqcap \exists\, has.(Invoice \sqcap \exists\, has.Payment)$). This is possible even without explicit pre- and post-conditions of *paid*, assuming that *pay* reads from a variable that is annotated with an *invoice* concept and it writes to a previously non-initialized variable that refers to a *payment* concept. Such inference is possible for most states which are defined over the existence of a general relation between data entities (as most states in the example are). However, more fine-grained state changes require explicit pre- and post-conditions of tasks. These may either be defined by directly annotating [11] the pre- and post-conditions of tasks with states of the ontology or they may be defined on the syntactical level, still allowing to infer the actual state in the ontology. For example the state *Shipped* is defined by the value *shipped* for the data-type property *hasShippingStatus* in the ontology. In this case read- or write accesses declarations of the activity *ship* are insufficient to infer the post condition state *shipped*. However, if the activity *ship* has the expression $a=$"*shipped*" as its post condition, where the variable a is annotated with the annotation path*/order/hasShippingStatus*, we can infer that the post condition is the *shipped* concept. Such pre- and post-conditions may be manually defined or heuristically derived from a log [22].

3.3   Taxonomy of Actions

The taxonomy of actions (ToA) describes abstract, well agreed actions that result in state changes of a specific business entity. Such actions are organized in a part of hierarchy. In this paper, we assume that such a taxonomy is provided by the user. However, it may be created with the help of existing clustering techniques such as [10] or by employing domain ontologies such as the MIT process handbook [1].

Each action in ToA is annotated with pre- and post-conditions. Both are DL expressions over states in the ontology. The semantics of the ToA is the following: If some action b is defined as a child-action of some action a, then b is considered as a potential part of a. Action b may be used to achieve the post condition of a but it is not required to use b to achieve a in every case. Therefore, the ToA can be considered as a general glossary of actions which can be reused for different processes of the domain. An example ToA is shown in Fig. 4. In the example the action $ProcessOrder$ has the precondition $Completed$ and the post condition $Processed$. In the ontology $Completed$ is defined as $AddressDefined$ $\sqcap ShipmentDefined$.

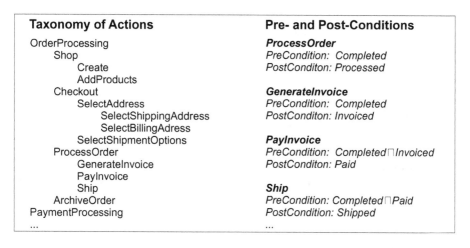

Fig. 4. An example taxonomy of actions

4   Ontology Guided Translations

After the inputs for an ontology assisted translation approach are defined in form of an annotated activity-centric process G, a reference ontology RO and a taxonomy of actions ToA, we can define what a desirable output of the translation is. The translation should use as much domain knowledge as possible. Therefore, obviously labels should be obtained from RO and ToA, for all matching stages, milestones and guards. Regarding the introduction of the state hierarchy as much hierarchic information from ToA should be added to the GSM process as possible. However, nesting should only be provided, when also groupings are performed. Therefore, nesting of a single stage into another stage is not considered as a desirable behavior.

4.1   Semantics-Based Translation Approach

We sketch how the proposed framework of an annotated process G, RO and ToA can guide the creation of a nested GSM process referring to agreed terms (guards, stages, milestones) of the domain. Our approach operates in three phases.

Phase 1: **Syntactic Translation.** First a syntactic translation is created that guarantees to preserve the behavior of the process in analogy to Sect. 2.3. We assume a 1:1 relation between activity-centric processes and artifacts. However, 1:n relations can be handled by first projecting the input process onto the different artifacts based on RO.

Phase 2: **Mapping Activities to States of RO and Actions of ToA:** Activities of the input process G are mapped with RO and ToA guided by the semantic annotations/data access definitions. This mapping has two purposes:

(1) Setting labels for guards (mapped states of preconditions in RO) and milestones (mapped states of post condition in RO) of atomic GSM stages. E.g. Figure 2(b), the label of the milestone of Pay can be set to $paid$ because the post condition of the activity Pay matches the $paid$ concept in RO (see Sect. 3.2 for details on this matching).

(2) Mapping of each activity $a \in G$ based on pre- and post-conditions with actions in ToA using RO. An activity a potentially matches an action t in ToA, if $t.pre \sqsubseteq a.pre \wedge a.post \sqsubseteq t.post$.

Phase 3: **Generation of Nested Stages:** After the activities of G and therefore, also the atomic stages of the target process are matched to RO and ToA, we create a nesting of atomic stages guided by ToA. A set of activities $A = \{s_1, s_2, ..., s_n\}$ can be nested into a parent stage p from ToA, if p is a parent of every $s \in A$ in ToA and if A matches the pre- and post-conditions of p and there exists no set of activities A', where $A \subset A'$ and A' matches p. Assuming that the ToA is generic and applicable for different processes, not all sub-actions of an action in ToA are necessarily required to realize the parent action p. Therefore, we propose the following matching criteria based on pre- and post-conditions:

Matching Post-Conditions: We require that the steps of A produce at least the post condition of p. Therefore, the combined post condition of A must be an equivalence or subclass of the post condition of p.

Matching Pre-Conditions: The combined post condition of all preceding steps of $first(A)$ in G must be an equivalence or subclass of $p.precondition$, where $first(A)$ defines the set of all steps $\subseteq A$ that are potentially executed first in G. Therefore, all preconditions for opening p are achieved in G before opening p.

Calculating Combined Post-Conditions: We propose to follow a similar approach for computing the combined post condition of multiple activities as [11, 22]. It depends on the control structures within the input process. We only discuss the case that A is a sequence in G here. The combined post condition of $< a, b >$ is *a.post* $\sqcap$ *b.post* unless *a.post* and *b.post* are disjoint. As [11, 22], we assume that contradicting effects of a are overwritten by b and consequently satisfiable solutions are generated by removing minimal sets of contradicting elements from *a.post*.

Example: In Fig. 2 the stages *GenerateInvoice*, *PayInvoice* and *Ship* have the same parent action *ProcessOrder* in *ToA*. *ProcessOrder.pre = Completed*, *ProcessOrder.post = Processed*. The combined post condition of the previous steps is *ProductSelectionCompleted* $\sqcap$ *Completed* which is obviously a subclass of *Completed*. The post-conditions of the child stages are *Invoiced, Paid, Shipped*, and *Invoiced* $\sqcap$ *Paid* $\sqcap$ *Shipped* $\equiv$ *Processed* (see def. of *Processed* in Fig. 3). Therefore, these stages can be nested into the stage *ProcessOrder*.

The nesting starts at the level of atomic stages/actions and subsequently also non atomic stages are nested based on the same principle. To ensure that as much of the structure of the *ToA* is reflected in the output process, the matching is done against the hierarchically nearest parents first and the procedure ends, when no nesting of two or more elements into a parent stage is possible.

Finally, the sketched translation approach allows to automatically generate the process shown in Fig. 2(c) based on the process shown in Fig. 2(a). The ontology and *ToA* should provide general descriptions of the domain of interest and they are not required to completely specify the input process. Therefore, the mapping of the activity-centric process to the ontology and *ToA* may only be partial. By starting with the syntactic translation we can still generate a complete and trace equivalent translation that takes advantage of the available knowledge.

5 Related Work

The translation of activity-centric processes to artifact centric models has been addressed in various works [8, 15, 17, 20, 21], where only [20, 21] and [8] generate GSM target processes. The approaches use different source models. While [8] takes UML activity diagrams as input (including data objects and state information), [21] is based on [20] and is used in combination with process mining and takes petri-nets as input. Our syntactic translation approach follows similar ideas as [20, 21]. However, since we use block-structured processes as input, a pattern based translation is directly possible for each block-type; references [20, 21] need to deal with more complex issues having petri-nets as input. The works in [15, 17] do not generate declarative GSM specifications but (synchronized) life cycle models. Reference [15] focuses on the identification of relevant business artifacts based on the concept of domination of explicitly defined data objects. Although, the generation of life-cycle models is sketched, naming of states and state hierarchies are not addressed in the work. The work in [17] discusses the roundtrip transformation of activity-centric and artifact centric processes (non GSM). For generating artifact-centric representations, the activity-centric process is augmented with attribute definitions for defining pre- and post- conditions, which are derived from the business rules of the (existing) artifact centric target process. All approaches above generate syntactic translations of activity-centric to artifact-centric processes. None of them utilizes domain knowledge and no nesting of stages in the GSM target process is supported.

Abstractions of activity-centric processes have been studied in works such as [10,16,23,24]. In particular knowledge-based approaches for the abstraction of activities such as [23] and [16] follow similar ideas, where a taxonomy of actions is used as input. However, these actions do not relate to business objects of the domain and they are defined by their label rather than by their pre- and post-conditions and an ontology.

Regarding efforts for the semantic enrichment of business processes, references [3,11,22] are closely related to our framework. In [11] business processes are annotated with semantic effects and cumulative effects are computed automatically, while [22] automatically derives post-conditions from log data. Ref. [3] assists the user in creating and augmenting process models by exploiting a domain ontology with a similar structure as our ontology framework but without a taxonomy of actions. Recently, an approach to represent GSM on the ontology level was presented in [5], leading to interesting future work such as the automatic translation to such models.

6   Conclusions

Syntactic translations cannot relate to relevant concepts and knowledge of the application domain and lead to poor results in comparison to translations provided by domain expert. In this paper we motivated and initiated the study towards a semantic translation approach to overcome this limitation. We developed a framework that allows to include the missing domain knowledge in the form of ontologies and semantic annotations. Based on this framework, we sketched a method for semantic translations that utilizes well agreed terms of the domain and that allows semantic nesting of stages in the target process. The resulting GSM models facilitate interoperation based on artifacts [2] syntactically and semantically. Current work includes the development of (semantic) quality metrics for GSM to further optimize and evaluate translation approaches.

References

1. Organizing Business Knowledge: The MIT Process Handbook, vol. 1. The MIT Press, 1st edn. (2003)
2. Boaz, D., Heath, T., Gupta, M., et al.: The ACSI hub: A data-centric environment for service interoperation. In: BPM 2014 Demos, p. 11, Septemper 2014
3. Born, M., Dörr, F., Weber, I.: User-friendly semantic annotation in business process modeling. In: Weske, M., Hacid, M.-S., Godart, C. (eds.) WISE Workshops 2007. LNCS, vol. 4832, pp. 260–271. Springer, Heidelberg (2007)

4. Damaggio, E., Hull, R., Vaculín, R.: On the equivalence of incremental and fixpoint semantics for business artifacts with guard-stage-milestone lifecycles. Inf. Syst. **38**(4), 561–584 (2013)
5. De Masellis, R., Lembo, D., Montali, M., Solomakhin, D.: Semantic enrichment of gsm-based artifact-centric models. J. Data Semant. **4**(1), 3–27 (2015)
6. Eder, J., Kerschbaumer, N., Köpke, J., et al.: View-based interorganizational workflows. In: Proceedings of CompSysTech 2011, Vienna, pp. 1–10 (2011)
7. Eshuis, R., Norta, A., Kopp, O., Pitkanen, E.: Service outsourcing with process views. IEEE T. Serv. Comput. **8**(1), 136–154 (2015)
8. Eshuis, R., Van Gorp, P.: Synthesizing data-centric models from business process models. Computing **98**, 1–29 (2015)
9. Gemino, A., Wand, Y.: A framework for empirical evaluation of conceptual modeling techniques. Requirements Eng. **9**(4), 248–260 (2004)
10. Günther, C.W., van der Aalst, W.M.P.: Fuzzy mining – adaptive process simplification based on multi-perspective metrics. In: Alonso, G., Dadam, P., Rosemann, M. (eds.) BPM 2007. LNCS, vol. 4714, pp. 328–343. Springer, Heidelberg (2007)
11. Hinge, K., Ghose, A., Koliadis, G.: A tool for semantic effect annotation of business process models. In: IEEE EDOC CONF 2009, pp. 55–63 (2009)
12. Hull, R., Damaggio, E., De Masellis, R., et al.: Business artifacts with guard-stage-milestone lifecycles: managing artifact interactions with conditions and events. In: Proceedings of DEBS 2011, pp. 51–62. ACM (2011)
13. Köpke, J., Eder, J.: Semantic annotation of XML-schema for document transformations. In: Meersman, R., Dillon, T., Herrero, P. (eds.) OTM 2010. LNCS, vol. 6428, pp. 219–228. Springer, Heidelberg (2010)
14. Köpke, J., Eder, J., Künstner, M.: Top-down design of collaborating processes. In: Proceedings of IIWAS 2014, pp. 336–345 (2014)
15. Kumaran, S., Liu, R., Wu, F.Y.: On the duality of information-centric and activity-centric models of business processes. In: Bellahsène, Z., Léonard, M. (eds.) CAiSE 2008. LNCS, vol. 5074, pp. 32–47. Springer, Heidelberg (2008)
16. Mafazi, S., Grossmann, G., Mayer, W., Schrefl, M., Stumptner, M.: Consistent abstraction of business processes based on constraints. JoDS **4**(1), 59–78 (2015)
17. Meyer, A., Weske, M.: Activity-centric and artifact-centric process model roundtrip. BPM Workshops, LNBIP **171**, 167–181 (2014)
18. Moody, D.L.: Theoretical and practical issues in evaluating the quality of conceptual models: current state and future directions. Data Knowl. Eng. **55**(3), 243–276 (2005)
19. W3C OWL Working Group. OWL 2 Web Ontology Language: Document Overview. W3C Recommendation, 27 October 2009
20. Popova, V., Dumas, M.: From petri nets to guard-stage-milestone models. BPM Workshops, LNBIP **132**, 340–351 (2013)
21. Popova, V., Fahland, D., Dumas, M.: Artifact lifecycle discovery. Int. J. Coop. Inf. Syst. **24**(01), 1550001 (2015)
22. Santiputri, M., Ghose, A.K., Dam, H.K., Wen, X.: Mining process task post-conditions. In: Johannesson, P., et al. (eds.) ER 2015. LNCS, vol. 9381, pp. 514–527. Springer, Heidelberg (2015). doi:10.1007/978-3-319-25264-3_38
23. Smirnov, S., Dijkman, R., Mendling, J., Weske, M.: Meronymy-based aggregation of activities in business process models. In: Parsons, J., Saeki, M., Shoval, P., Woo, C., Wand, Y. (eds.) ER 2010. LNCS, vol. 6412, pp. 1–14. Springer, Heidelberg (2010)
24. Smirnov, S., Reijers, H.A., Weske, M., et al.: Business process model abstraction: a definition, catalog, and survey. Distrib. Parallel DAT **30**(1), 63–99 (2012)

Applying Case Management Principles to Support Analytics Process Management

Fenno F. Heath III, Richard Hull$^{(\boxtimes)}$, and Daniel Oppenheim

IBM T.J. Watson Research Center, Yorktwon Heights, NY, USA
{theath,hull,music}@us.ibm.com

Abstract. Analytics Process Management (APM) is an emerging branch of Business Process Management that is focused on supporting Business Analysts and others as they apply analytics approaches, algorithms, and outputs in order to discover and/or repeatedly produce business-relevant insights and apply them into on-going business operations. While APM is now occurring in many businesses, it is typically managed in ad hoc ways using a variety of different tools and practices. This paper proposes to use principles from Case Management (or equivalently, Business Artifacts) to provide a foundational structure for APM. In particular, six key classes of Case Types are identified, that can model the vast majority of activities and data being manipulated in APM contexts. These Case Types can simplify support for managing provenance, auditability, repeatability, and explanation of analytics results. The paper also identifies two key adaptations of the classical Case Management paradigm that are needed to support APM. The paper validates the proposed Case Types and adaptations by examining two recent systems built at IBM Research that support Business Analysts in the use of analytics tools.

1 Introduction

The field of "Big Data Analytics" currently relies primarily on Data Scientists and Business Analysts. The Data Scientists develop and apply statistical and machine learning techniques to discover business insights and/or improve business operations performance, and the Business Analysts identify problem spaces where analytics can be beneficial, help interpret the raw data for the Data Scientists, and incorporate the analytics outputs into the broader business operations. Industries are increasingly more digitized and analytics tools are maturing and becoming more accessible to non-specialists. As a result there is an explosion in analytics-based applications, and the Business Analysts are taking a larger role in terms of applying statistical tools by themselves, without constant participation by Data Scientists. Analytics Process Management (APM) is now emerging as a new branch of Business Process Management (BPM) [4]. In APM, as with any form of BPM, a variety of business-relevant activities must be orchestrated amongst a variety of people and roles, sometimes with mission-critical outputs. Similar to Adaptive Case Management, the people performing and orchestrating APM tasks are knowledge-workers who require tremendous flexibility in choosing what tasks to perform and when. And unlike both traditional BPM and Case Management, APM involves tasks that manipulate and examine large data sets with rich implicit semantics, tasks that require time-consuming algorithms, tasks

© Springer International Publishing Switzerland 2016
M. Reichert and H.A. Reijers (Eds.): BPM Workshops 2015, LNBIP 256, pp. 376–388, 2016.
DOI: 10.1007/978-3-319-42887-1_31

that enable exploration of data and re-formulation of data processing steps, and tasks that involve integrating analytics outputs into other business processes.

The current paper describes how principles from Case Management and Business Artifact can be applied and extended for the design and development of analytics platforms that are intended for use by Business Analysts. The paper draws on knowledge of several analytics-based applications, and draws specifically on experiences with two analytics-based systems from IBM Research that aim at supporting Business Analysts. The two systems are LARIAT [1], which can be used to identify, prioritize, and nurture sales opportunities in a Business-to-Business (B2B) setting, and Alexandria [3], which supports Social Media Analytics as might be applied in Business-to-Consumer (B2C) applications. The main contribution of the paper is the identification of *six primary classes of Case Types* (or equivalently, Business Artifact types) that can be used as the conceptual and implementation skeleton for APM systems. In addition, the paper identifies *two key adaptations* to the Case Management paradigm that appear especially useful to support APM. The paper then provides an initial validation of these building blocks by describing how they arise in the LARIAT and Alexandria systems.

Organizationally, the Sect. 2 provides some background information and describes related work. Section 3 presents the six classes of Case Types and the two key adaptations. Section 4 overviews the LARIAT system and descripes how the Case Type classes arise there, and Sect. 5 does the same for Alexandria. Section 6 offers brief conclusions.

2   Background and Related Research

The connection between analytics and BPM has traditionally been found in the area of Business Intelligence [2], which is focused on applying analytics on process logs to improve operations within a business. However, with the increasing digitization of many industries, there is an explosion of analytics application areas, and a substantial increase in the need for data scientists to develop new algorithms, and for Business Analysts to apply those algorithms and guide their application to improve business efficiencies, increase business income, and more broadly, enable business transformations based on new analytics capabilities. For example, [7] in 2011 reported that in the United States the demand for deep analytical positions in the big data world could exceed the supply being produced by current trends by 140,000 to 190,000 positions. But, the report goes on to say that we project a need for 1.5 million additional managers and analysts in the United States who can ask the right questions and consume the results of the big data analytics effectively. Further, there is a need for ongoing innovation in technologies and techniques that will help individuals and organizations to integrate, analyze, visualize, and consume the growing torrent of big data.

Reference [4] provides an overall framework for Analytics Process Management (APM). As mentioned there, existing analytics processing suites, such as SPSS [14] and RapidMiner [11] (which is also available open source [12]) provide capabilities that are central to APM. In particular, they provide visual tools for specifying rich varieties of analytics flows, for storing and sharing them, and for version management. However, they do not emphasize a number of capabilities that are relevant to managing the overall lifecycle of these flows in the context of long-term production-level usage, maintenance and revision. Nor do they provide detailed support for iterative explorations a given application area, nor libraries of "derivation specifications" (e.g., text extractors or computed Decision Trees) that include meta-data on provenance, measurements, accuracy, and usages.

As discussed in [4], APM involves a broad range of capabilities, including: (i) support for business analysts in their search for useful insights; (ii) capabilities for incorporation of insights into surrounding business processes; (iii) measurement of value added by the insights; and (iv) support for increasing awareness about, and promotion of, the insights to different parts and executives of an overall business. These latter three aspects are expecially relevant for business insights of an on-going nature, e.g., weekly demand forecasts that would be incorporated into inventory management decisions. The current paper focuses on the first of these aspects, and provides an in-depth discussion about how Case Management principles can be applied and extended to support it.

The discussion in the current paper is significantly influenced by the Cross-Industry Standard Process for Data Mining (CRISP-DM) Reference Model [13]. That model is focused on the creation, refinement, and deployment of a data mining (i.e., analytics) project. It includes the following stages of activity:

1. Business Understanding of the problem to be explored;
2. Data Understanding, i.e., where is the data and how is it formatted
3. Data Preparation;
4. Modeling, i.e., creating a statistical model useful for understanding or prediction behaviors of the data;
5. Evaluation; and
6. Deployment.

There may be backtracking and cycles of these stages in a typical project. While there are a variety of tools to help with the CRISP-DM, including SPSS and RapidMiner mentioned above, and also MATLAB [8], and good old Python), the overall management of the CRISP-DM process is very often ad hoc. As a result, it is typically hard to find and/or reproduce the intermediate versions of the computation steps that ultimately lead to a deployed statistical model. Further, while the evaluation steps may be quite rigorous, again the archiving of the evaluation processes performed or data gathered is sporadic. Indeed, one of the goals of the current paper is to provide a systematic framework to support the coherent recording of processes performed and data obtained during the CRISP-DM method.

Another important input into the work of this paper is the book [10], which provides a very accessible top-down understanding of the primary styles of analytics that are most useful for improving business operations, along with best practices for applying them.

Up until now, the academic research community has focused largely on the challenges of statistical analysis, information extraction, and data "extract, transform, load" (ETL), and not on the challenge of managing analytics processes within the business context. Citation [2] provides an in-depth survey of techniques and challenges for applying analytics on the data produced by businesses. While numerous techniques for performing the analysis are provided, a framework to manage the analytics process is not present. Similarly, a recent survey on technical challenges in Big Data [5] describes highly scalable data storage techniques and distributed analytics processing algorithms, but the focus is on analytics outputs for human consumption, and a framework for APM is again not present. On a related note, [15] points out that "[r]esearch on how to manage analysis algorithms and how to provide an open platform for third parties to develop search and share algorithms is quite open."

3   Six Classes of Case Type

This section introduces the six primary *classes of Case Types* (or equivalently, classes of Business Artifact types) that can provide the conceptual and implementation skeleton for analytics processing support systems. It also identifies the two key ways that the Case Management paradigm needs to be extended to support APM.

Importantly, we are not saying that a Case Management system should be used to support an APM system in its entirety, nor are we saying that each of the Case Types identified below should be implemented literally as Case Types in a Case Management system. Rather, we are saying that it is useful to follow a discipline of modeling the overall APM system using Case Types, i.e., focusing on an information model and a lifecycle model for each identified Case Type. A secondary decision should be made, for each Case Type, concerning the best approach for actual implementation, including execution and persistent storage for each instance of the type.

A central benefit of adopting the Case-Management-centric view proposed here is that it will simplify the maintenance of provenance information. More specifically, as with Scientific Workflows, in a APM environment it is important to have available information about how an analytics insight was obtained. This will support explanation of results, and enable audits and verification of specified steps or the entire computation. The systematic management of information about the data and processing steps used, based on the Case Types given below, will enable a quite straightforward reconstruction of exactly where and how a given Insight came about.

The six classes of Case Types are as follows:

Project: Case types of this class are actively used by the Business Analyst. These are used to organize and record the steps taken and (intermediate and final) results created and/or derived during an investigation in search of useful business insights.

(Analytics) Derivation: There are typically several different case types of this class in a given analytics application. These are used to manage the production and application of statistical models (e.g., constructed using a regression analysis), perform text extractions (e.g., to determine the sentiment of a family of tweets, or the companies talking about plans for expansion into a new region), or perform other analytics-based processing. The details of many Derivation case types and instances may be largely hidden from the Business Analysts. But knowledge of the specific case instances involved is important for provenance, explanation, and repeatability.

(Derivation) Specification: This class of case types arises when a statistical model is created (e.g., a decision tree to guide matching of customer records with social media IDs, or a clustering specification based on a metric and centroids), and also when a rules-based approach is used to build an *extractor* (essentially a query) that guides the selection and annotation of documents that talk about specific topics of interest. There is typically a growing library of extractors, which includes multiple versions as they improve over time, and also information about evaluations, accuracy, and usages.

(Business) Insight: The class of case types is focused on the outputs from the investigations conducted by the Business Analysts. The outputs might be individual facts (e.g., company x, which performes knowledge-worker intensive investigation of insurance fraud, is planning a major expansion into the US southwest) or priortized lists (e.g., this week the top 50 sales leads for the IBM Case Manager product are as follows) or larger data sets with interactive visualizations (e.g., that support the interactive display of tweets and authors over the last 6 months that match a family of extractors, including various segmentations such as geographic location, gender, and recent life events of the authors). For a given Insight, it is important to track provenance information to support explanation, repeatability, and re-use. It is also useful to track usage, such as, which Insights were used to guide other business processes or support executive decisions, and if possible, what savings or income can be attributed to the insights.

Measurement: Measurement and refinement are central to the success of an analytics processing environment over time. Analytics environments are typically complex, involving the integration of multiple forms of analytics being applied to different parts of an overall situation, and being integrated together. Thus, there need to be measurements of various parts of the environment, and also measurements of the quality of the overall output. By using a Case Type for each kind of measurement that is conducted, it is possible to keep track in a coherent manner all of the following: the measurement goals, the data brought into specific measurements, the outcomes of the measurements, and finally the modifications made to the (sub)system to enable improvement of output quality.

(Data) Source: This class of case types is important to tracking the data sources in use, to support both *focal analytics* (which aim to provide insights about the focus of an investigation) and *support analytics* (which aim to provide insights, statistical models, text extractors, etc., that provide inputs into the focal analytics). Data sources may be *static*, *rolling* (e.g., updated in bulk once a day), or *streaming* (i.e., arriving continuously, typically for the purpose of continuous streamed processing and display).

The classical notion of "case" / "business artifact" needs some adaptation for use to support analytics processing applications. The two key adaptations needed for APM are as follows.

Templates and Executions: For most Derivation case types, a framework or "template" is set up (e.g., to create a statistical model such as a decision tree) and used multiple times to produce results (e.g., during weekly executions). However, the template itself might be revised periodically (e.g., re-compute the decision tree each 6 months). So, technically speaking, we actually use two case types for the one Analytics Derivation, one whose instances hold the different templates (e.g., what training data was used, what accuracy was achieved), and the second whose instances hold information about specific executions of one of those templates (information such as how was the template configured, when was the execution performed, who performed it, what where the outputs).

Support for Exploration: In traditional BPM and Case Management the end goal(s) of the business work are fairly clear, e.g., process this insurance claim, determine the root cause of this suspected fraudulent activity, or provide and manage over time appropriate social services for this person. While knowledge-workers may have substantial discretion over what tasks should be performed and when, the amount of iteration of individual activities is relatively low. In contrast, in Analytics Process Management there may be substantial iteration of families of activity while the Business Analyst is *exploring* the space of possibilities and refining various elements of a top-level Analytics Derivation. While the Project class of case types is intended to help manage these explorations, the amount of iteration in the specific case instances, and the need to revisit previously executed steps, adds the requirement for detailed access to case instance histories.

4   The Experience from LARIAT

This section briefly describes the LARIAT system for B2B sales opportunity identification, prioritization, and nurture [1], and then highlights how the six classes of Case Types can be used to manage the many activities and forms of data that are arise in systems such as LARIAT.

Figure 1 provides a high-level overview the LARIAT system in operation, focused on its use to generate prioritized listings of B2B sales leads. LARIAT is based on a model of continous ingestion of documents from the web, including newsfeeds, press releases, government filings, analyst blogs, etc. With each new document, "extractors" (i.e., queries) constructed using the rules-based text analytics language AQL [6] are used to determine whether any business patterns of interest are found, e.g., whether a company is expanding into a new region. Next, entity resolution is applied, to link the company as named in the document with other information about that company, including if available the Dunn & Bradstreet data about this company, and information from previously found documents about the company. This aggregated information may enable a match against a larger business pattern, which connects the observed company behavior or plan to an IBM product the company might need (e.g., an expanding company with knowledge-worker based processing might have need for the IBM Case

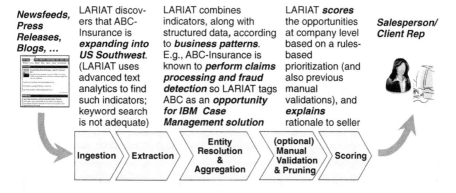

Fig. 1. Streamed flow of processing in LARIAT, from pulling a document from web, to extracting pre-specified "indicators", to Entity Resolution and Aggregation with structured data, to optional manual validation and pruning, to rules-based prioritization

Management product). Next there is an optional manual validation and pruning step, which is typically done in a periodic fashion against large collections of company records. Finally the company information is put through a configurable rules-based scoring engine. The company information with suggested products to sell can be sent to a Salesperson in the form of weekly prioritized listings, and also can be used to pro-actively alert a Salesperson if a certain priority level is achieved because of newly ingested documents.

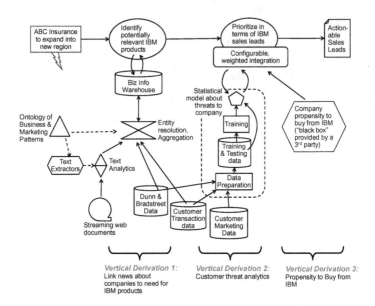

Fig. 2. Illustration of three "vertical" Analytics Derivations that are combined using a "horizontal" Analytics Derivation to construct prioritized lists of B2B sales leads, taking into account current news, competitive threat analytics, and propensity to buy analytics

Figure 2 shows a slight generalization of the LARIAT system, and highlights the general structure of analytics processes that are typical of APM systems aimed at Business Analysts. As shown in the picture, there are three "vertical" Analytics Derivations, focused on:

Interpreting web-accessible documents about companies: This Derivation involves the use of text analytics followed by Entity Resolution and Aggregation with available structured data. The text analytics itself is based on a family of AQL extractors which are built up, evaluated, refined, and extended over time. The Entity Resolution heuristics and algorithms are also evaluated, refined, and extended over time.

Determining competitive threats to a company: In this example the second vertical Derivation uses a traditional Supervised Learning approach to create a statistical model that can predict the level of competitive threat that a company is facing. In this case, training and testing data is prepared, which includes a notion of "ground truth" concerning threat levels. Once a statistical model is found (e.g., by classification or regression) it would be made available to the overall analytics process. It might be recomputed each 3 to 6 months to ensure a reasonable level of on-going accuracy.

Determining propensity of a company to buy from IBM: In the example here, the third vertical Derivation is focused on propensity to buy. It is assumed that this vertical is available from a third party, and so is somewhat a "black box" for IBM staff. However, the basic structure is probably similar to the second vertical Derivation.

The "horizontal" Derivation of Fig. 2 is illustrated by the 4 nodes across the top of the diagram. It is assumed that the Business Analyst is given flexibility in terms of which analytics capabilities are to be combined in order to find useful business insights. In this example, the choice was to first apply the pattern matching on web-accessible documents, and then combine that with the threat and propensity-to-buy analytics using a configurable, weighted integration. Even though the Business Analyst does not understand the details of the vertical Derivations, he is able to assemble them together to create one-off or re-usable analytics flows and reports.

We now turn to the six classes of Case Types and the two key adaptations. For each of these notions we describe how they arise on the LARIAT-inspired vision of Fig. 2.

Project: The horizontal Derivations can be modeled using Project Case Types or Derivation Case Types. For the discussion here we assume that a single Case Type with name "Project" is used. As mentioned above, Business Analysts might want to use different combinations of analytics capabilities; in such situations a different instances of Project would be used for the different combinations. (Actually, for Project we would have two case types, one for Project Templates and the other for Project Executions. Each Template instance might correspond to a different combination of the vertical Derivations, and each Execution instance would correspond to a single run of a given combination.)

(Analytics) Derivation: There would be a distinct Derivation Case Type for each of three kinds of vertical Derivation shown in Fig. 2, and additional derivation Dase Types if there were additional vertical Derivations available. As with the Project Case Type, these would actually have Template and Execution Case Types. Different Template instances would arise as the structure of the Derivation specification evolves, e.g., as new Text Extractors are incorporated into the text analytics Derivation, or if it is decided to use a different kind of training data for the threat analytics Derivation. Note that the text analytics Execution Case Type will have an execution per document processed whereas the threat analytics Derivation might have only a few executions a year. (On the other hand, there might be many Execution instances of the Project Case Type, and each of these might invoke the statistical model produced by a single execution of the threat analytics Derivation.)

(Derivation) Specification: In this example, Specification Case Types are used to hold things like the Text Extractors used in the text analytics Derivation, and the statistical models that are produced and used by the threat analytics Derivation. The reason we make them separate from the Template instances is that in many cases, especially with Text Extractors, there is a desire to re-use things either in whole or in part. Indeed, in systems such as LARIAT or

Alexandria it is helpful to build up a library of text extractors to enable sharing between efforts. Further, if a (family of) text extractor(s) will be used multiple times, then it is more affordable to increase the accuracy of the extractor(s). With the Specification Case Type, there should also be room to hold information about measurement of the accuracy of the specification, and perhaps also to record the situations where (different versions of) the specification have been used.

(Business) Insight: There may be several Case Types that correspond to the different kinds and grnularities of the analytics outputted by the system. At the most fine-grained level, there is a Case Type for managing the results of analyzing each individual document. For each document we should retain the provenance of how the extractions were done, the results from any manual evaluation, and also data on what it was merged into as a result of Entity Resolution. At the company level, the instance will include the continued extensions of the information about the company. Similarly, the outputs of the threat analytics and the propensity-to-buy analytics should be incorporated into the company instances. And at a more coarse-grained level, the weekly reports with prioritized listing of leads will serve as intances of another Insights Case Type.

Measurement: Each of the vertical Derivations involves areas where measurement is crucial, and there is also the need for measurement on the outputs of the Project level Case Types. In the text analytics Derivation two key areas are the quality of the text extractors (typically evaluated by manual examination of documents and what the extractors foiund) and the Entity Resolution heuristics (again typically evaluated by manual inspections). For the threat analytics Derivation, the idea of measuring the predicative accuracy by using testing data is well-known. For the propensity-to-buy Derivation, the internals cannot be measured, but the overall output information can be compared with the actual performance over a 6 month period following receipt of Propensity-to-Buy data. Finally, the overall output of prioritized sales leads can be tested over time, to compare the sales outcomes of companies that are near the top of the prioritized listing vs. the outcomes from companies that would be selected by previously used prioritization schemes.

(Data) Source: Numerous data sources are present in this example. This includes the streams of web-accessible documents, which may be adjusted over time. It includes the structured data about different customers, as shown in Fig. 2. Note that the structured data may be updated on a periodic or a more-or-less continuing basis. Also, a given data source might undergo cleaning or re-validation at different times. To support provenance, auditability, and explanation it is important to record this information about the data sources as they evolve.

Templates and Executions: The importance of using Case Types for both Templates of Derivations and Executions of Derivations was discussed above, in connection with Projects and Derivations.

Support for Exploration: As mentioned in the discussion of the Project Case Type above, the Business Analyst may explore different the use of different combinations of vertical Derivations in order to achieve Over time she may experiment with several different combinations, and also obtain measurements concerning their effectiveness. At some point she may want to create a Template (i.e., new combination of vertical Derivations) based on a handful of Template instances that she previously created. As such, the system should support the easy manipulation of existing Template instances, and splicing together of new

Template instances. It should also support what-if experiments based on historical data, e.g., what if I use a newly constructed Template instance – how would it have performed on data from the past 6 months?

5 The Experience from Alexandria

Alexandria [3] is an extensible platform that supports Business Analysts searching for insights in Social Media data. The current tooling is focused on Twitter, but other kinds of documents can be supported. As illustrated in Fig. 3, Alexandria includes tools to help Business Analysts (a) to rapidly scope the family of social media documents and authors that they will focus on, (b) to automatically invoke a variety of analytics routines on selected data, and (c) to visualize the sets of documents and authors found in a variety of ways. Although not discussed here in depth, the "rapid domain scoping" capability enables the user to rapidly build up *domain models*, that is, sets of text extractors that can focus in on social media documents and authors of interest for a particular investigation. Several tools are provided to help with the construction of the Topics, including tools to generate sets of similar terms (based on Word2Vec [9]) and sets of collocated terms.

Figure 4 shows the analytics processing steps current suppored. Here the squares represent processing steps, the circles represent repositories, and the hexagons visualization technologies. a systematic approach is needed to record and display what has been executed and what remains. Once the user is satisfied with a Domain Model, he can invoke the various analytics of Fig. 4 one-by-one or in a group. Due to space limitations we do not describe the particular kinds of analytics processes. But it is important to see that because of the sheer number, Recall that a domain model might include a number of extractors; it is planned that the analytics of Fig. 4 will be invokable at an incremental level, to enable incorporation of a single extractor at a time.

We briefly consider a subset of the six classes of Case Type and the two key adaptations.

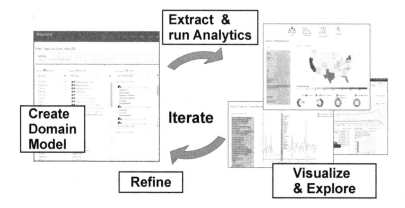

Fig. 3. Typical flow of Alexandria usage, including Rapid Domain Scoping, followed by automated data extraction and application of analytics, followed by exploration using interactive visualizations, and supporting iterations around the cycle multiple times

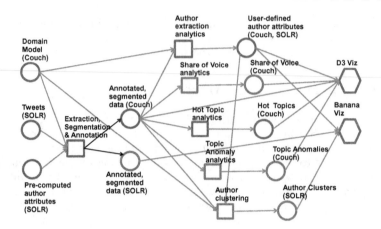

Fig. 4. DAG of current Alexandria analytics processing modules (squares), logical storage repositories (circles) and visualization capabilities (hexagons)

Project: In Alexandria there is one natural Project Case Type. Each instance of Project will correspond to the creation of one Domain Model followed by some number of extractions. Importantly, it is typical that once a first Domain Model has been built and the analytics derived and viewed, then there is a desire to make a clone of the Domain Model, make extensions and refinements, and then run the analytics again and visualize. Thus over time a family of related Project instances is created. Further, it is useful to create new instances by splicing together elements of previously constructed instances.

(Analytics) Derivations: As mentioned above, there are a handful of "vertical" Derivations used to support different forms of term generation and clustering, in support of the Rapid Domain Scoping. The use of different background corpora for these Derivations can yield results that are more or less useful when building Domain Models for contexts stemming from different industries (e.g., retail vs. travel vs. education). This suggests the need for maintenance of several different Derivation instances.

(Derivation) Specification: In Alexandria the Topics (clusters of similar terms) and Extractors (Boolean combinations of Topics used to identify a given set of documents of interest) are highly re-usable between Domain Models. As a result, a searchable library of Topics and Extractors is being created, organized around industry-specific ontologies. This is a clear example of how Specifications will have a long lifecycle, and be used in multiple, diverse Project instances.

Exploration: Alexandria has been designed to support iterative exploration by Business Analysts. Although not fully supported, the system will enable users to compare multiple Project instances (including both their Domain Models and the analytics outputs), in order to find the most accurate extractors, and also the most revealing combinations of extractors.

6 Conclusions

This paper identifies six important classes of Case Type that are central to supporting Analytics Process Management (APM). These Case Types can provide an overall structure for APM environments, can simplify the way that Business Analysts use the system, and can enable a very systematic and comprehensive approach for supporting provenance, auditability, repeatability, and explanation of analytics results and insights obtained.

The paper represents a preliminary and foundational step in the development of APM, and leaves many areas unexplored. The paper identified two areas where the Case Management paradigm needs to be extended, but only scratches the surface in terms of just how to extend Case Management. Also, while Case Management principles seem very useful to APM, it is still unclear which areas of APM should be supported by actual Case Management products vs. which areas should be supported using classical data management and programming techniques that are merely guided by a Case Management philosophy.

References

1. Callery, M., III, F.H., Hull, R., Linehan, M.H., Sukaviriya, P.N., Vaculín, R., Oppenheim, D.V.: Towards a plug-and-play B2B marketing tool based on time-sensitive information extraction. In: IEEE International Conference on Services Computing, SCC 2014, Anchorage, AK, USA, June 27-July 2, 2014, pp. 821–828 (2014)
2. Chaudhuri, S., Dayal, U., Narasayya, V.R.: An overview of business intelligence technology. Commun. ACM **54**(8), 88–98 (2011)
3. Heath III., F., Hull, R., Khabiri, E., Riemer, M., Sukaviriya, N., Vaculin, R.: Alexandria: extensible framework for rapid exploration of social media. In: Proceedings of the IEEE Big Data Congress (2015). to appear
4. Heath III, F.F., Hull, R.: Analytics process management: a new challenge for the BPM community. In: Fournier, F., Mendling, J. (eds.) Business Process Management Workshops. LNBIP, vol. 202, pp. 175–185. Springer, Heidelberg (2014)
5. Jagadish, H.V., Gehrke, J., Labrinidis, A., Papakonstantinou, Y., Patel, J.M., Ramakrishnan, R., Shahabi, C.: Big data and its technical challenges. Commun. ACM **57**(7), 86–94 (2014)
6. Krishnamurthy, R., Li, Y., Raghavan, S., Reiss, F., Vaithyanathan, S., Zhu, H.: Systemt: a system for declarative information extraction. SIGMOD Rec. **37**(4), 7–13 (2008)
7. Manyika, J., et al.: Big data: The next frontier for innovation, competition, and productivity, McKinsey Global Institute report, May 2011. http://www.mckinsey.com/insights/business_technology/big_data_the_next_frontier_for_innovation
8. MathWorks MATLAB official web site, Accessed June 5, 2015. http://www.mathworks.com/products/matlab/
9. Mikolov, T., Chen, K., Corrado, G., Dean, J.: Efficient estimation of word representations in vector space (2013). CoRR abs/1301.3781
10. Provost, F., Fawcett, T.: Data Science for Business: What You Need to Know About Data Mining and Data-Analytic Thinking. O'Reilly, Sebastopol, CA, USA (2013)
11. RapidMiner. RapidMiner Studio Manual. www.rapidminer.com/documentation/
12. RapidMiner Opensource Development Team. RapidMiner - Data Mining, ETL, OLAP, BI. http://sourceforge.net/projects/rapidminer/
13. Shearer, C.: The CRISP-DM model: The new blueprint for data mining. J. Data Warehouse. **5**(4), 13–22 (2000)

14. IBM SPSS official web site, accessed June 5, 2015. http://www-01.ibm.com/
    software/analytics/spss/
15. Truong, H.L., Dustdar, S.: A survey on cloud-based sustainability governance sys-
    tems. IJWIS **8**(3), 278–295 (2012)

A GSM-based Approach
for Monitoring Cross-Organization
Business Processes Using Smart Objects

Luciano Baresi, Giovanni Meroni[⊠], and Pierluigi Plebani

Dipartimento di Elettronica, Informazione e Bioingegneria, Politecnico di Milano,
Piazza Leonardo da Vinci, 32, 20133 Milano, Italy
{luciano.baresi,giovanni.meroni,pierluigi.plebani}@polimi.it

Abstract. The execution of cross-organization business processes often implies the exchange of physical goods without necessarily changing the ownership of such goods. Typical examples are logistic processes where goods are managed by shipping companies that are not the owner of the goods. To ensure that these goods are properly handled, while the service is executed, a monitoring system needs to be put in place.

The goal of this paper is to propose a novel approach for monitoring physical goods while executing cross-organization business processes. The approach envisions the usage of Smart Objects attached to the physical goods, or to their containers. To this aim, an extension of the Guard-Stage-Milestone framework is proposed to allow the Smart Objects to monitor the process execution and take into account the limitations of their power and computational resources.

Keywords: Guard-Stage-Milestone framework · Process-aware Smart Object · Process monitoring

1 Introduction

The exchange of goods in cross-organization business processes does not necessarily imply a change of ownership. Organizations could send goods to other organizations through a service provided by other organizations. A typical example is an order-to-delivery process: a seller company, which wants to send goods to the final customers, leaves their goods under the responsibility of a shipping company without transferring the property of these goods. At the same time, the owner of the goods (that could be either the seller or the receiver) wants to know how the goods are managed when they are under the responsibility of the shipping company. To this aim, Service Level Agreements (SLAs) are established among the parties. Although SLAs are commonly used in cross-organization business processes, the following limitations apply:

– Time consumption: the definition of SLAs is a long process where the quality of services, terms, conditions, and responsibilities need to be defined.

M. Reichert and H.A. Reijers (Eds.): BPM Workshops 2015, LNBIP 256, pp. 389–400, 2016.
DOI: 10.1007/978-3-319-42887-1_32

- Lack of flexibility: once defined, the SLA is valid for a specific service provider. Changing the provider usually requires the definition of a new SLA. Thus, this approach is not suitable for highly dynamic environments where parties change frequently.
- Information hiding: when resources are under the control of the service provider, the status of the goods are monitored by the provider according to its capabilities.
- Activity status hiding: the owners of the goods have limited visibility on what happens during the execution of the process by the service provider.

The goal of this paper is to investigate how the adoption of Smart Objects can improve the monitoring of business processes and solve the aforementioned limitations. The main idea is to equip the goods that move among the parties with Smart Objects to monitor their status independently of the service provider that is in charge of them. To this aim, we propose a framework based on an extension of the Guard-Stage-Milestone (GSM) notation [1] to model the external activities that need to be monitored. As the monitored processes can last for long periods, the proposed approach takes care of the limitations of Smart Objects (especially in terms of battery life) to maintain a sufficient quality of the monitoring activity.

The proposed solution enables the design and execution of more flexible multi-party business processes. The monitoring logic is executed on a Smart Object attached to monitored goods as defined by the party that owns the resource. When the resource is under the control of another party in the business process, only infrastructural capabilities can be required to that party, as the monitoring is exclusively under the control of the Smart Object. The resource owner can check the status of goods during the whole lifecycle by simply connecting — if a connection is available — to the Smart Object itself. Moreover, the Smart Object is able to detect anomalous situations that violate the agreement and to promptly report the problem to the owner.

The rest of the paper is structured as follows. Section 2 motivates the paper by introducing a running example about multi-modal transportation. Section 3 highlights the limitations of traditional process modeling notations and proposes a new one conceived specifically for Smart Objects. Section 4 proposes our solution to support the monitoring of multi-party business processes. Section 5 shows a possible application of our solution to the aforementioned example. Section 6 analyzes the state of the art, and Sect. 7 concludes the paper.

2   Processes and Smart Objects

Cross-organization business processes model the dependencies among processes performed by different organizations. An example is reported on the left-hand side of Fig. 1: it refers to a manufacturing company that, after completing the realization of a product, sends it to the customer. To achieve this objective, the company relies on a shipping company that enacts the related process once contacted by the manufacturing company.

Once the goods are under its responsibility, the shipping company has to monitor how the goods are managed and report to the client if critical situations occur. What to monitor, and how the communication among the parties occurs, is properly ruled by an SLA defined in advance. As mentioned in the previous section, usually the service provider (i.e., the shipping company) is in charge of monitoring the service execution. From a business process perspective, once the goods are under the responsibility of the organization that provides the service, the same organization has to put in place all the tools able to monitor the service provisioning to comply with the SLA. As a consequence, each service provider always gives the same structure and type of monitoring information to all of its consumers, regardless of their specific needs. For instance, the shipping company can inform the final customer that the goods are about to arrive only when the truck leaves the warehouse. For some of the customers of the shipping company, this information is too coarse-grained and a notification to the final customer is desirable when the truck is in the same city as the final customer.

Another issue concerns the visibility of what happens during service provisioning. Referring to our example, if the shipping process fails, the manufacturing company could not necessarily be aware of when exactly the problem occurred. Moreover, it might happen that the shipping company notifies problems with some delay, and this could affect the recovery mechanisms that the manufacturer company could put in place.

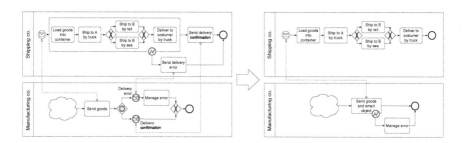

Fig. 1. As-is (left) and To-be (right) processes that adopt Smart Objects.

The approach proposed in this paper envisions the use of Smart Objects with the goal of making the relationship among the parties in cross-organization business processes simpler and more flexible.

A Smart Object is defined as *"an autonomous, physical digital object augmented with sensing/actuating, processing, storing, and networking capabilities"* [2]. Because of their diffusion, even in the domain of business processes, solutions based on Smart Objects are becoming more and more common.

In our approach, we assume that goods that are moving from different organizations are equipped with Smart Objects composed of: a computational unit able to run software, a sensing system, and a communication interface.

The use of Smart Objects permits to move from the situation reported on the left-hand side of Fig. 1 to what is represented on the right-hand side. The manufacturing company sends the goods along with the Smart Objects that have been properly configured to track the location of the goods with the required granularity. By doing so, if the activities that compose the process adopted by the shipping company are publicly described, the Smart Object will also detect the phase of such a process that is currently being executed. This way, and assuming that the Smart Object can communicate via a broadband network, the manufacturer company can monitor where the goods are, in which status they are, and in which (business) activity they are involved. The Smart Object can also identify violations in the process model and notify them to the user as soon as they happen (provided that a connection is available). By doing so, possible critical situations can be detected and managed directly by the owner of the goods, without asking the other organization to set up a specific monitoring infrastructure and to notify anomalies during the execution. Note that we may have the problem of having the Smart Object back once the shipping concludes. However, we decide not to address this problem in this paper, as it is similar to traditional ones like the management of pallets or shipping containers in the transportation domain.

The investigation on the adoption of Smart Objects for monitoring goods has been conducted in this paper by also considering the limitations of this technology. First of all energy consumption: most of these devices are battery-powered with limited autonomy and the battery is often difficult to recharge or replace. Fortunately, the amount of energy required by the computational part has dropped significantly in the last years, thus allowing Smart Objects to last longer and run more sophisticated software. For wireless data transmission, on the other hand, the reduction of energy requirements has not been as pronounced. For this reason, the proposed approach aims to increase the battery life by reducing the communication to the bare minimum. Secondly, the limitation of available computational resources on Smart Objects also influences the proposed solution. Monitoring the correct execution of the business process directly on board is not possible due to the requirements that usually characterize a business process management system. However, this paper envisions Smart Objects whose computational power is equivalent to the one of current Single Board Computing devices, such as Intel Galileo [3] or BeagleBoard [4].

Pairing a Smart Object with the goods to be monitored could have a significant impact on costs. A cost-benefit model is discussed in [5]. The authors propose a model to estimate the impact of introducing Smart Objects to monitor the supply chain with respect to adoption costs and gain in productivity. Even though we have not addressed cost-related problems yet in our work, we plan to do so in the future and we will use such a model as a starting point.

3   Extended Guard-Stage-Milestone

According to our approach, the main task of the Smart Object is to check if the monitored goods are managed according to the process agreed among the organizations. Although control-flow modeling languages are suitable for defining such an agreement (see Fig. 1), the same representation cannot be used to instruct the Smart Object about the process to be monitored for several reasons.

First of all, if the Smart Object were fed with a control-flow description and an activity were not executed in the right order, the Smart Object would raise an exception that would stop monitoring the rest of the process. In contrast, monitoring must continue, as the Smart Object could not always be connected and it could report anomalies in the process execution only at the end of the execution itself.

Secondly, control-flow languages assume the presence of an orchestrator that explicitly starts the execution of the activities. In our case, the Smart Object has to autonomously realize when activities start and terminate as a direct and continuous connection with the orchestrator could not exist.

Finally, control-flow languages lack constructs for explicitly defining conditions that detect the incorrect execution of an activity without necessarily implying a termination of such an activity. For example, during the shipment of a fragile item, the package could be dropped, condition that could cause a damage that would invalidate the whole process. Knowing exactly which activities did not execute correctly is critical for identifying responsibilities, and may also be useful to drive process changes.

Declarative languages, on the other hand, are well suited to our scenario. In fact, rather than relying on an explicit control flow definition, they mainly focus on defining which tasks should be performed under certain conditions, thus offering more flexibility with respect to control-flow languages. For this reason, the Guard-Stage-Milestone (GSM) [1] declarative notation was adopted and extended to properly instrument Smart Objects. We chose GSM because, with respect to other declarative languages, such as Declare [6], it provides constructs, namely *Guards* and *Milestones*, that explicitly define when an activity, which is named *Stage*, should start or end. Boolean formulas, named sentries, are associated with *Guards* and *Milestones*. They define conditions on captured events and, when they become true, determine the activation of the associated construct.

With respect to the standard definition of GSM, we introduce the following changes, as shown in Fig. 2:

Fig. 2. Standard GSM (left) versus Extended GSM (right). The Information Model element, which is part of the standard GSM specification, is not depicted as our extension does not make changes to that part.

– Guards are divided into *Process Flow Guards* and *Data Flow Guards*: Process Flow Guards define sentries only related to the activation of Data Flow Guards or Milestones, whereas Data Flow Guards define sentries only on external events. Defining conditions on both Milestones and data artifacts into the same sentry is not allowed. Moreover, Process Flow Guards do not determine the activation of the associated Stage. Instead, they specify which Stages are expected to start or end before the associated one.

For example, we know that an activity is executed whenever the Smart Object reaches a precise location. The Smart Object could be aware of the beginning of such an activity due to the associated Data Flow Guard. In fact, we can define a sentry that is triggered whenever the Smart Object's GPS coordinates change and are equal to the ones of such a location.

– For each Stage, it is possible to define *Fault Loggers*: such annotations allow us to define a sentry which, if true, marks the associated Stage as faulty. However, despite Milestones, the associated Stage is not closed once Fault Loggers are triggered. Analogously, Fault Loggers differentiate from invalidating sentries since they do not cause completed Stages to be started again, and are ignored once the associated Stage terminates.

For example, during the execution of an activity, we want to make sure that the Smart Object's temperature will not exceed 50°C. By defining a Fault Logger for such an activity with a Sentry that is triggered when the temperature changes and is above 50°C, we ensure the successful execution of the activity as long as the Fault Logger is not triggered.

These extensions allow us to use GSM to easily model process specifications suited for driving process-aware Smart Objects. Process Flow Guards model the process flow. Based on data gathered by the sensors installed on Smart Objects, Data Flow Guards define activity start conditions, Milestones activity end conditions, and Fault Loggers model activity constraints.

4   Process-Aware Smart Objects

After introducing our extended GSM for Smart Objects, we can now present the software architecture deployed on Smart Objects to allow them to monitor processes. Figure 3 shows its main software components and their relationships.

– *Trace Generator* is responsible for analyzing sensor data and external messages received by the Smart Object. It mainly consists of a Complex Event Processing (CEP) engine, which compares these data streams with the sentries defined in the process model to detect process events. The output of this module is a process trace, which records chronological information concerning the Data Flow Guards, Milestones, or Fault Loggers that are triggered by a specific event.

– *Violation Detector* compares the process trace with the process model to detect control flow violations and activity faults. When a connection is available, it informs the Smart Object's owner about violations by sending noti-

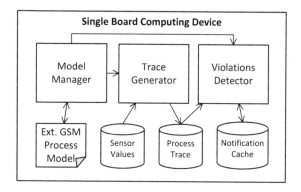

Fig. 3. Smart Object software architecture.

fications. A notification cache is also adopted to temporarily store unsent notifications.
- *Model Manager* is responsible for keeping the process model up to date. It accomplishes such a task by both receiving explicit updates by the process owners and requesting the process definitions to the involved parties that have not provided such definitions yet. It is also responsible for notifying changes on the process model to the other modules.

During process execution, changes in activity states are determined by Data Flow Guards and Milestones. Process Flow Guards and Fault Loggers, on the other hand, are used to determine violations on process flow and activity data, respectively.

Process-aware Smart Objects operate according to a GSM-based process model, while the agreement among organizations is usually defined by using a control-flow based model. The following steps must be performed to facilitate the definition of the GSM-based process model that is then deployed on the Smart Objects (see Fig. 4)[1]. The starting points are the control-flow based process and the to-be-monitored goods.

- *Identification of activities.* Starting from a standard BPMN process definition, the user identifies the activities that wants to monitor through Smart Objects. By doing so, a view on the main process is created and used as a reference for the subsequent phases. Such a view contains only the portion of the process definition related to the to-be-monitored activities.
- *Generation of extended GSM definition.* Starting from the process view of the previous phase, the system semi-automatically generates the process definition by using the extended GSM notation. This is obtained by automatically transforming activities in Stages, activity flows in Sentries for the Process

---

[1] For the sake of clarity, we assume that BPMN is adopted as control-flow process modeling language. Other control-flow languages can be adopted without affecting the validity of the approach.

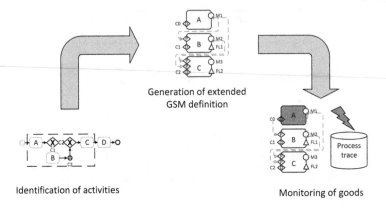

Fig. 4. Integration framework for GSM-based Smart Objects.

Flow Guards, and gateway conditions in Sentries for the Data Flow Guards. An empty Milestone is also inserted for each activity to allow for the definition of Sentries in Process Flow Guards. The translation rules for the message flow and process events are currently under investigation. Starting from the automatically generated model, the user manually enriches it by specifying Sentries for empty Milestones and optionally adding additional Data Flow Guards and Fault Loggers. The resulting GSM schema will be deployed on the Smart Objects.

– *Monitoring of goods.* In this phase the process definition is loaded onto the Smart Objects and executed. During execution, the Smart Objects keep track of the actual process trace: the actual Stage start and termination order is recorded, together with the list of Stages whose Fault Logger conditions are triggered, and those whose Data Flow Guards are triggered before Process Flow Guards become valid. With this information, process compliance can be assessed at runtime and violations can be promptly reported.

5   Validation

Back to the cross-organization process model introduced in Sect. 2, the manufacturing company wants to monitor the activities performed by the shipping company while the goods are moved to the final destination. As shown in Fig. 5, the shipping process to be monitored is composed of the following steps: (i) the goods are stored into a shipping container attached to a truck; (ii) the truck ships the goods to site A, more precisely to the railway station if the shipping takes place during holiday, or to the seaport if it takes place during a working day; (iii) the container is detached from the truck and either loaded onto a train, which carries it up to site B, or loaded onto a ship headed to site C; (iv) the container is unloaded from the train or the ship, and attached to a truck that finally ships the goods to the customer. This process has been simplified on purpose with respect to a real

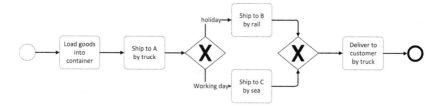

Fig. 5. Shipping process in BPMN notation.

world scenario to easily understand its transformation into extended GSM. Future work will take into consideration more complex process models.

From this process, the GSM-based process definition reported in Fig. 6 is obtained. Every Stage has a Data Flow Guard that defines the conditions on the data that determine the start of each activity. In this case, the Smart Object can identify the beginning of the goods loading phase by detecting that there is movement and their GPS coordinates identify the loading area of the producer's site as current location.

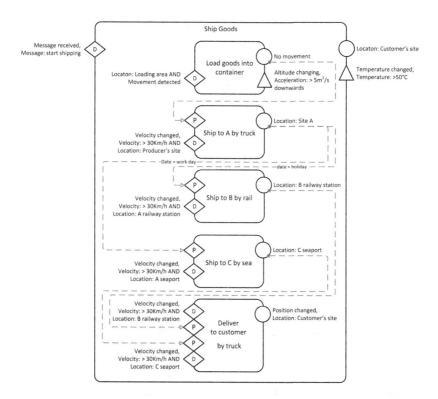

Fig. 6. Shipping process in extended GSM notation.

Also, every Stage has a Milestone that defines the condition on data that determines the end of each phase. In this case, the Smart Object can identify the end of the rail shipping phase by detecting that its position has changed and its GPS coordinates identify site B as current location.

The definition of Process Flow Guards allows us to define the expected activity execution order, which permits to assess process compliance with respect to the process flow directly onto the Smart Objects. In this case, Stage *Deliver to customer by truck* has two Process Flow Guards connected to the Milestones of Stages *Ship to B by rail* and *Ship to C by sea*, respectively. This way, we expect either the rail shipping to site B or the sea shipping to site C to precede the final delivery of the goods to the customer. Should the final delivery take place before either sea shipping or rail shipping, the Smart Object would immediately report a violation, but at the same time it would continue monitoring the process.

We also define Fault Loggers, conditions that if true mark the associated activity as invalid. We define a Fault Logger on the maximum vertical acceleration of the Smart Object on Stage *Load goods into container*. This permits to detect if the goods have been dropped and thus it identifies that the associated phase was not carried out correctly.

The obtained extended GSM schema is deployed on a Smart Object equipped with sensors monitoring the conditions that affect the shipping process (such as temperature, position and altitude). Indeed, these are the sensors required to realize if activities are skipped (e.g., the goods are shipped neither by rail nor by sea), executed in the wrong order, or not correctly performed (e.g., the goods were dropped during the loading operation).

The Smart Object can generate process traces during the execution of the shipping process. This way, both the producer and the shipping company can be notified whenever fault conditions are triggered or violations in the activity execution order are detected. Moreover, the shipping company can collect process traces from each Smart Object, and change its original BPMN process definition to reflect how the process is actually executed.

6   Related Work

Some research efforts have been spent on integrating Smart Objects with business processes. Meyer et al. [7] propose to extend the BPMN 2.0 notation to model smart devices as process components. This approach keeps the process knowledge on the information system, and no process fragments are introduced on smart devices.

Thoma et al. [8] propose to model the interaction with Smart Objects in BPMN 2.0 as activity invocations for simple objects, or as message exchanges with pools representing the whole Smart Object for more complex ones, thus leaving space for distributing parts of the process definitions on Smart Objects. The limitation of this work is the lack of details concerning how to deal with data uncertainty and how to define data requirements.

Tranquillini et al. [9] propose a framework that employs BPMN for driving the configuration of a Wireless Sensor Network (WSN). Since BPMN is used only at design time for defining the business process, and then it is converted into binary code executable by the WSN, introducing changes in the process definition at runtime is difficult. Also, simultaneously supporting multiple processes on the WSN is not feasible with this framework.

Schief et al. [10] propose a centralized framework that extends the process design and execution phases of BPM and that takes into consideration events generated by Smart Objects. Furthermore, such a framework provides data quality mechanisms for evaluating events and sensor data. However, this framework does not allow for the explicit definition of requirements for sensor data.

In particular, concerning goods tracking and monitoring among different parties, the solutions currently adopted by companies are limited to identifying when goods enter or exit a specific location by using passive RFID tags attached to them. For example, Brizzi et al. [11] propose a middleware that supports the exchange of RFID tag information across federated companies. However, in such solutions no process definition exists, therefore the task of identifying process violations is left to the information systems that belong to the involved parties.

Kunz et al. [12], on the other hand, propose a framework for monitoring goods that takes into consideration the involved business process. Such a framework, uses a CEP engine to collect and process sensor data coming from RFID tags attached to goods and to transform them into events. These events are then sent to a workflow engine that detects violations in the expected process flow and reacts by running compensation activities. However, such a solution requires the user to define process flow violation conditions at design time by specifying them with the BPMN Escalation event. Therefore, unpredicted violations cannot be handled during execution.

7   Conclusions and Future Work

This paper presents an approach for monitoring physical goods when they are exchanged among different parties according to a defined cross-organization business process. As control-flow models are not suitable to run on Smart Objects due to limited resources, and are not suitable for defining the behavior of the monitoring system due to their lack of flexibility, an extension of the Guard-Stage-Milestone framework is proposed. With this extension, a GSM-based definition of the portion of process to be monitored is deployed on Smart Objects. These objects, traveling along with the monitored physical goods, realize if and when anomalies in conducting the process occur.

Future work will mainly concentrate on a better definition of how to automatically derive the GSM process model that has to be deployed on the Smart Object starting from the control-flow process model agreed by the organizations. Moreover, an implementation of the modules that compose the process-aware Smart Object is planned to validate the approach on a real testbed.

Acknowledgments. This work has been partially funded by the Italian Project ITS Italy 2020 under the Technological National Clusters program.

References

1. Hull, R., et al.: Introducing the guard-stage-milestone approach for specifying business entity lifecycles. In: Bravetti, M., Bultan, T. (eds.) WS-FM 2010. LNCS, vol. 6551, pp. 1–24. Springer, Heidelberg (2011)
2. Fortino, G., Trunfio, P.: Internet of Things Based on Smart Objects. Technology, Middleware and Applications. Springer, Heidelberg (2014)
3. Intel Corporation. http://www.intel.com/content/www/us/en/do-it-yourself/galileo-maker-quark-board.html
4. BeagleBoard.org. http://beagleboard.org
5. Decker, C., et al.: Cost-benefit model for smart items in the supply chain. In: Floerkemeier, C., Langheinrich, M., Fleisch, E., Mattern, F., Sarma, S.E. (eds.) IOT 2008. LNCS, vol. 4952, pp. 155–172. Springer, Heidelberg (2008)
6. Pesic, M., Schonenberg, H., Van der Aalst, W.M.: Declare: Full support for loosely-structured processes. In: Proceedings of the 11th International Enterprise Distributed Object Computing Conference, p. 287. IEEE (2007)
7. Meyer, S., Ruppen, A., Magerkurth, C.: Internet of things-aware process modeling: integrating iot devices as business process resources. In: Salinesi, C., Norrie, M.C., Pastor, Ó. (eds.) CAiSE 2013. LNCS, vol. 7908, pp. 84–98. Springer, Heidelberg (2013)
8. Thoma, M., Meyer, S., Sperner, K., Meissner, S., Braun, T.: On iot-services: Survey, classification and enterprise integration. In: IEEE International Conference on Green Computing and Communications, pp. 257–260 (2012)
9. Tranquillini, S., et al.: Process-based design and integration of wireless sensor network applications. In: Barros, A., Gal, A., Kindler, E. (eds.) BPM 2012. LNCS, vol. 7481, pp. 134–149. Springer, Heidelberg (2012)
10. Schief, M., Kuhn, C., Rsch, P., Stoitsev, T.: Enabling business process integration of iot-events to the benefit of sustainable logistics. Technical report, Darmstadt Technical University (2011)
11. Brizzi, P., Lotito, A., Ferrera, E., Conzon, D., Tomasi, R., Spirito, M.: Enhancing traceability and industrial process automation through the virtus middleware. In: Proceedings of Middleware 2011 Industry Track Workshop, ACM (2011)
12. Kunz, S., Fabian, B., Ziekow, H., Bade, D.: From smart objects to smarter workflows-an architectural approach. In: Proceedings of the 15th Workshops of Enterprise Distributed Object Computing, pp. 194–203. IEEE (2011)

DeMiMoP Workshop

Preface to the Third International Workshop on Decision Mining and Modeling for Business Processes (DeMiMoP'15)

Jan Vanthienen[1], Bart Baesens[1], Guoqing Chen[2], and Qiang Wei[2]

[1] Department of Decision Sciences and Information Management,
KU Leuven, Naamsestraat 69 3000 Leuven, Belgium
{jan.vanthienen,bart.baesens}@kuleuven.be
[2] School of Economics and Management (SEM), Tsinghua University,
30 双清路, Haidian, Beijing, China
{chengq,weiq}@sem.tsinghua.edu.cn

Introduction

Most processes and business process models incorporate decisions of some kind. Decisions are typically based upon a number of business (decision) rules that describe the premises and possible outcomes of a specific situation. Since these decisions guide the activities and workflows of all process stakeholders (participants, owners), they should be regarded as first-class citizens in Business Process Management. Sometimes, the entire decision can be included as a decision activity or as a service (a decision service). Typical decisions are: creditworthiness of the customer in a financial process, claim acceptance in an insurance process, eligibility decision in social security, etc. The process then handles a number of steps, shows the appropriate decision points and represents the path to follow for each of the alternatives.

Business decisions are important, but are often hidden in process flows, process activities or in the head of employees (tacit knowledge), so that they need to be discovered using state-of-art intelligent techniques. Decisions can be straightforward, based on a number of simple rules, or can be the result of complex analytics (decision mining). Moreover, in a large number of cases, a particular business process does not just contain decisions, but the entire process is about making a decision. The major purpose of a loan process e.g., or an insurance claim process, etc., is to prepare and make a final decision. The process shows different steps, models the communication between parties, records the decision and returns the result.

It is not considered good practice to model the detailed decision paths in the business process model, because decisions and processes may change at different speeds and by different stakeholders. Separating rules and decisions from the process simplifies the process model (separation of concerns). Decision modeling allows to model the decision that is taken inside a process activity, to simplify nested decision paths, and to model decisions across activities (and even processes).

The aim of the workshop is to examine the relationship between decisions and processes, including models not only to model the process, but also to model the decisions, to enhance decision mining based on process data, and to find a good integration between decision modeling and process modeling.

Organizers

Jan Vanthienen	KU Leuven, Belgium
Bart Baesens	KU Leuven, Belgium
Guoqing Chen	Tsinghua University, China
Qiang Wei	Tsinghua University, China

Program Committee

Guoqing Chen	Tsinghua University, China
Qiang Wei	Tsinghua University, China
Jae-Yoon Jung	Kyung Hee University, South Korea
Dimitris Karagiannis	Universität Wien, Austria
Krzysztof Kluza	AGH University of Science and Technology, Krakow, Poland
Xunhua Guo	Tsinghua University, China
Hajo A. Reijers	Eindhoven University of Technology, The Netherlands
Robert Golan	DBmind technologies, USA
Markus Helfert	Dublin City University, Ireland
Pericles Loucopoulos	Loughborough University, England
Josep Carmona	Universitat Politècnica de Catalunya, Spain
Jochen De Weerdt	KU Leuven, Belgium
Seppe vanden Broucke	KU Leuven, Belgium
Johannes De Smedt	KU Leuven, Belgium

Integrated Process and Decision Modeling for Data-Driven Processes

Han van der Aa[1]($^{\boxtimes}$), Henrik Leopold[1], Kimon Batoulis[2],
Mathias Weske[2], and Hajo A. Reijers[1,3]

[1] Department of Computer Sciences,
VU University Amsterdam, Amsterdam, The Netherlands
`j.h.vander.aa@vu.nl`
[2] Hasso Plattner Institute, University of Potsdam, Potsdam, Germany
[3] Department of Mathematics and Computer Science,
Eindhoven University of Technology, Eindhoven, The Netherlands

Abstract. While business process models have been proven to represent useful artifacts for organizations, they are not suitable to represent the detailed decision logic underlying processes. Ignoring this limitation often results in complex, *spaghetti-like* process models for workflows driven by data-based decisions. To avoid this, decision logic should be isolated from process logic, following a *separation of concerns* paradigm. To support this practice, we present an approach that automatically derives process models for which this paradigm applies. It takes as input structural data-flow relations underlying a workflow and produces a process model that emphasizes the most important decisions in a process, while detailed decision logic is outsourced to dedicated decision models.

Keywords: Workflows · Process modeling · Decision modeling · Product based workflow design · Activity composition · BPMN · DMN

1 Introduction

A large amount of business processes, especially those found in the service domain, pursue the creation of an informational product, such as a mortgage offer, a decision on an insurance claim, or the assignment of social security benefits. The structure of these processes, which we here refer to as *workflows*, largely depends on the data-flow underlying them [2]. This data-flow consists of numerous elementary data processing steps that ultimately result in the computation of a desired end result. In most workflows, the exact steps necessary to determine this end result, i.e. the execution path of a process instance, depends on several decisions incorporated in the process. Typical decisions relate to the creditworthiness of a customer in a financial process, or eligibility decisions in social security assignments. For data-driven processes, these decisions are generally based on the evaluation of a set of data values. For instance, an applicant might only be entitled to social benefits if he or she is of a certain nationality and has a yearly income below a given amount.

© Springer International Publishing Switzerland 2016
M. Reichert and H.A. Reijers (Eds.): BPM Workshops 2015, LNBIP 256, pp. 405–417, 2016.
DOI: 10.1007/978-3-319-42887-1_33

Business process models have been proven to represent important artifacts to visualize an organization's workflows and other processes [4]. However, modeling languages such as the Business Process Model and Notation (BPMN) are not meant to represent the complex decision logic that is so important for these data-driven processes. Because the inclusion of detailed decision logic in process models often results in complex, *spaghetti-like* models, this is not considered good practice. Rather, rules and decisions should be separated from process logic, following a *separation of concerns* paradigm [3]. The recently standardized Decision Model and Notation (DMN) [9] provides a useful means to apply this paradigm in the context of business processes. Due to its declarative nature, DMN can be used to supplement BPMN models with a means to efficiently capture and structure decision logic [6].

Manually obtaining a so-called *BPMN/DMN* model, however, can be a difficult and time-consuming endeavor for processes with a complex underlying data-flow. In order to construct a correct and useful process model, one must be well-acquainted with the many elementary processing steps and their interrelations [2]. To overcome this problem, we present an approach that automatically achieves this. Our approach obtains a BPMN/DMN model for data-driven processes given the structural data-flow relations underlying a workflow. The resultant models emphasize the important decisions that determine the flow of a process, while at the same time outsourcing the decision details to the more appropriate DMN representation.

The remainder of this paper is structured as follows. Section 2 provides an example to motivate the goal of our work. Section 3 then presents our approach for automatically obtaining a BPMN/DMN model based on structural data-flow relations. We evaluate the complexity of the models generated using our approach in Sect. 4. Afterwards, we discuss related work in Sect. 5 and conclude the paper in Sect. 6.

2   Motivating Example

In order to illustrate the importance of our approach for separating process and decision logic, we first present a motivating example. To make our ideas operational, we capture the structural data-flow relations underlying a workflow in a Product Data Model (PDM). The concept of a PDM stems from *product based workflow design*, a methodology for the radical redesign of workflows [11]. A PDM describes the data elements, data processing steps, and their interrelations that together comprise the data-flow of a process. Figure 1 presents an example PDM. The example depicts the data-flow related to the process that deals with requests for governmental student grants in the Netherlands.

2.1   Product Data Model

A PDM contains a set of *data elements*, which are depicted as labeled circles. The top element $i42$, referred to as the *root* element, corresponds to the total

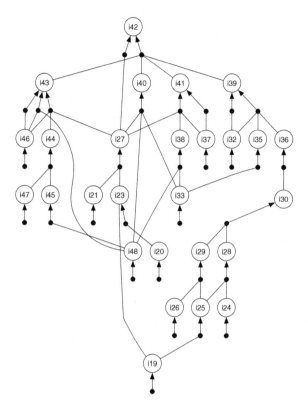

Fig. 1. Product Data Model of the student grants example

Table 1. Description of data elements present in the student grants example

ID	Description	ID	Description
i19	Date of request	i36	Parental contribution
i20	Birth date of applicant	i37	Requested amt. of loan
i21	Nationality of applicant	i38	Max. amt. of loan
i23	Age of applicant	i39	Amt. of supplementary grant assigned
i24	Social Security Number of father	i40	Amt. of basic grant assigned
i25	Reference year for tax authority	i41	Amt. of loan assigned
i26	Social Security Number of mother	i42	Total amt. of student grant assigned
i27	Applicant has the right to receive grant	i43	Amt. of tuition credit assigned
i28	Income of father of applicant	i44	Max. amt. of credit for tuition fees
i29	Income of mother of applicant	i45	Tuition fees of educational institution
i30	Income of parents of applicant	i46	Has requested credit for tuition fees
i32	Has requested a supplementary grant	i47	Tuition fees declared by law
i33	Living situation of applicant	i48	Kind of education of applicant
i35	Max. amt. of supplementary grant		

student grant assigned to an applicant. The other data elements in the PDM are relevant to the computation of $i42$, the ultimate goal of this workflow. A description of all data elements for the example is provided in Table 1. The values for data elements in a specific case are computed by executing *operations* on data elements. These operations are depicted as black dots in the figure. Each operation requires a set of input elements, and produces a single output data element. For example, Fig. 1 contains an operation that computes a value for $i27$ based on the values for $i21$ and $i23$.

The value for data element $i27$ forms the basis for the most important decision in the process: it determines if an applicant is eligible to receive a grant.[1] For ineligible applicants, i.e. when the value for $i27$ is negative, the application is directly rejected by executing the left-hand operation that has $i42$ as its output element. In this case the value for $i42$ is € 0, because an applicant will not receive any student grant. By contrast, if an applicant is eligible to receive a grant, the right-hand operation to compute $i42$ must be executed. This operation requires four data elements as input. Namely, the total amount of grant is computed by summing the values for four different sub-grants which eligible applicants may receive: (i) a basic grant ($i40$), (ii) a supplementary grant ($i39$), (iii) a student loan ($i41$), and (iv) any credit for tuition fees ($i43$). Three of these sub-grants also represent data-driven decisions in the workflow, because their computation follows a data-based choice in the PDM. This is recognizable because these data elements, i.e. $i39$, $i41$, and $i43$, can each be computed by multiple *alternative operations*. While any eligible applicant will receive the same basic grant, the amounts of the other sub-grants depend on the desire of applicants to receive them, as well as specific assignment criteria.

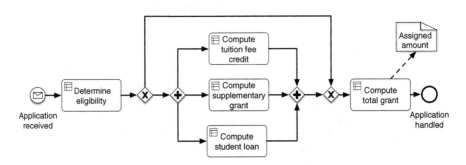

Fig. 2. BPMN/DMN model for the student grants example

2.2 BPMN/DMN Model

Due to the high number of atomic data-processing steps involved in a workflow and the complexity of their inter-dependencies, it is not feasible to directly transform

---

[1] An applicant must have the Dutch nationality (stored in $i21$) and may not be older than thirty ($i23$) in order to be eligible to receive a grant.

a PDM into a process model. For instance, a translation of the example PDM into a process model – using an automated approach from [16] – yields a process model with 87 activities and over 50 gateways. Process models of such size are difficult to understand and therefore of limited use [8].

To overcome this problem, we first group together elementary data processing steps into larger activities; an act we will refer to as *activity composition*. Process models based on composed activities are considerably smaller and therefore easier to understand. This is reflected by the process model depicted in Fig. 2, which is based on activities specifically designed to emphasize the main flow and decisions in the workflow. The representation of the detailed decision logic underlying this process is outsourced to DMN decision models which we associate with the BPMN model's activities.

Each of the activities in Fig. 2 conforms to a fragment of the data-flow structure underlying a workflow, i.e. a set of elementary data processing steps and data elements. The left-hand side of Fig. 3, for example, shows the PDM fragment that conforms to the activity *"Compute tuition fee credit"*. To efficiently represent the decision logic underlying an activity, a PDM fragment can be transformed into a DMN decision model.

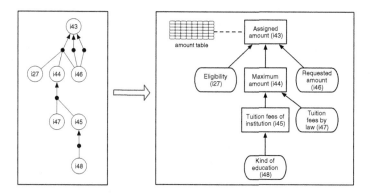

Fig. 3. Transformation of activity *"Compute tuition fee credit"* to decision model

DMN graphically depicts the inter-relations of the data values relevant to a particular decision in a *decision model*. We use two types of nodes for the graphical notation: (i) *decisions*, depicted by rectangles, and (ii) *input data*, represented by ellipses. The nodes are inter-connected by solid, directed *information requirement edges*. The right-hand side of Fig. 3 provides an example of a decision model related to the computation of the assigned amount of *tuition fee credit*. The model illustrates that the amount assigned to an applicant depends on the applicant's eligibility, the requested amount, and a maximum amount based on the tuition fees of the institution. To describe how these data values are actually used when determining the outcome of the decision, DMN uses decision tables.

A *decision table* describes which outcome results from a given set of values for the relevant data elements. Each row in a decision table represents a *decision rule*, having one or more conditions on the data values and an outcome, i.e. the conclusion. This conclusion determines the output value of the decision and, thus, also of the workflow activity. For instance, Table 2 shows that tuition fee credit is only assigned to applicants that are eligible and who have specifically requested credit for tuition fees.

Table 2. Decision logic to determine tuition fee credit (i43)

Eligibility	Requested amt.	Max. amt.	Assigned amt.
false	—	—	€ 0
—	€ 0	—	€ 0
true	€ x	€ y	min(x, y)

The example presented in this section demonstrates the impact that the separation of concerns paradigm can have on process model design. We transformed the complex data-flow structure underlying a workflow into an understandable BPMN/DMN model. The BPMN model depicts the main process flow, while detailed decision logic is outsourced to separate DMN models.

Manually obtaining a BPMN/DMN model from a complex data-flow structure is, however, a tedious and time-consuming endeavor. Most notably because the proper composition of activities requires an in-depth understanding of the elementary data processing steps and their inter-relations. To overcome this problem, Sect. 3 describes an approach that automatically achieves this.

3   Approach

In this section, we introduce our approach for automatically transforming a PDM into a BPMN model supplemented with DMN decision logic. Because the approach can take any PDM as input, it can be applied to any workflow for which the structure of its underlying data-flow is known. The approach sets out to design process models that emphasize the most important decisions in a workflow, while they outsource decision details to DMN. The remainder of this section describes the three consecutive steps that comprise our approach. In Sect. 3.1, we first consider the automated grouping of operations into activities. Second, Sect. 3.2 shows how DMN decision models can be automatically generated for the individual activities. Finally, Sect. 3.3 covers the conversion of a composed activity design into a BPMN/DMN model.

3.1   Activity Composition

To obtain process models that emphasize the main decisions taken in a workflow, we compose activities that play an important role from a decision-centric viewpoint. We achieve this by designing each activity such that it produces a data value that is important to the workflow's main process and decision structure.

We identify three classes of data elements that are important to this structure: (i) the root data element, (ii) decision outcomes, and (iii) reference values. The *root data element* of a PDM should straightforwardly be produced by an activity, because it represents the workflow's desired end result. *Decision outcomes*, which we define as those data elements that are created by multiple alternative operations, are also unmistakably important to the decision structure captured in a PDM. For each such data element, we therefore create an activity that determines the outcome of that decision. Lastly, we also define *reference values* as those data elements that play a role in multiple different decisions. We create separate activities that produce these reference values in order to avoid repeatedly expressing the same decision logic. Consider, for instance, data element $i27$, an applicant's eligibility to receive a student grant. This data element is required as input for the computation of all four decision outcomes in the student grant example ($i39$, $i41$, $i42$, and $i43$). By creating an activity that computes a value for this element, we do not have to express how an applicant's eligibility is determined for all these individual decisions. Furthermore, due to the involvement of $i27$ in multiple decisions, it is therefore arguably important to the workflow's decision structure. Consequently, we deem it worthwhile to emphasize the existence of this data element in the process model.

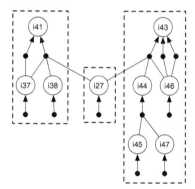

Fig. 4. Operations associated with $i27$, $i41$, and $i43$

Assuming D as the set of all data elements in a PDM, we define S_D as the set of data elements that fall into any of the above-mentioned classes of structurally important data elements. For the student grant example, this thus results in $S_D = \{i27, i39, i41, i42, i43\}$.

Next, for each data element d in S_D, we group together a set of operations into an activity that computes d. Similar to earlier activity composition approaches [1,2], we achieve this by recognizing that each operation is directly involved in the computation of exactly one element in S_D. For instance, in the fragment of the running example shown in Fig. 4, we observe that one operation relates to the computation of $i27$, four operations to the computation of $i41$, and seven to $i43$. We define the *associated data element* o_d of operation o as the sole data element $d \in S_D$ for which there exists a path p in the PDM from o to d, such that any data element contained in p is not a part of S_D.

Once the associated data elements have been identified, we compose activities by grouping together those operations with the same o_d. For data element $i43$, this for example results in the activity depicted in Fig. 3. Section 3.2 describes the subsequent transformation of composed activities into DMN models.

3.2   From Activity to Decision Model

To capture the decision logic underlying activities, we consider both the transformation of an activity into a graphical *decision model*, as well as the transformation of the actual decision logic into a *decision table*.

As illustrated in Fig. 3, the structure of a decision model is closely related to the internal structure of an activity. Both consist of a set of connected nodes leading up to a single root element. We transform a PDM fragment into a decision model as follows. We first create a single decision node that conforms to the root data element of the activity, i.e. the decision outcome. The activity's input data elements are converted into input data nodes. For each operation, we then draw an information requirement edge from all of its input elements to an (intermediary) decision node. We here avoid creating duplicate edges which occur when different alternative operations use the same input element. Finally, we create and associate *decision tables* to the decision node.

The decision tables linked to decision nodes describe the actual logic applied to determine the outcome of the decision. To transform the decision logic of an activity into a decision table, we translate the *execution conditions* attached to each operation into a single decision rule. For instance, Table 1 depicts the result of this transformation for the final decision node of the "*Compute tuition fee credit*" activity, based on the execution conditions specified in [14]. The table shows that an amount is only assigned to applicants that are eligible and who have specifically requested credit for tuition fees.

After this transformation, the decision models designed for individual activities can be incorporated into BPMN/DMN models in the form of *business rule tasks*. Section 3.3 considers the derivation of a process model based on the set of activities comprising the activity design.

3.3   Process Model Derivation

In the final step, we derive a process model based on the composed activity design. Similarly to existing algorithms that transform a PDM into a process model, there is no *one size fits all* solution for the derivation of a BPMN model based on an activity design. The exact derivation process depends on a modeler's preferences with respect to a number of design choices, among others, concurrency and execution efficiency [15]. For these reasons, we therefore refrain from introducing a specific process model derivation algorithm. Rather, we describe the main considerations when turning the activity design of the running example into the process model depicted in Fig. 2.

The main drivers of process model derivation are the data dependencies that exist between the individual activities. For example, the activity *"Determine eligibility"* which produces data element $i27$, must always occur prior to the activity *"Compute tuition fee credit"* in a process model, because the latter activity requires $i27$ as input. Data dependencies, similarly, play a crucial role when introducing alternative execution paths. The alternative paths in Fig. 2 are, for instance, necessary because the activity *"Compute total grant"* can be executed based on two sets of input elements, depending on an applicant's eligibility. Finally, when activities do not have any data inter-dependencies, no restrictions on their execution order are required. In these cases, parallel constructs can be used to allow them to be executed in an arbitrary order, such as seen for the three concurrent activities in the running example.

We here note that our automated approach obtains the exact process model depicted in the motivating example. This example illustrates that our approach can find a balance between the details captured in the process model and those captured in its accompanying decision models. To demonstrate the applicability of our approach beyond this example, Sect. 4 evaluates the approach in other workflow settings.

4   Evaluation

In this section, we evaluate the ability of our approach to provide a balance between details captured in the BPMN model and details captured in its accompanying DMN models. Achieving this balance is crucial, because an approach that fails to omit sufficient details at the process level, results in process models that are too large to be useful. By contrast, if the approach outsources too much detail to its decision models, process models will be too abstract to be informative. Furthermore, the DMN models can simultaneously become so large that also their usefulness is limited.

To asses the balance between details captured in a BPMN model and those captured in its DMN models, we compare the size of both types of models. This comparison is based on the premise that size is an important determinant for the amount of details a model contains. We therefore argue that our approach succeeds when both model types are of a comparable size.

4.1   Setting

We evaluate our approach for five cases obtained from literature, four of which represent real-world processes. The five cases, introduced in detail in [2], differ greatly in size and complexity. Table 1 provides additional information on the size of the PDMs.

For each case, we compare the size of the generated BPMN model with the average size of its DMN models. For BPMN models, we define size as the number of activities and gateways; for DMN models, we consider their number of data processing steps (Table 3).

Table 3. Overview of the PDMs included in the evaluation

ID	Description	Operations	Data elements	Decisions
1	Student grant (NL)	32	27	4
2	Bicycle manufacturing	36	29	3
3	Student grant (US)	48	45	3
4	Unemployment benefits	51	42	2
5	Fireworks license	81	46	4

4.2   Results

Figure 5 depicts the sizes of a case's original PDM, the generated BPMN model, and the decision models it contains. For each of the five cases it is clear that the size of all generated models is greatly reduced in comparison to the original PDM. Furthermore, it can be observed that the size of the BPMN models is generally well-comparable to the size of its DMN models.

The largest differences are found for cases 2 and 3. For the former case, the average size of the decision models is smaller than the one of the process model, because the generated process model includes a number of relatively small activities. That is because the process contains several different routing paths. The existence of these paths requires more process logic than decision logic when

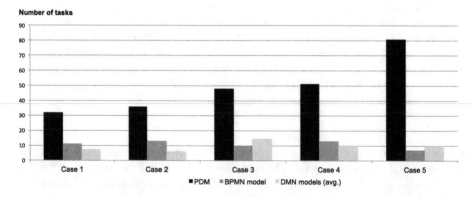

Fig. 5. Comparison of model sizes between a PDM, the generated BPMN model, and its largest DMN model

modeling the workflow. By contrast, the decision models in case 3 are on average larger than the process model for this case. We argue that also this imbalance is acceptable, because the difference results from the existence of a small number of complex decisions that take up to 25 different input elements. For the other cases, the size differences are even smaller and the results thus imply that the size of the models is overall well-balanced.

While these are just preliminary results, the evaluation indicates that our proposed approach distributes the complexity of a PDM over a BPMN model and its DMN models in a relatively even manner. As a result, the generated BPMN/DMN models provide a balance between process logic captured in the process model and detailed decision logic contained in its individual activities.

5   Related Work

The work presented in this paper mainly relates to process model abstraction and the separation of decision from process logic.

The goal of process model abstraction approaches is to group process model elements in an adequate way to increase understandability or to gain a different perspective. Existing approaches mainly focus either on structural properties, e.g. [10,13], or on semantic aspects such as activity labels [12].

The benefits of separating decision logic from process logic have been recognized by academic as well as rather practitioner-oriented contributions [5,7,17]. However, only recently researchers investigated how decision logic can be extracted from existing business process models. In [3], Batoulis et al. identify a number of control-flow patterns that indicate the presence of decision logic. Based on this analysis, they introduce a semi-automated approach to extract DMN models from BPMN process models. While our approach pursues a similar goal, we use PDMs as input. Hence, we have to deal with different challenges as, for example, activity composition.

6   Conclusions

This paper presented an approach to automatically derive a BPMN/DMN model based on the data-structure underlying a workflow. Our approach creates process models that emphasize the most important decisions in a workflow, while outsourcing the representation of the detailed decision logic to dedicated decision models. Due to its automated nature, the approach overcomes the time and effort involved in the manual transformation from complex data-flow structure to BPMN/DMN model. A preliminary evaluation furthermore revealed that the approach successfully provides a balance between the details captured in a BPMN model, and those captured in its DMN decision models.

In future work, we plan to extend the evaluation in order to further assess the effectiveness of our approach. For instance, we consider comparing the automatically generated process models to ones that have been manually created by modeling experts. The approach itself can furthermore be extended by incorporating other perspectives beyond the structural data-flow relations, e.g. by taking different organizational actors into account that are involved in the workflow execution.

References

1. van der Aa, H., Reijers, H.A., Vanderfeesten, I.: Composing workflow activities on the basis of data-flow structures. In: Daniel, F., Wang, J., Weber, B. (eds.) BPM 2013. LNCS, vol. 8094, pp. 275–282. Springer, Heidelberg (2013)
2. Van der Aa, H., Reijers, H.A., Vanderfeesten, I.: Designing like a pro: The automated composition of workflow activities. Computers in industry (2015 (in press))
3. Batoulis, K., Meyer, A., Bazhenova, E., Decker, G., Weske, M.: Extracting decision logic from process models. In: Zdravkovic, J., Kirikova, M., Johannesson, P. (eds.) CAiSE 2015. LNCS, vol. 9097, pp. 349–366. Springer, Heidelberg (2015)
4. Davies, I., Green, P., Rosemann, M., Indulska, M., Gallo, S.: How do practitioners use conceptual modeling in practice? Data Knowl. Eng. **58**(3), 358–380 (2006)
5. Debevoise, T., Taylor, J., Geneva, R., Sinur, J.: The Microguide to Process and Decision Modeling in Bpmn/Dmn: Building More Effective Processes by Integrating Process Modeling with Decision Modeling (2014)
6. Goedertier, S., Vanthienen, J., Caron, F.: Declarative business process modelling: principles and modelling languages. Enterp. Inf. Syst. **9**(2), 161–185 (2015)
7. Kluza, K., Kaczor, K., Nalepa, G.J.: Integration of business processes with visual decision modeling. presentation of the HaDEs toolchain. In: Fournier, F., Mendling, J. (eds.) BPM 2014 Workshops. LNBIP, vol. 202, pp. 504–515. Springer, Heidelberg (2015)
8. Mendling, J., Reijers, H.A., Cardoso, J.: What makes process models understandable? In: Alonso, G., Dadam, P., Rosemann, M. (eds.) BPM 2007. LNCS, vol. 4714, pp. 48–63. Springer, Heidelberg (2007)
9. OMG: Decision Model and Notation (DMN). FTF Beta 1 (2015)
10. Polyvyanyy, A., Smirnov, S., Weske, M.: The triconnected abstraction of process models. In: Dayal, U., Eder, J., Koehler, J., Reijers, H.A. (eds.) BPM 2009. LNCS, vol. 5701, pp. 229–244. Springer, Heidelberg (2009)
11. Reijers, H.A., Limam, S.: Product-based workflow design. J. Manage. Inf. Syst. **20**(1), 229–262 (2003)
12. Smirnov, S., Reijers, H.A., Weske, M.: A semantic approach for business process model abstraction. In: Mouratidis, H., Rolland, C. (eds.) CAiSE 2011. LNCS, vol. 6741, pp. 497–511. Springer, Heidelberg (2011)
13. Smirnov, S., Weidlich, M., Mendling, J.: Business process model abstraction based on behavioral profiles. In: Service-Oriented Computing, pp. 1–16. Springer, Heidelberg (2010)
14. Vanderfeesten, I.: Product-Based Design and Support of Workflow Processes. Ph.D. thesis, Eindhoven University of Technology (2009)
15. Vanderfeesten, I., Reijers, H.A., Aalst, W.V.D.: Case handling systems as product based workflow design support. In: Enterprise Information Systems, pp. 187–198 (2009)

16. Vanderfeesten, I., Reijers, H.A., van der Aalst, W.M.P., Vogelaar, J.: Automatic support for product based workflow design: generation of process models from a product data model. In: Meersman, R., Dillon, T., Herrero, P. (eds.) OTM 2010. LNCS, vol. 6428, pp. 665–674. Springer, Heidelberg (2010)
17. Von Halle, B., Goldberg, L.: The Decision Model: A Business Logic Framework Linking Business and Technology. CRC Press, New York (2009)

Enabling Dynamic Decision Making in Business Processes with DMN

Kimon Batoulis[(✉)], Anne Baumgraß, Nico Herzberg, and Mathias Weske

Hasso Plattner Institute at the University of Potsdam,
Prof.-Dr.-Helmert-Street 2–3, 14482 Potsdam, Germany
{Kimon.Batoulis,Anne.Baumgrass,Nico.Herzberg,Mathias.Weske}@hpi.de

Abstract. While executing business processes, regularly decisions need to be made such as which activities to execute next or what kind of resource to assign to a task. Such a decision-making process is often case-dependent and carried out under uncertainty, yet requiring compliance with organization's service level agreements. In this paper, we address these challenges by presenting an approach for dynamic decision-making. It is able to automatically propose case-dependent decisions during process execution. Finally, we evaluate it with a use case that highlights the improvements of process executions based on our dynamic decision-making approach.

Keywords: BPM · DMN · Decision modeling · Dynamic decision support

1 Introduction

Methodological and technological advances for managing businesses have been developed and evolved to help enterprises to improve their processes and minimize errors, i.e., in the discipline of Business Process Management (BPM) [24]. In this environment, the compounding complexity of business processes challenges current decision logic in order to achieve business goals efficiently and effectively [7]. For example, repeatable, numerous day-to-day decisions such as which activities to execute next or what kind of resource to assign are more often constrained from the outside, e.g., by legislative frameworks and norms [11,23]. At the same time, Service Level Agreements (SLAs) are negotiated among enterprises and customers to measure, ensure and enforce service fulfilment and quality in this dynamic context [22].

Processes can be automatized, controlled, improved and measured based on process models [24], which are usually designed using the industry standard: the Business Process Model and Notation (BPMN) [16]. However, misusing BPMN

The research leading to these results has received funding from the European Union's Seventh Framework Programme (FP7/2007-2013) under grant agreement 318275 (GET Service).

© Springer International Publishing Switzerland 2016
M. Reichert and H.A. Reijers (Eds.): BPM Workshops 2015, LNBIP 256, pp. 418–431, 2016.
DOI: 10.1007/978-3-319-42887-1_34

for representing complex decision logic results in models that are hard to comprehend, to implement, and to maintain, and violate the *separation of concerns* paradigm [2]. Therefore, we describe decisions based on the recently published Decision Model and Notation (DMN) standard [17], developed to support the separation of concerns paradigm in BPM.

In this paper, we present a novel approach that adapts the decision logic for each case dynamically based on previous and current running process executions in Business Process Management System (BPMS), i.e., supporting dynamic decision making during run-time. Thereby, we enable case-dependent predictions about process executions and empower the optimization of resource assignments and process utilities. It focuses on *(i)* automatically revealing decisions from historic process executions, *(ii)* automatically determining the dependencies between the decisions to enable optimal decision-making given SLAs, *(iii)* automatically translating the decisions to DMN decision models that can be used by a BPMS at run-time, and *(iv)* automatically adapting the decision logic in a DMN decision model dynamically dependent on current process executions. In particular, we build on previous work [1], which is extended in this paper by presenting the specific course of actions and an implementation enabling the proposed dynamic decision support as well its integration with DMN and its evaluation based on a use case. This use case is introduced as running example in Sect. 2. Next, Sect. 3 provides the formal foundation for our framework described in Sect. 4. Finally, we evaluate the framework in Sect. 5 that shows its suitability to improve decision-making.

2 Running Example

We will explain dynamic decision making along the example of a telephone company repairing phones, which is illustrated as a BPMN diagram in Fig. 1. The

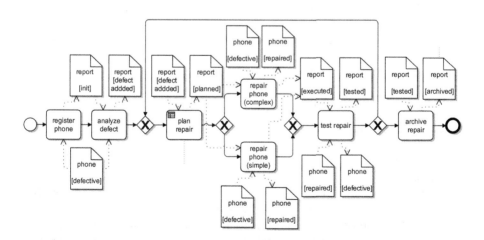

Fig. 1. Telephone repair process

defective phone and a repair report drive the process and are the basis for the decisions to make in this process. While the phone is either defective or repaired the report holds various kinds of information which are updated during process execution as shown in Fig. 2.

After we receive a defective phone, the phone is analyzed to determine the type of the defect. Note that the decisions taken during planning, i.e., which repair type (*repairType*) to choose and which technician is responsible to repair the phone (*solver*), are documented along the process in the report (see Fig. 2). If the repair was successful (*defectFixed*), it can be archived, otherwise a technician has to conduct another repair. Note, in this scenario, the number of attempts to repair a phone is limited to three so that it can be declared as *unrepairable* if it could not be fixed within this limit. Finally, when the process execution is finished (the phone is repaired or declared as unrepairable), its duration (*duration*) will be recorded in the repair report as well as the overall result (*finalDefectFixed*).

We assume two SLAs are requested by the customer and used by the telephone company to increase customer satisfaction:

SLA1. *The repair time is less than the mean repair time in at least* 70 % *of the cases.*
SLA2. 95 % *of the repair cases are successfully completed.*

Fig. 2. Repair report data model

In a naive approach, we could pursue this intent by first recognizing that, on average, the activity *repair phone (complex)* takes longer than *repair phone (simple)*. Hence, preferring the latter might be beneficial. However, the simple repair does not necessarily solve the defect so that the test afterwards reveals the repair procedure needs to be executed once again, thereby increasing the time to repair. Analyzing previous executions further, not only the type of the defect is crucial for deciding whether a simple or a complex repair should be executed, but also other context information like the experience, availability or success rate of the technicians. Thus, we need an automated approach that is able to propose a decision dynamically based on all data available from historic and current process executions.

3   Foundations

BPM aligns business and IT to support a company with realizing its business goals. In this context, several decision have to be made, ideally based on historic executions, various data and conditions. To cope with the increasing complexity, decisions are captured in decision models. Recently, DMN was introduced as standard by the Object Management Group (OMG) to support decision modeling, specification, implementation and monitoring [17]. DMN is used for describing decisions with respect to the prerequisites for a particular decision as well as the logic behind it on two levels. The decision requirements level consists of two basic notational elements defining which *input data*, and which sub-*decisions* need to be present to make a certain (top-level) *decision*. To express that a decision depends on input data or sub-decisions, these elements are connected by *information requirement edges*. The decision logic level could be represented by a decision table, a decision tree, an algorithm or simply by business rules.

Once BPMS are used to execute process models they log their execution in event logs [8]. In order to capture the dependencies between the events logged in the event log we decided to use Bayesian Networks (BNs) [21]. BNs can be used to query the probability of any variable (query variable) given the values of any other variables (evidence variables). Regarding the phone repair process given in Sect. 2, we may ask for the probability of a successful repair (query) given a simple repair is executed by solver $S1$ (evidence). In particular, BNs are directed acyclic graphs consisting of nodes representing random variables and edges indicating dependencies between those variables, see Definition 1.

Definition 1 (Bayesian Network). *A BN is a tuple $(\mathcal{N}, \mathcal{E})$ with*

- *a set of nodes $\mathcal{N} = \{n_1, \ldots, n_n\}$ called chance node, each representing a unique random variables x_i, and*
- *a set of directed edges $\mathcal{E} \subset \mathcal{N} \times \mathcal{N}$ where $(n_i, n_j) \in \mathcal{E}$ is an edge from parent node n_i to child node n_j representing a conditional dependency between nodes' variables x_i and x_j.*

Each node n_i is associated with a conditional probability distribution for its variable $P(x_i | Parents(x_i))$ that quantifies the effect of the parents on node' random variable, whereas the parents of n_i are the nodes that have an outgoing edge to n_i. If a node does not have any parents, it is associated with the random variable's prior distribution.

However, not all conditions of the process instance are available once the process started, but are rather set by the decisions made during the process execution. An Influence Diagram (ID) is an augmented BN that can be utilized to pursue this objective by including two additional types of nodes: decision nodes and utility nodes [15], formally defined in Definition 2. The values of the chance nodes are set by chance, as in BNs; the values of the decision nodes are set by the decision maker; the values of the utility nodes depend on the values of their parents (which can be chance, decision and utility nodes) and are functions thereof. In particular, IDs help in determining the decisions to be made in a process that have the largest *expected* utility [19]. The automatic generation of IDs and their usage to predict and decide about certain SLAs is detailed in the dynamic decision making framework in Sect. 4.

Definition 2 (Influence Diagram). *An ID is a tuple $(\mathcal{N}, \mathcal{E})$ with*

- *a set of nodes $\mathcal{N} = \{\mathcal{C}, \mathcal{D}, \mathcal{U}\} = \{n_1, \ldots, n_n\}$, where the set $\mathcal{C}$ consists of chance nodes, $\mathcal{D}$ of decision nodes and $\mathcal{U}$ of utility nodes, and*

- *a set of directed edges $\mathcal{E} \subset \mathcal{N} \times \mathcal{N}$, where $\mathcal{E} = \{\mathcal{P}, \mathcal{I}\}$, such that $(n_i, n_j) \in \mathcal{P}$ with $n_j \in \mathcal{C} \vee \mathcal{U}$ represents a conditional dependency between parent node n_i and child node n_j, and $(n_i, n_j) \in \mathcal{I}$ with $n_j \in \mathcal{D}$ represents an informational dependency between n_i and n_j.*

Each chance node $c_i \in \mathcal{C}$ is associated with a conditional probability distribution $P(x_i|Parents(x_i))$ of its random variable x_i it represents. The decision nodes $d_i \in \mathcal{D}$ are associated with a policy D_{d_i} specifying a decision given the parent nodes' values – a table indicating the best decision based on decisions' utilities. The utility nodes $u_i \in \mathcal{U}$ are associated with a utility function U_{u_i} determining its utility.

4   Dynamic Decision Making for BPM

The dynamic decision making framework shown in Fig. 3 is proposed as an extension to a BPMS. It is able to dynamically support the process execution by decision models. In particular, during the process executions data, namely event information, occurs that is stored in an event log repository. This event information is then used by our framework for adjusting the decision model dynamically, according to the current business process environment. The underlying concepts of this framework, i.e., the utilization of BNs, IDs, andDMN are explained in Sect. 4.1. Subsequently, Sect. 4.2 describes how our frameworkdeals with finite resources in this context. Section 4.3 demonstrates how DMN decision models are derived. Finally, a concrete implementation is presented in Sect. 4.4.

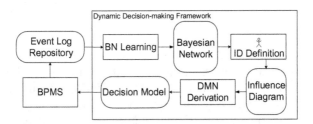

Fig. 3. System architecture

4.1   Concept

The dynamic decision making framework aims at guiding the actions and decisions of the BPMS, thus, automatically proposing decisions that have a behavioral character; i.e. they determine how a business reacts to business events [4]. An efficient way to determine such behaviour for a process is by the usage of a BN.

In our approach, the BN is derived automatically from an event log. Each event log contains information on the execution, e.g., the process instance, the duration of activities but also the data that is used and generated as well as the results of each task. In the example of the phone repair process, this might be the type of the defect or the fact whether the phone is fixed or not. This data is transformed into a database D of cases, in which each row represents an individual case with all information to it, structured into columns ($v \in D$), i.e., each column containing the values for a variable of the case.

Given the database D of cases, both the BN itself and the conditional probability distributions can be learned (qualitative and quantitative learning) using a BN learning algorithm. In particular, each column of the database (variables $v \in D$) is mapped to exactly one distinct node in the BN. Next, these nodes are connected by edges. Given Definition 1, an edge between two nodes represents their conditional dependency. To reveal this dependency, we rely on the $K2$-algorithm [6] (cf. Sect. 4.4). It reveals an edge between one node (parent node) that influences the value of another node (child node). The specific influence is measured by the probability of the network given the data, after connecting the child to the parent node.

As already mentioned in Sect. 3, BNs are acyclic, yet business processes often contain loops such as the repair loop of the phone repair process (cf. Fig. 1). In consequence, the event log contains events for all loop executions, which would result in as many database columns as there are executions of the loop. We tackle this problem by only putting the first, penultimate, and last value of a loop event into the database because these events yield the highest amount of information, a strategy which was proposed similarly in [10]. For example, for the *repairType* there will be nodes *firstRepairType*, *previousRepairType* and *repairType*.

Figure 4a shows an excerpt of the BN constructed for our running example. The "previous" loop variables, such as *previousRepairType* are not shown because often the phone could be repaired after two attempts such that *previousRepairType* equals *firstRepairType*, so that only the "first" loop variables are parent nodes of others (i.e., influence them).

The BN shows that the type of defect determines which repair type is used, represented by an edge from *defectType* to *firstRepairType* and *repairType*. To verify this dependency between the three, we inspected the corresponding event log (see Sect. 5). The data verifies the derived influences in the BN: For defect types 1–4 always a simple repair was executed, for defect types 7–10 only complex repairs were recorded, and for types 5 and 6 both repair types were used. Additionally, some defects seem harder to fix than others (e.g. parental dependency between *defectType* and *firstDefectFixed*), a successful repair depends on the technician (e.g. parental dependency between *firstSolver* and *firstDefectFixed*), and the duration is influenced by the choice of the first technician and the result of the last repair. Shown with this example, we see the first technician (*firstSolver*) plays a crucial role concerning the duration of the entire process, see Fig. 4a.

On the basis of the BN, we may pose queries about any decision in the process given knowledge about any conditions of the process. For example, we may want to decide which repair to conduct given a desired duration (less than

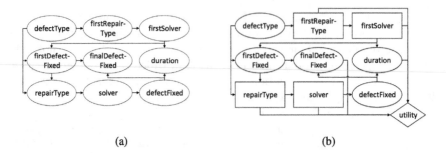

Fig. 4. Models for the phone repair use case: (a) learned BN, and (b) constructed ID from (a).

mean duration μ) and a certain type of defect (e.g., 4). In this case, we try all the different value assignments to $repairType$ to make the target value for $duration$ as likely as possible: $P(duration < \mu|defectType = 4, repairType)$.

In order to automate these tests and consider several predefined optimization criteria, the BN is transformed into an ID that serves this purpose. As IDs are augmented BNs, we use theBN as basis to construct anID. For the decision nodes, we analyze the process specification and its execution data to identify gateways and the decisions to be made. For example, the phone repair process model contains an exclusive gateway at which we are able to choose between a simple and a complex repair. Similarly, resources need to be assigned to activities in the process. Depending on the resource allocation strategy of a process execution, we furthermore decide which particular resource to assign to the activity. For instance, in the phone repair process there is a set of resources responsible for the simple repair ($S1$-$S3$) and another set ($C1$-$C3$) responsible for the complex repair. Utility nodes are constructed in a similar way. On the basis of the process model and its description, we can derive the costs of activities (e.g., duration) and also the different outcomes of the process (e.g., fines to be paid in case of SLA violations). Consequently, we can define one or more utility nodes in the ID and also their associated mappings as described in Definition 2. These utility nodes are added as additional nodes and represent the optimization criterion. In the phone repair process in Sect. 2, two decisions are required: (1) the type of repair and (2) the resource assigned to that repair.

The repair procedures and the technicians are associated with a cost, so these decision nodes are connected to the utility node in the ID. Furthermore, if the defect could not be fixed or the phone could not be repaired in less than mean repair time, the SLAs are violated and a fine must be paid. Consequently, the utility node is also connected to the $finalDefectFixed$ and $duration$ chance nodes. This is illustrated in Fig. 4b.

By $solving$ an ID, decision tables are constructed for each decision node in the ID. Thus, the ID yields an optimal function (wrt. utilities) D_{d_i} (see Definition 1) specifying the optimal decision for each decision node d_i based on each possible

Table 1. Utility table for *first-Solver* given *firstRepairType*

	S1	S2	S3	C1	C2	C3
simple	245	296	**333**	0	0	0
complex	0	0	0	**371**	354	257

Table 2. Decision table for *first-Solver* given *firstRepairType*

	S1	S2	S3	C1	C2	C3
simple	0	0	1	0	0	0
complex	0	0	0	1	0	0

decision's utility. For example, Table 2 is the decision table for the *firstSolver* decision based on the corresponding utility table shown in Table 1.

4.2 Dealing with Decisions About Finite Resources

The aim of our framework is to find optimal decisions automatically, based on historic and current process data. For instance, the framework should be used to identify which technician to assign to which running repair in our example such as *(i)* Assign technician *S3* for a *simple* repair, and *(ii)* Assign technician *C1* for a *complex* repair.

However, such rules are rigid, especially when assigning a restricted number of resources. It may happen that a resource is busy and thus not available at a particular moment. Hence, if *S3* is currently working on another case, assigning her to the repair at hand could actually delay the process execution and is usually not optimal. Consequently, we need some resource allocation strategy that is able to deal with such cases.

For this purpose, we incorporate the time that passes from assigning the resource to when it is actually required. In case the desired resource is unavailable, we consider how much time she already spent on the case she is currently working on. Additionally, we consider the probability density function of the time it takes this resource to complete her task. Based on this, we can compute the probability that the technician will be available when the next task is to be executed. Assuming that both the time until the resource is required and the time it takes the resource to complete its task are normally distributed, we can utilize the normal distribution function for each resource in the following way:

$$p_{available}(resource) = F(t^- + t^+ | \mu, \sigma) = \frac{1}{\sigma\sqrt{2\pi}} \int_{-\infty}^{t^- + t^+} e^{\frac{-(t-\mu)^2}{2\sigma^2}} dt, \quad (1)$$

where t^- is the time the resource already spent on the other case, t^+ is the estimated time until the resource is required, μ is the mean working time of the resource, and σ is its standard deviation. All four variables are based on previous executions of the process, either computed (μ and σ) or sampled (t^- and t^+). As a result, $p_{available}(resource)$ provides the probability that the resource will be available after $t^- + t^+$ time units. Having determined $p_{available}(resource)$, it is multiplied with the resource's "base" utility (cf. Table 1) to obtain its "present" utility (its utility given that it is presently unavailable) to construct a new utility table and therefore also a new decision table. The decisions to be made during

process execution are therefore adapted on the fly depending on the resources'
(un)availabilities and the resulting utility values.

4.3   Decision Model Derivation

To integrate the optimal decisions found by the ID
with the execution of the business process, we construct
a DMN decision model from the ID and its solution.
Thereby we cover the requirements level as well as the
logic level of DMN. Regarding the requirements level,
chance nodes are mapped to DMN input data, decision
nodes to decision elements and parent-child relationships to information requirements with the same direction. However, we do not map all nodes of the ID to
DMN nodes since we are only interested in nodes that
directly influence decisions. Since there may be many decision nodes in an ID,
not all of which are directly connected, we potentially derive several decision
models from an ID.

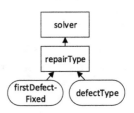

Fig. 5. Decision Model

Each decision model has exactly one top-level decision node. We identify such nodes in the ID by looking for decision nodes that do not influence any other
decision nodes. For example, the *solver* node in the
ID is mapped to a top-level decision node in a decision model, whereas *repairType* is not. After that,
we identify all decisions that are children of the top-
level decision and map them to sub-decisions in the
decision model. This procedure is repeated for every
decision node that is found with this strategy. For each decision node identified
as belonging to one decision model, we search the ID for chance nodes that are
direct children of it and connect them as input data nodes of the corresponding
decision in the decision model. One of the decision models constructed in that
way is illustrated in Fig. 5.

repairType	solver
simple	S3
complex	C3
none	none

Fig. 6. Decision table for
the *solver* decision

To construct the DMN logic level we simply map the decision tables found
by the ID solution to DMN decision tables. The table for the *solver* decision
is illustrated in Fig. 6. Note that, opposed to the *firstSolver* decision, *none* can
be chosen if the repair was successful after the first attempt. However, the outcome of this table deals with a finite resource, so that this table is not fixed.
Rather, each time it is to be evaluated, we apply the strategy proposed in the
previous section to it that dynamically updates the decision table depending
on the resource's availabilities and their resulting utility values. For example, in
another process execution *S2* might be proposed.

4.4   Implementation

Referring to the system architecture in Fig. 3, we implemented the approach as
shown in Fig. 7. Precisely, we transform the event log into a table that is required

by Kevin Murphy's Bayes Net Toolbox for MATLAB [14] to build a Bayesian network. This toolbox uses the *K2*-algorithm for the construction of Bayesian networks. Next, the network is converted to an influence diagram based on the mapping described in Sect. 4.1. For those possible, utilities are extracted from the event log, e.g. activity duration. Further utilities for the influence diagram may be derived from external databases and added manually, e.g. costs of resources. The algorithm for solving LIMIDS (limited memory in influence diagrams) as described in [13] is used to derive the utility table required to model the variables of a decision table in the decision model. This implementation and examples of the phone repair use case as well as its evaluation presented in the next section are available at http://bpt.hpi.uni-potsdam.de/Public/DecisionSupport.

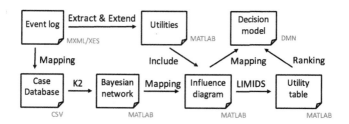

Fig. 7. Implementation

5   Evaluation

While the implementation in Sect. 4.4 shows the technical feasibility of the approach as proof-of concept, this section presents the application of the approach for the use case presented in Sect. 2 and thereby measures its benefits.

For the evaluation, we simulated new process instances based on the historic cases in the event log taken from a tutorial of the process mining tool ProM[1]. In the simulation, we evaluated the results and benefits for each instance one after another, yet considering the cases executed before. Essentially, we sampled new instances using the BN we constructed from the given event log and based on information we can derive from the event log, e.g., the average time it took a technician to repair a phone, his success rate and his probability of being available. Thus, we are able to probabilistically reproduce cases that historically occurred during process execution and manipulate them using different decision strategies. Hence, we have a mechanism to evaluate how the cases generated during process execution are affected by our dynamic decision making approach.

In particular, we evaluate the affects using the SLAs from Sect. 2. To fulfill $SLA1$, the probability that the process duration t of new process executions is less than the mean repair time ($\mu = 67$ min) must be at least 70 %. Currently, this objective is not met since only approximately 58 % of the phones are repaired

---

in less than mean repair time. Concerning SLA2, we identified that 3.6 % of the repaired cases failed in the past and the objective of at most 5 % failed repairs is actually met for the historic cases. For each sampled case, we assumed a phone is unrepairable after three unsuccessful repair attempts. Furthermore, we considered that a complex repair is more expensive than a simple repair represented by different utilities. Finally, we also incorporated different salaries for the solvers and fines for violating the SLAs (duration and fixed phone) as utilities.

A sampling of 10000 cases was done four times applying different decision strategies. First, we sampled without explicitly making any decisions, thereby reflecting the past process execution. Second, we used the ID solution with the calculated utilities derived from the historic process executions indicating which solver has to be taken for which repair type. In this case, we assumed resources were always available. Third, we added a simplistic resource allocation to this strategy to emulate that not all technicians are available at the same time and might work on other cases when a repair should start. To do so, each technician is assigned the same initial value at the start of the sampling and then subsequently we count in each case how many cases he has *not* worked on so far divided by the current total number of repairs, differentiating between simple and complex repairs. Hence, if a solver is assigned to the current repair case, it will be less likely that he will be available for the next case, and if a solver is not assigned his probability of being available will increase. Forth, we considered the approach presented in Sect. 4.2. Thus, we adapted the utilities for each solver after each case and incorporated the probability that he will be available when the repair starts instead of insisting that the solver is already available at process start. For each decision strategy, we computed the ratio of cases completed in less than mean repair time denoting the (non-)compliance with SLA1 and the ratio of cases completed successfully denoting the (non-)compliance with SLA2. Shown in Table 3, the unrealistic strategy yields very good results, because it assumes that the best solvers are always available. However, this changes dramatically if resource allocation is taken into account. Applying the adaptive strategy improves the results such that SLA1 and SLA2 are fulfilled.

Table 3. Results of evaluating the different allocation strategies

	Historic	Unrealistic	Unrealistic w/ allocation	Adaptive w/ allocation
SLA1 compliant (% being faster)	NO (58 %)	YES (88 %)	NO (1 %)	YES (71 %)
SLA2 compliant (% repaired)	YES (96 %)	YES (100 %)	NO (1 %)	YES (97 %)

In summary, this evaluation shows our approach is able to dynamically support the optimization of decisions during run-time to fulfil SLAs while considering all previous and current process execution data. Note that we could observe in our experiments that the specification of the utilities, the values of the SLAs, and process variables such as the number of attempts to repair a phone have an impact on the results of each case and our approach results, respectively. Thus, in future work, we aim to investigate this impact more precisely. Furthermore, we aim to rather consider real-world data with utilities checked by corresponding experts to verify the improved optimizations.

6   Related Work

By now, predictive and proactive behavior is researched in many areas of computer science, e.g., in compliance monitoring [22] or in the domain of dependable systems and fault management. In the latter area, literature has been published dealing specifically with predictive/proactive behavior that has been summarized in a survey [20].

Furthermore, similar research discusses the benefits of applying proactive techniques in event-driven systems. For example, [9] presents a system monitoring machinery that is critical for the successful completion of some business process. In this case, the proactive behavior manifests itself, because it is able to predict and avoid the failure of the machinery by applying preventive actions. Both examples provide insights to specific use cases, while we strive for a generic approach integrated into BPMSs and applicable in various domains. In the same vein, [18] targets on the analysis of the influence of various data attributes to choices made in business processes. These methods of decision mining identify the dependencies between data and paths within a business process. Our approach goes beyond the analysis and proactively affects the business process execution by influencing the process engine dynamically.

[12] describes an approach of building instance-specific probabilistic process models and their translation to Markov chains to enable predictions about future tasks. However, the approach focuses very case-oriented business processes. Similarly, Breuker et al. present an approach based on probabilistic finite automata (PFA) to predict future events in running process instances [5], which they further refine and implement in [3]. Their application of PFAs is similar to the Bayesian network approach in that events are encoded as states or nodes and dependencies as directed edges between these nodes, thereby forming a probabilistic model of the event log. However, the inference of optimal decisions from these models is not taken into account.

7   Conclusion

In this paper, we presented an approach to automatically support decision-making during business process execution in order to achieve optimal process execution and to ensure SLA compliance. It is based on the construction of a decision model in DMN from historic and current process execution data. In addition to a proof-of-concept implementation, we evaluated our approach on a use case. The evaluation shows our dynamic decision making approach enables significant improvements for process executions, e.g., regarding process duration, costs or resource allocation.

In future work, we will evaluate our concept on real-world scenarios in which actual utilities are defined and checked by experts in order to proof that we can positively, automatically, and dynamically support decision-making in process executions at run-time. Furthermore, we will investigate other techniques to find optimal decisions in business processes such as Markov decision processes to be able to compare them with each other.

References

1. Batoulis, K.: Proactive decision support during business process execution. In: EMoV+MinoPro@Modellierung, pp. 35–41 (2014)
2. Batoulis, K., Meyer, A., Bazhenova, E., Decker, G., Weske, M.: Extracting decision logic from process models. In: Zdravkovic, J., Kirikova, M., Johannesson, P. (eds.) CAiSE 2015. LNCS, vol. 9097, pp. 349–366. Springer, Heidelberg (2015)
3. Becker, J., Breuker, D., Delfmann, P., Matzner, M.: Designing and implementing a framework for event-based predictive modelling of business processes. In: EMISA, pp. 71–84 (2014)
4. Boyer, J., Mili, H.: Agile Business Rule Development - Process, Architecture, and JRules Examples. Springer, Heidelberg (2011)
5. Breuker, D., Delfmann, P., Matzner, M., Becker, J.: Designing and evaluating an interpretable predictive modeling technique for business processes. In: DeMiMoP (2014)
6. Cooper, G.F., Herskovits, E.: A Bayesian method for the induction of probabilistic networks from data. Mach. Learn. **9**(4), 309–347 (1992)
7. Debevoise, T., Taylor, J.: The Microguide to Process and Decision Modeling in BPMN/DMN. CreateSpace Independent Publishing Platform (2005)
8. Dumas, M., van der Aalst, W., ter Hofstede, A.: Process-Aware Information Systems. Wiley, New York (2005)
9. Engel, Y., Etzion, O., Feldman, Z.: A Basic Model for Proactive Event-driven Computing. In: ACM, DEBS (2012)
10. Grigori, D., Casati, F., Castellanos, M., Dayal, U., Sayal, M., Shan, M.C.: Business process intelligence. Comput. Indus. **53**(3), 321–343 (2004)
11. ISO: IEC 27002: 2013 (EN) Information technology-Security techniques - Code of practice for information security controls, Switzerland (2013)
12. Lakshmanan, G., Shamsi, D., Doganata, Y., Unuvar, M., Khalaf, R.: A Markov prediction model for data-driven semi-structured business processes. KAIS **42**(1), 97–126 (2015)
13. Lauritzen, S.L., Nilsson, D.: Representing and solving decision problems with limited information. Manage. Sci. **47**, 1235–1251 (2001)
14. Murphy, K.P.: The Bayes net toolbox for MATLAB. Comput. Sci. Stat. **33**, 2001 (2001)
15. Neapolitan, R.: Learning Bayesian Networks. Prentice Hall, Upper Saddle River (2004)
16. OMG: Business Process Model and Notation (BPMN), Version 2.0, January 2011
17. OMG: Decision Model And Notation (DMN), Version 1.0 - Beta 1, February 2014
18. Rozinat, A., Aalst, W.M.P.: Decision mining in business processes. Beta, Research School for Operations Management and Logistics (2006)

19. Russell, S., Norvig, P.: Artificial Intelligence: A Modern Approach, 3rd edn. Prentice Hall Press, Upper Saddle River (2009)
20. Salfner, F., Lenk, M., Malek, M.: A survey of online failure prediction methods. ACM Comput. Surv. **42**(3), 1–42 (2010)
21. Sutrisnowati, R.A., Bae, H., Park, J., Ha, B.H.: Learning Bayesian network from event logs using mutual information test. In: SOCA, pp. 356–360 (2013)
22. Thullner, R., Rozsnyai, S., Schiefer, J., Obweger, H., Suntinger, M.: Proactive business process compliance monitoring with event-based systems. In: EDOCW, pp. 429–437. IEEE (2011)
23. United States Code: Sarbanes-Oxley Act of 2002, PL 107–204, 116 Stat 745. Codified in Sections 11, 15, 18, 28, and 29 USC, Jul 2002
24. Weske, M.: Business Process Management - Concepts, Languages, Architectures, 2nd edn. Springer, Heidelberg (2012)

Gamification of Declarative Process Models for Learning and Model Verification

Johannes De Smedt$^{(\boxtimes)}$, Jochen De Weerdt, Estefanía Serral,
and Jan Vanthienen

KU Leuven Faculty of Economics and Business Department of Decision Sciences and
Information Management, Naamsestraat 69, 3000 Leuven, Belgium
{johannes.smedt,jochen.weerdt,estefania.serral,jan.vanthienen}@kuleuven.be

Abstract. Recently, a surge in the use of declarative process models
has been witnessed. These constraint-driven models excel at representing and enacting flexible and adaptable decision processes in application
areas such as scheduling and workflow management. This work exam-
ines the intricacies of the most widespread declarative process language,
Declare, which are commonly referred to as hidden dependencies. These
dependencies typically increase the steepness of the learning curve of
Declare models and making them explicit can lower the threshold for
modelers to use Declare in a sense-making and intuitive way. This work
proposes a way to gamify Declare models for novice users by annotating
such models with extra constraint and dependency information, and feedback. Hence, it offers the ability of discovering Declare and its intricacies
in a game-like fashion which lowers the threshold for learning these cog-
nitively demanding models, as well as to use them for assessing modeling
efforts by verifying that the desired behavior is present.

Keywords: Declarative process modeling · Declare · Gamification ·
Hidden dependencies

1 Introduction

Business process modeling has traditionally focused on explicitly representing
the workflow of companies' decision-making, capturing fixed process paths which
leave little room for flexibility and ad-hoc process adaptation. This setup has
been labeled the procedural process paradigm, reflecting its prescriptive nature.
Lately, a shift towards activity- and rule-centric approaches can be witnessed in
literature. Modeling languages, such as Declare [1], use constraints in-between
activities which allows everything that is not forbidden. Hence, these models
leave more options for deviation and adaptation, enabling more flexible enactment. A full comparison of languages and techniques can be found in [2].

Users of declarative process models, especially novice modelers and readers,
face the struggle of understanding all the implications of such models. As there is
no fixed process sequence, and since the interdependencies of different constraints

© Springer International Publishing Switzerland 2016
M. Reichert and H.A. Reijers (Eds.): BPM Workshops 2015, LNBIP 256, pp. 432–443, 2016.
DOI: 10.1007/978-3-319-42887-1_35

contain implicit behavior that is not immediately visible [3], it becomes hard to start using them without a thorough education.

This work tackles this issue by offering a proof-of-concept approach for expliciting hidden dependencies, and offer them to the user in game-like fashion, i.e., by coloring Declare models with this information in a simulation environment, that also supports a guessing functionality. This approach goes beyond the coloring of separate constraints [4], as it constitutes sets of interrelated constraints.

The paper is structured as follows. In the next section, an overview of the state-of-art including flexible process modeling approaches and Declare is given, followed by a small motivating example in Sect. 3. Next, Sect. 4 explains which activation and resolution strategies each of the separate constraints inflict. Section 5 shows how to construct dependency sets in-between constraints, which is implemented in a tool in Sect. 6. Finally, a conclusion and a discussion of future work can be found in Sect. 7.

2   Related Work

The introduction of flexibility into workflows has led to the proposal of many different approaches, languages, and techniques. Most notably, pockets of flexibility [5], worklets [6], and the guard-stage-milestone approach [7] have either introduced more flexibility into procedural workflows, or a new language altogether.

Next, Declare is a well-established framework for the support of both modeling and enacting flexible process models [8] and has become one of the standards for declarative process modeling. Originally, the set of templates was expressed in Linear Temporal Logic (LTL) and was called DecSerFlow and ConDec [1,9]. The constraints are enacted by using Büchi automata [10]. Later, a shift towards expressing the constraints in regular expressions was made, which is currently used in the Declare modeler [11]. Regular expressions are executed by using Finite State Automata (FSA), which enjoy the benefit of being better able to cope with finite executions. For the sake of completeness, both execution semantics as well as a verbose description of the constraints can be found in Table 1.

The downside of Declare, however, is the fact that modelers and readers witness a higher threshold for understanding all behavior present in the model, as extensively researched in [3,12,13]. The behavior that is not forbidden is not always explicit, which introduces a higher cognitive barrier for understanding all the implications of the constraints in a model. This has led researchers to introduce the concept of coloring constraints [4] which indicates the current state of constraints in the model, and to aid users with experts explaining hidden dependencies [14].

Gamification is a concept that recently has spiked the interest of researchers. It is a way of including gaming constructs in non-gaming contexts towards user engagement, understanding, and motivation [15]. An overview of previous applications and its effectiveness has been described in [16]. Gamification is used for creating a playful environment for learning and has been supported by a surge in human-interaction research and the impact of video gaming. More specifically, ludic systems [17,18] comprise of interactive productions that incorporate constructs of game play, simulation, or modeling and can be used towards transforming certain topics into easily-approachable games.

In business process modeling, work exists that enables gamification in some way. Most notably, human-centric BPM efforts such as [19], which use 3D virtual world technology for visualizing work places, or the advanced process simulation capabilities based on tokens for BPMN [20], or the BRITNeY Suite for Petri nets in CPN Tools [21] are improving user understanding by offering an advanced graphical user interface. These approaches focus mainly on procedural models. For declarative process models, true gamification approaches are sparse.

3   Motivating Example

A small example of a Declare model which contains hidden dependencies is included in Fig. 1. *Exclusive choice(Buy bonds, Buy stock)* implies that, when executing *Buy bonds*, not only *Buy stock* becomes disabled, but also *Withdraw money* and *Deposit money*. If *Buy stock* becomes permanently disabled, it can never activate *Withdraw money*, as they are connected by a *Precedence* relationship. This also implies that *Response(Deposit money, Withdraw money)* can never be resolved, as *Withdraw money* is now permanently disabled. Hence *Deposit money* is also permanently disabled. Firing any of these activities also disables *Buy bonds* for the same reason.

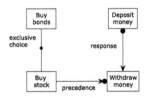

Fig. 1. An example of a small Declare model with hidden dependencies.

The proposed approach annotates a Declare model, showing these hidden dependencies by applying colors to the activities involved in dependent constraints. It also offers a setup which gives the user the opportunity to guess which activities are enabled, after which he/she receives feedback and a score. They can also replay Declare models that they made themselves, to verify whether the envisioned behavior is present, supporting model-driven development [23].

4   Declare Constraints

The body of Declare constraints consists of both unary, binary, and *n*-ary constraints. A full overview can be found in Table 1. In this work, we focus on

Table 1. An overview of Declare constraint templates with their corresponding LTL formula, regular expression, and verbose description.

Template	LTL Formula [1]	Regular Expression [22]	Description
Existence(A,n)	$\Diamond(A \wedge \bigcirc(existence(n-1, A)))$	.*(A.*){n}	Activity A happens at least n times
Absence(A,n)	$\neg existence(n, A)$	[^A]*(A?[^A]*){n-1}	Activity A happens at most n times
Exactly(A,n)	$existence(n, A) \wedge absence(n+1, A)$	[^A]*(A[^A]*){n}	Activity A happens exactly n times.
Init(A)	A	(A.*)?	Each instance has to start with activity A
Last(A)	$\Box(A \implies \neg X \neg A)$	.*A	Each instance has to end with activity A
Responded existence(A,B)	$\Diamond A \implies \Diamond B$	[^A]*((A.*B.*) |(B.*A.*))?	If A happens at least once then B has to happen or happened before A
Co-existence(A,B)	$\Diamond A \impliedby \Diamond B$	[^AB]*((A.*B.*) |(B.*A.*))?	If A happens then B has to happen or happened after after A, and vice versa
Response(A,B)	$\Box(A \implies \Diamond B)$	[^A]*(A.*B)*[^A]*	Whenever activity A happens, activity B has to happen eventually afterward.
Precedence(A,B)	$(\neg B \: U \: A) \vee \Box(\neg B)$	[^B]*(A.*B)*[^B]*	Whenever activity B happens, activity A has to have happened before it
Succession(A,B)	$response(A, B) \wedge precedence(A, B)$	[^AB]*(A.*B)*[^AB]*	Both Response(A,B) and Precedence(A,B) hold
Alternate response(A,B)	$\Box(A \implies \bigcirc(\neg A \: U \: B))$	[^A]*(A[^A]*B[^A]*)*	After each activity A, at least one activity B is executed. A following activity A can be executed again only after the first occurrence of activity B
Alternate precedence(A,B)	$precedence(A, B) \wedge \Box(B \implies \bigcirc(precedence(A, B)))$	[^B]*(A[^B]*B[^B]*)*	Before each activity B, at least one activity A is executed. A following activity B can be executed again only after the first next occurrence of activity A
Alternate succession(A,B)	$altresponse(A, B) \wedge precedence(A, B)$	[^AB]*(A[^AB]*B[^AB]*)*	Both alternative response(A,B) and alternate precedence(A,B) hold
Chain response(A,B)	$\Box(A \implies \bigcirc B)$	[^A]*(AB[^A]*)*	Every time activity A happens, it must be directly followed by activity B (activity B can also follow other activities)
Chain precedence(A,B)	$\Box(\bigcirc B \implies A)$	[^B]*(AB[^B]*)*	Every time activity B happens, it must be directly preceded by activity A (activity A can also precede other activities)
Chain succession(A,B)	$\Box(A \iff \bigcirc B)$	[^AB]*(AB[^AB]*)*	Activities A and B can only happen directly following each other
Not co-existence(A,B)	$\neg(\Diamond A \wedge \Diamond B)$	[^AB]*((A[^B]*) |(B[^A]*))?	Either activity A or B can happen, but not both
Not succession(A,B)	$\Box(A \implies \neg(\Diamond B))$	[^A]*(A[^B]*)*	Activity A cannot be followed by activity B, and activity B cannot be preceded by activity A
Not chain succession(A,B)	$\Box(A \implies \neg(\bigcirc B))$	[^A]*(A+[^AB][^A]*)*A*	Activities A and B can never directly follow each other
Choice(A,B)	$\Diamond A \vee \Diamond B$	.*[AB].*	Activity A or activity B has to happen at least once, possibly both
Exclusive choice(A,B)	$(\Diamond A \vee \Diamond B) \wedge \neg(\Diamond A \wedge \Diamond B)$	([^B]*A[^B]*) |.*[AB].*([^A]*B[^A]*)	Activity A or activity B has to happen at least once, but not both

the interplay of binary constraints. A Declare model is a tuple $DM = (A, \Pi)$ consisting of the set of activities A, and the constraints $\Pi : (A, A) \to \Theta$, with Θ the set of predefined Declare constraints. For the sake of brevity, all $p \in \Pi$ with image *Precedence* are written as Π_{Prec}. The other constraints are referred to in that fashion as well. An execution sequence is denoted as $\sigma = s_1, s_2, ..., s_n$ with $s_i \in A, i = 1..n$. A Declare graph is a directed graph $DG = (N, E)$, where $N = A$ and $E = \Pi$ only if Π consists of binary constraints, $\Pi = \Pi_{Resp/CoEx} \cup \Pi_{(A/C)Resp(onse)} \cup \Pi_{(A/C)Prec(edence)} \cup \Pi_{NotCoEx} \cup \Pi_{NotSuc} \cup \Pi_{NotChainSuc} \cup \Pi_{(Excl)Choice}$. Note that, by definition, $\Pi(a,b)_{Suc} = \Pi(a,b)_{Resp} \cup \Pi(a,b)_{Prec}, a,b \in A$.

Binary constraints consist of an antecedent (a), and a consequent (b), $a, b \in A$. The antecedent is the activating construct, the consequent the resolving construct [24]. The constraints are organized in a hierarchy-like fashion. At the base of the hierarchy, a *Responded existence(a,b)* enforces that, when a occurs,

Table 2. Activation and resolution of separate binary constraints.

Constraint	Activates	Resolves
Responded Existence(A,B)	A	B
Co-existence(A,B)	A,B	A,B
Precedence(A,B)	A	
Response(A,B)	A	B
Succession(A,B)	A	B
Alternate precedence(A,B)	A	
Alternate response(A,B)	A	B
Alternate succession(A,B)	A	B
Chain precedence(A,B)	A	
Chain response(A,B)	A	B
Chain succession(A,B)	A	B
Choice(A,B)		A,B
Exclusive Choice(A,B)	A,B	
Not co-existence(A,B)	A,B	
Not succession(A,B)	A	
Not chain succession(A,B)	A	not A,B

b has to happen, or has happened already, hence a activates the need for b. *Co-existence* is the reciprocal version of the former constraint, where both a and b act as activator and resolver at the same time. Next, these two constraints are used in an ordered fashion. *Precedence(a,b)* extends *Responded existence(a,b)* with the requirement that a has to happen before b, *Response(a,b)* is only fulfilled when a string contains at least one occurrence of b after any a. The alternate constraints extend this principle in a circular fashion, while chain constraints take this one step further and enforce the immediate occurrence of *Precedence*, and *Response*.

Other binary constraints include, *Choice(a,b)*, $\forall s \in \sigma, a \in s \lor b \in s$, and *Exclusive choice(a,b)*, $\forall s \in \sigma, (a \in s \lor b \in s) \land \neg(a, b \in s)$, and are temporarily violated at the start of a new execution sequence, as well as the negative constraints *Not co-existence(a,b)*, *Not succession(a,b)*, and *Not chain succession(a,b)*.

These different constraints lead to different violation profiles: a constraint can either be permanently violated, i.e., there exists no solution anymore to satisfy the constraint, temporarily violated, the constraint is currently violated, but there exists an execution sequence s which can still satisfy it in the future, and satisfied. Some constraints are always satisfied, such as every *(A/C) Precedence* constraint. *Response* constraints can be resolved as long as the consequent can fire. *Choice* constraints are temporarily violated by default, but can be resolved by either antecedent and consequent. *Exclusive choice*, *Not co-existence*, and *Not succession* are the only constraints that can permanently disable an activity. A summary of the activation and resolution profiles is given in Table 2.

5 Combining Constraints and Constructing Dependency Sets

In this section, we merge the insights of the previous section to establish dependency sets that interrelate different constraints in a model, rather than a set of separate constraints.

5.1 Constructing Dependency Sets

Using the activation and resolution profiles of each constraint, it is possible to travel through a Declare graph to constitute dependency structures for a certain constraint.

As pointed out in the previous section, only three constraints can permanently disable an activity. If this activity is involved in any other constraint that it resolves, the permanently disabling constraint cannot become fulfilled anymore. *Not co-existence* disables either the antecedent or the consequent, depending on which of the two fires first. Hence, if any of them is in a, e.g., *Response* relationship as a consequent, this means that either the *Response* has not been triggered, or that the other activity involved in the *Not co-existence* becomes permanently disabled, as otherwise the *Response* can never become satisfied. The same holds for *Exclusive choice* as well. *Not succession* disables the consequent after executing the antecedent. This infers that all constraints that need to be resolved by the consequent b must be satisfied before executing the antecedent a of *Not succession(a,b)*. When b activates activities, e.g., b is an antecedent in *Precedence(b,c)*, then a is rendered disabled until all the constraints for which c is a consequent have been fulfilled, and b has fired to fulfill the *Precedence* constraint.

To tackle these interrelations, a set of dependency structures are built to keep track of the current state of a certain constraint. We define a dependency structure DS as a tuple of $DS = (\Psi, SDS)$ with $\Psi \subseteq \Pi$. These structures are built for every $p \in \Pi_{ExclChoice} \cup \Pi_{NotCoEx} \cup \Pi_{NotSuc}$ and contain constraints influencing them, as well as substructures of the same structure. The algorithm explaining how this is done can be found in Algorithm 1. By back and forward tracking (lines 9–10) starting from both the antecedent and consequent in case of *Exclusive Choice* and *Not co-existence*, and from the consequent for *Not succession* (line 8), dependency structures are constructed by the recursive function (Algorithm 2). Backward searching is done by considering an activity $a \in A$, and scanning its inputs $\bullet a$ for constraints for which it serves as a consequent, and thus as a resolving activity. This is the case for $\Pi_{Resp/CoEx} \cup \Pi_{(C/A)Resp}$. Every constraint that satisfies this description is put in the dependency structure of the original constraint (lines 6–11). Forward searching is somewhat more complicated. For every constraint in the output of an activity $a\bullet$ for which is

---

Algorithm 1. Retrieving Dependent Activities for Binary Constraints

---

Input: $DM = (A, \Pi)$ ▷ A is the set of activities, Π the set of constraints
1: **procedure** RETURNDEPTRANS(PN)
2:     $BW = \Pi_{Resp/CoEx} \cup \Pi_{(C/A)Response}$
3:     $FW = \Pi_{Resp/CoEx} \cup \Pi_{(C/A)Precedence}$
4:     $DS \leftarrow \emptyset$ ▷ The set of all dependency structures
5:     **for** $a \in A$ **do**
6:         $DP \leftarrow \emptyset$ ▷ The set of dependent constraints for a
7:         $V = \emptyset$ ▷ Visited activities
8:         **if** $a \in \Pi_{ExlcChoi} \vee a \in \Pi_{NotCoEx} \vee a \in \Pi(A, a)_{NotSuc}$ **then**
9:             $DP \leftarrow Search(PN, t, V, \emptyset, BW, FW, true)$ ▷ Search left
10:            $DP \leftarrow Search(PN, t, V, \emptyset, BW, FW, false)$ ▷ Search right
11:            $DS \leftarrow DP$
12:         **end if**
13:     **end for**
14: **end procedure**

---

serves as an antecedent in case of $\Pi_{Resp/CoEx} \cup \Pi_{(C/A)Prec}$, a new dependency structure is created (lines 16–19) and added to the main dependency structure of the constraint. Note that there is no limitation on this nesting behavior, and that multiple levels can be found in one structure.

5.2   Using Dependency Sets

After creating the dependency sets, they can be put to use to aid user understanding of the interrelations of constraints as follows. For *Not co-existence(a,b)* and *Exclusive choice(a,b)*:

- Firing any activity in the dependency set of either a or b, or a or b themselves, will render the other activity and all the activities in its dependency set permanently disabled. E.g., if an activity in the dependency set of a fires, a needs to fire eventually to resolve the activity as a consequent. If an activity in a dependency set within the dependency set of a fires, a is needed to serve as an antecedent for the activity constituting the nested set, for that activity has to serve as a consequent. By definition, b cannot fire anymore, thus it can also not resolve or activate any activity in its dependency set anymore.
- This implies that, if the dependency sets of a and b overlap, none of the activities in the sets can ever fire, as they would require resolving and disabling at the same time. In case of *Exclusive choice*, the net has a faulty setup as the *Exclusive choice* requires the occurrence of either a or b to become satisfied.
- If a $Choice(c, d)$ constraint contains activities that are both included in one dependency set (or any of the nested sets), the other activity in *Not co-existence* or *Exclusive choice* and all the activities in its dependency set become disabled, as the $Choice(c, d)$ requires that at least either c or d is executed to become satisfied.

For *Not succession*:

- The antecedent of the constraint cannot be fired until all constraints dependent of the consequent are resolved. After executing the antecedent of *Not*

Algorithm 2. Search for Dependent Transitions and Places

1: **procedure** SEARCH(DM, a, V, DP, BW, FW, ls)   ▷ ls is a boolean for determining the search direction
2:     **if** $\neg(a \in V)$ **then**
3:         $V \leftarrow a$
4:         **if** ls **then**
5:             **for** $p \in \bullet a$ **do**   ▷ Scan all incoming Declare constraints
6:                 **if** $p \in BW$ **then**
7:                     $DP \leftarrow p$
8:                     **for** $s \in \bullet p$ **do**
9:                         $Search(PN, s, V, DP, BW, FW, true)$
10:                        $Search(PN, s, V, DP, BW, FW, false)$
11:                    **end for**
12:                **end if**
13:            **end for**
14:        **else**
15:            **for** $p \in a\bullet$ **do**   ▷ Scan all outgoing Declare constraints
16:                **if** $p \in FW$ **then**
17:                    $DL \leftarrow \emptyset$
18:                    **for** $s \in p\bullet$ **do**
19:                        $DL \leftarrow Search(PN, s, V, DP, BW, FW, true)$
20:                        $DL \leftarrow Search(PN, s, V, DP, BW, FW, false)$
21:                    **end for**
22:                    $DS \leftarrow DL$
23:                **end if**
24:            **end for**
25:        **end if**
26:    **end if**
27: **end procedure**

---

succession, all constraints and activities related to those constraints that reside in the top level of the dependency structure become disabled.

- The activities in any dependency structure nested in the main structure of *Not succession*, become disabled after executing the antecedent if there has not been an occurrence of the constraint inflicting the dependency. In the case of *Precedence*, executing the antecedent once enables the whole structure indefinitely, for *Alternate/chain precedence*, executing the antecedent grants the structure only one more occurrence as the antecedent of that structure can never fire again. This implies that any temporary violations within the structure need to be resolved before executing the consequent in a similar fashion to the antecedent of *Not succession*. This principle propagates through the whole chain of dependency structures.

Furthermore, any cycle of chained *Precedence* or *Response* constraints disables any activities involved, as it will never be possible to resolve any activation within this cycle.

5.3   Example Model

Consider the example given in Fig. 2. The model contains a *Not succession* constraint between D and F. Following the algorithms described in the previous section, the following dependency structure is built for *Not succession(F,D)*: $DS_{NotSuc(F,D)} = (Resp(C, D), Resp(Cc, C), \{DS_{Prec(Cc,Ccc)}, DS_{Prec(C,Bb)}, DS_{AltPrec(D,E)}\})$ with $DS_{Prec(Cc,Ccc)} = (\emptyset, \emptyset)$, $DS_{Prec(C,Bb)} =$

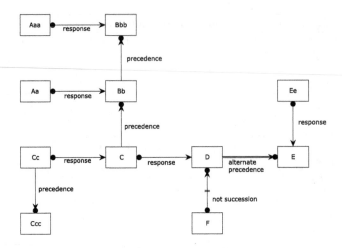

Fig. 2. An example of a Declare model with numerous hidden dependencies.

$(Resp(Aa, Bb), \{DS_{Prec(Bb,Bbb)}\})$, $DS_{Prec(Bb,Bbb)} = (Resp(Aaa, Bbb), \emptyset)$, and $DS_{AltPrec(D,E)} = (Resp(Ee, E), \emptyset)$. Using the dependency sets, the information provided goes beyond coloring constraints with violation, as it can indicate which constraints are actually related and influence the violation status. Also, the approach allows for getting the influence on an activity-level as well.

In Fig. 2, executing Cc and C will render F, the antecedent of *Not succession(F,D)*, disabled. For Cc, a chain of C, D is needed to resolve the *Reponse* constraints, given that the antecedents do not fire again. Firing Aa disables F as well, and F becomes enabled only after executing C, the antecedent that makes Bb in their *Precedence* relationship, which is included as a separate dependency structure $DS_{Prec(C,Bb)}$, enabled. The same holds for Ccc and Ee. If Aaa fires, again, it is enough for C to fire, which makes it possible to fire Bb, Bbb.

6   Towards Gamification and Proof-Of-Concept Implementation

The building of dependency sets as described in the previous section, has been implemented in the open-source process mining framework ProM[1] and is publicly available[2]. The execution semantics of Declare are based on the product of separate constraints expressed in regular expressions, and offer the global automaton as a finite state machine which is constructed with [25].

The plugin displays a Declare model which is set up as a guessing game, as shown in Fig. 3. The first state of the model is given, by coloring enabled activities in green. Next, the user can fire an activated activity and guess which activities are enabled after this execution. Finally, this guess is evaluated and the correctly

---

[1] http://www.promtools.org.
[2] http://j.processmining.be/declaregame.

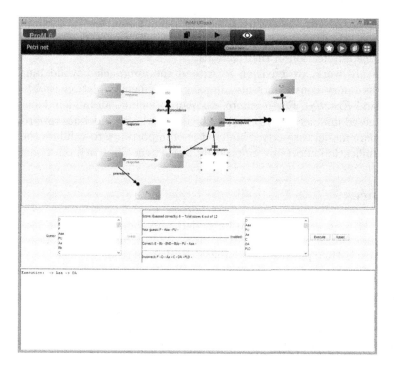

Fig. 3. An example of a Declare model with numerous hidden dependencies visualized in the proof-of-concept ProM implementation. (Color figure online)

and incorrectly classified activities are then displayed. The visualization of the model is updated to show the state after the execution. The model is annotated as follows:

- Red arcs indicate temporarily violated constraints.
- The user can select activities or constraints, after which the model displays these activities in blue, and the activities in the dependency sets in lighter blue for backward-dependent activities, and red for forward-dependent activities. A nested forward-dependent activity is indicated in a lighter shade of red and its dependent activities again in light blue.

The game can keep going, until the user fires an artificial *End* activity, which is only enabled if all constraints are satisfied. The user can also reset the net and start all over again. As such, the user can consult hidden dependencies between constraints at any time, which improves the understandability, and a playful aspect is added for he/she can obtain a score based on the guessing attempts.

7   Conclusion and Future Work

In this work, we improve the understanding of Declare constraints by making hidden dependencies between binary constraints explicit. This goes beyond coloring constraints with constraint-level granular information, and can act as an expert system guiding users towards executing a Declare model while understanding the implication of their actions.

For future work, we envision to extend the approach beyond binary constraints, as unary constraints also impact permanent violation (most notably *Absence* and *Exactly*). Furthermore, we plan to include all hidden dependencies in a text-based manner, hence offering the user verbose guidelines towards enacting a Declare model correctly. Finally, it is of importance to validate the impact of the gamification efforts by empirically testing the approach on modelers.

References

1. Pesic, M., van der Aalst, W.M.P.: A declarative approach for flexible business processes management. In: Eder, J., Dustdar, S. (eds.) BPM Workshops 2006. LNCS, vol. 4103, pp. 169–180. Springer, Heidelberg (2006)
2. Goedertier, S., Vanthienen, J., Caron, F.: Declarative business process modelling: principles and modelling languages. Enterprise IS **9**(2), 161–185 (2015)
3. Haisjackl, C., Zugal, S., Soffer, P., Hadar, I., Reichert, M., Pinggera, J., Weber, B.: Making sense of declarative process models: common strategies and typical pitfalls. In: Nurcan, S., Proper, H.A., Soffer, P., Krogstie, J., Schmidt, R., Halpin, T., Bider, I. (eds.) BPMDS 2013 and EMMSAD 2013. LNBIP, vol. 147, pp. 2–17. Springer, Heidelberg (2013)
4. Maggi, F.M., Montali, M., Westergaard, M., van der Aalst, W.M.P.: Monitoring business constraints with linear temporal logic: an approach based on colored automata. In: Rinderle-Ma, S., Toumani, F., Wolf, K. (eds.) BPM 2011. LNCS, vol. 6896, pp. 132–147. Springer, Heidelberg (2011)
5. Sadiq, S.K., Sadiq, W., Orlowska, M.E.: Pockets of flexibility in workflow specification. In: Kunii, H.S., Jajodia, S., Sølvberg, A. (eds.) ER 2001. LNCS, vol. 2224, pp. 513–526. Springer, Heidelberg (2001)
6. Adams, M., ter Hofstede, A.H.M., Edmond, D., van der Aalst, W.M.P.: Worklets: a service-oriented implementation of dynamic flexibility in workflows. In: Meersman, R., Tari, Z. (eds.) OTM 2006. LNCS, vol. 4275, pp. 291–308. Springer, Heidelberg (2006)
7. Hull, R., et al.: Introducing the guard-stage-milestone approach for specifying business entity lifecycles (invited talk). In: Bravetti, M. (ed.) WS-FM 2010. LNCS, vol. 6551, pp. 1–24. Springer, Heidelberg (2011)
8. Pesic, M., Schonenberg, H., van der Aalst, W.M.: Declare: full support for loosely-structured processes. In: 11th IEEE International Enterprise Distributed Object Computing Conference, EDOC 2007, pp. 287–287. IEEE (2007)
9. van der Aalst, W.M.P., Pesic, M.: Decserflow: Towards a truly declarative service flow language. In: The Role of Business Processes in Service Oriented Architectures, 16.07.2006–21.07.2006 (2006)
10. Somenzi, F., Bloem, R.: Efficient Büchi automata from LTL formulae. In: Emerson, E.A., Sistla, A.P. (eds.) CAV 2000. LNCS, vol. 1855, pp. 248–263. Springer, Heidelberg (2000)
11. Westergaard, M., Maggi, F.M.: Declare: a tool suite for declarative workflow modeling and enactment. BPM (Demos) 820 (2011)

12. Reijers, H.A., Slaats, T., Stahl, C.: Declarative modeling–an academic dream or the future for BPM? In: Daniel, F., Wang, J., Weber, B. (eds.) BPM 2013. LNCS, vol. 8094, pp. 307–322. Springer, Heidelberg (2013)
13. Fahland, D., Lübke, D., Mendling, J., Reijers, H., Weber, B., Weidlich, M., Zugal, S.: Declarative versus imperative process modeling languages: the issue of understandability. In: Halpin, T., Krogstie, J., Nurcan, S., Proper, E., Schmidt, R., Soffer, P., Ukor, R. (eds.) EMMSAD 2009. LNBIP, vol. 29, pp. 353–366. Springer, Heidelberg (2009)
14. Zugal, S., Pinggera, J., Weber, B.: Creating declarative process models using test driven modeling suite. In: Nurcan, S. (ed.) CAiSE Forum 2011. LNBIP, vol. 107, pp. 16–32. Springer, Heidelberg (2012)
15. Deterding, S., Dixon, D., Khaled, R., Nacke, L.: From game design elements to gamefulness: defining gamification. In: Proceedings of the 15th International Academic MindTrek Conference: Envisioning Future Media Environments, pp. 9–15. ACM (2011)
16. Hamari, J., Koivisto, J., Sarsa, H.: Does gamification work? - A literature review of empirical studies on gamification. In: 47th Hawaii International Conference on System Sciences (HICSS), 2014, pp. 3025–3034. IEEE (2014)
17. Selander, S.: Designs for learning and ludic engagement. Digital Creativity **19**(3), 145–152 (2008)
18. Lindley, C.A.: Ludic engagement and immersion as a generic paradigm for human-computer interaction design. In: Rauterberg, M. (ed.) ICEC 2004. LNCS, vol. 3166, pp. 3–13. Springer, Heidelberg (2004)
19. Brown, R., Rinderle-Ma, S., Kriglstein, S., Kabicher-Fuchs, S.: Augmenting and assisting model elicitation tasks with 3D virtual world context metadata. In: Meersman, R., Panetto, H., Dillon, T., Missikoff, M., Liu, L., Pastor, O., Cuzzocrea, A., Sellis, T. (eds.) OTM 2014. LNCS, vol. 8841, pp. 39–56. Springer, Heidelberg (2014)
20. Allweyer, T., Schweitzer, S.: A Tool for animating BPMN token flow. In: Mendling, J., Weidlich, M. (eds.) BPMN 2012. LNBIP, vol. 125, pp. 98–106. Springer, Heidelberg (2012)
21. Westergaard, M., Lassen, K.B.: The BRITNeY suite animation tool. In: Donatelli, S., Thiagarajan, P.S. (eds.) ICATPN 2006. LNCS, vol. 4024, pp. 431–440. Springer, Heidelberg (2006)
22. Westergaard, M., Stahl, C., Reijers, H.A.: UnconstrainedMiner: efficient discovery of generalized declarative process models. Technical Report BPM-13-28, BPMcenter (2013)
23. Pastor, O., España, S., Panach, J.I., Aquino, N.: Model-driven development. Informatik-Spektrum **31**(5), 394–407 (2008)
24. Maggi, F.M., Mooij, A.J., van der Aalst, W.M.: User-guided discovery of declarative process models. In: IEEE Symposium on Computational Intelligence and Data Mining (CIDM), 2011, pp. 192–199. IEEE (2011)
25. Møller, A.: dk.brics.automaton - Finite-state automata and regular expressions for Java (2010)

Deriving Decision Models from Process Models by Enhanced Decision Mining

Ekaterina Bazhenova[✉] and Mathias Weske

Hasso Plattner Institute at the University of Potsdam, Potsdam, Germany
{ekaterina.bazhenova,mathias.weske}@hpi.de

Abstract. Optimal decision making during the business process execution is crucial for achieving the business goals of an enterprise. Process execution often involves the usage of the decision logic specified in terms of business rules represented as atomic elements of conditions leading to conclusions. However, the question of using and integrating the process- and decision-centric approaches, i.e. harmonization of the widely accepted Business Process Model and Notation (BPMN) and the recent Decision Model and Notation (DMN) proposed by the OMG group, is important. In this paper, we propose a four-step approach to derive decision models from process models on the examples of DMN and BPMN: (1) Identification of decision points in a process model; (2) Extraction of decision logic encapsulating the data dependencies affecting the decisions in the process model; (3) Construction of a decision model; (4) Adaptation of the process model with respect to the derived decision logic. Our contribution also consists in proposing an enrichment of the extracted decision logic by taking into account the predictions of process performance measures corresponding to different decision outcomes. We demonstrate the applicability of the approach on an exemplary business process from the banking domain.

1 Introduction

Business process management is a widely adopted concept for managing an enterprise work. Making the right decisions during the business process execution is important for achieving the strategical and operational business goals [7,13]. The OMG group recently published the Decision Model and Notation (DMN) standard [17] that is supposed to complement BPMN for decision logic modeling and execution. However, an extra effort is needed to identify and implement integration of already existing and widely used process modeling and execution approaches with the new decision modeling standard. BPMN describes an end-to-end process as a flow of tasks, but the internal decision logic is often hidden in the process model in the form of implicit data dependencies, which makes it harder to derive the decision logic in an automated way [21].

In our paper, we address this issue by introducing an approach consisting of derivation of decision models from process models and execution logs on the examples of DMN and BPMN [16]. In particular, we derive the decision logic

© Springer International Publishing Switzerland 2016
M. Reichert and H.A. Reijers (Eds.): BPM Workshops 2015, LNBIP 256, pp. 444–457, 2016.
DOI: 10.1007/978-3-319-42887-1_36

in the form of decision tables from the event logs of a process model. Based on the derived decision logic, we show the way to construct a corresponding DMN decision model.

In the context of decision making in the business processes, often the strategic information is required, like, for example, knowledge about the time or risks associated with alternative actions to be taken. Deriving the decision logic, we also take into account the predictions of process performance measures corresponding to different decision outcomes, which is our another contribution.

2 Motivating Use Case

In this section we provide a description of the business process from the banking domain, to which we refer throughout the rest of the paper. The corresponding business process model is presented in Fig. 1; it is based on a step-by-step approach that is generally followed while assessing a personal loan [20].

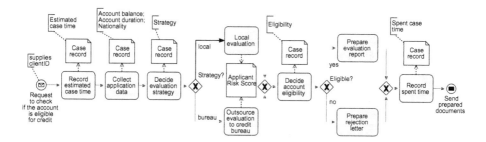

Fig. 1. Process model showing the example business process of assessing the credit

Upon receiving the request to check if the account is eligible for a credit, the bank worker firstly enters the estimated case time in the case record and then collects application data such as account balance, account duration, nationality, and registers it in the same case record. Afterwards, an expert decision is made about the evaluation strategy of the case: should it be done locally, or outsourced to a credit bureau. Presumably, there are guidelines identifying how the application risk score is assigned in the case of local evaluation; in the case of the credit bureau evaluation, the algorithm is not known. The process follows with an account eligibility decision, noted by a corresponding case recording. In case of a positive decision, the worker prepares an evaluation report, otherwise, a rejection letter. The process finishes after the worker sets the spent case time in the case record.

Figure 1 is a typical representation of a process model that is not aware of decisions. For example, the model contains textual annotations and decision activities which incorporate the business logic that is not represented explicitly in the model. It is not difficult to imagine that upon expanding, such process models quickly become complex, and the business logic management becomes tedious.

For understanding what would be a decision-aware process model in this case, we need to refer to the context of the business process. Nowadays there exist two main types of credit evaluation: (1) judgmental credit-evaluation systems, which may rely on the subjective evaluation of loan officers; and (2) credit-scoring systems that are empirically derived [5]. Basically, it has been settled in literature that using scoring in credit evaluation rules out personal judgment. In credit scoring systems, the decision are taken, depending on the applicant's total score, whilst in personal judgment this issue is neglected. The decision here depends on decision-makers' personal experience and other cultural issues, which vary from market to market [1]. With that, the brute force empiricism that characterizes the development of credit scoring systems can lead to a treatment of the individual applicant in an unjust manner; an example of such an occasion is judging the applicant's creditability by the first letter of a person's last name [6]. Thus, it seems reasonable to use automated credit scoring systems complemented with an explanatory model. The derivation of DMN decision model corresponding to this process model could provide such an explanatory model considering the past experiences, as the goal of the DMN standard is to provide basic principles and rules of thumb for organizing process models to maximize agility, reuse, and governance of decision logic in BPM solutions [21]. We demonstrate the derivation of such a model specific for the use case in Sect. 5.

3   Formal Framework

With respect for deriving the decision model from the process model and its execution log, we firstly review the most common ways to express decisions in process models. One of the most widely used decision construct is the exclusive gateway. It has pass-through semantics for exactly one out of a set of outgoing paths if the associated condition, a Boolean expression, evaluates to true [16]. Thus, a gateway does not "decide" anything; it just specifies the path taken by a process instance based on existing process data. For example, in Fig. 1 the evaluation strategy decision is taken in the activity preceding the corresponding gateway, which only uses the result of this decision.

Additionally, in our previous work [4], we identified further decision structures in process models, through analysis of 956 industry process models from multiple domains. We discovered that a single splitway pattern is a common decision pattern, which was used in 59 % of the models. For this paper, we use the notion of a *Decision point* [19], which corresponds to this single split gateway from our previous work. With that, we assume that the decision task preceding any decision gateway refers to the same business decision (the omission of this decision task is a common mistake made by inexperienced BPMN users [21]). Next, we provide the formal grounding distinguished into process modeling and decision modeling formalisms. We formally define the concepts of process model and decision point as follows.

Definition 1 (Process Model). *Process model* $m = (N, D, \Sigma, C, F, \alpha, \xi)$ consists of a finite non-empty set N of control flow nodes, a finite set D of data nodes, a finite set Σ of conditions, a finite set C of directed control flow edges, and a finite set F of directed data flow edges. The set of control flow nodes $N = J \cup E \cup G$ consists of mutually disjoint sets $J \subseteq T \cup S$ of activities being tasks T or subprocesses S, set E of events, and set G of gateways. $C \subseteq N \times N$ is the control flow relation such that each edge connects two control flow nodes. $F \subseteq (D \times J) \cup (J \times D)$ is the data flow relation indicating read respectively write operations of an activity with respect to a data node. Let Z be a set of control flow constructs. Function $\alpha : G \rightarrow Z$ assigns to each gateway a type in terms of a control flow construct. Function $\xi : (G \times N) \cap C \nrightarrow \Sigma$ assigns conditions to control flow edges originating from gateways with multiple outgoing edges. ◇

Definition 2 (Decision Point). Let $m = (N, D, \Sigma, C, F, \alpha, \xi)$ be a process model. Then $dp = (N', D', \Sigma', C', F', \gamma, \sigma)$ is a *decision point* of process model m if the following holds:

1. dp is a connected subgraph of process model m such that $N' \subseteq N$, $D' \subseteq D$, $\Sigma' \subseteq \Sigma$, $C' \subseteq C$, and $F' \subseteq F$;
2. Functions γ and σ are restrictions of functions α and ξ respectively with corresponding new domains;
3. $|G_{dp}| = 1 \wedge |g \bullet| \geq 2 \wedge (\gamma(g) = XOR \vee \gamma(g) = IOR)$, $g \in G_{dp}$ (the decision point contains exactly one split gateway),
4. $|J_{dp}| = |g\bullet| + 1$ (the number of activities of dp equals the number of outgoing edges[1] of the split gateway g plus 1),
5. $\bullet g = t \wedge |\bullet g| = 1, t \in T_{dp}$ (task t is the only predecessor of the split gateway),
6. $|\bullet t| = 0$ (task t is the start node of dp),
7. $\forall j \in J_{dp} \backslash t : \bullet j = g$ (all activities other than the one preceding the split gateway g directly succeed g),
8. $\forall j \in J_{dp} \backslash t : |j \bullet| = 0$ (all activities other than the one preceding the split gateway g are end nodes of dp), and
9. $\forall j \in J_{dp} \backslash t, c \in C_{dp}$ such that $(g, a) = c : \sigma(c) \in \Sigma_{dp}$ (all outgoing edges of the split gateway are annotated with a condition). ◇

We use subscripts, e.g., J_m or N_{dp}, to denote the relation of sets and functions to process model m, decision point dp, etc., and omit the subscripts where the context is clear.

Figure 2 presents two corresponding decision points with two alternative paths at the split gateway from the use case presented in the previous section. According to our assumption, the decisions are taken in the tasks preceding the gateways. In both of the decision points, since the gateway is of the type XOR, only one alternative can be chosen. In Decision Point 1 (dp_1, left part of the figure), based on the result of the task *Decide evaluation strategy*, different credit evaluation strategies are chosen (local or outsourcing to credit bureau).

---

[1] The number of outgoing (incoming) edges directly translates to the number of direct successors (predecessors) and vice versa.

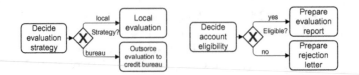

Fig. 2. Decision Points 1 and 2 referring to Fig. 1

In Decision Point 2 (dp_2, right part of the figure), based on the result of task *Decide account eligibility*, only one of the alternative activities is executed: the preparation either of the evaluation report, or of the rejection letter.

As decisions are happening within the scope of process models, it is important to take into account the process-related context. For deriving decisions, we propose to take into account in the context of a particular decision rule the quantifiable measures called *Key Performance Indicators* or *KPIs*. In our approach, we assume that the values of the KPIs are associated with the single activities of all the decision points of a process model.

Definition 3 (KPIs of Alternatives in a Decision Point). Let $DP = \{dp_1, \ldots, dp_M\}$ be a set of M decision points of a process model m. Then $K = \{K_1, \ldots, K_i\}$ is a set of $i \in \mathbb{N}^+$ *key performance indicators (KPIs)* if there is a function $\psi : (t_{dp_j} \bullet \times K) \twoheadrightarrow \mathbb{R}$, $1 \leq j \leq M$, which assigns the value of a given KPI to the tasks succeeding a gateway (alternatives) in each of the decision points of the process model. ◇

Our proposal is to enrich the business rules obtained by the decision mining in the previous section, by considering the values of the KPIs corresponding to the activities of a decision point. We will look at this in detail in Sect. 4.

DMN defines two levels for modeling decision logic, the *decision requirements level* and the *decision logic level*. The first one represents how *decisions* depend on each other and what *input data* is available for the decisions; these nodes are connected with each other through *information requirement edges*. A decision may additionally reference the decision logic level where its output is determined through an undirected association. The decision logic level describes the actual decision logic applied to take the decision. Decision logic can be represented in many ways, e.g. by a function or a decision table. In this paper, we utilize decision tables.

Definition 4 (Decision Requirement Diagram). *Decision requirement diagram* $drd = (D_{dm}, ID, IR)$ consists of a finite non-empty set D_{dm} of nodes called decisions, a finite set ID of input data nodes, and a finite set of directed edges representing information requirements: $IR \subseteq \{ID, D_{dm}\} \times D_{dm}$. ◇

Definition 5 (Decision Table). *Decision table* $dt = (I, O, R)$ consists of a finite non-empty set I of inputs, a finite non-empty set O of inputs, and a list of rules R, where each rule is composed of the specific input and output entries of the table row. ◇

Examples of the decision models will be given further in the paper (e.g., in Fig. 4); *decisions* are rectangles, *input data* are ellipsis, *information requirement edges* are solid, and the decision table associations are dashed.

4   Derivation of the Decision Model

In this section we propose the following step-by-step approach to derive decision models from process models. We demonstrate each step of the approach on the examples of BPMN process models and DMN decision models. The algorithm is expressed through BPMN process model, as shown in Fig. 3.

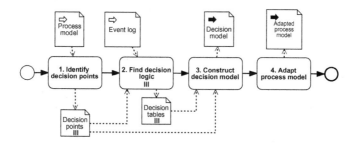

Fig. 3. Algorithm of derivation of the decision model and adaptation of the process model

The inputs to the algorithm are the process model m and the corresponding event log which contains the values of data object attributes assigned during the process execution. For concrete example of logs, see Sect. 5. The goal of the algorithm is to get the outputs: (1) The decision model consisting of one decision requirements diagram and corresponding decision tables; and (2) The adapted process model m', in which the described decisions are referenced by a *business rule* task. In order to simplify the algorithm explanation, we assume for the rest of this chapter, that each decision point of the input process model m contains only two outgoing control flow paths and, correspondingly, two alternative tasks to be executed, so that $|g \bullet| = 2$. The extrapolation of the algorithm for an arbitrary finite set of control flow paths and corresponding tasks will be presented in future work. Below we describe the actual algorithm step-by-step.

Step 1: Identify Decision Points. Firstly, the decisions points are identified in the input process model, accordingly to Definition 2: given a process model m, we determine constructs of directly succeeding control flow nodes that represent a gateway preceded by a task and succeeded by a task on each of the outgoing paths. The step output is a set of M decision points $DP = \{dp_1, \ldots, dp_M\}$ corresponding to a process model m.

Step 2: Find Decision Logic. The decision logic is extracted in the form of decision tables from a given process model m and a corresponding execution log by following the substeps below:

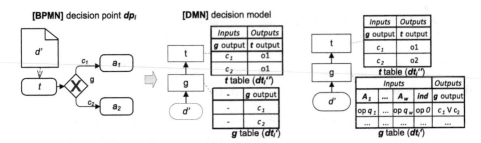

Fig. 4. Control-flow based mapping of a BPMN decision point and DMN decision model

Fig. 5. Enhanced decision model in case of 2 alternatives

2-A. We firstly build a *control-flow based skeleton* of the decision model to be derived, therefore utilizing the algorithm from our previous work [4], see Fig. 4.

The skeleton of the DMN decision model extracted from the arbitrary decision point dp_i of the process model m in Fig. 4 demonstrates that there are two decision tables to be considered. The first one is a decision table dt'_i which basically does not "decide" anything, as there are no rules for that; it reflects that the decision is chosen non-automatically (e.g., the case of judgmental credit evaluation systems). The second decision table dt''_i refers to the top-level decision and reflects the rule of process routing (o1 and o2 would be labels of the edges following the gateway of the decision point in the refactored model) after the strategy output was determined. What is of interest, is how to mine the meaningful explanatory business rules which will replace the dashes in dt'_i table (see Fig. 4).

2-B. Given is a process model m containing corresponding set $DP = \{dp_1, \ldots, dp_M\}$ of M decision points. Let $d' = (A_1, \ldots, A_v), v \in \mathbb{N}^*$ be a data node of the decision point which consists of the attributes $A_i, 1 \le i \le v$. The concrete values of these attributes are stored in the process execution log. The decision outcomes of the decision point $c_l \in C_{dp} = (c_1, \ldots, c_s)$, where $s, l \in \mathbb{N}^+, 1 \le l \le s$ are associated with control flow edges following the decision point gateway. The step outcome to be achieved is the *identification of the attributes* $(A_1, \ldots, A_w), 1 \le w \le v$ which have statistical correlation with the variable c in the log, which can be done, e.g., with the help of the correlation analysis.

2-C. Following the identification of the attributes which statistically correlate with the variable c, is the *decision rule extraction* in the following form: A_1 op $q_1, \ldots, A_w$ op $q_w \longrightarrow c_l$, where op is a comparison predicate and q is a constant. The concrete implementation of such extraction, e.g., with the help of the decision trees, can be found in [19]. This step is concluded with plain *transformation of the decision rules into a decision table* dt' (decision table dt'' contains user-made decisions, which can not be automatized with the help of rules as described above). The obtained table can be further contracted and minimized, e.g., following the techniques from [3].

2-D. The rules extracted at the previous step *explain what happened in the past.* However, taking into account the predictions of the values of KPIs of the alternatives to be taken based on their historical values recorded event log, can potentially *improve what will happen.* To achieve this, *the enrichment of the rules utilizing the KPIs* of the alternatives in the decision point (see Definition 3) is done at this step.

Given is $K = \{K_1, \ldots, K_i\}$, a set of $i \in \mathbb{N}^+$ key performance indicators (KPIs) which assigns the value of a given KPI to the tasks succeeding a gateway in each of the decision points of the process model. Let ind be a variable indicating the performance of which alternatives in the decision point is better: $ind = P(sum_{a_2}) - P(sum_{a_1})$, where $P(sum_{a_i})$ is a predicted value calculated as the expected value of the KPIs based on the historical records in the event log. In order to aggregate the values of KPIs, it is common to use the total performance function which sums them [18]: $sum = \sum_{j=1}^{i} K_j$. Taking into account the business goal is to maximize the total performance function, the decision rules extracted at the previous step, can be modified in the following way:

1. A_1 op $q_1, \ldots, A_w$ op $q_w, \boldsymbol{ind > 0} \longrightarrow c_l, l = 1, 2$
2. A_1 op $q_1, \ldots, A_w$ op $q_w, \boldsymbol{ind < 0} \longrightarrow \neg c_l, l = 1, 2$

In such a case, the mapping of the BPMN decision point from Fig. 4, will be refined as shown in Fig. 5. The concrete numerical examples for the rules enriched with predictions of the KPIs of alternatives in the decision point can be found in Sect. 5.

Step 3: Construct Decision Model. After the decision tables are identified for each decision point, the compound decision model of the whole process model can be constructed. The basic structure of the DMN elements corresponding to the decision point in the process model, is shown in Figs. 4 and 5. However, this mapping is not considering yet the data and decision dependencies in the process model. We suggest three complementing steps for completing the decision model, as described below.

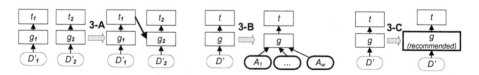

Fig. 6. Improvement of mapped elements of decision points

3-A. Let us assume that 2 arbitrary decision points dp_1 and dp_2 are found in a process model m, and dp_2 follows dp_1. The attributes which strongly correlate to the corresponding variables c_{dp_1} and c_{dp_2} were identified as an output from the previous step: $A_{dp_1} = (A_1, \ldots, A_{w_{dp_1}})$ and $A_{dp_2} = (A_1, \ldots, A_{w_{dp_2}})$. If there exist at least one attribute $y \in \mathbb{N}^+$, such that $A_y \in A_{dp_2} \backslash A_{dp_1}$ and $A_y \equiv o_x, x \in \mathbb{N}^+$, where o_x is the output of dp_1, then there is a data dependency between the top level decision t_{dp_1} and the gateway (data-based) decision g. In such a case, in the resulting DMN diagram there should be a corresponding information requirement (directed edge) inserted (left fragment in Fig. 6).

3-B. As the decision model needs to be explanatory, we suggest to replace the input data node corresponding to the mapping of a decision point to a decision model (described on the previous step) by w input data nodes, the names of which correspond to the attributes $(A_1, \ldots, A_w)$, $w \leq v$ which correlate statistically with the decision (central fragment in Fig. 6), in this manner they "explain" the decision.

3-C. At last, we suggest to concatenate the name of the gateway decision g in the resulting decision model with the string "recommended", so that the difference between the gateway and the top-level decision is clearer for the user: in the first case, the business rule is triggered, and in the second case, the actual decision is taken (either automatically, or manually), and the automated process routing happens (right fragment in Fig. 6).

Step 4: Adapt Process Model. After deriving the decision logic from a process model to a decision model, the process model needs to be adapted in order to be consistent together with the decision model. Basically, the entire decision logic is hidden inside of the first decision task of the decision point. For that purpose, BPMN offers *business rule tasks* that can be linked to decision models and that will output the value of the top-level decision of the decision model.

5   Application to Use Case

The approach is evaluated by showing its applicability to a credit assessment use case introduced in Sect. 2. An exemplary process execution log can be seen in Fig. 7; it is constructed analogously to the real-life German credit data set publicly available[2].

   For applying the algorithm introduced in the previous section, we consider two KPIs associated to the alternatives of the decision points. The first one is the time spent for the execution of the alternative task in a decision point, a very common performance measure for analyzing processes [10]. The second KPI which we will utilize, is the risk score. For making the credit decision, the credit scoring serves as a relevant performance measurer: by providing a low-cost and standardized metric of credit risk which strengthen the scrutiny of lending activities [5]. As one can see from Fig. 1 depicting the process model, there are two alternative activities representing the evaluation strategies. The result of their execution are records of the *Applicant Risk Score* data object. An instance of local evaluation and risk score assignment could be summing the points received on the various application characteristics to arrive at a total

---

[2] https://archive.ics.uci.edu/ml/datasets/Statlog+(German+Credit+Data).

caseID	esT	accB	accD	ifF	strategy	eligibility	KPI$_1$ (time)	KPI$_2$ (risk score)
1	20	2500	3	≠ F	local	Y	0.35	0.15
2	18	4720	1	F	bureau	N	0.42	0.42
3	22	1600	1	≠ F	local	N	0.41	0.25
4	19	150	5	≠ F	local	Y	0.37	0.21
5	20	800	1.5	F	bureau	N	0.45	0.43
6	21	590	3	F	bureau	N	0.42	0.31
7	22	430	1	≠ F	local	Y	0.31	0.23
8	17	4200	4	F	local	Y	0.33	0.12

Parameter	Risk score points
Account balance	
≥500	0.02
<500	0.01
Account duration	
≥0.5	0.03
<0.5	0.01
Nationality	
non-foreigner	0.02
foreigner	0.01

Fig. 7. Exemplary event log referring Fig. 1: *esT* - estimated case time, *accB* - acc. balance, *accD* - acc. duration, *ifF* - nationality

Fig. 8. Example of risk scoring guideline

score. An example of scoring guidelines is presented in Fig. 8. In the alternative evaluation strategy, the credit bureau can give their own estimations of risk score, based both on the applicants data sent, and their own data (like information whether the person was bankrupt or not). It is assumed that introduced KPIs are measured in abstract time units. Below we apply to the use case the step-by-step approach from the previous chapter.

Step 1. The identification of the decision points was done by using the Decision Miner plug-in of the ProM Framework[3]. The detailed explanation of the elements of the decision points is given in Sect. 3, as well as their visualization (Fig. 2).

Step 2. The analysis of the decision points with the help of Decision Miner showed that the parameters strongly correlating with the decision variable *Strategy* are *accB, accD, ifF*, and the parameters influencing the decision *Eligibility* are *accB, accD, ifF, strategy*. It is expectable that the parameter *esT* (estimated case time) does not correlate with the decision whether to give the credit or not. As well, with the help of the Decision Miner, we extract the business rules which we demonstrate on the example of the decision *Strategy*, see Fig. 9. We manually

Rule No	Inputs accB	Inputs accD	Inputs ifF	Outputs strategy
1	> 1000	> 2	≠ F	local
2	> 1000	> 2	= F	bureau
3	> 1000	< 2	≠ F	bureau
4	> 1000	< 2	= F	bureau
5	< 1000	> 2	≠ F	local
6	< 1000	> 2	= F	bureau
7	< 1000	< 2	≠ F	local
8	< 1000	< 2	= F	bureau

Rule No	Inputs accB	Inputs accD	Inputs ifF	Outputs strategy
1	> 1000	> 2	≠ F	local
2	> 1000	> 2	= F	bureau
3	> 1000	< 2		bureau
4	< 1000		≠ F	local
5	< 1000		= F	bureau

Rule No	Inputs ifF	Inputs accB	Inputs accD	Outputs strategy
1	≠ F	> 1000	>2	local
2		> 1000	<2	bureau
3		< 1000		local
4	= F			bureau

Fig. 9. Expanded, contracted, and minimised decision tables for the use case (Strategy decision)

---

[3] The Decision Miner, which is embedded in the ProM framework, can be downloaded from www.processmining.org.

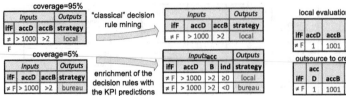

Fig. 10. Mined decision rules enriched with predictions of KPI values

Fig. 11. Execution log containing KPI values for two evaluation strategies

minimized the number of columns of a resulting decision table, according to the techniques from [3]. In the expanded table, every column comprises the derived decision rule. The contracted table is derived from the expanded decision table by combining logically adjacent columns that lead to the same action configuration. The number of columns in a contracted decision table can be further minimized by changing the order of the condition rows.

The enhancement of the obtained decision table with the help of KPIs associated to the alternatives of the decision points of a process model, is demonstrated in example shown in Fig. 10. Imagine that one of the candidate rules to be extracted is as shown in the figure, so that the coverage of the rule "$ifF \neq F \wedge accD > 2 \wedge accB > 1000 \longrightarrow strategy = local$" is 95 %, and the coverage of the rule "$ifF \neq F \wedge accD > 2 \wedge accB > 1000 \longrightarrow strategy = bureau$" is 5 %. In the classical mining, only one rule with the highest coverage that satisfies a given threshold will be chosen. However, let us consider the process instance execution, recorded in the event log as shown in Fig. 11. The case of local evaluation whether the client is eligible for a credit takes less time than in the case of requesting credit bureau to do the evaluation. With that, the risk score assigned by the credit bureau is lower than the risk score which would be assigned by local evaluation. We assume as described in the previous section, that the total performance is measured by summing the KPI values, and in such a case, it can be seen that outsourcing the evaluation to a credit bureau results in a better process performance. With that, if we simply followed the rule obtained by classical mining (Fig. 10, top right), then we would have to execute the process in a way which would result in a worse performance. However, an enrichment of the decision rules with the KPIs predictions (Fig. 10, bottom right), a rule leads to a better process performance.

Step 3. The consequent application of the suggestions from the previous section, yields the following decision model shown in Fig. 12 for our use case. The skeleton of the decision points was built analogously to the mapping depicted at Fig. 4. Then, it was established during the decision logic extraction (which we partly omit) that there are data dependencies between decision points dp_1 (Strategy) and dp_2 (Eligibility). Therefore, an information requirement is added to the decision model (directed edge between "Decide evaluation strategy" and "Eligibility" decisions). Also, input data "case record" was replaced by the attributes which statistically were correlated based on the records from the event log to the corresponding decisions (*Account balance*, *Account duration*, and *Nationality*). At last, the labels of the gateway data-based decisions *Strategy* and *Eligibility* were concatenated with the strings "recommended" so as to reflect that the decision logic in the form of business rules was related to them.

Step 4. Adaptation of the process model in our use case works as follows: in the Fig. 1, the types of the tasks *Decide evaluation strategy* and *Decide account eligibility* will be changed into *business rules* tasks. These business rules will be referencing the corresponding decision tables, e.g. the Strategy table shown in Fig. 9.

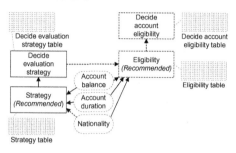

Fig. 12. Constructed decision model referring to Fig. 1.

The extracted decision model in Fig. 12 reflects explicitly the decisions corresponding to the process model from Fig. 1, and therefore, could be served as an explanatory model, e.g., for compliance checks. Another advantage of the derived decision model is that it permits changes in the decision model without changing the process model, and vice versa, which supports the principle of separation of concerns [21].

6   Related Work

Lately, both scientific and commercial communities shared increasing interest towards exploring the decision support in organizations demonstrated by an increasing number of emerging approaches on different decision ontologies [12] and decision service platforms [2,22]. Similarly to our point of view, the motivation to separate decision from process logic is discussed in [9,21].

Improving business process decision making based on past experience is described in [11], but without considering the specifics of DMN standard. Another approach explores possibilities of improving the decisions within a DMN model [15], but is not concerned with the problem of the integration of BPMN and DMN. Additionally, [8] puts forward a general technique to discover branching conditions where the atoms are linear equations or inequalities involving multiple variables and arithmetic operators; it can be used for enhancing our approach.

With respect to the algorithm for mining the decision rules, there are multiple works done, among them three approaches to solve the rules classification problem are prominent [3,14,19]. The first one – solving the decision mining by constructing a neural network – gives very accurate classifications, but the output rules might be quite complex which is then hard to translate into a self-explanatory decision model [3]. The second one – mining the decision rules with the help of support vector machines – also provide very accurate classifications, however, there are no existing solutions of translating the output support vector machines into the business rules [14]. With that, the application of the third approach (shown in our paper) – solving the rule classification problem with the help of the decision trees – allows easy creation of business rules from the output decision trees, although the classification accuracy is worse in this case than in two approaches mentioned above [19].

7   Conclusion

Following the motivation of separation of concerns, in this paper we provided a formal framework to derive decision models from process models on the examples of DMN and BPMN notations. In particular, we provided an approach to firstly identify the decision points in a process model, then to extract the decision logic containing the data dependencies derived from the process model, followed by the construction of decision requirements diagram and adaptation of the process model with respect to the derived decision logic. We demonstrated that the decision rule extraction can be enriched by taking into account the predictions of process performance measures corresponding to different decision outcomes. The approach was evaluated by showing its applicability to a use case from a banking domain.

The presented approach is our first step in investigating the possibility of derivation of DMN process model from process model and its execution log. For that, we assumed that each decision point of the input process model contains only two outgoing control flow paths and, correspondingly, two alternative tasks to be executed. In future, we plan to generalize this for an arbitrary finite set of control flow paths and corresponding tasks. Secondly, we plan to include into the framework the extraction of the decision rules by discovering branching conditions where the atoms are linear equations or inequalities involving multiple variables and arithmetic operators, as in [8]. Further, we will do an implementation of the provided framework and provide the extended approach evaluation by applying it to business processes from multiple domains.

References

1. Abdou, H.A., Pointon, J.: Credit scoring, statistical techniques and evaluation criteria: a review of the literature. Int. Syst. Account. Finance Manage. **18**(2–3), 59–88 (2011)
2. SAP AG: http://scn.sap.com/docs/DOC-29158. Accessed 13 Nov 2014
3. Baesens, B., Setiono, R., Mues, C., Vanthienen, J.: Using neural network rule extraction and decision tables for credit - risk evaluation. Manage. Sci. **49**(3), 312–329 (2003)
4. Batoulis, K., Meyer, A., Bazhenova, E., Decker, G., Weske, M.: Extracting decision logic from process models. In: Zdravkovic, J., Kirikova, M., Johannesson, P. (eds.) CAiSE 2015. LNCS, vol. 9097, pp. 349–366. Springer, Heidelberg (2015)

5. Board: report to the congress on credit scoring and its effects on the availability and affordability of credit. Technical report, August 2007
6. Capon, N.: Credit scoring systems: a critical analysis. J. Mark. **46**(2), 82–91 (1982)
7. Catalkaya, S., Knuplesch, D., Chiao, C., Reichert, M.: Enriching business process models with decision rules. In: Lohmann, N., Song, M., Wohed, P. (eds.) BPM 2013 Workshops. LNBIP, vol. 171, pp. 198–211. Springer, Heidelberg (2014)
8. de Leoni, M., Dumas, M., García-Bañuelos, L.: Discovering branching conditions from business process execution logs. In: Cortellessa, V., Varró, D. (eds.) FASE 2013 (ETAPS 2013). LNCS, vol. 7793, pp. 114–129. Springer, Heidelberg (2013)
9. Debevoise, T., Taylor, J.: The MicroGuide to Process Modeling and Decision in BPMN/DMN. CreateSpace Independent Publishing Platform (2014)
10. Dumas, M., La Rosa, M., Mendling, J., Reijers, H.A.: Fundamentals of Business Process Management. Springer, Heidelberg (2013)
11. Ghattas, J., Soffer, P., Peleg, M.: Improving business process decision making based on past experience. Decis. Support Syst. **59**, 93–107 (2014)
12. Kornyshova, E., Deneckère, R.: Decision-making ontology for information system engineering. In: Parsons, J., Saeki, M., Shoval, P., Woo, C., Wand, Y. (eds.) ER 2010. LNCS, vol. 6412, pp. 104–117. Springer, Heidelberg (2010)
13. Lohrmann, M., Reichert, M.: Modeling business objectives for business process management. In: Stary, C. (ed.) S-BPM ONE – Scientific Research. LNBIP, vol. 104, pp. 106–126. Springer, Heidelberg (2012)
14. Lovell, B.C., Walder, C.J.: Support vector machines for business applications. In: Business Applications and Computational Intelligence, p. 267 (2006)
15. Mertens, S., Gailly, F., Poels, G.: Enhancing declarative process models with DMN decision logic. In: Gaaloul, K., Schmidt, R., Nurcan, S., Guerreiro, S., Ma, Q. (eds.) BPMDS 2015 and EMMSAD 2015. LNBIP, vol. 214, pp. 151–165. Springer, Heidelberg (2015)
16. OMG: Business Process Model and Notation (BPMN) v. 2.0.2 (2013)
17. OMG: Decision Model and Notation (DMN) v. 1 (2014)
18. Pufahl, L., Bazhenova, E., Weske, M.: Evaluating the performance of a batch activity in process models. In: Fournier, F., Mendling, J. (eds.) Business Process Management Workshops. LNBIP, vol. 202, pp. 277–290. Springer, Heidelberg (2014)
19. Rozinat, A., van der Aalst, W.M.P.: Decision mining in business processes. Technical report, BPM Center Report BPM-06-10 (2006)
20. Sathye, M., Bartle, J., Vincent, M., Boffey, R.: Credit Analysis and Lending Management. Wiley, Milton (2003)
21. Von Halle, B., Goldberg, L.: The Decision Model: A Business Logic Framework Linking Business and Technology. Taylor and Francis Group, Boca Raton (2010)
22. Zarghami, A., Sapkota, B., Eslami, M.Z., van Sinderen, M.: Decision as a service: separating decision-making from application process logic. In: EDOC. IEEE (2012)

A Framework for Recommending Resource Allocation Based on Process Mining

Michael Arias[(⊠)], Eric Rojas, Jorge Munoz-Gama, and Marcos Sepúlveda

Computer Science Department, School of Engineering,
Pontificia Universidad Católica de Chile, Santiago, Chile
{m.arias,eric.rojas}@uc.cl, {jmun,marcos}@ing.puc.cl

Abstract. Dynamically allocating the most appropriate resource to execute the different activities of a business process is an important challenge
in business process management. An ineffective allocation may lead to
an inadequate resources usage, higher costs, or a poor process performance. Different approaches have been used to solve this challenge: data
mining techniques, probabilistic allocation, or even manual allocation.
However, there is a need for methods that support resource allocation
based on multi-factor criteria. We propose a framework for recommending resource allocation based on Process Mining that does the recommendation at sub-process level, instead of activity-level. We introduce a
resource process cube that provides a flexible, extensible and fine-grained
mechanism to abstract historical information about past process executions. Then, several metrics are computed considering different criteria
to obtain a final recommendation ranking based on the BPA algorithm.
The approach is applied to a help desk scenario to demonstrate its usefulness.

Keywords: Resource allocation · Process mining · Business processes ·
Recommendation systems · Organizational perspective · Time perspective

1 Introduction

Dynamic resource allocation is an important and challenging issue within business process management [8,20]. It can contribute significantly to the quality and
efficiency of business processes, improve productivity, balance resource usage,
and reduce execution costs. This article describes a framework that supports
resource allocation based on multi-factor criteria, considering both resources
capabilities, past performance, and resources workload.

An initial strategy is to assign to a given activity a resource whose profile is
closest to the profile required by the activity. However, this strategy does not
consider the current workload of the resource or how successful the resource
has been performing similar tasks in the past. To fill this gap, it is possible to
take advantage of historical information stored by today's information systems
about business processes execution, knowing who executed what activity, when,

M. Reichert and H.A. Reijers (Eds.): BPM Workshops 2015, LNBIP 256, pp. 458–470, 2016.
DOI: 10.1007/978-3-319-42887-1_37

and how long it took. Moreover, recently it has been proposed to use historical information stored in event logs to improve resource allocation using process mining techniques [20].

Different mechanisms have been proposed to allocate resources to activities [6,8–12,16,18]. In [18], several workflow resource patters are identified. For example, three allocation types defined are: capability-based allocation, history-based allocation and role-based allocation. Capability-based allocation provides a mechanism for allocating a resource to an activity through matching specific requirements for an activity with the capabilities of the potential range of resources that are available to undertake it. History-based allocation involves the use of information on the previous execution history of resources when determining which of them to allocate to a given activity. Role-based allocation assigns a resource to an activity based on their position within the organization and their relationship with other resources. In this article we consider the first two and assume role-based allocation can be used a priori to filter the potential resources. In capability-based allocation, usually a profile is defined for specifying resources capabilities and activities requirements (cf. Table 1). Organizational models [13,16], and resource meta-models [6,10,18], have also been used to represent resources capabilities. Among the resource allocation algorithms, we can highlight: data mining techniques and machine learning algorithms to derive allocation rules based on log events [9,11,12,16], and dynamic context-based resource allocation based on Markov decision process [8] or resource allocation based on hidden Markov models [10]. A more recent approach [6] allows specifying preferences for different resources using expressions based on a Resource Assignment Language (RAL), and generating a resources ranking considering a meta-model.

Table 1. Comparison with the related work.

	[18]	[16]	[12]	[8]	[10]	[9]	[11]	[6]	Proposed
Activity profile		✓							✓
Resource profile	✓	✓			✓			✓	✓
Performance & quality									✓
Resource meta-model	✓				✓			✓	✓
History	✓	✓	✓	✓	✓	✓	✓	✓	✓
Process mining tool		✓			✓				✓
Allocation at sub-process level									✓

In this article, we propose a framework for recommending resource allocation based on process mining. We introduce a resource process cube that provides a flexible, extensible and fine-grained mechanism to abstract historical information about past process executions, extracted from process event logs. One difference between our approach and the approaches proposed in the literature is that we consider sub-processes as the target allocation unit; however, it can also be used to allocate resources at the activity level or at the process level, as a whole (see Sect. 2). Also, several metrics are computed over the cube, considering different criteria: fitting between resources capabilities and the expertise required to perform an activity, and past performance (frequency, duration, quality and cost). These metrics are combined to obtain a final recommendation ranking based on the Best Position Algorithm (BPA). The request to recommend the allocation of a resource is described as follows:

Definition 1 (Recommended Resource Allocation Request). *A recommended resource allocation request function is a function $req(c, i, w) = rank$, that given a process characterization c, a resource allocation information (historical and contextual) of the process execution i, and the weights describing the importance of each criterion w, returns a ranking of the most suitable resources to be assigned.*

The remainder of the article explains the different elements of this request, and it is structured as follows: in Sect. 2 the characterization of a resource allocation request is presented. Section 3 proposes the use of historical and contextual information to measure six different process criteria for an accurate resource allocation request. Section 4 presents the weighting of the different criteria and the recommendation algorithm. The implementation of the approach and its experimental evaluation is discussed in Sect. 5. Finally, the paper is concluded and future work is discussed in Sect. 6.

2   Resource Allocation Characterization

The first necessary step for a proper resource allocation is to characterize the request, i.e., what part of the process is the resource request for, and how similar is this request to others in the past. Most of the approaches in the literature limit that characterization to a simple *activity* level [9,10,12,16], i.e., a resource is always assigned to a single activity of the process, and only historical information of the execution of that activity is considered for future allocations.

In this article we propose a more flexible resource allocation characterization, where the allocations are not done at an activity-level or a process-level, but at a *sub-process-level*, i.e., the overall process is decomposed into sub-processes, and a resource is allocated for the execution of each sub-process. The decomposition of the process may be done manually using the own semantics of the process. For instance, let us consider a help-desk process (`HelpDesk`), for a company that provides support for both printers and servers. The process is decomposed by the two levels of customer interaction: first-contact level 1 and expert level 2. Each one of the two levels may correspond with a different sub-process. The decomposition may also involve an automatic process decomposition [1], using some of the decomposition approaches proposed in the literature, like Passages [3] or Single-Entry Single-Exit (SESE) [14]. Notice that, by definition, an activity or the overall process are also sub-processes. Therefore, the flexible resource allocation characterization proposed allows also the classical allocations at the activity or process levels. The usage of context dependent activity ordering is seen as a current challenge within intention-centric business process domain [5]. Considering the execution context can be useful for selecting the appropriate sub-process or select the required tasks for each process instance, allowing the optimization of resource allocation. Additionally, the sub-process characterization is combined with a typology characterization, i.e., the historical information is classified and used depending on the typology of the request. For instance, different typologies of processes may distinguish between normal/VIP clients, English/Spanish/German languages, or Internet/call-center interactions. In the HelpDesk example we consider two types of requests: printer-related and server-related problems. Note that, increasing the number of typologies may narrow the focus, but it may cause also a scarcity problem, i.e., not having enough information of each typology for a proper recommendation.

Definition 2 (Characterization of a Resource Allocation Request). *A resource allocation request characterization $c = (f_1, \ldots, f_n)$ is a multi-factor representation of the request properties. The two-factor characterization proposed is a tuple $c = (SP, T)$, where SP defines the sub-process where the resource is being requested, and T is the typology of the process execution that request the resource.*

In HelpDesk, $c_1 = (level1, printer)$ and $c_2 = (level2, server)$ represent two different request characterizations for the same help-desk process.

3 Resource Allocation Criteria

The simplest resource allocations rely on pure random assignments between resources and requests. As it is shown in Table 1, more advanced systems base their decisions on specific criteria, e.g., the resource that is estimated to spend less time, or the one with more experience performing a task. In this article we propose a six-dimension recommended allocation that uses both historical and contextual information. The proposed dimensions are:

- Frequency Dimension: measures the rate of occurrence that a resource has completed the requested characterization.
- Performance Dimension: measures the execution time that a resource has achieved performing the requested characterization.
- Quality Dimension: measures the customer evaluation of the execution of the requested characterization performed by a resource.
- Cost Dimension: measures the execution cost of the requested characterization performed by a resource.
- Expertise Dimension: measures the ability level at which a resource is able to execute a characterization.
- Workload Dimension: measures the actual idle level of a resource considering the characterizations executed at the time.

Notice that the flexible nature of the proposed framework allows the inclusion of new dimensions, and the extension with other metrics proposed in the literature. In the remainder of this section we formalize the historical and contextual information used on the resource allocation request, in terms of resource process cubes and expertise matrices, respectively (Sect. 3.1), and we propose metrics to assess each one of the dimensions (Sect. 3.2).

3.1   Resource Process Cube and Expertise Matrices

We define the *resource process cube* $\mathbb{Q}$ as the semantic abstracting all the historical execution information of the process to be analyzed. The resource process cube is inspired by the process cubes presented in [2], and its definition is closer to the well-known OLAP cubes [7], providing slice and dice operations for the analysis of each specific characterization and resource.

Definition 3 (Resource Process Cube). *Let r, c, and d, be a resource, resource allocation request characterization, and dimension, respectively. A resource process cube $\mathbb{Q}[r][c][d]$ abstracts all the historical information about the resource r and the characterization c necessary to analyze the dimension d. Similarly, $\mathbb{Q}[\ ][c][d]$ abstracts the historical information about all resources for the execution of the characterization c, and $\mathbb{Q}[r][\ ][d]$ abstracts the information for all the characterizations performed by r.*

For example, in `HelpDesk`, given a characterization $c_1 = (level1, printer)$ and a resource $r_1 = mike$, $\mathbb{Q}[r_1][c_1][p]$ provides all the historical information related about the performance, such as, what is the maximal and minimal time *mike* needed to perform c_1 (denoted as $\mathbb{Q}[r_1][c_1][p].max$ and $\mathbb{Q}[r_1][c_1][p].min$, respectively), or the average time required by *mike* to perform c_1 (denoted as $\mathbb{Q}[r_1][c_1][p].avg$). Similarly, $\mathbb{Q}[\ ][c_1][p].max$ represents the maximal time required considering all the resources.

Note that, the resource process cube is a high-level semantic abstraction of the historical information, rather than an implementational definition. Therefore, the cube can be implemented using any database (relational or non-relational) or OLAP technology, and including, for example, pre-calculated values, or shared values among cells.

Besides historical information, the expertise dimension requires contextual information, i.e., it compares the current level of expertise of each resource with the desired level of expertise for the characterization to be performed. In [15] the authors propose a Human Resource Meta-Model (HRMM) where the expertise of the resources is classified by competencies, skills, and knowledge. Based on that model, we represent the expertise of a resource r as an array of naturals $\mathbb{E}_r[1 : n]$, where each position represents a specific competence, skill or knowledge, and the value of $\mathbb{E}_r[i]$ range from $\perp_i$ (usually 0 indicating the lack of competence/skill/knowledge i) to $\top_i$ (complete expertise on the competence/skill/knowledge i). The set of arrays for all the resources is known as the expertise resource matrix. Similarly, we represent the desired level of expertise required for performing a characterization c as the array $\mathbb{E}_c[1:n]$. For instance, given the characterization $c_1 = (level1, printer)$ and a resource $r_1 = mike$, $\mathbb{E}_{c_1} = [2,2]$ denotes a mid-high required level (assuming $\top = 3$ and $\bot = 0$ for both positions) on printer hardware (position 1) and printer software (position 2), while $mike$ has a low or non existent knowledge on printers denoted as $\mathbb{E}_{r_1} = [0,1]$.

3.2 Resource Allocation Metrics

In this subsection we present metrics for each one of the six before mentioned dimensions. All the metrics proposed are normalized between 0 and 1, and they satisfy the set of properties proposed in [17]: *validity* (i.e., metric and property must be sufficiently correlated), *stability* (i.e., stable against manipulations of minor significance), *analyzability* (i.e., measured values should be distributed between 0 and 1 with 1 being the best and 0 being the worst), and *reproducibility* (i.e., the measure should be independent of subjective influence).

In the remainder of the section we consider a resource process cube $\mathbb{Q}$ representing the historical information of the process, and expertise matrices $\mathbb{E}_r$ and $\mathbb{E}_c$ representing the expertise information.

Frequency Dimension: Let $\mathbb{Q}[r][c][f].total$ be the number of times a resource r has performed the characterization c. Let $\mathbb{Q}[\ ][c][f].total$ be the number of cases of characterization c. We define the metric as (1):

$$Frequency\_Metric(r,c) = \frac{logarithm(\mathbb{Q}[r][c][f].total) + 1}{logarithm(\mathbb{Q}[\ ][c][f].total) + 1} \quad (1)$$

We use a logarithmic scale since we are mainly interested in measuring different magnitude orders between potential resources.

Performance Dimension: Let $\mathbb{Q}[r][c][p].avg$ be an operation that returns the average duration, considering only cases in which the resource r has taken part in executing the characterization c. Let $\mathbb{Q}[\ ][c][p].min$ and $\mathbb{Q}[\ ][c][p].max$ be the minimum and maximum duration for executing the characterization c. We define the metric as (2):

$$Performance\_Metric(r,c) = \frac{\mathbb{Q}[\ ][c][p].max - \mathbb{Q}[r][c][p].avg}{\mathbb{Q}[\ ][c][p].max - \mathbb{Q}[\ ][c][p].min} \quad (2)$$

Quality Dimension: Let $\mathbb{Q}[r][c][q].avg$ be an operation that returns the average quality, considering only cases in which the resource r has taken part in executing the characterization c. Let $\mathbb{Q}[\ ][c][q].min$ and $\mathbb{Q}[\ ][c][q].max$ be the minimum and maximum quality evaluation for the executed characterization c. We define the metric as (3):

$$Quality\_Metric(r,c) = \frac{\mathbb{Q}[r][c][q].avg - \mathbb{Q}[\ ][c][q].min}{\mathbb{Q}[\ ][c][q].max - \mathbb{Q}[\ ][c][q].min} \quad (3)$$

Cost Dimension: Let Q[r][c][co].avg be an operation that returns the average cost, considering only cases in which the resource r has taken part in executing the characterization c. Let Q[ ][c][co].min and Q[ ][c][co].max be the minimum and maximum cost for the executed characterization c. We define the metric as (4):

$$Cost\_Metric(r, c) = \frac{Q[\ ][c][co].max - Q[r][c][co].avg}{Q[\ ][c][co].max - Q[\ ][c][co].min} \tag{4}$$

Expertise Dimension: To determine if a resource r is qualified to execute a characterization c, we present two metrics that uses the expertise matrices explained in Sect. 3.1. To evaluate this dimension, we compare the value of each level of expertise $\mathbb{E}_r$ with the corresponding value in $\mathbb{E}_c$, in order to measure the under-qualification or the over-qualification level of a resource. To define the under-qualification metric, we first calculate an under-qualification degree comparing each value as follows in (5):

$$under(i) = \begin{cases} \frac{\mathbb{E}_c[i] - \mathbb{E}_r[i]}{\mathbb{E}_c[i] - \bot_i} & \text{if } \mathbb{E}_c[i] \geq \mathbb{E}_r[i] \\ 0 & \text{otherwise} \end{cases} \tag{5}$$

Then the metric to measure the under-qualification is defined as (6):

$$UnderQualification\_Metric = 1 - \frac{1}{n}\sqrt{\sum_{i=1}^{n}\left(under(i)\right)^2} \tag{6}$$

Symmetrically, to determine the over-qualification metric, we define (7):

$$over(i) = \begin{cases} \frac{\mathbb{E}_r[i] - \mathbb{E}_c[i]}{\top_i - \mathbb{E}_c[i]} & \text{if } \mathbb{E}_r[i] \geq \mathbb{E}_c[i] \\ 0 & \text{otherwise} \end{cases} \tag{7}$$

The metric to measure the over-qualification of a resource is then defined as (8):

$$OverQualification\_Metric = 1 - \frac{1}{n}\sqrt{\sum_{i=1}^{n}\left(over(i)\right)^2} \tag{8}$$

In both qualification metrics, n represents the number of expertise elements in the matrix. We use the Euclidean distance because all expertise features are equally relevant, are defined in the same scale, and to favor smaller differences in all features at the same time. Notice that if the expertise of a resource r perfectly match with the expertise required for a characterization c, the value for both metrics will be 1.

Workload Dimension: Let Q[r][ ][w].total be a function that returns the number of cases in which a resource r is working at the moment when a new resource allocation request is required. Let Q[r][ ][w].top and Q[r][ ][w].bottom be the maximum and minimum number of cases that a resource can attend simultaneously. We define the metric as (9):

$$Workload\_Metric(r,c) = \frac{Q[r][\ ][w].top - Q[r][\ ][w].total}{Q[r][\ ][w].top - Q[r][\ ][w].bottom} \qquad (9)$$

4   Recommended Resource Allocation

We face the challenge of allocating appropriate resources to execute characterizations dynamically. We propose a recommendation system to create a final resource ranking, considering the six dimensions presented in Sect. 3. The recommendation system is inspired on the portfolio-based algorithm selection [19]. To accomplish this goal, we consider the top-k queries, a technique that allows to obtain the k most relevant items in a dataset. According with [4], to give an answer to top-k queries we use m lists of n data items, so that each data item has a local score in each list, and the lists are ordered accordingly to the local score of its data items. With those lists, the BPA algorithm [4] can be used to get the top-k results.

In order to obtain the most appropriate resource, we need to generate an ordered list of resources according to their metric scores in every dimension. Before applying the algorithm, we need to combine all ordered metric score lists considering the weights specified for each dimension, e.g., we could give more importance to the cost and frequency dimensions, rather than quality or expertise. If the user does not want to incorporate weights for the recommendation, each m list is not modified; otherwise, each local score is multiplied by the respective weight, generating updated m lists.

Giving the m lists, the final ranking can be calculated by applying the BPA algorithm, which is used to find the k-data items that have the highest overall score. BPA calculates the overall score for each data item, registering the best seen positions, and maintain in a set Y the k-data items with the highest overall score. The algorithm allows an iterative approach to access and evaluate the resources based on their local score and the position in each list. If at same point the set Y contains k-data items whose overall scores are higher than or equal to a generated *threshold*, then there is no need to continue scanning the rest of the lists. The output of the algorithm is an ordered list, where the final score for each resource is stored. The first value represents the resource with the highest overall score and therefore the best recommendation. For details on the algorithm we refer the reader to [4].

5   Implementation and Experimental Evaluation

A real-life help desk process (HelpDesk) was selected to evaluate our approach. We focused on two typologies: printers and servers. The HelpDesk process includes two attention levels and their corresponding activities (sub-process 1 and sub-process 2). For the executed experiments, event logs with different amount of cases were simulated. The attributes for each case include Case ID, Subprocess group, Process Typology, Resource, Cost, Customer Satisfaction (Quality), Creation date, Closing date and Priority. Three experiments were performed:

- **Experiment 1:** Calculate the top 3-queries processing over the sorted lists, considering each single metric by itself.
- **Experiment 2:** Reproduce an scenario for 3 types of companies: a large size called General Consulting, a small size called Service Guide, and a mid size company named DeskCo. Specific weight values were defined for each scenario.
- **Experiment 3:** A similar scenario as the described in experiment 2, but both the event log size and the amount of resources were increased. Due to the variety in the resource quantity, we calculated the top-2 queries with 28 resources, preserve the top-3 with 20, and use top-5 queries with 70 resources.

Discussion: Table 2 specifies the parameters used in the different experiments and their results. For experiments 1 and 2 (with 20 resources), an event log was simulated, which includes 3 resources whose frequency of participation in

Table 2. Resource recommendations for the 3 experiments

Exp.	Weights (%)	# Cases	#R SP1	#R SP2	Ranking	Time (sec)
1.1	F:100 - others:0	1200	20	20	R06: 0.601 - R04: 0.593 - R05: 0.554	0.954
1.2	P:100 - others:0	1200	20	20	R03: 0.851 - R02: 0.833 - R01: 0.832	0.954
1.3	Q:100 - others:0	1200	20	20	R09: 0.913 - R07: 0.864 - R08: 0.808	0.954
1.4	C:100 - others:0	1200	20	20	R18: 0.962 - R20: 0.962 - R19: 0.959	0.954
1.5	U:100 - O:100 - others:0	1200	20	20	R12: 1.000 - R13: 1.000 - R14: 1.000	0.954
2.1	F:010 - P:050 - Q:010 C:100 - U:015 - O:000	1200	20	20	R20: 0.647 - R03: 0.635 - R18: 0.632	11.122
2.2	F:025 - P:015 - Q:100 C:030 - U:075 - O:065	1200	20	20	R19: 0.802 - R14: 0.758 - R13: 0.754	11.565
2.3	F:050 - P:050 - Q:050 C:050 - U:050 - O:050	1200	20	20	R19: 0.725 - R03: 0.712 - R02: 0.675	10.897
3.1.1	F:010 - P:050 - Q:010 C:100 - U:015 - O:000	1200	14	14	R01: 0.795 - R02: 0.788 - R14: 0.784	10.942
3.1.2	F:010 - P:050 - Q:010 C:100 - U:015 - O:000	10000	14	14	R13: 0.769 - R02: 0.567 - R14: 0.758	17.160
3.1.3	F:010 - P:050 - Q:010 C:100 - U:015 - O:000	100000	14	14	R13: 0.767 - R14: 0.765 - R02: 0.764	59.063
3.2.1	F:010 - P:050 - Q:010 C:100 - U:015 - O:000	1200	20	20	R19: 0.649 - R20: 0.647 - R03: 0.635	11.122
3.2.2	F:010 - P:050 - Q:010 C:100 - U:015 - O:000	10000	20	20	R01: 0.586 - R03: 0.582 - R02: 0.573	17.642
3.2.3	F:010 - P:050 - Q:010 C:100 - U:015 - O:000	100000	20	20	R01: 0.834 - R20: 0.784 - R18: 0.783	58.913
3.3.1	F:010 - P:050 - Q:010 C:100 - U:015 - O:000	1200	35	35	R03: 0.626 - R05: 0.618 - R04: 0.572	11.014
3.3.2	F:010 - P:050 - Q:010 C:100 - U:015 - O:000	10000	35	35	R04: 0.608 - R05: 0.603 - R01: 0.599	17.739
3.3.3	F:010 - P:050 - Q:010 C:100 - U:015 - O:000	100000	35	35	R04: 0.593 - R02: 0.580 - R11: 0.428	58.637

F= Frequency, P= Performance, Q= Quality, C= Cost, U= Underqualified, O= Overqualified, R= Resource and others= Other dimensions the case resolution in `HelpDesk` is higher compared to the other resources of the same level. Equally, it was simulated the existence of 3 resources that have better resolution time resolving cases, 3 resources that perform better in quality, 3 resources that present the lowest costs, and 3 resources that fit the expertise level required.

In **experiment 1**, it is possible to observe that the best specified resources for each dimension are the expected, existing a clear correlation between the proposed metric for each dimension.

In **experiment 2**, for each company different weights are specified, according to the priorities for each one (e.g., General Consulting (exp. 2.1) has an interest for cheaper and faster solutions; Service guide (exp. 2.2) gives more importance to quality services and DeskCo (exp. 2.3) prefers giving a medium value to all dimensions). Considering the criteria established in the Resource Allocation Request function, complex and high calculation results are obtained faster and simpler. If top-3 queries are applied, the results for each company establish a ranking with the recommended resources, different from experiment 1. The recommended resources are different for each company, proving that our approach produces resource recommendations based on the given requests. For example, for the General Consulting Company, R20, R03 and R18 are recommended under the criterion of low cost but balanced with the resolution mean time. For DeskCo, R19, R03 and R02, are the suitable ones to accomplish the activities based on the criteria established in the request.

In **experiment 3** (exp. 3.1.1 to exp. 3.3.3) a similar scenario to the experiment 2 was executed, but with changes on the amount of cases and resources per attention level. Logs with 1.200, 10.000, 100.000 and 500.000 cases were considered; and the amount of resources are 28, 40 and 70. Figure 1a displays the behavior of the processing time according to the amount of cases. As it can be seen, when more historical data is used to make the recommendation, a linear relation appears between the time and the log size. If the log size is larger, the information to be processed by the cube is larger and higher is the time to generate the ranking, but this dependency is linear. This proves that it is possible to process large amounts of information through the technique and get quick response times, and if its required, it is possible to include additional dimensions to get a better recommendation. Figure 1b displays that the result of using the BPA algorithm is not dependent of the number of resources used at the allocation request moment. It was proven, in an experimental way, it is possible to obtain the recommended resources ranking without having to visit all positions in the ordered list, thanks to the threshold management and the early stop condition of the BPA algorithm. This confirms that the results of the BPA algorithm are constant regarding the amount of resources given to resolve the top-k queries problem, which could be very useful for companies with high quantity of resources.

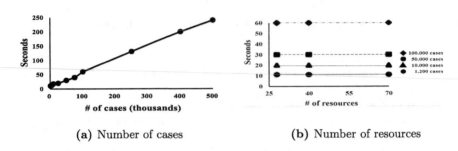

(a) Number of cases   (b) Number of resources

Fig. 1. Performance analysis

6   Conclusions and Future Work

We proposed a flexible framework for dynamically allocating the most appropriate resources to execute a sub-process. Our contributions are fourfold. First, while other approaches focus only on a single process perspective, the proposed framework considers the organizational, time and case perspectives. We define specific dimensions to assess different resource features: frequency, performance, quality, cost, expertise, and workload. Secondly, unlike others approaches in the literature that consider resource allocation only at an activity level, the proposed framework considers it at a generic sub-process level (an activity can be seen as a specific-case). Third, the resource allocation request, together with a precise characterization of both resources and activities, provide a fine-grained degree of customization. Finally, the conceptual framework is designed to be generic and extensible, being able to adapt to any company-specific scenario.

Our work has been implemented and tested in a `HelpDesk` scenario, and the experimental results show that given a specific characterization it is possible to obtain a final ranking of recommended resources based on multi-factor criteria. We tested the BPA algorithm with different event log sizes and resource amounts. We observed a linear relation between the algorithm performance and the log size. Moreover, the BPA algorithm confirms its efficiency to compute top-k results independent of the amount of resources.

As future work, we plan to extend the comparison with existing works in order to generate a comprehensive theoretical analysis and enhance the experimental evaluation. We aim to evaluate the effectiveness and the efficiency of alternative approaches and compare them with our framework in a partial or complete way. We plan to use artificial scenarios and case studies with real data to validate our recommendation technique. This could be useful to compare the results obtained by other approaches and real resource allocations, with the ones proposed by our framework. Incorporate new dimensions to the resource process cube for improving the analysis may also be considered. This work attempts to encourage organizations to use real performance time, quality and cost data, to generate better resource allocations.

Acknowledgments. This work is partially supported by Comisión Nacional de Investigación Científica – CONICYT – Ministry of Education, Chile, Ph.D. Student Fellowships, and by University of Costa Rica Professor Fellowships.

References

1. van der Aalst, W.M.P.: Decomposing petri nets for process mining: a generic approach. Distrib. Parallel Databases **31**(4), 471–507 (2013)
2. van der Aalst, W.M.P.: Process cubes: slicing, dicing, rolling up and drilling down event data for process mining. In: Song, M., Wynn, M.T., Liu, J. (eds.) AP-BPM 2013. LNBIP, vol. 159, pp. 1–22. Springer, Heidelberg (2013)
3. van der Aalst, W.M.P., Verbeek, H.M.W.: Process discovery and conformance checking using passages. Fundam. Inform. **131**(1), 103–138 (2014)
4. Akbarinia, R., Pacitti, E., Valduriez, P.: Best position algorithms for efficient top-k query processing. Inf. Syst. **36**(6), 973–989 (2011)
5. van Beest, N., Russell, N., ter Hofstede, A.H.M., Lazovik, A.: Achieving intention-centric BPM through automated planning. In: 7th IEEE International Conference on Service-Oriented Computing and Applications (SOCA 2014), Matsue, Japan, November 17–19, 2014, pp. 191–198 (2014)
6. Cabanillas, C., García, J.M., Resinas, M., Ruiz, D., Mendling, J., Ruiz-Cortés, A.: Priority-based human resource allocation in business processes. In: Basu, S., Pautasso, C., Zhang, L., Fu, X. (eds.) ICSOC 2013. LNCS, vol. 8274, pp. 374–388. Springer, Heidelberg (2013)
7. Chaudhuri, S., Dayal, U.: An overview of data warehousing and OLAP technology. ACM Sigmod Rec. **26**(1), 65–74 (1997)
8. Huang, Z., van der Aalst, W.M.P., Lu, X., Duan, H.: Reinforcement learning based resource allocation in business process management. Data Knowl. Eng. **70**(1), 127–145 (2011)
9. Huang, Z., Lu, X., Duan, H.: Mining association rules to support resource allocation in business process management. Expert Syst. Appl. **38**(8), 9483–9490 (2011)
10. Koschmider, A., Yingbo, L., Schuster, T.: Role assignment in business process models. In: Daniel, F., Barkaoui, K., Dustdar, S. (eds.) Business Process Management Workshops. Lecture Notes in Business Information Processing, vol. 99, pp. 37–49. Springer, Heidelberg (2012)
11. Liu, T., Cheng, Y., Ni, Z.: Mining event logs to support workflow resource allocation. Knowl. Based Syst. **35**, 320–331 (2012)
12. Liu, Y., Wang, J., Yang, Y., Sun, J.: A semi-automatic approach for workflow staff assignment. Comput. Ind. **59**(5), 463–476 (2008)
13. Ly, L.T., Rinderle, S., Dadam, P., Reichert, M.: Mining staff assignment rules from event-based data. In: Bussler, C.J., Haller, A. (eds.) BPM 2005. LNCS, vol. 3812, pp. 177–190. Springer, Heidelberg (2006)
14. Munoz-Gama, J., Carmona, J., van der Aalst, W.M.P.: Single-entry single-exit decomposed conformance checking. Inf. Syst. **46**, 102–122 (2014)
15. Oberweis, A., Schuster, T.: A meta-model based approach to the description of resources and skills. In: AMCIS, p. 383 (2010)
16. Rinderle-Ma, S., van der Aalst, W.M.P.: Life-cycle support for staff assignment rules in process-aware information systems (2007)
17. Rozinat, A., van der Aalst, W.M.P.: Conformance testing: measuring the alignment between event logs and process models. BETA Research School for Operations Management and Logistics (2005)

18. Russell, N., van der Aalst, W.M.P., ter Hofstede, A.H.M., Edmond, D.: Workflow resource patterns: identification, representation and tool support. In: Pastor, Ó., Falcão e Cunha, J. (eds.) CAiSE 2005. LNCS, vol. 3520, pp. 216–232. Springer, Heidelberg (2005)
19. Xu, L., Hutter, F., Hoos, H.H., Leyton-Brown, K.: Satzilla: portfolio-based algorithm selection for SAT. CoRR abs/1111.2249 (2011)
20. Zhao, W., Zhao, X.: Process mining from the organizational perspective. In: Wen, Z., Li, T. (eds.) Foundations of Intelligent Systems. Advances in Intelligent Systems and Computing, vol. 277, pp. 701–708. Springer, Heidelberg (2014)

Context and Planning for Dynamic Adaptation in PAIS

Vanessa Tavares Nunes[1,2(✉)], Flávia Maria Santoro[3], Claudia Maria Lima Werner[2], and Célia Ghedini Ralha[1]

[1] Computer Science Department, Institute of Exact Sciences, University of Brasilia,
P.O. Box 4466, Brasilia, 70904-970, Brazil
{vanessanunes,ghedini}@cic.unb.br
[2] COPPE/PESC – Systems Engineering and Computer Science Program – UFRJ, P.O. Box 68511,
Rio de Janeiro, 21945-970, Brazil
werner@cos.ufrj.br
[3] Department of Applied Informatics, UNIRIO, Rio de Janeiro, Brazil
flavia.santoro@uniriotec.br

Abstract. The need for constant adaptation to address emerging demands or undesired events within organizations has grown. Unplanned situations may occur at any time during process execution and the design of a process model that predicts all paths should give place to flexible "organic" design. This paper addresses the problem of how to provide mechanisms for dynamic adaptation in Process-Aware Information Systems. On top of a theory for context-aware information systems, we propose a context management framework that aims to automate dynamic process adaptation by re-planning a process instance. The proposal was partially implemented and evaluated in a real case scenario.

Keywords: Dynamic adaptation · Context-aware process · Process-Aware Information Systems · Planning

1   Introduction

Information technology has changed business process within enterprises as they increasingly depends on Information Systems (IS) driven by process models (Process-Aware Information Systems - PAIS) [1, 2]. Besides, the need for constant adaptation of work to address emerging demands has grown. This research focuses on structured and interactive processes like automotive engineering, healthcare or product change management where there are a set of activities and resources that have a dependency among each other over time (state changes). In this view we make use of imperative languages in order to describe the process in terms of its state space and how to identify and get from one state to another, as discussed by [3]. Nevertheless, describing all possible paths in a process model can harm its understanding and stability due to the high degree of complexity and changes required [4, 5]. The design of a process model predicting all possibilities has given place to a flexible design based on reuse and adaptation [2].

An important strategy is the ability to react to (complex) situations that may occur at runtime by dynamically adapting the process when required. In this scenario there are many concurrent process instances in execution in which human intervention is less

© Springer International Publishing Switzerland 2016
M. Reichert and H.A. Reijers (Eds.): BPM Workshops 2015, LNBIP 256, pp. 471–483, 2016.
DOI: 10.1007/978-3-319-42887-1_38

acceptable because it can be time-consuming, high costly and error-prone [6]. However, dynamic process adaptation is still not fully addressed in literature.

This paper addresses the problem of providing mechanisms for dynamic adaptation in PAIS through a systematic approach. A framework to handle process instance adaptations at runtime and improve knowledge about process definition, variations and goals is proposed. The approach is built on the concept of context and planning techniques and a prototype for the adaptation reasoning was developed. We argue that a situation is characterized by a number of contextual elements that should guide the task of re-planning a process instance keeping it aligned to predefined goals.

The paper is organized as follows. Section 2 presents the research background; Sect. 3 discusses related work; Sect. 4 describes the proposed solution with the GCAdapt prototype; Sect. 5 evaluates the prototype in a real scenario; and, Sect. 6 concludes the paper and discusses further research perspectives.

2 Research Background

In this section, we present the three pillars of this research work: context, a design theory for context-aware information systems and automated planning.

Context is related to how a social and cultural phenomenon is interpreted within a perspective or interpretation. We adopt the definition proposed by [7]: context is a complex description of the shared knowledge about physical conditions, social, historical and others in which actions and events occur. We also adopt the conceptual models proposed by [8] for the representation of context in business process. Context is the set of contextual elements (CE) instantiated and combined that are necessary to characterize a situation occurred during the execution of a process activity.

A theory-driven design of Context-Aware Information System (CAIS) was taken as a conceptual foundation [9] to serve as basis to operationalize context and business process concepts. In this work, a set of prescriptive statements with guidelines were derived from a set of five meta-requirements (MR) based on the extensions of design propositions for work system theory [10] and theory of adaptive systems [11]. These MR describe the class of problems addressed by context-aware IS design theory, intending to provide prescriptions to: model domain work system and relevant context; specify strategies for context-based adaptations; and increase work system and context models by learning. From each MR, we derived a set of meta-design features (MD), which describes the prescriptions that a CAIS needs to implement, in order to support dynamic adaptation. MR-03 relates to strategies for implementing context reasoning, which is related to the third pillar of our approach (planning).

Dynamic process adaptation could be conceived as a planning task [12]. Planning is a proceeding that chooses and organizes actions by anticipating their expected outcomes. Planning algorithms search for plans of actions that succeed not only for a given initial state, but also under potential circumstances, aiming at achieving as best as possible specified goals. Then, a process and its possible adaptations can be considered as a set of actions and resources that may have constraints among them (e.g., action A must be performed before action B), and manipulate a set of data, aiming at achieving a desired goal according to a desired performance. In this scenario, the context that characterizes situations during process execution may provide insights for planners when producing a plan for a given problem.

3 Related Work

Many proposals focusing on process adaptation have been described in literature. In [13], the authors propose a methodology and a prototype toolkit to address process variability at runtime under the concept of context-aware software product lines based on the configuration of a standard process, its variations and the use of constraint satisfaction problem to reason on adaptation decision.

Regarding workflow-based systems, [14] propose a temporal rule-based system for deciding and performing automated adaptations at runtime. Among the PAIS proposals that deal with different types and levels of adaptation stand out: YAWL [15], FLOWer [2], Declare [16], ADEPT [17] and AristaFlow [18]. All of them support dynamic adaptation in some degree at design-time, by deviation, by under specification or by change, mostly considering the control flow perspective, using a rule-based reasoning approach [19]. The main drawback of these approaches is that, despite being aligned with organizational goals, rule-based adaptations require constant maintenance efforts due to their static nature.

In [20], the authors propose the use of PLANLETS within YAWL that are self-contained specifications with pre-conditions, desired effects and post-conditions. PLANLETS adapts process flow automatically at runtime, by handling exceptions without human interaction. It assumes dynamic adaptation management to be integrated to the PAIS. In [21], the authors propose an approach for automating business process reconfiguration at runtime by using AI planning techniques. This works has a similar approach to our research, although planning algorithms, planner tools and domain/problem language representation of business process are different. We claim that a domain (processes, components, constraints, rules, etc.) is always in constant evolution. Thus, it may also be modified, demanding the planners to reason over it, and re-plan process instances. Our scenario is a PAIS dealing with a structured flow. In this setting, the process and its alignment to organizational needs, demands and self-characteristics should be considered when a situation occurs, i.e., a change in the domain needs to be considered in the process as a whole.

4 GCAdapt

GCAdapt is a context management framework that addresses dynamic process adaptation life-cycle based on context and planning concepts. In this section the conceptual basis, design and implementation of GCAdapt are presented.

4.1 Concepts Operationalization

Based on the theory-driven design for CAIS proposed by [9] and the Multilayer Context
Metamodel proposed by [8], we propose a class diagram of the Goal-Process-Context
concepts to illustrate the concepts and the relationships (Fig. 1). Classes are explained
(highlighted in text) as follows.

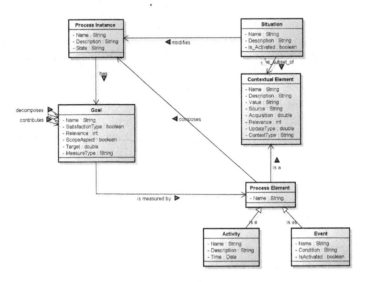

Fig. 1. Goal-process-context concepts

A **Process Instance** represents one specific execution of a process and it has one or
more **Goals** (restricted goals) to achieve. A Process Instance is composed of a number
of **Process Elements**, which are all the concepts represented in the Business Process
Metamodel (e.g., the concepts Activity and Event were represented in the figure). Each
Process Element value can be a **Contextual Element (CE)** (i.e., data value and resource
status), depending on its relevance to the process monitoring. A set of specific CE values
(or range of values) constitutes a **Situation** that indicates the need to modify and re-plan
a specific process instance.

We assume PAIS is a type of CAIS, so all properties defined by [9] apply, and we
extended each of the five MR, based on the analysis of the context-process concepts
operationalization. As an example, MR-03 defines how tasks, technology, structure and
people are adapted in response to a context change. The rule-based adaptation strategy
was substituted by the planning approach. We extended the MD designed to solve the
problems proposed for each MR. For each of the 20 MD we defined the operationalization prescriptions for a context-aware PAIS stating how PAIS and GCAdapt should
operate. As an example: MD-12 defines prescriptions for control adaptation strategies
that come from and trigger a system-internal or an environmental change. We extended
those definitions by defining operationalization for each strategy considering a context-
ware PAIS. As for in MD-12, a **Situation** may characterize a change in the environment
(**CE** values). So GCAdapt must be able to: computationally represent the Situation

within domain and problem; reason and decide adaptations in control flow. Considering self-self adaptation, GCAdapt monitors, decides and sends to PAIS the order to adapt the process instance.

4.2   The Procedures

We proposed procedures to support the context management life cycle for dynamic process adaptation which is an evolution of preliminary versions presented in [22, 23]. The steps are divided in two main phases: Design Time and Run Time.

At design time, the domain infrastructure is elicited and configured. The process model is defined (the **process elements** are modeled), **CE** related to the process is elicited, process variants are identified, **situations** already known are modeled and everything is linked to represent domain and problem definitions of the world. Initially, experts' opinion and historical data may be used to define the first set of information that PAIS and GCAdapt should work with. As instances are executed, learning abilities act to enhance GCAdapt reasoning abilities.

At runtime, instances are executed, monitored and adapted. Context identification occurs from the combination of CE values captured during the execution of process instance activities that trigger process instance re-plan. Based on the new situation at hand (which may modify domain and/or problem definitions through changes in resources, environmental conditions, policies, constraints and goals), GCAdapt reasons over the new reality and decides for the optimal procedure in order to make the process instance more effective.

4.3   The GCAdapt Design

CGAdapt (Fig. 2) (preliminary version presented in [23]) provides a central server supporting the whole context management life cycle for dynamic process adaptation. The context-reasoning engine was designed separately from the running process through a PAIS approach. Thus, PAIS becomes less rigid, more easily maintained, and only concerned with process implementation. The framework comprises services that provide distributed intelligence, and allows interactivity between capturing mechanisms and implementation, having autonomous and proactive behavior. The framework has four main components: Aggregator, Mediator, Maintainer and Actuator. They interface with Context and Processes repositories, with the capturing and implementation mechanisms, and the PAIS.

CE capturing can vary from manual to fully automated, through independent *CE Capturing Mechanisms*, depending on the available infrastructure and type of information. *Aggregator* receives a collection of CE, and verifies if a **Situation** is to be activated. Situations identified during **process instance** execution are stored in the log *Repositories* for future process learning. *Aggregator* can be seen as a middleware between the *CE Capturing Mechanisms* and the *Mediator;* it is not concerned on how to collect CE and identify Situations, but only on how to interface with *Mediator*.

Mediator is responsible for deciding an adaptation when a situation occurs during process instance execution, when the adaptation should be performed and its impact in

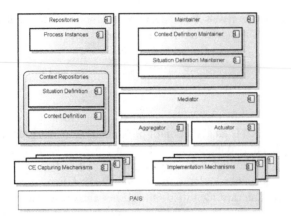

Fig. 2. GCAdapt - context management framework for dynamic process adaptation

the process and organizational **goals**. Its key features are intelligent behavior and decision-making support skills. *Mediator* reasons over a situation that will not lead the process instance to a stable state or will not lead the process instance into its best performance, in order to decide if an adaptation should be taken. When a Situation is activated, *Mediator* represents the world current status (i.e., work system including process, systems, people, organization and inside/outside data) redefining domain and problem definitions. It then reasons over the new definitions in order to continue satisfying, at best, process and organizational goals.

Maintainer is responsible for keeping *Context Definition* and *Situation Definition* updated through the *Context Definition Maintainer* and the *Situation Definition Maintainer*, respectively.

Actuator receives the adaptation reasoned by the Mediator, and sends the appropriate commands to perform the necessary adaptations in the process through the implementation mechanisms. The *Implementation Mechanisms* are responsible for the interface between GCAdapt and PAIS to implement the necessary changes.

4.4   The GCAdapt Implementation Details

Aggregator and *Actuator* were partially implemented together with *Mediator*, as a unique service, to work with the processes used in the observational study described in Sect. 5. The implementation was built on top of YAWL [15], that provides support for flexibility through the concept of worklets, which are self-contained processes associated to rules. The Planner adopted was SAPA [24]. SAPA is a domain-independent planner with a forward chaining algorithm that can handle durative actions, metric resource constraints and deadline goals. In summary, it is a multi-objective metric temporal planner. SAPA is developed using JAVA Technology, and handles Planning Domain Definition Language (PDDL) 2.1. Figure 3 depicts the interface among YAWL PAIS, the GCAdapt modules and SAPA Planner.

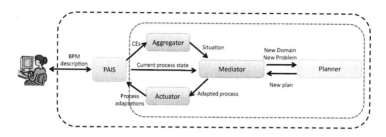

Fig. 3. Architecture for the association among PAIS, GCAdapt main modules and planner

The implementation works as follows: (i) the process instance is executed in YAWL, which manages flow control, resources and data; (ii) *Aggregator* receives CEs data from YAWL and sends it to the *Mediator*, if relevant; (iii) *Mediator* changes PDDL problem description based on CEs values and/or PDDL domain description if there are changes in rules, goals, constraints or variants. It generates new process definitions as a PDDL description for SAPA Planner to reason, receiving the new plan in return. Based on each adaptation informed by the *Mediator*, *Actuator* enables the implementation mechanisms related to one of the existing adaptation strategies. We proposed a parser between YAWL process and worklets XML definitions in domain and problem PDDL description, where we assume the tasks of a process and each worklet specification as planning actions. One contribution of this work is the construction of *Mediator* as a Yawl Custom Service. It interfaces with *Interface X* available in YAWL architecture (it notifies process current status), before the execution of each activity, to reason over process instance, goals and constraints without the need to maintain adaptations rules based on variable statements.

The integration of *Mediator* with YAWL was made based on the YAWL Worklet Service implementation. The conditions and worklets execution rules were defined through customized functions. So five new functions were developed and used as conditions expressions in rule nodes (through the class *RdrConditionFunctions*) and, together with *Mediator* (a standalone application) track and trigger the selected worklets. So, worklets are created as defined by YAWL, and Mediator Service receives information updated from process instance execution, modifies domain and problem XMLs files, transforms them into PDDL files, and call SAPA to re-plan it. *Mediator* enables worklets based on the new plan generated.

5   Observational Study

In this section, we present a real case scenario evaluation of the proposal. The goal was to **analyze** dynamic process adaptation using the GCAdapt prototype, **regarding** adaptation feasibility and effectiveness, **from the viewpoint of** the Researcher and the Domain Expert, **in the context of** a real aircraft takeoff process scenario.

The conditions under which the observational study was executed were: (i) The study was conducted using an Aircraft Takeoff process modeled within the Galeão International Airport in Rio de Janeiro, Brazil. It runs on large scale, with many instances executing simultaneously. The process was modeled and a subset of relevant CE was elicited in [8] based on interviews with two air traffic controllers, each with over 30 years of experience, and a pilot with 29 years of experience adding up more than 2,500 flight hours; (ii) The CE and Situations were elicited with a domain expert at the Brazilian Airspace Traffic Control (ATC) during this research; (iii) The process was modeled using BPMN notation attending the organization BPM methodology. Afterwards they were converted to the YAWL notation based on Petrinets; (iv) In order to simulate possible Situations, CEs values were generated randomly; (v) Situations were presented to other specialists (different from the previous ones) so as to be evaluated by them; (vi) The research proposal was presented to the specialists and they were asked about its benefits.

5.1   The Aircraft Takeoff Process

A simplified Aircraft Takeoff is represented in BPMN to depict the process model (Fig. 4). A sample of real data regarding instances of the Aircraft Takeoff Process was used as a base to elicit situations in order to carry on the study in this research. It presents information about rates of flight delays, weather conditions at airports, weather conditions during flight, airport infrastructure (inoperativeness of technical equipment, problems on runways), flow management measures and other occurrences in order to reason over the main goal: guarantee passengers and aerodrome safety. Based on the CEs presented in [8], in this work, 9 situations and 7 worklets were elicited and modeled (an example is shown in Fig. 5.).

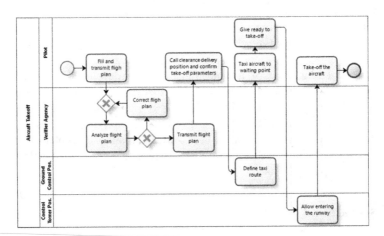

Fig. 4. Aircraft takeoff process model

As an example, Situation S2, is presented: Unfavorable meteorological condition under equipment unavailability. After the execution of activity "Transmit flight plan" the situation could be triggered. S2 = {"Fill and transmit fight plan" activity status = completed, Amount of rain fall in destination (RainfallLevelDestination) = high, EquipmentAvailability = false}.

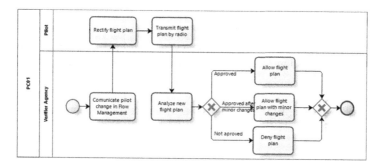

Fig. 5. BPMN designed worklet PC_01

5.2 Evaluation and Discussion

Four research questions, focusing on a performance and organizational suitability point of view, were defined: RQ1: Was GCAdapt-Mediator able to adapt the process correctly? This question aims to determine if it is possible to generate adapted processes using the proposed approach (GCAdapt + SAPA + YAWL) implementation. The results obtained from the analysis of this issue allow the discussion of the applicability of the approach to adapt processes that continue to run properly; RQ2: Are the adapted instances more adherent to current demands (the goals) than the standard process? This question seeks to evaluate if the adapted process may have a better performance than the standard one; RQ3: Is the process representation (process and variations separately) within the proposed approach more efficient than the conventional one contained in a unique model? This question seeks to evaluate if the process models structure is considered more efficient compared to traditional approaches; RQ4: Do the models produced by the approach require less time to be adapted in comparison to a manual analysis? RQ1 was evaluated by checking the running instances after adaptation; RQ2, RQ3 and RQ4 were evaluated through data collected from an interview with four pilots.

The independent variables considered are related to: (a) The specialists who validated process models, components, CE and Situations: They work in the process, not being possible to increase control over the level of experience and knowledge; (b) Size, complexity and relevance of the domain: The ATC scenario was chosen due to its remarkable relevance, highly dynamic, and because it presents a number of factors that could possibly interfere with the process execution.

Threats to the study validity are: (i) Internal validity: Simulation of situations were randomized (it is not possible to confirm the combinations of CE is a real possibility) so the study was not biased; Situation elicitation was partial and simplified. But, it was still considered by the interviewed experts as possible; choosing YAWL and SAPA, limits the approach to: the level of flexibility in adaptation supported by YAWL and the richness of PDDL notation supported and the reasoning algorithm implemented by SAPA; (ii) External Validity: The study is not exhaustive. Further evaluations with a larger number of processes in different domains have to be performed; (iii) Construct Validity: Participants were chosen for convenience. They could be biased by the expected results and towards researcher's intentions although during interviews they were first presented with Situations and only after their decisions they had access to GCAdapt findings; (iv) Conclusion Validity: the processes goals adherence analysis was not ideal, because other experts from different process roles are needed. Therefore, this study presents a limitation related to the results, which will be considered only as evidence.

Table 1 summarizes the four questions, variables analyzed, and results that are detailed in the sequence. RQ1 was evaluated by checking the running instances after adaptation; RQ2, RQ3 and RQ4 were evaluated through data collected from an interview with four pilots.

Table 1. Aircraft takeoff process – summarized questions, variables and results

RQn	Variable	Results
RQ1	Model correctness	All situations were correctly reproduced. All models were considered correct accordingly to YAWL quality model checking
RQ2	Process performance	Answers adherent to situations presented. 9 situations (7 adherents). Many more factors may impact in decision making
RQ3	User satisfaction	Evidence that the approach was considered useful in supporting the accomplishment of the research goals
RQ4	Reasoning time	$T < 2$ s; Reaction time considered fast when $T < 5$ min; PSPACE-Complete problem; Precedence relations among actions; Evidence: $T < 8$ min (500 s)

RQ1: 5 process instances were randomly created, and through each adaptation the new process structure was analyzed. All 5 tests worked as planned. Worklets were enacted as soon as they appeared in the plan, considering that all of them were supposed to be executed right after situations that triggered them were activated.

RQ2: The pilots were presented to the 9 Situations and 4 possible actions to react on them. In general, they choose *Mediator* suggestions as a possibility. 2 not matched situations could be related to other not modeled CE that must be taken into consideration. Pilot P3 observed that situations were correctly elicited, and the adaptations applied, but decisions are made based on a more complex combination of CE. Pilot P1 reported that data such as type of mission (commercial or military), distance from destination, destination airport infrastructure and aircraft technology, are to be taken into account when reasoning on the situations. At the end, they all agreed with the Mediator suggestions, considering the CE at hand.

RQ3: 10 questions related to the GCAdapt approach (procedure execution and CE awareness, reasoning and learning) where made. Pilots were also asked to assign a score from 1 (strongly disagree) to 5 (strongly agree) to the benefits of GCAdapt: decrease in time perception of unexpected events (average: 4.5), dissemination of information to all participants of the takeoff procedure (av.: 3.5); decision making and suggestion of actions to react to unexpected events (av.: 5); maintenance of standard process documentation, simple, easy to understand and independently representation of different (re)actions to be taken depending on the situation (av.: 4.75); and learning based on previous takeoff over actions related to unexpected events and the outcome of the takeoff procedure in order to improve computational reasoning (av.: 5). All the pilots envisioned potential in the research approach (total average: 4.55). A disagreement from Pilots P1 (av.: 3.5 on one benefit) comes from the fact that he flies commercial flights and the others pilots are militaries. Due to companies' interests, some decisions are not in pilot's hands as in military aviation. For him, being aware of information that he has "no managerial power" brings a sense of frustration.

RQ4: The total time to reason and act on situations was under 2 s. In general, computational complexity from propositional STRIP planning, to determine if a given planning instance has any solution, is PSPACE-complete [25] which is seen as "efficient". The performance of SAPA [26] was tested using complex domain and problems as Zeno Travel [27]. Results show that most of the problems are solved within 500 s. When considering imperative processes as a planning problem, one has to take into consideration that domain represents actions with precedence rules among them. So complexity is mostly subject to the objects (resources and data) that are to be manipulated in the problem instance. Discussing response time, the four pilots said that for the situations presented, 5 min to decide is considered fast enough.

6 Conclusion

This paper presented: GCAdapt, a framework for dynamic process adaptation addressing context management; and a prototype for GCAdapt-Mediator, to reason and decide process adaptations. GCAdapt identifies situations that demand process behaviors not defined by default; and as so, understands how context affects process, reasoning about the adaptation through planning in a goal-oriented way. In order to enhance PAIS abilities to dynamically adapt process instances, we improve context-awareness about the organizational environment in which a process instance is inserted so as to reason autonomously. The motivation for planning is very practical: it is concerned with choosing and organizing actions based on changes in the state of a work system. It is able to reason over variables, possible actions, goals, policies, constraints, and preferences that exist in a given moment. Since PAIS deals with this information, there is not the burden of maintaining rules and constraints.

Based on the real application scenario, we obtained evidences about the feasibility of the proposal since the outcomes from the execution of the inferences and tasks of the planner resulted in a coherent process, whose instance could achieve the desired goals. From pilots' viewpoint, it is feasible to perform computational reasoning based on context monitoring in spite of dealing with a very complex environment.

Our main contribution relies on the proposed framework, which addresses context management (capturing, analyzing context and adapt the running instance) integrated within a PAIS. The prototype also made possible to get contributions from a practical perspective since we provide an operational environment that could be used and tested in organizations. Future work includes mechanisms for analyzing the process along time, as situations evolve, to improve by learning.

References

1. Aalst, W.M.P.: Process-Aware Information Systems: Design, Enactment, and Analysis. Wiley Encyclopedia of Computer Science and Engineering, pp. 2221–2233. Wiley, Hoboken (2009)
2. Dumas, M., Aalst, W.M.P., Hofstede, A.H.M.T.: Process Aware Information Systems: Bridging People and Software Through Process Technology. Wiley-Interscience, Hoboken (2005)
3. Fahland, D., Lübke, D., Mendling, J., Reijers, H., Weber, B., Weidlich, M., Zugal, S.: Declarative versus imperative process modeling languages: the issue of understandability. In: Halpin, T., Krogstie, J., Nurcan, S., Proper, E., Schmidt, R., Soffer, P., Ukor, R. (eds.) Enterprise, Business-Process and Information Systems Modeling. LNBIP, vol. 29, pp. 353–366. Springer, Heidelberg (2009)
4. Bider, I.: Masking flexibility behind rigidity: notes on how much flexibility people are willing to cope with. In: Proceedings of the CAiSE 2005 Workshops, Workshop on Business Process Modeling, Development and Support, Porto, Portugal, pp. 7–18 (2005)
5. Kumar, K., Narasipuram, M.M.: Defining requirements for business process flexibility. In: Proceedings of the CAiSE 2006 Workshop on Business Process Modeling, Development, and Support (BPMDS 2006), Luxembourg, pp. 137–148 (2006)
6. Reichert, M., Weber, B.: Enabling Flexibility in Process-Aware Information Systems - Challenges, Methods, Technologies. Springer, Heidelberg (2012)
7. Bazire, M., Brézillon, P.: Understanding context before using it. In: Dey, A.K., Kokinov, B., Leake, D.B., Turner, R. (eds.) CONTEXT 2005. LNCS (LNAI), vol. 3554, pp. 29–40. Springer, Heidelberg (2005)
8. Mattos, T.C., Santoro, F.M., Revoredo, K., Nunes, V.T.: A formal representation for context-aware business processes. Comput. Ind. **65**, 1193–1214 (2014)
9. Ploesser, K.: A Design Theory for Context-Aware Information Systems. Ph.D. thesis, Queensland University of Technology (2013)
10. Alter, S.: Metamodel for understanding, analyzing, and designing sociotechnical systems. In: Sprouts: Working Papers on Information Systems, vol. 9, no. 59, pp. 1–47 (2009)
11. Ackoff, R.L.: Towards a system of systems concepts. Manage. Sci. **17**(11), 661–671 (1971)
12. Ghallab, M., Nau, D., Traverso, P.: Automated Planning: Theory and Practice. Morgan Kaufmann Publishers Inc., Elsevier, San Francisco (2004)
13. Murguzur, A., De Carlos, X., Trujillo, S., Sagardui, G.: Context-aware staged configuration of process variants@runtime. In: Jarke, M., Mylopoulos, J., Quix, C., Rolland, C., Manolopoulos, Y., Mouratidis, H., Horkoff, J. (eds.) CAiSE 2014. LNCS, vol. 8484, pp. 241–255. Springer, Heidelberg (2014)
14. Müller, R., Greiner, U., Rahm, E.: AgentWork: a workflow system supporting rule-based workflow adaptation. Data Knowl. Eng. **51**, 223–256 (2004)
15. Aalst, W.M.P., Hofstede, A.H.M.T.: YAWL: yet another workflow language. Inf. Syst. **30**, 245–275 (2005)
16. Pesic, M., Schonenberg, H., Aalst, W.M.P.: DECLARE: full support for loosely-structured processes. In: Proceedings of the 11th IEEE International Enterprise Distributed Object Computing Conference, Washington, pp. 287–300 (2007)
17. Reichert, M., Dadam, P.: Enabling adaptive process-aware information systems with ADEPT2. In: Handbook of Research on Business Process Modeling, pp. 173–203. Hershey, Information Science Reference, New York (2009)

18. Lanz, A., Kreher, U., Reichert, M.: Enabling process support for advanced applications with the AristaFlow BPM Suite. In: Proceedings of the Business Process Management 2010 Demonstration Track, Hoboken (2010)
19. Weber, B., Sadiq, S., Reichert, M.: Beyond rigidity – dynamic process lifecycle support. Comput. Sci. Res. Dev. **23**, 47–65 (2009)
20. Marrella, A., Russo, A., Mecella, M.: Planlets: automatically recovering dynamic processes in YAWL. In: Meersman, R., et al. (eds.) OTM 2012, Part I. LNCS, vol. 7565, pp. 268–286. Springer, Heidelberg (2012)
21. van Beest, N.R.T.P., Kaldeli, E., Bulanov, P., Wortmann, J.C., Lazovik, A.: Automated runtime repair of business processes. Inf. Syst. **29**, 45–79 (2014)
22. Nunes, V.T., Santoro, F.M., Borges, M.R.: A context-based model for knowledge management embodied in work processes. Inf. Sci. **179**, 2538–2554 (2009)
23. Nunes, V.T., Werner, C.M.L., Santoro, F.M.: Dynamic process adaptation: a context-aware approach. In: 15th International Conference on Computer Supported Cooperative Work in Design, Lausanne, Switzerland, pp. 97–104 (2011)
24. Talamadupula, K., Benton, J., Kambhampati, S., Schermerhorn, P., Scheutz, M.: Planning for human-robot teaming in open worlds. ACM Trans. Intell. Syst. Technol. (TIST) **1**(2), 14 (2010)
25. Bylander, T.: Complexity results for planning. In: Proceedings of the Twelfth International Joint Conference on Artificial Intelligence, Sydney, pp. 274–279 (1991)
26. Do, M.B., Kambhampati, S.: SAPA: a multi-objective metric temporal planner. J. Artif. Intell. Res. **20**(1), 155–194 (2003)
27. Penberthy, S., Weld, D.: Temporal planning with continuous change. In: Proceedings of the 12th National Conference on Artificial Intelligence, pp. 1010–1015 (1994)

IWPE Workshop

Preface to the International Workshop on Process Engineering (IWPE'15)

Mathias Weske[1] and Stefanie Rinderle-Ma[2]

[1] Hasso Plattner Institute, University of Potsdam,
Prof.-Dr.-Helmertstr. 2-3 14482 Potsdam, Germany
weske@hpi.de
[2] University of Vienna, Währingerstraße 29 1090 Vienna, Austria
stefanie.rinderle-ma@univie.ac.at

Motivation

Business process management as a scientific discipline has been very successful in developing concepts, languages, algorithms, and techniques in different aspects of the domain. Many of those concepts and techniques, however, did not yet find their way to the operational business of companies. One of the reasons for the weak uptake of research results in business process management is the lack of research in engineering aspects of process oriented information systems. Engineering focuses on the entire value chain of system development, from the elicitation of business requirements to the engineering of suitable architectures, components and user interfaces of process systems, as well as their testing, deployment, and maintenance.

To identify novel engineering challenges and, more generally, to strengthen engineering aspects in business process management, researchers from both academia and industry met at the first International Workshop on Process Engineering at BPM 2015.

Overview

In his keynote, Manfred Reichert provided a concise introduction to engineering challenges when building process aware information systems. By looking at research results in the database domain, Manfred identified a major shortcoming in BPM research, which is related to implementation concepts. Implementation concepts have been an active area in database research. Unfortunately research related to the design of process systems has not been sufficiently acknowledged as a research area by the BPM community.

In the first paper session, Olena Skarlat from the University of Vienna looked at engineering challenges related to the energy efficiency in BPM cloud applications. Anne Baumgrass from HPI at the University of Potsdam presented a methodology for engineering event-driven process applications in the logistics domain. Faiz Ul Muram from the University of Vienna introduced an approach to improve business processes based on counterexample analysis. In a panel on Novel Platforms for Process Engineering organized by Mathias Weske, panelists Manfred Reichert, Cesare Pautasso, and Antonio Ruiz-Cortès discussed general research directions and concrete challenges in process engineering. The discussion with a lively participation of the audience carved out the strong need for research on process engineering. Particularly, the demand for benchmarks, advanced implementation concepts, and the realization of cross-organizational process settings was emphasized.

Conclusions

The workshop was attended by up to 50 researchers, which shows the interest of the community in process engineering as a research discipline. The workshop was perceived as an important and timely starting point to further develop the research portfolio of the business process management community. The organizers express their gratitude to the members of the program committee for their detailed and timely reviews that were instrumental in compiling the program.

Potsdam and Vienna, November 2015
Mathias Weske and Stefanie Rinderle-Ma

On Energy Efficiency
of BPM Enactment in the Cloud

Olena Skarlat[✉], Philipp Hoenisch, and Schahram Dustdar

Distributed Systems Group, Institute of Information Systems, TU Wien,
Argentinierstr. 8/184-1, 1040 Vienna, Austria
{o.skarlat,p.hoenisch,dustdar}@infosys.tuwien.ac.at
http://www.infosys.tuwien.ac.at

Abstract. Today, a new infrastructure provisioning approach called Cloud Elasticity is evolving, covering three dimensions of elasticity: resource, cost, and quality. Recently, Cloud Elasticity has been utilized for Business Process Enactment in the Cloud as the involved services face highly volatile demand levels. Through treating the three dimensions equally, so-called Elastic (Business) Processes can be achieved, i.e., by leasing and releasing resources on-demand, and customer's requirements regarding quality and cost can now be met more easily. However, information technology infrastructures are now counted as a problem linked to global warming, and accounting for energy efficiency is an adequate response towards "Green" initiatives. This paper is focused on the fulfillment of the principles of Green Computing and Green Business Process Management on the basis of Cloud Elasticity to support Elastic Processes. We describe an approach for the enactment of energy-efficient Elastic Processes by means of the ViePEP platform.

Keywords: Energy efficiency · Elastic processes · Business Process Enactment · Cloud Computing

1 Introduction

Contemporary data centers are complex systems that allow to organize the uninterrupted operation of server and telecommunication facilities. Data centers have to meet the demands of highly converged infrastructures. These can be represented as a fusion of two current trends in Information and Communication Technologies (ICT) – maximization of efficiency and improving the ability to adapt to business dynamics. Cloud Elasticity is an approach used to identify and to implement on-demand runtime adjustment of infrastructural components of Cloud-based data centers through three dimensions: resource, quality, and cost elasticity [1]. Business Process Enactment describes the execution of (potentially resource-intensive) tasks that become dominating in business and scientific domains. ICT infrastructures featuring Cloud Elasticity allow to deploy resource-intensive tasks on-demand and provide a foundation for so-called "Elastic Processes" [2].

© Springer International Publishing Switzerland 2016
M. Reichert and H.A. Reijers (Eds.): BPM Workshops 2015, LNBIP 256, pp. 489–500, 2016.
DOI: 10.1007/978-3-319-42887-1_39

The resource dimension of Cloud Elasticity has a correlation with Quality of Service (QoS), i.e. quality elasticity, in a sense that on-demand leasing and releasing of resources has to be done with regard to QoS constraints. The third dimension is cost elasticity which implies using dynamic pricing to change the costs for the provisioned resources meeting QoS constraints [1].

In the last decade, the problem of energy efficiency of ICT infrastructures has gained much attention by both the software industry and the research community. This can be traced back to a noticeable growth of ICT infrastructures and an increase of energy prices. Hence, a necessity for the analysis of energy efficiency is obvious. In fact, aspects of environmental sustainability, reduction of use of harmful materials, and minimization of energy consumption are the main goals of an evolving paradigm named Green ICT [3]. European research and innovation programmes involve considerable efforts and funding for energy, resource, and waste efficiency of Green ICT area. For example, the FP7 project *Adapting Service lifeCycle towards EfficienT Clouds* (ASCETiC)[1] is aimed at minimizing energy consumption by means of optimization of design, implementation, and monitoring of the software in Clouds. *Experimental Awareness of CO_2 in Federated Cloud Sourcing* (ECO2Clouds)[2] also aims at the optimization of CO_2 emissions and of energy consumption. Another project, *Context-Aware Cloud Topology Optimization and Simulation* (CACTOS)[3] is focused on the heterogeneity of data center hardware and on the delivery of Cloud-based applications taking into account overall energy consumption. Finally, EU Horizon2020 project *Self-Organizing, Self-Managing Heterogeneous Cloud* (CloudLightning)[4] plans to implement resource provisioning approaches within Clouds to reduce power consumption and deliver savings to Cloud providers and Cloud consumers.

Still, energy efficiency aspects of Business Process Enactment using Cloud-based computational resources are not explicitly addressed, since the aforementioned EU projects are concentrated around the idea of optimization of the use of Cloud resources, without addressing Business Process Management (BPM) aspects.

Cloud-based BPM offers to companies Platform-as-a-Service or Software-as-a-Service solutions for process support within agile Cloud infrastructures [4]. Consolidation of Cloud and BPM follows a MinMax optimization approach: minimization of capital and infrastructure expenses and maximization of flexibility and reaction towards rapid changes of the demands of the customers [5]. Green BPM [3,6] is based on mapping the requirements of Green Computing to BPM. The novelty of this approach is emphasized by the non-existence of sophisticated approaches, and potential challenges in the area do not take into consideration Cloud-based aspects.

This paper is aimed at investigating the principles of Green BPM, especially in the field of energy management techniques. In an earlier work, we described the

---

[1] http://ascetic-project.eu/.

[2] http://eco2clouds.eu//.

[3] http://www.cactosfp7.eu/.

[4] http://cloudlightning.eu/.

Vienna Platform for Elastic Processes (ViePEP) [5,7,8] – a BPM-driven system that allows to model and enact Elastic Processes taking into account the whole BPM lifecycle. ViePEP provides the functionality to select services for service orchestration, i.e., business processes, with regard to Cloud Elasticity. ViePEP performs optimization of scheduling and resource provisioning. In this work we extend the components of ViePEP to meet the requirements of Green BPM, specifically to address the energy efficiency problem.

Our contributions in this work are: (1) we consider the state-of-the-art in the area of consolidation of the Cloud and BPM technologies meeting "Green" principles, in particular, energy efficiency; (2) we discuss extensions to the Elastic Process lifecycle with regard to Cloud Elasticity and energy efficiency; (3) we show how extensions to the components can be implemented in ViePEP.

The remainder of this work is organized as follows: we give our comment on the related work in the field of energy efficiency in the Cloud with regard to "Green" principles (Sects. 2 and 3). We propose an extension to our former work on Elastic Process scheduling to integrate energy efficiency techniques (Sect. 4), which is followed by an overview of the implementation of the reasoning mechanism by means of ViePEP (Sect. 5). Last but not least, we identify open challenges in the area and present an outlook on our future work (Sect. 6).

2   Related Work

The interest towards Cloud Elasticity is characterized by a rapid change of the demands to ICT services and is enforced by Service Level Agreements (SLAs). Elasticity in power consumption based on the automatic predictive and reactive policies for resource resizing is considered in [9]. The problem of autonomous resource provisioning in Cloud Computing is addressed in [10], where service deployment is introduced as a control system with a closed loop, and Virtual Machines (VMs) are allocated in a way the total count of VMs is minimized. Dynamic reallocation of VM proposed in [11] shows how to migrate VMs and shut down servers using heuristics.

Research work in the area of Cloud and BPM integration regarding Green ICT aspects is still at the beginning. State-of-the-art research in energy efficiency in Cloud Computing can be divided into three main directions: hardware-, software-, and communication-oriented. Crucial research questions within these directions are virtualization and abstraction in data centers, mechanisms for soft turning-off system network components and design of new communication protocols, and elaboration of new replication and data storage algorithms, implementation of plug-in applications and energy-control centers [12]. The same approach of virtualization in data centers for energy consumption minimization, but with respect to the requirement to maintain high QoS levels, is considered in [11].

Management issues on Green ICT, namely an infrastructure for Cloud monitoring [13], a Green Cloud framework [14], and a data center architecture [15] present the concept of VM consolidation to collect from physical servers data dealing with energy consumption. The first step of server consolidation management is to analyze server workload and then to decide on which physical machine to migrate servers and which to shut down. There are energy management schemes to be considered as challenging in the area: voltage scaling [16,17], frequency scaling [11], and dynamic turn-off [11,12]. These energy management schemes are intended to reactively change the voltage and frequency during the operation time of CPUs depending on their utilization level.

Green ICT's main objective is to reduce carbon emissions. The correlation between CO_2 emissions and power consumption is shown in [18]. Two metrics dealing with energy (and CO_2 emissions) are considered: per bit of data transfer and per second of task execution. However, there is no suggestion how to apply this model and how to measure these two energy parameters.

Another point of view of workload management [19] considers temperature awareness and focuses on the analysis of geo-specific temperature regimes, i.e. how outdoor temperature affects cooling system efficiency. The energy consumption of cooling systems, which is about 30 % [16,20] of the consumption of the whole data center, may be optimized applying a joint optimization algorithm. Another localization approach on the basis of local thermal profiles is discussed in [21], where an optimization using a placement function is performed. The placement of virtual resources on the basis of thermal-awareness finds its reflection in workload profiles, thus leading to a reduction in energy consumption. In an earlier work [20], a power-thermal management framework is proposed on the basis of a server consolidation approach to achieve overall minimization of power consumption by means of a thermal manager. In this framework, thermal measurement is presented to maintain one temperature threshold level in the whole data center. The dependency between latency, power consumption, and temperature is discussed in [22]: power consumption has a linear correlation with latency of CPUs, but as far as CPU temperature and frequency parameters are concerned, the relationship turns to be quadratic.

The paradigm of Green BPM deals with the achievement of overall infrastructural and collaborative sustainability and creation of new BPM standards, yet with step-by-step evolution of existing standards and mechanisms [23]. In addition, Berl et al. [12] mention that the popularity of business processes within the business environment places an emphasis on the question of mapping business processes to the software and hardware resources regarding energy-aware constraints and, therefore, becomes a novel research problem. According to the authors, enhancement of existing models by adding environmental metrics and by enrichment of planning optimization algorithms by additional *Energy Indicators* (EIs) are the key challenges to be addressed.

The adaptation towards environmental saving strategies may be considered through four phases: strategy investigation in terms of EIs, process model adaptation and application of dynamic provisioning techniques, analysis of the runtime to meet green metrics, and monitoring of the indicators and metrics [24]. To perform such adaptation and to optimize business processes in terms of the environmental impact the use of environment-aware business process patterns is proposed in [25]. The authors state that the explicit application of Green BPM

Table 1. An overview of related work

Ref.	Technology	Method	Component	Metrics
[9]	Clusters, Amazon EC2	Prediction, policy	Elastic site prototype	Workload
[10]	Cloud	Proactive, reactive scaling	Elastic Cloud controller	Performance, workload
[11]	Data center	Heuristics, policy	Fast heuristics algorithms	Performance
[13]	IBM Cloud	Server consolidation	Monitoring infrastructure	Performance
[14]	Data center	Temperature, image management	Green Cloud framework	Performance
[15]	Data center	Server consolidation, live migration	VM-based energy-efficient data center	Performance
[16]	Data center	Voltage, frequency scaling, dynamic shutdown	GreenCloud	Performance, workload
[17]	Clusters, Cloud	Voltage, frequency scaling	Smart metering system	Performance
[18]	Data center	CO_2 optimization	Carbon efficient green policy	Performance, workload
[19]	Data center	Outside aircooling optimization	Empirical cooling efficiency model	Workload, temperature
[20]	Data center	Temperature-aware resource provisioning	Power thermal management Framework	Performance, temperature
[21]	Clusters	Thermal-aware heuristics	Thermal-aware placement algorithm	Workload, temperature
[22]	Map-reduce clusters	Periodic optimization with latest CPU temperatures	Temperature-aware power allocation framework	Workload, temperature

research is still in its beginning and the evaluation of the ecosystem sustainability, that can be achieved by means of green initiatives, remains a challenge.

In Table 1, we summarize approaches investigated in related research in Cloud Computing regarding energy efficiency. Common methods can be distinguished here: server consolidation and live migration, proactive and reactive resource allocation, as well as voltage and frequency scaling, i.e. energy management. The correlation between temperature, workload, and power consumption is explicitly regarded: Optimization deals with the business model of data centres and their ability to provide services in a way that reduces the trade-off between saving energy and performance and workload metrics, decreasing cost expenses from the user and data center sides. These approaches can be used to achieve energy efficiency on the physical and virtual levels of Cloud infrastructures by affecting the scheduling and reasoning mechanisms in the Cloud.

3   Problem Statement

Green BPM implies the adaptation of existing Cloud Computing and BPM solutions by aggregating them with "green components". On the basis of our investigation of the related work in the domain of energy efficiency and Green Computing initiatives, we are now able to set research objectives towards the extensions of components that we use in ViePEP. We consider Cloud-based data centers in terms of ICT infrastructure, and ViePEP as the basis towards the optimized enactment of Elastic Processes. Accounting for the investigated variability of used techniques to approach green metrics, the main objective of resource allocation in Clouds remains the priority of a service delivery to the customers with regard to SLAs and QoS.

In Sect. 1 we discussed that energy awareness is a major trend in European research projects. One of the objectives of the ASCETiC project is to develop a framework that considers energy efficiency metrics in the Cloud and to deal with energy as a part of quality dimension of elasticity elaborated within SLAs. The approach is to obtain an estimation of the energy consumption of particular elements of the infrastructure during runtime. Here, EIs are divided into three levels: application, virtual, and physical. The migration strategy is based on accounting for energy probes, i.e. actual energy measurements.

Another project (CACTOS) uses heuristic algorithms to optimize the cost function on the basis of predicted cost of energy consumption of VMs and on the node level. This becomes a foundation for deployment planning. They propose to use an EIs model that takes into account power consumption of starting VMs, during migration process, and shutdowns.

The ECO2Clouds project considers different metrics of power consumption of VMs and infrastructure through monitoring. The set of metrics include infrastructural, virtualization, and application layer metrics. Data that is collected by these metrics is used to adapt the deployment and the runtime of an application. The overall optimization process here is concentrated on maximization of use of the single physical resources, i.e. allocating VMs on the host that features the highest energy consumption.

The overview of the European projects and related work showed common approaches towards achieving energy efficiency. The purpose of the related work analysis was to extract trends to improve ViePEP, which is a research Business Process Management System (BPMS). Our previous work on ViePEP presented a reasoning mechanism for scheduling and optimal resource leasing and releasing from the user point of view, i.e. the overall optimization was conducted in order to minimize cost [5]. We extend our previous work by extending Elastic Process scheduling and resource allocation by the notion of energy efficiency. For this, we also need to extend ViePEP by dedicated components which take into account the energy efficiency problem from the service provider side.

4   Extension Mechanism for Energy Efficiency of BPM

ICT infrastructural resources can be classified into computational, storage, and network resources. Elastic Processes are business processes that are realized on the basis of such ICT infrastructural solutions and are able to react to dynamic changes in the computational and business environment [2].

To realize Elastic Processes, a well-known approach from Autonomic Computing, namely the MAPE-K cycle [27] can be applied: to Monitor, Analyze, Plan, and Execute processes based on a Knowledge Base. To map these steps of the MAPE-K model onto a business process lifecycle, the following phases are considered, which are performed by the administration of the used BPMS and

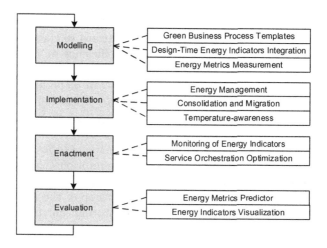

Fig. 1. Extensions to the elastic process lifecycle phases to meet energy efficiency demands (adapted from [6])

owners of the business processes: *Plan* step: process identification and modelling along with the overall process and single process step implementation; *Execute* step: process enactment; *Monitor* step: process monitoring; *Analyze* step: post-enactment evaluation. By applying the suggestions of the green business process lifecycle to the work of Nowak et al. [6], we extend our current approach towards optimization of Elastic Processes as it can be seen in Fig. 1.

The process of leasing and releasing of resources needs to be fulfilled by adaptivity means of the BPMS (here: ViePEP). Thereby, decision making by the BPMS regarding the use of ICT infrastructural resources must follow a Min-Max approach: minimizing resource and cost, and maximizing quality. Energy efficiency can be attributed to the QoS, while energy consumption expenses affect the overall cost optimization function. The *Plan* step includes the actual process modeling and its implementation. Process modeling is the first phase in the Elastic Process lifecycle. The main task of this phase is to perform energy-aware design of business processes. To compose a business process, a *Green BP Templates* selector will be used with predefined energy-aware metrics. A new BPM stakeholder, the *energy management officer*, should be considered here. Her main responsibility is to perform an energy audit within the enterprise, identify Key Performance Indicators (KPIs) dealing with energy consumption (i.e., EIs), and to take appropriate measures to fulfill these specified indicators. Single process steps as well as the service orchestration need to have methods to incorporate the values of EIs within the design-time environment. EIs of various types will be stored in the *Energy Indicators Registry*, applying to the application level, VMs and physical machines. During business process composition, usage of energy metrics will be indicated via data that is received from sensors (*Energy Metrics Controller*) regarding specific parts of the infrastructure. Depending on the design of the business process, a pricing model will be adapted to different energy profiles. During the business process implementation phase, the optimization of the resource use with regard to energy efficiency can be configured. The approaches to achieve energy efficiency on the physical level (as shown in Table 1) can be associated with single process steps. Within this phase, energy-aware scheduling and live migration can be performed, i.e. choosing physical hosts to deploy VMs. The energy-aware operation of VMs involves dynamic management of VMs on the basis of EIs values. Energy metrics data has to be associated with the business process instances, i.e. to be annotated. Another optional phase of the process lifecycle is the certification of a certain business process model to confirm its energy-consumption characteristics, e.g., by an accredited external party.

The *Execute* step correlates with the *Monitor* step of the MAPE-K model. The enactment phase will involve extended monitoring. For process optimization at runtime, the executions of business process steps (in terms of Cloud-based services) are monitored. Monitoring data is available in the form of data streams. This is followed by EI-driven process data analysis integrated with service composition re-planning which results in a near-optimal process service plan with partial re-deployment at runtime. To achieve quantitative analysis, periodic monitoring is to be performed during design-time, runtime, and post runtime.

The evaluation phase of the Elastic Process lifecycle corresponds to the *Analyze* step of the MAPE-K model. The phase uses received monitoring data to reconfigure business processes. Runtime optimization based on the energy consumption allows dynamically changing a running process instance while being executed. Alternatively, the data acquired at runtime of an instance can be analyzed for future runs of other instances of the process model. To accomplish this, statistical processing will consider historical data and aim at the analysis of real-time data streams and events produced by the environment. The other need is to establish the ability to customize process visualization according to user needs and based on EIs. Future green initiatives may lead to a trade-off in cost and quality of the provided services in terms of penalties which apply if a process deadline can not be met. An according cost optimization function reflects the financial streams that are generated from the activities that are arranged to gain energy efficiency.

5 Enactment of Energy-Efficient Elastic Processes by Means of ViePEP

In general, ViePEP aims at the cost-efficient enactment of Elastic Processes. For an overview of the main components, refer to [5, 7].

In order to take into account energy-efficiency, it is necessary to extend ViePEP by according software components (see Fig. 2) as well as enable energy-efficient scheduling and resource allocation.

On the lowest level, an additional output from the *Backend VMs* regarding energy metrics will be received by the *Energy Metrics Controller*. The monitoring aspect will be regarded during design-time: The *Process Manager* will be

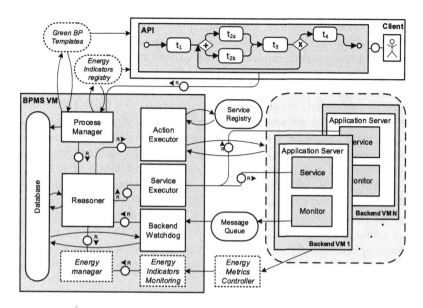

Fig. 2. Extensions to ViePEP to meet energy efficiency demands

extended by an interface to an energy-aware *Green BP Templates* selector in order to have the possibility to choose another alternative of a business process, taking into account energy considerations. The *Energy Indicators Registry* aims at the integration of the information about EIs into a business process instance. The *Backend Watchdog* will be supplemented by the subcomponent *Energy Indicators Monitoring* to specify the influence on the energy efficiency and to monitor dependencies of various actions on the Elastic Process steps. The *Reasoner* component performs the optimization of the complete business process and overall Cloud infrastructure landscape. The *Energy Manager* is a supplement component to the *Reasoner*, and will consider an energy-efficient execution of business processes by allocating resources on-demand with regard to EIs and objective energy profiles.

6   Conclusions and Future Work

The use of Cloud-based Elastic Processes provides the means of dynamic deployment of business processes onto ICT infrastructural resources. To address the problem of consolidation of Cloud and BPM, an application of a MinMax optimization approach is needed: minimization of capital and infrastructure expenses, maximization of flexibility and reaction towards rapid changes of the demands of the customers.

The comment on the related research in the field of Business Process Enactment on the basis of Cloud Elasticity established a foundation for the research plan of improving our research BPMS for Elastic Processes – ViePEP – with the means to take into account energy efficiency aspects. A mechanism of consolidation of Cloud Elasticity to use energy efficiency techniques was discussed on the basis of the general requirements of Green Computing and Green BPM principles.

The general barriers towards green initiatives can be explicitly divided into structural and financial. Structural barriers describe the fragmentation of the Cloud market. Small data centers are not cost-effective enough to invest in energy efficiency aspects. Therefore, a union of small data centers may be financially more attractive. The other major problem is the lack of an international protocol document regarding measurement of energy efficiency in data centers. This leads to the absence of real stimulus to use energy-efficient domain equipment and controllers. High initial expenses to reconfigure old and buy new equipment and long pay-off period are also considered as a barrier. Additionally, data centers do not account for the financial benefits dealing with the energy efficiency in their financial streams. Consequently, success in achieving energy efficiency is implied by evolutionary approaches of comfortable step-by-step integration of green principles into existing systems.

In our future work, we want to take into account energy efficiency during the Plan and Execute steps of the MAPE-K model. The design of energy-efficient business processes is challenging in terms of the application of Green Business Process patterns [25, 26]. During enactment energy efficiency needs to be taken into account as another constraint for scheduling and resource allocation. Finally, the Monitor and Analyze steps of the MAPE-K model should be improved by means of accounting for KPIs of green initiatives, namely EIs.

Acknowledgment. This paper is supported by TU Wien research funds.

References

1. Copil, G., Moldovan, D., Truong, H.-L., Dustdar, S.: Multi-level elasticity control of cloud services. In: Basu, S., Pautasso, C., Zhang, L., Fu, X. (eds.) ICSOC 2013. LNCS, vol. 8274, pp. 429–436. Springer, Heidelberg (2013)
2. Dustdar, S., Guo, Y., Satzger, B., Truong, H.-L.: Principles of elastic processes. IEEE Internet Comput. **15**(5), 66–71 (2011)
3. Houy, C., Reiter, M., Fettke, P., Loos, P.: Towards green BPM – sustainability and resource efficiency through business process management. In: Muehlen, M., Su, J. (eds.) BPM 2010 Workshops. LNBIP, vol. 66, pp. 501–510. Springer, Heidelberg (2011)
4. Baeyens, T.: BPM in the cloud. In: Daniel, F., Wang, J., Weber, B. (eds.) BPM 2013. LNCS, vol. 8094, pp. 10–16. Springer, Heidelberg (2013)
5. Hoenisch, P., Schuller, D., Schulte, S., Hochreiner, C., Dustdar, S.: Optimization of complex elastic processes. IEEE Trans. Serv. Comput. **PP**(99), 1–8 (2015). IEEE Press
6. Nowak, A., Leymann, F., Schumm, D.: The differences and commodities between green and conventional business process management. In: 9th IEEE International Conference in Dependable, Autonomic and Secure Computing, pp. 569–576. IEEE Press (2011)

7. Schulte, S., Hoenisch, P., Venugopal, S., Dustdar, S.: Introducing the vienna platform for elastic processes. In: Ghose, A., Zhu, H., Yu, Q., Delis, A., Sheng, Q.Z., Perrin, O., Wang, J., Wang, Y. (eds.) ICSOC 2012. LNCS, vol. 7759, pp. 179–190. Springer, Heidelberg (2013)
8. Hoenisch, P., Schulte, S., Dustdar, S.: Workflow scheduling and resource allocation for cloud-based execution of elastic processes. In: 6th International Conference on Service-Oriented Computing and Applications, pp. 1–8. IEEE Press (2013)
9. Marshall, P., Keahey, K., Freeman, T.: Elastic site: using clouds to elastically extend site resources. In: 10th International Conference on Cluster, Cloud and Grid Computing, pp. 43–52. IEEE Press (2010)
10. Ali-Eldin, A., Tordson, J., Elmroth, E.: An adaptive hybrid elasticity controller for cloud infrastructures. In: IEEE Network Operations and Management Symposium, pp. 204–212. IEEE Press (2012)
11. Beloglazov, A., Buyya, R.: Energy efficient allocation of virtual machines in cloud data centers. In: 10th International Conference on Cluster, Cloud and Grid Computing, pp. 577–578. IEEE Press (2010)
12. Berl, A., Gelenbe, E., Di Girolamo, M., Giuliani, G., De Meer, H., Dang, M.Q., Pentikousis, K.: Energy-efficient cloud computing. Comput. J. **53**(7), 1045–1051 (2010)
13. Corradi, A., Fanelli, M., Foschini, L.: Increasing cloud power efficiency through consolidation techniques. In: Symposium on Computers and Communications, pp. 129–134. IEEE Press (2011)
14. Younge, A.J., von Laszewski, G., Lizhe, W., Lopez-Alarcon, S., Carithers, W.: Efficient resource management for cloud computing environments. In: International Green Computing Conference, pp. 357–364. IEEE Press (2010)
15. Ye, K., Huang, D., Jiang, X., Chen, H., Wu, S.: Vitrual machine based energy-efficient data center architecture for cloud computing: a performance perspective. In: International Conference on Green Computing and Communications and International Conference on Cyber, Physical and Social Computing, pp. 171–178. IEEE Press (2010)
16. Kliazovich, D., Bouvry, P., Khan, S.U.: GreenCloud: a packet-level simulator of energy-aware cloud computing data centers. J. Supercomput. **62**, 1263–1283 (2012)
17. Tu, C.-Y., Kuo, W.-C., Teng, W.-H., Wang, Y.-T., Shiau, S.: A power-aware cloud architecture with smart metering. In: 39th International Conference on Parallel Processing Workshops, pp. 497–503. IEEE Press (2010)
18. Garg, S.K., Yeo, C.S., Buyya, R.: Green cloud framework for improving carbon efficiency of clouds. In: Jeannot, E., Namyst, R., Roman, J. (eds.) Euro-Par 2011, Part I. LNCS, vol. 6852, pp. 491–502. Springer, Heidelberg (2011)
19. Xu, H., Feng, C., Li, B.: Temperature aware workload management in geo-distributed datacenters. In: ACM SIGMETRICS/International Conference on Measurement and Modeling of Computer Systems, pp. 373–374. ACM (2013)
20. Pakbaznia, E., Ghasemazar, M., Pedram, M.: Temperature-aware dynamic resource provisioning in a power-optimized datacenter. In: Design, Automation, and Test in Europe Conference and Exhibition, pp. 124–129. IEEE Press (2010)
21. Kaushik, R.T., Nahrstedt, K.: T*: a data-centric cooling energy costs reduction approach for big data analytics cloud. In: International Conference for High Performance Computing, Networking, Storage and Analysis, pp. 1–11. IEEE Press (2012)
22. Li, S., Wang, S., Abdelzaher, T., Kihl, M., Robertsson, A.: Temperature aware power allocation: an optimization framework and case studies. Sustain. Comput. J. **2**, 117–127 (2012)

23. Jakobi, T., Castelli, N., Nolte, A., Stevens, G., Schonau, N.: Towards collaborative green business process management. In: 28th EnviroInfo ICT for Energy Efficiency Conference, pp. 683–690. BIS-Verlag (2014)
24. Nowak, A., Leymann, F., Schumm, D., Wetzstein, B.: An architecture and methodology for a four-phased approach to green business process reengineering. In: Kranzlmüller, D., Toja, A.M. (eds.) ICT-GLOW 2011. LNCS, vol. 6868, pp. 150–164. Springer, Heidelberg (2011)
25. Nowak, A., Leymann, F., Schleicher, D., Schumm, D., Wagner, S.: Green business process patterns. In: 18th Conference on Pattern Languages of Programs, article no. 6. ACM, New York (2011)
26. Nowak, A., Breitenbücher, U., Leymann, F.: Automating green patterns to compensate CO_2 emissions of cloud-based business processes. In: 8th International Conference on Advance Engineering Computing and Applications in Sciences, pp. 132–139. IARIA (2014)
27. Kephart, J.O., Chess, D.M.: The vision of autonomic computing. Computer **36**(1), 41–50 (2003)

Towards a Methodology for the Engineering of Event-Driven Process Applications

Anne Baumgraß[1]([✉]), Mirela Botezatu[2], Claudio Di Ciccio[3], Remco Dijkman[4],
Paul Grefen[4], Marcin Hewelt[1], Jan Mendling[3], Andreas Meyer[1],
Shaya Pourmirza[4], and Hagen Völzer[2]

[1] Hasso-Plattner-Institut, University of Potsdam, Potsdam, Germany
anne.baumgrass@hpi.de
[2] IBM Research – Zurich, Zurich, Switzerland
[3] Institute for Information Business at WU Vienna, Vienna, Austria
[4] Eindhoven University of Technology, Eindhoven, The Netherlands

Abstract. Successful applications of the Internet of Things such as smart cities, smart logistics, and predictive maintenance, build on observing and analyzing business-related objects in the real world for business process execution and monitoring. In this context, complex event processing is increasingly used to integrate events from sensors with events stemming from business process management systems. This paper describes a methodology to combine the areas and engineer an event-driven logistics processes application. Thereby, we describe the requirements, use cases and lessons learned to design and implement such an architecture.

Keywords: Event-driven process applications · Business process management · Architecture design · Methodology · Logistics

1 Introduction

Traditionally, Business Process Management Systems (BPMSs) execute and monitor business process instances based on events that stem from the process engine itself or from connected client applications. However, recently, successful applications of the Internet of Things such as smart cities, smart logistics, and predictive maintenance emerge that include and provide sensors tracking objects via Global Positioning System (GPS) or Radio-Frequency Identification (RFID), measuring the temperature, the energy consumption, or other types of data. Thus, information from the environment in which processes are executed is available but often not considered in the design of traditional (BPMSs) [1].

Such external applications offer new possibilities to control and evaluate the business process execution, yet they require a novel concept of integration with

The research leading to these results is part of the GET Service project and has received funding from the European Commission under the 7th Framework Programme (FP7) for Research and Technological Development under grant agreement 2012-318275.

M. Reichert and H.A. Reijers (Eds.): BPM Workshops 2015, LNBIP 256, pp. 501–514, 2016.
DOI: 10.1007/978-3-319-42887-1_40

a BPMS. Complex Event Processing (CEP) is often considered as a suitable technique for tackling this challenge [2], especially in logistics [3].

In the GET Service project[1], we analysed typical logistics scenarios, explored their environments, and evaluated BPMSs for their execution and monitoring. GET Service aims at techniques and systems to plan transportation routes more efficiently and to respond quickly to unexpected events such as adverse weather or strikes, during transportation. In recent studies [4], disruptions due to such events mainly cause a loss of productivity and revenue as well as an increased cost of working. Therefore, timely notifications are important in logistics to reduce the impact. Nowadays, these disruptions are handled manually and often by phone – an ineffective and not reliable (in terms of fast reaction and prevention) source of interaction. In this paper, we document how the aim of the project to automate these notifications is addressed, specifically by the selection of a process engine in combination with a CEP system and a process modelling tool that got extended to support the required functionalities like automatic event query generation.

In particular, we present – in terms of a methodology – the course of actions we conducted from the description of the logistics scenarios to the iterative design and implementation of the systems supporting these scenarios. In this line, we present an architecture that supports the execution and monitoring of the business processes across distributed BPMSs and the consideration of heterogeneous event sources. It is mainly based on an analysis of transportation scenarios from practice. Although stemming from logistics, the architecture can be generalized and also used in further domains. Its core components make use of novel concepts for annotating process models with which the event subscription can be automated. As a proof-of-concept, we implemented the architecture such that progress and violations during process execution can be effectively monitored for process-internal and environmental events; the implementation may be found in [5].

Against this background, the remainder of this paper is structured as follows: Sect. 2 briefly introduces the methodology used before Sect. 3 discusses the use case for this paper. Section 4 presents an architectural overview of our process-based real-time execution and monitoring approach which is mainly based on use cases similar to the one presented in Sect. 3. Thereby, Sects. 4.1, 4.2, and 4.3 zoom in to three important components of our architecture: process modeller, process engine, and event processing engine. Finally, Sect. 5 presents the conclusion and outlook.

2   Methodology

The proposed methodology results from the GET Service project that aims to improve transport planning and execution in terms of transport costs, CO_2-emission, and customer service. Thus, it requires the design of a service platform

---

[1] http://www.getservice-project.eu.

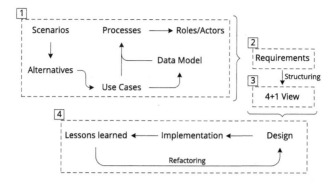

Fig. 1. Procedure of stepwise refinement of information towards the final artefact: the implemented software system

for joint transport planning and execution. As starting point, a basic understanding of the logistics domain and its scenarios were established. In total, five usage scenarios were identified, each one depicting a particular logistics chain from different industries and focusing on different transport modes and stakeholders [6]. For each scenario, several use cases, influences of events, and success criteria were defined. These served as input to specifically define processes including its data model, roles, and actors. For further investigation in the project, we specifically decided to support three use cases [7]: (1) Export of containers through a port requiring an efficient synchronization of transport participants, (2) Airfreight transportation including the possibility of shifts from one airport to another, and (3) Synchromodal transport synchronizing multiple transports for the same order at once. In the remainder of the paper, we consider the process of a freight-shift in use case (2) to reflect our requirements, the corresponding architecture, and its implementation. It is presented in Sect. 3.

Figure 1 shows the procedure of our methodology. The main input for the requirements analysis (step 2) were the process models we created together with domain experts and users from this field in step 1. Using those we were able to exactly identify the right roles and actors as well as a joint data model for all use cases. In the requirement analysis, we determined the functional and non-functional aspects of the GET Service platform necessary for transportation planning. Specifically, we defined how planning relies on historic and real-time information and in which way this information should serve as its input. For example, how real-time information like an accident of a truck is recognized, correlated with a transport plan and changing it as well as how this information is forwarded to the user.

After eliciting the requirements, they need to be transitioned into a system architecture. Thereby, views on processes, system interfaces, domain model, system functionality, and the utilized physical hardware must be considered – a wide spectrum of information.

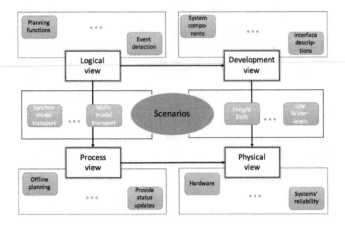

Fig. 2. Kruchten's 4+1 [8] model applied to GET Service

We used Kruchten's 4+1 view model [8] to structure all requirements in step 3 as input to design, implement, and refactor GET Service's architecture in step 4. This model combines aspects of architectural models, layers, and principles from the field of software and systems engineering. As such, it is used to create distinct views for each of the stakeholders' viewpoints. Figure 2 shows the application of this model to our project and the above mentioned views.

Considering the example of the functional requirement to provision real-time information, the description of such is dealt with in the logical view. From those, the process models are constructed in the process view to deal while the scenarios are used to derive the specific behaviour. The components enabling the functionality are designed in the development view. Finally, the physical view shows the concrete implementation and the set-up of the infrastructure to enable the provisioning of real-time information. To meet the interests of this workshop, we focus, in the remainder of this paper, on the parts of GET Service that deal with execution and monitoring of logistics processes.

3   Running Example of a Freight-Shift in Transportation

As a example, we consider the part of a logistic process instance pertaining to the transportation of a container from a storage area in Nice to a distribution centre located in Frankfurt. The whole multi-modal transport plan comprises a first truck-based leg from the French storage area to Nice Côte d'Azur Airport, then a second aircraft-based leg brings the cargo to Frankfurt Airport, and finally a truck-based leg towards the distribution centre in Germany. Such a transport is managed by a logistics service provider (LSP) that can utilise a fleet of trucks of its own, distributed Europe-wide, or some subcontractor, another LSP. Air-freight, however, is usually handled from a commercial cargo airline company which thus is in charge of the air-based leg of the transport.

From recent studies [4] and the scenarios we surveyed in the GET Service project we learned that numerous disruptions might occur even in such simple transports as described here. Not all of them are known a-priori but happen unexpectedly. For example, an air-plane may have to unexpectedly land at a different airport due to adverse weather or a strike. Alternatively, an air-plane might suddenly have more transportation capacity available, because of transportation order cancellations. In the end, both occurrences lead to a shift of transportation capacity or demand from one location to another. However, nowadays, real-time information of transport progress or disruptions are often communicated late, incomplete, or by no means at all among the affected actors.

In our process, for instance, a strike at Frankfurt airport could force the pilot to divert the flight to another location, namely Brussels Airport. This would certainly compromise the successful completion of the multi-modal transportation activity, because empty trucks would wait for the air-plane to land in Frankfurt, since the logistics service provider did not get informed about the diversion. This would not happen before the actual landing in Brussels, with clear negative effects on *(i)* productivity, due to the longer waiting times and empty trucks, *(ii)* costs, caused by the re-routing or re-booking of additional trucks to move the containers from Brussels to Frankfurt, and *(iii)* timeliness of the delivery, due to the fact that compensation actions would be taken after landing.

Obviously, freight-shifts and other events influencing the completion of the process should be detected as quickly as possible to properly act on them. This means, they have to be considered by the process engine enacting the process model. In consequence, the possible occurrence of events and a reaction to them have to be integrated into the process model. With current technology, this would restrict the monitoring only to events known at design time, require the determination of a reaction, which might differ from instance to instance, and increase the complexity of process models drastically. Furthermore, the process engine must collect events relevant for the process during execution of a process and evaluate the impact of them. In contrast to the freight-shift, for example, a small congestion on a road might only cause a delay for the truck that does not influence the transport chain, while a problem with the motor of the truck might enforce the planner to pick another truck for the transport. Section 4 details the architecture and highlights the requirements leading to its design and the corresponding implementation. The system including the interaction between different components is provided as screencast at http://youtu.be/JE2Df7iaERk.

4   Design of an Architecture for Event-Driven Logistics Processes

The Workflow Management System (WfMS) Reference architecture [9] served as blueprint for the design of our event-driven logistics process architecture. As central component it shows the workflow enactment service that is connected via 5 interfaces to other components for modelling (IF1), for controlling client applications and devices (IF2), for invoking external applications (IF3), for monitoring and administration (IF4), and also for invoking other WfMSs (IF5). Currently, WfMSs are designed to operate with static control structures. Dynamic environments, such as logistics with a lot of events (e.g. weather, congestions, or strikes influencing the process execution), require more flexibility and interfaces to consider external events. Therefore, dynamism is the key requirement in our architecture.

Based on investigations on the connection between events and process models in [3], we added a new interface from the workflow enactment service to the event engine fostering flexibility. In this setup, for each task in a process model, not only the workflow execution semantics need to be evaluated, but also the associated event notifications have to be considered. Therefore, this design alternative may reduce the performance of the whole system. However, it can increase the dynamism of our architecture. This design allows all the tasks in a process model to communicate with the event processing engine, and consequently, one task can be executed 'both' manually by a user in the user interface of the process engine or automatically based on high-level events.

From this high-level we designed the architecture for connecting environment sources and consider them during process execution as shown in Fig. 3. This architecture also shows the necessary components to enable event-driven logistics processes and their interfaces: (i) The *Event Engine*, responsible for event processing, definition of high-level events, and provisioning of subscriptions mechanisms, (ii) the *BPMS*, which allows to model (*Modeller*) and enact (*Process Engine*) processes, and (iii) the set of *Event Sources* providing the information processed by the event engine.

This architecture shows how real-time event data can be correlated automatically to real-time process data and vice versa through publish subscribe mechanisms. Several event sources provide event streams, e.g. GPS locations, which input event data into the *Event Engine*. This may happen constantly or in chunks. The *BPMS* allows to model business processes which are then enacted within a *Process Engine*. The event information is automatically correlated to

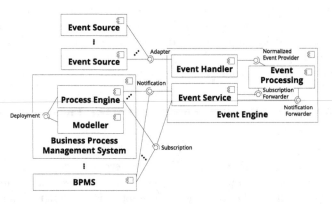

Fig. 3. High-level architecture for real-time monitoring of business processes through CEP

the actual process instances – the run-time equivalents of process models – such that subscriptions must be defined that are provided to the *Event Service* which in turn provides notifications to the affected process instances for each set of events corresponding to a subscription.

In the following sections, we discuss the requirements, the design, the implementation, and the lessons learned for the three main components in our architecture: the modeller, the process engine, and the event engine. This is in line with the steps displayed in the lower part of Fig. 1 and the logical, development, and physical views in Fig. 2.

4.1   Process Modelling

In general, a process model can be used to integrate different IT systems and services based on Service-Oriented Architecture (SOA) and a process execution engine.

Requirements. Based on the use case described in Sect. 3, the process modelling language must *(1)* support modelling of tasks, events and messages occurring in a supply chain, *(2)* have execution semantics and suitable engines supporting this semantics, *(3)* introduce roles for different parts in the process model to specify the responsible client or external IT system for its execution, *(4)* include a specification that the progress of some tasks is determined by external information, *(5)* provide means to specify time- and location-related constraints in the process model that are relevant for the process engine to reveal the adherence of process execution with the process model, and *(6)* support semantics for a process engine to use process models not only for execution but also for status tracking and visualization of disruptions.

In our literature review, we observed that there is no *off-the-shelf* process modelling language that fully supports all requirements [10]. Thus, we decided to extend the industry standard Business Process Model and Notation (BPMN) [11], since it is widely supported by tools and engines, has a suitable expressiveness, provides standard mechanisms for its extension, and has high emphasis on both, the design and analysis as well as the process automation of use cases. BPMN provides a XSD-specification of its metamodel. Thus, BPMN-conform process models can be exchanged via XML.

Design. To adequately address the requirements of logistics processes, such as the detection of a flight diversion from our use case, we enriched the BPMN metamodel with annotations that capture the time and location constraints of a logistics process as well as annotations to consider the internal and external event sources either driving the process or influencing its execution. Details on the extension are provided in [10].

The annotations may be explained using the automatic generation of event subscriptions from process models. For the purpose of automation, we pre-define various event subscription templates that are then filled by the modeller component with process model information (e.g. the deadline to execute a task) and extended by the process engine with process instance information (e.g. the truck that actually transports the cargo). Note that these templates are written in Esper [12] to be conform with the event processing language of the event engine. An example of such a subscription template is shown in Listing 1. It aims at notifying about strikes (type="strike") at a specific destination airport before a certain deadline is reached. Case-dependent information is marked by preceding '$'. Thus, while the name of the destination airport ($destination) and the deadline ($deadline) in this example should be extracted from the process model, the specific case for which this query is relev ant ($caseId) must be set by the process engine itself. Given the specific task "Drive to destination" in Fig. 4 the process engine uses the annotations in the process model and subscribes to be notified about strikes at 'Frankfurt' before '2015-07-04T08:00' (resp. latest arrival of the truck in Frankfurt).

Listing 1. Event subscription template for strikes at an airport.

```
1   SELECT type,timestamp,description,url,title,latitude,longitude, $caseId as caseId FROM
        Warning where type="strike"and description like"%$destination%"and timestamp.
        before($deadline)
```

An event subscription is associated with a BPMN element, encapsulated in the documentation. The types of events that result from an event subscription are determined by the event type given in the documentation ((<eventType>Warning</eventType>)). It furthermore includes a scope defining when the query has to be activated and how the responses of the event engine to this query have to be interpreted, see Listing 2. The scope in this example does not trigger any status update of

Fig. 4. Annotated task "Drive to destination".

the task (trigger="false") and the observation of corresponding events is within the task execution (<startTask>Task2</startTask> <endTask>Task2</endTask>), i.e. the subscription starts when the truck starts driving and ends when the truck arrives at the airport, which can be captured in further queries. Obviously, in this example, the modeller, the process engine and the event engine have to have a common understanding of the annotations and how to understand their content.

Lessons Learned. The provisioning of subscription templates is essential in our approach, since the low level of modelling competence of modellers in process documentation projects is a well-known problem in the Business Process Management (BPM) field [13]. From the practical experience in the GET Service project, further challenges arise when users are not used to model process models at all. Furthermore, closely related to our event engine (see

Listing 2. Excerpt of an event subscription in the XML-based T-BPMN process model.

```
1   <task id="Task2"name="Drive to destination">
2    <documentation> <queryAnnotation> <query>
3     <queryText> [Query of Listing 1] </queryText>
4     <eventType>Warning</eventType>
5     <scope trigger="false">
6      <startTask>Task2</startTask>
7      <endTask>Task2</endTask>
8     </scope>
9   </query> </queryAnnotation> </documentation> ... </task>
```

Sect. 4.3), we defined aggregation rules that hide the complexity of event processing from the user to ease the utilization and understanding of event subscriptions. For instance, we specify rules in the event engine that produce high-
level events whenever a truck reaches a destination. Thus, the modeller does
not need to define queries comparing all truck positions to reason about destination arrival himself. Instead, she can simply subscribe via "Select * from
ArrivedAtTransportNode(operatorId=$truckId)".

4.2   Executing Annotated Process Models

In this section, we review the features that need to be supported by our process
engine.

Requirements. We employed a systematic review approach to create a list
of all possible process engines that can execute any kind of process model. We
considered both service orchestration engines or business process management
execution engines. Based on the general requirements derived from the components functionality, the architecture, and the required interfaces, we identified
6 generic criteria the 36 identified engines are evaluated against: *(i)* Does the
system have an open-source license? *(ii)* Does the system have an in-depth documentation? *(iii)* Does the system support BPMN language? *(iv)* Has the system
been implemented in Java? *(v)* Does the system have an active developer community for communication? *(vi)* Does the system support runtime adaptability?
    The third criterion considers our decision for BPMN as business process mod-
elling language as discussed in Sect. 4.1. The sixth criterion evaluates the ability
to change the process model during runtime of the system. This is required due
to re-planning activities in logistics. In [14], we discussed the process engine evaluation in detail. Summarized, based on our requirements, we chose the Activiti[2]
process engine as our base process engine.

Design. The *process engine* requires algorithms to parse and interpret the annotated process models (cf. Sect. 4.1) and needs to ensure that activities specified

---

[2] http://www.activiti.org/.

therein are properly executed and monitored. To achieve this, the process engine enacts process models, by generating *process instances*. A process instance captures for each activity *(i) when*, *(ii)* by *whom*, and *(iii) how* its state can be updated.

Most interesting for the interaction between the introduced systems, all notifications the process engine receives are extracted from the annotated process model and extended with process instance information. While notifications about progress or status updates do not affect the design of the process model, the process engine may receive notifications about violations in the business process, as either actual or predicted ones. Please note that violations often involve updates both in the design and execution of the process model. Thus, we require the implementation of a dynamic reconfiguration of process instances which we discuss in detail in [15].

Implementation. We extended the Activiti [16] process engine in three main aspects: (i) We allow full support of runtime adaptations of the process; (ii) we integrate the process engine with the event processing engine in order to react to the external events; and (iii) we provide additional access to the process engine through external devices, e.g. mobile clients. As mentioned in the previous section, an algorithm has been developed in order to apply the instance migration after process adaptation and address extension (i).

Extension (ii) was discussed in Sect. 4, where we discussed the integration of a WfMS with an event processing engine. We designed an additional interface to facilitate this extension. As consequence of this integration, the Activiti engine can subscribe to listen to predefined *query notifications* (e.g. position update of a vehicle) it can produce events about the executions (e.g. status of each task). Therefore, the process engine can always publish events; however in order to listen to a specific event, the prerequisite is the existence of a process model that is sufficiently annotated with the query notifications (cf. [10]).

Extension (iii) to the Activiti engine provides different RESTful services that contain both: information about the execution of a process instance and query notifications. Therefore, any web-based client (e.g. mobile device) can employ these services in order to interact with the WfMS remotely.

Lessons Learned. We revealed that the assignment of tasks to users may differ from the user who is interested in the notifications for a task; e.g. a driver executes some driving while the planner monitors this execution. For the former, we utilize the concept of swimlanes (provided by BPMN and Activiti) while for the latter, we introduced additional policies by extending the developed interface IF6 (cf. Fig. 3) such that it now supports both: user specific event queries and an integration of our WfMS with our event processing engine (extension (iii)).

4.3   Event Processing

Event sources are meant to provide streams of data, i.e. a series of updated digital information objects (henceforth, *events*). In our context, events pertain to the applicants, devices, and means of transportation under control that are utilized for executing a logistics process. Knowledge can be extracted from events that *(i)* permits to monitor the carry-out of related activities, *(ii)* detects anomalies in their execution, and *(iii)* predicts possible disruptions in the process execution.

Requirements. Corresponding to [17] and the use case and requirements described before, an event engine must provide: *(1)* a generic interface to different sources which streams events concerning trucks, air-planes and their environment, *(2)* technologies to normalize data in heterogeneous formats for processing, *(3)* support to define high-level events, *(4)* a publish-subscribe interface for other systems to receive events or respective notifications about events, and *(5)* perform ex-ante predictions on the future evolution of the process instance.

Design. The *Event Handler* is designed to read multiple sources by means of dedicated *Adapters* to publish them as uniform events for event processing. This entails that the event engine not only has to provide the possibility to register queries to be informed on events of interest, but it also needs to be capable of automatically correlating events to transport processes. In our architecture, event processing is based on the subscriptions forwarded by the process engine that derived them from sufficiently annotated process models, e.g. for progress updates and violation detection. For a correlation with external event data, instance-specific information is required in the subscriptions, e.g. the container id or the destination of a transport.

To match high-level events to subscriptions of the process engine, the event engine must also be capable of aggregating events of finer granularity, such as the subsequent positional updates of the air-planes, to more informative ones, such as the changes of speed, altitude, and direction in a time interval. To this end, techniques coming from the area of Complex Event Processing [18] are exploited.

Finally, the event engine is demanded to predict diversions ahead of time. While predicting violations based on deterministic events such as congestions can be done through subscriptions as shown above, probabilistic predictions correspond to exceptional situations that turn out to be hard to encode by means of human-specified subscriptions. Therefore, we resort on automated classification and regression techniques, well established in the research field of Machine Learning [19]. The objective is to make the event processing module capable of automatically classifying anomalies in harmful or not significant for the correct process execution based on conditions learned through analysis of past executions. When possible, the quantification of foreseen effects on the process are also expressed in terms of, e.g. of delays.

Implementation. Technically, the core functionality of event processing is provided by the open source platform Esper[3], which we extended based on the requirements identified. We included an event hierarchy and aggregation rules

---

[3] http://www.espertech.com/.

for the logistics domain. Additionally, we included custom function calls for geographic calculations and to access static data on transport nodes. For the management of event sources, aggregation rules, subscriptions, and logistics process specific services, we built a framework around Esper [12]. The event engine, in which Esper is embedded and used in the GET Service project, is called UNICORN[4]. UNICORN is implemented in Java and devises several ways to receive events: through a web service, using the web-based UI, through ActiveMQ[5], and through configurable adapters that pull events from different sources. Consumers, like the process engine in our scenario, subscribe to events by sending Esper queries via a web service. Another web service allows to register transports by passing their parameters, in which case the event engine handles all subscriptions. Notifications are distributed via ActiveMQ queues. Alternatively, the web UI of the event engine can be used to display notifications.

Consider the air-plane from our use case in Sect. 3. The processing and analysis of events tracing its position would contribute to observe its anomalous behaviour by changing the route and to foresee the disruption of the transportation process [20]. The event monitoring, the anomaly detection, and the disruption prediction are the functionalities that are also encapsulated in the event service component (see Fig. 3).

Lessons Learned. Rather than be unified under a single general-purpose component to derive or predict high-level events, the dedicated modules can be plugged in. Each module adopts its own algorithm to interpret the current status and recent history of the process instance according to the scope of its predictive analysis. For instance, the module that raises alerts in case of delays of trucks differs from the one utilised for the flight route anomalies. At the same time, they also act as event sources that publish their outcomes as fine-granular events that are then aggregated and retransmitted as prediction events. In the scenario, a diversion prediction would be notified when a given number of consecutive flight route anomalies were received and aggregated by the Event Processing component. This actually reflects the technique adopted in [21], a technique applying event processing in the context of flight diversions within logistics transports.

5   Conclusion

Guided execution and monitoring the status of business processes is of vital importance, if an organization needs to promptly react to occurring problems. We presented a methodology to engineer a logistics process application that is driven by events for execution and monitoring. This allows utilization of information from several event sources, pre-processed and refined by an event engine, to not only execute or monitor processes, but also predict potential problems. We argue that the event subscriptions, necessary for such purposes, must be

---

[4] http://bpt.hpi.uni-potsdam.de/UNICORN.
[5] http://activemq.apache.org/.

contained as annotations in the process model which are automatically registered by a process engine with the event engine. Exemplified, we discussed the design of such a system, presented the corresponding implementation, and highlighted lessons learned for the modelling, execution, and monitoring. The complete implementation and the interaction between the components is provided as screencast provided at http://youtu.be/JE2Df7iaERk.

In future work, we aim to establish a reference model for the whole process and describe it along the whole architecture of the GET Service project. We also expect our approach to be generalizable to other domains such as manufacturing or healthcare, in which external events play a central role in the proceeding of business processes.

References

1. Dumas, M., Rosa, M.L., Mendling, J., Reijers, H.A.: Fundamentals of Business Process Management. Springer, Heidelberg (2013)
2. Luckham, D.C.: Event Processing for Business: Organizing the Real-Time Enterprise. Wiley, Hoboken (2011)
3. Cabanillas, C., Baumgrass, A., Mendling, J., Rogetzer, P., Bellovoda, B.: Towards the enhancement of business process monitoring for complex logistics chains. In: Lohmann, N., Song, M., Wohed, P. (eds.) BPM Workshops. LNBIP, vol. 171, pp. 305–317. Springer, Heidelberg (2013)
4. Business Continuity Institute: Supply Chain Resilience 2014 - An International Survey to Consider the Origin, Causes & Consequences of Supply Chain Disruption (2014)
5. Baumgrass, A., Di Ciccio, C., Dijkman, R., Hewelt, M., Mendling, J., Meyer, A., Pourmirza, S., Weske, M., Wong, T.: GET controller and UNICORN: event-driven process execution and monitoring in logistics. In: BPM Demo track, CEUR Workshop Proceedings (2015)
6. Treitl, et al.: Use Cases, Success Criteria and Usage Scenarios, Deliverable report 1.1, GET Service (2014)
7. Baumgrass, A., Dijkman, R., Grefen, P., Pourmirza, S., Voelzer, H., Weske, M.: A software architecture for transportation planning and monitoring in a collaborative network. In: Camarinha-Matos, L.M., Bénaben, F., Picard, W. (eds.) Risks and Resilience of Collaborative Networks. IFIP AICT, vol. 463. Springer, Heidelberg (2015)
8. Kruchten, P.: Architectural blueprints - the "4+ 1" view model of software architecture. Tutorial Proc. Tri-Ada 95, 540–555 (1995)
9. Hollingsworth, D., Hampshire, U.: Workflow management coalition the workflow reference model. Workflow Manag. Coalition 68, 26 (1993)
10. Botezatu, M., Völzer, H.: Language and meta-model for transport processes and snippets. In: Deliverable D4.1, GET Service (2014)
11. Object Management Group: Business process model and notation (BPMN) v2.0 (2011)
12. Bernhardt, T., Vasseur, A.: Esper: Event Stream Processing and Correlation (2007)
13. Mendling, J., Reijers, H., van der Aalst, W.: Seven process modeling guidelines (7PMG). Inf. Softw. Technol. 52(2), 127–136 (2010)
14. Pourmirza, S., Dijkman, R.: A Survey of Orchestration Engines. In: Deliverable report 7.1, GET Service (2014)

15. Pourmirza, S., Dijkman, R., Grefen, P.: Switching parties in a collaboration at run-time. In: EDOC, pp. 136–141. IEEE (2014)
16. Rademakers, T.: Activiti in Action: Executable business processes in BPMN 2.0. Manning Publications, Shelter Island (2012)
17. Baumgrass, A., Breske, R., Cabanillas, C., Ciccio, C.D., Eid-Sabbagh, R., Hewelt, M., Meyer, A., Rogge-Solti, A.: Conceptual architecture specification of an information aggregation engine, Deliverable report 6.2, GET Service (2014)
18. Mühl, G., Fiege, L., Pietzuch, P.: Distributed Event-Based Systems. Springer, Heidelberg (2006)
19. Mitchell, T.M.: Machine Learning, 1st edn. McGraw-Hill Inc, New York (1997). McGraw Hill series in computer science
20. Baumgrass, A., Hewelt, M., Meyer, A., Raptopoulos, A., Selke, J., Wong, T.: Prototypical Implementation of the Information Aggregation Engine. In: Deliverable D6.3, GET Service, September 2014
21. Cabanillas, C., Di Ciccio, C., Mendling, J., Baumgrass, A.: Predictive task monitoring for business processes. In: Sadiq, S., Soffer, P., Völzer, H. (eds.) BPM 2014. LNCS, vol. 8659, pp. 424–432. Springer, Heidelberg (2014)

Counterexample Analysis for Supporting Containment Checking of Business Process Models

Faiz UL Muram[(✉)], Huy Tran, and Uwe Zdun

Software Architecture Group, University of Vienna, Vienna, Austria
{faiz.ulmuram,huy.tran,uwe.zdun}@univie.ac.at

Abstract. During the development of a process-aware information system, there might exist multiple process models that describe the system's behavior at different levels of abstraction. Thus, containment checking is important for detecting unwanted deviations of process models to ensure a refined low-level model still conforms to its high-level counterpart. In our earlier work, we have interpreted the containment checking problem as a model checking problem and leveraged existing powerful model checkers for this purpose. The model checker will detect any discordance of the input models and yield corresponding counterexamples. The counterexamples, however, are often difficult for developers with limited knowledge of the underlying formal methods to understand. In this paper, we present an approach for interpreting the outcomes of containment checking of process models. Our approach aims to analyze the input models and counterexamples to identify the actual causes of containment inconsistencies. Based on the analysis, we can suggest a set of countermeasures to resolve the inconsistencies. The analysis results and countermeasures are visually presented along with the involved model elements such that the developers can easily understand and fix the problems.

Keywords: Counterexample analysis · Containment checking · Consistency checking · BPMN · Process model · Behavior model · Model checking · Countermeasure

1 Introduction

Model checking is a powerful verification technique for detecting inconsistencies of software systems [8]. In general, especially in the context of business process management, behavior models are transformed into formal specifications and verified against predefined properties. The model checker then exhaustively searches for property violations in formal specifications of a model and produces counterexample(s) when these properties do not satisfy the formal specifications. The ability to generate counterexamples in case of consistency violations are considered as one of the strengths of the model checking approach. Unfortunately, counterexamples

© Springer International Publishing Switzerland 2016
M. Reichert and H.A. Reijers (Eds.): BPM Workshops 2015, LNBIP 256, pp. 515–528, 2016.
DOI: 10.1007/978-3-319-42887-1_41

produced by existing model checkers are rather cryptic and verbose. In particular, there are two major problems in analyzing counterexamples. First, the developers and non-technical stakeholders who often have limited knowledge of the underlying formal techniques are confronted with cryptic and lengthy information (e.g., states numbers, input variables over tens of cycles and internal transitions, and so on) in the counterexample [11]. Second, because a counterexample is produced as a trace of states, it is challenging to trace back the causes of inconsistencies to the level of the original model in order to correct the flawed elements [9]. As a result, the developers have to devote significant time and effort in order to identify the cause of the violation, or they get confused about the relevance of a given trace in the overall explanation of the violation. Besides that, in order to raise the practical applicability of model checking, there is a need for an automated approach to interpret the counterexamples with respect to containment checking and finding the causes of a violation.

There is a certain amount of approaches that target counterexample analysis for model checking [4,9,11]. Out of these existing approaches, only a few are aiming at supporting counterexample analysis of behavioral models [11]. Most of these approaches focus on fault localization in source programs for safety and liveness properties or generation of proofs to aid the understanding of witnesses. As these approaches focus on model checking in a generic context, their analysis techniques can be applied in a wide range of application domains. However, this comes with a price: the analysis outcomes are rather abstract and far from helping in understanding the specific causes of a violation in a particular domain. Furthermore, these techniques have not considered to provide any annotations or visual supports for understanding the actual causes nor suggest any potential countermeasures.

In this paper, we propose to focus on a specific context, which is the *containment checking problem*, in order to achieve better support for understanding and resolving the inconsistencies. The goal of containment checking is to ensure that the specifications in high-level models created, for instance, by business analysts early in the development lifecycle, are not unwittingly violated by refined (one or more low-level) models of the high-level model created, for instance, by developers during the detailed design phase [13]. The containment checking problem can be interpreted as a model checking problem, in which the behavior described in the high-level model are used as the constraints that the low-level counterpart must satisfy [13]. In case of a containment violation, the model checkers will generate corresponding counterexamples.

We have developed an approach that supports the interpretation of the generated counterexamples and reports typical possible causes of a containment inconsistency. In particular, we have constructed a counterexample analyzer that automatically extracts the information from the counterexample trace file generated by containment checking using the NuSMV model checker [5]. Based on the extracted information along with formalization rules for the containment relationship, our counterexample analyzer identifies the cause(s) of the violation(s) and produces an appropriate set of guidelines to countermeasure the containment violations. Our approach allows the developers to focus on the immediate cause of an inconsistency without having to sort through irrelevant information. In order to make our approach more usable in practice, we devise visual supports that can highlight the involved elements in the process models. Furthermore, it provides annotations containing causes of inconsistencies and potential countermeasures shown in the input process models. In the scope of this study, we consider BPMN[1] process models because they are widely used for the description of business processes and the majority of process developers are familiar with their syntax and semantics.

The paper is structured as follows. In Sect. 2, we provide background information on our model-based containment checking approach. Section 3 describes the counterexample interpretation approach in detail. Section 4 presents a use case extracted from an industrial case study to illustrate our approach. In Sect. 5, we review the related approaches regarding behavioral consistency checking and counterexamples interpretation. Finally, we conclude on our main contributions and discuss future work in Sect. 6.

2   Model Checking Based Containment Checking Approach

This section briefly introduces important aspects of our model checking based approach for containment checking [13]. Containment checking aims to verify whether the elements and structures (e.g., activities, events and/or gateways) of a high-level BPMN model correspond to those of a refined low-level model. An example of a high-level model is a specification produced by a business analyst together with a customer early in the software development lifecycle. Later during architecting and detailed design, this model is usually gradually refined for subsequent implementation. Containment checking can ensure that the high-level behavior model is completely contained in the refined models and that developers did not (unwittingly) introduce deviations (aka consistency violations). According to the definition of containment relationship, the opposite direction is not essential because the low-level behavior models are often constructed by refining and enriching the high-level model. An overview of the approach is shown in Fig. 1.

As shown in Fig. 1, the high-level process model under study will be automatically transformed into Linear Temporal Logic (LTL) rules [14] whilst the low-level counterpart will be automatically transformed into a SMV specification (input language of NuSMV model checker) [6]. Then, containment checking is performed by leveraging the NuSMV model checker [5]. In particular, the model checker takes the generated LTL rules and the SMV specification as inputs to verify whether they are satisfied. In case the SMV specification satisfies the LTL rules, it implies that the low-level process model conforms to the corresponding high-level model. If, however, the low-level process model deviates improperly

---

[1] http://www.omg.org/spec/BPMN/2.0.

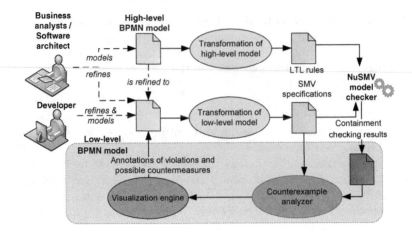

Fig. 1. Overview of the containment checking approach (Color figure online)

from the high-level counterpart, NuSMV will generate a counterexample that consists of the linear (looping) paths of the SMV specification leading to the violation. The main focus of this paper is shown in the big grey box.

The counterexample essentially shows the progress of the states from the beginning (i.e., all variables are initialized) until the point of violation along with the corresponding variables' values. Hence, it is time consuming and error-prone to locate relevant states because the developers may have to exhaustively walk through all of these execution traces. We note that counterexamples generated by the NuSMV model checker may contain different information depending on the selected model checking options, model encoding techniques, and the input LTL rules. Thus, it is crucial to provide useful feedbacks to the developers and non-technical stakeholders that can reveal the causes of containment inconsistencies and suggest potential resolutions.

In the subsequent sections, we present in detail our approach for counterexample interpretation that is able to help identifying the causes of containment inconsistencies. It also provides an appropriate set of guidelines to developers containing countermeasures to address the deviations from the containment relationship. The low-level model is updated based on the guidelines and re-mapped to its formal specification, and then will be re-verified. This process iterates until no containment violations are detected.

3   Interpretation of Containment Inconsistencies

Containment inconsistencies may occur due to a variety of reasons, such as missing or misplaced elements in the low-level model, and so on. We propose a two-step approach for locating the causes of containment inconsistencies. In the first step, the counterexample analyzer extracts the information from the output trace file generated by the NuSMV model checker and identifies the actual causes of the unsatisfied containment relationship and produces appropriate suggestions. In the second step, the information provided by the counterexample analyzer will be annotated in the low-level process model along with concise descriptions of the violation's causes and potential countermeasures.

3.1   Counterexample Analyzer for Locating Causes of Containment Inconsistencies

The counterexample analyzer investigates the causes of an unsatisfied containment relationship with respect to the LTL-based primitives. Initially, the counterexample analyzer reads the output trace file and parses the counterexamples that represent the unsatisfied LTL rules. Afterwards, the counterexample analyzer traverses the extracted information, LTL-based primitives and SMV specification to find out why the elements and control flow structures of the high-level model are not matched by their corresponding low-level counterparts. Note that the elements that are described in the high-level model but missing or misplaced in the low-level model can be the causes of the containment inconsistencies. The counterexample analyzer inspects and addresses all possible causes of an unsatisfied containment relationship defined by a specific LTL-based primitive and possible countermeasures.

In order to locate the causes of the inconsistency, the counterexample analyzer first verifies whether all the elements (e.g., activities, events and/or gateways) that exist in the high-level model are also present in the low-level model. For this, the counterexample analyzer locates the missing element cause (either one, multiple, or all elements could be missing) and suggests the countermeasure (i.e., insert missing element at a specific position in the model).

After that a number of rules related to unsatisfied LTL rules for different possible kinds of elements in the BPMN model are checked. For this, the counterexample analyzer matches the exact position of the corresponding elements in the high-level model related to unsatisfied LTL rules with elements present in the low-level model. Specifically, the counterexample analyzer reads the sequence (of elements of the low-level model) from the SMV specification and identifies corresponding element (i.e., activity or a gateway) causing the violation of the LTL rules. The preceding and succeeding elements of that element are matched with the elements of LTL rules to locate the causes of inconsistencies.

The descriptions of the possible causes for each LTL-based primitive and relevant countermeasures to resolve these causes are presented in Table 1. The right-hand side column contains the informal description of elements and second column contains the corresponding LTL-based primitives for formally representing these constructs. Let us consider the first one as an example: sequential order, which describes the relation that one element A2 eventually follows another element A1. As in the other rules in Table 1, violations occur due to a misplacement of elements. For instance, in the case of the sequence described by the LTL rule $(G (A1 \rightarrow F A2))$, a violation might happen because the element A2 (transitively) exists in the low-level model as a preceding element of the element A1, but not as

Table 1. Tracking back the causes of containment violations and relevant countermeasures

Elements	LTL-Based Primitives	Causes of Unsatisfied Rule	Possible Countermeasures
Sequence: A set of elements (transitively) executed in sequential order.	`(G (A1 -> F A2))`	The sequential rule is violated, if element A2 does not eventually follow element A1 in the low-level model, but A2 exists as a preceding element of A1.	• Swap the occurrence of A2 and A1. • Add A2 after A1 in the low-level BPMN model.
Parallel Fork (AND-Split): The execution of a Fork leads to the parallel execution of subsequent activities or events (A1, A2...An). Please note that the activities or events may be executed one after the other or possibly may be executed in a real parallel enactment.	`G (ParallelFork -> F (A1 & A2 & ...& An))`	The Parallel Fork rule is unsatisfied, if a Fork gateway is not eventually followed by either one or all the activities/events (A1, A2,...An), or either one or all the activities/events exist as a preceding element of a Fork gateway.	• Put elements (A1 and/or A2 ...and/or An) after the Parallel Fork in the low-level model. • Elements (A1, A2...An) shall be triggered from the Parallel Fork.
Parallel Join (AND-Join): The execution of two or more parallel elements (A1, A2...An) leads to the execution of a Join gateway. The semantics is represented that all elements must complete before the execution of a Join gateway.	`(G (A1 & A2 & ...& An) -> F ParallelJoin)`	The Parallel Join rule is violated, because either one or all the elements (A1, A2 ... An) exist as succeeding elements of a Join gateway, but are not followed by a Join gateway.	• Replace flawed elements(s) ("element's name") with the correct elements ("element's name"), respectively. • Remove flawed element(s) ("element's name") from the low-level BPMN model. • Elements (A1, A2...An) shall be followed by a Parallel Join.
Exclusive Decision (XOR-Split): The execution of an Exclusive Decision eventually followed by the execution of at least one of the elements among the available set of elements based on condition expressions for each gate of the gateway.	`(G (ExclusiveDecision -> F (A1 xor A2)))`	The Exclusive Decision rule is violated, if both of the branches return either FALSE or TRUE exclusively. It means that the Exclusive Decision gateway is not followed by elements (i.e., A1 and A2).	• Replace flawed elements ("element's name") with correct elements ("element's name") after the Exclusive Decision, respectively. • Remove flawed elements ("element's name") from the low-level BPMN model.
Exclusive Merge (XOR-Join): The execution of at least one element among a set of alternative elements will lead to the execution of an Exclusive Merge gateway.	`( G (A1 xor A2) -> F ExclusiveMerge)`	The Exclusive Merge rule is unsatisfied, because activity A1 and activity A2 are not followed by an Exclusive Merge, but one or both elements exist as the succeeding elements of an Exclusive Merge in the low-level model.	• Put the Exclusive Merge after A1 and A2 in the model. • Replace the flawed elements ("element's name") with correct elements ("element's name") before the Exclusive Merge, respectively.

a succeeding element of A1. In this context, the counterexample analyzer generates the relevant countermeasures to resolve the violation (in this case: "*swapping the occurrence of A2 to A1*" or "*add A2 after A1*"). Nevertheless, our approach provides promising results for composite controls, for instance, combinations of two or more control structures, like G (ParallelFork -> F (ExclusiveDecision & A1 & .... & An)).

3.2 Visual Support for Understanding and Resolving Inconsistencies

In this section, we explain how the containment checking results can be presented to the developers in a user friendlier manner in comparison to the counterexamples. The visual support aims at shows the developer the causes of containment inconsistencies that occur when the elements and structures (e.g., activities, events and/or gateways) of the high-level process model do not have corresponding parts in the low-level model and also provides relevant countermeasures to resolve the violations.

The visual support is based on the information provided by the counterexample analyzer along with the input low-level process model. In particular, the element(s) that indicates the first element causing the violation of the LTL rule is highlighted in blue whilst the elements that are causes of containment violations are visualized in red, and the elements that satisfied the corresponding LTL rule appear in green. In order to improve the understandability of the counterexamples, we create annotations at the first element causing the violation to show the description of the cause(s) of the containment violation and relevant potential countermeasures to address the violation. Once the root cause of a containment violation is located, the cause is eliminated by updating the involving elements of the low-level process model. To differentiate more than one unsatisfied rule, shades of the particular color are applied, for instance, the first unsatisfied rule is displayed in the original shade while others are gradually represented in lighter tones. The low-level process model displaying highlighted involving elements and annotation of the actual causes of the containment inconsistencies and relevant countermeasures is shown in Fig. 3.

4 Use Case from Industrial Case Study

This section briefly discusses a use case from an industrial case study on a billing and provisioning system of a domain name registrar and hosting provider to illustrate the validity of our technique. The Billing Renewal process is taken from our previous industry projects [18]. The Billing Renewal process comprises a wide variety of services, for instance, credit bureau services (cash clearing, credit card validation and payment activities, etc.), hosting services (web and email hosting, cloud hosting, provisioning, etc.), domain services (domain registration, private domain registration, transfer, website forwarding, etc.), and retail services (customer service and support, etc.). Figure 2 shows the high-level Billing Renewal process modeled as a BPMN model. The model is devised to capture essential control structures such as sequence and parallel execution, exclusive decision, and so on. Similarly, the low-level model of the Billing Renewal process containing detailed information is also modeled.

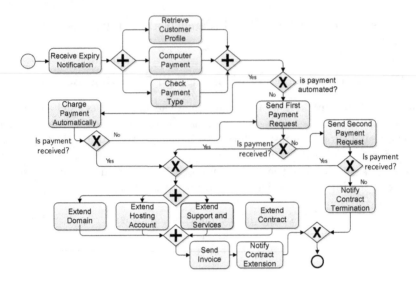

Fig. 2. High-level BPMN model of the Billing Renewal process

Formal consistency constraints (i.e., LTL rules) are automatically generated from the high-level BPMN model whilst the low-level BPMN model is transformed into SMV specification. Next, NuSMV verifies whether the formal SMV specification is consistent with the generated LTL rules. The NuSMV model checker generates a counterexample demonstrating a sequence of permissible state executions leading to a state in which the violation occurs in LTL rule. Finally, our approach for counterexample interpretation is applied to process the violation traces and visualize the involved elements in the low-level BPMN model along with annotations containing containment violation causes and suggestions. We opt to omit the verbose generated LTL rules and SMV specifications and focus more on the interpretation of the generated counterexample.

Listing 1.1 shows an excerpt of a violation trace generated by NuSMV including the list of satisfied and unsatisfied LTL rules, i.e., a counterexample. Despite the size and execution traces of this counterexample, the exact cause of the inconsistency is unclear, for instance, is the containment violation caused by a missing element, or a misplacement of elements, or both of them? It is time consuming and human labor intensive to locate the relevant states because the developers may have to exhaustively walk through all of these execution traces. The counterexample presents symptoms of the cause, but not the cause of the violation itself. Therefore, any manual refinement to the model could fail to resolve the deviation and may introduce other violations.

Figure 3 shows the low-level Billing Renewal process displaying the actual causes of the containment inconsistency and relevant countermeasures to address them. Using the visualizations of the violation, it is easy to see which elements of the low-level model involve in the containment inconsistency. In this case, the containment relationship is not satisfied due to the

violation of a parallel fork rule and a sequential rule. The parallel fork rule
G (ParallelFork1 -> F ((ComputerPayment & CheckPaymentType) & Retrie
veCustomerProfile)) is unsatisfied because ParallelFork1 is not followed by
the parallel execution of the subsequent tasks (i.e., ComputerPayment, Check-
PaymentType and RetrieveCustomerProfile) in the low-level model, which is the
actual cause of the containment violation. This violation can be addressed by triggering ComputerPayment from ParallelFork1 as shown in the attached comment
to ParallelFork1. Similarly, the root cause of second violation is mainly because
SendInvoice does not lead to ParallelJoin4. This might be a symptom of a misplacement of SendInvoice in the model as the primary cause that led to the containment inconsistency.

Listing 1.1. NuSMV containment checking result of the billing renewal process

```
$ NuSMV BillingRenweal.smv
...
-- specification  G (StartEvent ->  F ReceiveExpiryNotification)  is  true
-- specification  G (ReceiveExpiryNotification ->  F ParallelFork1)  is
   true
-- specification  G (ParallelFork1 ->  F ((ComputerPayment &
   CheckPaymentType) & RetrieveCustomerProfile))  is false
-- as demonstrated by the following execution sequence
Trace Description: LTL Counterexample
Trace Type: Counterexample
-> State: 1.1 <-
  StartEvent = TRUE
  ReceiveExpiryNotification = FALSE
  ParallelFork1 = FALSE
  RetrieveCustomerProfile = FALSE
  ComputerPayment = FALSE
.....
-- Loop starts here
-> State: 1.6 <-
  CheckPaymentType = FALSE
  ParallelJoin2 = TRUE
  SendLastPaymentRequest = FALSE
  ExclusiveDecision5 = TRUE
  ParallelJoin3 = TRUE
.....
```

The use case illustrates that a rich and concise visualization of the inconsistency
causes can allow for an easy identification of the elements that cause the violation
and helps developers correct the process model accordingly. In the particular case,
after following the suggested countermeasures, rerunning the containment checking process yielded no further violations. Without these supports, the developers
would have to study and investigate the syntax and semantics of the trace file in
order to determine the relationship between the execution traces and the process
model, and then locate the corresponding inconsistency within the model, meaning
that the complex matching between the variables and states in the counterexample
and the elements of the models must be performed manually.

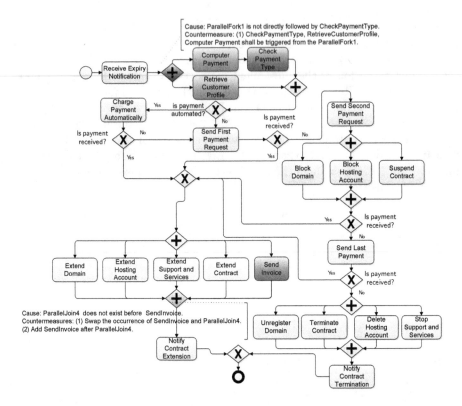

Fig. 3. Visual support for understanding and resolving containment violations (Color figure online)

5   Related Work

The work presented in this paper relates to the two main research areas: behavior model consistency checking and analysis of the model checking results (i.e., counterexamples) for identifying the causes of inconsistencies.

5.1   Behavior Model Consistency Checking

In the literature, many approaches tackle different types of models and/or model checking techniques [12]. However, very few of these studies focus on the consistency of behavior models; for instance, van der Straeten et al. [15] present an approach for checking the consistency of different UML models by using description logic. This approach considers model-instance, instance-instance, and model-model conflicts, instead of containment checking. Van der Aalst presents a theoretical framework for defining the semantics of behavior inheritance [1]. In this work, four different inheritance rules, based on hiding and blocking principles, are defined for UML activity diagram, state-chart and sequence diagram. Similar ideas have been presented in [16]. In [10] a general methodology is presented to deal with consistency problem of state-chart inheritance, which involves state-charts as well as the corresponding class diagrams. Communicating Sequential Processes (CSP) is used as a mathematical model for describing the consistency requirements and the FDR tool[2] is used for checking purposes. Weidlich et al. consider the compatibility between referenced process models and the corresponding implementation based on the notion of behavior inheritance [19]. Awad et al. introduce an approach for automated compliance checking of BPMN process models using BPMN-Q queries [3]. They adopted the reduction approach to verify the correctness of process models, instead of performing the detailed analysis using model checker. Unlike our approach, the aforementioned techniques do not aim at providing the analysis of the violation results for identifying the causes of inconsistencies and a set of countermeasures to resolve inconsistencies. Thus, these approaches are very useful for finding similar or alternative behavioral descriptions but not applicable for verifying the containment relationship.

5.2   Generating and Analyzing Counterexamples

The problem of generating and analyzing model-checking counterexamples are classified as follows: generating the counterexample efficiently, automatically analyzing the counterexample to extract the exact cause of violations, and creating a visualization framework suitable for interactive exploration.

Several existing approaches have addressed the idea of generating proofs from the model-checking runs. Many of these techniques focus on building evidence in form of a proof and controlling the generation of information to aid the understanding of counterexamples [7,17]. One of the drawbacks of these approaches is their size and complexity, which can be polynomial in the number of states of the system and of exponential length in the worst case. The proof-like witness techniques also require manual extrapolation, and the developers still need certain knowledge of the underlying formalisms in order to understand the proofs.

The problem of the automated analysis of counterexamples was addressed by many researchers, for instance, Ball et al. [4] describe an error trace as a symptom of the error and identify the cause of the error as the set of transitions in an error trace that does not appear in a correct trace of the program via the SLAM model checker. Kumazawa and Tamai present an error localization technique LLL-S for a given behavior model. The proposed technique identifies the infinite and lasso-shaped witnesses that resemble the given counterexample [11]. However, these approaches focus on finding the error causes in the program, such as deadlocks, assertion violations, and so on, but they are not applicable for verifying the causes of unsatisfied containment relationships.

Visual presentation of generated counterexamples is explored by Dong et al. [9]. The authors developed a tool that simplifies the counterexample exploration by presenting evidence for modal μ-calculus through various graphical views.

---

[2] https://www.cs.ox.ac.uk/projects/fdr/.

In particular, the highlighting correspondence between the generated counterexample and the analyzed property is addressed in their visualization process. Armas-Cervantes et al. [2] developed a tool for identifying behavioral differences between pairs of business process models by using Asymmetric Event Structure (AES) and verbalization of the results.

The above discussed approaches focus on general consistency checking. In contrast to our work, none of these techniques focuses on the diagnosis of counterexamples generated by a model checker with respect to containment checking. Note that, in our approach we do not need nor modify the source code of the model checker. Our interpretation process automatically extracts the information from the generated counterexample. In addition, another differentiating factor of our approach in comparison to aforementioned approaches is that our framework provides a compact and concise representation of the failure causes (such as missing or misplacement of elements) and countermeasures that are easily understandable for non-expert stakeholders. Finally, the counterexample interpretation steps are fully automated and do not require developer intervention.

6   Conclusion and Future Work

In this paper, we presented an approach for interpreting the causes of inconsistencies in behavior models based on the output results (i.e., counterexamples) of the model checker. In our work, the counterexample analyzer will help locating the actual causes of a containment inconsistency and producing appropriate guidelines as countermeasures based on the information extracted from counterexample trace file, formalization rules (i.e., LTL-based primitives), and the SMV specification of the low-level models. The visual support will show the involving elements along with annotations of causes and countermeasures in the low-level model. The advantage of this interpretation technique is twofold. On the one hand, the technique supports users who have limited knowledge of the underlying formalisms, and therefore, are not proficient in analyzing the cryptic and verbose counterexamples. On other hand, by locating actual cause(s) of the inconsistency and providing the relevant countermeasures to alleviate the inconsistencies to the user, it significantly reduces the time of manually locating the causes of an inconsistency. To the best of our knowledge, we investigated and presented almost all possible causes of a containment inconsistency and relevant countermeasures represented by a specific LTL-based primitive.

Currently, our approach supports output generated by the NuSMV model checker with respect to containment checking. Nevertheless, it is possible to adapt the presented techniques to support the other behavior models such as state machines, sequence diagrams[3], and BPEL[4] with reasonable extra efforts. In our future work, we plan on extending our approach for additional constructs (rather than the set of essential widely used constructs presented in this paper) and evaluate our approach with larger case studies. Another direction for future work is

---

[3] http://www.omg.org/spec/UML/2.4.1.
[4] https://www.oasis-open.org/committees/tc_home.php?wg_abbrev=wsbpel.

to quantitatively evaluate the counterexample interpretation approach in order to explore the pragmatic usability of the approach. Finally, we are looking into ways to extend our approach, in particular to support the interpretation and visualization of the analysis results from model checkers such as SPIN[5] that employ different underlying model checking techniques and data structures. The counterexample analyzer depends on the formalization rules and the options used in the model checker for generating output trace file. Extending our approach for SPIN is also possible as NuSMV and SPIN share several similar concepts regarding the state based counterexamples.

Acknowledgments. The research leading to these results has received funding from the Wiener Wissenschafts-, Forschungs- und Technologiefonds (WWTF), Grant No. ICT12-001.

References

1. Van der Aalst, W.M.: Inheritance of dynamic behaviour in UML. MOCA **2**, 105–120 (2002)
2. Armas-Cervantes, A., Baldan, P., Dumas, M., García-Bañuelos, L.: Behavioral comparison of process models based on canonically reduced event structures. In: Sadiq, S., Soffer, P., Völzer, H. (eds.) BPM 2014. LNCS, vol. 8659, pp. 267–282. Springer, Heidelberg (2014)
3. Awad, A., Decker, G., Weske, M.: Efficient compliance checking using BPMN-Q and temporal logic. In: Dumas, M., Reichert, M., Shan, M.-C. (eds.) BPM 2008. LNCS, vol. 5240, pp. 326–341. Springer, Heidelberg (2008)
4. Ball, T., Naik, M., Rajamani, S.K.: From symptom to cause: localizing errors in counterexample traces. In: Proceedings of the 30th ACM SIGPLAN-SIGACT Symposium on Principles of Programming Languages, POPL 2003, pp. 97–105. ACM, New Orleans (2003)
5. Cimatti, A., Clarke, E., Giunchiglia, F., Roveri, M.: NuSMV: a new symbolic model checker. Int. J. Softw. Tools Technol. Transfer **2**(4), 410–425 (2000)
6. Cimatti, A., Clarke, E., Giunchiglia, F., Roveri, M.: NuSMV: a new symbolic model verifier. In: Halbwachs, N., Peled, D.A. (eds.) CAV 1999. LNCS, vol. 1633, pp. 495–499. Springer, Heidelberg (1999)
7. Clarke, E.M., Grumberg, O., McMillan, K.L., Zhao, X.: Efficient generation of counterexamples and witnesses in symbolic model checking. In: Proceedings of the 32nd Annual ACM/IEEE Design Automation Conference, DAC 1995, pp. 427–432. ACM, New York (1995)
8. Clarke, E.M., Grumberg, O., Peled, D.A.: Model Checking. MIT Press, Cambridge (1999)
9. Dong, Y., Ramakrishnan, C.R., Smolka, S.: Model checking and evidence exploration. In: Proceedings of 10th IEEE International Conference and Workshop on the Engineering of Computer-Based Systems, 2003, pp. 214–223, April 2003
10. Engels, G., Heckel, R., Küster, J.M.: Rule-based specification of behavioral consistency based on the uml meta-model. In: 4th International Conference on The Unified Modeling Language. Modeling Languages, Concepts, and Tools, pp. 272–286. Springer, London (2001)

---

[5] http://spinroot.com/spin/whatispin.html.

11. Kumazawa, T., Tamai, T.: Counterexample-based error localization of behavior models. In: Bobaru, M., Havelund, K., Holzmann, G.J., Joshi, R. (eds.) NFM 2011. LNCS, vol. 6617, pp. 222–236. Springer, Heidelberg (2011)

12. Lucas, F.J., Molina, F., Toval, A.: A systematic review of UML model consistency management. Inf. Softw. Technol. 51(12), 1631–1645 (2009)

13. Uesaka, Y., Manalo, E.: How communicative learning situations influence students' use of diagrams: focusing on spontaneous diagram construction and protocols during explanation. In: Dwyer, T., Purchase, H., Delaney, A. (eds.) Diagrams 2014. LNCS, vol. 8578, pp. 93–107. Springer, Heidelberg (2014)

14. Pnueli, A.: The temporal logic of programs. In: Proceedings of the 18th Annual Symposium on Foundations of Computer Science, SFCS 1977, pp. 46–57. IEEE Computer Society, Washington (1977)

15. Van Der Straeten, R., Mens, T., Simmonds, J., Jonckers, V.: Using description logic to maintain consistency between UML models. In: Stevens, P., Whittle, J., Booch, G. (eds.) UML 2003. LNCS, vol. 2863, pp. 326–340. Springer, Heidelberg (2003)

16. Stumptner, M., Schrefl, M.: Behavior consistent inheritance in UML. In: Laender, A.H.F., Liddle, S.W., Storey, V.C. (eds.) ER 2000. LNCS, vol. 1920, pp. 527–542. Springer, Heidelberg (2000)

17. Tan, L., Cleaveland, W.R.: Evidence-based model checking. In: Brinksma, E., Larsen, K.G. (eds.) CAV 2002. LNCS, vol. 2404, pp. 455–470. Springer, Heidelberg (2002)

18. Tran, H., Zdun, U., Dustdar, S.: Name-based view integration for enhancing the reusability in process-driven SOAs. In: Muehlen, M., Su, J. (eds.) BPM 2010 Workshops. LNBIP, vol. 66, pp. 338–349. Springer, Heidelberg (2011)

19. Weidlich, M., Dijkman, R., Weske, M.: Behaviour equivalence and compatibility of business process models with complex correspondences. Comput. J. 55(11), 1398–1418 (2012)

Transforming Process Models
to Problem Frames

Stephan Faßbender[1]([⊠]) and Banu Aysolmaz[2]

[1] paluno - The Ruhr Institute for Software Technology, Duisburg-Essen, Germany
stephan.fassbender@paluno.uni-due.de
[2] Department of Computer Science, VU University, Amsterdam, The Netherlands
b.e.aysolmaz@vu.nl

Abstract. An increase of process awareness within organizations and advances in IT systems led to a development of process-aware information systems (PAIS) in many organizations. UPROM is developed as a unified BPM methodology to conduct business process and user requirements analysis for PAIS in an integrated way. However, due to the purpose, granularity and form of UPROM artifacts, one cannot analyze the software requirements in detail with (semi-)formal methods for properties such as completeness, compliance and quality. In contrast, Problem Frames modeled using the UML4PF tool can be used for such analysis. But using the Problem Frames notation and corresponding methods alone does not cover a direct support for building a PAIS. Hence, in this work we propose to integrate UPROM and UML4PF using model transformation. We use eCompany, a project which is part of an e-government program, as running example.

Keywords: Requirements engineering · Transformation · UPROM · Problem Frames

1 Introduction

With the rise of process awareness and IT systems, more and more organizations develop process-aware information systems (PAIS) to automate their processes [1]. Business process modeling (BPM) is the key instrument to analyze, design and identify the user requirements of a PAIS [2,3]. However, process functions need to be further analyzed for their behavior, data usage and operations during PAIS execution to identify user requirements in the business domain [2–5]. Moreover, those requirements need to be represented in a structured form so that they can be systematically exploited for detailed requirements analysis and software development.

UPROM is developed as a unified BPM methodology to conduct business process and user requirements analysis for PAIS in an integrated way [6]. Process models of UPROM are then used to automatically generate artifacts for PAIS development [4]. To provide a seamless link between business process analysis and software development, methods to systematically utilize business process

© Springer International Publishing Switzerland 2016
M. Reichert and H.A. Reijers (Eds.): BPM Workshops 2015, LNBIP 256, pp. 529–542, 2016.
DOI: 10.1007/978-3-319-42887-1_42

knowledge for PAIS development are necessary. UPROM already provides structured representation of process and requirements knowledge in business domain in the form of models. However, due to their purpose, granularity and form, we cannot analyze them with formal methods for properties, such as completeness and compliance. Moreover, the treatment of software qualities in a structured way is neglected in UPROM right now as qualities are only added as textual notes or high level goal. Hence, UPROM focuses on the functionality right now. To improve this situation, we need to refine these models in such a form that they can be used in the subsequent phases, specifically detailed software requirements analysis, and can be (semi-)formally analyzed.

The Problem Frames method based on the Problem Frames notation, as introduced by Jackson [7], decomposes the overall problem of building the system-to-be into small sub-problems. Using the Problem Frames approach to define software requirements provides various benefits. First of all it allows a thorough analysis and rigid definition of requirements [8]. Moreover, Problem Frames models have a semi-formal structure, which allows an (semi - automated) analysis of different qualities, such as, for example, privacy [9], security [10], and compliance with laws and standards [11,12], and an (semi - automated) interaction analysis for functional [13] as well as quality [14] requirements. Additionally, several topics such as aspect-orientation [15], variability [16], and requirements reconciliation and optimization [14] can be treated if necessary. Last but not least, Problem Frame models allow a seamless transition to the architecture and design phase [17]. Moreover, the overall system-to-be is decomposed using the requirements, which makes the usage of problem diagrams scalable even for large systems, because the complexity of single problem diagrams is independent of the system size.

The UML4PF tool which facilitates the modeling in the Problem Frames notation is used for all the aforementioned analysis. Typically, problem frame models are developed from scratch for each software project. This requires a considerable amount of effort and makes it difficult to establish the trace links between problem diagrams and business processes. Such a traceability is the key to ensure the completeness of software requirements from a business perspective, specifically when developing a PAIS.

In this paper, we propose a method to utilize business process and user requirements models of UPROM to create Problem Frame models. As a result, the Problem Frame models are directly based on process models, which ensures that the Problem Frame model covers the user requirements of the business domain. In this way, process knowledge elicited in the business domain is systematically transferred to subsequent phases of software development and the definition of process aware requirements is ensured. The integration of Problem Frames and UPROM also lowers the obstacles of using Problem Frames within a company. First of all, it relates a notation which is already well known with Problem Frames. Second, the transformation lowers the effort of using Problem Frames and assures that information which is already available in the form of process descriptions can be actually reused. Therefore, this integration enables a detailed requirements analysis using semi-formal Problem Frame models, but at the same time lowers the obstacles and effort to be taken for using the Problem Frame notation.

In the following section (Sect. 2) we introduce the background on UPROM and Problem Frames, which is necessary to comprehend the rest of the paper. Next, we introduce our case study in Sect. 4. Then, we describe our method (Sect. 3), which consists of two phases. In Sect. 4 we show the results of applying our method to our case study. In the last section (Sect. 6), we conclude our paper and present the future work.

2   Background

UPROM is a unified BPM methodology to conduct business process and user requirements analysis in an integrated way. Event-driven process chain diagram (EPC) is the core of UPROM notation for business process analysis. To conduct user requirement analysis, the functions in EPC diagrams to be automated by a PAIS are identified. If the function is to be (semi-) automated, a functional analysis diagram (FAD) is created as a sub-diagram. An FAD is used to analyze the requirements by identifying the responsibilities, related entities, operations on entities, and constraints applicable during the execution of the related function.

An FAD includes elements of the types function, entity, cluster, application, organizational elements (position, organizational unit, external person), and constraint. An example FAD is shown in Fig. 4. The function element, which is the same element as in the EPC diagram, is in the center of the FAD. Organizational elements are connected to the function named with the involvement types of "carries out", "approves", "supports", "contributes to", "must be informed on completion". In this way, the responsibilities to conduct the function in PAIS are identified. Entities or clusters which are required for or during the execution of the function, are connected to the function. The operations executed on these entities are defined by the connection name. The possible operations are uses, views, creates, changes, reads, deletes, and lists. Each entity is also connected to the application on which it resides. If there are further constraints that restrict how the system operates, they are modeled as constraints and connected to the related application. During the development of FADs, conceptual level entity definitions are discovered. The general aggregation and generalization relations between those entities are modeled in Entity Relationship (ER) diagrams.

The UPROM tool is developed to support the method. By using the tool, one can automatically generate textual user requirements, functional size estimation and process documentation from the EPCs and FADs developed.

Problem Frames. The objective of requirements engineering is to construct a *machine* (i.e., system-to-be) that controls the behavior of the environment (in which it is integrated) in accordance with the requirements. For this purpose, Jackson proposes to use the so called problem frame notation and approach [7]. The first step towards understanding and defining the problem to be solved by the machine is to understand the context of the machine. The context of the machine is given by the environment in which the problem to be solved is located, and in which the machine will be integrated to solve the problem. The environment is defined by means of domains and interfaces between these domains and the machine. Note that we use a UML-based adaption of problem frames, which is implemented as a specific UML profile for problem frames (UML4PF) as proposed by Hatebur and Heisel [8]. Hence, the graphical representation differs from the original representation proposed by Jackson [7], but the semantics remain the same. To be able to annotate problem diagrams with quality requirements, we extended the problem frames notation [17]. This enables us to complement functional requirements with quality requirements. Jackson distinguishes the domain types *machine* (Class with the stereotype ≪machine≫) which is the thing to be built, *biddable domains* (Classes with the stereotype ≪biddableDomain≫) that are usually people, *causal domains* (Classes with the stereotype ≪causalDomain≫) that comply with some physical laws or the specification is known, and *lexical domains* (Stereotype ≪lexicalDomain≫) which represent data. In the Problem Frames notation, *interfaces* connect domains and they contain *shared phenomena*. Shared phenomena may, for example, be events, operation calls or messages. They are observable by at least two domains, but controlled by only one domain, as indicated by "!". In Fig. 1 the notation $BM!C1$ (between the machine domain *BuldingMachine* and the causal domain *Sensor*) means that the phenomena $C1$ are controlled by the machine *BuildingMachine*. All other domains which are connected by the interface the phenomenon is part of can observe it. In our case, $BM!C1$ is observed by the domain *Sensor*. The information about the machine and its environment is modeled in a so called *context diagram*. An example is given in Fig. 3.

Problem frames are a means to describe and classify software development problems. A problem frame is a kind of pattern representing a class of software problems. It is described by a frame diagram, which consists of *domains, interfaces* between them, and a

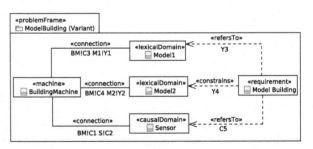

Fig. 1. Problem Frame model building

requirement. Figure 1 shows the problem frame for a model building variant. This variant contains the machine *BuildingMachine* which is the software or system which shall later fulfill the described requirement *Model Building*. The causal domain *Sensor* represents information about the real world from which the model is built. The lexical domain *Model1* provides the information necessary for the model building. The lexical domain *Model2* shall then reflect the result of the model building.

Requirements analysis with problem frames provides decomposition of the overall problem into sub-problems, which are represented by *problem diagrams*. A problem diagram is an instance of a *problem frame*. When we state a requirement we want to change something in the environment of the machine. Therefore, each requirement talks about and *constrains* at least one domain. Thus, these domains have to be influenced or changed to fulfill the requirement. For example, the domain *Model 2* (Class *Model 2* with stereotype ≪lexicalDomain≫) is constrained by the requirement *Model Building* (Class *Model Building* with stereotype ≪requirement≫) as shown in Fig. 1 (Dependency with stereotype ≪constrains≫ between class *Model Building* and class *Model2*). A requirement may also *refer to* several other domains in the environment of the machine which provide necessary information for fulfilling the requirement. The requirement *Model Building* refers to the domains *Sensor* (Class *Sensor* with stereotype ≪causalDomain≫) and *Model1* (Class *Model 1* with stereotype ≪lexicalDomain≫) (Dependency with stereotype ≪refersTo≫ between class *Model Building* and classes *Model1* and *Sensor*).

3   Method

The method to transform a UPROM model into a Problem Frames model consists of two phases. First, the EPC process model is turned into a context diagram. Then, each FAD bound to a function in the EPC is turned into one or more problem diagram(s).

Create a Context Diagram from an EPC. An EPC, which describes the business process which shall be supported by the system-to-be, is transformed into one or more context diagrams through a series of steps which are described in the following. The expected output is an initial *Problem Frame Model* which includes *machines, causal domains, biddable domains, lexical domains, phenomena* and *context diagrams*.

Create Machines: In the first step we investigate the *applications* in the *EPC*. If this application is to be developed, we add a *machine* to our *problem frame model*. Decision rules for separating machines and external applications are described in [6].

Aggregate Machines: In many cases there are several *applications* to be developed, thus several machines, as part of an *EPC*. Now, we aggregate those to one *aggregated machine*. It might happen that there are several independent systems-to-be and therefore several *aggregated machines*. For each of them, we create a separate *context diagram*.

Create Causal Domains: For those *applications* which are not to be developed, we add *causal domains* to the *context diagram(s)*. We will refer to such applications as external or existing applications.

Create Biddable Domains: In this step, we consider elements which are of the types *position, group, organizational unit* or *external person*. Those elements have in common that their behavior is not predictable and they can be influenced only to some extent. Hence, we turn them into *biddable domains* and add them to the *diagram(s)*.

Create Lexical Domains: In this step, we transform the *EPC* elements that represent information (*document, list, log* or *files*) to *lexical domains*. We then check if ERDs contain any information to aggregate them. If so, we add this joined element as lexical domain and create a mapping diagram for relation between that and its parts. We add all lexical domains which are not part of another lexical domain to the *context diagrams*.

Create Phenomena: Only those functions that are connected to an application to be developed are used to create *phenomena*. *Phenomena* do not exist on their own but in relation to domains which control and observe them. Hence, we also have to take into account the elements of the *EPC* connected to the functions. We distinguish four different cases for transformation depending on the type of elements connected to the functions. Table 1 shows a transformation table for one of the cases[1]. The first part of the table defines the input required for the transformation. The first mandatory input is *part of the EPC* which defines elements and relations that have to be present in the EPC at hand to enable the transformation. Note that some elements can be exchanged: e.g. the actor can be modeled in different ways. The *Questions* part defines the questions to determine the correct option for transformation and is optional. The second main part defines the output. The output can differ as there are different options for the transformation. An option is described by the answers given (☑ stands for the answer yes, ☒ stands for the answer no, and ☐ stands for no answer or an indifferent answer). Underneath, the resulting output is given in the UML4PF notation. In case of a fully automated transformation, the default option is used, rather than expecting answers to the questions. Note that the complete transformation covers a combination of the four cases and different options. Hence, some phenomena might be created several times. In case a phenomenon already exists, it is not created a second time.

Create Problem Diagrams. The input for the process of *creating problem diagrams* are the *FADs* developed in the business analysis phase. For each FAD we create a problem diagram including the according *requirement*. For each *application* which does not already exist and is part of the corresponding FAD, we add a new *machine* to the problem diagram. Each *machine* created this way has to be *mapped* to the corresponding machine that is part of the context diagram or to one of the already known sub-machines which were aggregated to the machine in the context diagram.

For all *entities* in the FAD, we *add a lexical domain* to the problem diagram. If we add a not already known *lexical domain* this way, we search for a *mapping* of the corresponding entity to existing entities in the ERDs. If we find such a mapping, we also model the mapping in the problem frame model. In case we

---

[1] All transformation tables can be found in a technical report available under http://www.uml4pf.org/publications/TR20150306_UPROM2UML4PF.pdf.

Table 1. (Context diagram) Create phenomena: Case 1 (option 2 and 5 out of 5 options)

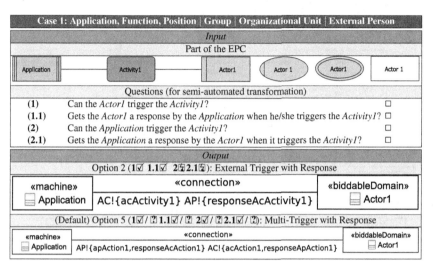

cannot find such a mapping, we have to create one or we have to add the new lexical domain to the related context diagram. In the same manner we *add a biddable domain* for each *position, group, organizational unit, internal person, or external person* and *map* these *biddable domains* whenever necessary. We also *add causal domains* for the *existing applications* and *map* them if necessary.

Up to this point we added machines and domains using the entities in FAD. Next, we need to *add the connections (associations), phenomena and dependencies* between them. We distinguish five cases with different options for transformation. An example transformation table for problem diagrams is given in (Table 2) (see Footnote 1). In case of a fully automated transformation, always the default option is used, while for semi-automated transformation answers to the questions is used to identify the transformation option. Note that the involvement types of the actors, if present, might indicate certain answers to the questions. Another aspect is that the transformation might not generate valid or complete problem diagrams in the first place. This has to be corrected in a later step.

After adding the phenomena, we also *create a textual* description of the *requirement*. Frequently, textual requirements are needed in PAIS projects for domain expert reviews, contract preparation and project management purposes. In UPROM, textual requirement sentences are generated automatically using FADs [18]. These textual requirements might contain more information than represented by the transformed problem diagram. Hence, they are of use for further refinements of the problem diagrams.

Table 2. (Problem diagram) Create phenomena: Case 1 (option 4 out of 5 options)

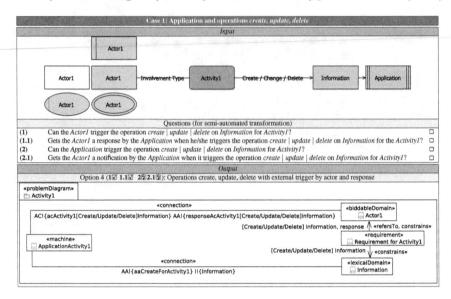

After creating and adding the textual requirement to the problem diagram for the FAD at hand, the transformation itself is finished. Now the resulting problem diagram needs to be analyzed further. First, we have to *adjust the problem diagram to be valid*. As mentioned, the combination of different transformation options might not result in a valid problem diagram. For example, it can happen that a requirement only refers to domains but no domain is constrained. Such invalid problem diagrams point out missing information, which we now have to add. Even if valid, the problem diagrams which are created from FAD tend to be rather big. The reason is that a business activity might combine different system functions. Hence, it might be possible to *decompose a problem diagram* into smaller sub-diagrams. Note that the last two steps can only be applied if doing a semi-automated transformation.

As the information about desired quality requirements is only modeled in an unstructured and high level way in UPROM, the information about quality requirements is missing up to this point. But as the functionality as described by the UPROM models is now turned into a Problem Frames model, for example, the UML4PF extension PresSuRE can be used to turn a high level goal (such as "System shall be secure") into related security requirements. In the same manner all other UML4PF extensions can be used to add quality requirements, as the extensions only require a detailed model of the functionality and some high level quality goals such as performance, compliance, and so forth.

4   Application

In this section, we briefly introduce our case study. Afterward, the application of our method for creating a context diagram and problem diagrams is explained on our case.

Case Study. The Company Central Registration project (eCompany) was initiated as part of an e-government program to develop an online workflow management system to automate life cycle processes of companies such as such as citizen application for company establishment, management of new establishments and updates by officers. The initial phase of the project included the analysis of business processes and user requirements and preparation of the technical contract. In this phase, three analysts from the integrator, three from the subcontractor and two domain experts cooperated. UPROM was used for process and requirements analysis. 15 EPCs and 82 FADs were created. 363 generated textual requirement statements were used in the technical contract.

A part of the process for establishing a company is shown in Fig. 2. The FAD for the last function *Define company name* of this EPC is shown in Fig. 4. The *Company Establishment Applicant carries out* this function. To accomplish the function, the *Company Establishment Application* has to *create* the *company name* and the *name alternatives* ensured not to match the *list* of existing *company names*, and the *name control fee*, which is calculated based on the number of *name alternatives* identified by the company establishment applicant. The company establishment application sends (*creates*) the name control fee to an external application called *finance office web service*. To identify the later payment it *uses* the *application number*. In the end, the company establishment application *changes* the *application status*. Restrictions on the function to be considered during its execution, which cannot be expressed directly in the FAD, are attached as constraint elements in dark green.

Fig. 2. Part of the EPC for the process "Establish Company" (Color figure online)

Create Context Diagram. In the following, we will explain how to create the context diagram for our case as shown in Fig. 3. In the first step, we *create the machines*. The EPC contains two applications we need to consider: The *Company Establishment Application* and the *Company Establishment Approval* application. We *aggregate the machines* found to the *eCompanyApplication* machine.

Table 3. (Context diagram) Create phenomena: Case 1 for "Define company name"

Case 1: Application, Function, External Person		
Input		
Part of the EPC		
Company Establishment Application	Define company name	Company Establishment Applicant
Questions (for semi-automated transformation)		
(1) Can the *Company Establishment Applicant* trigger the *Define company name*?		☑
(1.1) Gets the *Company Establishment Applicant* a response by the *Company Establishment Application* when he/she triggers the *Define company name*?		☑
(2) Can the *Company Establishment Application* trigger the *Define company name*?		▣
(2.1) Gets the *Company Establishment Application* a response by the *Company Establishment Applicant* when it triggers the *Define company name*?		▣
Output		
Option 2 (1☑ 1.1☑ 2▣2.1▣): External Trigger with Response		
«machine» eCompanyApplication	«connection» CEA!{ceaDefineCompanyName} ECA!{responseCeaDefineCompanyName}	«biddableDomain» CompanyEstablishmentApplicant

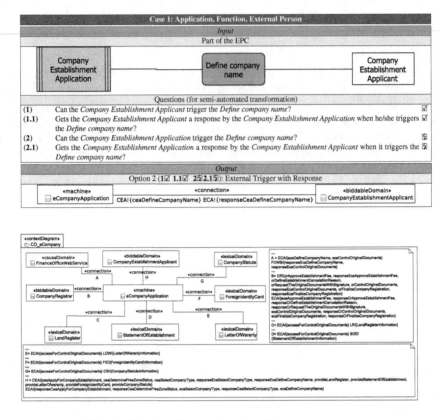

Fig. 3. Context diagram for the eCompany system

Next, we *create the causal domains*. In case of the EPC alone we do not have to model a causal domain as the external applications, such as *Finance Office Web Service*, only relate to external processes. For the causal domains we also have to consider the FAD related to the functions in the EPC at hand. The external application finance office web service is also part of the FADs for the functions "Define company name" and "Control original docs". Hence, we add the causal domain *FinanceOfficeWebService* to our context diagram. Next, we *create the biddable domains*. According to the EPC, we create the biddable domains *CompanyRegistrar* and *CompanyEstablishmentApplicant*.

Afterward, we also create the lexical domains *LandRegister*, *StatementOfEstablishment*, *LetterOfWarranty*, *ForeignIdentityCard*, and *CompanyStatute*. As described in Sect. 3, we also examine the ERD and create according mapping diagrams.

Last, we *create the phenomena*. We exemplify the creation of phenomena using the function "Define company name". We conduct a semi-automated transformation. Table 3 shows the transformation case for the function which matches

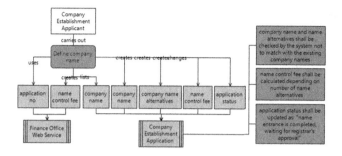

Fig. 4. FAD for the activity "Define company name"

the first case. The function is triggered by the company establishment applicant who gets a response, while the company establishment application remains passive. Note that in the resulting output the company establishment application is replaced by the eCompanyApplication, which aggregates the different applications which have to be developed to support the EPC at hand. The function "Define company name" matches also further cases which are not shown for sake of brevity but explained in the technical report[2]. The resulting complete context diagram is shown in Fig. 3.

Create Problem Diagrams. The FAD which we use to exemplify the creation of a problem diagram is the one bound to the function "Define company name" as shown in Fig. 4. We create a problem diagram for the FAD which contains the *requirement "Requirement For Define Company Name"*. We *add the application ApplicationDefineCompanyName* as machine domain to the problem diagram. This *machine* we created is *mapped* to the CompanyEstablishmentApplication machine which itself is mapped to the eCompanyAppSlication machine in the context diagram. We *add the lexical domains Application Status, Name Control Fee, Application No, Company Name and Company Name Alternatives* to the problem diagram as the corresponding entities are part of the FAD at hand. The *biddable domain CompanyEstablishmentApplicant* is also *added* to the problem diagram. Last, we *add a causal domain* for the external application *Finance Office Web Service*.

Up to this point, we prepared the elements of a problem diagram reflecting an FAD. Next, we need to add the *connections (associations), phenomena and dependencies* between them. Will only discuss the transformation for the creation of the *company name* by the *Company Establishment Applicant* using the *Company Establishment Application* in detail. The creation is triggered by the company establishment applicant who gets a response by the company establishment application. Hence, we use *option 4* of *case 1* for the transformation (see Table 2). We get the phenomena for triggering the company name creation and the according response between the biddable domain *CompanyEstablishmentApplicant* and the machine *ApplicationDefineCompanyName*. Furthermore, we

---

[2] http://www.uml4pf.org/publications/TR20150306_UPROM2UML4PF.pdf.

get the phenomena for the actual creation of the company name between the machine and the lexical domain *Company Name*. The *Requirement For Define Company Name* constrains the company name, and refers to and constrains the company establishment applicant. The FAD "Define company name" matches also six further cases and options which are not shown for the sake of brevity but are explained in the technical report (see footnote 2). After adding the phenomena, we also *create a textual* description of the *requirement*. The resulting problem diagram is shown in Fig. 5.

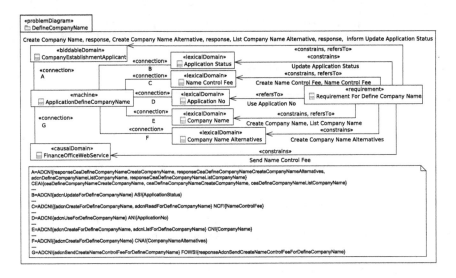

Fig. 5. Problem diagram for "Define company name"

Next, we would have to *adjust the problem diagram to be valid*. Moreover, as the problem diagram is quite big, we might *decompose a problem diagram* into smaller sub-diagrams. Those two steps are currently under research.

5   Related Work

BPM is frequently used for requirements analysis of PAISs. However, process models are not expressive enough for requirements engineering [2]. Yet, there exist a few studies that integrate process and requirements modeling [18] or derive requirements from process models [5]. Examples are goal modeling approaches utilized in early phases [19] and data-centric approaches [3]. The only study integrating problem frames and process modeling is tne by Cox et al., who link process models to problem frames via Role-Activity Diagrams [20]. However, this study does not systematically handle derivation of requirements from process models.

6   Conclusion

In this paper we have presented a method to integrate the UPROM method with the Problem Frames method via a transformation approach. The motivation is the need to systematically transfer process knowledge to software requirements analysis and further phases. Currently, the business and requirements analysis phases are quite separated, which makes it hard to ensure that a system developed is really able to support the business processes. The integration of UPROM and UML4PF ensures conformance to business processes and enables the use of all the methods offered by UML4PF for various analysis and the seamless transition to following software engineering phases.

Our contributions in this paper are: **(1)** A guided method for creating a context diagram and problem diagrams based on process models is presented. **(2)** This method lays the foundation for tool support enabling the (semi-) automated transformation from process to Problem Frame models. **(3)** In case of semi-automated transformation, additional information is elicited that enriches the Problem Frame diagrams in a lightweight way. **(4)** The generated problem diagrams are suitable for further analysis, such as completeness and quality. **(5)** Tracing from business processes to software development artifacts is enabled. **(6)** The obstacles and effort for using Problem Frames may be lowered.

Currently, we are finishing the development of a tool which supports the (semi-) automated transformations[3] and we are preparing a validation within an ongoing project.

References

1. Sinur, J., Hill, J.B.: Magic Quadrant for Business Process Management Suites (2010)
2. Monsalve, C., April, A., Abran, A.: On the expressiveness of business process modeling notations for software requirements elicitation. In: IECON 2012, pp. 3132–3137 (2012)
3. de la Vara, J.L., Fortuna, M.H., Sánchez, J., Werner, C.M.L., Borges, M.R.S.: A requirements engineering approach for data modelling of process-aware information systems. In: Abramowicz, W. (ed.) BIS 2009. LNBIP, vol. 21, pp. 133–144. Springer, Heidelberg (2009)
4. Aysolmaz, B., Demirörs, O.: Modeling business processes to generate artifacts for software development: a methodology. In: MISE Workshop, Hydarabad, India (2014)
5. Nicolás, J., Toval, A.: On the generation of requirements specifications from software engineering models: a systematic literature review. Inf. Softw. Technol. **51**(9), 1291–1307 (2009)
6. Aysolmaz, B.: UPROM: A Unified Business Process Modeling Methodology. Phd, Middle East Technical University (2014)
7. Jackson, M.: Problem Frames: Analyzing and Structuring Software Development Problems. Addison-Wesley, Boston (2001)

---

[3] The tool and used models are available under http://www.uml4pf.org/ext-uprom/index.html.

8. Hatebur, D., Heisel, M.: Making pattern- and model-based software development more rigorous. In: Dong, J.S., Zhu, H. (eds.) ICFEM 2010. LNCS, vol. 6447, pp. 253–269. Springer, Heidelberg (2010)

9. Beckers, K., Faßbender, S., Heisel, M., Meis, R.: A problem-based approach for computer-aided privacy threat identification. In: Preneel, B., Ikonomou, D. (eds.) APF 2012. LNCS, vol. 8319, pp. 1–16. Springer, Heidelberg (2014)

10. Faßbender, S., Heisel, M., Meis, R.: Functional requirements under security pressure. In: Proceedings of ICSOFT-PT 2014 (2014)

11. Faßbender, S., Heisel, M.: A computer-aided process from problems to laws in requirements engineering. In: Cordeiro, J., Sinderen, M. (eds.) ICSOFT 2013. CCIS, vol. 457, pp. 215–234. Springer, Heidelberg (2014)

12. Beckers, K., Côté, I., Faßbender, S., Heisel, M., Hofbauer, S.: A pattern-based method for establishing a cloud-specific information security management system. RE J. (2013)

13. Alebrahim, A., Faßbender, S., Heisel, M., Meis, R.: Problem-based requirements interaction analysis. In: Salinesi, C., van de Weerd, I. (eds.) REFSQ 2014. LNCS, vol. 8396, pp. 200–215. Springer, Heidelberg (2014)

14. Alebrahim, A., Choppy, C., Faßbender, S., Heisel, M.: Optimizing functional and quality requirements according to stakeholders' goals. In: System Quality and Software Architecture (SQSA), pp. 75–120. Elsevier (2014)

15. Faßbender, S., Heisel, M., Meis, R.: Aspect-oriented requirements engineering with problem frames. In: Proceedings of ICSOFT-PT 2014 (2014)

16. Alebrahim, A., Faßbender, S., Filipczyk, M., Goedicke, M., Heisel, M., Konersmann, M.: Towards a computer-aided problem-oriented variability requirements engineering method. In: Iliadis, L., Papazoglou, M., Pohl, K. (eds.) CAiSE Workshops 2014. LNBIP, vol. 178, pp. 136–147. Springer, Heidelberg (2014)

17. Alebrahim, A., Hatebur, D., Heisel, M.: Towards systematic integration of quality requirements into software architecture. In: Crnkovic, I., Gruhn, V., Book, M. (eds.) ECSA 2011. LNCS, vol. 6903, pp. 17–25. Springer, Heidelberg (2011)

18. Aysolmaz, B., Demirörs, O.: Deriving user requirements from business process models for automation: a case study. In: IEEE REBPM Workshop, pp. 19–28 (2014)

19. Pourshahid, A., Amyot, D., Peyton, L., Ghanavati, S., Chen, P., Weiss, M., Forster, A.J.: Toward an integrated user requirements notation framework and tool for business process management. In: 2008 International MCETECH Conference on e-Technologies (2008)

20. Cox, K., Phalp, K.T., Bleistein, S.J., Verner, J.M.: Deriving requirements from process models via the problem frames approach. Inf. Softw. Technol. 47(5), 319–337 (2005)

TAProViz Workshop

Preface to the 4th International Workshop on Theory and Application of Visualizations and Human-Centric Aspects in Processes (TAProViz 2015)

Ross Brown[1], Simone Kriglstein[2], and Stefanie Rinderle-Ma[3]

[1] Science and Engineering Faculty,
Queensland University of Technology, Brisbane, Australia
r.brown@qut.edu.au
[2] Faculty of Informatics, Vienna University of Technology, Vienna, Austria
kriglstein@cvast.tuwien.ac.at
[3] Faculty of Computer Science, University of Vienna, Vienna, Austria
stefanie.rinderle-ma@univie.ac.at

Introduction

This is the fourth TAProViz workshop being run at the 13th International Conference on Business Process Management (BPM). The intention this year is to consolidate on the results of the previous successful workshops by further developing this important topic, identifying the key research topics of interest to the BPM visualization community. Towards this goal, the workshop topics were extended to human computer interaction and related domains.

Submitted papers were evaluated by at least three program committee members, in a double blind manner, on the basis of significance, originality, technical quality and exposition. Three full and one position papers were accepted for presentation at the workshop. In addition, we invited a keynote speaker, Jakob Pinggera, a postdoctoral researcher at the Business Process Management Research Cluster at the University of Innsbruck, Austria.

The papers address a number of topics in the area of process model visualization, in particular:

- Visualizing Human Behavior and Cognition
- A Research Agenda for Invigorating Process Models
- Visual Design of Process Model Element Labels
- Visually Navigating Process Execution Data

The keynote, *Visualizing Human Behavior and Cognition: The Case of Process Modeling* by Jakob Pinggera, provides an overview on how visualizations have been and will be utilised to gain a deeper understanding of the process of process modeling.

In their position paper, *Towards an Integrated Framework for Invigorating Process Models: A Research Agenda*, Banu Aysolmaz and Hajo A. Reijers present their plan to use eight components to enhance process comprehension, viz., animation and visualization techniques for 2D and 3D models, 2 Brown, Kriglstein, and

Rinderle-Ma identification/design of animation scenarios, animations for process model layouts, user controls, usage of narration and on-screen text, embedding process perspectives, mode of operation and tailoring for personal factors.

Romain Emens, Irene Vanderfeesten and Hajo A. Reijers, present their full paper *The Dynamic Visualization of Business Process Models: A Prototype and Evaluation*. They present a new conceptual design for dynamic visualization of process models, whereby the user is dynamically guided to relevant parts of the diagram. A prototype implementation is presented with an evaluation by process participants.

Agnes Koschmider, Kathrin Figl and Andreas Schoknecht present a *Comprehensive Overview of Visual Design of Process Model Element Labels*. The paper includes findings in existing literature, analysis of the status quo of visual design of element labels, and finally, recommendations regarding the visual design of element labels.

In the final full paper, *Business Process Models for Visually Navigating Process Execution Data*, Jens Gulden and Simon Attfield present an analysis approach for navigating multi-dimensional process instance execution logs based on business process models. By visually selecting parts of a business process model, a set of available log entries is filtered to include only those entries that result from selected process branches.

Organizers

Ross Brown	Queensland University of Technology
Simone Kriglstein	Vienna University of Technology
Stefanie Rinderle-Ma	University of Vienna

Program Committee

Ralph Bobrik (Switzerland)
Massimiliano De Leoni (Netherlands)
Remco Dijkman (Netherlands)
Phillip Effinger (Germany)
Kathrin Figl (Austria)
Hans-Georg Fill (Austria)
Jens Kolb (Germany)
Agnes Koschmider (Germany)
Maya Lincoln (Israel)
Jürgen Mangler (Austria)
Silvia Miksch (Austria)
Margit Pohl (Austria)
Rune Rasmussen (Australia)
Pnina Soffer (Israel)
Irene Vanderfeesten (Netherlands)
Eric Verbeek (Netherlands)
Günter Wallner (Austria)

Visualizing Human Behavior and Cognition: The Case of Process Modeling

Jakob Pinggera[✉]

University of Innsbruck, Innsbruck, Austria
Jakob.Pinggera@uibk.ac.at

1 Introduction

Nowadays, business process modeling is heavily used in various business contexts. For instance, process models help to obtain a common understanding of a company's business processes [1], facilitate inter–organizational business processes [2], and support the development of information systems [3]. Still, process models in industrial process model collections often display a wide range of quality problems [4], calling for a deeper investigation of process model quality.

In response to the demand of process models of high quality, researchers recently have begun to take into account the processes involved in their creation. In this context, the *process model development lifecycle* involves several stakeholders, who drive the creation of the process model in *elicitation phases* and *formalization phases* [5]. In *elicitation phases*, information from the domain is extracted and used in the *formalization phase* by *process modelers* for creating a formal process model [6]. Since requirements evolve over time, model development usually comprises several iterations of elicitation and formalization, resulting in an evolving process model.

This extended abstract can be attributed to research on the formalization of process models intended to provide a brief overview on how visualizations have been utilized in the past and will be used in the future in order to gain a deeper understanding of the *formalization* of process models—the *process of process modeling (PPM)*. For this, two existing visualizations will be briefly sketched (cf. Sect. 2). Further, an outlook on how such visualizations can be extended toward more advanced concepts, i.e., cognitive load, is provided (cf. Sect. 3). The paper is concluded with a brief summary in Sect. 4.

2 Visualizing the PPM

In order to investigate the formalization of process models, i.e., PPM, we started by recording all interactions of modelers with the modeling environment in an event log (cf. [7]). These interactions provide the basis for both visualizations illustrated in this section.

This work has been funded by Austrian Science Fund (FWF): P26609–N15.

M. Reichert and H.A. Reijers (Eds.): BPM Workshops 2015, LNBIP 256, pp. 547–551, 2016.
DOI: 10.1007/978-3-319-42887-1_43

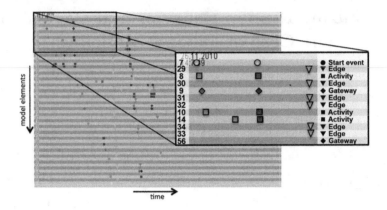

Fig. 1. Example of PPMChart

PPMCharts. [8,9] propose a visualization of all interactions during the PPM based on Dotted Charts (cf. Fig. 1). Each interaction is represented as a dot on the canvas. Dots on the same line indicated interactions to the same element, e.g., creating a node and moving it later. This visualization is used in [10] for identifying a correlation between structured modeling and the quality of the resulting process model. This direction is further pursued as described in [11] to derive the Structured Process Modeling Theory (SPMT). A detailed description of PPMCharts can be obtained from [9].

Modeling Phase Diagrams (MPD). Modeling Phase Diagrams (MPDs) were proposed to abstract from the interactions with the modeling environment to gain a better overview of the PPM [12]. For this, MPDs abstract from the interactions by forming phases of the PPM. Interactions indicating modeling, such as adding content by creating nodes and edges, are mapped to *modeling* phases. Similarly, interactions indicating clean–up, such as laying out the process model, are mapped to *reconciliation* phases. Finally, phases of inactivity usually indicate cognitive activities like understanding the problem, and hence are mapped to *comprehension* [12]. In Fig. 2, the different phases are represented by different types of lines. While the horizontal axis represents time, the vertical axis indicates the number of elements in the process model. Similar to PPMCharts, MPDs have evolved into a series of PPM measures that allow quantifying the various aspects of the PPM (cf. [13]). A detailed description of MPDs can be obtained from [12,13].

3   Cognitive Load—Adding a New Dimension to the PPM

In the future, additional data sources could be explored to provide additional perspectives on the PPM. For instance, *cognitive load*, i.e., the mental load for

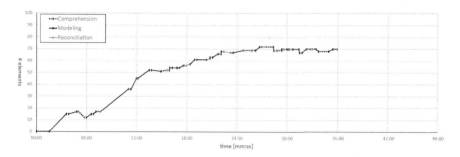

Fig. 2. Example of a modeling phase diagram

performing a task, could be integrated into MPDs (cf. Fig. 3). This could be promising since overstraining the capacity of the modeler's working memory by a mental task likely results in errors [14] and therefore may affect how process models are created. By continuously measuring mental effort, deeper insights should be possible into how and why errors occur while creating process models. Various techniques for measuring cognitive load can be applied, such as the measurement of the diameter of the eyes' pupil (*pupillometry*), heart–rate variability, and rating scales [15]. Pupillometric data and rating scales (i.e., self–rating mental effort) have especially been shown to reliably measure mental effort and are widely adopted [16]. As illustrated in Fig. 3, phases of high cognitive load could be identified in order to understand their causes. A more detailed description on how continuous cognitive load measurement might be used for analyzing the PPM is provided in [17].

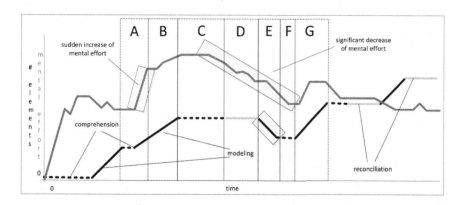

Fig. 3. MPD including mental effort visualization

4 Conclusion

While providing only a glimpse of information on visualizations and their use in the context of the PPM, this extended abstract provides an indication regarding the usefulness of such visualizations. Each of the two existing visualizations has been essential for the development of more complex theories. Without such visualizations, the development of respective theories would not have been possible.

References

1. Bandara, W., Gable, G.G., Rosemann, M.: Factors and measures of business process modelling: model building through a multiple case study. Eur. J. Inf. Syst. **14**(4), 347–360 (2005)
2. Zhao, X., Liu, C., Yang, Y., Sadiq, W.: Aligning collaborative business processes–an organization-oriented perspective. Trans. Syst. Man Cybern. Part A: Syst. Hum. **39**(6), 1152–1164 (2009)
3. Dumas, M., van der Aalst, W.M.P., ter Hofstede, A.H.M.: Process Aware Information Systems: Bridging People and Software Through Process Technology. Wiley-Interscience, Hoboken (2005)
4. Mendling, J.: Metrics for Process Models: Empirical Foundations of Verification, Error Prediction, and Guidelines for Correctness. Springer, Heidelberg (2008)
5. Hoppenbrouwers, S.J., Proper, E.H., van der Weide, T.P.: Formal modelling as a grounded conversation. In: Proceedings of LAP 2005, pp. 139–155 (2005)
6. Hoppenbrouwers, S.J.B.A., Proper, H.A.E., van der Weide, T.P.: A fundamental view on the process of conceptual modeling. In: Delcambre, L.M.L., Kop, C., Mayr, H.C., Mylopoulos, J., Pastor, Ó. (eds.) ER 2005. LNCS, vol. 3716, pp. 128–143. Springer, Heidelberg (2005)
7. Pinggera, J., Zugal, S., Weber, B.: Investigating the process of process modeling with cheetah experimental platform. In: Proceedings of ER-POIS 2010, pp. 13–18 (2010)
8. Claes, J., Vanderfeesten, I., Pinggera, J., Reijers, H.A., Weber, B., Poels, G.: Visualizing the process of process modeling with PPMCharts. In: Rosa, M., Soffer, P. (eds.) BPM Workshops 2012. LNBIP, vol. 132, pp. 744–755. Springer, Heidelberg (2013)
9. Claes, J., Vanderfeesten, I., Pinggera, J., Reijers, H.A., Weber, B., Poels, G.: A visual analysis of the process of process modeling. Inf. Syst. e-Business Manage., 1–44 (2014)
10. Claes, J., Vanderfeesten, I., Reijers, H.A., Pinggera, J., Weidlich, M., Zugal, S., Fahland, D., Weber, B., Mendling, J., Poels, G.: Tying process model quality to the modeling process: the impact of structuring, movement, and speed. In: Barros, A., Gal, A., Kindler, E. (eds.) BPM 2012. LNCS, vol. 7481, pp. 33–48. Springer, Heidelberg (2012)
11. Claes, J., Vanderfeesten, I., Gailly, F., Grefen, P., Poels, G.: The structured process modeling theory (spmt) a cognitive view on why and how modelers benefit from structuring the process of process modeling. Inf. Syst. Front., 1–25 (2015)
12. Pinggera, J., Zugal, S., Weidlich, M., Fahland, D., Weber, B., Mendling, J., Reijers, H.A.: Tracing the process of process modeling with modeling phase diagrams. In: Daniel, F., Barkaoui, K., Dustdar, S. (eds.) BPM Workshops 2011, Part I. LNBIP, vol. 99, pp. 370–382. Springer, Heidelberg (2012)

13. Pinggera, J.: The Process of Process Modeling. Ph.D. thesis, University of Innsbruck, Department of Computer Science (2014)
14. Sweller, J.: Cognitive load during problem solving: effects on learning. Cogn. Sci. **12**(2), 257–285 (1988)
15. Paas, F., Renkl, A., Sweller, J.: Cognitive load theory and instructional design: recent developments. Educ. Psychol. **38**(1), 1–4 (2003)
16. Zugal, S., Pinggera, J., Reijers, H., Reichert, M., Weber, B.: Making the case for measuring mental effort. In: Proceedings of EESSMod 2012, pp. 37–42 (2012)
17. Pinggera, J., Zugal, S., Furtner, M., Sachse, P., Martini, M., Weber, B.: The modeling mind: behavior patterns in process modeling. In: Bider, I., Gaaloul, K., Krogstie, J., Nurcan, S., Proper, H.A., Schmidt, R., Soffer, P. (eds.) BPMDS 2014 and EMMSAD 2014. LNBIP, vol. 175, pp. 1–16. Springer, Heidelberg (2014)

Towards an Integrated Framework for Invigorating Process Models: A Research Agenda

Banu Aysolmaz[✉] and Hajo A. Reijers

VU University Amsterdam, De Boelelaan 1105, 1081 HV Amsterdam, The Netherlands
{b.e.aysolmaz,h.a.reijers}@vu.nl

Abstract. Process models abstract a dynamic phenomenon in the form of a static representation. This contrast makes them difficult to comprehend. Innovative usage of dynamic multimedia techniques in combination with static process model visualization knowledge remains an opportunity to address this problem. In this paper, we unfold our research plan to invigorate process models through the development of eight different embellishment components to enhance process comprehension.

Keywords: Business process models · Process model comprehension · Process model visualization · Process model animation

1   Introduction

Business processes are among the most critical organizational assets and their optimization is perceived as the key to cost efficiency and competitiveness [1]. Business processes modeling is used for various practices, such as process improvement, process reengineering, project management, knowledge management and for the analysis and design of process aware information systems (PAIS) [2]. Business process models, or *process models* for short, provide a means of communication for various communities. Process models can be utilized only if related stakeholders can comprehend them well [3]. Among business professionals, many process stakeholders with different backgrounds and levels of expertise can be found: business analysts, domain experts, process owners and process actors. It is not easy for stakeholders of different backgrounds to understand static process models, as processes are dynamic in nature and carry various types of information [4].

There are many research studies on analysing and enhancing comprehension of process models [3–5]. However, existing research mainly focuses on visualization techniques for static process representations. The need for 3D visualization and the animation of process models was already identified [5, 6], yet there are few – albeit promising – studies. Moreover, we observe an emerging trend in the industry to utilize modern multimedia techniques to visualize operations. Some organisations even started to investigate new ways for visualizing process models [7].

Multimedia techniques are utilized in innovative ways (i.e. animation, game, simulation, virtual environment) to recreate static representations in a dynamic way. This happens in various domains, such as biological processes, physical phenomena, science,

© Springer International Publishing Switzerland 2016
M. Reichert and H.A. Reijers (Eds.): BPM Workshops 2015, LNBIP 256, pp. 552–558, 2016.
DOI: 10.1007/978-3-319-42887-1_44

health, mechanical devices, historical information, where they have shown great potential to improve learning [8]. Similar techniques can be exploited in the process modeling field to enhance human comprehension. We foresee an opportunity to combine existing knowledge of static process model visualization with model animation and other dynamic invigoration techniques from the multimedia domain to enhance model comprehension. In our preparatory studies, we identified eight different embellishment components that can add value to invigorate process models. Each component represents a different aspect of a process model that can be invigorated by multimedia techniques. Through usage of these embellishment components in an integrated way, models can be dynamically invigorated and presented to business professionals in a more comprehensible manner. In this paper, we unfold our research plan on invigorating process models so that we can inspire other researchers and motivate them to team up with us to pursue this line of research.

Research related to existing work on enhancing process model comprehension and multimedia usage for process modeling is provided in the following section. In Sect. 3, the embellishment components for which invigoration techniques can be developed are described. Conclusion and the research agenda is described in the final section.

2   Related Work

A process model is considered as comprehended if: (1) a mental model of the presented information built by the reader accurately corresponds to what is meant by the modeler, (2) the reader is able to transfer the related information to other tasks, and (3) the mental model is created in the least amount of time possible. Visualization and animation techniques for models can enhance all three aspects.

The basic building blocks of any process model are its nodes and edges. Visualization techniques on static process models change how nodes and edges are displayed. These can be grouped into two categories of techniques that affect the layout and dimensions of a process model (2D vs. 3D): The layout of a process model affects either (1) *concrete syntax* [9]; i.e. symbols, colours and position of nodes; or (2) *abstract syntax* [10]; i.e. process elements and their structural relations. Some visualization techniques that affect the abstract syntax are *block structuring, duplication, compacting, modularization, and others that affect the concrete syntax are layout guidance, highlighting, annotation.* In studies, *syntax highlighting* for block structures proved to enhance comprehension [11] and a third dimension allowed for more information to be integrated in an understandable way [12, 13].

There is limited research on dynamic process representation. Mainly two animation techniques are used; *continuous movement* by letting tokens flow from one node to another [14] and *highlighting* of the objects [15]. These studies provide a qualitative judgement that the techniques indeed enhance understanding. The design of animation scenario is another topic of study. In the existing studies, the sequence of steps to be animated was defined in either a script by means of a graphical interface [14], or defined by the analysts [16, 17]. Design of animation sequence can be based on event logs, too, either using simulation data or by observed behavior [14, 15].

Cognitive theory of multimedia learning and its principles provide valuable insights on how to animate process models to enhance their comprehension [8]. The theory guides us on how to utilize human working memory to present information, engage readers in cognitive process and use multiple sensory pathways. We found studies indicating benefits as well as inconclusive results on using animation for multimedia learning. One study shows that when animation effects are used, such as highlighting or cueing, listeners *do* direct their attention better [18, 19]. In other studies, different conclusions are reached for the effect of three cueing types on a process retention and transfer task and perceived ease of use [19, 20]. A meta-analysis reports on the overall advantage of instructional animations over static pictures for acquiring knowledge [14]. Yet another study reports that a combination of animation and narration yields better results [21]. User controls (such as rewind, pause, play, jump, rotating and scaling of 3D models) and pacing style of the animation also affect comprehension [18]. Personal factors is a final dimension worth mentioning that affects understanding of process models [3].

In summary, there has been a lengthy debate on benefits of learning from animations or dynamic representations [22]. In contrast to studies in multimedia learning, the results for using animation in process models are restricted in terms of coverage for different techniques and their effect on enhancing comprehension. Further research is required to examine which techniques regarding process model invigoration could enhance process model comprehension.

Dynamic visualization of process models by means of diverse embellishment components may affect comprehension positively in various ways. When the user reads a static diagram, she has to create a mental model of the overall diagram and alternative sequence of steps. When animation is used, the construction of this mental model is supported. Multiple process executions can be visualized by using one dynamic model, since animation effects can appear and disappear. Combining process model animation with narration may result in even more effective learning due to simultaneous usage of both sensory pathways.

To our knowledge, there exists no research up to date which evaluated the effects of animations using a popular process modeling notation or methods or guidelines on how to define animated scenarios. Most important of all, there are limited amount of techniques used for each component we identified for invigorating process models, and the results for evaluation of these techniques are very scarce.

3 Embellishment Components

We aim to combine existing knowledge of static process model visualization with knowledge of model related animation techniques and dynamic media in multimedia learning and reveal possible innovative ways of dynamic media applications on process models. For this, we plan to develop invigoration techniques for control-flow oriented modeling notations. We identified 8 potential embellishment components that can be used in an integrated way to invigorate process models.

Component 1-Animation and Visualization Techniques for 2D and 3D Models:
Animation and visualization techniques that can be used to enhance process model comprehension will be examined in detail. Although there are existing techniques such as *continuous movement, highlighting and cueing*; there is still room to develop other techniques and use them in an integrated way to cover different needs of process models for diverse purposes. Principles from multimedia and learning fields, such as cognitive theory of multimedia learning, will be utilized to develop the techniques. We aim to develop and compare animations for 2D and 3D visualization. In collaboration with the studies of *Component 6*, visualization of additional information added to third dimension will be identified.

Component 2-Identification/Design of Animation Scenario: For any animation technique used, an animation scenario also needs to be defined to determine how the animation runs. Multiple methods for scenario definition may not be sufficient under different conditions. When event logs are available, the scenario can be defined automatically by using historical information. If data is not available, it may be designed by an analyst or identified by the user during animation. This component includes the design of different animation scenario identification techniques.

Component 3-Animations for Process Model Layout: Visualization techniques will be developed for process model layout. Example patterns for which visualization techniques will be developed are; for concrete syntax, highlighting and annotations; for abstract syntax, block structuring and modularization.

Component 4-User Controls: Possible user controls during an animation affect how the user interacts with the model. Depending on the aim, lack of user control or rather various user control options and pacing may be helpful to enhance understanding. User controls specific to the visualization techniques developed will be designed.

Component 5-Usage of Narration and On-Screen Text: This component includes the integration of narration and on-screen text with animation and visualization techniques. However, narration may not be applicable at all times and will be substituted with on-screen text.

Component 6-Embedding Process Perspectives: This component is highly correlated with *Component 1*. Integration of data, organisation and other perspectives (such as time, performance) for different animation techniques will be investigated. Other possible perspectives that can add value to the models (such as time, performance) and their visualization will also be examined.

Component 7-Mode of Operation: A majority of people using process models consist of PAIS users. They often complain that they get lost as to the big picture and state that they feel the need to understand the overall system in greater detail. When the users consult to process models to develop an understanding of the system, a link between the

PAIS can provide information on where the user is in the process models. This component includes the design of modes of operation (offline and in interaction with PAIS) to provide context-awareness to a user while she uses a PAIS.

Component 8-Tailoring for Personal Factors: No matter how "good" we design our visualization methods, it may not be as efficient for users of different types and with various levels of expertise. This component includes an investigation of how personal factors affect the comprehension and tailor the techniques defined in other components for personal factors. Specifically, the needs of different target groups will be examined: business analysts and process owners.

When the techniques developed for all these components are aggregated, they are expected to constitute various ways to invigorate the process models. These can be utilized by users for different conditions and purposes. An important contribution of this line of research will be the evaluation of the effect of different invigoration techniques on process model comprehension. There are a few studies proposing dynamic visualization techniques on process models, yet systematic evaluations for impact of these techniques on understanding are even more limited. Experiments to understand the effect of different invigoration techniques on comprehension of process models using evaluation techniques from multimedia learning and instruction are valuable. Methods such as eye tracking, retention, and transfer tasks will be used.

4 Conclusion and Future Work

In the presented line of research, we aim to investigate and develop techniques to enhance the comprehension of process models by embellishing them in various ways, combining process modeling and multimedia techniques, thus invigorating what are up till now *static* process models. In our preparatory studies, we identified eight different embellishment components. We explained potential techniques to be developed for these components to invigorate processes from different aspects.

Our findings from the previous section reveal that systematic evaluations for impact of process model visualization techniques on comprehension are limited. An important contribution of this research will be the evaluation of the effect of different invigoration techniques on process model comprehension. Experiments will be designed using methods from multimedia learning and instruction, such as eye tracking, conduct of retention and transfer tasks. Lastly, to enable widespread application of the invigoration techniques in real life settings, an open source tool will be developed as part of mainstream process modeling platforms.

We hope that this paper inspires other investigators to develop innovative ways to improve the understanding of process models and welcome proposals for collaboration.

Acknowledgments. This project has received funding from the European Union's Horizon 2020 research and innovation programme under the Marie Sklodowska-Curie grant agreement No. 660646. We thank Romain Emens for his review of the literature that has been incorporated in this study.

References

1. Bobs Guide: BPM more important to UK businesses than the rest of Europe. http://www.bobsguide.com/guide/news/2006/Oct/17/bpm-more-important-to-uk-businesses-than-the-rest-of-europe-but-lags-behind-on-delivery-filenet-survey-reveals.html

2. Becker, J., Rosemann, M., von Uthmann, C.: Guidelines of business process modeling. In: van der Aalst, W.M., Desel, J., Oberweis, A. (eds.) Business Process Management. LNCS, vol. 1806, pp. 30–49. Springer, Heidelberg (2000)

3. Reijers, H.A., Mendling, J.: A study into the factors that influence the understandability of business process models. IEEE Trans. Syst. Man Cybern. Part A Syst. Hum. **41**, 449–462 (2011)

4. Recker, J., Reijers, H.A., van de Wouw, S.G.: Process model comprehension: the effects of cognitive abilities, learning style, and strategy. Commun. Assoc. Inf. Syst. **34**, 199–222 (2014)

5. Mendling, J., Strembeck, M., Recker, J.: Factors of process model comprehension—findings from a series of experiments. Decis. Support Syst. **53**, 195–206 (2012)

6. Rosemann, M.: Potential pitfalls of process modeling: part A. Bus. Process Manag. J. **12**, 249–254 (2006)

7. Shell: Strategic Report - Business Overview. http://reports.shell.com/annual-report/2013/strategic-report/our-businesses.php

8. Mayer, R.E., Moreno, R.: Animation as an aid to multimedia learning. Educ. Psychol. Rev. **14**, 87–99 (2002)

9. La Rosa, M., Hofstede, A.H.M.Ter, Wohed, P., Reijers, H.A., Mendling, J., van der Aalst, W.M.P.: Managing process model complexity via concrete syntax modifications. IEEE Trans. Ind. Inform. **7**, 255–265 (2011)

10. La Rosa, M., Wohed, P., Mendling, J., Ter Hofstede, A.H.M., Reijers, H.A., van der Aalst, W.M.P.: Managing process model complexity via abstract syntax modifications. IEEE Trans. Ind. Inform. **7**, 614–629 (2011)

11. Reijers, H.A., Freytag, T., Mendling, J., Eckleder, A.: Syntax highlighting in business process models. Decis. Support Syst. **51**, 339–349 (2011)

12. Betz, S., Eichhorn, D., Hickl, S., Klink, S., Koschmider, A., Li, Y., Oberweis, A., Trunko, R.: 3D representation of business process models. In: MobIS 2008, pp. 79–93 (2008)

13. Schönhage, B., van Ballegooij, A., Eliens, A.: 3D gadgets for business process visualization—a case study. In: Proceedings of the Fifth Symposium on Virtual Reality Modeling Language (Web3D-VRML), pp. 131–138 (2000)

14. Philippi, S., Hill, H.J.: Communication support for systems engineering – process modelling and animation with APRIL. J. Syst. Softw. **80**, 1305–1316 (2007)

15. Günther, C.W.: Process Mining in Flexible Environments (2009)

16. Nawrocki, J., Nedza, T., Ochodek, M., Olek, L.: Describing business processes with use cases. Bus. Inf. Syst. BIS **2006**, 13–27 (2006)

17. Gemino, A.: Empirical comparisons of animation and narration in requirements validation. Requir. Eng. **9**, 153–168 (2003)

18. Jamet, E., Gavota, M., Quaireau, C.: Attention guiding in multimedia learning. Learn. Instr. **18**, 135–145 (2008)

19. Boucheix, J.-M., Lowe, R.K., Putri, D.K., Groff, J.: Cueing animations: dynamic signaling aids information extraction and comprehension. Learn. Instr. **25**, 71–84 (2013)

20. Jamet, E.: An eye-tracking study of cueing effects in multimedia learning. Comput. Hum. Behav. **32**, 47–53 (2014)

21. Morett, L.M., Clegg, B.A., Blalock, L.D., Mong, H.M.: Applying multimedia learning theory to map learning and driving navigation. Transp. Res. Part F Traffic Psychol. Behav. **12**, 40–49 (2009)
22. Höffler, T.N., Leutner, D.: Instructional animation versus static pictures: a meta-analysis. Learn. Instr. **17**, 722–738 (2007)

The Dynamic Visualization of Business Process Models: A Prototype and Evaluation

Romain Emens[1], Irene Vanderfeesten[1(✉)], and Hajo A. Reijers[1,2]

[1] Eindhoven University of Technology, Eindhoven, The Netherlands
romain.emens@gmail.com, i.t.p.vanderfeesten@tue.nl
[2] VU University, Amsterdam, The Netherlands
h.a.reijers@vu.nl

Abstract. Business process models are commonly used for communication purposes among stakeholders. They are often distributed by means of web portals in the form of images. As the organizational population accessing these web portals has diverse needs and prior knowledge, the process models should be *intuitive*, *likeable*, *well-accepted*, and *easily understandable* [8] to reach their communication goal. Up to now, process models are mostly represented in a graphical but *static, one-size-fits-all* way. Visualization techniques have been applied at design time only to improve on the communication power of the model and support the model user in reading the model. The opportunity to *dynamically* guide model users to relevant parts of the diagram when reading the model is missed, and model users may not know where to focus their attention on. This paper provides a conceptual design for the *dynamic visualization* of process models. Our design is implemented in a prototype for a case study and evaluated by process participants. From this we conclude that such a dynamic visualization is preferred over a static visualization.

Keywords: Business process model · Dynamic visualization · Highlighting · Animation · User-interaction

1 Introduction

Nowadays, many organizations engage in Business Process Management (BPM) initiatives. An integral part in these BPM initiatives are (business) process models [1], which serve as a basis for activities associated with the business process management lifecycle [2]. During these activities, one of the purposes of a process model is to serve as a communication vehicle for various stakeholders [3, 4]. Since communication processes are vital during the lifecycle of BPM initiatives [5] and a process model is the best way to support communication in these initiatives [6], the process model employed should sufficiently support all parties involved. For instance, process models are used in employee training [3] or published in internet portals [7, 8] to inform employees about e.g. the activities in the process, their order, and involved resources.

Business processes are usually presented in a rather static manner, e.g. as simple drawings or textual descriptions [7], and the processes are displayed to users in the same

M. Reichert and H.A. Reijers (Eds.): BPM Workshops 2015, LNBIP 256, pp. 559–570, 2016.
DOI: 10.1007/978-3-319-42887-1_45

way as drawn by the process designer [9]. Furthermore, model users have different needs and require personalized views [9]; process owners, for instance, require an overview of the general flow of activities, whereas process actors are primarily interested in the details of which tasks they should execute. However, when process models are published in a static form and employed as described above, the opportunity to guide process actors to relevant parts of the business process model is missed. Furthermore, most casual staff members who are inexperienced in terms of process modeling lack confidence to interpret visual process diagrams [10], and model users may be overwhelmed with information [11]. The feeling of being overwhelmed by the scale and complexity of a model is labelled '*map shock*' and may cause a degradation of motivation and incomplete processing of the map elements by the model reader [12]. In the instance described above, the communication vehicle employed is not sufficiently supporting all communication purposes involved. Therefore, process models should reveal their content in an *intuitive* [8, 13] and *easy to understand* [1, 14] manner. Furthermore, the visualization of the process models should be *likeable* and *well-accepted* by the model-users [8].

Although there exists a considerable body of literature on process model understandability and complexity, e.g. [15], to fulfill the needs described above, the proposed mechanisms to deal with complexity are often applied at design time only to ensure *Understandability-by-Design* (cf. [6]). However, the application of these (research) efforts to realize suitable process models ends at design time, which results in a *static, one-size-fits-all* visualization of process map images. Therefore an approach is explored in this paper which encompasses a *dynamic* visualization of a process model to ensure a form of '*Understandability-by-Presentation*'. The proposed dynamic visualization consists of two elements. First of all, a dynamic model diagram publication implies the for the user visible alteration of a process model in terms of visual representation (i.e. secondary notation) or inner structure. Secondly, the alteration during diagram inspection may be system or user imposed. To provide support for a dynamic visualization approach, multiple general designs are described, implemented in a prototype, and evaluated in the remainder of this paper.

We proceed as follows. Firstly, Sect. 2 describes related work regarding business process model visualization. Next, a set of conceptual designs for the dynamic visualization of process models is presented in Sect. 3, and the implementation and evaluation of these designs in the context of a case study is described in Sect. 4. Finally, a discussion and conclusion is provided in Sect. 5.

2   Related Work

Apart from the work on measuring quality, understandability, complexity and readability of process models, e.g. [38] some prior works have also focused on improving the communication power of process models. Research was done on improving the static representation of a process model, and on visualizing model dynamics as is summarized below.

In terms of static visualizations, most research efforts involve the application of a single visualization technique and a comparison with respect to model understandability between both process models. Techniques modifying the visual representation of a process model (i.e. without changing the underlying relationships) include layout guidance, highlighting, representation, naming guidance [15], size, position, orientation, texture [16], and dimensionality [17, 18]. Furthermore, techniques which alter the underlying model relationships (cf. [19, 20]) and thereby changing the visual model, can be best summarized as techniques that either add or remove model elements. The application of these techniques occurs at design time, which introduces multiple limitations. First of all, the techniques selected by the process designer may not be optimal for all (groups of) model users. For instance, to show the route of a specific process instance, one may prefer all irrelevant elements to be removed from the model, but one may also choose to show the original process model containing the corresponding process instance highlighted. The former would help an inexperienced model reader to find the relevant information while the latter may help a more experienced reader to keep the overview. Secondly, given the elements a process model may consist of (i.e. tasks, events, sequence flows, information flows, data, systems, and so on), groups of model users may not be interested in all model elements. Although a process designer generating simple drawings may anticipate the needs described so far during design time, this quickly becomes infeasible for large numbers of process models and users. Hence, compared to simple, static drawings, a more sophisticated publication of process models is required to meet the needs of different type of model users.

In terms of dynamic process model visualization, Philippi and Hill [21], Günther [22], and Allweyer and Schweitzer [23] make use of (continuous) token flow animation to show model dynamics. Also, Nawrocki et al. [24] demonstrate an animation approach that consists of showing successive frames of model diagrams in which each diagram contains a new node which is highlighted. These works on dynamic visualizations all use a certain form of animation without any user interaction.

Given the broad basis of general visualization techniques available in literature [18] and the limited related work of using advanced visualizations for process models as described above, it is worthwhile to examine whether a combination of several static and dynamic visualization techniques is beneficial to support the model user. The design for a dynamic visualization of a process model that is presented in this paper combines several visualization techniques with the dynamic alteration of the static process model. It therefore integrates and extends current process visualization techniques that were discussed in literature before.

3 Dynamic Visualization

In this section we describe the development of a dynamic visualization for process models as an integration of different (static and dynamic) visualization techniques in order to create personalized views on the process model for different model users.

3.1 Methodology

For the design of our dynamic visualization approach, a design-oriented methodology [25, 26] was followed. First, use cases and corresponding requirements were defined for scoping purposes based on a real life case of process model use in a web portal. Next, several theoretical visualization techniques [18] were reviewed, selected and integrated to fulfill the requirements in a conceptual design. As a dynamic visualization may be realized by altering a single model diagram, the techniques described by previous research may be applied, either system or user imposed, during diagram inspection. The following visualization techniques were deemed a candidate for selection [18] *dimensionality*, *representational notation*, *highlighting*, and *zooming* (i.e. removal or addition of model elements). In addition, since our definition of what a dynamic visualization consists of includes whether the visual alteration is system or user imposed and since one criterion to assess innovative visualization approaches is the level of interaction [18], *user-interaction* was considered during the design process as well.

After the selection of visualization techniques and the development of the conceptual design, the dynamic visualization approach was technically realized in the form of a prototype web environment for a specific case. This web environment was evaluated by process actors working for a case study company, both in a quantitative (survey) and qualitative form (semi-structured interviews and think-aloud sessions). In order to incorporate user feedback in the refinement of the design, the aforementioned approach was repeated once and a final prototype was realized.

Below we will only discuss the main results of this design process, i.e. we describe the use cases and the main design decisions. For more details on the design process and justification of the selected visualization techniques we refer to [37].

3.2 Use Cases

A use case is a description of the interactions and responsibilities of a system with actors [27] and describes the requirements the system should fulfill. In light of this research, the system is an environment which enables users to inspect business process models in a dynamic manner, and the actor that interacts with the system is the user group of process participants. Note that although different user groups (e.g. managers, process participants, or external collaborators) access process models with varying motivations and needs [9], the scope in this research is limited to process participants who are assigned to process roles executing the visualized business process. This user group was selected on the grounds that a critical practice for successful BPM initiatives is that employees understand the entire process [28]. As business processes can be seen from a number of perspectives [29], understanding the entire process implies apprehending, first of all, the control-flow perspective and the resource perspective. Therefore, the following use cases were implemented.

Use case 1: Inspection of control flow
This use case refers to model users who inspect a process model to learn how process instances may be executed given the sequence flow of activities from start to end.

Use case 2: Inspection of process flow in terms of resource responsibilities
Besides acquiring knowledge regarding process instance execution, for process actors
it is highly relevant to learn what activities are executed per process role.

3.3 Design

Based on the above use cases and theory on cognitive psychology, visualization techniques and multimedia learning, a number of design decisions were proposed that should
help a model reader in a dynamic way to inspect and understand the process model.

Decision 1:Constrained User-Interaction. In light of use case #1, the simulation and
tracing of process instances along the arcs of a process model may be user-imposed (i.e.
user decides what nodes are inspected) or system-imposed (e.g. token flow animation
by Günther [22]). In order to prevent feelings of 'map shock', the first design includes
a node-by-node inspection constraint that forces model users to inspect the process
model node-by-node as "by animating discrete portions of the overall node-link map in
a node-by-node manner, one directs the viewer's attentional focus, thereby eliminating
map shock" [12]. Also, the animation is broken into short meaningful segments that can
be processed on a pace set by the user, which is a guideline for animated images [30].
To illustrate this, in Fig. 1(a), when the user is inspecting node $\mu6$, one may only proceed
with the instance simulation to either node $\mu3$ (backward) or $\mu7$ (forward).

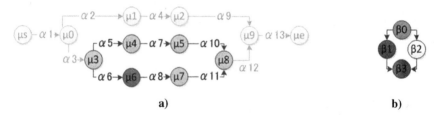

a)   b)

Fig. 1. Illustration of conceptual designs for (a) use case #1, and (b) use case #2 (Color figure
online)

Decision 2: Active Activity Highlighting. During the execution of a process instance,
the state of the model adjusts according to the control flow defined. To facilitate tracing
of process instances, this design includes highlighting the activity that is being inspected
(i.e. user-imposed) or executed (i.e. system imposed), as highlighting creates a visual
referent. A visual referent may function as an external memory or cognitive trace [31],
which is one way to reduce the load on working memory [32]. As can be seen in Fig. 1(a),
the active node ($\mu6$) is highlighted by a red color, thereby omitting the need for a "mental
token" [33].

Decision 3: Active Process Segment Highlighting. In addition to the accentuation of
the activity that is active or being inspected, this design decision involves greying out
the process segments which do not contain the active activity to create a highlighting
effect; a process segment is defined as a set of model elements which can be aggregated

in one single node. As "the goal of highlighting is to make some small subset of a display clearly distinct from the rest" [30], the user's attention is guided to a coherent piece of process model information. Also, a feeling of 'map shock' [12] is avoided as attention is guided to a subset of all model elements, which may be beneficial in terms of understandability as well [34]. For instance, in Fig. 1(a), all model elements except those belonging to the relevant process segment (nodes µ3–µ8) are greyed out.

Decision 4: Token Flow Animation. Besides the previous three designs to support use case #1, token flow animation was introduced as well. The animation has both a representing and directing function [35]. In terms of the representing function, the moving token represents the shifts between states of the process model, thereby eliminating implicit processing of this shift within model-user's working memory. Additionally, the moving token directs the learner's attention pre-attentively as the model-user's eyes may lock onto it and track it [30]. Moreover, the need for a "mental token" is eliminated [33]. In Fig. 1(a), a moving token would flow along arcs α6 or α8, depending on what node the user selected to inspect next (i.e. as result from design 1).

Decision 5: Role-Responsibilities Highlighting. To fulfill use case #2, an extension of the highlighting approach described by Müller and Rogge-Solti [36] was selected; the design involves the use of greying out all model elements and color highlighting to accentuate, using unique colors, role-specific model elements in terms of resource responsibilities (responsible, accountable, consulted, or informed). This highlighting approach generates benefits as elaborated above as well as one also generated by 3D process models as described by Betz et al. [17], which is that "users can easily catch the position of a specific role, e.g. always at the beginning/in the middle/at the end of a process or if the role appears in several parts of the process". To illustrate in Fig. 1(b), given three process roles and a visualization of responsibilities, we see that two roles are responsible for the execution of node β3, one role for β1, and another single role for β0. Note that the decision of what role responsibilities to visualize can be user-imposed or system imposed.

4   Application

To illustrate and evaluate the general design outlined in the previous section, a prototype implementation was developed for a specific process model in a case study.

4.1   Case Study Example

The case study consists of the application of the visualization designs to a specific process of managing hardware and software changes on an IT department of a major financial services provider in the Netherlands. The common way of communicating process model in this company is by modeling them as EPC models and publishing them in an off-the-shelve (OTS) web environment offered by a major software vendor. Process actors working for this company access the web portal to learn and get information about the process. A small group of employees was asked to evaluate our prototype with our dynamic visualization as compared to the static OTS representation of the same process model.

The prototype web portal containing the dynamic visualization approach[1] consisted of two sections to support each use case individually. A screenshot illustration of the implementation of the designs can be found in Figs. 2 and 3. The five design decisions are labeled accordingly. As can be seen in Fig. 2, the active activity (design 2) is highlighted by a blue color, the corresponding process segment is highlighted and the other segments are greyed out (design 3), and the user is able to proceed to the next or previous activity node only (design 1). When this occurs, the token follows the control flow path accordingly in a small animation (design 4). In terms of use case #2, Fig. 3 illustrates that the activities at which a certain process role is consulted are yellow, informed are blue, and activities directly succeeding or preceding these activities hold the original EPC color (design 5). In addition, a refined version of our prototype includes an option for model users to visualize, *user-imposed*, the responsibilities of *multiple* roles in one diagram.

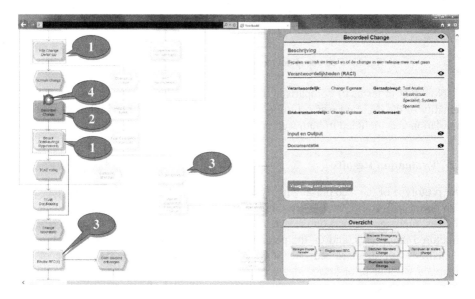

Fig. 2. Web portal developed showing designs for use case #1

The existing OTS web portal published a static process model image as drawn by the process designer and corresponding process annotation (e.g. textual activity descriptions) without any visual guidance to support model users. The only non-static elements of the business process models were that users were able to click on individual model elements to view the textual process annotation.

---

[1] See http://is.ieis.tue.nl/staff/ivanderfeesten/Papers/TAProViz2015/ for more details.

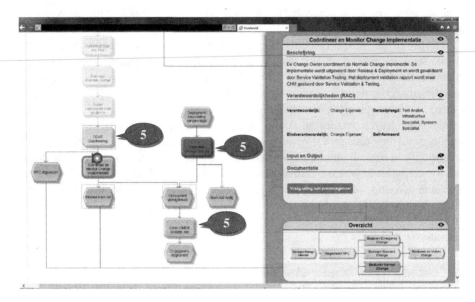

Fig. 3. Web portal developed showing design for use case #2

Note that in terms of comparison, the process modelling language and the dimensionality of the diagram was set to be equivalent, and textual (activity-based) process annotation was included in both web portals.

4.2   Evaluation Results

Our prototype of the web portal with dynamic visualization as well as the existing OTS web portal with static process representation have been evaluated by 11 employees (5 novices, 6 process actors) on the user experience and understandability through semi-structured interviews, and on the perceived usefulness and ease of use through questionnaires with standardized questions. A novice was seen as an employee of the company without prior knowledge regarding process modeling, the extensive use of process models in practice, and the domain knowledge of the business process modeled. The same characteristics hold for the process actors group, with the exception of domain knowledge. Below we discuss the main outcomes from the semi-structured interview evaluation as they give the most insightful conclusions. For a detailed overview of all evaluation results we refer to [37].

As a result from *constrained user-interaction*, the model diagram is processed more consciously (reported by 46 % of the participants) and more actively per activity (37 %). It is also reported that it slows down diagram inspection (noted by 55 % of participants), but this is not necessarily seen as a disadvantage. According to 37 % of the participants, constrained user-interaction is more suitable for people who are learning the process model (novices), than for experienced process actors having domain knowledge or model language knowledge. Node-by-node inspection of model elements which are yet to be inspected would be sufficient according to four out of five process actors (80 %).

Furthermore, *active activity* and *process segment highlighting* is reported as being useful (73 % and 64 % respectively). For instance, the activity highlighting serves as a visual referent (as indicated by 46 % of the participants), and process segment highlighting provides clarification of relevant areas (92 %). In addition, *token flow animation* is perceived as funny (46 %), and the hypothesized directing function has been confirmed by respectively 64 % and 55 % of the participants.

Finally, there is promising support for *color highlighting* of relevant model elements which are assigned to individual process roles (73 %). Also, the use of color is said to be helpful even if the process becomes more complex. Four out of five (80 %) process actors would use a visualization approach to inspect the responsibilities of multiple roles. All in all, we conclude from this evaluation that the use of dynamic visualizations as an integrated set of visualization techniques is beneficial to model readers, regardless of whether they are novices or more experienced process actors, as compared to the static representation in the existing process web portal. However, the exact impact of each of the techniques should be further investigated.

5   Discussion and Conclusion

In contrast to the traditional use of visualization techniques applied at design time, which result in static diagrams, this paper examined an approach which encompasses the *dynamic* application and integration of several visualization techniques to process model images during end-user inspection. Five design decisions that alter the model's secondary notation were introduced to dynamically support model readers: (i) constrained user-interaction, (ii) token flow animation, (iii) active activity high-lighting, (iv) process segment highlighting, and (v) role-responsibilities highlighting.

From the evaluation of our prototype implementation, we conclude that a dynamic visualization of a process model as proposed by our designs is preferred over the static alternative. All our design decisions appeared to provide added value in supporting the model reader to inspect the model leading to an *intuitive*, *likeable*, *well-accepted*, and *easily understandable* representation of the process model. The token flow animation and the highlighting of the current activity, relevant process segment and role responsibilities was found useful by the majority of our participants. For the constrained user-interaction the opinions were more diverse. This seems a suitable technique for novices to reading process models but process actors with more modeling knowledge or domain knowledge find this technique too restricting. This is in line with the multimedia instruction learner control principle that learners with lower levels of prior knowledge benefit from system-controlled instruction and users with more prior knowledge benefit from user-controlled environments [35].

Further research may include additional forms of adaptive control or machine learning to adjust the freedom of user-control for more experienced model users. Also, other, more specific use cases for the interaction with the process model in a web portal may be investigated and elaborated in dynamic visualization design, such as the view on work-handovers for a process actor, the projection of performance information on the process for a process owner, and the status and execution trace of a specific process instance, cf. the suggestions by [33].

In addition to the evaluation of the user experience and perceived usefulness and ease of use, we also plan a further objective evaluation of the comprehensibility of dynamic visualizations as compared to static visualizations by e.g. testing the number of correctly answered questions on the content of the process model, and the time needed for answering them. Finally, our current prototype implementation requires quite some manual work to transform a static EPC into a dynamic visualization of the process. Research efforts on automatically applying the visualization techniques to an arbitrary process model would make our approach easier to use on a large scale.

References

1. Schrepfer, M., Wolf, J., Mendling, J., Reijers, H.A.: The impact of secondary notation on process model understanding. In: Persson, A., Stirna, J. (eds.) PoEM 2009. LNBIP, vol. 39, pp. 161–175. Springer, Heidelberg (2009)
2. Mendling, J.: Managing structural and textual quality of business process models. In: Cudre-Mauroux, P., Ceravolo, P., Gašević, D. (eds.) SIMPDA 2012. LNBIP, vol. 162, pp. 100–111. Springer, Heidelberg (2013)
3. Melcher, J., Mendling, J., Reijers, H.A., Seese, D.: On measuring the understandability of process models. In: Rinderle-Ma, S., Sadiq, S., Leymann, F. (eds.) BPM 2009. LNBIP, vol. 43, pp. 465–476. Springer, Heidelberg (2010)
4. Becker, J., Rosemann, M., von Uthmann, C.: Guidelines of business process modeling. In: van der Aalst, W.M., Desel, J., Oberweis, A. (eds.) Business Process Management. LNCS, vol. 1806, pp. 30–49. Springer, Heidelberg (2000)
5. Guo, H., Brown, R., Rasmussen, R.: A theoretical basis for using virtual worlds as a personalised process visualisation approach. In: Franch, X., Soffer, P. (eds.) CAiSE Workshops 2013. LNBIP, vol. 148, pp. 229–240. Springer, Heidelberg (2013)
6. Reijers, H., Mendling, J., Recker, J.: Business process quality management. In: vom Brocke, J., Rosemann, M. (eds.) Handbook on Business Process Management 1, pp. 167–185. Springer, Heidelberg (2015)
7. Hipp, M., Mutschler, B., Reichert, M.: Navigating in complex business processes. In: Liddle, S.W., Schewe, K.-D., Tjoa, A.M., Zhou, X. (eds.) DEXA 2012, Part II. LNCS, vol. 7447, pp. 466–480. Springer, Heidelberg (2012)
8. Rosemann, M.: Potential pitfalls of process modeling: part A. Bus. Process Manag. J. **12**, 249–254 (2006)
9. Bobrik, R., Reichert, M., Bauer, T.: View-based process visualization. In: Alonso, G., Dadam, P., Rosemann, M. (eds.) BPM 2007. LNCS, vol. 4714, pp. 88–95. Springer, Heidelberg (2007)
10. Leopold, H., Mendling, J., Polyvyanyy, A.: Generating natural language texts from business process models. In: Ralyté, J., Franch, X., Brinkkemper, S., Wrycza, S. (eds.) CAiSE 2012. LNCS, vol. 7328, pp. 64–79. Springer, Heidelberg (2012)
11. Rinderle, S.B., Bobrik, R., Reichert, M.U., Bauer, T.: Business process visualization - use cases, challenges, solutions. In: Proceedings of the 8th International Conference on Enterprise Information Systems (ICEIS 2006): Information System Analysis and Specification, pp. 204–211. INSTICC (2006)

12. Blankenship, J., Dansereau, D.F.: The effect of animated node-link displays on information recall. J. Exp. Educ. **68**, 293–308 (2000)
13. Becker, J., Kugeler, M., Rosemann, M.: Process Management: A Guide for the Design of Business Processes: With 83 Figures and 34 Tables. Springer, Heidelberg (2003)
14. Dehnert, J., van der Aalst, W.M.: Bridging the gap between business models and workflow specifications. Int. J. Coop. Inf. Syst. **13**, 289–332 (2004)
15. La Rosa, M., ter Hofstede, A.M., Wohed, P., Reijers, H.A., Mendling, J., Van der Aalst, W.M.P.: Managing process model complexity via concrete syntax modifications. IEEE Trans. Industr. Inf. **7**, 255–265 (2011)
16. Bertin, J.: Semiology of graphics: diagrams, networks, maps. The University of Wisconsin Press, Madison (1983)
17. Betz, S., Eichhorn, D., Hickl, S., Klink, S., Koschmider, A., Li, Y., Oberweis, A., Trunko, R.: 3D representation of business process models. In: Proceedings of Modellierung betrieblicher Informationssysteme (MobIS 2008). Köllen Verlag, Saarbrücken (2008)
18. Fill, H.-G.: Survey of existing visualisation approaches. In: Visualisation for Semantic Information Systems, pp. 39–159. Gabler (2009)
19. La Rosa, M., Wohed, P., Mendling, J., ter Hofstede, A.M., Reijers, H.A., Van der Aalst, W.M.P.: Managing process model complexity via abstract syntax modifications. IEEE Trans. Industr. Inf. **7**, 614–629 (2011)
20. Hipp, M., Mutschler, B., Reichert, M.: Navigating in process model collections: a new approach inspired by Google earth. In: Daniel, F., Barkaoui, K., Dustdar, S. (eds.) BPM Workshops 2011, Part II. LNBIP, vol. 100, pp. 87–98. Springer, Heidelberg (2012)
21. Philippi, S., Hill, H.J.: Communication support for systems engineering – process modelling and animation with APRIL. J. Syst. Softw. **80**, 1305–1316 (2007)
22. Günther, C.W.: Process mining in flexible environments. Technische Universiteit Eindhoven (2009)
23. Allweyer, T., Schweitzer, S.: A tool for animating BPMN token flow. In: Mendling, J., Weidlich, M. (eds.) BPMN 2012. LNBIP, vol. 125, pp. 98–106. Springer, Heidelberg (2012)
24. Nawrocki, J.R., Nedza, T., Ochodek, M., Olek, L.: Describing business processes with use cases. In: Proceedings of BIS 2006, pp. 13–27 (2006)
25. van Aken, J., Berends, H., Van der Bij, H.: Problem Solving in Organizations: A Methodological Handbook for Business and Management Students. Cambridge University Press, Cambridge (2012)
26. Johannesson, P., Perjons, E.: A design science primer. CreateSpace Independent Publishing Platform (2012)
27. Adolph, S., Cockburn, A., Bramble, P.: Patterns for Effective Use Cases. Addison-Wesley Longman Publishing Co., Inc., Boston (2002)
28. Škrinjar, R., Trkman, P.: Increasing process orientation with business process management: critical practices'. Int. J. Inf. Manage. **33**, 48–60 (2013)
29. Jablonski, S., Bussler, C.: Workflow Management: Modeling Concepts, Architecture and Implementation (1996)
30. Ware, C.: Information Visualization: Perception for Design. Elsevier, Waltham (2012)
31. Scaife, M., Rogers, Y.: External cognition: how do graphical representations work? Int. J. Hum. Comput. Stud. **45**, 185–213 (1996)
32. Johnson, S.D.: A framework for technology education curricula which emphasizes intellectual processes. Journal of Technology Education **3**, 29–40 (1992). Reprint Series

33. Zugal, S., Pinggera, J., Weber, B.: Assessing process models with cognitive psychology. In: Proceedings of the 4th International Workshop on Enterprise Modelling and Information Systems Architectures, EMISA 2011, Hamburg, Germany, 22–23 September 2011, vol. 190, pp. 177–182. GI (2011)
34. Mendling, J., Reijers, H.A., Cardoso, J.: What makes process models understandable? In: Alonso, G., Dadam, P., Rosemann, M. (eds.) BPM 2007. LNCS, vol. 4714, pp. 48–63. Springer, Heidelberg (2007)
35. Mayer, R.E.: The Cambridge Handbook of Multimedia Learning. Cambridge University Press, Cambridge (2014)
36. Müller, R., Rogge-Solti, A.: BPMN for healthcare processes. In: Proceedings of the 3rd Central-European, vol. 705 (2011)
37. Emens, R.: A dynamic visualisation of business process models for process participants. Master thesis, Eindhoven University of Technology (2014). http://is.ieis.tue.nl/staff/ivanderfeesten/Papers/TAProViz2015/Master%20thesis%20Romain%20Emens.pdf
38. Reijers, H., Mendling, J.: A study into the factors that influence the understandability of business process models. Syst. Man Cybern. Part A **41**(3), 449–462 (2011)

A Comprehensive Overview of Visual Design of Process Model Element Labels

Agnes Koschmider[1][(⊠)], Kathrin Figl[2], and Andreas Schoknecht[1]

[1] Institute of Applied Informatics and Formal Description Methods,
Karlsruhe Institute of Technology, Karlsruhe, Germany
{agnes.koschmider,andreas.schoknecht}@kit.edu
[2] Institute for Information Systems and New Media,
Vienna University of Economics and Business, Vienna, Austria
kathrin.figl@wu.ac.at

Abstract. Process model element labels are critical for an appropriate association between a symbol instance in a model and the corresponding real world meaning. Disciplines, in which an efficient presentation of text labels is crucial (e.g., cartography) have continuously improved their visualization design techniques for labels since they serve as effective cognitive aids in problem solving. Despite the relevance of labels for information exploration, surprisingly little research has been undertaken on the visual design of element labels of business process models. This paper fills this gap and provides a comprehensive overview of visual design options for process model element labels. First, we summarize the findings existing in the diverse areas of literature relevant to visual display of process model element labels. Second, we analyze the status quo of visual design of element labels in common business process modeling tools indicating only little layouting support. Third, we give recommendations regarding the visual design of element labels. To our knowledge, this is the first comprehensive analysis of visual design of process model element labels.

Keywords: Information visualization · Layout · Process model · Text labeling

1 Introduction

"Labels play a critical role at the sentence (diagram) level, in distinguishing between symbol instances (tokens) and defining their correspondence to the real world domain" [1, p. 764]. Thus, if users do not (fully) understand the tokens (text labels of process model elements), an improper notion of the real process might arise. In the same vein, [2, p. 203] denote that the "Tagging [of] graphical objects with text labels is a fundamental task in the design of many types of informational graphics." Research in the field of informational graphics has made a high effort to identify the best strategies to label areas (such as oceans in cartography), lines and points (e.g., in graphs) and to find efficient algorithms to solve these tasks (e.g., to find the maximum possible number of labels and the maximum size for labels while avoiding label-label overlaps [2, 3]).

Against this background, surprisingly little articles address the visual design of labels of process model elements, while semantic issues of labeling process model

© Springer International Publishing Switzerland 2016
M. Reichert and H.A. Reijers (Eds.): BPM Workshops 2015, LNBIP 256, pp. 571–582, 2016.
DOI: 10.1007/978-3-319-42887-1_46

elements have received higher attention. Semantic issues tackled in these articles [4–7] are either related to recommendations on labeling styles or to the revision of the vocabulary of process model element labels. Although process modelers follow these modeling guidelines recommended for labeling process elements[1], the reader can still be handicapped in his/her task execution due to an improper recognition of the label (as a result of an improper visual design). In order to support appropriate task execution of model readers, both issues (semantics and visual design of labels) must be addressed. This paper is dedicated to the investigation of visual design of process model element labels since no modeling guidelines exist for this issue so far.

To identify relevant influence factors for an efficient visual design, first, a solid analysis of related disciplines emphasizing text labels is required. Process model element labels are a concatenation of words with its own style conventions and they can be considered as a specific form of natural language text. There is a long tradition of research on word recognition in natural language text. However, it is open which findings from reading research can be transferred to visualization criteria of modeling labels. Experimental research in the area of source code comprehension has for instance shown that there are fundamental differences between reading source code and reading natural language prose [8]. Similarly, the generalizability of reading research to process model element labels might be limited; there could for instance be interaction effects between the underlying graphical modeling language and the use of natural language in the labels.

To study the status quo of practical implementations of visual design we firstly describe visual variables to define the frame of our study. Afterwards, we analyze the layouting support for labels offered by common business process modeling tools, in Sect. 3. Section 4 describes which recommendations from related disciplines can be applied to the visual design of process model element labels. Based on this discussion we identified several open issues on visual variables of element labels, which need to be addressed by research. The open issues are discussed in Sect. 5. Section 6 highlights how our contribution complements related work. Finally, the paper ends with a summary and outlook in Sect. 7.

2   Visual Design of Process Model Element Labels

The business process task represented by a process element in a visual model is described through a label typically using natural language. The label can be expressed with different linguistic styles. Current modeling guidelines advocate using a verb-object style [4], in which the object is described by a noun (or noun compound) and the action is described by a verb in infinitive. Further common labeling styles for process model elements are a deverbalized-noun + "of" + noun (e.g., evaluation of

---

[1] In the context of this paper, we subsume active (activities) and passive (events) elements of the modeling language under the term 'process model elements', but disregard labels of gateways.

flights), a noun + deverbalized-noun (e.g., flight evaluation) or a gerund + noun (e.g., evaluating flights).[2]

The natural language used to label the process model element can be designed in different visual ways. The visual design options are best discussed by the "graphic design space" [1], which bases on the visual variables of Bertin. There are 8 visual variables: horizontal and vertical position, shape/form, size, brightness (originally termed "value"), direction/orientation, texture (hue) and color. These variables can be applied to any form of graphic object, and also to textual objects like labels [9]. Most of Bertin's variables (shape/form, size, direction/orientation and color) are applicable for process model element labels.[3] Beside these visual variables, depending on the process modeling notation the label placement (e.g., within, above, below) might vary. We characterize this specificity of process model element labels by adding the new variable "position". The perception of the label might also be influenced by the space specified to enter letters. We consider this issue in our context by adding a further new visual variable termed "segmentation". Table 1 displays related visual variables for process model element labels, which are discussed in detail in Sect. 4.

Table 1. Visual variables (visual encoding) on process model element labels

Visual Variable	Example		
Shape/Form	evaluate flight	Evaluate Flight	EVALUATE FLIGHT
Size	evaluate flight	evaluate flight	evaluate flight
Direction/ Orientation	evaluate flight	evaluate flight	evaluate flight
Color	evaluate flight (red)	evaluate flight (blue)	evaluate flight (green)
Position	evaluate flight	evaluate flight	evaluate flight
Segmentation	evaluate flight immediately	evaluate flight immediately	evaluate flight immediately

To study the implementation of visual design of process model element labels in practice, seven common process modeling tools were investigated. The results are summarized in the next section.

---

[2] The role who executes the task might also be attached to the label (e.g., check flight by clerk).

[3] Texture and brightness are not elaborated separately in our context. Brightness and texture (hue) are considered as components of color aesthetic (color is scaled down to hue and brightness). Consequently, identical assumptions are applied for hue and texture as for color.

3 Visual Design Support in Business Process Modeling Tools

In this section, the support for visual design of process model element labels of seven business process modeling tools is summarized. These tools have been selected as they are a representative subset of the market leaders according to the 2010 Gartner Report [46]. Additionally, these tools provide sophisticated support for the process modeling phase as identified in [47]. At least one representative of widely used notations such as BPMN, EPC and Petri Nets has been investigated. The analysis results are summarized in Table 2.

Table 2. Results of business process modeling tool analysis.

Modeling Tool	Notation	Shape / Form	Size	Color	Orientation	Position	Segmentation
ARIS Business Architect	EPC	Calibri bold font, *changeable*	9 pt, *changeable*	black text on multiple backgrounds, *changeable*	centered, horizontal, *not changeable*	inside of element, *changeable*	restricted by element / label border
BizAgi Process Modeler	BPMN	Segoe UI plain font, *changeable*	8 pt, *changeable*	black text on multiple backgrounds, *changeable*	centered, horizontal, *not changeable*	inside activity, below event and gateway, *not changeable*	restricted by element / label border
BOC Adonis	BPMN	unknown plain font, *not changeable*	unknown, *not changeable*	black text on multiple backgrounds, *not changeable*	centered, horizontal, *not changeable*	inside activity, below event and gateway, *changeable*	restricted by element / label border
Horus Enterprise	Petri Net	Arial bold transition font, plain place font, *changeable*	18 pt transition label, 16 pt place label, *changeable*	black text on white background, *changeable*	left aligned, horizontal, *not changeable*	above transition, below place, *changeable*	no automatic segmentation, manual sizing of text label, segmentation on label border
Intalio Designer	BPMN	Verdana plain font, *changeable*	8 pt, *changeable*	black text on white or blue background, *changeable*	centered, horizontal, *not changeable*	inside activity, below event and gateway, *not changeable*	restricted by element / label border
Microsoft Visio 2013	BPMN / EPC	Calibri plain font, *changeable*	12 pt, *changeable*	black text on white background, *changeable*	centered, horizontal, changeable *(also rotation)*	inside activity and gateway, below event, inside element in EPC, *changeable*	restricted by element / label border
Signavio Process Editor	BPMN / EPC	unknown plain font, *not changeable*	unknown, *not changeable*	black text on white background, *partly changeable*	centered, horizontal, *not changeable*	inside activity, below event and gateway, inside element in EPC, *partly changeable*	restricted by element border

The analysis shows that these process modeling tools offer basic layouting support for process model element labels but do not provide any sophisticated label segmentation features. The tools typically provide users with options to adjust *shape and form* of model element labels, i.e. the font type and form can be changed. Also the *size and color* of labels can be modified in general. The standard text color is black while the background color of labels differs. The background color of labels outside a shape is typically white while it corresponds to the shapes' color if the label is placed inside a shape. With respect to the *orientation* of process model element labels the analyzed modeling tools do not provide such a rich feature set, which offers all possible options. While the alignment of labels can be changed, e.g. from the most common option 'centered' to 'left'- or 'right-aligned', the typical horizontal orientation can only be changed in Microsoft Visio. The implementation of *positioning* of element labels depends on the modeling notation. In general, most tools allow for a free positioning of labels. As a presetting, the BPMN modeling tools place the labels of an activity inside its shape, while the label of an event or gateway is typically placed below the shape. The EPC-based modeling tools place the labels inside the model elements and the Petri Net based modeling tool places them below places and above transitions. Finally, no sophisticated support for label *segmentation* is provided. For instance, no tool uses any approach to segment labels into chunks that might ease the understanding or reading fluency of a label. In general, all analyzed modeling tools wrap the words of a label as soon as the border of the corresponding shape or label form is reached - i.e. no words can poke out of their corresponding form. The Horus Enterprise tool does not apply an automatic segmentation leading to one-line labels. However, the label size can be segmented manually resulting in the same segmentation "behavior" as used in the other modeling tools.

To sum up, only rudimentary layouting is supported in existing modeling tools.

4   Recommendations for Visual Design in Literature

Next, we studied potential effects of each visual variable as described in literature. The analysis unveils that each visual variable can serve as a cognitive aid when used appropriately.

Shape/Form. The realization of this variable is achieved by choosing an appropriate letter type (uppercase, lowercase or mixed) and font type. Generally, a conventional and consistent usage of upper and lowercase letters is recommended (for the English language) [10]. However, the lowercase usage of letters is more promoted than uppercase. Tinker and Fisher [11, 12] showed that text displayed in uppercase suffers readability compared to text in lowercase. Text in lowercase is found to be read faster [13]. This result is explained by the unfamiliarity of the higher text size of uppercases for readers leading to higher reading difficulty. However, in case of low resolution uppercases might be advantageous [14]. Based on this consideration, an element label such as "Receive Order" should be transformed to "receive order" since upper cases are not common for both words. Process modelers presumably have more practice in reading lowercase words and letters should not distract attention from its neighboring letters in order to better form a coherence [13]. Research in the field of software comprehensibility has demonstrated that the identifier style camel-case (e.g., employeeName) is superior to the underscore style (e.g., employee_name). Although it took programmers higher visual effort to read camel-case identifiers, they performed better in a variety of experimental tasks when using camel-case [8]. This result gives a hint that uppercase might also have advantages when used for labels consisting of few words, which do not show in natural language prose reading. In practice, however, we can often find labels in which each word starts with an uppercase letter, e.g., [15].

With respect to font type, Verdana and Arial are considered to be the most legible fonts [16] (usage of sans-serif is recommended over serif). Readability is reduced when plain text is used instead of italicized [17]. Regarding text highlighting words in bold are not harder to read than non-bold words [18]. In the area of cartography [19, p. 642] states that "it is considered good practice to select one typeface, but allow several variants of a type family, e.g., allow Times Roman and italic, variation in weight (light, medium, bold), and a small number of font sizes." However, it is questionable whether it makes sense to transfer this practice to process modeling, since in process models lower variability than in maps is needed to distinguish between labels. Such a variation is not typically used for visualizing semantically different types of process elements. Consequently, we recommend a sans-serif, non-bold font text for process elements labels.

Size. Next, we turn to considerations for choosing an appropriate font size. The recommendation for reading text on software displays is 10 points (9 pixels) [16]. Moody [20] advocates the use of constant symbol size, symbol form and font size. Thus, he suggests to determine the optimal size of a symbol based on the amount of text that should fit inside (e.g., 2×3 cm as a size for symbols to be large enough to fit in labels of around 50 characters in 11-point font) [20]. The main argument behind this suggestion is that a variation in a visual variable (font size, symbol shape) may introduce the misunderstanding that the respective element is different to the other element, for instance of higher importance. The model reader might perceive the model element as significant or special although the variation is random due to a longer label and the model creator did not intend to communicate such a message. This reasoning is also reflected in labeling rules of other domains, which use variations in font size to indicate differences. For instance in the area of map labeling it is suggested that "larger cities should have their name in a larger font than smaller cities" [19, p. 642].

However, the optimal length for an element label is unclear and empirical evidence for the choice of 50 characters as maximum value is missing. Research in word recognition [21] has demonstrated that there is a u-shape relationship between word length (varying from 3 to 13 letters in the respective study) and word recognition. Words between 5 and 8 letters seem to be easiest to recognize, shorter words are skipped and longer words need more fixations. It may be possible that for process model element labels a similar medium label length is optimal. Yet, further research is needed to determine the "optimal" average label length.

Direction/Orientation. This variable is implemented through the alignment of the text label (e.g., horizontal vs. vertical, left-aligned vs. right-aligned). Agreement exists that a straight-on text orientation shows the best reading speed [22, 23]. Horizontal text is superior to vertical text [24]. In collaborative settings in which the (mobile) workbench is rotated between different users and thus the orientation is not directed towards all users, Wigdor and Balakrishnan [25] have shown that rotation does not impair readability as assumed in previous studies. Another aspect related to the visual variable direction is text alignment. An empirical study demonstrated that left-aligned text leads to higher task performance than justified text for web pages [26]. The word spacing that is forced by justified text was found to impair readability. It is open if a general warning for a justified alignment should be given for process element labels. While in the modeling notation BPMN a justified alignment is common, for Petri Nets typically left-aligned text labels are used.

Color. Color is a powerful and effective visual variable because it is detected in parallel by the human visual processing system [27]. Differences in color are perceived faster than differences in shape. Generally, color facilitates information processing [28], when used effectively. Readability is increased when colors with higher levels of contrast are used [29]. In the context of process modeling, empirical studies have demonstrated higher model comprehension when using color for syntax highlighting [30]. The prevailing color for text of process model element labels is black and the most widely-used font and background color combination is black text on a white background. Although a better performance was detected for other font/background color combinations, e.g., light blue on dark blue pages [29], we still advocate to use black text on a white background for modeling labels due to the higher familiarity with black on white.

Position. Generally, element labels can be positioned left, right, inside, above or below a process model element. Standard documents as BPMN [31] remain vague and give no clear recommendation for the label position. It is stated that "BPMN elements (e.g. Flow objects) MAY have labels (e.g., its name and/or other attributes) placed inside the shape, or above or below the shape, in any direction or location, depending on the preference of the modeler or modeling tool vendor." Based on cartography literature as e.g., [32], Moody [20] suggests the following positions for line labeling: close, but not behind a line, centered, above horizontal and to the right of vertical lines. Moody suggests placing labels centered in model shapes [20]. This is because, if labels are located within the label, the Gestalt law of common region is best exploited [33, 34]. The principle of common region is "the tendency for elements that lie within the same bounded area to be grouped together" [34, p. 312]. Thus, the reader can recognize without conscious effort which label belongs to which referent modeling element and the label-element association is non-ambiguous [20]. Therefore, labels should be placed spatially close to corresponding graphic objects (modeling symbols) to reduce cognitive resources needed for scanning and searching the model. This recommendation is also backed up by the 'spatial contiguity effect' [35], saying that students learn better when textual and graphical information belonging to each other are placed spatially close to each other.

Finally, the textual placement also depends on the length of the text and the node type. In the non-normative BPMN examples published by OMG [15], textual descriptions of the process element "activity" are typically positioned inside the elements while the descriptors of "event" elements (which usually have short descriptors) are positioned above or below. It is open whether long textual descriptions of process elements should be placed inside (which is common for BPMN) or outside the element.

To sum up, a placement spatially close to corresponding graphic objects is recommended.

Segmentation. An element label usually consists of several words that require an appropriate visual segmentation. Prior research on learning with text has demonstrated that text segmentation "facilitates the identification of meaningful units in the text" and improves text retention [36, p. 217]. In contrast to a process description in narrative text format, process models already break down the overall text into segments, as each label belongs to a specific business activity. Still, the segmentation on the lower level of words is relevant, too. A great deal of literature has already investigated whether phrase-cued text can help readers to improve reading performance resulting in mixed results [37]. In comparison to usual written text, which has no cues on phrase boundaries, phrase-cued text is typographically segmented into meaningful "chunks", phrases or "units of thoughts" e.g., by printing spaces between phrases or using line breaks. Negative consequences of wrongly placed line breaks can result from the 'immediacy assumption' in text reading, which assumes that the "reader tries to interpret each content word of a text as it is encountered, even at the expense of making guesses that sometimes turn out to be wrong" [38, p. 330]. Additionally, appropriate text segmentation has an influence on reading fluency. [40] showed that when English phrases are interrupted by a line break, readjustment to non-anticipated words in the next line is especially harder for non-native English speakers. Thus, text should be formatted (e.g., by line breaks) in a way that avoids phrase-disrupting and preserves clausal units in order to promote reading fluency [39]. Therefore, a goal in setting line breaks should be to "help readers avoid incorrect anticipation, while also considering those moments in the text where readers tend to pause in order to integrate the meaning of a phrase" [40, p. 720]. This visual variable has been widely neglected. Empirical evidence is missing how to best segment a text label.

5   Discussion

Based on the analysis of both perspectives (literature and modeling tools) we identify areas for future research and potential improvement of existing tools as follows. Table 3 summarizes our discussion on visual design of process element labels. It indicates which recommendations from literature on informational graphics can be adopted for process element labels and for which visual variables no appropriate recommendations could be found and a validation is outstanding.

Specifically, a deeper understanding of the characteristics size and direction/orientation is needed in order to support an appropriate perception of the process elements. In addition, the research to date has not yet addressed "segmentation" in a way relevant to the context of process model labels. A solution to an appropriate segmentation of text labels into chunks is essential since it highly impacts the lexical access (activation of the meanings of a language) of the label. If the lexical access is hampered, readers cannot understand the process model element label and thus an inappropriate association of the real process might arise. With respect to the tool support, on the one hand some variables are already widely implemented as e.g., options for changing font type and size or text alignment. On the other hand label segmentation is neglected and only implemented rudimentary. What might also be a nice-to-have feature of process modeling tools is an automatic conversion of letters from lower- to uppercase and vice versa. This functionality was not found in any tool.

Table 3. Recommendations for the visual design of process model element labels

Visual variable	Recommendation
Shape/form	Lowercase usage of letters, sans-serif, non-bold fonts
Size	Words between 5 to 8 letters seem to be easiest to recognize; "optimal" average length is an open research issue
Direction/orientation	Left-alignment is superior, but has not been empirically validated for process element labels
Color	Usage of high levels of contrast for font/background colors
Position	Placement spatially close to corresponding graphic objects
Segmentation	Open issue

6 Related Work

The visualization of process element labels impacts the understandability of a business process model. Therefore, related approaches are those, which intend to improve process model understandability. Two complementary streams of research related to this goal can be found. The first one deals with improving the visual design of process modelling languages and "secondary" language issues of process models. Prior research in this vein has for instance compared different languages and symbol choices [41] or suggested improvements to visual syntax [42]. However, available studies have addressed label design only as a side issue.

The second research stream relevant to this paper focusses on improving semantics of process model labels. In this context, prior research has put a specific focus on improving the fit between the actual semantic interpretation of process model labels and their intended meaning [7]. For instance, the semantic quality of element labels can be promoted through a controlled assistance for labeling of process model elements [44, 45] and recommending superior naming conventions [4].

All these works, however, do not consider the visual design of the process model element label. Therefore, to the best of our knowledge, no theoretical or empirical work investigating the visual design of element labels have so far been undertaken. Findings from disciplines where visual word recognition is central such as graph drawing, cartography and linguistics can be adopted to process element label visualization. These related approaches have been discussed in Sect. 4.

7 Summary and Outlook

To sum up, this paper has presented the first discussion of theoretical issues of the visual design of process model element labels. The paper integrated relevant research findings of multiple disciplines concerned with efficient presentation of text labels to identify a cumulative body of label layout-related knowledge. Recommendations for font, size and color can be transferred to labels of process model elements, while identification of appropriate recommendations for size (label length), direction/ orientation, position and segmentation is still an open research goal.

In addition, we investigated the as-is situation of visual design support in common process modeling tools indicating only little support for automatic layouting and fine tuning of labels. We advise future tool revisions to take visual variables for process model element labels into account. Furthermore, we suggest extending related modeling guidelines with relevant aspects on visual design of labels. This research has thrown up many questions in need of further investigation. Considerably more work will need to be done to define heuristics for the visual design of labels for all common labeling styles in our future research effort. In addition, we encourage empirical research to investigate the actual effects of label design on human understanding.

References

1. Moody, D.L.: The "physics" of notations: towards a scientific basis for constructing visual notations in software engineering. IEEE Trans. Software Eng. **35**, 756–779 (2009)
2. Christensen, J., Marks, J., Shieber, S.: An empirical study of algorithms for point-feature label placement. ACM Trans. Graph. (TOG) **14**, 203–232 (1995)
3. Wagner, F., Wolff, A., Kapoor, V., Strijk, T.: Three rules suffice for good label placement. Algorithmica **30**, 334–349 (2001)
4. Mendling, J., Reijers, H.A., Recker, J.: Activity labeling in process modeling: empirical insights and recommendations. Inf. Syst. **35**, 467–482 (2010)
5. Leopold, H., Smirnov, S., Mendling, J.: On the refactoring of activity labels in business process models. Inf. Syst. **37**, 443–459 (2012)
6. Leopold, H., Eid-Sabbagh, R.-H., Mendling, J., Azevedo, L.G., Baião, F.A.: Detection of naming convention violations in process models for different languages. Decis. Support Syst. **56**, 310–325 (2013)
7. Koschmider, A., Ullrich, M., Heine, A., Oberweis, A.: Revising the vocabulary of business process element labels. In: Zdravkovic, J., Kirikova, M., Johannesson, P. (eds.) CAiSE 2015. LNCS, vol. 9097, pp. 69–83. Springer, Heidelberg (2015)
8. Binkley, D., Davis, M., Lawrie, D., Maletic, J.I., Morrell, C., Sharif, B.: The impact of identifier style on effort and comprehension. Empirical Softw. Eng. **18**, 219–276 (2013)
9. Deeb, R., Ooms, K., De Maeyer, P.: Typography in the eyes of Bertin, gender and expertise variation. Cartographic J. **49**, 176–185 (2012)
10. Moody, D.L., Sindre, G., Brasethvik, T., Sølvberg, A.: Evaluating the quality of process models: empirical testing of a quality framework. In: Spaccapietra, S., March, S.T., Kambayashi, Y. (eds.) ER 2002. LNCS, vol. 2503, pp. 380–396. Springer, Heidelberg (2002)
11. Tinker, M.A.: Legibility of Print. Iowa State University Press, Ames (1963)
12. Fisher, D.F.: Reading and visual search. Mem. Cogn. **3**, 188–196 (1975)
13. Sanocki, T., Dyson, M.C.: Letter processing and font information during reading: beyond distinctiveness, where vision meets design. Atten. Percept. Psychophys. **74**, 132–145 (2012)
14. Arditi, A., Cho, J.: Letter case and text legibility in normal and low vision. Vision. Res. **47**, 2499–2505 (2007)

15. Object Management Group: BPMN 2.0 by Example (2010)
16. Sheedy, J.E., Subbaram, M.V., Zimmerman, A.B., Hayes, J.R.: Text legibility and the letter superiority effect. Hum. Factors J. Hum. Factors Ergon. Soc. **47**, 797–815 (2005)
17. Hill, A., Scharff, L.: Readability of websites with various foreground/background color combinations, font types and word styles. In: Proceedings of 11th National Conference in Undergraduate Research, pp. 742–746 (1997)
18. Tullis, T.S., Boynton, J.L., Hersh, H.: Readability of fonts in the windows environment. In: Conference Companion on Human Factors in Computing Systems, pp. 127–128. ACM (1995)
19. Dijk, S.V., Kreveld, M.V., Strijk, T., Wolff, A.: Towards an evaluation of quality for names placement methods. Int. J. Geogr. Inf. Sci. **16**, 641–661 (2002)
20. Moody, D.L.: The art (and science) of diagramming: communicating effectively using diagrams (tutorial). In: IEEE Symposium on Visual Languages and Human-Centric Computing. IEEE (2012)
21. New, B.: Reexamining the word length effect in visual word recognition: new evidence from the English Lexicon Project. Psychon. Bull. Rev. **13**, 45–52 (2006)
22. Kruger, R., Carpendale, S., Scott, S.D., Greenberg, S.: How people use orientation on tables: comprehension, coordination and communication. In: Proceedings of the 2003 International ACM SIGGROUP Conference on Supporting Group Work, pp. 369–378. ACM (2003)
23. Tang, J.C.: Findings from observational studies of collaborative work. Int. J. Man Mach. Stud. **34**, 143–160 (1991)
24. Yu, D., Park, H., Gerold, D., Legge, G.E.: Comparing reading speed for horizontal and vertical English text. J. Vis. **10**, 21 (2010)
25. Wigdor, D., Balakrishnan, R.: Empirical investigation into the effect of orientation on text readability in tabletop displays. In: Gellersen, H., Schmidt, K., Beaudouin-Lafon, M., Mackay, W. (eds.) ECSCW 2005, pp. 205–224. Springer, Heidelberg (2005)
26. Ling, J., van Schaik, P.: The influence of line spacing and text alignment on visual search of web pages. Displays **28**, 60–67 (2007)
27. Treisman, A., Souther, J.: Illusory words: The roles of attention and of top–down constraints in conjoining letters to form words. JExPH **12**, 3 (1986)
28. Lohse, G.L.: A cognitive model for understanding graphical perception. Hum.-Comput. Interact. **8**, 353–388 (1993)
29. Hall, R.H., Hanna, P.: The impact of web page text-background colour combinations on readability, retention, aesthetics and behavioural intention. Behav. Inf. Technol. **23**, 183–195 (2004)
30. Reijers, H.A., Freytag, T., Mendling, J., Eckleder, A.: Syntax highlighting in business process models. Decis. Support Syst. **51**, 339–349 (2011)
31. Object Management Group: Business Process Model and Notation (BPMN) Version 2.0.2 (2013)
32. Imhof, E.: Positioning names on maps. Am. Cartographer **2**, 128–144 (1975)
33. Palmer, S.E.: Common region: a new principle of perceptual grouping. Cogn. Psychol. **24**, 436–447 (1992)
34. Palmer, S.E., Brooks, J.L., Nelson, R.: When does grouping happen? Acta Psychol. **114**, 311–330 (2003)
35. Mayer, R.E., Moreno, R.: Nine ways to reduce cognitive load in multimedia learning. Educ. Psychol. **38**, 43–52 (2003)
36. Florax, M., Ploetzner, R.: What contributes to the split-attention effect? The role of text segmentation, picture labelling, and spatial proximity. Learn. Instr. **20**, 216–224 (2010)

37. Rasinski, T.V.: The effects of cued phrase boundaries on reading performance: a review (1990)
38. Just, M.A., Carpenter, P.A.: A theory of reading: from eye fixations to comprehension. Psychol. Rev. **87**, 329 (1980)
39. Levasser, V., Macaruso, P., Palumbo, L.C., Shankweiler, D.: Syntactically cued text facilitates oral reading fluency in developing readers. APsy **27**, 423–445 (2006)
40. Salama, A., Oflazer, K., Hagan, S.: Typesetting for improved readability using lexical and syntactic information. In: Proceedings of the 51st Annual Meeting of the Association for Computational Linguistics, pp. 719–724 (2013)
41. Figl, K., Mendling, J., Strembeck, M.: The influence of notational deficiencies on process model comprehension. J. Assoc. Inf. Syst. **14**, 312–338 (2013)
42. Genon, N., Heymans, P., Amyot, D.: Analysing the Cognitive Effectiveness of the BPMN 2.0 Visual Notation. In: Malloy, B., Staab, S., Brand, M. (eds.) SLE 2010. LNCS, vol. 6563, pp. 377–396. Springer, Heidelberg (2011)
43. La Rosa, M., Wohed, P., Mendling, J., ter Hofstede, A.H.M., Reijers, H.A., van der Aalst, W.M.P.: Managing process model complexity via abstract syntax modifications. IEEE Trans. Industr. Inf. **7**, 614–629 (2011)
44. Leopold, H., Mendling, J., Reijers, H.A., La Rosa, M.: Simplifying process model abstraction: techniques for generating model names. Inf. Syst. **39**, 134–151 (2014)
45. Delfmann, P., Herwig, S., Lis, L., Stein, A.: Supporting distributed conceptual modelling through naming conventions-a tool-based linguistic approach. Enterp. Model. Inf. Syst. Architect. **4**, 3–19 (2009)
46. Sinur, J., Hill, J.B.: Magic quadrant for business process management suites. Technical report, Gartner RAS Core Research (2010)
47. Koschmider, A., Fellmann, M., Schoknecht, A., Oberweis, A.: Analysis of process model reuse: where are we now, where should we go from here? Decis. Support Syst. **66**, 9–19 (2014)

Business Process Models for Visually Navigating Process Execution Data

Jens Gulden[1]([⊠]) and Simon Attfield[2]

[1] University of Duisburg-Essen, Universitätsstr. 9, 45141 Essen, Germany
`jens.gulden@uni-due.de`
[2] Middlesex University London, The Burroughs, London NW4 4BT, UK
`s.attfield@mdx.ac.uk`

Abstract. To analyze large amounts of data, visual analysis tools offer filter mechanisms for drilling down into multi-dimensional information spaces, or slicing and dicing them according to given criteria. This paper introduces an analysis approach for navigating multi-dimensional process instance execution logs based on business process models. By visually selecting parts of a business process model, a set of available log entries is filtered to include only those entries that result from execution instances of the selected process branches. Using this approach allows to exploratively navigate through process execution logs and analyze them according to the causal-temporal relationships encoded in the underlying business process model. The business process models used by the approach can either be created using model editors, or be statistically derived using process mining techniques. We exemplify our approach with a prototypical implementation.

Keywords: Visual analysis · Business analysis · Business intelligence · Business process modeling · Process mining · Big data

1 Navigating Large Amounts of Data Along Process Paths

Existing analysis methods for navigating large amounts of data primarily focus on multi-dimensional navigation along the structures and relationship of business objects [1]. Distributed enterprise systems, however, often embed a process-based nature in the way they interoperate [3]. Data created and used by operative systems is not only structured along the objects it represents, but also along the causal-temporal relationships of the processes in which data plays a role [13]. To gain insight into the meaning of available data, and to derive valuable knowledge with relevance for business decisions from existing data, business analysis tools should offer means for analyzing data according to the causal-temporal relationships among the existing data objects, because these data objects have been created and used in procedural contexts shaped by the underlying business processes.

© Springer International Publishing Switzerland 2016
M. Reichert and H.A. Reijers (Eds.): BPM Workshops 2015, LNBIP 256, pp. 583–594, 2016.
DOI: 10.1007/978-3-319-42887-1_47

Interactive visualizations put the human in the loop. This is an appropriate solution when the solution to a problem cannot be achieved by automation alone [11]. Such situations rely on the human ability for recognizing the important problems and interpreting the meaning of data not just in virtue of the data itself but also through a nuanced understanding of context – something which humans tend to do well. They are also appropriate when the problems are not clearly defined. Thus interactive exploration of the data led by human interpretation and scent following [11] can make for an effective combination of capabilities.

It is the goal of the work at hand to sketch an approach for making business process models feasible as a visual navigation element for allowing causal-temporal drill downs into multi-dimensional sets of data in a visual business analysis environment.

In the next Sect. 2, known concepts and existing research which relate to the presented approach are discussed. Subsequently, Sect. 3 describes the fundamentals of the proposed solution. A running prototype operating on widely known test data is presented in Sect. 4 as an evaluation of the concept, and a short conclusion in Sect. 5 sums up the presented work.

2   Related Research

The presented approach makes use of business process models for expressing causal-temporal relationships that can be applied as a filter to navigate mass data and perform analyses on it. Consequentially, core principles from the fields of business process modeling and business process management (e.g. [2,15]) are underlying our approach. Business process modeling spans the area of abstracting over actions, actors and resources in organizations, usually by representing business process types as visual models with a flow-like notation. Business process models can serve as means of communication among humans to get a common understanding of the described processes. Due to their high level of abstraction and formalization compared to natural language, they can also be a basis for system design and development [8], e.g., the development of enterprise information systems [9], to support the tasks of an organization described with the respective business process models.

Closely related to analyzing process-related mass data is the field of process mining (e.g. [13]). As an alternative to manually creating business process models, process mining techniques can serve as a source of business process models that describe the causal-temporal structures which the presented approach uses for filtering data. As it will be discussed, the approach presented may serve as an extension to process mining procedures, and act as a feedback-loop, in which mined processes can be examined for their suitability in terms of properly reflecting causal-temporal relationships of the related data.

Our proposal involves an approach called 'coordinated multiple views' (CMV), which represent a class of dashboards. CMV has become something of a standard in information visualization design and is incorporated into several off-the-shelf tools and tool kits [14]. For an overview of some of the main ideas underpinning CMV we direct the interested reader to [12]. [12] characterizes the premise motivating CMV to be that users understand data better if they interact with its presentation and view it through different representations. In CMV the user is supported in an interactive dialogue with data by allowing them to interact with different views of the data such that interaction is coordinated across the views. There are a number of view patterns which are particularly common, including choropleth maps [4], timelines, network graphs, scatter plots, bar charts, line graphs, and parallel coordinate plots [10].

By using multiple forms, CMV allows the user to examine data from two or more perspectives simultaneously. [12] gives the examples of Overview and Detail, Focus and Context, Difference views, Master/Slave and Small Multiples. These multiple views are then coupled with a large variety of interaction strategies. For example, these might include brushing in which elements are selected and highlighted in one display. This can result in these elements being highlighted in another display, thus showing element values at different resolutions or according to different parameters. It may also include cross-filtering, panning or zooming in which the filtering applied to one view affects how another view is displayed. Overall, the aim is to support the user in an exploratory and interactive dialogue with the data.

3   Utilizing Business Process Models for Navigating in Coordinated Multiple Views Environments

Our approach comprises an analysis setting composed of coordinated multiple views (CMV) [12], with each view showing different aggregate information derived from the set of currently selected process instances filtered from process instance log data. Figure 1 shows a mockup of an analysis application which provides CMV with individual data displays. Each display offers a different view on the selected data entries, e.g., by presenting performance indicators calculated from the selected set of data entries.

When an element in the business process model view is selected, this process element and all following ones in the same sub-branch are highlighted, to mark the set of elements on which data gets filtered. After any change to the selection of the business process model, the CMV components get immediately updated to show current information derived from the newly selected set of process instances and their related cases. By watching the displays' content at real-time and simultaneously performing selections on the business process model, causal-temporally related differences in the selected sets of data become intuitively visible, and can provide insight into valuable knowledge for business-relevant decisions.

To match process instance logs against the selection filter, each log entry must contain at least one reference to a case-id which uniquely identifies objects that flow through the modeled business process [13]. Based on such a case-id, chains of log entries which belong to the same process instance are discovered during process mining. When filtering according to selected process elements, only case-ids from process instances which during their execution have passed

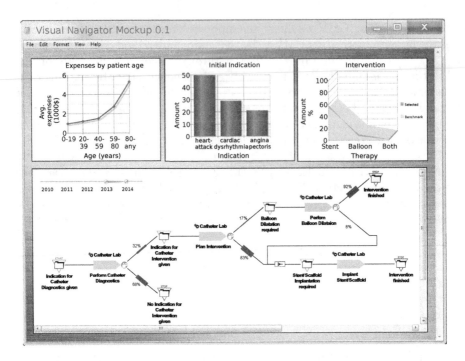

Fig. 1. Mockup in its initial state with no filtering selected (Color figure online)

any of the selected elements at least once, will be considered in the analyzed data set. Loops and repetitions during process instance execution do not affect how this mechanism works, because the filter criterion is whether a process instance has at least once passed any of the selected elements, independent from how often this actually happens.

To specify constraints on the overall time span from which data entries are to be looked at, the business process model view contains an alphaslider in its upper left corner which allows for specifying a start and an end time to pre-select entries from the specified range of time for further filtering.

The approach can be used both with business process models originating from manual business process modeling activities [2,15], as well as with automatically derived models that result from applying process mining techniques [13] to the analyzed set of log data entries. When used with process models resulting from process mining, an iterative analysis procedure can be applied. It starts with mining an initial process model, which subsequently is used in a CMV analysis as causal-temporal structure to filter data on. This analysis step may reveal information about the suitability of the underlying process model, thus the quality of the mining, which in turn may lead to the decision to repeat the mining step which different parameters, again apply the result in the CMV analysis, and iterate until a desired setting is achieved.

Figure 2 shows the already introduced example view with two different selected sub-paths of the business process model. While the business process model is a representation of an actual healthcare guideline used in practice, the figures displayed in the example are purely fictional, and may not make any sense from a medical point of view. What gets demonstrated by comparing the two different selection states are the dynamic changes in the dashboard displays when different parts of the business process model get selected.

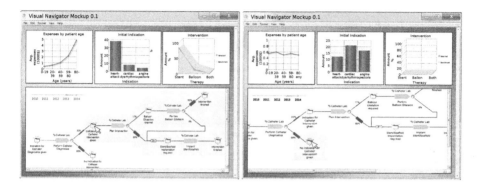

Fig. 2. Mockup with selected sub-branch "apply heart catheter" (left), in contrast to selected sub-branch "do not apply heart catheter" (right) (Color figure online)

4   Prototype Implementation and Application to Real Data

We have implemented the suggested approach inside an ECLIPSE tooling environment by combining an extended version of the MEMO ORGML [7,8] business process model editor with the BUSINESS INTELLIGENCE AND REPORTING TOOLS (BIRT) [6] toolkit. Figure 3 shows how the environment looks like.

4.1   Example Analysis Case

As an example of a large set of real-world data, we have chosen to use a set of demonstration data shipped with a well known process mining application, which is the CallcenterExample.csv data set included in the DISCO [5] process mining application. The reason for this decision is that this test data has already served for other demonstration purposes and is thus known throughout the BPM community. The presented example can thus better be understood and be compared to other use cases involving the same data set.

The example data represents information about call center events that are related to each other in a process structure, with each event type being identified by the entry in the data column Operation. Among other information, the

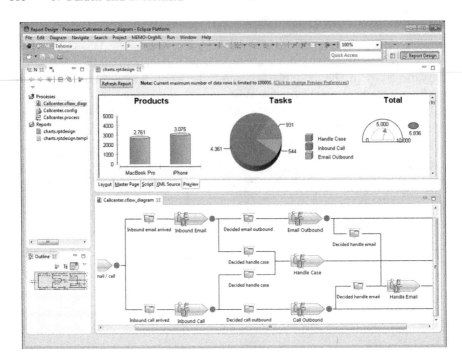

Fig. 3. The implemented prototype, combining the BIRT reporting tools with an enhanced MEMO ORGML editor (Color figure online)

data set also contains information about the topic of the callcenter event in the `Product` column, and about the involved agent in the `Agent` column. Information about the start and end time of each task are stored in the columns `Start Date` and `End Date`. Listing 1 shows the first lines of the data set in CSV representation, which in total has 7548 entries.

```
Service ID,Operation,Start Date,End Date,Agent Position,Customer ID,Product
    ,Service Type,Agent
Case 1,Inbound Call,9.3.10 8:05,9.3.10 8:10,FL,Customer 1,MacBook Pro,
    Referred to Servicer,Helen
Case 1,Handle Case,11.3.10 10:30,11.3.10 10:32,FL,Customer 1,MacBook Pro,
    Referred to Servicer,Helen
Case 1,Call Outbound,11.3.10 11:45,11.3.10 11:52,FL,Customer 1,MacBook Pro,
    Referred to Servicer,Henk
Case 2,Inbound Call,4.3.10 11:43,4.3.10 11:46,FL,Customer 2,MacBook Pro,
    Referred to Servicer,Susi
Case 3,Inbound Call,25.3.10 9:32,25.3.10 9:33,FL,Customer 3,MacBook Pro,
    Referred to Servicer,Mary
```

Listing 1. Callcenter example data

From this data, a rudimentary process structure can be derived using DISCO's process mining capabilities. This process structure can then in turn be used to filter the log data according to the relationships among tasks given in the process model. The model serves as an auxiliary structure to automatically select the transitive hull of elements until the end of the process is reached. However, the approach does not require to use this mechanism, because a manual multi-selection can be also applied as filter configuration. For this reason, the underlying model also does not necessarily have to be entirely precise in reflecting the causal-temporal relationships in the real data, and an imprecise "mined" version of a business process model may be sufficient to serve for filtering purposes. The result processed by DISCO, which is further used in this example as the underlying process structure, is shown in Fig. 4.

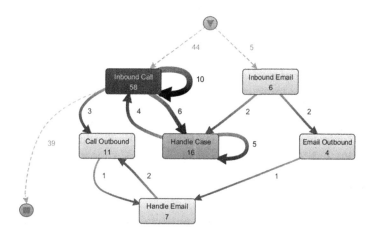

Fig. 4. Process model derived from the example data set using the DISCO tool, the numbers attached to events and transitions represent the amount of event log entries that have been interpreted by the mining algorithm as the respective model element

The model derived by DISCO has been made the basis to manually create a business process model in the MEMO ORGML language, which reflects the structure of the mined process. Due to the comparably strict syntax of MEMO ORGML, the representation requires several intermediate events to be included in the model. Also, for purposes of demonstrating the selection and highlighting mechanism, a single start task has been added which initially distinguishes between inbound e-mails vs. phone calls. The MEMO ORGML model is shown in Fig. 5.

Again it is important to notice that the aforegoing mining step is optional, and that any manually modeled BPM can be used for analysis navigation, even BPMs which do not perfectly reflect the causal-temporal relationships of the analyzed data entries.

The BIRT report for this example analysis comprises of three chart elements. The first one is a bar chart displaying the number of different products involved in those callcenter events that went through the currently highlighted process elements. The second chart is a pie chart, which shows the distribution of execution runs among all selected process elements. As a third widget, a gauge element displays the total number of events that occurred at the selected event

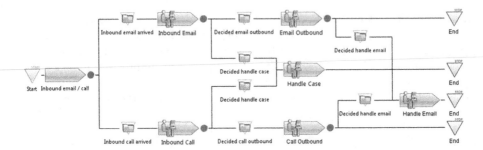

Fig. 5. Process model in the MEMO ORGML language used for analysis navigation

types. This collection of visualization widgets demonstrates how information of different kinds can be queried and visualized using BIRT in combination with the proposed approach.

The example setup shows how different selections in the business process model lead to diverse outputs of the chart visualizations, which can reveal knowledge from the analyzed data which is not obvious a priori. E.g., the example selection in Fig. 6 highlights those business process model elements that are related to processing inbound e-mails.

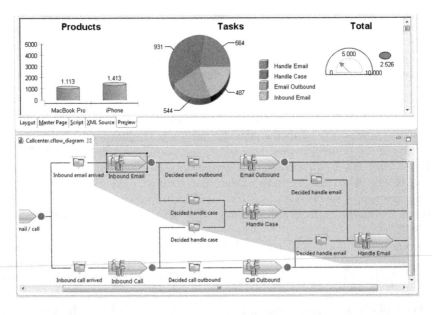

Fig. 6. Filtering on business process model elements that are related to processing inbound e-mails (Color figure online)

In comparison to Fig. 6, in Fig. 7 the lower BPM branch which processes inbound calls is highlighted. Comparing the "Products" analysis charts, it becomes visible that a much larger absolute number of incidents is covered by this branch. Additionally, there is a noticeably unequal distribution among the frequencies with which the individual selected tasks have been executed, as the "Tasks" pie chart reveals. These differences might, e.g., lead to the business-related conclusion that in the lower branch, when handling inbound calls, optimizations are required.

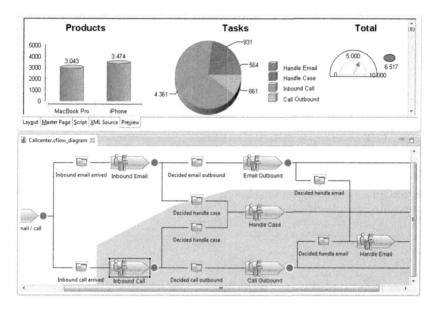

Fig. 7. Filtering on business process model elements that are related to processing inbound calls (Color figure online)

By selecting a common start element, the entirety of all process nodes gets highlighted, as shown in Fig. 8. This kind of selection resembles the filter state where no highlighting is set at all, i.e., after having cleared the selection by clicking somewhere on a free white diagram region.

As mentioned previously, the highlighting mechanism can manually be controlled to explicitly select highlighted model elements and disable the automatic transitive hull detection. When selected together with the shift key pressed, multiple elements can individually be added to the set of highlighted filter elements. This configures the filter to include all those process instances that passed any of the selected process elements during their execution. Figure 9 shows an example of a manual filter configuration without automatic transitive hull detection.

Given the demonstrated flexibility of the report design and BPM creation, which allows for virtually any kind of data extraction and visualization with traditional reporting elements, this running prototype setup proves the effective applicability of the approach in real world analysis scenarios.

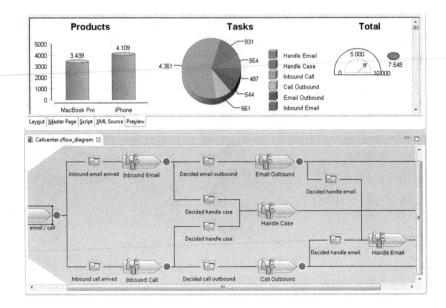

Fig. 8. Filtering on all elements by selecting a common start element, which resembles the filter state after clearing the selection (Color figure online)

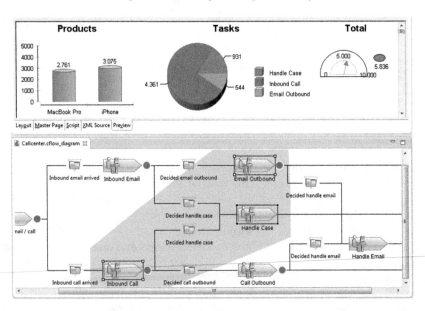

Fig. 9. Explicit selections of the elements "Inbound Call", "Email Outbound", and "Handle Case" (Color figure online)

5   Conclusion and Future Work

With the sketched approach, a concept for visually exploring data has been introduced that links characteristics of business process models to tasks of dynamically filtering and exploring multi-dimensional process-related instance data. Given the demonstration use case, a setting has been described which is applicable to any real-world domain where multi-dimensional data sets are analyzed with regard to their procedural characteristics.

Up to now the approach is primarily justified by being based on prior research on coordinated multiple views displays in interaction design, as well as business process management covering business process modeling and business process mining approaches. Further evaluation, preferably embedded in a setting with other data visualization techniques adapted to a specific use case as a whole, is required.

One future conceptual extension would be to allow multiple selection modes, represented by different highlighting colors. These modes could be used to mark distinct sets of data that can be compared to each other in the analysis.

A few limitations apply to the prototype in its current state of implementation. At first, the alphaslider suggested in the design concept to limit the processed range of events to a specific time span is not implemented, because the pre-filtering of events according to their start and end times can be realized independent from the essential visual parts of the suggested approach.

By using a convex polygon algorithm to determine the shape of the yellow selection marker, it may happen that the highlighting also appears behind elements which actually do not belong to the semantically following elements, or a set of multiple manually selected elements. This could be overcome by applying a more sophisticated algorithm which also removes areas around unselected elements by making the polygon concave at these locations. For the time being, in such cases the traditional selection markers provided by the original model editor, which appear as black rectangles around selected elements, can be used to determine the selection state of an element in addition to the striking yellow highlighting marker.

References

1. Berson, A., Smith, S.J.: Data Warehousing, Data Mining, & OLAP. McGraw-Hill, New York (2004)
2. Dumas, M., La Rosa, M., Mendling, J., Reijers, H.: Fundamentals of Business Process Management. Springer, Heidelberg (2013)
3. Dumas, M., van der Aalst, W.M.P., ter Hofstede, A.H.: Process-Aware Information Systems: Bridging People and Software Through Process Technology. Wiley, Hoboken (2005)
4. Dykes, J.: Exploring spatial data representation with dynamic graphics. Comput. Geosci. **23**(4), 345–370 (1997)
5. Fluxicon. Disco. 22 March 2015. http://fluxicon.com/disco/
6. Eclipse Foundation. Business intelligence and reporting tools (BIRT). 22 March 2015. http://www.eclipse.org/birt/

7. Frank, U.: Memo organisation modelling language (2): focus on business processes. ICB Research Report 49, University of Duisburg-Essen, Institute for Computer Science and Business Information Systems (ICB) (2011)

8. Frank, U.: Multi-perspective enterprise modeling: foundational concepts, prospects and future research challenges. J. Softw. Syst. Model. **13**, 941–962 (2013)

9. Gulden, J.: Methodical Support for Model-Driven Software Engineering with Enterprise Models. Ph.D. thesis, Universität Duisburg-Essen, Berlin (2013)

10. Inselberg, A.: Parallel Coordinates: Visual Multidimensional Geometry and its Applications. Springer, Heidelberg (2009)

11. Munzner, T.: Visualization Design and Analysis: Abstractions, Principles, and Methods. CRC Press, Boca Raton (2014)

12. Roberts, J.C.: State of the art: coordinated & multiple views in exploratory visualization. In: CMV 2007 Proceedings of the Fifth International Conference on Coordinated and Multiple Views in Exploratory Visualization, pp. 61–71. IEEE Computer Society, Washington, DC (2007)

13. van der Aalst, W.M.P.: Process Mining: Discovery, Conformance and Enhancement of Business Processes. Springer, Heidelberg (2011)

14. Weaver, C.: Building highly-coordinated visualizations in improvise. In: Ward, M.O., Munzner, T. (eds.) 10th IEEE Symposium on Information Visualization (InfoVis 2004), Austin, TX, USA, 10–12 October. IEEE Computer Society (2004)

15. Weske, M.: Business Process Management: Concepts, Languages, Architectures. Springer, Heidelberg (2007)

Author Index

Printed in the United States
By Bookmasters